LANDSCAPE ARCHITECTURE

LANDSCAPE ARCHITECTURE

An Illustrated History in Timelines, Site Plans, and Biography

William A. Mann

School of Environmental Design
University of Georgia

JOHN WILEY AND SONS, INC.
New York / Chichester / Brisbane / Toronto / Singapore

This text is printed on acid-free paper.

This publication is designed to provide accurate and authoritative information in regard to the subject matter covered. It is sold with the understanding that the publisher is not engaged in rendering legal, accounting, or other professional services. If legal advice or other expert assistance is required, the services of a competent professional person should be sought. *From a Declaration of Principles jointly adopted by a Committee of the American Bar Association and a Committee of Publishers.*

Library of Congress Cataloging in Publication Data:

Mann, William A., 1941–
Landscape architecture : an illustrated history in timelines, site plans, and biography / William A. Mann.
p. cm.
Rev. ed. of: Space and time in landscape architectural history. © 1981.
Includes bibliographical references (p.) and index.
ISBN 0-471-59465-2 (paper)
1. Landscape architecture—History. 2. Landscape architecture—Designs and plans. 3. Landscape architecture—Biography. I. Mann, William A., 1941– Space and time in landscape architectural history. II. Title.
SB470.5.M37 1993
712—dc20 92-41489

Printed in the United States of America

10 9 8 7 6

Contents

FIVE

Acknowledgments

For this author, *Landscape Architecture* has been a labor of love. It grew out of the materials that I felt compelled to prepare for myself as I needed to learn the subject of landscape architecture history when I first began to teach it at the University of Georgia in 1971.

Many friends and colleagues have helped and I want to use this opportunity to thank them in print. Without the aid of the following this work could never have been completed: Charles McDaniel, of The SWA Group, Dallas, Texas, for a plan of Williams Square; Garrett Eckbo, Dan Kiley, Ted Osmundson, Robert Royston, Hideo Sasaki, and John Simonds for information about their careers. Also, I want to express my admiration for the late James Rose, who spent a whole day with me a few years ago, sharing his stories about the profession and driving me around to several of his gardens in New Jersey. Mrs. Maggie Baylis, wife of the late Doug Baylis, was kind to send information about his career.

The following people helped immensely by reading and making suggestions about portions of the manuscript: Thomas Nieman, professor at the University of Kentucky–Lexington; Jot D. Carpenter, professor at Ohio State University; Kenneth I. Helphand, professor at the University of Oregon; E. Lynn Miller, professor emeritus at Pennsylvania State University; Lance M. Neckar, associate professor at the University of Minnesota; Constance A. Webster, assistant professor at Rutgers University, Department of Landscape Architecture; Nancy J. Volkman, associate professor at Texas A & M University; Arnold R. Alanen and William H. Tishler, both professors at the University of Wisconsin; George F. Thompson of the Center for American Places in Harrisonburg, Virginia; and Malcolm Cairns, associate professor at Ball State University.

Miriam E. Rutz, professor at Michigan State University, helped with advice and data about the many women who have been important in the history of environmental concerns. John Lyle and Jeff Olson at California State Polytechnic University furnished information about California landscape architects; John Burgess of the Landscape Architecture Unit at the Royal Melbourne Institute of Technology in Australia and John Oldham, of Perth, Western Australia helped to supply data about their countrymen and women; Denise Royle of Stockton, New Jersey, sent vital data about New Jersey designers. Both Cameron Man of Mississippi State University and Robert Grese of the University of Michigan furnished me with many good contacts in Canada, including Patrick Mooney at the University of British Columbia, Susan Donaldson at the University of Oregon, and Pleasance Crawford of Toronto, Ontario. I also appreciate the thoughtful and constructive criticism I received from the three anonymous reviewers of my manuscript, whoever they are.

My editor at John Wiley & Sons, Daniel Sayre, has been a most helpful and patient person to work with. I thank Dan very much for being so supportive of this effort from the first time we discussed it.

A special thank you goes to my graduate assistants at the University of Georgia, Terry DeMeo and Stephanie Gibbs, who helped with proofreading most of my manuscript. Over the past three years, Michael Del Giudice, Kathy Gager-Davis, and Cristine Johnson also helped with information gathering.

I appreciate all the support and encouragement I received during the process of my revising this volume from my indispensable Macintosh ally, Masha Parks-Grizzle, and Darrel G. Morrison, dean of the School of Environmental Design at the University of Georgia for the past nine years. I also want to thank the new dean of the School of Environmental Design, Kerry Dawson, for information and encouragement on this project.

For help on the first edition, I again want to thank my assistants and those whose moral support I still appreciate and without which I could not have pulled it all together: Helen Brandenburg, Charles Brenton, Jon Spence, Ian Firth, Claris Ingersoll, Deanna Kent, Tilda Wall, Robert P. Nicholls, Michael D. (Iver) Wahl, and Natalie B. Alpert of the University of Illinois.

Most of all to my wife, Barbara, and my boys, Anthony and James, I want to say thank you for tolerating all my weekends in "that room."

Landscape Architecture Defined

What is *landscape architecture,* when did it have its beginning as a profession, and how is it defined? In an undated letter from Henry Hill Elliot, one of the New York City street commissioners, to the city council, the designers of Central Park, Frederick Law Olmsted and Calvert Vaux, were appointed "landscape architects and designers." According to Olmsted's biographers, Charles E. Beveridge and David Schuyler, "This [letter, written some time in 1860] is the first instance [they] have found of the use of the term 'landscape architects' to describe Olmsted and Vaux's professional design activity" (Beveridge and Schuyler, 1983, p. 267). Prior to that time, *landscape gardening* was the most widely accepted term used for the creative activity in which Olmsted was to engage for half a century.

Three years later, on May 12, 1863, Olmsted and Vaux used the term *landscape architect* for the first time in a letter of resignation to the New York Park Commission—due to the intolerable political interference they were made to endure in the course of developing their grand "greensward" plan for Central Park. This was the first official documented use in America of that professional title. It is also thought to have been used casually in Great Britain at an earlier time. But that was in personal correspondence rather than in connection with an official communiqué between professionals and their client.

Calvert Vaux was satisfied with the title *landscape architect;* Olmsted was not but consented to its use for lack of a more suitable term. Vaux said, "I think it is the art title we want to set art out ahead & make it command its position . . ." Similarly, Horace William Shaler Cleveland, a friend of Olmsted's and practicing landscape architect, resisted calling himself or his profession by that name, opting instead for *landscape engineer* or *landscape designer.* Yet in 1870 he wrote his superb little book, *Landscape Architecture as Applied to the Wants of the West.*

A century later, in 1971, Norman T. Newton, wrote in *Design on the Land* that landscape architecture is "the art—or the science, if preferred—of arranging land, together with the spaces and objects upon it, for safe, efficient, healthful, pleasant human use" (Newton, p. xxi). This was followed in 1977 by the American Society of Landscape Architects (ASLA) which defined *landscape architecture* as:

> *a science and an art [which] embraces those professional activities relating to the systematic planning of land areas, the design of outdoor places and spaces, the conservation of our natural resources and the creation of a more useful, safe and pleasant living environment.* (*ASLA Handbook of Professional Practice,* 1981, p. 19)

Six years later, on November 18, 1983, the following expanded definition was adopted by the trustees of the ASLA:

> *Landscape architecture is the profession which applies artistic and scientific principles to the research, planning, design and management of both natural and built environments. Practitioners of this profession apply creative and technical skills and scientific, cultural and political knowledge in the planned arrangement of natural and constructed elements on the land with a concern for the stewardship and conservation of natural, constructed and human resources. The resulting environments shall serve useful, aesthetic, safe and enjoyable purposes.*
>
> *Landscape architecture may, for the purposes of landscape preservation, development and enhancement, include: investigation, selection, and allocation of land and water resources for appropriate use; feasibility studies; formulation of graphic and written criteria to govern the planning and design of land construction programs; preparation, review, and analysis of master plans for land use and development; pro-*

duction of overall site plans, landscape grading and landscape drainage plans, irrigation plans, planting plans, and construction details; specifications; cost estimates and reports for land development; collaboration in the design of roads, bridges, and structures with respect to the functional and aesthetic requirements of the areas on which they are to be placed; negotiation and arrangement for execution of land area projects; field observation and inspection of land area construction, restoration and maintenance. (*ASLA Members Handbook,* 1990–1991, p. 1)

The International Federation of Landscape Architects (IFLA) defines the landscape architect as one who:

plans and designs the aesthetic layout of land areas for such projects as parks and other recreational facilities, roads, commercial, industrial and residential sites and public buildings: consults with clients, engineers and architects on overall programme; studies site conditions such as nature of soil, vegetation, rock features, drainage and location of buildings; designs landscape, harmonizing improvements with existing land features and buildings and proposed structures; prepares working drawings, specifications and cost estimates for landscaping, including vegetation to be planted and other related site development work; supervises landscaping to ensure that work is carried out according to specifications. The Landscape Architect may specialize in a particular type of landscape architecture such as parks landscaping. (*IFLA Yearbook, 1989,* p. 26)

SECTION 1

INTRODUCTION

Introduction

While teaching landscape architectural history over the past twenty years, countless probing questions have been asked of me by my students. The most challenging were those that caused me to pause and question my own understanding or beliefs about a particular point of inquiry. Such exciting stimulation has been the sustaining force in my continued fascination with the subject of humankind's role in affecting the physical environment around us, particularly those consciously designed accomplishments that are the focus of landscape architectural history.

The frequency with which certain questions are asked ("what," "where," "why," "how," and "by whom?") is the reason "why" this book evolved. It is not always possible for historians to answer with precision a simple question such as "where" or "when." It is even more difficult to be certain about "why" or "how" some of human environmental creations came into existence. How were the great pyramids of Egypt created? When was Stonehenge built, or where, if at all, was Atlantis?

The purpose of this collection of information is to aid students of environmental design history in visualizing and perhaps thereby better understanding certain heretofore undistilled bits of information obtained from the many fine books on this vast area of the history. One can use this book to gain a better sense of the space–time continuum as well as the geographical location or the scale and character of works executed and their chronological relationship to exemplary precedents and antecedents. Within these pages are plans representing a majority of the varied project types which are generally classified as *environmental design* or *landscape architecture*. These include gardens, urban civic spaces, architectural structures, parks, and campuses. At a common scale, one can study and compare an ancient Roman garden with its twentieth-century counterpart or a nineteenth-century park with the plan of a Renaissance villa.

USE OF THIS BOOK

This work was compiled as an aid to those who may have been exposed to many types of history courses during their schooling but have yet to knit all the scattered miscellany together into a whole cloth—to make a correlation of the myriad facts and dates. It is comprised of sections: a series of *timelines* or chronological matrixes that reference the major political, philosophical, technological, and environmentally significant events and creations; an *outline of history* relative to environmental design; *maps* that locate the major environmental design works; *design plan drawings* at two scales, 1 inch equals 100 feet and 1 inch equals 2000 feet; *biographical sketches* of a wide selection of people who have been important in shaping the environment through the recorded history of humankind; and a *glossary* of terms related to landscape architecture, architecture, planning, botany, engineering, and art.

The material included here is not claimed to be all-inclusive but to suggest the major events, intellectual accomplishments, social and political circumstances, and creations relative to each general time period and geographical region. Space does not allow for the many other significant historical facts to be included. Furthermore, if more items were incorporated in the tables, they would suffer an even greater loss of clarity than they may have in their present crowded form. The author hopes that those using this book for review or reference will not be disappointed in not finding specific events or creative works included. This compilation has been a somewhat personal work, with the major items identified for all others who might make use of it.

The separation of events into political, cultural, artistic and scientific pigeonholes is an expedient that fails to convey the real-world interrelationship of all human activities. Each happening or natural occurrence begets other reactions or responses to that fact. There are many overlapping, indivisible relationships that here may seem arbitrary. Please forgive the analogy, but like reading sheet music, one should scan the tables both vertically and horizontally—and from page to page. How fascinating it has been for this author to find, for example, that in the year that Jamestown was founded (1607), Santa Fe (New Mexico) was two years old, and elsewhere, Francis Bacon, Ben Jonson, Shakespeare, and Cervantes were in their most creative years. In the midst of the aesthetic bruhaha surrounding the different camps of landscape garden stylists in England during the third quarter of the eighteenth century (the "picturesque" versus the "beautiful"), we may momentarily lose sight of what was happening in America. Lancelot "Capability" Brown's career (1740–1783) paralleled the American colonists in the midst of their own battle, the struggle to win their independence from British authority. Interestingly, despite Brown's intimacy with the aristocracy, he was opposed to the war with the American colonies—characterizing it an "unfortunate and disgraceful war."

Another point that must be made here is that this volume is admittedly biased toward Western civilization—a risky approach. At the time of this writing, Western society is taking a more holistic world view, and as a result more and more attention is being given to the myriad contributions to human civilization made by peoples from all over the globe. In acknowledgment of that fact, this edition has included a number of citations of non-Western design examples and information about significant thinkers and designers from around the world. In the decade since the previous edition of *Space and Time* (published by the Landscape Architecture Foundation) was published, the important role that members of racial and ethnic minorities and women have played in our nation's history and in landscape architecture have come to the fore. This revised edition includes all the available information about these people and their place in our history.

IMPORTANCE OF DATES

1066, 1215, 1492, 1776, 1787, 1861, 1865, 1917, 1941, 1957, 1963—these dates are indelibly etched into the memory of most Western minds. Almost immediately they recall to consciousness such occurrences as the Battle of Hastings, the Magna Carta, Columbus's "discovery of America," the Declaration of Independence, the U.S. Constitution, the outbreak of the American War Between the States, the assassination of Lincoln, the Bolshevik Revolution (the same year as the birth of John F. Kennedy), the bombing of Pearl Harbor, the first Sputnik, the assassination of Kennedy, and so on.

The Roman philosopher Marcus Aurelius (emperor, A.D. 161–180), wrote, "Time is a river of passing events, aye a rushing torrent." Ninety generations later, the American philosopher Henry David Thoreau wrote, "Time is but the stream I go fishing in." His New England contemporary, Henry Wadsworth Longfellow, said: "What is Time? The shadow on the dial, the striking of the clock, the running of the sand, centuries—these are but arbitrary and outward signs, the measure of Time, not Time itself. Time is the life of the soul." Stephen W. Hawking, the brilliant professor of mathematics at Cambridge University, wrote an entire book about time, *A Brief History of Time* (1988). He compared three concepts of time: *absolute time,* as it was thought to be *prior* to Albert Einstein's theory of relativity ($E = mc^2$); *imaginary time,* of the world of physics, which, like movements in space, allows one to go either forward or backward in time; and *real time,* which holds that the subjective sense of the direction of time, "the direction in which we feel time passes [permits us to] remember the past but not the future." The latter he also called "the psychological arrow of time" (Hawking, pp. 144–145).

Dates—points in time—are abstract fabrications too easily attached to happenings that occurred as a result of a continuum, flowing like Thoreau's stream or Hawking's arrow. *Chronology* is defined as the study of the arrangement of events in time. Real history cannot be pinned down to the ticks of some huge clock. The "fall" of the Roman Empire did not actually happen in a day, on a specific date, but the erosion of the old order moldered away slowly, over several generations during the fifth century A.D. Similarly, the Dark Ages did not begin one morning. Instead, the culture of the Roman era, like a rich tapestry, became both threadbare and unraveled around its edges. The bright threads of the social order wore thin from within the cloth, and the edges of the entire piece began to fray as they were clawed at by the "barbaric" outside forces from the far-flung provinces. The thin intellectual fabric of the Classic times was ultimately set afire, and with the flames went most of the fibers of the former glorious past. The knowledge base was all but destroyed with the destruction of the great libraries, repositories of the world's great writings in Egyptian and Greek as well as Latin.

The various cultures each measure time by their own system. The Jewish calendar marks time from the creation of the world, 3761 B.C. on the Gregorian calendar. Therefore, our year 1993 is year 5754 according to Judaism. The Moslem year 1 is the date of Mohammed's Hegira, his flight from Mecca to Medina—called *annus hegirae* (A.H.)—about the year A.D. 622 on the Gregorian calendar. Thus 1993 is 1371 A.H. on the Moslem calendar. The Egyptian calendar begins in our year 4236 B.C. The Mayan calendar was 3372 years old at the birth of Christ and is therefore in the year 5365 at the time of this writing. The Chinese lunisolar calendar, with its year of the cow, dog, tiger, horse, and so on, based on the Chinese zodiac, was established 2637 years before Christ.

We in the Western world, itself a chauvinistic, abstract, conceptual invention of a very geocentric point of view, mark time by the system conceived by a sixth-century monk, Denis the Little, as taking place either before or after the time of Jesus of Nazareth, Christ—*before Christ* (B.C.) or *anno Domini* (A.D.)—and yet the very birth and crucifixion of Christ is uncertain. We use not His birth or last days on earth; rather, the year 1 is when He was about 6 years old! In fact, there is no year zero in the Christian era since the first year of the era is designated A.D. 1, and the year preceding it is 1 B.C. Despite its Christian basis, the international community today marks time by the Gregorian calendar (365 days, six hours per year). This system was devised by Pope Gregory III in 1582.

TIMELINES OF LANDSCAPE ARCHITECTURAL HISTORY

Section 2 consists of a series of timelines or chronological charts that attempt to relate a selection of environmental design creations with many other significant human events. Creative acts do not simply happen. They occur not in isolation but as a response to certain needs or desires of their time. As Sigfried Giedion stated in 1941, in *Space, Time and Architecture:*

> History is a process; a pattern of living and changing attitudes and interpretations . . . history carries our lives into a wider time dimension [architecture] can give us insight into the consciousness of a period because it is so bound up with the way of life of the period as a whole. Everything in it—fondness for shapes, approaches to building problems—reflects the conditions of the age from which it springs. Design is a product of social, economic, scientific, technological and ethnological factors (p. 7).

For the foregoing reasons the timelines have identified other human events—politics/economics, society/environment, and geography/technology. In addition, style periods and the careers of important designers have been charted.

Few of humankind's creations can be said to be truly original. More often they have tended to be re-creations and adaptations of similar works executed for similar purposes but of another time and place. Such cross-influences, whether by inheritance, borrowing, or outright copying, have enriched the cumulative total of human environmental compositions. The challenge for the devotee of history is to recognize those features and qualities which distinguish that which is truly original while appreciating the meaning of the trade-offs and adaptations of ideas applied elsewhere.

The environmental design works and related events in the series of charts represent, to this author, the real landmarks of quality design or influential human history and have thus been chosen. Within the available literature dealing with historical events, particularly environmental design history, there exists considerable inconsistency regarding the dating of major events. This results, in part, from a genuine lack of verifiable data as well as a certain degree of "author's license" in designating dates of origin. Certain authors tend to indicate the date of completion, while other references represent the date of a design that may not have been constructed until a later date. This author has attempted to determine the most verifiable dates through as wide a search of the literature as practicable.

The timelines have been categorized in such a way as to enable the most expeditious, at-a-glance, visual reference to related information. Although not the most satisfactory arrangement for a comprehensive study of environmental history, the major headings—Ancient Times (4000 B.C.–A.D. 400), The Middle Ages (400–1400), Italy (1400–1700), France (1500–1800), England (1500–1900), and America (1600–2000)—do lend themselves to a manageable review of material already studied in other excellent historical reference texts.

Each page has been organized to display as great a span of time as space permits. The first section, dealing with ancient times, includes listings from earliest human communal living to nearly the fall of the Roman Empire—from 4000 B.C. to A.D. 400. Out of necessity the time scale had to be adjusted so that the greatest number of years could be displayed in a reasonable number of pages. Therefore, each line on the first two charts represents a period of 40 years. On the next two pages (19 and 21) each line represents 10 years. The same scale applies to the medieval section—one line equals 10 years. The sections dealing with Italy, France, England, and the United States to the year 1900 (page 26–51) are at a scale of one line per two years. The twentieth century (1900–2000) (pages 52–56) is at a scale of one line per year.

The fragmentation of historically simultaneous events into geographical subdivisions can be overcome, if the reader desires, by photocopying or even cutting out each chart and splicing them together both longitudinally and latitudinally to form a mosaic as shown in the diagram to the right. In the case of the DESIGNERS and CAREERS portions of each chart, the length of each dark vertical line is intended to correspond to the earliest date of design work attributable to that designer. When lines are shown extending beyond the top or bottom margins, the symbolized period or career is continued on the adjoining page. Whenever possible, historical events have been displayed in the appropriate columns in each section, such as GEOGRAPHY, "Pompeii founded by Greeks"; TECHNOLOGY, "wheeled vehicle invented"; and so on. In certain cases such data may be recorded in a column entitled POLITICS/ECONOMICS or SOCIETY/ENVIRONMENT when its occurrence may have been of significance in a number of circumstances.

A selection of examples from the visual arts and literature have been used to designate important creative works other than environmental designs. These are referenced on the timelines in either the column entitled SOCIETY/ENVIRONMENT or GEOGRAPHY/TECHNOLOGY and are identified by the symbols

Illiad, HOMER	(literature)
David, sc, MICHELANGELO	(sculpture)
Mona Lisa, pt, LEONARDO	(painting)

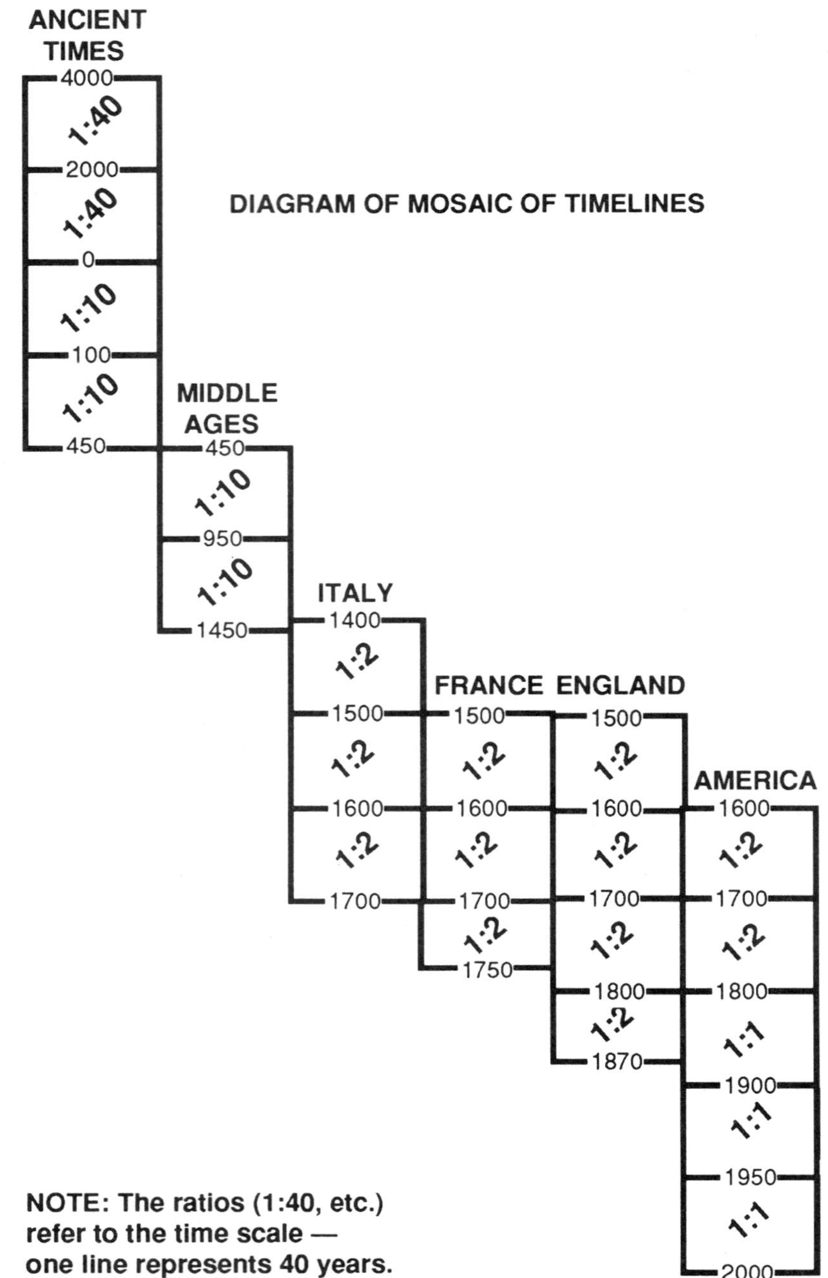

OUTLINE OF LANDSCAPE ARCHITECTURAL HISTORY

To render the breadth and complexity of environmental design history more manageable, the author has distilled Western civilization's environmental design accomplishments into an outline format that comprises Section 3 of the book. The outline of each historical period deals with the environmental and cultural contexts as well as the design expressions and exemplary project types within each period. Also listed in the outline are significant terms relative to the vocabulary of each time frame.

MAPS OF MAJOR WORKS OF LANDSCAPE ARCHITECTURE

Section 4 of the book is comprised of maps of each of the major geographical areas and locations of the important cities and environmental design works of historical relevance. Thus one can easily determine the location and the proximity, or remoteness, of associated design examples. Also, through an examination of the various maps, an interpretation of the influence of geography, latitude, and resultant climatic conditions can be made. The maps may also be of assistance to persons wishing to visit places of special interest since it is often difficult elsewhere to fix locations of many of the examples cited.

IMPORTANCE OF SCALE AND SCALED GROUND PLANS

Section 5 consists of a compilation of scaled ground plans representing a selection of the most important historical environmental design projects. Within the available literature on the history of environmental design and landscape architecture there exists a wealth of pictorial and design plan material to illustrate the character and planimetric organization of nearly all the historically important compositions. Many of these were the original plans drawn by the actual designer or drawn under his or her direction. These not always being available, other design drawings were sometimes produced by contemporary delineators, who may have portrayed a scheme as it appeared to them upon completion. Typically, such drawings were executed in very laborious detail, with remarkable accuracy. Yet since the delineators may have not worked from a ground survey or with scaled architectural documents, the final results sometimes lack true measurable scale. In addition, the variety with which common design elements such as vegetation or water were delineated limits the observer in making comparative use of the renderings. Because, in spatial design, a sense of the scale of a project is so important to understanding its overall character and evaluating its success, the intent here is to represent each composition at a common scale and, as far as possible, with a consistent graphic delineation technique.

Unfortunately, given the wide disparity in the dimensions of the major works, no single scale is suitable to display the vastness of Versailles or the intimacy of Paley Park. Therefore, two scales are used to allow for the variation in sizes of the projects illustrated. The scales are, for the smaller projects, 1:1200, or 1 inch equals 100 feet; and for the larger projects, 1:24,000, or 1 inch equals 2000 feet. The former was chosen because it allowed for the optimum degree of detail to be shown and it is a commonly used working scale among designers and students of design. The latter scale was chosen because it is the most basic scale that the U.S. Department of the Interior uses for its U.S. Geological Survey (USGS) 7.5-minute quadrangle maps. Since these maps are so widely available and on them one can locate nearly all large-scale American design projects, they readily allow for a comparison of overall sizes. More interestingly, if examined along with the appropriate USGS sheet, a comparison can be made between an original composition and any subsequent modifications occurring between the time of its origin and today. On the pages opposite each plan drawn at 1:1200 scale is shown a dimensioned square representing 1 acre, or 0.4047 hectare. This provides a means of relating each of the schemes drawn at that scale. Each of the 1:24,000 scale plans can be related by referring to the square opposite them, which represents 100 acres, or 40.47 hectares.

To facilitate comparisons between plans, a common orientation has been used when possible. Most of the plans have been oriented with north at the top of the page, with the exception of the few whose dimensions or configuration required that they be realigned rather than cropped. Listed to the left of each of the scaled plan drawings are the basic data relative to each, such location and date or dates of the design or development of each example, together with the names of the designer(s), client(s), and approximate size of each in both acres and hectares.

Due to limitations of space, not all historically important design creations that this writer believes should be included are to be found in this book. Those omitted were either too large to be accommodated at the 1:1200 scale (where dimensions of even a representative portion of the overall plan exceeded 850 feet by 1100 feet and therefore could not be accommodated on the standard 8½ by 11-inch page) or were not sufficiently grand to be of any consequence if displayed at a scale of 1:24,000 (where dimensions were less than approximately 5000 feet square).

Through the historical perspective presented here, perhaps the reader can incorporate a sense of time and space not only with the works of humankind's past but also with his or her own contemporary work and surroundings.

BIOGRAPHICAL SKETCHES

The section of biographical sketches (Section 6) is a new addition to this revised edition of *Space and Time*. It grew out of the author's concern that the major contributors of the creative works that comprise this book be better understood and recognized for their contribution to the history of environmental design. At the beginning of the process of compiling these data, it was thought that the number of notables that would comprise the list might perhaps be four or five dozen names. As the research continued and the field of inquiry expanded, the author was encouraged by several reviewers of the biographical sketches not to overlook the contributions of this person or that person until it swelled to the present size. There are, at this writing, over 280 people included in the group.

It is hoped that no major figure in the broad field of landscape architectural history has been slighted by being left out of this study. It was difficult to decide who among those living and still actively practicing landscape architecture to include and who to leave out. It was assumed that perhaps in another few years this work can be revised and the list of names increased to include those deserving persons who, for lack of space, were not included here.

A number of entries may at first seem obscure to some readers, but when the role of such persons is considered in the wider context of environmental design, their contribution is significant. Most people cited were, or are, shapers of the environment: planners, architects, or landscape architects. A few persons included were important in their time through their influence as patrons or clients who commissioned the great designers. Among that former group are Queen Hatshepsut and Amenhotep III, Egyptian rulers and among the first patrons of the arts we know by name; members of the Medici family; Pope Sixtus V; King Louis XIV of France; and many others. The activities of many amateur designers in both England and America who designed the residences and grounds of their own country seats during the eighteenth and nineteenth centuries are summarized. That group includes a number of leading statesmen in the United States, such as Sir Francis Nicholson, George Washington, and Thomas Jefferson. Other people included have been important to the field of landscape architecture through the immeasurable effect that each had upon our ecological thinking, aesthetic taste, and art appreciation in their time. Examples of such persons are Leone Battista Alberti during the Italian Renaissance; Jean-Jacques Rousseau, Edmund Burke, and Joseph Addison during the formative stages of the English landscape gardening movement; and in our own day, Jane Jacobs, Aldo Leopold, and Ian McHarg. Artists such as the landscape painters Claude Lorrain, Nicolas Poussin, and Salvator Rosa were also important in the English design reform period, and therefore brief biographical sketches of their careers are included in this portion of the book. In the United States during the first half of the nineteenth century, many members of the Hudson River school of landscape painters helped to sensitize our eyes to the beauties of the natural wilderness; therefore, the roles of these persons have been documented in brief biographical sketches. Architects and sculptors, from ancient times to the present, have played a very large role in the changes made in humankind's design on the land. Among the architect-sculptors to be found in these pages are such Renaissance artists as Michelangelo, Raphael, and Bernini of the sixteenth and seventeenth centuries, and the Japanese-American Isamu Noguchi and Brazilian Roberto Burle Marx of the twentieth century.

A substantial portion of the information presented in this section has been brought together in one volume for the first time. It is hoped that readers will think of it as what it is, a beginning. This is the basis of a larger work, already in progress: that of compiling the information on many persons whose efforts have been overlooked for too long in our history of landscape architecture.

GLOSSARY

The specialized vocabulary of the design fields, together with the confusion one experiences when dealing with multicultural and multidisciplinary information, can be overwhelming without a means of clarification. Thus a glossary of related terms has been compiled which includes definitions from the fields of landscape architecture, architecture, planning, history, art, engineering, ecology, and horticulture, as well as those significant foreign language words or expressions that are critical to an understanding of the subject.

REFERENCES

This book has only been possible because of the tremendous wealth of good reference material relative to the field of landscape architecture available today. This was not so true just a few decades ago. As one can tell by examining the references listed at the back of this book, many of the sources available were published within the past twenty years. This volume is not intended to be *the* history, but is *another* history—albeit one with a particular, if somewhat personal point of view.

It might be of help to the reader to know which authors and titles were most helpful in assembling the data between these covers. Therefore, at the risk of leaving out some equally worthy books, I suggest below sources that I recommend as a point of beginning—certainly not an all-inclusive library for the student of landscape architecture history. One should read as many of those cited as one's interest and time permit. Through exposure to these other authors' thoughts, one may gain as wide a perspective as possible and thus profit from the points of view of the various thinkers on the subject. Perhaps needless to say in a visual field of study such as this, upon consulting the great range of literature sources, one cannot help but benefit from the rich assortment of pictorial information to be enjoyed in the library of works in the field of landscape architecture. Probe as widely and deeply as your appetite for learning permits.

Among the best general introductions to the field of landscape architecture are John Simond's *Landscape Architecture,* second edition (McGraw-Hill, 1983) and his *Earthscape: A Manual of Environmental Planning* (McGraw-Hill, 1978). The former was almost the only substantial textbook available for those of us who were students in the 1960s, and *Earthscape* is excellent because of the many case studies included and its fine illustrations throughout. Michael Laurie's *An Introduction to Landscape Architecture* (American Elsevier, 1986) has a good historical overview and a very well-rounded summation of the field. First published in 1917, *An Introduction to the Study of Landscape Design* by Henry Hubbard and his wife, Theodora Kimball (Hubbard Educational Trust, revised edition, 1967), provides a good insight into the mode of thinking among practicing and teaching landscape architects in the United States seventy-five years ago. *Gardens Are for People* by Thomas Church (McGraw-Hill, revised edition, 1983) is also an excellent source of inspiration from the California perspective of one of this country's greatest designers of the landscape. Ian McHarg's *Design with Nature* (John Wiley & Sons, revised edition, 1992) is a classic among the literature on ecologically based planning and design. With its many historical examples, this is essential reading for all persons interested in contemporary issues as well as historical landscape architecture.

For a solid international historical overview of garden design and landscape architecture, the definitive work is by Baroness Marie Louise Gothein, *A History of Garden Art* (J.M. Dent & Sons, 1928), first published in 1917. This work, although finished before the twentieth century unfolded, is comprised of some of the most solid text and illustrations available today. Among the many outstanding British histories are Derek Clifford's *A History of Garden Design* (Praeger, revised edition, 1967); *The Garden: An Illustrated History* by Julia Berrall (Viking Penguin, 1978), with its many vivid color plates; Christopher Thacker's *The History of Gardens* (University of California Press, 1979); and *The Landscape of Man* by Geoffrey and Susan Jellicoe (Thames & Hudson, second edition, 1987). The Australian husband and wife co-authors John and Ray Oldham wrote *Gardens in Time* (Lansdowne Press, 1980), which has an especially convincing discussion of the importance of Asian design in Western garden design.

American works on landscape architecture history are regrettably few in number. The best and most complete among them are *Design on the Land: The Development of Landscape Architecture* by Norman T. Newton (Harvard/Belknap, 1971). This 700-page tome is the most inclusive book we have to date. It is well written, even though it rings with Professor Newton's Harvard Square accent on the subject.

John R. Stilgoe's *Common Landscape of America, 1580 to 1845* (Yale University Press, 1982), is the most substantial piece of U.S. history to be written about the vernacular landscape of this country. It is crammed with a remarkable volume of information and is extremely readable for either the layperson or the scholar. John Brinkerhoff Jackson's *American Space* (W.W. Norton, 1972) is a marvelous work of literature about the American landscape, and it covers much of the time period not encompassed by Stilgoe.

Rudy J. and Joy P. Favretti's *Landscapes and Gardens for Historic Buildings* (American Association for State and Local History, 1978) is a major contribution to the area of colonial American gardens, and Walter L. Creese's *The Crowning of America: Eight Great Spaces and Their Buildings* (Princeton University Press, 1985) is a fascinating examination of the wonders of such locales as the Hudson River Valley, the Yosemite Valley, and the University of Virginia. John Reps' *The Making of Urban America* (Princeton University Press, 1965) is the standard reference for the history of urban form in the United States. It is also a gold mine of city plans and early views of towns and cities in all sections of the country.

The recently published *American Landscape Architecture: Designers and Places,* edited by William H. Tishler (The Preservation Press of the National Trust for Historic Preservation, 1989), is a well-rounded compilation of brief biographies of twenty-one of this country's most notable shapers of the landscape. Included are some of the too often overlooked worthies, such as Thomas Jefferson, Ellen Biddle Shipman, Charles A. Platt, Jacob Weidenmann, and Henry V. Hubbard. This author owes much to the vault of information to be found within the pages of Tishler's compact book.

H. W. Janson's *History of Art* (Prentice Hall, 1969) is a work that must not be neglected by those persons searching for information about the influence that the fine arts have had on this field. Elizabeth B. Kassler's *Modern Gardens and the Landscape* (Museum of Modern Art, revised edition, 1984) is one of the best collections of descriptions and pictures of modern landscape architectural design.

Two general history sources that this author has found indispensable are *The Outline of History* by H. G. Wells (Doubleday, 1971), and *The Timetables of American History,* Laurence Urdang, editor (Simon and

Schuster, 1981). Another two books that this author has enjoyed and turned to for many important points of clarification about our world are Jacob Bronowski's *The Ascent of Man* (Little, Brown and Company, 1973) and Stephen W. Hawking's *A Brief History of Time: From the Big Bang to Black Holes* (Bantam Books, 1988).

Encyclopedic references that are musts include John Claudius Loudon's *An Encyclopaedia of Gardening* (Garland Publishing, 1822, reprinted 1982), *A Dictionary of Landscape Architecture* by Baker H. Morrow (University of New Mexico Press, 1987), and Warner Marsh's *Landscape Vocabulary* (Miramar, 1964). The most comprehensive reference work summarizing the breadth and depth of the history of garden design and landscape architecture all over the globe is *The Oxford Companion to Gardens* by Geoffrey and Susan Jellicoe with Patrick Goode and Michael Lancaster (Oxford University Press, 1986). This monumental collection of essays, garden descriptions, biographies, and definitions is the best volume of its kind anywhere. Its bibliography (pages 629–635) is categorized according to over 120 headings, from geographical to biographical to technical topics. The indispensable source for definitions included in the glossary at the back of this book was the *Oxford English Dictionary, Second Edition,* edited by J. A. Simpson and E. S. C. Weiner (Clarendon Press, 1989).

Several good biographical information references worth noting are *The Dictionary of American Biography,* Dumas Malone, editor (Charles Scribner's Sons, 1936); *The Macmillan Encyclopedia of Architects,* edited by Adolf K. Placzek (Macmillan, 1982); Laura Wood Roper's *FLO: A Biography of Frederick Law Olmsted* (Johns Hopkins University Press, 1973); *Park Maker: A Life of Frederick Law Olmsted* (Macmillan, 1977) by Elizabeth Stevenson; and *Landscape and Gardens, Women Who Made a Difference,* Miriam Rutz, editor (Proceedings of the Conference on Women in Landscape Architecture, Michigan State University, East Lansing, 1987).

Architectural sources of unshakable repute are Sigfried Giedion's *Space, Time and Architecture* (Harvard University Press, 1941) and Sir Bannister Fletcher's *A History of Architecture,* 19th edition, (Butterworth, 1987). Edmund Bacon's *The Design of Cities* (Viking Penguin, revised edition 1974) is one of the best works relative to urban design and is beautifully illustrated.

CONCLUSION

The author hopes that those using this book will find its content a useful resource for the review of material previously learned elsewhere and informative on a number of historical facts that one may not have read or seen before. Students of landscape architecture history should read a number of the very comprehensive reviews of world history and art history as well as textbooks assigned for a specific class. Only by reading as wide a diversity of books as possible can one obtain a variety of viewpoints. In doing so, one will also avail oneself of a rich assortment of visual information. Through ground plans, paintings, sketches, sections, and elevations, the student of history can gain a reasonably clear mental picture of the organization and character of places far, far away and long, long ago.

Practicing landscape architects might find the scaled plans in this book useful, as they can compare exemplary historical precedents with their own work "on the boards," as well as other contemporary design projects. With very little effort, proposed plans can be enlarged or reduced in scale by many of our widely available photocopying machines. The cost of color reproduction of plans and illustrations in this book would have made it prohibitive for use as a study reference. However, the practicing landscape architect could color-render plans from this book in the same scheme as used on their own plans and review these with clients for purposes of comparison.

It is hoped that persons other than students of landscape architecture will also find this book of value. Architects, planners, and civil engineers might see opportunities for using the scaled plans, the timelines, the glossary, and even the reference list.

SECTION 2

TIMELINES OF LANDSCAPE ARCHITECTURAL HISTORY

Timelines of Landscape Architectural History

ANCIENT (4000 B.C.–A.D. 450)

In this section two different time scales are used. The period 4000 B.C. to the year 1 (pages 15 and 17) is at a scale of one line per 40 years. The section 600 B.C.–A.D. 450 (pages 19 and 21) is at a scale of one line per 10 years. Included in this section are the following design style periods:

- Golden age of Egypt
- Pyramid age
- Golden age of Babylon
- Golden age of Crete
- Golden age of Greece
- Hellenic
- Hellenistic
- "Greco-Roman"
- Golden age of Rome
- Persian

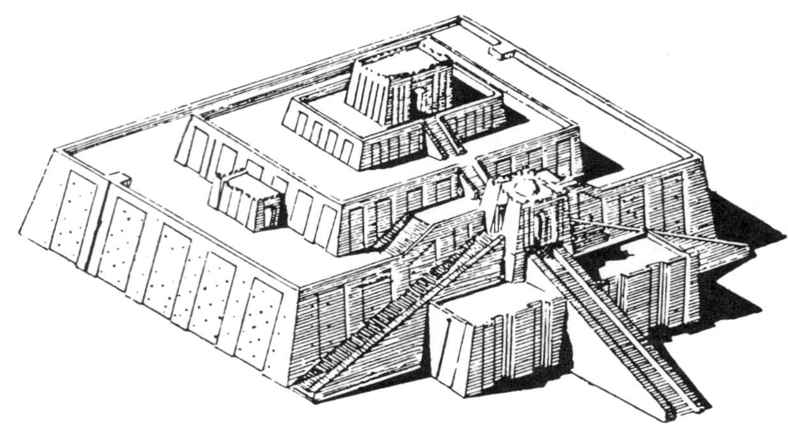

Figure 1. *Ziggurat of Ur, Sumeria.*

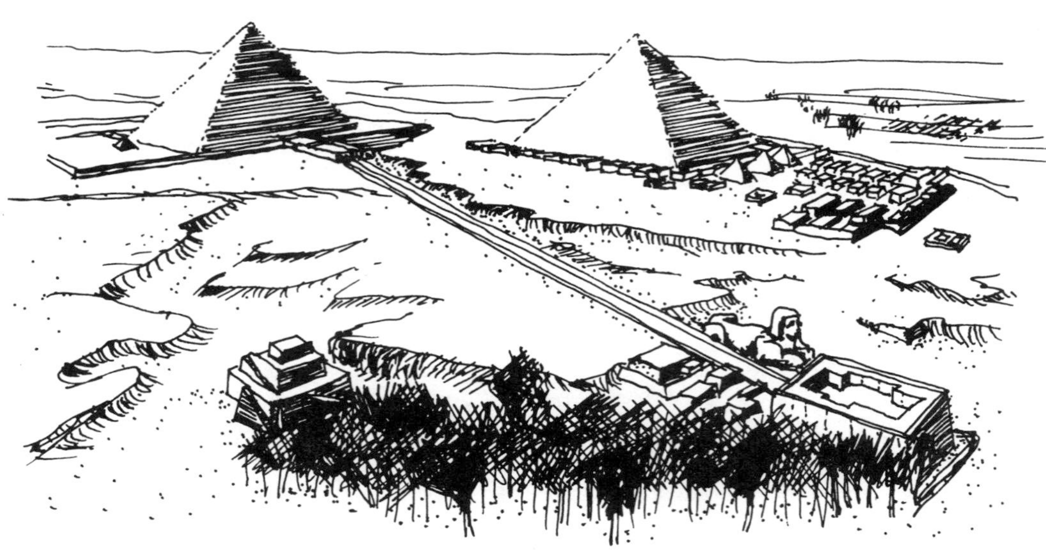

Figure 2. *The Pyramids of Giza, Egypt.*

ANCIENT TIMES (Egypt, Mesopotamia) 4000BC - 2000BC

Politics Economics	Society Environment	Geography Technology	Date	Historical Period	Environmental Design	Designers
	NEOLITHIC PERIOD 4000-3300 EASTERN MEDITERRANEAN MESOLITHIC PERIOD, NORTHERN EUROPE NEOLITHIC EASTERN MEDITERRANEAN	SUMERIANS SETTLE MESOPOT.	4000			
		COPPER USED, EGYPT & MESO.	3900			
	JEWISH CALENDAR, 1st DAY, 3760 BC		3800			
			3700			
			3600			
	PROTO-LITERATE PERIOD, 3500-3000 BC PROTO-LITERATE PERIOD	CUNEIFORM WRITING, SUMERIA	3500			
	MAYAN CALENDAR, 1st DAY, 3372		3400			
		BRONZE TOOLS BRONZE AGE	3300			
			3200			
FIRST DYNASTY, EGYPT 3100-2181 1st DYNASTY		MEMPHIS FOUNDED HIEROGLYPHICS INV'D, EGYPT WHEEL INVENTED, ASIA MINOR PAPER INVENTED, EGYPT	3100			
	NEOLITHIC 3000-1500 SPAIN & NORTHERN EUROPE	CALENDAR INVENTED, EGYPT STONE CONSTRUCTION BRICK MAKING, EGYPT	3000		ZIGGURATS BUILT IN SUMER (MESOPOTAMIA) STONE ALIGNMENTS, CARNAC, FRANCE	SUMERIANS
			2900			
OLD KINGDOM, EGYPT OLD KINGDOM EGYPT TRADING w/ BABYLON		WHEELED VEHICLE, SUMER UR, SUMER (IRAQ) FOUNDED 1st TOTALLY STONE BUILDING	2800		STEPPED PYRAMID OF ZOSER, SAQQARA, EGYPT	EGYPTIANS
			2700	PYRAMID AGE	GREAT PYRAMID OF CHEOPS, GIZA, EYGPT	IMHOTEP
		COPPER MINED, SINAI SAILING BOATS, EGYPT	2600		GREAT SPHINX, GIZA, EGYPT	EGYPTIANS
FIRST DYNASTY OF UR, 2500-2350			2500			
SUMERIAN EMPIRE			2400			
			2300		ZIGGURAT AT UR, SUMERIA (IRAQ)	SUMERIANS
			2200			
MIDDLE KINGDOM-EGYPT 2065-1785			2100	EGYPT GOLDEN AGE OF ART		
	MACEDONIANS SETTLE IN GREECE		2000		MORTUARY TEMPLE OF MENTUHOTEP, DEIR EL-BAHRI, EGYPT	MENTOHOTEP II

Figure 3. Residential gardens of an official of Amenhotep III, Egypt.

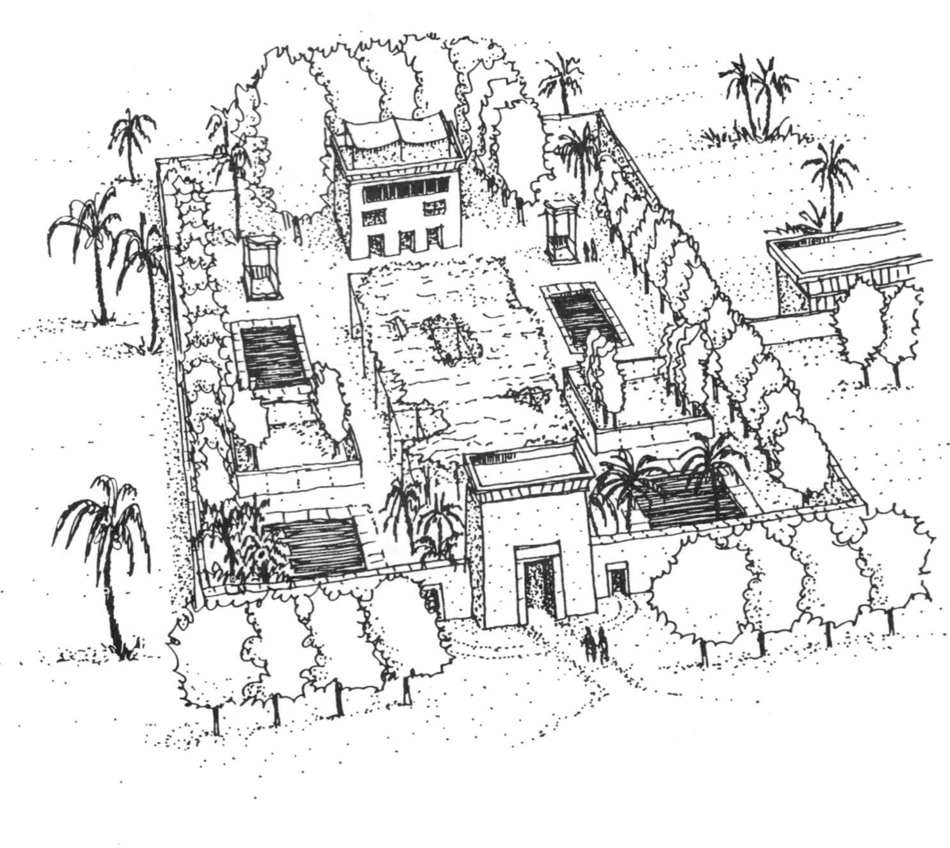

Figure 4. Hanging Gardens of Babylon.

ANCIENT TIMES (Mesopotamia, Greece, Rome) 2000BC - 1BC

Politics Economics	Society Environment	Geography Technology	Date	Historical Period	Environmental Design	Designers
MIDDLE KINGDOM	NEOLITHIC AGE	HORSE FIRST RIDDEN, PERSIA; BRONZE AGE	2000	GOLDEN AGE OF ART, EGYPT	STONE CIRCLE, AVEBURY, ENGLAND	
FIRST DYNASTY BABYLON, 1900-1600			1900			
					STONEHENGE, WILTSHIRE, ENGLAND	DRUIDS
HAMMURABI RULED BABYLON	BABYLON THE CULTURAL CENTER OF SUMER	JERUSALEM	1800		ROCK-CUT TOMBS, BENI HASAN, EGYPT	
	Written Law Codes, HAMMURABI, 1750					
		KNOSSOS, CRETE LEVELED BY EARTHQUAKE	1700			
		HORSE USED IN EGYPT				
	GOLDEN AGE OF CRETE 1600-1400		1600	GOLDEN AGE OF CRETE	PALACE AT KNOSSOS, CRETE	MINOANS
EGYPTIAN EMPIRE, 1567-1085	*Snake Goddess*, sc, KNOSSOS				ISFAHAN	SHAH ABBAS I
					TEMPLE OF AMUN, KARNAK, THEBES, EGYPT	EGYPTIANS
QUEEN HATSHEPSUT,1503-1450		IRON TOOLS, HITTITES	1500		MORTUARY TEMPLE OF QUEEN HATSHEPSUT, DEIR EL-BAHRI, EGYPT	SENEMUT
EYGPTIAN EMPIRE						
AMENHOTEP III, 1411-1375	HEIGHT OF EGYPTIAN PROSPERITY					
1st METAL COINS, ASSYRIA	*Ten Commandments*, MOSES	IRRIGATION INVENTED, ASSYRIA	1400		TEMPLE TO AMUN-RE, LUXOR, THEBES, EGYPT	AMENHOTEP III
AMENHOTEP IV, 1375-1362	SUN WORSHIP BEGINS, EGYPT	PULLEY INVENTED, ASSYRIA			RESIDENTIAL GARDENS, OFFICER OF AMENHOTEP III	EGYPTIANS
TUTANKAHMUN, 1361-1352					TEMPLE OF AMUN-RE, KARNAK, THEBES, EGYPT	EGYPTIANS
RAMESSES II, 1304-1237	*Ramesses II*, sc, ABU SIMBEL		1300		ABU SIMBEL ROCK TEMPLES	RAMESSES II
EXODUS OF HEBREWS FROM EGYPT					LION GATE, CITADEL OF TIRYNS, MYCENAE	
		IRON USED IN EGYPT	1200			
TROJAN WAR, GREECE						
		GREEKS COLONIZE ASIA MINOR	1100			
KING SAUL, 1072-1032						
KING DAVID, 1032-992						
ASSYRIAN EMPIRE, 1000-612	*Old Testament*, HEBREWS	CONCEPT OF "PARADISE" OR "GARDEN OF EDEN," MESOPOTAMIA	1000		ROYAL HUNTING PARKS, ASSYRIA	ASSYRIANS
SOLOMON RULED ISRAEL, 973-933						
ASSYRIAN EMPIRE			900			
	Iliad & Odyssey, HOMER	CARTHAGE FOUNDED BY PHOENICIANS			GREAT MOSQUE, SAMARRA	AL-MUTAWAKKIL
	FIRST OLYMPIC GAMES, GREECE	BAGHDAD	800		LA VENTA, MEXICO	OLMECS
		ROME				
		SYRACUSE, SICILY			CITADEL OF SARGON II, KHORSABAD, ASSYRIA	ASSYRIANS
ATTICA (ATHENS) UNIFIED			700	GREEK COLONIZATION 700-200	BABYLON REBUILT	BABYLONIANS
ASSYRIANS INVADE EGYPT		BYZANTIUM			TIKAL, GUATEMALA	MAYANS
BABYLONIAN EMPIRE, 625-538					TOWER OF BABEL, BABYLON	BABYLONIANS
NEBUCHADNEZZER, 605-561	NINEVEH (ASSYRIAN CAPITAL) DESTROYED	DORIC ORDER	600		HANGING GARDENS, BABYLON	BABYLONIANS
		WINDMILLS GRIND CORN, PERSIA			BASILICA, PAESTUM, ITALY	GREEKS
PERSIAN EMPIRE, 539-331					AGORA, ATHENS	GREEKS
LAST EGYPTIAN DYNASTY	ROMAN REPUBLIC, 510-27	CONFUCIUS BORN, 551			TEMPLE OF APOLLO, DELPHI	GREEKS
PERSIA CONQUERS EYGPT, GREECE, SUMERIA, BABYLON	SOPHICLES, 496-406		500		TEMPLE OF POSEIDON, PAESTUM, ITALY	GREEKS
	The Discus Thrower, sc, MYRON			AGE OF PERICLES 460-429	PALACE OF DARIUS, PERSEPOLIS	PERSIANS
GREECE INDEPENDENT OF PERSIA	HIPPOCRATES, 460-370	POMPEII FOUNDED BY GREEKS			PARTHENON, ACROPOLIS, ATHENS, GREECE	ICTINUS
PELOPONESIAN WARS, GREECE	PLATO, 424-347	SOCRATES, 469-399	400		ERECHTHEUM, ACROPOLIS, ATHENS, GREECE	MNESICLES
		IONIC ORDER			OLYNTHUS & RHODES PLANNED	GREEKS
ALEXANDER THE GREAT, 336-323	ARISTOTLE, 384-322	GREECE OCCUPIES PERSIA, SYRIA, EGYPT & INDIA			THEATER OF EPIDAURUS	GREEKS
					1st AQUEDUCT, ROME	ROMANS
		EUCLID BORN, 323	300		APPIAN WAY, ROME	ROMANS
ROME CONTROLS ITALIAN PENINSULA		CORINTIAN ORDER			GREAT WALL OF CHINA STARTED	
ROME CONQUERS SPAIN	*Dying Gaul*, sc	ROSETTA STONE CARVED, EGPYT			TEMPLE OF HURUS, EDFU, EGYPT	EGYPTIANS
			200		POMPEII REBUILT	ROMANS
	Nike of Samothrace, sc				ALTAR OF ZEUS & ATHENA, PERGAMON	GREEKS
ROME CONQUERS GREECE	*Venus de Milo*, sc	CONCRETE, ROMANS			GREAT STUPA, SANCHI, INDIA	
ROME INVADES BRITAIN	CICERO, 106-43		100		FORUM ROMANUM, ROME	ROMANS
	VERGIL, 70-19				TEMPLE OF DEVINE JULIUS, ROME	ROMANS
JULIUS CAESAR, DICTATOR 48-44	HORACE, 65-8				CAESAR'S IMPERIAL FORUM, ROME	ROMANS
CAESAR AUGUSTUS, 27BC-14AD	VITRUVIUS, 31BC-14AD				HORACE'S VILLA, ROME	ROMANS
	JESUS OF NAZARETH, 6BC-29AD		0			

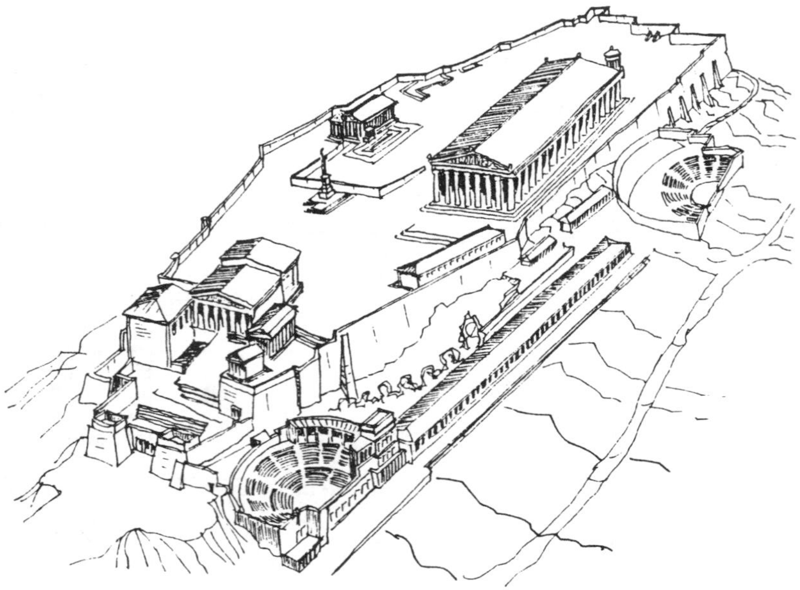

Figure 5. *Acropolis, Athens, Greece.*

Figure 6. *Agora, Assos, Turkey.*

ANCIENT TIMES (Mesopotamia, Greece, Rome) 600BC-100BC

Politics Economics	Society Environment	Geography Technology	Date	Historical Period	Environmental Design	Designers
BABYLONIAN EMPIRE 625-538		GREEK COLONIZATION 700-200	600	GOLDEN AGE OF BABYLON	HANGING GARDENS OF BABYLON	BABYLONIANS
			590		TIKAL, GUATEMALA	MAYANS
		1st URBAN SEWERS, ROME	580			
			570			
			560		BASILICA, PAESTUM, ITALY	GREEKS
PERSIAN EMPIRE			550		AGORA, ATHENS	GREEKS
					TEMPLE OF APOLLO, TREASURY OF SIPHNIAUS, DELPHI	GREEKS
					TEMPLE OF DEMETER, PAESTUM	GREEKS
BATTLE OF MARATHON	SOPHICLES 496-406 PERICLES, 490-429		500			
	CLASSICAL PERIOD, 480-323			HELLENIC / CLASSICAL; GOLDEN AGE OF GREECE		
GREECE GAINS INDEPEND. FROM PERSIA					MILETUS REBUILT	HIPPODAMUS
	SOCRATES 469-399				PIRAEUS PLANNED (PORT CITY OF ATHENS)	HIPPODAMUS
	AGE OF PERICLES 460-429			AGE OF PERICLES; GOLDEN AGE	TEMPLE OF POSEIDON, TEMPLE OF HERA, PAESTUM	GREEKS
	HIPPOCRATES 460-370					
			450		POMPEII FOUNDED AS GREEK COLONY	GREEKS
					ACROPOLIS, ATHENS, 450-400BC	CALLICRATES
PELOPONESIAN WARS ATHENS,SPARTA,CORINTH					PARTHENON 447-432BC	ICTINUS
					OLYNTHUS, PLANNED CITY	GREEKS
	PLATO 427-347				ERECHTHEUM, ACROPOLIS, ATHENS	GREEKS
					SELINUS REBUILT	GREEKS
					RHODES, PLANNED CITY	GREEKS
	TRIAL OF SOCRATES		400			
	ARISTOTLE 384-322	IONIC ORDER				
		PLATO FOUNDS ACADEMY, ATHENS				
		ARISTOTLE JOINS ACADEMY				
			350		PRIENE, PLANNED CITY	GREEKS
					THEATER OF DIONYSOS, ATHENS	GREEKS
ALEXANDER THE GREAT, 336-323		GREECE OCCUPIES PERSIA, SYRIA, EGYPT, INDIA			OSTIA PLANNED (PORT CITY OF ROME)	ROMANS
					CIRCUS MAXIMUS, ROME	ROMANS
	EUCLID 323-285	CORINTHIAN ORDER		HELLENISTIC	1st AQUEDUCT, AQUA APPIA, ROME	ROMANS
					APPIAN WAY, ROME TO BRINDISI	ROMANS
			300			
					DURA EUROPUS, PLANNED FORTRESS COLONY	GREEKS
ROME CONTROLS ITALIAN PENINSULA 265						
PUNIC WARS 264-201						
ROMAN REPUBLIC			250			
ROME CONQUERS SPAIN 206						
			200		PYRAMIDS OF TEOTIHUACAN, MEXICO	MAYANS
	Nike of Samothrace, sc(Winged Victory)				POMPEII, REBUILDING, 200-100BC	ROMANS
	Aphrodite of Milo, sc (Venus de Milo)	CONCRETE, ROMANS	150	"GRECO-ROMAN"		
		AQUEDUCT 60 MILES LONG, ROME			AQUA MARCIA, ROME	ROMANS
ROME CONQUERS GREECE 146						
ROME INVADES BRITAIN						
	CICERO 106-43		100		FORUM ROMANUM, 100-29BC	ROMANS

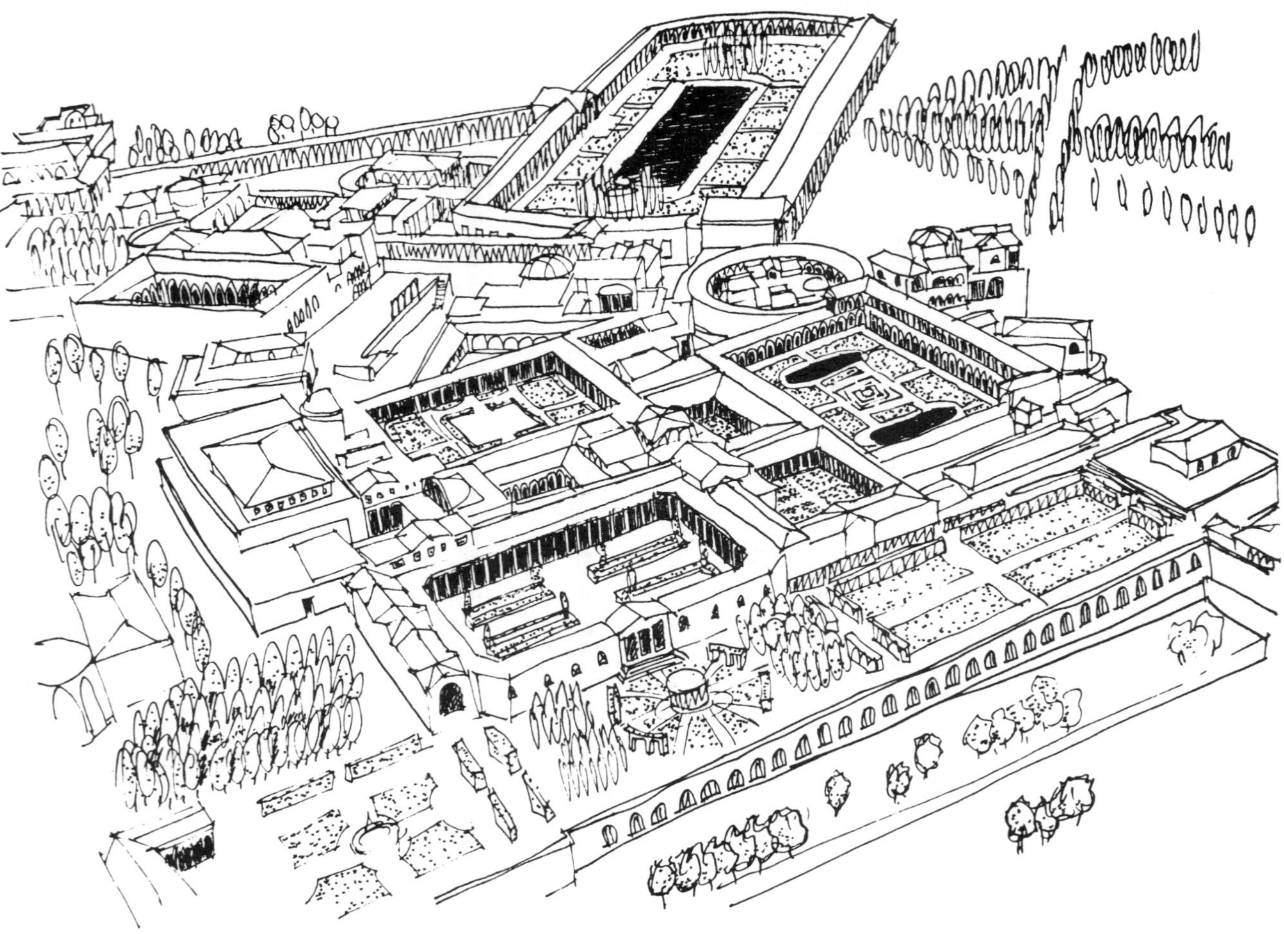

Figure 7. *Hadrian's Villa, Tivoli, Italy.*

ANCIENT TIMES (Rome) 100BC - 400AD

Politics Economics	Society Environment	Geography Technology	Date	Historical Period	Environmental Design	Designers
ROMAN REPUBLIC			100	HELLENISTIC; "GRECO-ROMAN"		
			90		TEMPLE OF VESTA (SIBYL), TIVOLI	ROMANS
			80		TABULARIUM, FORUM ROMANUM,	ROMANS
PALESTINE BECOMES ROMAN PROVINCE	HORACE, 65-8		70			
		ROME INVADES BRITAIN	60		BASILICA AEMELIA, FORUM ROMANUM,	ROMANS
JULIUS CAESAR, DICTATOR, 48-44			50		BASILICA JULIA. FORUM ROMANUM	ROMANS
ASSASSINATION OF CAESAR					CAESAR'S IMPERIAL FORUM	ROMANS
EYGPT MADE ROMAN PROV.	VITRUVIUS, 31BC-14AD				CIRCUS MAXIMUS, ROME	ROMANS
CAESAR AUGUSTUS 27BC-14AD 1st EMPEROR					HORACE'S VILLA	
					TEMPLE OF DIVINE JULIUS, FORUM ROMANUM	ROMANS
					MAISON CARREE, NIMES, FRANCE	ROMANS
SPAIN CONQUERED BY ROMANS	JESUS OF NAZARETH, 6BC-29AD		0			
PAX ROMANA					AUGUSTUS'S IMPERIAL FORUM	ROMANS
	de Architectura, VITRUVIUS				CLAUDIAN AQUEDUCT, ROME	ROMANS
	CRUCIFIXION OF JESUS					
CALIGULA, 37-41	*New Testament*				LONDON FOUNDED	ROMANS
CLAUDIUS, 41-54		ROME CONQUERS BRITAIN				
			50		PONT DU GARD, NIMES, FRANCE	ROMANS
NERO, 54-68					HOUSE OF VETTII, POMPEII	ROMANS
					GOLDEN HOUSE OF NERO, ROME	ROMANS
	GREAT FIRE OF ROME, 64	EARTHQUAKE DAMAGES POMPEII			PLINY THE YOUNGER'S VILLA, TUSCANY	ROMANS
JERUSALEM DESTROYED BY ROMANS		MT. VESUVIUS ERUPTS, POMPEII			POMPEII REBUILT AFTER EARTHQUAKE	ROMANS
		GLASS 1st USED IN WINDOWS		GOLDEN AGE OF ROME	ARCH OF TITUS, ROME	ROMANS
	PLINY THE ELDER, 23-79				COLOSSEUM, ROME 75-82	ROMANS
TRAJAN, 98-117		ROMAN EMPIRE'S MAXIMUM SIZE	100		PLINY THE YOUNGER'S VILLA, LAURENTINUM	ROMANS
					TRAJAN'S IMPERIAL FORUM 98-113	ROMANS
					TRAJAN'S COLUMN	ROMANS
HADRIAN, 117-138	PLINY THE YOUNGER, 62-113				HADRIAN'S VILLA, TIVOLI 117-138	ROMANS
					PANTHEON, ROME 120-124	ROMANS
					HADRIAN'S WALL, ENGLAND	ROMANS
ROMAN EMPIRE	POPULATION OF ROME 1,200,000					
			150			
					STADIUM, ATHENS	
MARCUS AURELIUS, 161-180	*Marcus Aurelius*, sc, (ROMAN)					
BEGINNING OF COLLAPSE OF ROMAN EMPIRE						
					TIMGAD, ALGERIA, PLANNED	ROMANS
SEPTIMUS SEVERUS, 193-221					COLUMN OF MARCUS AURELIUS, ROME	ROMANS
CARACALLA, 198-217			200		ARCH OF SEPTIMUS SEVERUS, ROME	ROMANS
					BATHS OF CARACALLA, ROME	ROMANS
HANNIBAL INVADES ITALY	EDICT OF CARACALLA, 212					
			250		PYRAMIDS OF TEOTIHUACAN, MEXICO	MAYANS
	PERIOD OF PERSECUTION OF CHRISTIANS				SANCTUARY OF JUPITER, BAALBEK, SYRIA	CATACOMBS, ROME
DIOCLETIAN (EAST), 284-305						
					BATHS OF DIOCLETIAN, ROME	ROMANS
			300		PALACE OF DIOCLETIAN, YUGOSLAVIA	ROMANS
CONSTANTINE, 308-337					BASILICA OF CONSTANINE, ROME	ROMANS
					ARCH OF CONSTANTINE, ROME	ROMANS
	EDICT OF MILAN, 313, CHRISTIANITY RECOGNIZED				CHURCH OF HOLY SEPULCHRE, JERUSALEM	ZENOBIUS
ROMAN EMPIRE RULED FROM CONSTANTINOPLE		CONSTANTINOPLE, CAPITAL OF EASTERN ROMAN EMPIRE			OLD ST. PETER'S BASILICA, ROME	ROMANS
			350	BYZANTIUM		
ROMAN EMPIRE DIVIDED INTO EAST AND WEST					ST. PAUL'S OUTSIDE THE WALLS, ROME	ROMANS
		ROMANS EVACUATE BRITAIN	400			

MEDIEVAL (450–1450)

This section continues from the ancient period at the same scale: one line equals 10 years. Included are the following design style periods:

- Romanesque
- Early Gothic
- Late Gothic ("High Gothic")
- Iconoclastic period

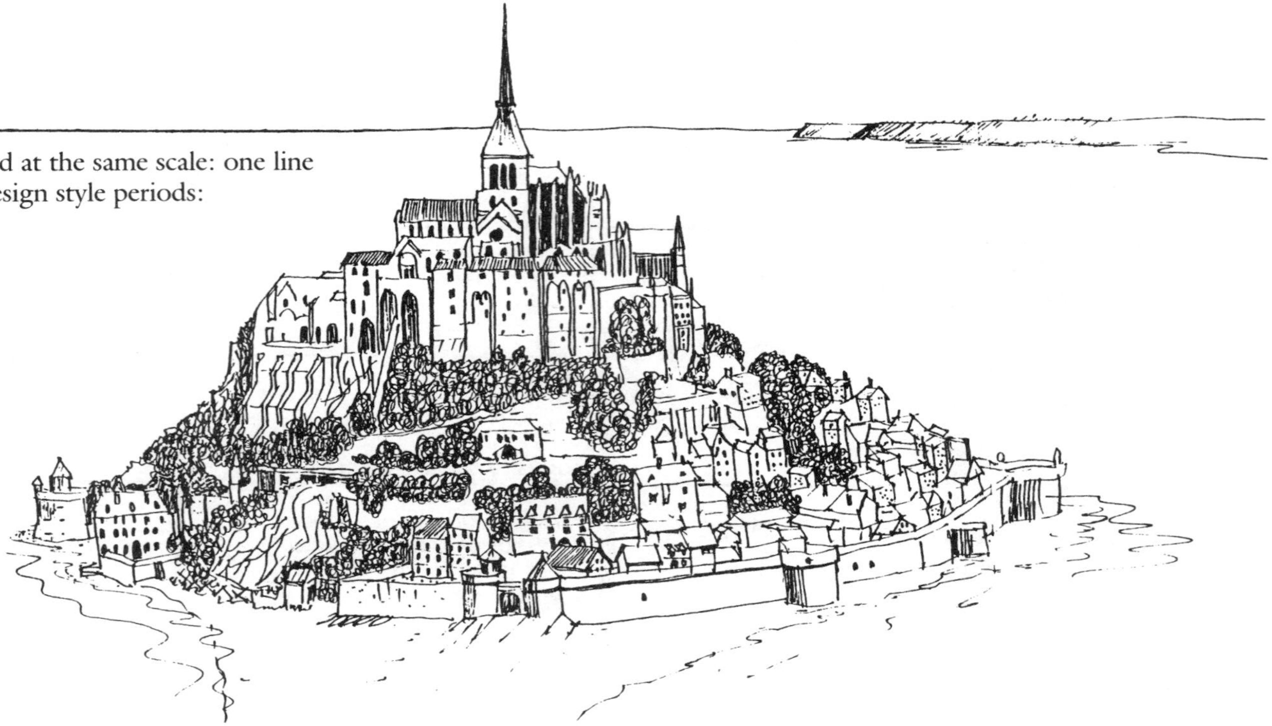

Figure 8. *Mont St. Michel, France.*

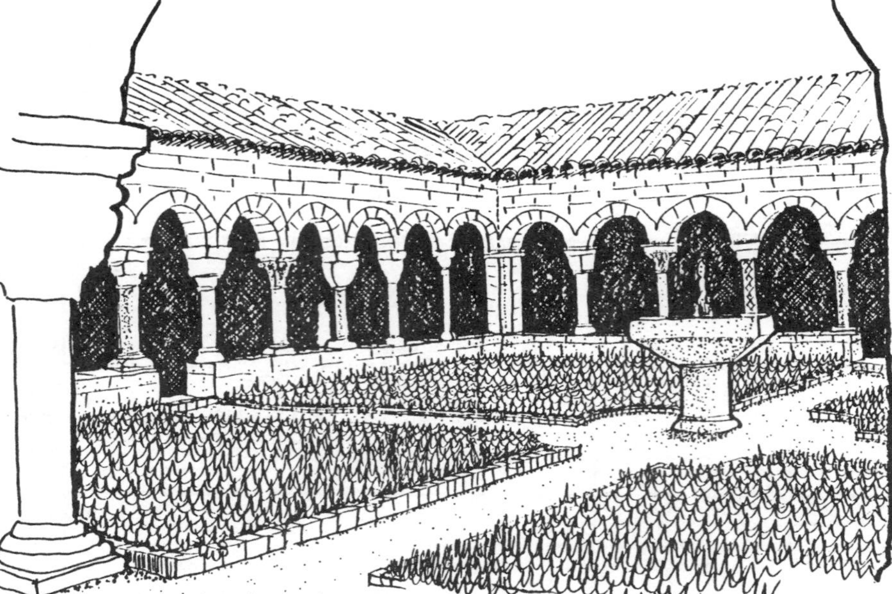

Figure 9. *Medieval cloister garden.*

THE MIDDLE AGES 400AD - 900AD

Politics Economics	Society Environment	Geography Technology	Date	Historical Period	Environmental Design	Designers
ROME SACKED BY VISIGOTHS			400	BYZANTIUM (EASTERN ROMAN EMPIRE)		
ROME SACKED BY BARBARIANS ROME SACKED BY VANDALS FALL OF ROMAN EMPIRE, 476 OSTRAGOTHS OCCUPY ITALY			450		ST. APOLLINARE IN CLASSE, RAVENNA, ITALY	BYZANTINES
JUSTINIAN, EMPEROR OF EAST RAVENNA REUNITED WITH BYZANTIUM	ACADEMY OF ATHENS CLOSED		500		ST. APOLLINARE NUOVO, RAVENNA HAGIA SOPHIA, CONSTANTINOPLE SAN VITALE, RAVENNA	BYZANTINES ATHEMUS ANTHEMIUS
	BENEDICTINE ORDER BUDDHISM OFFICIALLY RECOGNIZED MOHAMMED, 586-632 SHINTO RELIGION ESTABLISHED		550		GREAT WALL OF CHINA, 585-608 COPAN, MEXICO, c.600	CHINESE MAYANS
MOSLEM CONQUESTS (SYRIA, MESOPOTAMIA, PERSIA, EGYPT)	VISION OF MOHAMMED, 610 ISLAMIC (MOSLEM) RELIGION *Koran*, MOHAMMED	HEGIRA, MOHAMMED FLEES FROM MECCA TO MEDINA	600		MONTE ALBAN, MEXICO, 600-900 PALENQUE, MEXICO GREAT PARK OF EMPEROR YANG DI, BEIJING	ZAPOTECS MAYANS
BYZANTIUM LOSING CONTACT WITH WESTERN ROMAN EMPIRE MOSLEM CONQUEST OF N. AFRICA			650		HORYUJI TEMPLE, NARA, JAPAN TEMPLE OF MAMALLAPURAM, INDIA	
MOORS CLAIM SOUTHERN SPAIN, 712-1492 MOSLEM ADVANCES INTO EUROPE STOPPED IN FRANCE BY CHARLES MARTEL			700	ICONOCLASTIC PERIOD	XING QING PALACE, XIAN, CHINA	XUAN ZONG
RAVENNA FALLS TO LOMBARDS CORDOBA BECOMES WESTERN "MECCA," 755-1031			750		STUPA OF BARABUDUR, JAVA MOSQUE, CORDOBA, SPAIN	MOORS
CHARLEMAGNE, HOLY ROMAN EMPEROR, 800-814, RESISTS MOSLEMS IN SPAIN	HOLY ROMAN EMPIRE 800-1806 MONASTERIES ARE CENTERS OF LEARNING		800		ITSUKUSHIMA SHRINE, JAPAN PIAZZA SAN MARCO, VENICE, 830-1810 ST. GALL, MONASTERY, SWITZERLAND	VENETIANS BENEDICTINES
ALFRED THE GREAT, ENG. 871-901			850		TIKAL, GUATAMALA, COLLAPSED 600BC-900AD UXMAL, MEXICO	MAYANS MAYANS
			900			

Figure 10. *Court of the Myrtles, the Alhambra, Granada, Spain.*

Figure 11. *Court of the Lions, the Alhambra, Granada, Spain.*

THE MIDDLE AGES 900AD - 1400AD

Politics / Economics	Society / Environment	Geography / Technology	Date	Historical Period	Environmental Design	Designers
FEUDAL SYSTEM 500 - 1400	HEIGHT OF EUROPEAN FEUDALISM		900	BYZANTIUM (EASTERN ROMAN EMPIRE)	UXMAL, MEXICO	MAYANS
					MONT ST. MICHEL, FRANCE	BENEDICTINES
			950			
					COURT OF ORANGES, CORDOBA	MOORS
		ERIC THE RED COLONIZES GREENLAND				
VIKINGS DOMINATE NORTHERN EUROPE	*Optics*, AL HAZEN, TOLEDO, SPAIN					
	PERSPECTIVE UNDERSTOOD BY MOORS	LIEF ERICSON IN N. AMERICA	1000	ROMANESQUE PERIOD		
		GUNPOWDER USED IN CHINA				
		MUSICAL NOTATION				
			1050		CATHEDRAL GROUP, PISA	
BATTLE OF HASTINGS, ENG.					ST. MARK'S BASILICA, VENICE	VENETIANS
NORMAN CONQUEST	TOLEDO, SPAIN, CITY OF MOORS, JEWS & CHRISTIANS				AVILA, SPAIN, WALLED TOWN	SPANISH
WILLIAM THE CONQUERER	SCHOOL OF TRANSLATORS				ABBEY, CLUNY, FRANCE	CLUNIACS
					TOWER OF LONDON	ENGLISH
	1st CRUSADE TO HOLY LANDS				DURHAM CATHEDRAL, ENGLAND	ENGLISH
HEIGHT OF GUILD SYSTEM	RISE OF MERCHANT CLASS & GUILDS		1100	CASTLE BUILDING	JIN SHAN, BEIJING, CHINA	
					GEN YUE, KAIFENG, CHINA	ZHAO JI
					ANGKOR WAT, CAMBODIA	
					MONT ST. MICHEL ABBEY, FRANCE	BENEDICTINES
					RIEVAULX ABBEY, YORKSHIRE , ENGLAND	CISTERCIANS
	2nd CRUSADE 1147-1149			CASTLE GARDENS	FOUNTAINS ABBEY, YORKSHIRE, ENGLAND	CISTERCIANS
			1150	EARLY GOTHIC		
					NÔTRE DAME, PARIS	
	OXFORD UNIVERSITY				LAON CATHEDRAL, FRANCE	
					BEIHAI PARK, BEIJING, CHINA	
	3rd CRUSADE 1187-1192	ST. FRANCIS OF ASSISI, 1182-1226			CHARTRES CATHEDRAL, FRANCE	
	BEGINNINGS OF REPRESENTATIVE INSTITUTIONS		1200		COURT OF THE ORANGES, CORDOBA, SPAIN	MOORS
GENGHIS KHAN	CAMBRIDGE UNIVERSITY					
MAGNA CARTA, JOHN I	ROGER BACON 1214-1294				SALISBURY CATHEDRAL, ENGLAND	ENGLISH
	FRANCISCAN ORDER	ST. THOMAS AQUINAS, 1225-1274		HIGH GOTHIC	AMIEN CATHEDRAL, FRANCE	FRENCH
CORDOBA REGAINED BY CHRISTIANS					REIMS CATHEDRAL, FRANCE	FRENCH
SEVILLE REGAINED BY CHRISTIANS					ALHAMBRA PALACE, GRANADA, SPAIN	MOORS
			1250			
	DANTE	MARCO POLO IN CHINA			SAIHO-JI TEMPLE (MOSS GARDEN), KYOTO, JAPAN	KOKUSHI
	GIOTTO	*Summa Theologica*, AQUINAS			PIAZZA DELLA SIGNORIA, FLORENCE	FLORENTINES
					PIAZZA DEL CAMPO, SIENA	SIENESE
					FLORENCE CATHEDRAL	FLORENTINES
	Divine Comedy, DANTE		1300	LATE GOTHIC TO 1500		
	BOCCACCIO				GENERALIFE, GRANADA, SPAIN	MOORS
	PETRARCH	GUNPOWDER USED IN EUROPE			SHI ZI LIN CITY GARDENS, SUZHOU, CHINA	NI ZAN
					ALCAZAR PALACE, SEVILLE, SPAIN	MOORS
100 YEARS WAR (ENG-FRANCE) / 100 YEARS WAR	BLACK DEATH / BUBONIC PLAGUE (1/3 EUROPEAN POPULATION KILLED)				DOGES PALACE, VENICE	VENETIANS
					COURT OF THE MYRTLES, ALHAMBRA, GRANADA	MOORS
	CHAUCER		1350		TENOCHTITLAN, MEXICO CITY	AZTECS
					GARDEN OF SAIHO-JI TEMPLE, KYOTO, JAPAN	MUSO SOSEKI
					MEI YUAN (PLUM TREE GARDEN), WUXI, CHINA	
					COURT OF THE LIONS (ALHAMBRA), GRANADA	MOORS
					NEW COLLEGE, OXFORD UNIVERSITY	
	Canterbury Tales, CHAUCER				MILAN CATHEDRAL	
					KINKAKU-JI (GOLDEN PAVILION), KYOTO, JAPAN	YOSHIMITSU
			1400		CERTOSA DI PAVIA, MILAN, ITALY	CARTHUSIANS

ITALY (1400–1700)

In this section, the scale changes from the preceding two sections: each line represents 2 years. Included are the following design style periods:

- Beginnings of Renaissance
- "Philosopher's" gardens
- High Renaissance
- Post High Renaissance ("mannerism")
- Baroque

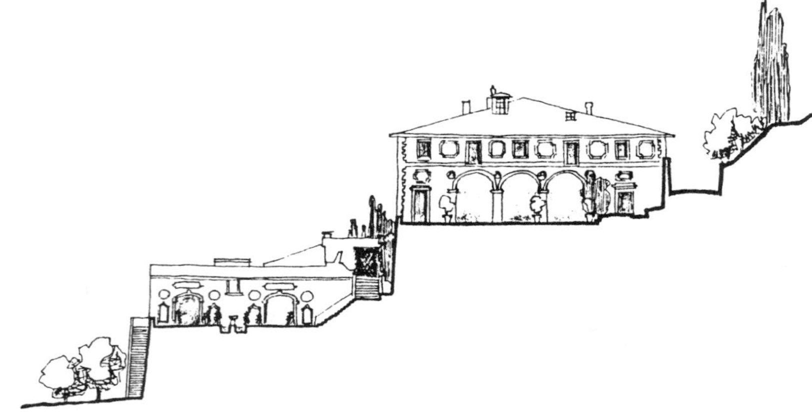

Figure 12. *Villa Medici, section view.*

Figure 13. *Villa Medici, Fiesole, Italy.*

Politics Economics	Society Environment	Geography Technology	Date	Style Period	Environmental Design	Designers	Careers
			1400		SHINJU-AN GARDEN, KYOTO, JAP.		
	Bronze Doors, sc, BAPTISTRY, FLORENCE, GHIBERTI		1402		GREAT WALL OF CHINA		
			1404		FORBIDDEN CITY, BEIJING, CHINA		
			1406				
			1408				
JOHN XXIII, "ANTI-POPE"			1410	BYZANTIUM			
					PIAZZA DEL CAMPO, SIENA COMPLETED (1288-1413)		
	VITRUVIUS' *de Architectura* FOUND						
					DOME, FLORENCE CATHEDRAL	BRUNELLESCHI	
	SCHOOL OF PERSPECTIVE, FLORENCE	LAWS OF PERSPECTIVE, BRUNELLESCHI	1420	LATE GOTHIC	ALTAR OF HEAVEN, BEIJING, CHINA		
					FOUNDLING HOSPITAL, FLORENCE	BRUNELLESCHI	
	Gates of Paradise, sc, BAPTISTRY, FLORENCE, GHIBERTI				DOGE'S PALACE COMPLETED, PIAZZA SAN MARCO, VENICE	VENETIANS	BRUNELLESCHI
		AZTECS DOMINATE MEXICO					
JOAN OF ARC BURNED AT STAKE	*David*, sc, DONATELLO		1430				
COSIMO DEI MEDICI RULES FLORENCE 1434-1469	*de Pittura* (Perspective), ALBERTI				VILLA CAREGGI, FLORENCE (REMODELED)	MICHELOZZO	
	de Architectura, ALBERTI	MOVEABLE TYPE	1440		PAZZI CHAPEL, FLORENCE	BRUNELLESCHI	
					ALPHONSO V OF SPAIN INTRODUCED ISLAMIC USE OF WATER TO ITALY		MICHELOZZO
POPE NICHOLAS V	PLAGUES				DUCAL PALACE, URBINO	LAURANA	
	de re Aedifacatoria, ALBERTI	COLUMBUS BORN, LEONARDO DA VINCI BORN	1450		RECONSTRUCTION OF ST. PETER'S VATICAN		
FALL OF CONSTANTINOPLE TO TURKS	END OF BYZANTINE EMPIRE & END OF MIDDLE AGES. BYZANTINE SCHOLARS & ARTISTS FLEE TO EUROPE. REVIVAL OF CLASSICAL KNOWLEDGE & BEGINNING OF RENAISSANCE	*Gutenburg Bible* (1st PRESS)			YU HUA YUAN, BEIJING, CHINA		
					GINKAKU-JI(SILVER PAV.), KYOTO	YOSHIMASA	ALBERTI
POPE PIUS II					VILLA PALMIERI, FLORENCE REMODELED	MICHELOZZO	
					VILLA MEDICI, FIESOLE	MICHELOZZO	
			1460		PIAZZA DEL POPOLO, CATHEDRAL, PALAZZO & GARDEN, PEINZA	ROSSELLINO	
POPE PAUL II				BEGINNINGS OF RENAISSANCE			
WAR OF THE ROSES, ENG. / MEDICI DOMINANCE IN FLORENCE							
LORENZO DEI MEDICI							
POPE SIXTUS IV			1470				
		FIRST BOOK PRINTED IN ENGLISH		"PHILOSOPHERS' GARDENS"			
	SPANISH INQUISITION						
	Birth of Venus, pt, BOTTICELLI		1480		PROCURATIE VECCHIE BEGUN, P. SAN MARCO, VENICE		
	Delivery of the Keys, pt, PERUGINO				VILLA POGGIO A CAIANO, FLOR.	SANGALLO	
POPE INNOCENT VIII	*Plato Translated*, FICINO						
KING HENRY VIII, ENGLAND	*Virgin of the Rocks*, pt, LEONARDO				VILLA BELVEDERE, VATICAN		SANGALLO
					RYOAN-JI, KYOTO, JAPAN	SOAMI	
			1490		VILLA CELSA		
POPE ALEXANDER VI	CHRISTIANS REGAIN SOUTH'N SPAIN	COLUMBUS LANDS IN NEW WORLD					
KING CHARLES VIII OF FRANCE INVADES ITALY, MEDICIS EXPELLED FROM FLORENCE					AMBOISE, FRANCE	PACELLO	BRAMANTE
	Last Supper, pt, LEONARDO				SILVER PAVILION, KYOTO, JAPAN	SOAMI	LEONARDO
	SAVONAROLA BURNED AT STAKE	NEWFOUNDLAND, CANADA, EXPLORED BY CABOT			CLOCK TOWER, S. MARCO, VENICE		
WAR WITH FRANCE (K. LOUIS XII)	*The Garden of Earthly Delights*, pt, BOSCH		1500		MACHU PICCHU, PERU	INCAS	

Figure 14. *Villino Farnese (Villa Caprarola), Caprarola, Italy.*

Figure 15. *Cortile del Belvedere, Vatican City (Rome), Italy.*

ITALY 1500 - 1600

Politics Economics	Society Environment	Geography Technology	Date	Style Period	Environmental Design	Designers	Careers
POPE JULIUS II	*David*, sc, MICHELANGELO *Mona Lisa*, pt, LEONARDO *Sistine Chapel Ceiling*, pt, MICHELANGELO *School of Athens*, pt, RAPHAEL MACHIAVELLI	BRAZIL DISCOVERED, VESPUCCI	1500	ITALIAN INFLUENCE IN FRANCE HIGH RENAISSANCE	CORTILE DEL BELVEDERE, ROME *David*, sc, BY MICHELANGELO, PLACED IN PIAZZA, FLORENCE PLAN FOR ST. PETER'S ZHUO ZHENG YUAN, SUZHOU, CH.	BRAMANTE, RAPHAEL, et al BRAMANTE WANG ZIAN CHEN	BRAMANTE RAPHAEL LEONARDO SANGALLO, THE ELDER
FRENCH EXPELLED FROM ITALY POPE LEO X PART OF ITALY CAPTURED BY FRENCH FRENCH EXPELLED FROM ITALY	*The Prince*, MACHIAVELLI *Moses*, sc, MICHELANGELO *95 Theses*, MARTIN LUTHER INDEX OF PROHIBITED BOOKS LEONARDO DA VINCI DIED AT AMBOISE CHARLES V, HOLY ROMAN EMPEROR	FLORIDA DISCOVERED, PONCE DE LEON PACIFIC DISCOVERED, BALBOA	1510		DAISEN-IN MONAST., KYOTO, JAP. PIAZZA ANNUNZIATA, FLORENCE ("THE SECOND MAN") VILLA MADAMA, ROME	SOAMI SANGALLO, ELDER RAPHAEL	
POPE HADRIAN VI POPE CLEMENT VII FRANCE RETAKES MILAN	VITRUVIUS' *de Architectura* PUBLISHED TURKS DEFEATED IN VIENNA	CIRCUMNAVIGATION OF THE EARTH, MAGELLAN COPERNICUS	1520	"POST HIGH RENAISSANCE"	JI CHANG YUAN (GARDEN OF ECSTACY), WUXI, CHINA		MICHELANGELO
POPE PAUL III	CHURCH OF ENGLAND SEPARATES FROM ROME COUNTER REFORMATION	PERU CAPTURED, PIZZARO	1530		LIBRARY, PZA. S. MARCO, VENICE CAMPIDOGLIO, ROME	SANSOVINO MICHELANGELO	
REFORMATION IN ENGLAND	COUNCIL OF TRENT	MISSISSIPPI RIV. DISCOVERED, DE SOTO COPERNICUS REFUTES GEOCENTRIC VIEW OF EARTH	1540		VILLA CASTELLO, FLORENCE VILLA MEDICI, ROME ST. PETER'S CATH. DOME, ROME PALAZZO FARNESE, CAPRAROLA VILLA D'ESTE, TIVOLI BOBOLI GARDENS, FLORENCE	TRIBOLO LIPPI MICHELANGELO VIGNOLA, PERUZZI LIGORIO, OLIVIERI TRIBOLO, et al	
POPE JULIUS III POPE PAUL IV	*Antiquities of Rome*, PALLADIO		1550		VILLA GIULIA, ROME VILLA CAPRA, VICENZA UFFIZI, FLORENCE *Neptune Fountain*, sc, PZA SIGNORIA PALAZZO FARNESE PALAZZO PITTI, FLORENCE	VIGNOLA PALLADIO VASARI AMMANATI VIGNOLA AMMANATI	VIGNOLA
POPE PIUS V	*Five Orders of Architecture*, VIGNOLA *de Architectura*, PALLADIO	ST. AUGUSTINE, FLORIDA ESTAB.	1560		PORTA DEL POPOLO, ROME VILLA PIA, VATICAN VILLA ORSINI, BOMARZO VILLA LANTE, BAGNAIA VILLA ROTUNDA, VICENZA VILLA MONDRAGONE, FRASCATI	VIGNOLA LIGORIO VIGNOLA PALLADIO LUNGHI, FONTANA	PALLADIO
POPE GREGORY XIII			1570		VILLINO FARNESE, CAPRAROLA VILLA RUSPOLI, VIGNANELLO AN LAN YUAN, YAN GUAN, CHINA	VIGNOLA ORSINI CHEN	
POPE SIXTUS V	GREGORIAN CALENDAR		1580	BAROQUE MANNERISM	TEATRO OLIMPICO, VICENZA PROCURATIE NUOVE, PIAZZA SAN MARCO, VENICE OBELISK, PIAZZA SAN PIETRO, VATICAN (FROM NERO'S CIRCUS) OBELISK, PZA DEL POPOLO, ROME (FROM CIRCUS MAXIMUS)	PALLADIO SCAMOZZI & LONGHENA FONTANA FONTANA	DELLA PORTA
POPE CLEMENT VIII		MICROSCOPE THERMOMETER GALILEO	1590		PALMA NUOVA (IDEAL CITY PLAN) VILLA ALDOBRANDINI, FRASCATI	DELLA PORTA, FONTANA, OLIVIERI	
			1600				

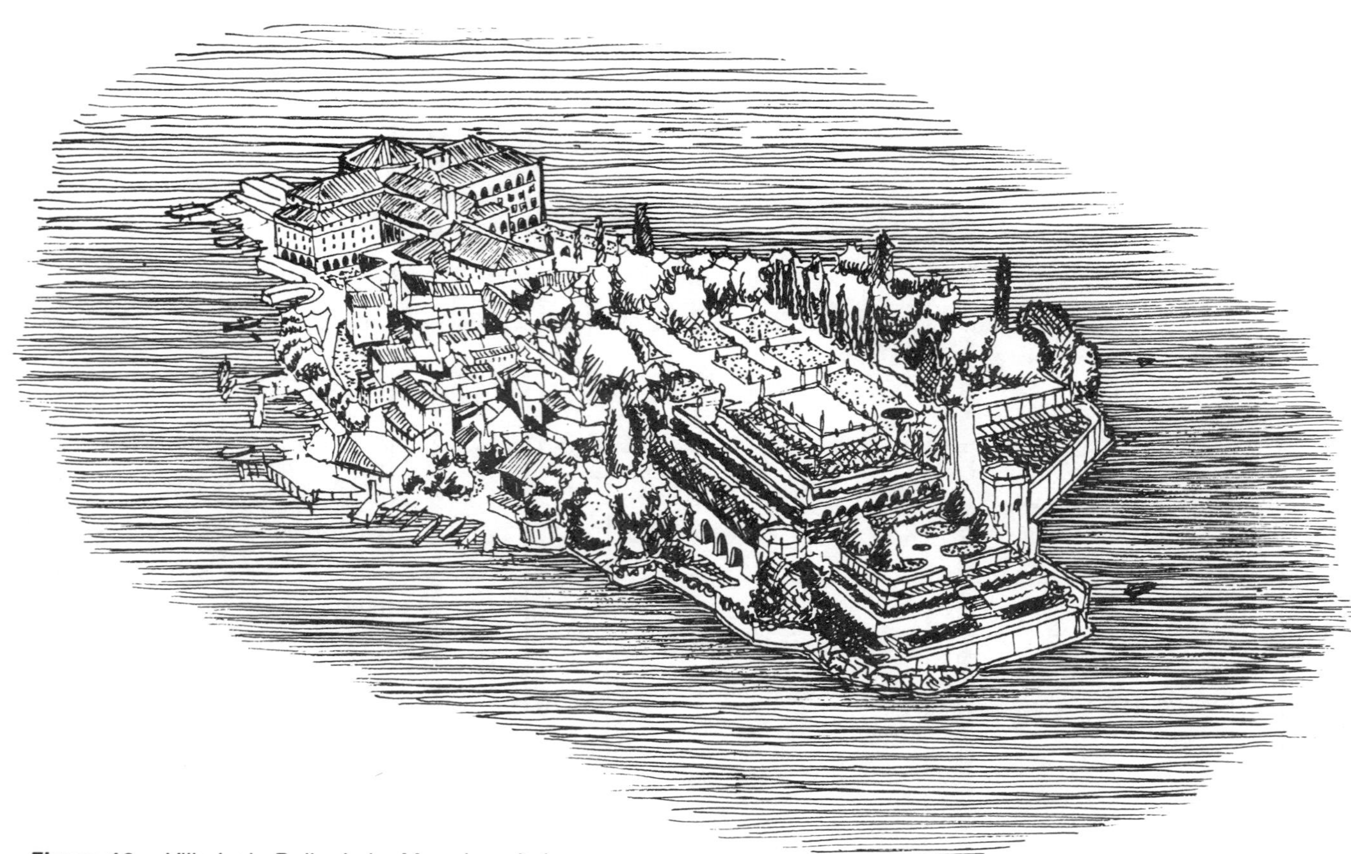

Figure 16. *Villa Isola Bella, Lake Maggiore, Italy.*

Politics Economics	Society Environment	Geography Technology	Date	Style Period	Environmental Design	Designers	Careers
			1600				
					KORAKU-EN, KYOTO, JAPAN	YORIFUSI	
POPE PAUL V					VILLA BORGHESE, ROME	VASANZIO	
		JAMESTOWN, VIRGINIA			FACADE OF ST. PETER'S, ROME	MADERNO	
		TELESCOPE, GALILEO	1610		VILLA GAMBERAIA, FLORENCE	GAMBERELLI	
	MATTHIAS, HOLY ROMAN EMPEROR						
					GARDEN, SHAH OF ASHRAR, IRAN	MOGHUL	
					PALACE OF 40 COLUMNS, ISFAHAN, IRAN	MOGHUL	
	FERDINAND II, HOLY ROMAN EMPER'R				SHALIMAR BAGH, LAHORE, INDIA	MOGHUL	
		PLYMOUTH COLONY	1620		KATSURA PALACE, KYOTO, JAPAN	KOBURI ENSHU	
		INDUCTIVE REASONING, BACON			VILLA TORLONIA, FRASCATI	MADERNO	
		PROHIBITION OF COPERNICUS' VIEWS					
			1630		TAJ MAHAL, AGRA, INDIA	SHAH JAHAN	
POPE GREGORY XV					VILLA ISOLA BELLA, LAKE MAGGIORE	CRIVELLI	
POPE URBAN VIII					SENTO GOSHO GARDENS, KYOTO	KOBURI ENSHU	
	FERDINAND III, HOLY ROM. EM	ANALYTICAL GEOMETRY, DECARTES					
			1640		RED FORT, NEW DELHI, INDIA	SHAH JAHAN	
		GALILEO'S TRIAL & CENSURE					
					LIU GARDEN, SOOCHOW, CHINA		
	Fountain of Four Rivers, sc, ROME, BERNINI						
			1650				
		BAROMETER					
					SHUGAKU-IN IMP. VILLA, KYOTO	GOMITSUNOÓ	
					PIAZZA SAN PIETRO, ROME	BERNINI	
	LEOPOLD I, HOLY ROM. EMP.						
			1660				
POPE ALEXANDER VII		BERNINI MEETS WREN IN PARIS					
					TWIN CHURCHES, SANTA MARIE PIAZZA DEL POPOLO, ROME	RAINALDI	
			1670				
			1680		BAN MU YUAN , BEIJING, CHINA	LI YU	
POPE INNOCENT XI							
			1690				
			1700				

Vertical bars — Society Environment: REMBRANDT, CLAUDE LORRAIN, NICOLAS POUSSIN; Geography Technology: GALILEO; Style Period: MANNERISM, BAROQUE TO 1750; Careers: DELLA PORTA, BERNINI, RAINALDI.

FRANCE (1500–1800)

In this section each line represents 2 years. Included are the following design style periods:

- Italian influence
- Mannerism
- Beginnings of French national style
- French national style
- Baroque
- Rococo

Figure 17. Chenonceaux, River Cher (Loire Valley), France.

Politics Economics	Society Environment	Geography Technology	Date	Style Period	Environmental Design	Designers	Careers
CHARLES VIII 1483-1498 LOUIS XII 1498-1515	WAR WITH ITALY & SPAIN FRANCE & SPAIN OCCUPY NAPLES FRANCE CEDES NAPLES TO SPAIN	COLUMBUS DIES	1500	ITALIAN INFLUENCE (begins) EARLY FRENCH RENAISSANCE	AMBOISE 1495 BLOIS	PACELLO PACELLO & DA CORTONA	LEONARDO DA VINCI MICHELANGELO
FRANCIS I 1515-1547 NORTHERN ITALY CAPTURED BY FRANCE 30 YEARS WAR WITH ITALY (begins)	*95 Theses,* LUTHER LEONARDO DIES AT AMBOISE CHARLES V, HOLY ROMAN EMPEROR	REFORMATION IN GERMANY	1510		CHENONCEAUX AZAY-LE-RIDEAU CHAMBORD	PACELLO DE L'ORME DA CORTONA	
FRANCE SURRENDERS ITALY	LUTHER EXCOMMUNICATED		1520	MANNERISM (begins)	CHANTILLY FONTAINEBLEAU	SERLIO	
FRANCE AT WAR WITH SPAIN	REFORMATION LED BY CALVIN JESUIT ORDER ESTABLISHED	COPERNICUS REFUTES GEOCENTRIC VIEW OF EARTH CARTIER EXPLORES ST. LAWRENCE RIVER, CANADA	1530				
WAR BETWEEN FRANCIS I & CHARLES V 1542-1544 REFORMATION IN ENGLAND HENRI II (Q. CATHERINE DE MEDICI & MISTRESS DIANE DE POITIERS)	ENGLAND & SCOTLAND INVADE FRANCE		1540		PALAIS DE LOUVRE, PARIS CHENONCEAUX (FOR DIANE DE POITIERS) VILLANDRY		ANDREA PALLADIO JACQUES MOLLET I DU CEARCEAU PHILIBERT DE L'ORME
FRANCIS II (Q. MARY, ENGLISH)	ENGLAND EXPELLED FROM FRANCE FERDINAND I, HOLY ROMAN EMP'R		1550		ANET (FOR DIANE DE POITIERS) CHENONCEAUX (CATH. DE MEDICI)	DE L'ORME DE L'ORME	
CHARLES IX	RELIGIOUS WARS, CATHOLICS vs HUGUENOTS MAXIMILIAN I, HOLY ROMAN EMP'R		1560		CHANTILLY TUILERIES (CATH. DE MEDICI)	BULLANT DE L'ORME	
HENRI III	RUDOLF I, HOLY ROMAN EMPEROR PROTESTANTISM FORBIDDEN LE NOTRE VISITS ITALY	PORTUGESE EXPEL FRENCH FROM BRAZILCOLONY, FOUND RIO DE JANEIRO	1570		CHARLEVAL		
			1580				
HENRI IV (Q. MARIA DE MEDICI) HOUSE OF BOURBON, 1589-1792	PROTESTANTISM ACCEPTED		1590		ST. GERMAIN-EN-LAYE (FOR MARIA DE MEDICI)	MOLLET, FRANCINI	
			1600		TUILERIES (COURS DE LA REINE)	MOLLET, BOYCEAU	

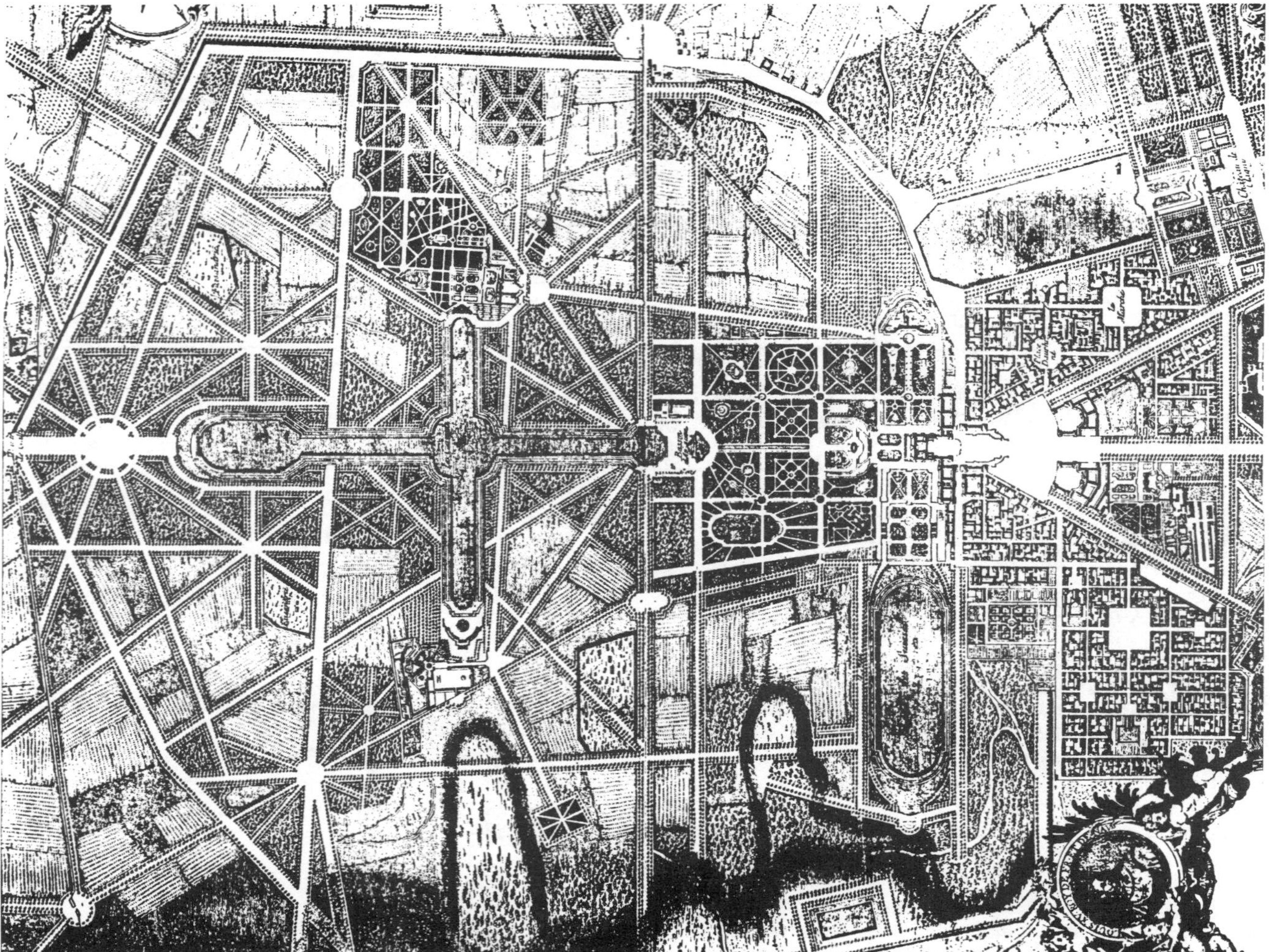

Versailles,France
(1:24000/1"=200')

Figure 18. *Versailles, France (1 : 24,000/1 inch = 200 feet).*

FRANCE 1600 - 1700

Politics Economics	Society Environment	Geography Technology	Date	Style Period	Environmental Design	Designers	Careers
	le Theatre d'Agriculture, DE SERRES		1600	BAROQUE	TUILERIES (COURS DE LA REINE)	MOLLET, BOYCEAU	
	RELIGIOUS WARS				PLACE ROYAL, PARIS	CHASTILLON	
KING LOUIS XIII FRANCE A EUROPEAN POWER			1610				
					LUXEMBOURG PALACE, PARIS	DE BROSSE, BOYCEAU	
			1620				
CARDINAL RICHELIEU, PRIME MIN.					VERSAILLES, HUNTING LODGE	BOYCEAU	
	PROTESTANTS SURRENDER TO RICHELIEU						
			1630				ANDRE MOLLET; CLAUDE MOLLET II
					CHEVERNY		
WAR WITH SPAIN							
			1640				
		MONTREAL, CANADA					
LOUIS XIV, KING AT AGE 5 KING CHARLES, ENG. EXECUTED	ENGLISH ROYAL FAMILY IN FRANCE						GABRIEL MOLLET
	Traite du Jardinage, BOYCEAU						
	le Jardin de Plaisir, A. MOLLET		1650				
	le Theatre...Jardinage, C. MOLLET						
LOUIS XIV COMES OF AGE							
					VAUX-LE-VICOMTE	LE NOTRE, LE VAU	LE NOTRE
LOUIS XIV BECOMES ABSOLUTE RULER "le Roi Soleil"			1660	FRENCH GRAND STYLE	ST. CLOUD	LE NÔTRE	
RESTORATION, ENGLAND					VERSAILLES	LE NÔTRE, LE VAU	
					HAMPTON COURT, LONDON	MOLLET BROS.	
					TUILERIES	LE NÔTRE	
					CHANTILLY REMODELED	LE NÔTRE	
		WREN MEETS BERNINI IN PARIS			PARC DE LA VILLETTE	MANSART	
					CHAMPS-ELYSEES	LE NÔTRE	
			1670		HERRENHAUSEN, HANOVER, GER.	CARBONNIER	
					SCEAUX	LE NÔTRE	
					CLAGNY	LE NÔTRE	
					FONTAINEBLEAU REMODELED	LE NÔTRE	
					TUILERIES REMODELED	LE NÔTRE	
		LE NÔTRE VISITS ITALY			MARLY	LE NOTRE	
			1680		DROTTNINGHOLM, STOCKHOM	TESSIN	
					PLACE VENDÔME, PARIS	MANSART	
	LOUIS XIV FORBIDS ALL BUT CATHOLICISM, HUGUENOTS FLEE				GRAND TRIANON, VERSAILLES	LE NÔTRE	
					HAMPTON COURT, LONDON	WISE & MAROT	
			1690		HET LOO, HOLLAND	MAROT, DE MARAIS	
					SCHLEISSHEIM, MUNICH	EFFNER	
					SCHONBRUNN, VIENNA	VON ERLACH	
					ANNAPOLIS, MARYLAND PLANNED	NICHOLSON	
					BELVEDERE, VIENNA	HILDEBRANDT	
					WILLIAMSBURG, VIRGINIA PLAN'D	NICHOLSON	
			1700				

Figure 19. *Palazzo Reale, Caserta, Italy.*

FRANCE 1700 - 1800

Politics Economics	Society Environment	Geography Technology	Date	Style Period	Environmental Design	Designers	Careers
			1700	FRENCH GRAND STYLE; BAROQUE	WILHELMSLOHE, GERMANY	GUERNIERO, PAPIN	
					RIKUGI-EN, TOKYO, JAPAN	YOSHMASA	
					BI SHU SHAN ZHUANG, CHINA	QIAN LONG	
BATTLE OF BLENHEIM, ENGLAND DEFEATS FRANCE	JOSEPH II, HOLY ROMAN EMPEROR				BLENHEIM, ENGLAND	VANBRUGH & WISE	
	la Theorie...Jardinage, D'ARGENVILLE						
	CHARLES VI, HOLY ROMAN EMPEROR	STEAM ENGINE, NEWCOMEN	1710	LANDSCAPE GARD., ENGLAND	KARLSRUHE IDEAL CITY,GERMANY	NEUMANN	
KING LOUIS XV					PETERHOF, PETERSBURG, RUSSIA	LE BLOND	
					BELVEDERE, VIENNA	GIRARD	
					NYMPHENBURG, MUNICH	GIRARD, EFFNER	
					LA GRANJA, SEGOVIA, SPAIN	CARTIER, BOUTELET	
	la Theorie...du Jardinage, LE BLOND		1720		FREDERIKSBORG PAL., DENMARK	KRIEGER	
	Brandenburg Concertos, BACH						
					SPANISH STEPS, ROME	SPECCHI & SANCTIS	
WAR WITH ENGLAND & SPAIN							
			1730				
			1740		YUAN MING YUAN (GARDEN OF PERFECT BRIGHTNESS), BEIJING	CHI'IEN LUNG	
	CHARLES VII, HOLY ROMAN EMPEROR						
WAR WITH ENGLAND IN CANADA	FRANCIS I, HOLY ROMAN EMPEROR						
					SUMMER PALACE, BEIJING, CHINA	QIAN LONG	
					PLACE DE LA CARRIERE, NANCY	HERE	
			1750		PALAZZO REALE, CASERTA, ITALY	VANVITELLI	
					PLACE DE LA CARRIERE, NANCY	HERE	
					PLACE DE LA CONCORDE, PARIS	GABRIEL	
					SANS SOUCI, POTTSDAM, GERM.	VON KNOLESDORF	
FRENCH & INDIAN WAR					VILLA ALBANI, ROME	WINCKLEMAN	
					QUELUZ, LISBON, PORTUGAL	ROBILLON	
					TREVI FOUNTIAN, ROME	VALLE & BRACCI	
			1760		WINTER PALACE, PETERSBURG	RASTRELLI	
	The Social Contract, ROUSSEAU						
	JOSEPH II, HOLY ROMAN EMPEROR				PARC D'ERMENONVILLE	GIRARDIN & MOREL	
			1770				
					HAMEAU, CHANTILLY	LEROY	
KING LOUIS XVI, MARIE ANTOINETTE					PARC MONCEAU	CARMONTELLE	
FRANCE AIDS AMER. REVOLUTION					DESERT DE RETZ	BARBIER	
					BAGATELLE	BELANGER	
					HAMEAU, PETIT TRIANON	MIQUE	
			1780				
		HOT AIR BALLOON					
	JEFFERSON LIVES IN PARIS				HOTEL LANGEAC, PARIS	JEFFERSON	
U. S. CONSTITUTION							
FRENCH REVOLUTION					ENGLISCHE GARTEN, MUNICH	THOMPSON	
			1790				
	FRANCIS II, HOLY ROMAN EMPEROR						
KING LOUIS XVI BEHEADED							
NAPOLEON CAPTURES ITALY							
NAPOLEON CAPTURES EGYPT NAPOLEON CAPTURES SYRIA	NAPOLEON RULES FRANCE, 1799-1804	ROSETTA STONE FOUND	1800		MORTEFONTAINE, FRANCE	JOS. BONAPARTE	

ENGLAND (1500–1900)

In this section each line represents 2 years. Included are the following design style periods:

- Tudor
- Elizabethan
- Jacobean
- English Renaissance
- Classic Revival
- Informal: "romanticism"; "picturesque"; "English landscape gardening school"
- Victorian
- Edwardian

Figure 20. *The Pond Garden, Hampton Court, London, England.*

ENGLAND 1500 - 1600

Politics Economics	Society Environment	Geography Technology	Date	Style Period	Environmental Design	Designers	Careers
KING HENRY VII; WAR OF ROSES			1500		[HADDON HALL, 1480]		
KING HENRY VIII							
			1510				
CARDINAL WOLSEY. LORD CHANCELLOR	MARTIN LUTHER POSTS 95 THESES REFORMATION IN GERMANY				HAMPTON COURT BUILT FOR CARDINAL WOLSEY		
			1520	TUDOR	COMPTON WYNATES		
	HENRY VIII CLAIMS HAMPTON COURT						
HOUSE OF TUDOR	HENRY VIII DIVORCES FIRST WIFE, CATHERINE OF ARAGON		1530		CHAPULTAPEC PARK, MEXICO	KING PHILIP II, SPAIN	
	HENRY VIII REMARRIES, ANN BOLEYN						
REFORMATION	CHURCH OF ENGLAND ESTABLISHED						
	HENRY VIII DISSOLVES MONASTERIES REDISTRIBUTES CHURCH PROP. TO "LANDED GENTRY"						
			1540				
MARY, QUEEN OF SCOTS							
ENG. & SCOT. INVADE FRANCE		COPERNICUS REFUTES GEOCENTRIC VIEW OF EARTH					
KING EDWARD VI	HENRY VIII MARRIES SIXTH TIME				MONTECUTE, 1st STAGE		
	Book of Common Prayer, ANGLICAN						
			1550				
QUEEN MARY I, "BLOODY MARY"	*Antiquities of Rome*, PALLADIO; ENGLAND RETURNS TO CATHOLICISM, PROTESTANTS PERSECUTED						
QUEEN ELIZABETH I EXPELLED FROM FRANCE					PACKWOOD HOUSE		
			1560		CHATSWORTH, Q. MARY'S BOWER		
	CHURCH OF ENGLAND FORMED				LONGLEAT		
					ST. CATHERINE'S COURT		PALLADIO
ELIZABETHAN	*de re Architectura*, PALLADIO		1570				
	LAW OF THE INDIES, SPANISH						
			1580	EARLY ENGLISH RENAISSANCE; ELIZABETHAN	MONTECUTE ENLARGED		
		GREGORIAN CALENDAR					
MARY, QUEEN OF SCOTS EXECUTED	WAR WITH SPAIN						
	SPANISH ARMADA DEFEATED						
			1590				
					ALAMEDA PARK, MEXICO	SPANISH	
	SHAKESPEARE						
	EAST INDA COMPANY		1600				

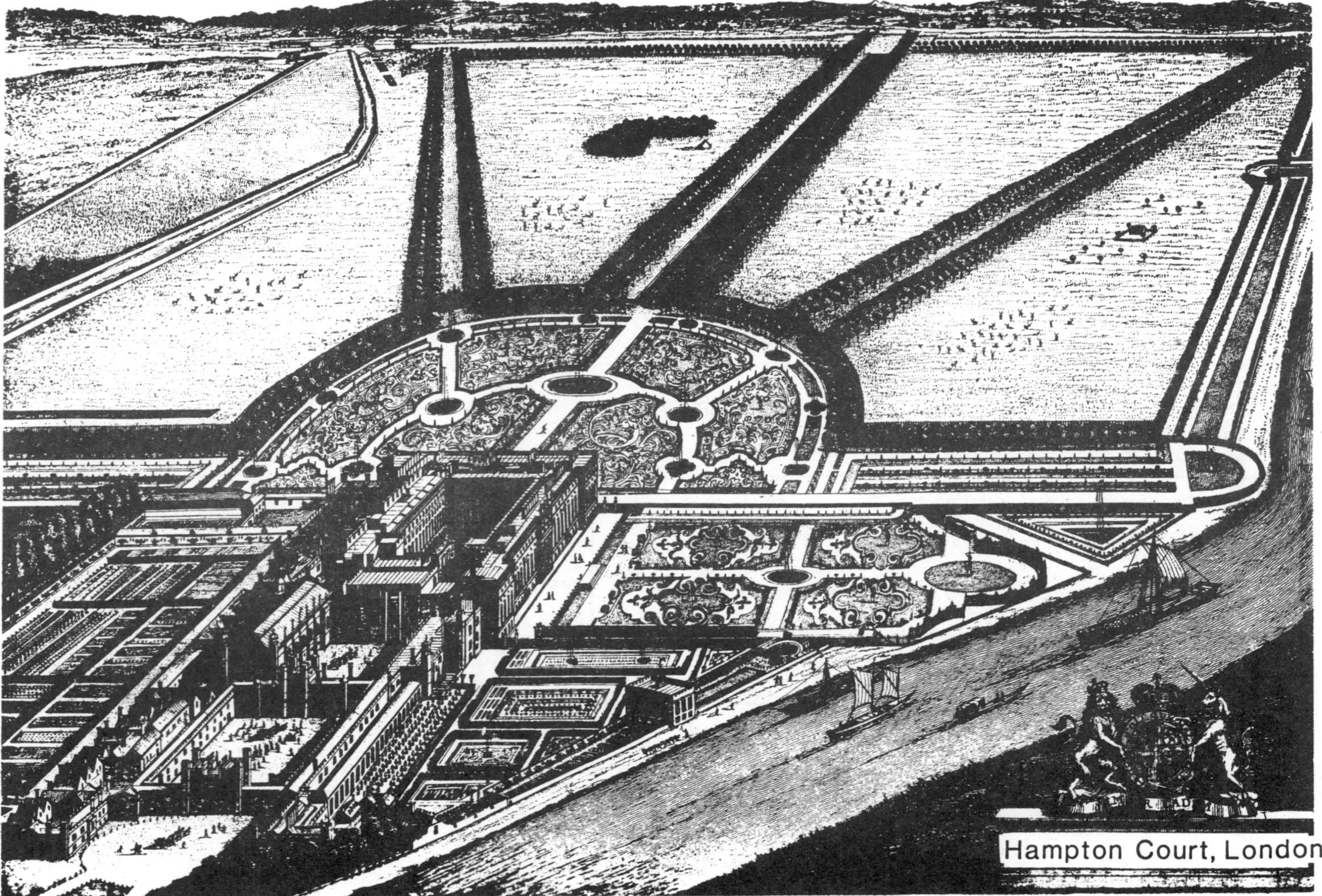

Figure 21. *Hampton Court, London, England.*

Politics Economics	Society Environment	Geography Technology	Date	Style Period	Environmental Design	Designers	Careers
	EAST INDIA COMPANY		1600				
KING JAMES I (JAMES VI, SCOTLAND)							
	PLAGUE, LONDON						
	LAWS AGAINST CATHOLICS	JAMESTOWN, VIRGINIA			HATFIELD HOUSE	DE CAUX	
		HUDSON RIVER EXPLORED					
		LAWS OF PLANETARY MOTION	1610				
	King James Bible	TELESCOPE, GALILEO, IN ITALY					
		TEA INTRODUCED INTO EUROPE					
JAMES I DISSOLVES PARL.							
	INIGO JONES RETURNS FROM ITALY						
	TOBACCO FROM VIRGINIA						
	SLAVES IMPORTED INTO VIRGINIA						
		PLYMOUTH COLONY, MASS.	1620				
	BOTANIC GARDEN, OXFORD						
	Vitruvius Britanicus, WOTTON						
KING CHARLES I	*Of Gardens*, BACON				BLICKLING HALL		
PARLIAMENT DISSOLVED							
RULE w/o PARLIAMENT			1630		CANON'S ASHBY		
	MASSACHUSETTS POP. 16,000		1640				
CIVIL WAR		AUSTRALIA & NEW ZEALAND EXPLORED					
KING CHARLES EXECUTED							
MONARCHY ABOLISHED							
COMMONWEALTH ESTABLISHED	ROYAL FAMILY LIVES IN FRANCE				PACKWOOD HOUSE		
WAR WITH HOLLAND	*le Jardin de Palaisir*, MOLLET		1650				
O. CROMWELL, LORD PROTECTOR							
					VAUX-LE-VICOMTE, FRANCE	LE NÔTRE	
RICHARD CROMWELL, LORD PROT.	COLONIAL POPULATION, 84,000						
KING CHARLES II, RESTORATION	WREN STUDYING ARCH. IN PARIS		1660		VERSAILLES REMODELLED	LE NÔTRE	
SCOTLAND UNITED w/ ENG.					BLOOMSBURY SQUARE, LONDON		
	Sylva...Forest Trees, EVELYN				ST. JAMES PARK, LONDON	MOLLET BROS.	
	PARLIAMENTARY ENCLOSURE ACTS				HAMPTON COURT, LONDON	MOLLET BROS.	
	PLAGUE, LONDON	WREN MEETS BERNINI IN PARIS			ROYAL HOSPITAL, GREENWICH	WEBB & WREN	
		GREAT FIRE, LONDON			LONDON PLANNED AFTER FIRE	WREN	
			1670				
					ST. PAUL'S CATHEDRAL, LONDON	WREN	
			1680		SOHO SQUARE, LONDON	G. KING	
					CHATSWORTH	LONDON, WISE & GRILLET	
KING JAMES II, ENG. & SCOT.	*Upon the Gardens of Epicurus*, TEMPLE						
WILLIAM III & MARY II	DUTCH INFLUENCE, TOPIARY				HAMPTON CT., FOUNTAIN GARDEN	MAROT	
			1690		LEVENS HALL	BEAUMONT	
MARY DIES							
					BRAMHAM PARK, YORKSHIRE	LORD BINGLEY	
					GREENWICH HOSPITAL	WREN	
	COLONIAL POPULATION, 1,000,000		1700		CASTLE HOWARD	VANBRUGH	

Period bars — Politics/Economics: JACOBEAN; HOUSE OF STUART. Society/Environment: SHAKESPEARE. Style Period: JACOBEAN; CLASSIC REVIVAL / PALLADIAN. Careers: JONES; ANDRE MOLLET; CLAUDE MOLLET II; GABRIEL MOLLET; S. ROSA; CLAUDE LORRAIN; N. POUSSIN; WREN; LONDON; WISE.

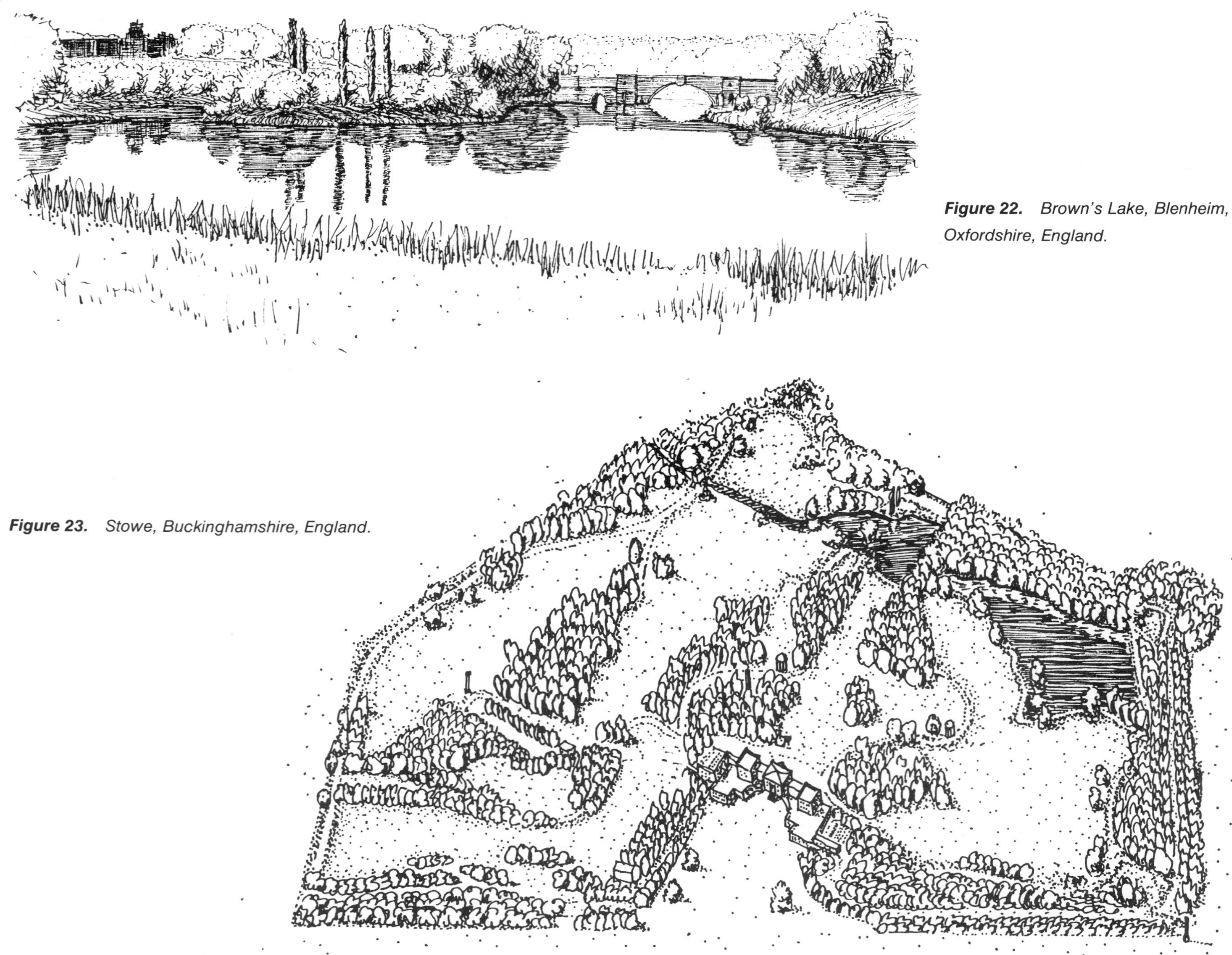

Figure 22. *Brown's Lake, Blenheim, Oxfordshire, England.*

Figure 23. *Stowe, Buckinghamshire, England.*

ENGLAND 1700 - 1800

Politics Economics	Society Environment	Geography Technology	Date	Style Period	Environmental Design	Designers
QUEEN ANNE			1700		LONGLEAT	LONDON & WISE
ENG. DEFEAT FR. AT BLENHEIM					ST. JAMES PARK, LONDON	MOLLET BROS.
	PINUS STROBUS INTRO. FROM N. AM.				MELBOURNE HALL	LONDON & WISE
SCOTLAND REUNITED w/ ENG.	*The Moralist*, SHAFTESBURY				BLENHEIM, OXFORDSHIRE	VANBRUGH & WISE
	Essay on Criticism, POPE				NIEBOROW, LOWICZ, POLAND	GAMEREN
					WREST PARK	
	The Spectator, ADDISON & STEELE		1710		BRAMHAM PARK	
		STEAM ENGINE, NEWCOMEN			WILTON HOUSE	
KING GEORGE I	*The Guardian*, POPE	*The Architecture of Palladio*, LEONI			STOWE PARTERRES REMOVED	BRIDGEMAN
	Vitruvius Britanicus, CAMPBELL				STOWE FOLLIES	VANBRUGH
					DUNCOMBE PARK, YORKSHIRE	DUNCOMBE III
	Ichnographia Rustica, SWITZER (USED TERM, *ferme ornée*)					
	KENT STUDIES IN ITALY, 1710-1718				POPE'S GARDEN, TWICKENHAM	POPE
			1720		LONGLEAT "IMPROVED"	
	BRIDGEMAN RETURNS FROM CHINA					
		HA-HA AT STOWE, BRIDGEMAN				
KING GEORGE II	*New Princ. of Gardening*, LANGLEY				CLAREMONT	BRIDGEMAN
BRIDGEMAN & WISE ANALYZE COST OF ROYAL GARD. MAINT.	*New Princ. of Gard. Des.*, BRIDGEMAN				QUEEN SQUARE, BATH	WOOD, SR.
					CHISWICK HOUSE, LONDON	LORD BURLINGTON
					KEW GARDENS, LONDON	KENT
	Epistle to Lord Burlington, POPE	*Gardener's Dictionary*, MILLER	1730		PRIOR PARK, BATH	WOOD, Sr.
		Gardener's Kalendar, MILLER			BIALYSTOK, WARSAW, POLAND	
					PALLADIAN BRIDGE AT WILTON	LORD PEMBROKE
					PAINESHILL, SURREY	HAMILTON
					ROUSHAM	KENT
			1740		STOWE FOLLIES & BRIDGE,	KENT & BROWN
					STOURHEAD	HOARE
					CLAREMONT	KENT
					THE LEASOWES	SHENSTONE
	POMPEII EXCAVATIONS BEGIN				WARWICK CASTLE	BROWN
			1750			
	The Analysis of Beauty, HOGARTH	*Species/Genera Plant'm*, LINNAEUS			THE CIRCUS, BATH	WOOD, Sr
	Design of Chinese Bldgs, CHAMBERS					
					LONGLEAT	BROWN
KING GEORGE III	*Julie*, ROUSSEAU					
	Elements of Criticism, LORD KAMES	INDUSTRIAL REVOLUTION, 1760 - 1840	1760		BLENHEIM	BROWN
	Unconnected Thoughts..Gard'g, SHENSTONE				KEW GARDEN	BROWN
AMER. COLONIAL STAMP ACT	"CAP." BROWN, ROYAL GARDENER				CHATSWORTH	BROWN
					PARC D'ERMENONVILLE, FRANCE	GIRARDIN & MOREL
	Observ. on Modern Gardn'g, WHATELY				KEW GARDEN PAGODA	CHAMBERS
					PRIOR PARK, BATH	BROWN
BOSTON MASSACRE	*History of Mod. Taste in Gard.*, WALPLE	AUSTRALIA EXPLORED, COOK	1770		ROYAL CRESCENT, BATH	WOOD, Jr
	Diss. on Oriental Gardens, CHAMBERS				PORTLAND PLACE, REGENT'S PRK	NASH
					SYON HOUSE	BROWN
AMERICAN REVOLUTION		STEAM ENGINE, WATT			BAGATELLE, PARIS	BELANGER
	Wealth of Nations, ADAM SMITH				PETIT TRIANON, VERSAILLES, FR.	MIQUE
		HAWAII EXPLORED, COOK			SCHWETZINGEN, GERMANY	VON SCKELL
					TSARSKOYE SELO, PETERSBURG	CAMERON
FRENCH REVOLUTION		CAST IRON BRIDGE			ARKADIA, POLAND	ZUG & ITTAR
	Observations of Pict. Beauty, GILPIN		1780		HAREWOOD	BROWN
	PICTURESQUE CULT vs BROWNIAN	HOT AIR BALLOON			PAVLOVSK, PETERSBURG, RUSSIA	CAMERON
U. S. CONSTITUTION	JEFFERSON TOURS ENGLISH GARD'S				HÔTEL DE LANGEAC, PARIS	JEFFERSON
FEDERATION OF AMER. STATES	*On the Picturesque*, PRICE				ENGLISCHE GARTEN, MUNICH	THOMPSON
					SHEFFIELD PARK	REPTON
	Remarks on Forest Scenery, GILPIN		1790		LANDSCDOWNE CRESCENT, BATH	PALMER
KING LOUIS XVI BEHEADED	*The Landsc...a Didactic Poem*, KNIGHT	LANDSCAPE GARDEN STYLE CRITICIZED BY THE PICTURESQUE SCHOOL			TATTON PARK	REPTON
	Essay on the Picturesque, PRICE				WEMBLY PARK	REPTON
					CREWE HALL	REPTON
					CORSHAM	REPTON
	Sketches..on Landsc. Gard'g, REPTON				WENTWORTH HOUSE	REPTON
IRELAND UNITED w/ ENGLAND	*Essay on Population*, MALTHUS		1800		DROTTNINGHOLM PARK, SWEDEN	PIPER

Period bars: GEORGIAN; INDUSTRIAL REVOLUTION

Style Period: PALLADIANISM; EXPERIMENTAL PERIOD IN LANDSCAPE GARDENING; CHINOISERIE; ROMANTICISM; LAND. GARD. CRITICISM

Careers: VANBRUGH; LONDON; WISE; WREN; POPE; KENT; BROWN; GILPIN; NASH; REPTON; KNIGHT; PRICE

Figure 24. *Cumberland Terrace, Regent's Park, London, England.*

Figure 25. *Regent's Park, London, England.*

ENGLAND 1800 - 1900

Politics Economics	Society Environment	Geography Technology	Date	Style Period	Environmental Design	Designers	Careers
			1800		PULAWY, POLAND	DIONIZY	
NAPOLEON EMPEROR OF FRANCE	*Observations..Landsc. Gard.*, REPTON				NYMPHENBURG PALACE, MUNICH	VON SCKELL	
					CHAUX	LEDOUX	
	Anal. Inq...Principles of Taste, KNIGHT	ROYAL HORTICULTURAL SOCIETY			LONGLEAT	REPTON	
					BLOOMSBURY SQUARE, LONDON	REPTON	
	BRIT. MUSEUM TAKES *Elgin Marbles* FROM PARTHENON				ARC DE TRIOMPHE, PARIS	CHALGRIN	
			1810		VILLA BORGHESE, ROME	MOORE	
					REGENT'S PARK, LONDON	NASH & J. REPTON	
					REGENT'S STREET, LONDON	NASH	
BATTLE OF WATERLOO	*Fragments on..Landsc. Gard.*, REPTON	STEAM LOCOMOTIVE					
KING GEORGE IV			1820				
	Encyclopedia of Gardening, LOUDON						
		RAILWAY SYSTEM			PARC DE LA VILLETTE, OISE, FR.	LALOS	
		STEAM POWERED ATL. CROSS'G					
		PHOTOGRAPHY					
KING WILLIAM IV			1830				
	Practical Hints..Landsc. Gard., GILPIN				TIERGARTEN, BERLIN	LENNE	
	Hints on Landsc. Gardening, MUSKAU				PARK-MUSKAU, EAST GERMANY	PUCKLER-MUSKAU	
QUEEN VICTORIA	NEW LANARK PLANNED, OWEN				VICTORIA PARK, LONDON	PENNETHORNE	
					CHATSWORTH CONSERVATORY	PAXTON	
	Landsc. Gard. of H. Repton, LOUDON		1840				
					PRINCE'S PK (SEFTON), LIVERP'L	PAXTON	
					BIRKENHEAD PARK, LIVERPOOL	PAXTON	
	Communist Manifesto, MARX, ENGELS				HAREWOOD TERRACES	BARRY	
	DOWNING TOURS ENGLAND				BRANITZ PARK, EAST GERMANY	PUCKLER-MUSKAU	
	OLMSTED TOURS ENGLAND	FIRST WORLD'S FAIR, LONDON	1850		CRYSTAL PALACE, LONDON	PAXTON	
	VAUX EMIGRATES TO AMERICA	*Walks and Talks of an American Farmer in England*, OLMSTED			BOIS DE BOULOGNE, PARIS	ALPHAND	
	The Origin of the Species, DARWIN						
	OLMSTED TOURS ENGLISH PARKS	INTERNAL-CUMBUSTION ENGINE, LENOIR	1860				
					PARC DU BUTTES CHAUMONT, PARIS	ALPHAND	
		SUEZ CANAL OPENED					
			1870				
					BODNANT GARDEN, GWYNEDD, WALES	MILNER	
	The Wild Garden, ROBINSON		1880				
					BOTANIC GARDENS, REGENTS PK	ROBINSON	
			1890				
			1900				

Periods (vertical bars): GEORGIAN PERIOD; QUEEN VICTORIA

Style Period (vertical bars): "LANDSC. GARDEN STYLE" CRITICIZED BY "PICTURESQUE SCHOOL"; VICTORIAN STYLE CARPET BEDDING

Careers (vertical bars): KNIGHT; PRICE; GILPIN; LOUDON; NASH; REPTON; PAXTON; ROBINSON; JEKYLL

AMERICA (1600–1981)

In this section the charts for 1600–1900 (pages 47, 49, and 51) are at a scale of one line per 2 years. The charts for 1900–2000 (pages 53 and 55) are at a scale one line equals 1 year. Included are the following design style periods:

- English formal: "Elizabethan"; "Jacobean"
- Federal
- Classic Revival
- Greek Revival ("antebellum")
- Eclecticism
- City Beautiful Movement
- Country Place Era
- Functionalism
- Contemporary
- Postmodern

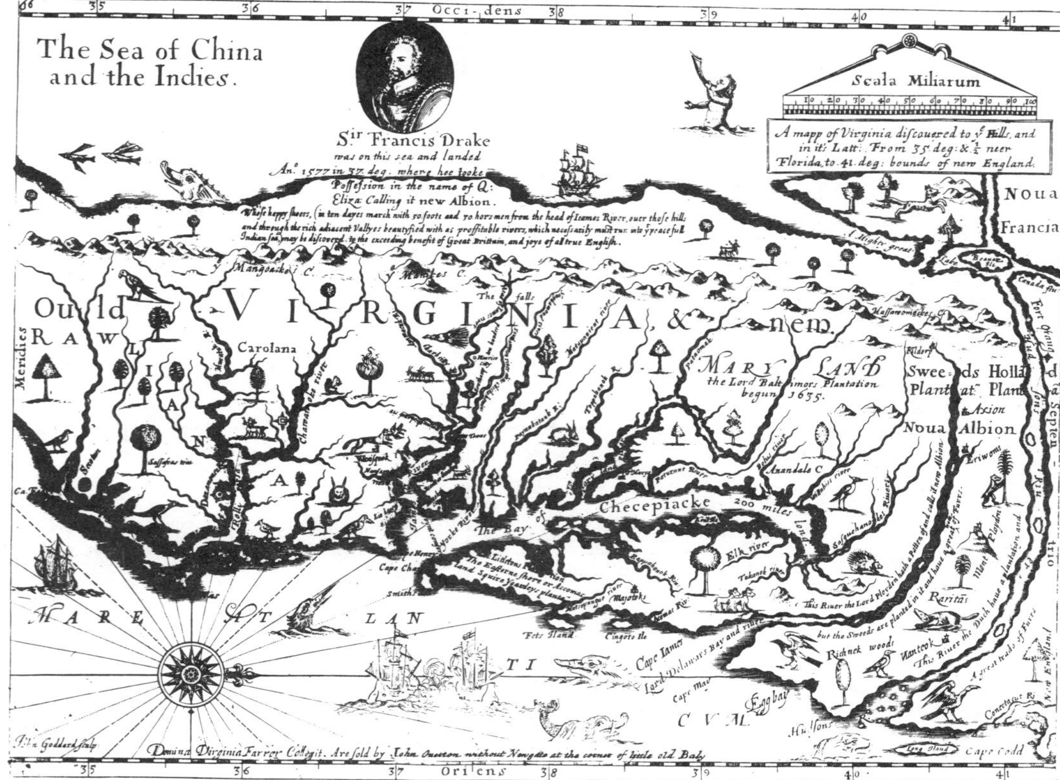

Figure 26. *Virginia Colony, 1650.*

Politics Economics	Society Environment	Geography Technology	Date	Style Period	Environmental Design	Designers	Careers
	EAST INDIA COMPANY	ST. AUGUSTINE, FL EST 1565	1600				
KING JAMES I	DUTCH EAST INDIA COMPANY	ST. LAWRENCE RIVER EXPLORED					
		SANTA FE, NM					
		JAMESTOWN, VA					
	HUDSON RIVER EXPLORED	QUEBEC CITY, CANADA					
	CORN CULTIVATION LEARNED, VA	TELESCOPE, GALILEO, IN ITALY					
	TOBACCO CULTIVATION LEARNED, VA	HUDSON BAY EXPLORED	1610				
	TOBACCO EXPORTED TO ENGLAND						
1st COLONIAL PARLIAMENT, VA	SLAVES IMPORTED INTO VA	PILGRIMS LAND, PLYMOUTH, MA	1620	DOORYARD GARDENS; ELIZABETHAN			
	DUTCH WEST INDIA COMPANY	1st USE OF BRICK IN COLONIES					
	CORN CULTIVATION LEARNED, MA	NEW AMSTERDAM, (N. YORK CY)					
KING CHARLES I	TIMBER PERMITS ORDINANCE, MA	SALEM, MA					
		FLOUR MILL, NEW NETHERLAND					
		PATROON SYSTEM EST., N.NETH.					
		BOSTON, MA	1630				
		MIDDLE PLANTATION, VA					
		MARYLAND COLONY					
	HARVARD COLLEGE, MA	CONN. RIVER VALLEY SETTLED					
	HUNTING REGULATIONS, RI	PRINTING PRESS, VA					
	GREAT PONDS ACT, MA		1640	JACOBEAN			
		MONTRÉAL, CANADA					
		WOOLEN MILL, MA					
		IRON WORKS, MA					
BRITISH MONARCHY ABOLISHED	ROYAL FAMILY LIVES IN FRANCE	SHIP BUILDING, BOSTON					
COMMONWEALTH ESTABLISHED	COLONIAL POPULATION 52,000		1650				
O. CROMWELL, LORD PROTECTOR		MAINE COLONY					
		NORTH CAROLINA COLONY					
RESTORATION OF MONARCHY			1660				
KING CHARLES II		CONNECTICUT COLONY					
ENGLISH SEIZE NEW NETHERLAND		RHODE ISLAND COLONY					
	HUDSON BAY COMPANY	SOUTH CAROLINA COLONY	1670		CHARLESTON, SC PLANNED		
	COLONIAL POPULATION 114,500						
BACON'S REBELLION, VIRGINIA							
		OHIO & MISSISSIPPI RIVERS & GREAT LAKES EXPLORED					
	COLONIAL POPULATION 155,000		1680				
	TREE CLEARANCE ORDINANCE, PA	PENNSYLVANIA COLONY			PHILADELPHIA PLANNED	PENN & HOLME	
KING JAMES II							
WILLIAM & MARY	TREES RESERVED FOR ROYAL SHIP MASTS, MA		1690				
	COLLEGE OF WILLIAM & MARY, VA				COLLEGE OF WILLIAM & MARY, VA	WREN ?	
		RICE INTRODUCED, CAROLINAS			ANNAPOLIS PLANNED	NICHOLSON	
		1st COLONIAL MAIL					
	COLONIAL POPULATION 275,000	TRADE w/ W. INDIES & AFRICA	1700		WILLIAMSBURG PLANNED	NICHOLSON	

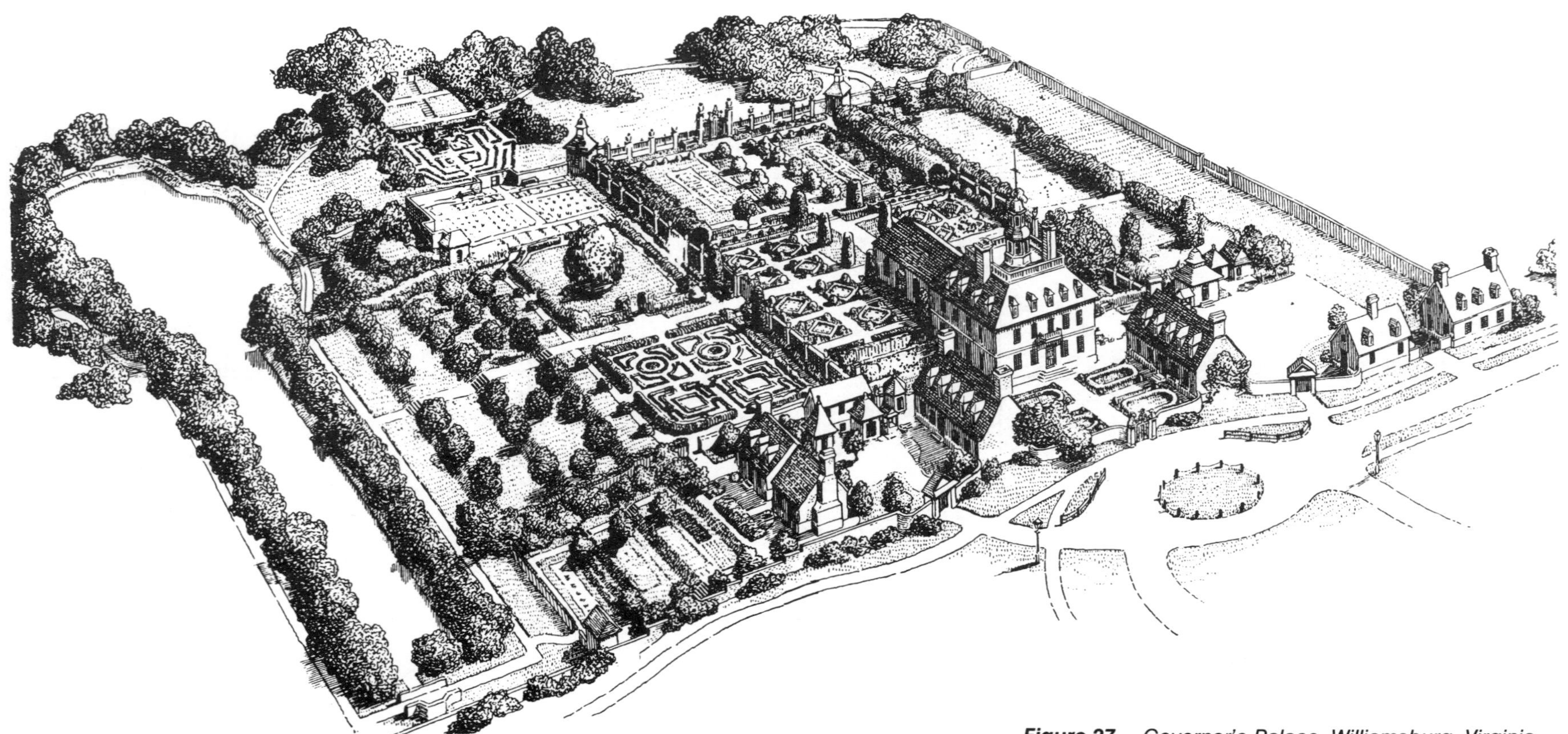

Figure 27. *Governor's Palace, Williamsburg, Virginia.*

AMERICA 1700 - 1800

Politics Economics	Society Environment	Geography Technology	Date	Style Period	Environmental Design	Designers	Careers
QUEEN ANNE		FRONTIER AT APPALACHIANS	1700				
	PINUS STROBUS INTRO. TO ENGLAND						
		GERMAN SETTLE IN PENNSYLV.					
	COLONIAL POPULATION 357,000		1710				
KING GEORGE I					GOVERNOR'S PAL., WILLIAMSBURG	SPOTSWOOD	
		SCOTS-IRISH EMIGRATION POTATO INTRODUCED, N.H.			MARGRAVATE OF AZILIA, GA NEW ORLEANS PLANNED	MONTGOMERY	
		LEAD MINES, MISSOURI	1720				
	COLONIAL SLAVE POP. 75,000						
KING GEORGE II					WESTOVER, VA	BYRD	
					BOTANICAL GARDENS, PHILA. PA	BARTRAM	
	COLONIAL POP. 655,000		1730	GEORGIAN	STRATFORD HALL, VA		
					SAVANNAH, GA PLANNED	OGLETHORPE	
	JOHN BARTRAM TOURS SOUTH, 1736-1766				FREDERICA, GA PLANNED	OGLETHORPE	
	METHODISM FOUNDED, SAVANNAH						
	INDIGO PLANT PROCESSED, SC		1740		MIDDLETON PLACE, CHARLESTON		
	SUGAR CANE INTRODUCED, LA AMER. PHILOS. SOCIETY, PHILA.				MAGNOLIA GARDENS, CHARLEST.		
	BRITAIN PROHIBITS COLONIAL MANUFACTURE OF FINISHED IRON		1750				
	COLONIAL POPULATION 1,500,000						
FRENCH AND INDIAN WAR	WILLIAM BARTRAM TOURS SOUTH, 1753-1800				GUNSTON HALL, VA	MASON	
					BELMONT, CHARLESTON, SC	PINCKNEY	
KING GEORGE III		INDUSTRIAL REVOLUTION, ENG.	1760				
	COLONIAL POPULATION 1,650,000	TREATY OF PARIS EXPANDS ENGLAND'S N. AMER. TERR. TO FLORIDA & THE GREAT LAKES					
BRITISH STAMP ACT					PACA HOUSE, ANNAPOLIS MORVEN, PRINCETON, NJ	PACA STOCKTON	
	SEA ISLAND COTTON, GA						
BOSTON MASSACRE	AMERICAN ACADEMY OF FINE ART	AUSTRALIA EXPLORED, COOK	1770				WASHINGTON
		AMERICA'S 1st MUSEUM, PHILA.					
BOSTON TEA PARTY CONTINENTAL CONGRESS		STEAM ENGINE, WATT IN ENG. QUEBEC ACT GIVES GREAT LAKES AND OHIO TO CANADA					
DEC. OF INDEPENDENCE REVOLUTIONARY WAR, 1775-83		HAWAII EXPLORED, COOK					
FRENCH REVOLUTION		SPANISH EST. CALIF. MISSIONS					
ARTICLES OF CONFEDERATION RATIFIED		OHIO TERR. CEDED TO U. S. A. TURNPIKE, VIRGINIA	1780		STATE HOUSE GARDEN, PHILA.	VAUGHAN	JEFFERSON
		NORTHWEST TERR. SURVEYED		DUTCH & JACOBEAN FORMALSIM EXPERIMENTATION w/ LANDSC. GARDEN	NATIONAL SURVEY GRID	JEFFERSON, ET AL	
U. S. CONSTITUTION FEDERATION OF 13 STATES	JEFFERSON TOURS ENG. GARDENS NORTHWEST ORDINANCE	PATOMACK CANAL, VA			MOUNT VERNON, VA (1759-1786) THE WOODLANDS, PHILADELPHIA	WASHINGTON HAMILTON	
WASHINGTON , PRES. 1789-97	*The Rights of Man*, PAINE	STEAMBOAT ON POTOMAC RIV.			VIRGINIA ST. CAPITAL, RICHMOND	JEFFERSON	
VERMONT, KENTUCKY & TENNESSEE STATEHOOD	1st U.S.A. POP. CENSUS 3,929,627 SLAVE POP., APPROX.694,280	1st U. S. PATENT LAW	1790	FEDERAL	FED. CAPITAL PLANNED, WASH.DC	L'ENFANT, JEFFS'N	
	UNITED STATES BANK, PHILA.	COTTON GIN, SAVANNAH			WHITE HOUSE	HOLBAN	
	Travels Through No. & So. Carolina, Georgia & Florida, Wm BARTRAM	TURNPIKE, PHILA. - LANCASTER SANTEE CANAL, SC			FEDERAL CAPITOL YALE ROW AND GARDEN	THORNTON TRUMBULL	
JOHN ADAMS PRES. 1797-1801							
		LAND ACT 320 ACRES / SETTLER	1800				

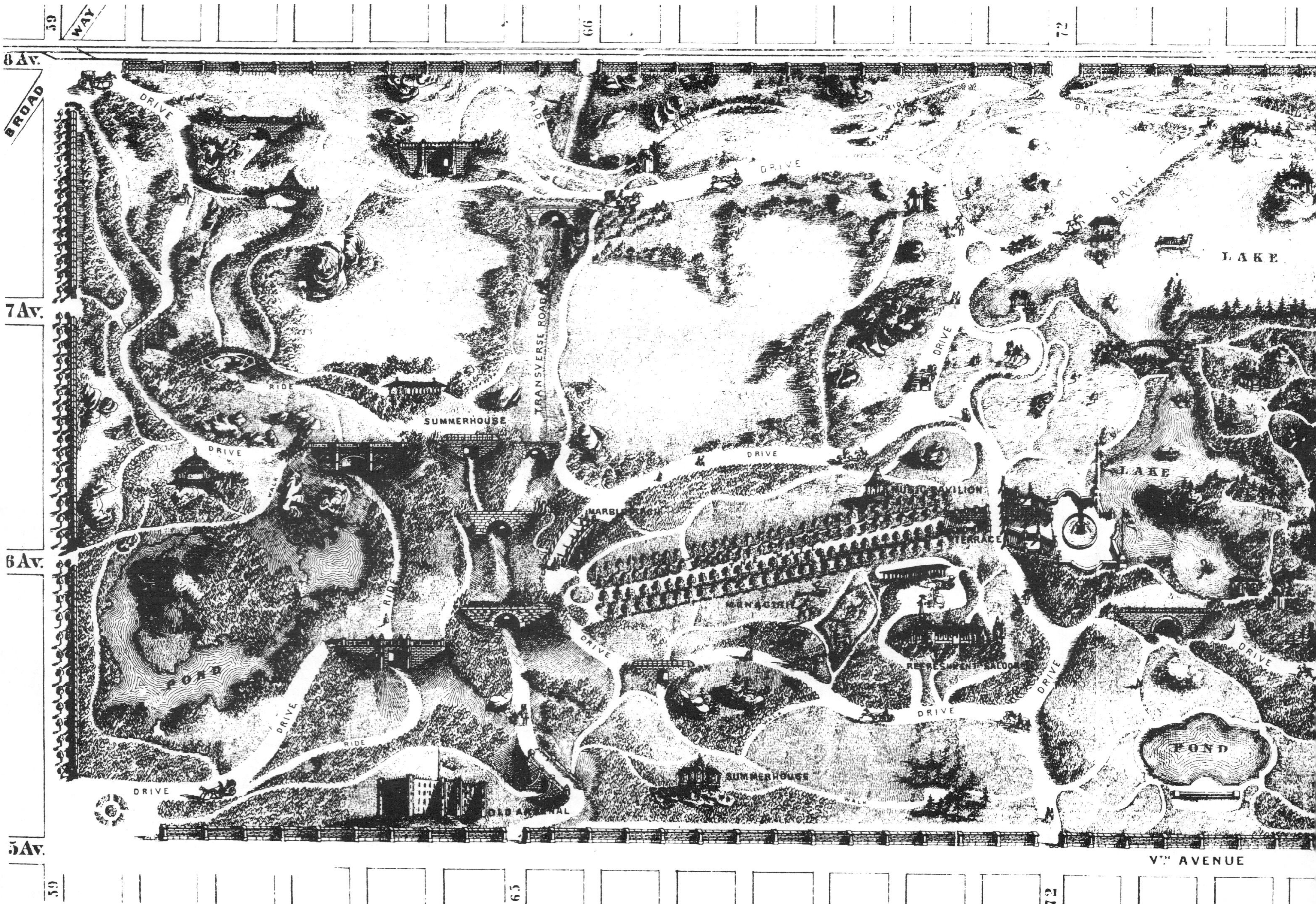

Figure 28. *Central Park, New York.*

Politics Economics	Society Environment	Geography Technology	Date	Environmental Design	Designers
JEFFERSON, PRES. 1801-1809 FRENCH BLOCKADE N. ORLEANS EMPEROR NAPOLEON I 1804-1814 MADISON, PRES. 1809-1817	WASH. D.C. BECOMES NAT'L CAPITAL 1st LAND GRANT SCHOOL, OHIO CATTLE DRIVE, OHIO—EAST COAST *Amer. Gardener's Calendar*, M'MAHON	LOUISIANA PURCHASE LEWIS & CLARK EXPEDITION STEAMBOAT, *CLAREMONT*	1800	MONTICELLO REMODELLED BUFFALO, NY PLANNED PERE-LACHAISE CEMETERY, PARIS GORE PLACE, BOSTON DETROIT PLANNED	JEFFERSON BRONGNIART LA GRAND WOODWARD
WAR OF 1812 (1812-1814) vs ENG. BATTLE OF WATERLOO, BELGIUM MONROE, PRES. 1817-1825 KING GEORGE IV, 1820-1830 MEXICO GAINS INDEPENDENCE	*Thanatopsis*, W. C. BRYANT LOUISIANA STATEHOOD STEAMBOAT DOWN OHIO & MISS. RIV. ANDREW JACKSON DOWNING BORN *Rip Van Winkle*, IRVING UNIV. OF VIRGINIA FOUNDED	GAS STREET LAMPS, PHILADEL. NAT'L ROAD, CUMBERLAND, MD-WHEELING, WV IND., ILL., MISS. STATEHOOD CUMBERLAND ROAD VIA MTS. ALABAMA STATEHOOD	1810	UNION COLLEGE, SCHENECTADY WASHINGTON MONUMENT, BALT. UNIVERSITY OF VIRGINIA DESIGNED POINT BREEZE, BORDENTOWN, NJ	RAMÉE MILLS JEFFERSON JOS. BONAPARTE
JOHN Q. ADAMS, PRES. 1825-1829 JACKSON, PRES. 1929-1837 KING WILLIAM IV, 1830-1837	HUDSON RIVER SCHOOL OF PAINTING U.S.A. POP. 9,638,453 FREDERICK LAW OLMSTED BORN *Dictionary of American English*	MISSOURI STATEHOOD SANTA FE TRAIL ERIE CANAL, BUFFALO-ALBANY HORSE-DRAWN RAILROAD, MA STEAM-POWERED ATL. CROSSING	1820	BROOKLYN BOTANIC GARDEN U.S. CAPITOL COMPLETED	PARMENTIER BULFINCH
REP. OF TEXAS GAINS INDEPEND. QUEEN VICTORIA, 1837-1901	INDIANS DRIVEN WEST OF MISS. RIV. G. CATLIN PROPOSED NAT'L PARK DE TOCQUEVILLE VISITS AMERICA *Nature*, EMERSON NEW ENGLAND FORESTS EXHAUSTED	EASTERN TEXAS SETTLED STEAM-POWERED RAILROAD, PA CLIPPER SHIP LAUNCHED, BALT. STEEL PLOW, JOHN DEERE COLT REVOLVER	1830	MT. AUBURN CEMETERY, BOSTON LAUREL HILL CEM., PHILADELPHIA	BIGELOW & DEARBORN NOTMAN DOUGLASS
TEXAS ANNEXED BY U.S. A. MEXICAN-AMERICAN WAR,1846-48 GOLD DISCOVERED, CALIFORNIA TEXAS, N. MEX., CALIFORNIA CEDED BY MEXICO TO U.S.A.	*Treatise on ... Landsc.Gard.*, DOWNING TREE PLANTING SOCIETIES, MASS. DICKENS VISITS AMERICA *The Horticulturist Magazine*, DOWNING MICH., WISC., IOWA, ARK., STATEH'D C. VAUX ARRIVES IN AMERICA CENTRAL PARK ACT, NEW YORK CTY	WAGON TRAINS TO CALIFORNIA RAIL MILES EXCEED CANALS TELEGRAPH, BALT.—WASH.DC LAWN GRASS IMPROVED IRRIGATION IN UTAH OREGON TRAIL LAND GRANTS TO RAILROADS	1840	SPRING GROVE CEM., CINCINNATI WASHINGTON MONUMENT, 1848-84	DANIELS MILLS
U.S.A. POP. 31,443,321	CRYSTAL PALACE, LONDON *Walks & Talks of an American Farmer* *Seaboard Slave States*, OLMSTED *Walden*, THOREAU PIKE'S PEAK GOLD RUSH, COLORADO *Origin of the Species*, DARWIN	RAIL LINK, CHICAGO TO N. YORK ELEVATOR, OTIS CANAL, LAKE SUPERIOR-HURON ELECTRIC TROLLEY, WASH. DC SILVER DISCOVERED, NEVADA OIL WELL, PA	1850	WASH. MALL/SMITHSONIAN GRNDS LLEWELLYN PARK, W. ORANGE,NJ SLEEPY HOLLOW CEMETERY LAKE FOREST, IL CENTRAL PARK, NEW YORK CITY SPRING GROVE CEM. REDESIGNED	DOWNING DAVIS &HASKELL COPELAND & CLEV. HOTCHKISS OLMSTED & VAUX STRAUCH
LINCOLN, PRESIDENT CIVIL WAR, 1861-1865 BURNING OF ATLANTA	F.L.O. HEADS U.S. SANITARY COMM. HOMESTEAD ACT OF 1862 MORRILL LAND GRANT COLLEGE ACT YOSEMITE VALLEY CEDED TO CA *Man and Nature*, MARSH FRANK LLOYD WRIGHT BORN *Handbook of Landsc Gardening*	PONY EXPRESS, ST LOUIS TO CA 15 MILL. BUFFALO KILLED 1863-78 ALASKA BOUGHT FROM RUSSIA TRANSCONTINENTAL RAILROAD BROOKLYN BRIDGE	1860	GRACELAND CEM. CHICAGO 1st USE OF TERM "LANDSC. ARCH" MT. VIEW CEM., OAKLAND, CA UNIV. OF CALIFORNIA, BERKELEY PROSPECT PARK, BROOKLYN PARKWAY PLANNED, CHICAGO RIVERSIDE, CHICAGO	CLEVELAND & SIMONDS OLMSTED & VAUX OLMSTED OLMSTED OLMSTED & VAUX CLEVELAND OLMSTED & VAUX
U. S. POP. 50,155,783	YELLOWSTONE NATIONAL PARK *Landsc. Arch... West*, CLEVELAND *The Earth as Modified...*, MARSH	BARBED WIRE TELEPHONE, BELL U.S. GEOLOGICAL SURVEY EST. LIGHT BULB, EDISON	1870	FAIRMOUNT PARK, PHILADELPHIA GOLDEN GATE PARK, SAN FRAN. MT. ROYAL PRK, MONTREAL, CAN. U.S. CENTENNIAL EXPO, PHILA. U.S. CAPITOL GROUNDS, WASH.DC "EMERALD NECKLACE", BOSTON	OLMSTED HALL & McLAREN OLMSTED OLMSTED OLMSTED
	NIAGARA FALLS RESERVATION WORLD'S FAIR, PARIS YOSEMITE NATIONAL PARK	1st AUTOMOBILE, GERMANY ESTIMATED BUFFALO POP. 3,000 EIFFEL TOWER, PARIS MOVIE CAMERA WAINWRIGHT BLDG, ST LOUIS	1880	METRO PRK SYST, MINN / ST PAUL STANFORD UNIV CAMPUS, CA BILTMORE ESTATE, ASHEVILLE, NC PARK SYSTEM, LOUISVILLE, KY	CLEVELAND OLMSTED OLMSTED OLMSTED
GOLD RUSH, KLONDIKE, ALASKA SPANISH - AMERICAN WAR U. S. POP. 76,094,000	TRUSTEES OF RESERVATIONS, BOST. SEQUOIA NATIONAL PARK *Italian Villas*, PLATT FREUD'S 1st WORK BILTMORE SCHOOL OF FORESTRY AMER. SOC. OF LANDSC. ARCH., NYC	1st GARDEN CLUB, ATHENS, GA SIERRA CLUB, JOHN MUIR AMERICAN ACADEMY IN ROME 1st RADIO, MARCONI RADIUM DISCOVERED, CURIES	1890	FRANKLIN PARK, BOSTON COLUMBIAN WORLD'S EXPO, CHIC. DRUID HILLS SUBDIV, ATLANTA FAULKNER FARM EST., BOSTON METRO PARK SYSTEM, BOSTON CARSON, PIRIE, SCOTT BLDG, CHIC	OLMSTED OLMSTED OLMSTED PLATT ELIOT SULLIVAN
			1900		

Style Period: FEDERAL STYLE; TURNPIKE AND CANAL BUILDING; CLASSIC REVIVAL; GRECO-ROMAN TOWN NAMES; DUTCH AND JACOBEAN FORMALISM; EXPERIMENTATION WITH "LANDSCAPE GARDEN"; ANTE-BELLUM; GREEK REVIVAL; MOORISH, EGYPTIAN; GOTHIC, ITALIANATE; VICTORIAN ERA; ECOLE DES BEAUX ARTS; COUNTRY PLACE ERA; ART NOUVEAU; ROMANESQUE REVIVAL

Careers: JEFFERSON; PARMENTIER; DOWNING; CLEVELAND; OLMSTED; ELIOT

Figure 29. *Donnell residence, Sonoma, California.*

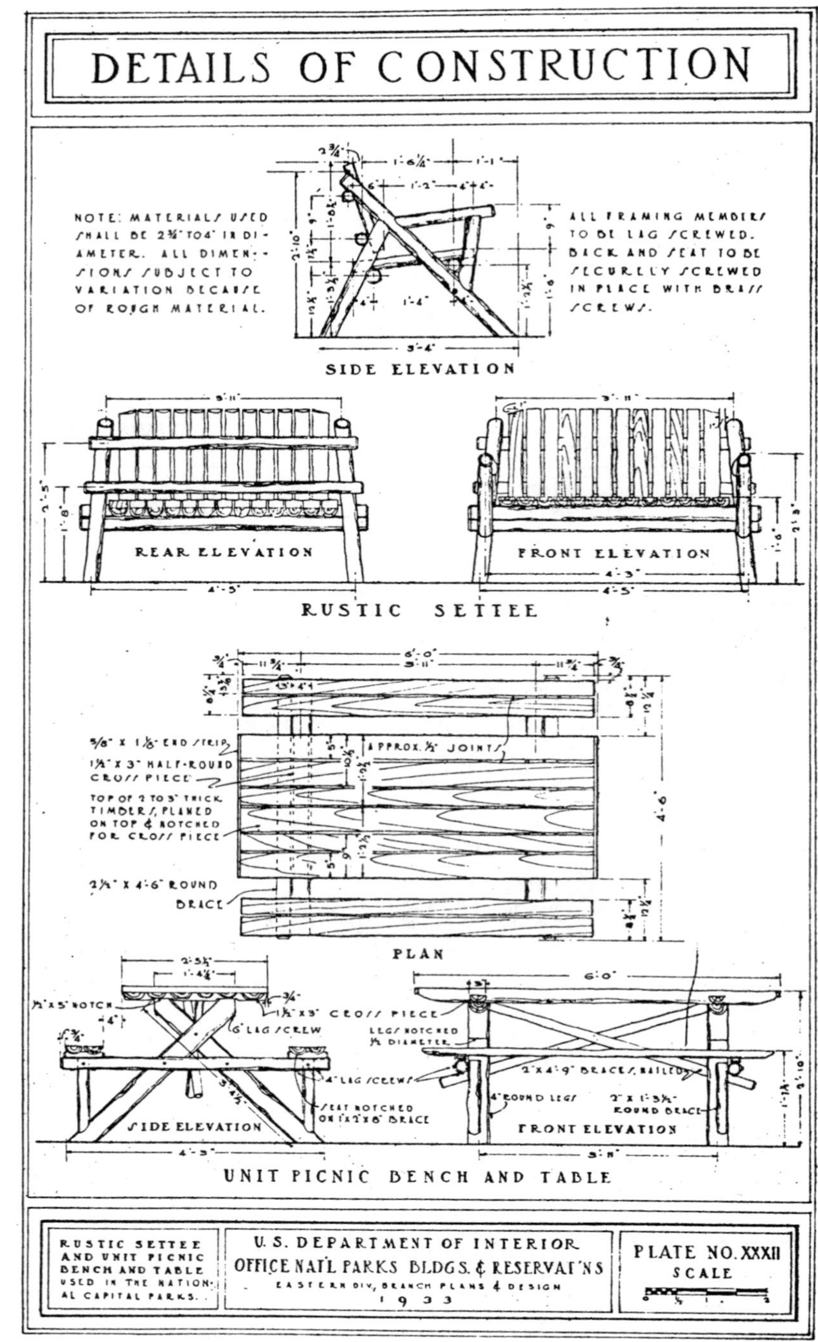

Figure 30. *Park furniture details (U.S. National Park Service).*

AMERICA 1900 - 1950

Politics Economics	Society Environment	Geography Technology	Date	Environmental Design	Designers
THEO. ROOSEVELT, PRESIDENT	LAND. ARCH. COURSES AT HARVARD		1900		
	LOWTHORPE SCHOOL, GROTON, MA	OIL DISCOVERED, TEXAS	1901	McMILLAN COMM. PLAN, WASH. DC	FLO, JR., BURNHAM
	CITY PLANNING PROFESSION		1902	PARK GUELL, BARCELONA, SPAIN	GAUDI
	Garden Cities of To-morrow, HOWARD	WRIGHT BROTHERS' FLIGHT, NC	1903		
			1904		
		Theory of Relativity, EINSTEIN	1905		
	NATIONAL AUDUBON SOCIETY	ASSEMBLY LINE, FORD MOTORS			
	EARTHQUAKE, SAN FRANCISCO			SAN FRANCISCO PLAN	BURNHAM
				MANILA, PHILIPPINES PLANNED	BURNHAM
	CITY PLANNING COURSES, HARVARD			BRONX RIVER PARKWAY, NYC	CLARKE
				UNION STATION, WASHINGTON	BURNHAM
	1st NATIONAL CONSERVATION CONF.			CHICAGO PLAN	BURNHAM
	CUBISM, PICASSO & BRACH			ROBIE HOUSE, CHICAGO	WRIGHT
				FOREST HILLS, NYC	OLMSTED BROS.
	U.S.A. POP. 91,972,266	468,000 AUTOMOBILES REGISTR'D	1910	LINCOLN MEMORIAL, WASH. D.C.	BACON
				TIMBERLINE, PA / GWINN, CLEVEL.	PLATT
	Nude Descending a Stair, pt DUCHAMP			CANBERRA, AUSTRALIA, PLANNED	GRIFFIN
	Gardens for Country Houses, JEKYLL			COUNTRY CLUB DIST., KANSAS CY	HARE AND HARE
				KILLENWORTH, LONG ISL., NY	GREENLEAF
		PANAMA CANAL COMPLETED			
WORLD WAR I BEGINS, EUROPE	1st ZONING LAW, NEW YORK CITY			SWAN HOUSE, ATLANTA	SCHUTZE
			1915	PANAMA PACIFIC EXPO, S. FRAN.	GOODHUE
	NATIONAL PARK SERVICE			VILLA VIZCAYA, MIAMI	SUAREZ
U.S.A. ENTERS WORLD WAR I RUSSIAN REVOLUTION				COLUMBUS PARK, CHICAGO	JENSEN
	GRAND CANYON NATIONAL PARK				
TREATY OF VERSAILLES	ZION NATIONAL PARK	BAUHAUS-GROPIUS, MIES, CORB.			
WOMEN GET RIGHT TO VOTE		9,000,000 AUTOS REGISTERED	1920		
HARDING, PRESIDENT	*Three Musicians,* pt , PICASSO	RADIO STAT'N *KDKA*-PITTSBURG		MARIEMONT, OHIO	NOLEN
				DUMBARTON OAKS, WASH. D.C.	FARRAND
				ORMSTON, LONG ISLAND, NY	OLMSTED BROS
				TRIBUNE TOWER, CHICAGO	
COOLIDGE, PRESIDENT TEAPOT DOME SCANDAL				SAGRADA FAMILIA CATHEDRAL BARCELONA, SPAIN	GAUDI
	FLORIDA LAND BOOM PEAKS	SCOPES "MONKEY TRIAL"	1925	WILLIAMSBURG RESTOR. BEGUN	SHURCLIFF, ET AL
		LINDBERGH FLIES ATLANTIC		RADBURN, NJ	STEIN & WRIGHT
		TELEVISION BROADCASTS		CHICOPEE, GA	DRAPER
	PENICILLIN, FLEMING	*The Jazz Singer,* 1st SOUND FILM		JONES BEACH, LONG ISLAND, NY	COMBS
STOCK MARKET CRASH HOOVER, PRESIDENT	DEPT. OF CITY PLANNING, HARVARD	DUST STORMS - KS, CO, OK, TX			
	U.S.A. POP. 122,775,046	EMPIRE STATE BUILDING-NYC	1930		
				TACONIC STATE PARKWAY, NY	CLARKE
		1st HISTORIC ZONING ORDINAN.			
HITLER, CHANCELLOR				SKYLINE DRIVE, VA	NAT'L PARK SERV.
ROOSEVELT, PRESIDENT	TENNESSEE VALLEY AUTHORITY	H.A.B.S. - NAT'L PARK SERVICE		BLUE RIDGE PARKWAY, VA & NC	ABBOTT
"NEW DEAL"	CIVILIAN CONSERVATION CORPS	DUST STORMS & DROUGHTS		CENT. OF PROGRESS EXPO, CHIC	
SEC. & EXCHANGE COMM.	GRT SMOKY MOUNTAINS NAT'L PRK			NORRIS, TN	DRAPER
				GREENBELT, MD	BURSLEY &WALKER
WORKS PROG. ADMIN.			1935	GRENHILLS, OH	HARTZOG &STRONG
SOCIAL SECURITY SYST.	SOIL CONSERVATION SERVICE	BOULDER (HOOVER) DAM COMPL		FALLING WATER, BEAR RUN, PA	WRIGHT
	WILDLIFE RESTORATION ACT	GROPIUS AT HARVARD		TALIESIN WEST, SCOTTSDALE, AZ	WRIGHT
	MONDRIAN PAINTINGS	ECKBO, KILEY, ROSE REVOLT		GREENDALE, WI	PETERS & CRANE
	Guernica, pt, PICASSO			BALDWIN HILLS VILLAGE, LS ANG	STEIN & BARLOW
				JEFFERSON MEMORIAL, WASH.	POPE
				ST. ANN'S HILL, CHERTSEY, ENG.	TUNNARD
	Siftings, JENS JENSEN			GOLDEN GATE INT'L EXPO, S. F.	
GERMANY IN POLAND		*Gone With the Wind,* COLOR FILM		WORLD'S FAIR, NEW YORK CITY	
	U.S.A. POP. 131,669,275		1940	WOODLAND CREMATORIUM STOCKHOLM, SWEDEN	ASPLUND
	U.S. FISH & WILDLIFE SERVICE				
PEARL HARBOR, U.S. IN WW II					
		DDT INTRODUCED INTO USA		UNION SQUARE, SAN FRANCISCO	PFLEUGER
		ATOMIC CHAIN REACTION, FERMI			
	URBAN RENEWAL ACT				
TRUMAN , PRESIDENT		ATOMIC BOMB ON HIROSHIMA	1945		
JAPAN BOMBED, W. WAR II ENDS				GEN MOTORS TECH CNTR, DETROIT	SAARINEN & CHURCH
UNITED NATIONS FORMED AT DUMBARTON OAKS, WASH. DC	BUREAU OF LAND MANAGEMENT			LEVITTOWN, NY	LEVITT & SONS
				FRESH MEADOWS, NEW YORK CTY	GEIFFERT
				DONNELL RESIDENCE, SONOMA,CA	CHURCH&HALPRIN
	Sand County Almanac, LEOPOLD	NAT'L TRUST FOR HIST. PRESERV		PALISADES PARKWAY, NJ	CLARKE
PEOPLE'S REPUBLIC OF CHINA				RONCHAMP CHAPEL, FRANCE	LE CORBUSIER
	U. S. A. POP. 150,697,000		1950		

Politics bars: W W I; PROHIBITION; DEPRESSION; ROOSEVELT, PRESIDENT; WW II

Style Period: BEAUX-ARTS; COUNTRY PLACE ERA; CITY BEAUTIFUL MOVEMENT; ART NOUVEAU; BAUHAUS; L.A. "MODERNISM"/"FUNCTIONALISM"

Careers: F.L.O.; PLATT; BURNHAM; F. L. OLMSTED, Jr.; CLARKE; FARRAND; NOLEN; O.C.SIMONDS; COFFIN; JENSEN; FLANDERS; DRAPER; ECKBO, KILEY, ROSE; CHURCH

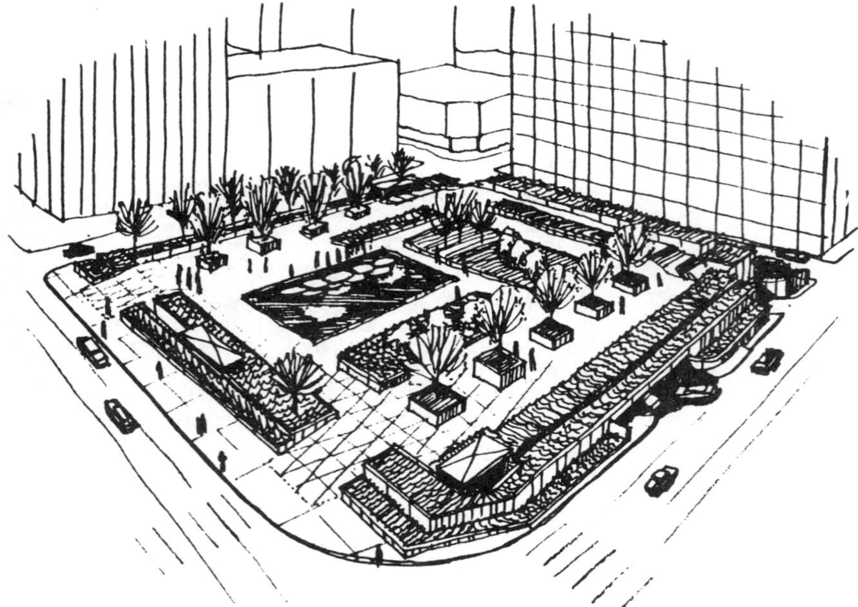

Figure 31. *Mellon Square, Pittsburgh, Pennsylvania.*

Figure 32. *Freeway Park, Seattle, Washington.*

AMERICA 1950 - 2000

Politics Economics	Society Environment	Geography Technology	Date	Style Period	Environmental Design	Designers
KOREAN WAR McCARTHY HEARINGS QUEEN ELIZABETH II EISENHOWER , PRESIDENT KOREAN WAR ENDS *BROWN VS. BRD OF EDUC.*	U. S. A. POPULATION 150, 697,000 POLLACK'S FIRST "DRIP" PAINTING *The Sea Around Us*, CARSON *The Silent World*, COUSTEAU MT. EVEREST CLIMBED SALK POLIO VACCINE	GUAM MADE U. S. TERRITORY COLOR TELEVISION UHF TELEVISION HYDROGEN BOMB TESTED DNA MOLECULE MAPPED 3-D MOVIES *NAUTILUS*, NUCLEAR SUB	1950		LEVER HOUSE, NEW YORK TAPIOLA NEW TOWN, FINLAND MELLON SQUARE, PITTSBURG MUS. OF MOD. ART SCULPT. GARDEN, NYC	SOM SIMONDS BROS. JOHNSON
NAACP BUS BOYCOTTING USSR INVADES HUNGARY CASTRO TAKES OVER CUBA U.S.A. POPULATION 179.3 MILL.	4 MINUTE MILE, R. BANNISTER WATER POLLUTION ACT INTERSTATE HIGHWAYS BEGAN COMMERCIAL JET TRAVEL USSR LANDS *LUNA II* ON MOON NASA LAUNCHES TWO MONKEYS	CONTACT LENSES BRASILIA PLANNED TRANSATLANTIC TELEPHONE *SPUTNIK*, USSR PENICILLIN XEROX MACHINE NASA EST. ALASKA & HAWAII STATEHOOD ST. LAWRENCE SEAWAY OPENS	1955		GARDEN STATE PARKWAY, NJ CIGNA/CONN. GENERAL, BLOOMFIELD, CT FOOTHILL COLLEGE, LOS ALTOS, CA AIR FORCE ACAD., COLORADO SPRINGS IBM RESEARCH CNTR, YORKTOWN HTS,NY	CLARKE NOGUCHI SASAKI, WALKER KILEY SASAKI, WALKER
NAACP BOYCOTTING KENNEDY, PRESIDENT CUBAN MISSLE CRISIS M.L.KING: "I HAVE A DREAM" KENNEDY ASSASSINATED JOHNSON, PRES.	U-2 SPY PLANE CAPTURED BY USSR BIRTH CONTROL PILL BERLIN WALL BUILT *Silent Spring*, CARSON CLEAN AIR ACT LAND & WATER CONSERV. FUND CLEAN RIVER ACT	LASER BEAM MANNED SPACE FLIGHT, USSR PEACE CORPS FOUNDED JOHN GLENN ORBITS EARTH FIRST WOMAN IN SPACE, USSR POLAROID CAMERA NEW YORK WORLD'S FAIR	1960		SEA PINES PLANTATION, HILTON HD, SC UPJOHN CO. , KALAMAZOO, MI McINTIRE GARDEN, HILLSBOROUGH, CA SEA RANCH, CA CONSTITUTION PLAZA, HARTFORD, CT CHASE MANHATTAN BANK PLAZA, NYC JACOB RIIS PLAZA, NYC	SASAKI, WALKER SASAKI, WALKER HALPRIN HALPRIN SASAKI, WALKER NOGUCHI FRIEDBERG
H.U.D. CREATED U.S.A. POPULATION 2 MILLION M. L. KING SHOT SEN. ROBT KENNEDY SHOT NIXON, PRESIDENT (VIETNAM WAR)	NAT'L REGISTER OF HIST. PLACES STATE LAND USE PLAN, HAWAII *The Population Bomb*, ERLICH *Design With Nature*, McHARG WOODSTOCK FESTIVAL NATIONAL ENVIRON. POLICY ACT	ASTRODOME, HOUSTON USSR SATELLITE HITS VENUS NASA "SOFT LANDS" ON MOON HUMAN HEART TRANSPLANTS EXPO '67, MONTREAL SANTA BARBARA OIL LEAK MANNED LUNAR LANDING *CONCORDE* SST FLIGHT	1965		RESTON, VA COPLEY SQUARE, BOSTON NICOLLET MALL, MINNEAPOLIS FORD FOUNDATION HEADQUARTERS, NYC PALEY PARK, NYC GHIRARDELI SQUARE, SAN FRANCISCO OAKLAND MUSEUM, OAKLAND, CA	ROUSE CO. SASAKI, DAWSON HALPRIN KILEY ZION & BREEN HALPRIN KILEY
FIRST EARTH DAY U.S. POP. 203,235,298 WATERGATE SCANDAL AGNEW RESIGNS NIXON RESIGNS FORD, PRESIDENT.	COUNCIL OF ENVIRON. QUAL. (EPA) DDT BANNED CLEAN AIR ACT *Limits to Growth*, CLUB OF ROME *Small Is Beautiful*, SCHUMACHER A.I.M. SEIZES WOUNDED KNEE *Amarillo Ramp*, sc SMITHSON "STREAKING" IN PUBLIC	*Spiral Jetty*, *sc* SMITHSON AMTRAK CREATED *MARINER 9* ORBITS MARS 6TH AND LAST LUNAR LANDING SYDNEY OPERA HOUSE WORLD TRADE CENTER, NYC SEARS TOWER, CHICAGO "TEST-TUBE" BABIES, ENGLAND	1970		IRA KELLER FOUNTAIN, PORTLAND, OR WALT DISNEY WORLD, ORLANDO, FL BOSTON CITY HALL PLAZA SUNY AT BUFFALO, NY AMELIA ISLAND, FL INNER HARBOR, BALTIMORE	HALPRIN W. DISNEY PROD. KALLMAN, ET AL SASAKI, DAWSON WMRT WMRT
CARTER, PRESIDENT 50 HOSTAGES TAKEN BY IRAN INFLATION IS 13.3% USSR INVADES AFGANISTAN EGYPT-ISRAEL TREATY	CHINA EARTHQUAKE KILLS 655,000 *Running Fence*, sc, CRISTO "LEGIONNAIRE'S DISEASE," PHILA. JONESTOWN MURDER-SUICIDES THREE MILE ISLAND DISASTER 125,000 CUBAN REFUGEES IN U. S.	USA/USSR SPACE RENDEZVOUS ALASKAN OIL PIPELINE FLUOROCARBONS BANNED *VOYAGER I & II* TO JUP. & SAT. CIGARETTES CAUSE CANCER VIKING COINS FOUND IN MAINE LOVE CANAL EMERGENCY	1975		FREEWAY PARK, SEATTLE WINTER GARDEN, NIAGARA FALLS, NY FANEUIL HALL/QUINCY, MARKET BOSTON WOODLANDS, TEXAS GASWORKS PARK BAGEL GARDEN WOODLAND PARK ZOO, SEATTLE	HALPRIN FRIEDBERG ROUSE CO. McHARG HAAG SCHWARTZ JONES & JONES
HOSTAGE RESCUE FAILS U.S. POPULATION 226.6 MILLION REAGAN, PRESIDENT FALKLAND ISLANDS WAR GRENADA ISLAND "RESCUE" 1ST WOMAN V. P. NOMINATED	MOUNT ST. HELENS ERUPTION AIDS IDENTIFIED ALASKAN OIL SPILL	SPACE SHUTTLE ARTIFICIAL HEART 1ST AMER. WOMAN IN SPACE BHOPAL, INDIA GAS LEAK	1980	POST-MOSERNISM	FDR MEMORIAL, WASHINGTON, DC PIAZZA D'ITALIA, NEW ORLEANS VIETNAM VETERANS MEMORIAL, WASH. HARLEQUIN PLAZA, ENGLEWOOD, CO SKID ROW PARKS, LOS ANGELES SEASIDE NEW TOWN, FL	HALPRIN MOORE LIN SWA POD, INC. DUANY/ PLATER-ZYBERK
GORBACHEV, SOVIET LEADER U.S. CONSTITUTION 200 YEARS STOCK MARKET CRASH BUSH, PRESIDENT BERLIN WALL REMOVED	MEXICO CITY EARTHQUAKE CHERNOBYL NUKE PLANT DISASTER LOS ANGELES EARTHQUAKE SAN FRANCISCO EARTHQUAKE	*CHALLENAGER* EXPLOSION *VOYAGER* PLNE CIRCLES EARTH *PIONEER*, VENUS PROBE LANDS	1985		WILLIAMS SQUARE, IRVING, TX BLOEDEL GARDENS, SEATTLE COPLEY SQUARE REDESIGN, BOSTON TANNER FOUNTAIN, CAMBRIDGE BATTERY PARK CITY ESPLANADES, NYC REGIS GARDENS, MINNEAPOLIS CODEX WORLD HDQRTRS, CANTON, MA	SWA HAAG ABBOTT WALKER HANNA / OLIN VAN VALKENBERG HANNA / OLIN
PANAMA INVASION PERSIAN GULF WAR USSR DISSOLVED	EUROPEAN ECONOMIC COMMUNITY U. S. A. POPULATION 253.5 MILLION		1990		KOREAN WAR VETERANS MEMORIAL, WASH., DC WOMEN IN VIETNAM MEMORIAL, WASH.,DC EURO DISNEYLAND, PARIS, FRANCE NATIONAL PEACE GARDEN, WASHINGTON	COOPER-LECKY DICKIE / HOK POD, INC. / EDAW ROYSTON
			1995			
			2000			

Careers: CHURCH, ROSE, ECKBO, KILEY, SIMONDS, SASAKI, McHARG, HALPRIN, FRIEDBERG

Figure 33. *Locational score, Sea Ranch, California.*

SECTION 3

OUTLINE OF LANDSCAPE ARCHITECTURAL HISTORY

Outline of Landscape Architectural History

- I. **Prehistory** (20,000–3300 B.C.)
  - A. **Paleolithic:** Old Stone Age (20,000–8000 B.C.)
    1. First tools (stone axe, knife)
    2. Hunting skills evolving
    3. Food gathering
    4. Nomadic lifestyle
    5. Worship of fertility goddess
    6. Burial monuments considered sacred
    7. Various races evolved
  - B. **Mesolithic:** Middle Stone Age (8000–4000 B.C.)
    1. More advanced hunting skills developed
    2. Plant collecting techniques advanced
    3. Semisettled lifestyle
  - C. **Neolithic:** New Stone Age (4000–3300 B.C.)
    1. Earliest agriculture (barley and wheat: domestication of pigs, sheep, goats; use of fire to clear fields)
    2. Formation of villages and towns
    3. Evolution of power and design to express authority
    4. Toolmaking techniques improved
    5. Weaving and pottery developed
  - D. **Bronze Age** (3300–1600 B.C.)
    1. Transition from villages to cities
    2. Ability to produce food in abundance led to surpluses and means of storing surplus
    3. Writing developed
    4. Social organization; specialists gained power over laboring force
    5. Technology advancing (metallurgy—bronze and copper tools, pottery refined, mathematics, astronomy, calendar)
- II. **Ancient Times** (4000 B.C.–A.D. 476)
  - A. **Egypt** (4000–500 B.C.)
    1. **Environment:** desert environment protected and stabilized social system; annual flooding of Nile Valley led to fertile agricultural lands
    2. **Culture:** strong central government with pharaoh worshipped as god; slave labor maintained vital irrigation network; strong belief in afterlife
    3. **Design expressions:**
       - a. Monumental structures
         - (1) Zigguarts
         - (2) Pyramids (tombs, astronomical observatories, calendar, survey device)
         - (3) Axial funerary or mortuary temples (reflect periodic religious processional, enclosed within walls, aligned toward rising sun; monumental, terraced, trees transplanted and irrigated)

           Example:
           - Queen Hatshepsut's mortuary temple, Deir el-Bahri, c. 1480 B.C.
       - b. Formal residential estates and gardens (enclosed in walls,

included utilitarian plantings of trees, shrubs, and vines; formal orderly ground plan influenced by irrigation system; included fish tanks or pools, residence enclosed within a gardenlike setting)

Example:

- Residential estate of high official of Amenhotep III, c. 1400 B.C.

4. **Vocabulary:**
   - Acacia
   - Al fresco
   - Arbor
   - Axis (axes)
   - Bas-relief
   - Bilateral symmetry
   - Cromlech and Dolmen
   - Floodplain
   - Hieroglyphics
   - Lotus
   - Oasis
   - Obelisk
   - Orthogonal
   - Papyrus
   - Pergola
   - Pylon
   - Shaduf
   - Topiary
   - Topography
   - Ziggurat

B. Mesopotamian Civilizations (3,500–538 B.C.): Sumerian (3500–900 B.C.), Assyrian (900–625 B.C.), neo-Babylonian (611–538 B.C.)

1. **Environment:** the "fertile crescent" between the Tigris and Euphrates rivers, a broad flood plain; more temperate climate than Egypt
2. **Culture:** urbanized populations; social organization
3. **Design expressions:**
   a. Royal hunting parks (enclosed, formal ground plan, stocked with game animals, imported plant materials, artificial "mounts," temples, and palaces)
   b. Concepts of "paradise" or "garden of Eden" (the notion that "heaven" was capable of being created by human beings on the earth and that such was to be quadrilaterally symmetrical, divided by four water channels flowing forth from a central point)
   c. Hanging Gardens of Babylon (605 B.C.) (created for the wife of King Nebuchadnezzar as a "green mountain" of a seven-storied palace with gardens planted on each terrace level)
   d. Walled cities were "organic" in form
   e. Residences were of sun-baked brick with interior courtyards to provide open-air ventilation while separated from undesirable street conditions
4. **Vocabulary:**
   - Cedar of Lebanon
   - Eden
   - Mount
   - Paradise
   - Post and lintel
   - Spiral pump

C. Persia (539–331 B.C.)

1. **Environment:** empire extended from Egypt to Indus River (India); characterized by hot, arid desert landscape with few fertile river valleys
2. **Culture:** synthesis of Assyrian, Egyptian, and Ionian Greek; religion of mysticism; ban on figurative art led to geometric abstract patterns; open-air worship; under Darius I and Xerxes (523–465 B.C.) the height of the empire; in 331 B.C. Alexander the Great ended Persian dominance
3. **Design expressions:**
   a. Idealization of the world as "paradise gardens"
      (1) Geometric ground plan
      (2) Biaxially divided into "four quarters of the universe" or "four rivers of heaven"
      (3) Enclosed within architectural walls
      (4) Water in reflecting pools, cascades, and small fountains
      (5) Lush plant material for shade, scent; symbolism of flowers and fruit
   b. Origin of Islamic ("Moorish") style such as created in Spain during the fourteenth century (Alhambra, Generalife, Alcazar)
4. **Vocabulary:**
   - Bagh
   - Chadar
   - Qanat

D. Greece (700–136 B.C.)

1. **Environment:** rugged, mountainous indented peninsulas and islands that made land travel difficult, leading to maritime travel and communications; isolation of people into separate political units (polis); hot, arid climate; little arable land area
2. **Culture:** philosophy based on notion of pure reason and truth derived from scientific evidence; belief in a basic order and idealized harmonies of forms ("golden mean" or "golden

section"); polytheistic religion with many gods associated with natural phenomena

3. **Design expressions:**
   a. The polis or city-state as urban focus of agricultural community
      (1) Governmental, commercial, and religious functions incorporated into central civic marketplace or "agora"
         (a) Formal unity and rectangularity
         (b) Pedestrian traffic only
      (2) Walled towns with gridiron street pattern, two major streets oriented north-south and east-west
      (3) Private residences clustered behind walls with south-facing, open "atrium" courtyards for fresh air and sunlight
         (a) Restrictions on building heights and number of windows
         (b) "Adonis gardens" within the home
   b. Planned colonial settlements; principles of planning codified by Hippodamus c. 450 B.C.; orderliness and regularity the established mode of development
      Examples:
      - Miletus
      - Olynthus
      - Priene
   c. Acropolis: the religious symbolic center of the community; usually atop a lofty promontory ("the high city"); enclosed within walls; comprised of the temple(s) to local patron deity; the site considered sacred; nonaxial grouping of structures that were arrived at obliquely, thus seen "in the round," expressed harmony with site
      Examples:
      - Acropolis, Athens
      - Acropolis, Delphi
   d. Sacred grove: places in their natural condition imbued with sacred significance; places of worship and meditation that became the setting for the academy
   e. Academy evolved from natural setting in sacred grove to more formalized architectural complex with facilities for schooling and development of the body as well as the mind (the "gymnasium" for athletic events has an open-air "peristyle" courtyard as its focus)
4. **Vocabulary:**
   - Academy
   - Acropolis
   - Adonis garden
   - Agora
   - Animism
   - Anthropomorphic
   - Atrium
   - Basilica
   - Bouleterion
   - Capital
   - Caryatid
   - Classic, classical
   - Colonnade
   - Cyclopean
   - Entablature
   - Entasis
   - Erectheum
   - Exedra
   - Fluting
   - Frieze
   - Gymnasium
   - Hellenic
   - Hellenistic
   - Hippodamian
   - Nymphaeum
   - Orders (Doric, Ionic, Corinthian)
   - Panathenaic way
   - Parthenon
   - Pediment
   - Peristyle
   - Polis
   - Polytheism
   - Portico
   - Space (negative/positive)
   - Stoa
   - Term
   - Xystos

E. **The Roman World** (510 B.C.–A.D. 476)

1. **Environment:** originated in the hot, arid central Italian peninsula in the city of Rome (510 B.C.) and expanded by second century A.D. westward to Spain and Scotland and eastward to the Persian Gulf
2. **Culture:** Roman Republic (510–27 B.C.) based on Greek democracy and religion; Roman Empire (27 B.C.–A.D. 476), class system under dictatorship of emperor, who was worshipped as a god; Christianity, initially opposed by paganism, was legalized as official religion in A.D. 313 by Emperor Constantine; in A.D. 395 empire was split into Western (Roman) and Eastern (Byzantine) branches
3. **Design expressions:**
   a. Engineering and technology
      (1) Roads (Appian Way, Rome to the "heel" of Italy, 100 B.C.)
      (2) Bridges
      (3) Aqueducts (Pont du Gard, Nimes, France, A.D. 50)

(4) Fortresses and walls (Hadrian's Wall, England, c. A.D. 125)
(5) Walled towns (London, Pompeii), planned orderliness based on Greek gridiron scheme

b. Urban open-space development
(1) The Forum Romanum, Rome (c. 100–c. 46 B.C.)
(a) Urban open space evolves as "monumental" in its own right
(2) The Imperial Fora, Rome (44 B.C.–A.D. 112)
(a) Each succeeding Emperor created larger and more impressive forum
(b) Each was contiguous to the others and interrelated by a series of interlocking perpendicular axes
(c) Each rectangular space enclosed by four colonnaded sides

Examples:
- Forum of Julius Caesar, 44 B.C.
- Forum of Augustus, A.D. 14
- Forum of Trajan, A.D. 100–112

(c) Urban residential gardens
(1) Garden enclosed within house in a rectangular open-air space defined by colonnades; called a "peristyle court"
(2) Plants grown in the ground
(3) Atrium, as used by Greeks, retained as forecourt

Example:
- House of the Vettii, Pompeii, A.D. 65–79

d. Villas
(1) Urban—"villa urbana": enclosed within walls, included formal, geometric gardens

Example:
- Horace's Villa, Sabine Hills, 30 B.C.

(2) Country—"villa rustica": often expansive, yet walled, comprised of numerous structures for residence and entertainment; included many enclosed formal gardens as well as agricultural fields and orchards

Examples:
- Pliny the Younger's Villa, Laurentinum, A.D. 100
- Hadrian's Villa, Tivoli, A.D. 117–138

4. Vocabulary:
- Amphitheater
- Aqueduct
- Arcade
- Arch
- Bucolic
- Byzantine
- Cardo
- Castrum
- Circus
- Colosseum
- Cruciform
- Decumanus
- Domus
- Etruscan
- Exedra
- Forum
- Fresco
- Genius loci
- Gestatio
- Grotto
- Hippodrome
- Impluvium
- Insula
- Labyrinth
- Maze
- Mosaic
- Panorama
- Pastoral
- Topiary
- Vault
- Villa (rustica, urbana)

III. The Middle Ages—Medieval Period or Dark Ages (A.D. 476–c. 1350)

A. Christian Europe

1. Environment: The geographical area comprises today's Western European countries, spanning from the Mediterranean landscapes (hot, arid, mountainous, agriculturally poor) of Italy and Spain to the northerly lush temperate environments of Britain, France, Germany, and so on, with their varying topography from the Pyranees and Alps to the gentle, rolling hills and "low country" of the Netherlands

2. Culture: Following the ultimate collapse of the politically unified Western Roman Empire, the divergent ethnic peoples of medieval Europe reverted to the provincialism of pre-Roman times; numerous small kingdoms often at war with one another; Christianity was the common religious belief; the high level of technological achievement of the classical times was eroded by the destruction of libraries and classic works by the barbarians; monasteries were the institutions that preserved and perpetuated the knowledge of the classics; the majority of the population lived within or adjacent to fortified towns or on manors; the majority of creative effort was directed toward defensive or religious objectives

3. Design expressions:

a. Monasteries
(1) Frequently autonomous or semi-self-sufficient

(2) Orderly arrangement of facilities
(3) Central open space; focus of monastery complex was the cloister
  (a) Rectangular or square in shape
  (b) Enclosed, usually on all four sides
  (c) Usually located on the south side of the transept of the church
  (d) Surrounded by monks' dormitories, study rooms, library, and so on
  (e) Contained gardenlike "paradise," "garth," or "hortus conclusus" of evergreens or medicinal plants (hence called a "physic garden"), a water feature (well, fountain, pool, or baptismal font), central feature joined by four paved or gravel walks from the surrounding "ambulatory" corridor

Examples:
- St. Paul's Outside-the-Walls, Rome, fifth century
- St. Gall, Switzerland, A.D. 830

b. Walled towns
(1) Fortified with massive masonry walls
(2) Location chosen for security as well as means of access and availability of water
(3) Many first settled by Romans as fortresses
(4) Cramped, densely populated—growth by accretion
(5) Disease rampant
(6) Streets narrow and irregular in alignment
(7) Limited open space, usually near center with church or cathedral, town hall, and central public water well
  (a) Open space ("square," "piazza," "plaza") irregular in configuration
  (b) Often no streets passed straight through
  (c) The public gathering space of citizenry
  (d) Many evolved into harmonious and aesthetic urban works of art

  Examples:
  - Piazza del Popolo, Todi, Italy
  - Piazza della Signoria, Florence
  - Piazza del Campo, Siena
  - Piazza San Marco, Venice
  - Piazza della Cisterna and Piazza del Duomo, San Gimignano

c. Castle gardens
(1) Occupied limited and irregular space within the inner walls or between double walls
(2) Gardens began as plots for growing vegetables, herbs, or medicinal plants
(3) Gradually evolved, after Crusades (based on Middle Eastern "paradise" concept), into relatively harmonious pleasure gardens ("pleasance") with:
  (a) Wild flowers
  (b) Fruit and flowering trees
  (c) Walls or fences made of lattice or "wattle and daub"
  (d) Earthen seats formed of wattle and daub
  (e) Water features such as fountain or well
  (f) Gravel or stone pavement
  (g) Topiary work in evergreen plants
  (h) Mounts
  (i) Sundials
  (j) Carved wooden or stone figurines (called "beestes" in England)
  (k) Mazes and labyrinths

4. Vocabulary:

- Abbey
- Ambulatory
- Beeste(s)
- Bollard
- Campanile
- Castle
- Cathedral
- Chivalry
- Cloister
- Colonnette
- Feudalism
- Fief
- Font
- Garth
- Gothic
- Gothic arch
- Goths
- Heraldry
- Hermitage
- Hortus conclusus
- Keep
- Kitchen garden
- Knot (open/closed)
- L-shaped piazza
- Labyrinth
- Loggia
- Manor
- Maze
- Moat
- Monastery
- Mysticism
- Nave
- Organic
- Ostrogoths
- Parapet
- Parvis
- Physic garden
- Piazza, plaza, place, square
- Pinwheel piazza
- Pleasance
- Quadrilateral symmetry
- Raised beds
- Romanesque
- Serf
- Transept
- Vandal
- Vassal
- Visigoths
- Wattle and daub

B. Islamic (Moorish) Spain (eighth–fifteenth centuries A.D.)

1. **Environment:** similar to Moslem Middle East; extremely hot and dry with a rugged and inarable landscape
2. **Culture:** religion of Islam the unifying element in the lifestyle; originated in Mecca (Saudi Arabia) in early seventh century and expanded both east and west; by seventh century, southern Spain was predominantly Islamic; followers were called "Moors" in Spain because their ancestors had migrated from the Middle East through Morocco; Islam forbid portrayal or animal or human forms, hence the development of elaborate geometric decorative embellishment for buildings and gardens; belief in scientific evidence rather than miracles; paradise gardens created to prepare one for afterlife in heaven (after which gardens were modeled)
3. **Design expressions:**

a. Religious courtyard: A place of spiritual preparation prior to entering house of worship; mosque

(a) Enclosed within high walls
(2) Plant material arranged in straight rows
(3) Irrigation channels determined pattern of tree placement
(4) Pools of water reflected the mosque and brought Allah (God) and heaven down into the garden or court
(5) Ablution tanks for religious ritual cleansing before prayer
(6) Shade provided by trees

Example:

- Court of the Oranges, Cordoba, c. A.D. 750–987

b. Palace courtyards

(1) An expression of "paradise"; idealized universe with four rivers of heaven
(2) Elaborate abstract geometric decorative architectural wall
(3) Sequence of small cool interior chambers adjoining open hot sunny courts
(4) Cool air movement induced to flow through courts
(5) King or sultan carried through palace as if on "flying carpet"
(6) Interpenetration of indoor and outdoor space
(7) Central water feature

(a) Ablution tank with reflecting water
(b) Fountain with playful water
(c) Water "jokes" and water in handrails
(d) Microclimate cooled by ice-cold mountain water
(e) Minimal use of water for maximum effect

(8) Contrasts of light and shadow
(9) Window openings ("miradors") allowed outside views to surrounding landscape
(10) Use of colorful glazed tiles ("azulejos")

Examples:

- Canal Garden, Generalife, Granada, 1275
- Palace of the Alcazar, Seville, 1364
- Court of the Myrtles, Palace of the Alhambra, Granada, 1350
- Court of the Lions, Palace of the Alhambra, Granada, 1375

4. **Vocabulary:**

- Ablution
- Adobe
- Arabesque
- Azulejo
- Bagh
- Casa
- Chabutra
- Chadar
- Chadar-Bagh
- Chenar
- Filigree
- Glorieta
- Hegira
- Islam
- Koran
- Mecca
- Minaret
- Mirador
- Mohammed
- Moor
- Mosaic
- Mosque
- Muslim/Moslem
- Patio
- Plaza
- Qanat
- Rill
- Runnel

IV. The Renaissance (fourteenth–seventeenth centuries)

A. Italy (c. 1350–1675)

1. **Environment:** Italian peninsula varies from flat in the south to mountainous in the north, and extremely hot and dry in the south to lush, cool, and temperate in the Alps of the north; good agricultural lands abound throughout
2. **Culture:** many independent republics, some of which were continuously at war with one another; virtually all of Italy was Catholic, with allegiance to the Pope in Rome; a new class of merchants was becoming the aristocracy in trading centers such as Florence; humanism became the new philosophical outlook rather than the mysticism of the Middle

Ages; a fascination with the classical in the arts and lifestyle prevailed within the intelligentsia; Roman (Latin) and Greek literature were being rediscovered, translated, and enjoyed

3. **Design expressions:** Emulation of classical Roman orderliness adapted to relate to human dimensions
   a. Residential houses and gardens (villas) of the formative period; the "philosopher's garden" period (1430–1500)
      (1) Rural sites for ample space, fresh air, water, scenery
      (2) Evolved from medieval country castles
      (3) Revision of classical design concepts and forms
      (4) Developed as the venue of philosophical gatherings, the "Platonic academy," pleasure, entertaining, and display of art objects
      Example:
      - Villa Medici in Careggi, 1434, by Michelozzo

      (5) Systematized design theory articulated by Leonbatista Alberti, in his ten-volume book *De Re Aedificatoria* (1452), as he translated Vitruvius's *Ten Books on Architecture* (published in the first century A.D.)
         (a) Hillside sites
         (b) Terraced
         (c) Enclosed in walls
         (d) Elongated terraces for strolling
         (e) Geometric, symmetrical plan for each terrace
         (f) No axial interconnection between terraces
         (g) Central water feature (fountain or well)
         (h) Trees
         (i) Topiary of evergreen plants
         Examples:
         - Villa Medici, Fiesole (first newly built Renaissance villa), 1458, by Michelozzo
         - Villa Poggio a Caiano, Florence, 1482, Giuliano Sangallo

   b. High Renaissance villas (1500–1575)
      (1) Consistent axial arrangement
      (2) Terraced on hillsides
      (3) Central axis, symbolized by a water channel, began uphill in grove of trees ("bosco"), with the water source symbolized by "grotto"
      (4) Along watercourse were fountains, cascades, or pools
      (5) Integration of house and gardens: upper terrace; middle terrace, with residence structure ("casa" or "casino"); and lower terrace, with terminus of axis and water's flow
      (6) Distinct expression of enclosure and separation from surroundings achieved by walls or tall clipped hedges
      (7) Elaborate, ornate details such as statues, fountains, benches, gates, walls, stairs
      Examples:
      - Cortile del Belvedere, (Vatican) Rome, 1503, by Bramante
      - Villa Madama, Rome, 1519, by Raphael
      - Villa d'Este, Tivoli, 1550, by Ligorio and Olivieri
      - Boboli Gardens of the Pitti Palace, Florence, 1550, by Tribolo
      - Villa Giulia, Rome, 1550, by Vignola
      - Villa Lante, Bagnaia, 1566, by Vignola
      - Villino Farnese, Caprarola, 1573, by Vignola

   c. Baroque period villas (1575–1675)
      (1) A period of overelaboration of form and detail
      (2) Dramatic hillside terracing
      (3) Exaggeration of architectural retaining walls
      (4) Introduction of diagonal or radial patterns
         (a) Diagonal tree-lined avenues
         (b) Cross axes
      (5) Grotesque figures carved in in-situ stone
      (6) Greater degree of alteration of natural topography
      (7) Visual perspective deception ("false perspective")
      Examples:
      - Villa Aldobrandini, Frascati, 1598, by della Porta
      - Villa Gamberaia, Settignano, 1610
      - Isola Bella, Lake Maggiore, 1632, by Fontana

   d. Urban civic space design (piazzas)
      (1) Revival of classical orderliness
         (a) Rectangular or trapezoidal
         (b) Bilaterally symmetrical
         (c) Classic revival architectural motifs articulate edges of space
         (d) Axial approach route into civic space
      (2) Retained similar function to that of forum or medieval civic space

(a) Church or cathedral forecourt
Examples:
- Piazza del Popolo, Pienze, 1460, Rossolino
- Piazza della Santissima Annunziata, Florence, 1419, by Brunelleschi, and 1516, by Giuliano Sangallo

(b) Town hall forecourt (Piazza della Signoria, Florence)
(c) Mayor's residence formed one edge
(d) Served as marketplace
(e) Civic assembly place
(f) Religious assembly place

(3) Open-space proportions provided for viewing distance to major public building(s)
(4) Articulated with rich details and features
(a) Fountains
(b) Statues (Piazza del Campidoglio, Rome)
(c) Obelisks (Piazza del Popolo, Rome)
(d) Stairs (Spanish Steps, Rome)
(e) Paving (Piazza del Campidoglio, Rome)
(5) False perspective; visual deception
(6) Trapezoidal configuration (Piazza del Campidoglio, Rome, by Michelangelo, 1538)
(7) Blending of the old and the new
(8) Renaissance forms or details "grafted" onto medieval (Piazza della Signoria, Florence, 1503, the statue of "David" by Michelangelo)
Examples:
- Piazza della Santissima Annunziata, Florence, 1419, Brunelleschi, and 1516, Giuliano Sangallo
- Piazza del Campidoglio, Rome, 1537 by Michelangelo
- Piazza San Marco, Venice, c. 800–1810
- Piazza del Popolo, Rome, 1589, Fontana
- Piazza di San Pietro, Vatican City, 1585, by Fontana (after Pope Sixtus V's scheme for uniting Holy Pilgrimage churches of Rome) and 1656, by Bernini, the colonnaded elliptical enclosure

4. Vocabulary:
- Barco
- Baroque
- Belvedere
- Bosco, boschetto
- Byzantine
- Campagna
- Cascade
- Casino
- Cobblestone
- Cortile
- Cupola
- Finial
- Giardino segreto
- Grotto
- Herm
- Humanism
- Loggia
- Nymphaeum
- Orangery
- Palazzo
- Parterre
- Philosopher's Garden
- Piazza
- Podere
- Renaissance
- Rococo
- Rustication
- Sacro bosco
- Sgraffito
- Terra-cotta
- Villa
- Villeggiatura
- Vista
- Water theater

B. France (1495–1750)

1. Environment: continental European temperate climate with cold, snowy winters and warm, sunny summers supporting a rich agricultural productivity; landscape varies from the Alps in the southeast, to the flat marshes of the Mediterranean south coast, to the gently rolling hill country intersected by broad, flat river valleys and floodplains in central France

2. Culture: stable, politically unified country by mid-sixteenth century with the king as absolute ruler; predominantly Roman Catholic with a materialistic lifestyle for the aristocracy

3. Design expressions:

a. Royal palaces and gardens ("châteaux")
(1) Learned garden design from Italy
(2) Located in rural areas, often riverine locations
(3) Generally flat or gentle topography
(4) Early French Renaissance chateau gardens added onto existing medieval castles (1495–1550)
(a) Irregular in arrangement
(b) Not architecturally integrated with residence
(c) Gardens walled and often surrounded by moat
Examples:
- Amboise, 1495, for King Charles VIII, by Pacello
- Blois, 1500, for King Louis XII, by Pacello
- Fontainebleau, 1528, for King Francis I, by Serlio

- Chenonceaux, 1551, for Diane de Poitiers, and 1560, for Queen Catherine de Medici, by de L'Orme

(5) High Renaissance chateau conceived as axial union of residence and gardens (1550–1656)
  (a) Central axis linked forecourt, residence, and gardens
  (b) Gardens walled and surrounded by decorative moat
  (c) Elaborate patterns sculpted in shrubbery, "parterres"
  (d) Trees "pleached" or pruned to lend architectural character
  (e) Slightly raised strolling promenades allowed view over parterres
  (f) Water expressed in flat, reflecting pools of geometric shape
  (g) Few fountains, usually a single vertical jet, "jet d'eau"
  (h) Marble statuary distributed liberally

  Examples:
  - Anet, 1550, for Diane de Poitiers, by de L'Orme
  - Charleval, 1572, by du Cerceau
  - Tuileries, 1563, for Queen Catherine de Medici, by de L'Orme, and 1600, for Queen Marie de Medici, by Claude Mollet and Jacques Boyceau
  - St. Germain-en-Laye, 1592, for Queen Marie de Medici, by Claude Mollet and Francini
  - Luxembourg Gardens, 1615, for Louis XIII and Queen Marie de Medici, by Jacques Boyceau and De Brosse

(6) The French grand style, baroque, as developed by André Le Nôtre (1656–1720s)
  (a) Increased scale of gardens
  (b) Increased sense of clear, open spaciousness
  (c) Use of false perspective, trompe l'oeil
  (d) Radial avenues, allées
  (e) Cross axes meeting at rond points
  (f) Expanded use of standing water, grand canal
  (g) Elaboration of patterns in parterres
  (h) Orangeries, formal arrangements of citrus trees (lemons and oranges) in moveable tubs near a large greenhouse
  (i) Increased number of elaborate fountains and cascades
  (j) Frequent remodeling of preexisting châteaux

  Examples:
  - Vaux-le-Vicomte, 1656, for N. Fouquet, by Le Nôtre
  - Versailles, 1661, for King Louis XIV, by Le Nôtre
  - Chantilly, 1664, by Le Nôtre
  - Fontainebleau, 1675, by Le Nôtre
  - Tuileries, 1663–1678, by Le Nôtre

(7) French grand style adopted by royalty for palace gardens outside France
  (a) Slight adaptations in design expression to reflect local conditions such as topography, climate, plant materials, construction materials, and local architectural styles and taste

  Examples:
  - Herrenhausen, Hanover, Germany, 1670, Martin Charbonnier and Henry Wise
  - Hampton Court, London, 1661–1665, Wise and André Mollet
  - Schleissheim, Munich, Germany, 1692, J. Effner
  - Schönbrunn, Vienna, Austria, 1693, von Erloch
  - Belvedere, Vienna, 1696, Hildebrandt
  - Peterhof, Leningrad, Russia, 1714, Le Blond
  - La Granja, Segovia, Spain, 1719, Cartier and Boutelet
  - Palazzo Reale, Caserta, Italy, 1729, Vanvitelli

(b) Urban form as influenced by the grand formal style of Versailles
  (1) Le Nôtre remodeled gardens of the Tuileries (1678) to extend central axis westward beyond built-up portion of Paris
  (2) Tuileries axis lends form for subsequent urban

growth of Paris (Champs-Elysées and Place de la Concorde); reconstruction of Parisian streets, 1853–1870, by Baron G. Haussmann for Napoleon III

(3) Urban design adaptations beyond France:
   (a) Wren's plan for rebuilding of London after the great fire, 1666
   (b) Plan of Maryland colonial capital at Annapolis, 1695, by Governor Francis Nicholson
   (c) Plan of Virginia colonial capital at Williamsburg, 1699, by Nicholson
   (d) Plan of American national capital at Washington, DC., 1791, by L'Enfant with T. Jefferson and G. Washington
   (e) Plan for new or rebuilt American towns and cities

   Examples:
   - Buffalo, New York, 1804
   - Detroit, Michigan, 1807
   - Indianapolis, Indiana, 1821
   - Madison, Wisconsin, 1836

4. Vocabulary:

- Allée
- Arabesque
- Balustrade
- Bastide
- Bosquet
- Boulevard
- Broderie par terre
- Cabinet
- Château(x)
- Chinoiserie
- Clairevoie
- Cour d'honneur
- Cul-de-sac
- Espalier
- Facade
- Flying buttress
- Gargoyle
- Hameau
- Jardin
- Jet d'eau
- Le Grand Siecle
- Le Moyen age
- Le Roi Soleil
- Mannerism
- Mansard roof
- Niche
- Orangerie
- Parterre
- Patte d'oie
- Perron
- Place
- Pleasance
- Podium
- Pollard
- Potager
- Radial
- Riparian
- Rocaille
- Rond point
- Tapis vert
- Treillage
- Trompe l'oeil
- Vista
- Voile

C. England (1480–1715)

1. Environment: a small island with subtle landscape variations, from the rocky coasts of the southwest in Cornwall to the flatland expanses of the east coast in East Anglia to the Pennine moorlands of Yorkshire and Northumberland; the maritime climate is cool and moist with considerably less bright sunshine than in continental or Mediterranean countries; rich agricultural land abounds

2. Culture: during the majority of this period, England politically unified under a monarch (king or queen), with a parliamentary form of government; Roman Catholicism was the predominant religion until 1534, when Henry VIII, after divorcing his wife Catherine, was excommunicated from the Catholic church and subsequently reformed the church into the Church of England (Anglican); the Reformation period, 1536–1539; the period 1629–1660 was one of great political and social turmoil; Charles I abolished Parliament; he was executed in 1647 and the monarchy was abolished; the British Commonwealth was established in 1650 and run by Oliver and Richard Cromwell, as Lord Protectors; great austerity measures were imposed; the restoration of the monarchy took place in 1660 with the return of Charles II from exile in France to claim the throne of England; Scotland united with England; England became a world colonial power

(3) Design expressions:

a. Residential gardens of aristocracy or royalty
   (1) Tudor period (1480–1603)
      (a) Great increase in rural estate development following reformation and subsequent redistribution of monastic land holdings to Henry VIII's friends ("landed gentry")
      (b) Rural lowland settings
      (c) Compact, geometric, enclosed within masonary walls, hedges, or fences
      (d) Abundance of bright floral material
      (e) Limited use of water features
      (f) Garden components: lead statuary, carved wooden "beestes," sundials, grass turf, stone paved paths, minimal provisions for shade

      Examples:
      - Haddon Hall, 1480
      - Hampton Court (pond garden), 1515
      - Compton Wynates, 1520

   (2) Elizabethan period (1558–1603)

(a) Transition to larger, more formal, ornate gardens
(b) Axial master plans begin
(c) Increased influence from the European continent
(d) Increased use of topiary

Examples:
- St. Catherine's Court, 1570
- Montacute, 1558–1600

(3) Jacobean period (1603–1625)
(a) Increased influence from Italy (Inigo Jones returns from study in Italy, Vitruvius translated into English)

Examples:
- Hatfield House, 1611
- Canon's Ashby, 1632

(4) England in political turmoil (1629–1660)
(a) Reduced activity in development of rural homes and gardens due to dissolving of Parliament, 1629; aboliton of the monarchy, 1649; royal family lives in exile in France, 1649–1660; Commonwealth of Oliver and Richard Cromwell, 1650–1660

(5) English High Renaissance (1660–1715)
(a) Restoration of the royal family to the throne and their return from France with French habits and design taste
(b) Surge in development of country homes and gardens
(c) French formal landscape design becomes the fashion throughout Britain
(d) "Seeds are sown" for design revolution from formal to informal landscaping; large number of formal gardens and related environmental impacts lead to reduction of forest areas, game habitats, and game populations; parliamentary enclosure acts of the mid-seventeenth century

Examples:
- Hampton Court (and Bushy Park), 1663–1689
- Chatsworth, 1685
- Levens Hall, 1691
- Melbourne Hall, 1704
- Longleat, 1701
- Blenheim, 1705

V. The Modern World—Europe (1700–1900)

A. English natural or romantic period (1715–1837)

1. Social context: war with France; the American Revolutionary War; urbanization of population follows "industrial revolution"; age of enlightenment; social unrest and reform
2. Cultural aesthetic evolves from formal to informal:
   a. John Evelyn's book *Sylva, or a Discourse of Forest Trees* (1664) urged property owners to help reforest the treeless countryside, to "improve" their land
   b. Parliamentary enclosure acts of the 1660s enabled wealthy landowners to enclose their open land; stone walls and hedgerows brought about change in scale of rural landscape; reestablished small-game habitats
   c. Critical essays and other writing against formal gardens
      (1) Joseph Addison and Richard Steele, writings in *The Spectator,* 1712–1714, "Nature and art should imitate each other"
      (2) Alexander Pope, writings in the *Guardian,* 1714
      (3) William Kent stated in 1730, "Nature abhors a straight line"
      (4) William Hogarth stated in 1752, "The waving line is the way to beauty"
   d. Visits to China by Sir William Temple and Sir William Chambers; asymmetrical design, or "occult balance" ("Anglo-Chinese," "chinoiserie")
   e. The "Grand Tour" to Roman and Greek historic sites
   f. Seventeenth-century fashion of owning romantic landscape paintings by Claude Lorrain, Nicolas Poussin, and Salvator Rosa; principles of painting composition being applied to design of the landscape
   g. Royal cost assessment of maintenance of all royal formal gardens
   h. Queen Anne declared dislike of the smell of boxwood
   i. The book *The Architecture of Palladio* by Leoni (1714) generates renewed interest in Western classicism
   j. England, emerging as major world power, is desirous of its own national style as opposed to the French grand style

k. Authors such as Jean-Jacques Rousseau generate interest in return to nature
l. Age of Enlightenment and increase in scientific endeavors toward nature, which emphasized the character of the indigenous English landscape; the visual irregularity and beauty of nature; the laws of nature (ecology) as determinants of design elements and compositions

3. Landscape design became an expression of a sympathetic attitude toward nature which emphasized the character of the indigenous English landscape; the visual irregularity and beauty of nature; the laws of nature (ecology) as determinants of design elements and compositions
4. Design character:
   a. Creations of natural or picturesque pastoral scenery
   b. "Offskips" or "borrowed scenery" to surrounding countryside outside one's ownership
   c. Landscape components: open meadows, ponds, trees in masses
5. Creation of soft, "romantic" landscape scenery was frequently done at the expense of preexisting "grand formal" establishments; thousands of geometric gardens were removed and replaced by informal "naturalesque" scenery
6. The rejection of geometric formal style meant corresponding excesses in the new fashion; palatial rural mansions left to sit "amidst pastureland"
7. Contrived artifice: "follies" or "eyecatchers;" constructed "ruins"; temples or castles; dead trees "planted" to lend appearance of the natural; rustic hermitages with "hermits" employed to reside in forest huts or caves; deer herds
   Examples:
   - Castle Howard: 1699 by Sir John Vanbrugh
   - Stowe: 1713 by Charles Bridgeman, 1740 by William Kent, 1750 by "Capability" Brown
   - Pope's Garden in Twickenham: 1719–1744 by Alexander Pope
   - Longleat: 1720 by Bridgeman, 1757 by Brown
   - Chiswick: 1727 by Kent
   - Stourhead: 1743–1775 by Henry Hoare II
   - Blenheim: 1761 by Brown
   - Chatsworth: 1763 by Brown
   - Kew Garden: 1763 by Sir William Chambers
8. Following the era dominated by "Capability" Brown (1750–1783) and excessive ""pastoralism" was a period of compromise between informal and formal; Humphry Repton, first to call himself a "landscape gardener," 1780, urged the reinstatement of geometric gardens and terraces immediately surrounding the house; he used "red books" to convey his design proposals to clients
   Examples:
   - Holkham Hall, 1789, modified Kent's and Brown's landscape
   - Sheffield Park, 1789, modified Brown's landscape
   - Tatton Park, 1792, modified Brown's landscape
   - Harewood, 1795, modified Brown's landscape
   - Wimpole, 1801, modified Brown's landscape
   - Longleat, 1804, modified Brown's landscape
9. In the late eighteenth century, a debate arose between the admirers of Brown's soft, manicured landscapes and those opposed to the "beautiful" style, who advocated more "natural," more "picturesque," unkempt-looking landscapes; the three leaders of this picturesque cult were William Gilpin, Sir Uvedale Price, and Richard Payne Knight
10. Important books on the topic of landscape gardening and architecture:
    a. *Vitruvius Britanicus,* 1715, Colin Campbell
    b. *New Principles of Gardening,* 1728, Batty Langley
    c. *Epistle to Lord Burlington,* 1731, Alexander Pope
    d. *The Analysis of Beauty,* 1753, William Hogarth
    e. *Design of Chinese Buildings,* 1755, William Chambers
    f. *Elements of Criticism,* 1761, Lord Kames
    g. *Observations on Modern Gardening,* 1770, Thomas Whately
    h. *History of the Modern Taste in Gardening,* 1770, Horace Walpole
    i. *Observations on . . . Picturesque Beauty,* 1782, William Gilpin
    j. *An Essay on the Picturesque,* 1794, Uvedale Price
    k. *Sketches and Hints on Landscape Gardening,* 1795, Humphry Repton

B. Jardin anglais: adaptations of English landscape garden style on the European continent. Many examples were remodeled from earlier formal gardens or were situated adjacent to formal gardens that remained in place

Examples:
- Parc d' Ermenonville, France, 1770, by Louis-René Girardin
- Petit Trianon, "l'Hameau," Versailles, 1775, by Richard Mique
- Drotteningholm Park, Stockholm, 1780, by Fredrik Magnus Piper
- Englische Garten (public park), Munich, Germany, 1789, by Benjamin Thompson (Count Rumford)
- Villa Borghese, Rome, 1810, by Moore
- Tiergarten (public park), Berlin, 1818–1840, by Peter Josef Lenné
- Park-Muskau, East Germany, 1820–1845, by Prince von Pückler-Muskau
- Bois de Boulogne, Paris, 1852–1870 by Adolphe Alphand
- Parc du Buttes-Chaumont, Paris, 1864–1869 by Adolphe Alphand

C. **Urban residential squares:** speculative construction of a unified facade on a fashionable complex of row houses, with an open central square, with streets continuing through; designed to appear "palatial"; tenants were middle-class "nouveau riche" who sought the image of aristocratic housing in small parklike setting; each house provided a small garden plot to its rear

Examples:
- Place Royale, Paris, 1605, by Chastillon
- Place Vendôme, Paris, 1685, by Mansart
- Bloomsbury Square, London, 1660, by Lord Southampton
- Soho Square, London, 1681, by Gregory King
- Queen's Square, Bath, 1729, by John Wood, Sr.
- King's Circus, Bath, 1754, by John Wood, Sr.
- Royal Crescent, Bath, 1767, by John Wood, Jr.
- Lansdowne Crescent, Bath, 1790, by John Palmer
- Portland Place, London, 1810, by John Nash

D. **Urban "country parks" created from royal properties** Centuries-old royal hunting parks redesigned into fashionable pleasure parks in the English landscape garden style; surrounded by middle-class "terrace" houses; access was restricted to owners of abutting terrace houses and other aristocrats; often for horse riding rather than strolling; after Queen Victoria (1837) these were opened for public use

Examples:
- Regent's Park, London, 1811, by John Nash and John Repton
- St. James's Park, London, 1820, by Nash (remodeled from French formal garden by André and Gabriel Mollet in the 1660s)
- Green Park, London, 1820s, by Nash

E. **Urban "country parks" created on newly acquired public lands** Due to industrial revolution and influx of population into cities without public open-space amenities for leisure enjoyment; awakening social consciousness about living conditions for urban working class

1. Parks were financed by the development and sale of "terrace houses" or "villas" built around the edges but within park boundaries
2. Parks designed according to English landscape garden style principles
3. Influenced Frederick Law Olmsted substantially during his visit to England (1850–1852)

Examples:
- Victoria Park, London, 1841, by James Pennethorne
- Birkenhead Park, Liverpool, 1844, by Joseph Paxton

F. **Vocabulary:**
- Agrarian
- Alley
- Arbor
- Arboretum
- Arcadian
- Bailey
- Baluster
- Batter
- Battlement
- Beeste
- Berm
- Borrowed scenery
- Bower
- Bucolic
- Carpet bedding
- Carrying capacity
- Castellated
- Catch basin
- Chinoiserie
- Clerestory, clearstory
- Common
- Eclecticism
- Ecology
- Ecosystem
- Eye catcher
- Folly
- Fosse
- Gardenesque
- Giardino inglese
- Green
- Greensward
- Habitat
- Ha-ha
- Half-timber
- Hermitage
- Indigenous
- Jardin anglais
- Motte
- Naturalesque
- Naturalistic
- Open space
- Orientation
- Pastoral
- Picturesque
- Pilaster
- Serpentine
- Sharawadgi
- Sharawaggi
- Sublime

VI. American Environmental Design (1600–1993)

A. Environment: from the Atlantic to the Pacific, the Gulf of Mexico to the St. Lawrence River, the Great Lakes to Puget Sound; including landscapes as varied as the expansive coastal plains and rocky coasts to rolling Piedmont, vast prairies of the middle west to the mountain ranges extending north to south on both the east coast and entire western one-third of the continent; from rain forests to arid deserts and from boreal forests to the subtropics

B. Culture: a new civilization established by many peoples from the entire world who came to America for a great number of reasons, including religious freedom, political freedom, economic opportunities, resource exploitation, land speculation, and many others

C. Design expressions:

1. Colonial period, 1620s–1791
   a. Residential gardens in the New England colonies
      (1) Seventeenth century; modest, compact utilitarian "dooryard gardens" for growing of herbs, medicinal plants, flowers
         (a) Enclosed in stone walls, split-rail or paling fences
         (b) Located beside kitchen or front door
      (2) Eighteenth century pleasure gardens for the middle class
         (a) Use of native and imported vegetation
         (b) Use of decorative features such as fences, gates, benches, arbors, dovecotes, statuary, topiary, pleaching
   b. Residential gardens in the southern colonies
      (1) Plantations
         (a) Large land holdings for production of monoculture cash crops (tobacco, rice, cotton, indigo)
         (b) Discouragement of formation of towns by wealthy plantation owners (as a means of avoiding export tax if produce shipped through port towns)
         (c) Self-sufficiency of plantations
         (d) Palatial houses and grand, formal gardens with geometric patterns of clipped boxwood and other evergreens
         (e) Terrace gardens descending to the river (main transportation artery)
         (f) Mixture of indigenous and imported ornamental trees and shrubs
         (g) Design style mimicked that of English Jacobean, and to a lesser extent, the French grand style

         Examples:
         - Stratford Hall, Rappahannock River, Virginia, 1730
         - Middleton Place, Charleston, South Carolina, 1741
         - Mount Vernon, Potomac River, Virginia, 1759–1786
      (2) Townhouse gardens
         (a) Modest in size
         (b) Geometric patterns
         (c) Clipped boxwood mixed with native and imported plants
         (d) Design patterns obtained from itinerant gardeners or pattern books

         Examples:
         - Williamsburg gardens, c. 1720s–1730s
         - Paca House, Annapolis, Maryland, 1763, William Paca (the formal upper terraces)
   c. Early experiments with the natural or English landscape garden style; practiced by Americans who had large libraries of design books; had visited England and saw the "modern" style there; English and continental designers who came to America

      Examples:
      - Williamsburg Governor's Palace gardens, 1712–1720, Governor Alexander Spotswood (exploited "borrowed scenery" from the palace to meadows and the canal)
      - Westover, James River, Virginia, 1711–1740, William Byrd II (naturalistic tree plantings; "borrowed scenery" toward the James River; ha-ha wall; grotto)
      - Belmont, Charleston, S.C., 1758–1765, Eliza Lucas Pinckney (planted in the "modern" or "natural" style)

- William Paca House, Annapolis, Maryland, 1765 ("wilderness" on the lowest terrace)
- Morven, Princeton, N.J., 1766, Richard and Annis Stockton (modeled after Alexander Pope's garden in Twickenham, England; planted in the natural style; grotto)
- Monticello, Charlottesville, Virginia, 1771–1810, Thomas Jefferson (borrowed scenery; planted in the natural style; serpentine "roundabouts" and footpaths)

d. Town planning

(1) New England colonial towns egalitarian; formed by families of farmers and other tradesmen; property distributed by drawing lots to assure fairness

(a) Each family claim was to be of equal value for agricultural use (they were frequently unequal in physical size)

(b) Several parcels for different purposes or worth were allotted per family (town lot, farm lot, forest lot)

(c) Each family residence was approximately equidistant from town center

(d) Town settled along navigable river or inlet

(e) Central open space in the town was the "common," used for the drilling of militia, grazing of the family cow, or last stronghold if the town were attacked

(f) At center were church, school, meetinghouse, marketplace

(g) Animals allowed to forage, run loose in streets; necessitating the enclosure of dooryard gardens with fences or walls

(h) Settlement of families was based on a half-day's ride from home to town center and back

(i) Second-generation families, too far from town, formed a second town, called "hiving off"

(j) Towns were totally cleared from existing forests, thus were treeless

Examples:

- Plymouth, Massachusetts, 1620
- Salem, Massachusetts, 1625
- Boston, Massachusetts, 1630

(2) Capital towns were formed by governor or director appointed by the king

(a) Layout was an orderly, geometric gridiron pattern of streets and lots (followed ancient classical or baroque prototype)

(b) Lot survey and distribution to settlers was expedited by grid

(c) Standardized lot sizes and street widths

(d) Frequent occurrence of inequitable quality or worth of lots of equal size

(e) Regional plan schemes allowed for land granting to include an in-town house lot and an outlying farm plot; all properties were equal in size for everyone

Example: Savannah, Georgia, 1733, James Oglethorpe

(f) Growth of town was usually by expansion according to original street and lotting pattern

(g) Centralized civic facilities; market; churches; school; meetinghouse

Examples:

- Philadelphia, Pennsylvania, 1682, William Penn and Captain Thomas Holme, surveyor-general
- Annapolis, Maryland, 1695, Francis Nicholson
- Williamsburg, Virginia, 1699, Francis Nicholson
- Margravate of Azilia, Georgia, 1717, Robert Montgomery
- Savannah, 1733, James Oglethorpe

e. Vocabulary:

- Agrarian
- Common
- Crown colony
- Dooryard garden
- Hiving off
- Trust lots
- Tythings
- Wards

2. American National (Classic period, the Roman idiom), 1791–1830, after the war for independence, the new American nation ambitiously began to proclaim its new independent status by building governmental facilities in each of the new states

a. City planning; grand baroque master plans modeled on

the plan of Versailles, the Wren plan of London, and other foreign capitals

Examples:

- U.S. Federal Capital City (Washington, D.C.), 1791, by Pierre Charles L'Enfant, George Washington, and Thomas Jefferson
- Richmond, Virginia, 1790
- Jeffersonville, Indiana, 1802, by Thomas Jefferson
- Jackson, Mississippi, 1804, by Thomas Jefferson
- Buffalo, New York, 1804
- Detroit, Michigan, 1807, by Augustus B. Woodward

b. Institutional facilities; Classic Revival (Roman-style) buildings and complexes of buildings

Examples:

- State Capitol Building, Richmond, Virginia, 1790, by Thomas Jefferson
- President's House, the "White House," Washington, D.C., 1792–1819, by James Holban; porticoes, 1807–1808, by Benjamin Henry Latrobe
- "U.S. Congress House": the Capitol, Washington, D.C., 1793–1800, by Dr. William Thornton; the House wing, 1803–1817, by B. H. Latrobe; the central Rotunda, 1817–1829, by Charles Bulfinch; Capitol enlarged, 1857–1863, by Thomas Walter
- Fairmont Waterworks, Philadelphia, 1799–1822, by B. H. Latrobe
- University of Virginia, Charlottesville, Virginia, 1805–1825, by Jefferson, with advice from Latrobe and Thornton

c. Residential gardens continued to be designed as geometric compositions similar to colonial examples

(1) Beginnings of botanical gardens and horticultural nurseries; stimulation of interest in exotic plant materials

(2) Mail-order purchase of nursery plants and seeds

(3) Pattern books provided garden designs for homeowners

d. Continuing experiments with the "natural" or English landscape garden style by Americans who saw the "modern" style as an expression of American enlightenment and currency with the fashions in England and the continent

Examples:

- Monticello, Charlottesville, Virginia, 1789–1810, by Jefferson
- Mount Vernon, Potomac River, Virginia, 1785–1786, by George Washington
- The Woodlands, Philadelphia, 1789, by William Hamilton
- State House Garden, Philadelphia, 1785–1787, by Samuel Vaughan
- Yale College, New Haven, Connecticut, 1792, John Trumbull
- Union College, Schenectady, New York, 1813, by Joseph Jacques Ramée
- Point Breeze, Bordentown, New Jersey, 1817–1825, by Joseph Bonaparte

3. American Romantic, 1831–1869; the period of increased popularity of the English landscape gardening style, indicated a gradual shift from geometric formal design to informal or "naturalesque" images; these were often achieved more by the application of eighteenth-century formulas and rules of design than by the more site-sensitive approach that emerged after about 1869; new project types were beginning to appear

a. Public facilities (cemeteries, parks)

Examples:

- Mount Auburn Cemetery, Cambridge, Massachusetts, 1831–1871, by Dr. Jacob Bigelow and Henry A. S. Dearborn
- Laurel Hill Cemetery, Philadelphia, 1836–1839, by John Notman
- Spring Grove Cemetery, Cincinnati, 1845, by Howard Daniels, remodeled, 1855, by Adolph Strauch
- Green-Wood Cemetery, New York City, 1838, Major David Bates Douglass
- Smithsonian Museum grounds and the Mall, Washington, D.C., 1851, Andrew Jackson Downing
- Greensward plan for Central Park, New York City,

1858, Frederick Law Olmsted and Calvert Vaux
- Golden Gate Park, San Francisco, 1863 (plan recommended by Olmsted; revised and built 1870–1880 by William H. Hall)
- Mountain View Cemetery, Oakland, California, 1864, by Olmsted
- Yosemite Valley ceded to California as a state wilderness reservation, 1864; Olmsted wrote the management manual, 1865
- University of California at Berkeley, 1865, Olmsted
- Prospect Park, Brooklyn, 1865, Olmsted and Vaux

b. Residential developments; the term *suburb* coined in 1841 by writer Nathaniel Parker Willis relative to his proposed utopian community, Highland Terrace
  (1) Planned suburban communities in the romantic, naturalistic, picturesque style
    (a) At the edges of major cities
    (b) Within reasonable public transit commuting distance to central city
      i. Private carriage
      ii. Steamboat
      iii. Train
    (c) Parklike setting with relatively large private building lots, generous open space, and landscape amenities such as rolling topography, mature trees, water bodies
    (d) Public community facilities, usually of rustic character: foot paths; picnic shelters; benches; sculptural elements
    (e) Curvilinear street networks
    (f) Property lines that meandered in conformity with topography and streets

    Examples:
    - Highland Terrace, Cornwall, New York, 1851, by N. P. Willis (not executed)
    - Llewellyn Park, West Orange, New Jersey, 1853, by Alexander Jackson Davis and Eugene A. Baumann
    - Riverside, Illinois, 1868–1870, by Olmsted and Vaux

4. Expansion of the profession of landscape architecture, 1869–1960; a gradual shift away from reliance on the romantic idiom toward more systematic and rational design methodologies, based on a truer conformity to landforms, microclimate, and existing vegetation: increasing numbers of practicing landscape architects doing public projects along with an expansion in the number of private works
  a. Public urban parks and parkways

    Examples:
    - Mount Royal Park, Montréal, Canada, 1875, by Olmsted
    - The Fens and Back Bay network of parks (the "emerald necklace") and Franklin Park, Boston, 1878–1891, by F. L. Olmsted and John Charles Olmsted
    - Minneapolis park system, 1883, Horace W. S. Cleveland
    - Pope and Bushnell parks, Hartford, Connecticut, 1893, Jacob Weidenmann
    - Boston Metropolitan Park District, 1893, Charles Eliot

  b. Private work; "County Place Era," c. 1870–c. 1929; picturesque and single-track eclectic revivalism
    (1) Stimulated by the unprecedented industrial boom occurring in the United States, an era of tremendous rural residential construction swept the populated parts of the country; landscape architects were called upon to design the grounds for immense mansions whose designs were mimics of a wide range of historic styles, scaled-down models of European royal palaces

      Examples:
      - Armsmear, Hartford, Connecticut, 1855–1862, by Colonel Samuel Colt
      - Olana, Hudson, New York, 1870, by Calvert Vaux
      - Biltmore, Asheville, North Carolina, 1888–1895, by Richard Morris Hunt, architect; Olmsted, Sr., and John Charles Olmsted; and Gifford Pinchot, forester
      - Swan House, Atlanta, 1928, by Philip Shutze
      - Villa Vizcaya, Miami, 1914–1921, by Hoffman and Diego Suarez

    (2) Landscape architectural design advances
      (a) Greater care for detail, proportion, scale

(b) Clarity of spatial formation as positive element
(c) Refinements in comprehensive site planning of circulation, both horizontal and vertical
(d) Maturation of handling of materials and forms, both natural and human-made
(e) Increased ecological sensitivity, use of native plants
(f) General design restraint

Examples:

- Faulkner Farm, Boston, 1896, Charles A. Platt
- Timberline, Bryn Mawr, Pennsylvania, 1912, Platt and Olmsted Brothers
- Gwinn, Cleveland, Ohio, 1912, Platt
- Ormston, Long Island, 1922, Olmsted Brothers
- Killenworth, Long Island, c. 1925, James L. Greenleaf
- Thorne residence, Long Island, Vitale and Geiffert

(3) Residential and park work of landscape architect, Jens Jensen, in the American middle west, characterized by ecologically sensitive use of native plants in soft, natural planting schemes with minimal site disturbance

Examples:

- Edward L. Ryerson residence, Lake Forest, Illinois, 1912
- Fair Lane (Henry Ford estate), Dearborn, Michigan, 1914–1920
- West Chicago Park District (Union, Humboldt, Douglas, Garfield, and Columbus parks), Chicago, 1900–1918
- The Clearing, his "school of the soil," in Door County, Wisconsin, 1935–1951

(4) Emergence of women in landscape architecture; women in practice for themselves or working in established offices, often working on country estates; among the major practitioners:
(a) Marian Coffin
(b) Annette Flanders
(c) Beatrix Jones Ferrand
(d) Theodora Kimball Hubbard
(e) Ellen Biddle Shipman
(f) Florence Yoch

c. Expositions: Industrial expansion in the United States led to the nation's emergence as a world leader in technology and invention. Colossal international expositions were staged to show off this country's accomplishments. These extravaganzas exploited the talents of our leading designers. Environmental consequences were:
(1) Demonstration of the advantages of interprofessional collaboration between engineers, architects, landscape architects, and product designers
(2) The leadership role of landscape architects, serving as designers of the master land plan within which architects and engineers were to operate

Example:

- World's Columbian Exposition, Chicago, 1893, by the collaborative efforts of Olmsted; architects: McKim, Mead and White; Burnham and Root; Richard M. Hunt; Adler and Sullivan; Peabody and Stearns; and sculptors: Augustus Saint-Gaudens and Daniel Chester French

(3) An undesirable consequence of the Chicago Fair was the widespread influence that the fair's architectural motif had on many cities and civic architecture in the United States. The "classical" motif of the major pavilions of the "great white way" was adopted as emerging cities built courthouses, post offices, city halls, libraries, and so on. Thus while an aroused interest in civic design followed the fair, the model chosen was a step backward architecturally.
(4) This wave of interest in civic improvement generated the "City Beautiful Movement," which lead to:
(a) Heightened public awareness of the appearance of town centers
(b) A desire for impressive and grandiose public spaces and buildings
(c) Redesigning of central urban areas
(d) The formation of a new design profession—"civic design" or "urban planning"—led by

Daniel Burnham, John Nolen, Henry V. Hubbard, Charles M. Robinson, Warren Manning, and Walter Burley Griffin

Examples:

- The McMillan Commission Plan for Washington, D.C., 1901 (regeneration of interest in L'Enfant plan of 1791), by F. L. Olmsted, Jr., Daniel Burnham, and Charles McKim
- San Francisco Plan, 1906, Burnham
- Manila, Philippines Plan, 1906, Burnham
- Chicago Plan, 1909, Burnham
- Canberra, Australia Plan, 1912, Griffin

d. Planned residential communities

(1) The demand for an expanded housing supply to meet the population growth, migrating industries, and increased mobility made possible by the private automobile stimulated the development of comprehensively planned suburban communities. A major influence was English town planning and the garden city movement (Sir Ebenezer Howard's book *Garden Cities for To-morrow,* 1898). Landscape architects, working in collaboration with planners, architects, and engineers, master-planned numerous new communities during the decade preceding the stock market crash of 1929

Examples:

- Kingsport, Tennessee, 1915, John Notman
- Mariemont, Ohio, 1921–1923, John Nolen
- Sunnyside Gardens, New York, 1924–1928, Clarence Stein, Henry Wright, and Majorie S. Cautley
- Radburn, New Jersey, "a town for the motor age," 1927, Stein, Wright, and Cautley
- Chicopee, Georgia, 1927, Earle S. Draper

(2) Depression-era federally funded new garden cities or greenbelt towns planned under Franklin D. Roosevelt's New Deal administration

Examples:

- Greenhills, Ohio, 1933, Justin Hartzog and W. A. Strong
- Greenbelt, Maryland, 1935, Hale Walker and H. B. Bursley
- Greendale, Wisconsin, 1935, Elbert Peets and Jacob Crane
- Greenbrook, New Jersey, 1935 (not executed), Stein and Wright

(3) Post–World War II housing demand led to the construction of sprawling subdivisions near major urban centers

Examples:

- Levittown, Long Island, New York, 1946–1951, William Levitt and Sons
- Levittown, Bucks County, Pennsylvania, 1950–1958, William Levitt and Sons
- Levittown, Burlington County, New Jersey, 1955–1960, William Levitt and Sons

e. Public parks: Beginning with efforts in 1863 by F. L. Olmsted to secure the Yosemite Valley as a public land preserve (ultimately acquired in 1864 by the state of California as America's first state park), the movement grew to encompass not only large natural and scenic landscapes but historic sites, small and vital natural areas, forests, and Indian lands. Following the establishment of the first national park, the various states began to identify and acquire their own unique land areas for protection and/or recreational purposes

(1) National parks

(a) Yellowstone, Wyoming, 1872, the first national park

(b) Each park independently managed, no unified national system

(c) Stephen Mather, "father of the National Park Service," in 1915 initiated coordinated management policy of the thirteen independently administered national parks

(d) National Park Service established, 1916

(e) Landscape architects becoming involved as park planners/designers

(f) Park system expanded to twenty during the Depression as a result of public works project contributions, 1929–1933

(2) State parks

(a) Influenced by the National Park System and the example of Yosemite in 1864

(b) Niagara Falls became first state reservation in 1885 through the efforts of F. L. Olmsted

(c) Slow, sporadic progress until establishment of National Park Service, 1916

(d) Development of park facilities done by Civilian Conservation Corps under Roosevelt's New Deal program

(e) Landscape architects instrumental in planning and design

(f) The private automobile an impetus to expansion of state park system

(3) Small urban parks and recreational open-space networks

(a) Expansive central-city parks ("country parks") declined in importance due to increased personal mobility made possible by the automobile

(b) Vital open-space areas within urban environment of increased importance as result of sprawling growth of cities

(c) Numerous small play spaces, with easy access, dispersed into residential neighborhoods in closer proximity to users

Examples:

- Charlesbank, Boston, 1895
- Chicago South Parks, 1910

(4) Parkways

(a) Freedom of movement brought about by improved public transportation and the private automobile stimulated development of a recreational facility that had its precedent in many older, tree-lined boulevards in Europe and the United States

(b) Interconnection of varying open space, natural, scenic, or culturally significant landscapes

(c) Provided convenient and pleasant movement experience in protected, controlled-access linear network

Examples:

- "Emerald necklace," Boston, 1880–1887, F. L. Olmsted
- Minneapolis "parks and parkways," 1883, H. W. S. Cleveland
- Bronx River Parkway, 1913–1923, Gilmore Clarke
- George Washington Memorial Parkway, Washington, D.C., 1928, National Park Service
- Skyline Drive, Virginia, 1931–1940, National Park Service
- Blue Ridge Parkway, Virginia and North Carolina, 1930s, Stanley Abbott of the National Park Service
- Taconic State Parkway, New York, 1933, Clarke
- Henry Hudson Parkway, New York, Clarke
- Mount Vernon Memorial Parkway, Virginia, Clarke
- Merritt Parkway, Connecticut, 1934–1940, Clarke
- Mississippi River Parkway, from Minnesota to Louisiana, planned in 1950s, Abbott of the National Park Service
- Garden State Parkway, New Jersey, 1956

5. For the landscape architectural profession, the period of time from the Depression to the beginning of World War II (1929–1941) was one in which America was gradually showing indications of its eventual breaking away from the eclectic design influences of Europe

a. Traditionalism

(1) American Academy in Rome; prize-winning designs retained the "Beaux-Arts" appearance through the 1930s

(2) Landscape architectural education continued to emphasize traditional stylistic approach rather than site-specific problem-solving process

(3) Works executed were eclectic in character

Examples:

- Lincoln Memorial, Washington, D.C., 1910–1922, Henry Bacon
- Colonial Williamsburg, Virginia, "restored or replicated," 1928–1937, Rockefeller Foundation, and Arthur Shurcliff, landscape architect

- Meridian Hill Park, Washington, D.C., 1917–1936, Ferruccio Vitale
- U.S. Supreme Court Building, Washington, D.C., 1930
- Jefferson Memorial, Washington, D.C., 1939–1943, John Russell Pope

b. Transition to new attitudes about the environment, planning, and design
  (1) Regional environmental management done under the Federal New Deal program of 1933, which established the Tennessee Valley Authority to:
    (a) Provide hydroelectric power generation
    (b) Reforest devastated areas of seven southern states
    (c) Provide employment (largest employer of landscape architects after the National Park Service)
    (d) Develop recreational facilities
    (e) Initiate soil conservation practices
    (f) Improve navigation of the region's rivers
    (g) Introduce scientific farming practices such as contour plowing and crop rotation
  (2) Experimentation with nontraditional design approaches being attempted
    (a) Thomas Church in California residential design
    (b) Dan Kiley, James Rose, and Garrett Eckbo, graduate students at the Harvard Graduate School of Design, under the influence of cubism and Walter Gropius and the international style of architecture; went public with their avant-garde design ideas, publishing many journal articles in *Pencil Points* (now *Progressive Architecture*) and elsewhere
    (c) Work by Frank Lloyd Wright that expressed uniqueness of the site, indigenous materials, spatial flow, human scale
    Examples:
      - Fallingwater, Bear Run, Pennsylvania, 1936
      - Taliesin West, Scotsdale, Arizona, 1937
    (d) San Fransisco Museum of Art Exhibition, "Contemporary Landscape Architecture," 1937; publicized the new "curvilinear" or "moderne" expression in design; much of the work was by Thomas Church
    (e) New York World's Fair, 1939, displayed to the world the new departure in architecture and landscape architectural design characterized by:
      i. Flowing, curving lines
      ii. No apparent beginning or end
      iii. Cohesive and pleasing when viewed from any vantage point
      iv. Asymmetrically balanced
      v. Simplicity of forms that were derived from function and/or the use of nontraditional materials: concrete; glass blocks; asbestos paneling; mirrors; stainless steel; redwood; fiberglass; and so on
      vi. Unique design solutions resulting from the unique requirements of program and site
    Examples:
      - Exhibition Garden for Golden Gate Exposition, San Francisco, 1940, T. Church
      - Donnell residence, "El Novillero," Sonoma, California, 1948, T. Church and Lawrence Halprin

6. The landscape architecture profession during the post–World War II period, 1945–1993, made a major shift in project types and clients. Commissions for the design of residential grounds for the wealthy, once the mainstay of many practices, dwindled to a very small proportion of the profession's expanding scope of work. This period marked by:
  a. Major population increases (the U.S. population nearly doubled, from 131.7 million in 1940 to 253.5 million in 1992)
  b. Population shift from predominantly rural to urban and concomitant growth of cities
  c. Urban sprawl into the suburbs as a result of cheaper land, expanding number of private automobiles, and perception of greater safety outside urban centers
  d. Many previously urban-based institutions relocated to the suburbs on cheaper, open land, with space for expansion and with many intangible assets and amenities, such as mature vegetation, natural scenery, fresh air, and tranquility

7. Profession of landscape architecture evolved to handle a diversity of project types and at the same time, renewed its commitment to the fundamental concern for the environment—the stewardship of the land—working with ecological conditions in the most sensitive ways possible. Contemporary scope includes:
   a. Planned residential communities ["planned unit development" (PUD)]
      Examples:
      - Sea Pines Plantation, Hilton Head Island, South Carolina, 1960s–1980s, Sasaki, Walker and Associates
      - Reston, Virginia, 1964, James Rouse and Co.
      - Sea Ranch, Sonoma Co., California, 1967, Lawrence Halprin & Associates
      - Columbia, Maryland, 1965, James Rouse and Co.
      - Woodlands, Texas, 1972–1980, Wallace, McHarg, Roberts and Todd
      - Seaside, Florida, 1980s–1990s, Duany and Plater-Zyberk
      - Laguna West, Sacramento, California, 1980s–1990s, Peter Calthrope and Associates
   b. Suburban shopping centers
      Examples:
      - Cherry Hill Shopping Center, Haddonfield, New Jersey, 1962, Victor Gruen and Associates
      - Northwest Plaza, St. Louis, Missouri, 1965, Lawrence Halprin & Associates
   c. Urban renewal: redevelopment of deteriorating inner-city sections into new and/or adaptive land uses (occasionally at the expense of displacing low-income urban residents while bringing about much needed rejuvenation of deteriorating city centers)
      Examples:
      - Mellon Square, Pittsburg, 1955, Simonds and Simonds Associates
      - Constitution Plaza, Hartford, Connecticut, 1963, Sasaki, Walker and Associates
      - Ghirardelli Square, San Francisco, 1964–1968, Lawrence Halprin & Associates
      - Jacob Riis Plaza, New York City, 1964, M. Paul Friedberg and Partners
      - Inner Harbor, Baltimore, 1973, James Rouse and Wallace McHarg, Roberts and Todd
      - Fanueil Hall, Quincy Market, Boston, 1978, Rouse and Co.
      - Battery Park City Esplanades, New York City, 1988, Hanna/Olin Ltd.
   d. Suburban college campuses
      Examples:
      - Foothill College, Los Altos, California, 1959, Sasaki, Walker and Associates
      - U.S. Air Force Academy, Colorado Springs, 1968, architects, Skidmore, Owings and Merrill and landscape architect, Dan Kiley
      - State University of New York at Buffalo, 1968–1978, Sasaki, Dawson, De May and Associates
      - University of California at Santa Cruz, 1960–1992, Thomas Church, Lawrence Halprin, Robert Royston, Dan Kiley, Garrett Eckbo
      - University of New Mexico, 1962–1992, Garrett Eckbo
   e. Urban plazas and vest pocket parks
      Examples:
      - Paley Park, New York City, 1966, Zion and Breen Associates
      - Jacob Riis Plaza, New York City, 1964, M. Paul Friedberg and Partners
      - Copley Square, Boston, 1966, Sasaki, Dawson, De May, redesigned and rebuilt 1984–1990, Dean Abbott
      - Lovejoy Plaza, Portland, Oregon, 1965–1966, Lawrence Halprin & Associates
      - Auditorium Forecourt (now Ira Keller Foundation) Plaza, Portland, Oregon, 1965–1970, Lawrence Halprin & Associates and Angela Danadjieva
      - Williams Square, Las Colinas, Irving, Texas, 1983–1985, The SWA Group
      - Fountain Place, Dallas, Texas, 1985, Dan Kiley
   f. Rooftop plazas and gardens
      Examples:
      - Mellon Square, Pittsburgh, 1953, Simonds and Simonds Associates

- Kaiser Center Roof Garden, Oakland, California, 1960, Osmundson and Staley Associates
- Constitution Plaza, Hartford, Connecticut, 1963, Sasaki, Walker and Associates
- Ghirardelli Square, San Francisco, 1964–1968, Lawrence Halprin & Associates
- Oakland Museum, Oakland, California, 1969, Kiley
- Freeway Park, Seattle, 1976–1990, Lawrence Halprin & Associates and Angela Danadjieva
- Harlequin Plaza, Englewood, Colorado, 1982, George Hargreaves of The SWA Group

g. Industrial, corporate, and institutional office parks
Examples:
- Connecticut General Life Insurance (CIGNA), Bloomfield Hills, Connecticut, 1957, Dan Kiley and Isamu Noguchi
- Upjohn Co. Headquarters, Kalamazoo, Michigan, 1960–1961, Sasaki, Walker and Associates
- Deere and Company Headquarters, Moline, Illinois, 1963–1970, Sasaki, Dawson, De May and Associates
- Pepsico World Headquarters, Purchase, New York, 1965, Edward D. Stone, Jr. Associates
- Carlson Center, Minnetonka, Minnesota, 1988, EDAW Design Group
- TRW World Headquarters Lyndhurst, Ohio, 1985, Sasaki Associates
- Codex World Headquarters, Canton, Massachusetts, 1986–1989, Hanna/Olin Ltd.

h. Memorials
Examples:
- Vietnam Veterans Memorial, Washington, D.C., 1981, Maya Ying Lin
- Franklin Delano Roosevelt Memorial, Washington, D.C., designed 1974 (under construction 1991–1995), Lawrence Halprin
- Women in Vietnam Memorial, Washington, D.C., 1992 (not built to-date), landscape architect, George Dickie of Helmuth, Obata and Kassabaum, Inc.
- Korean War Veterans Memorial, 1992 (not built to-date), Cooper-Lecky Associates

i. Historic landscape preservation/restoration
Examples:
- Gas Works Park, Seattle, Washington, 1970–1975, Richard Haag Associates
- Pioneer Square, Seattle, 1979, Jones and Jones
- Monticello Garden Terrace, Charlottesville, Virginia, 1983, Rudy Favretti and William Kelso
- Afton Villa, St. Francisville, Louisiana, 1980–1990, Neil Odenwald
- Springside, Poughkeepsie, New York, 1980s, Charles Birnbaum
- Central Park, New York City, 1980s–1990s, Kelly, Varnell Associates and the Central Park Conservancy

j. Natural landscape restoration
Examples:
- Midwestern prairie restoration, Morton Arboretum, Lisle, Illinois, 1960s, Roy Schulenburg
- Kansas City International Airport entrance road, native prairie grasses and wildflowers, 1973, Fred Markham and Associates
- Lincoln Memorial Garden, Springfield, Illinois, reestablishment of native vegetation, 1970s, Darrel G. Morrison
- CUNA Mutual Insurance Co., Madison, Wisconsin, 1970s, reestablishment of native prairie grasses and wildflowers, Darrel G. Morrison
- Morris County, New Jersey, 1980s, restoration of native wetland vegetation, Andropogon Associates
- National Wildflower Research Center, Austin, Texas, 1992–1994, Darrel Morrison and J. Robert Anderson

k. Environmental/visual resource analysis and planning
Example:
- The Hanalei Valley, Kauai, Hawaii, 1980s, 1000 Friends of Kauai and Land and Community Associates

l. Reclamation of disturbed lands
Examples:
- Chief Logan State Park, West Virginia, 1980s, Environmental Design Group, Inc.

- Oakbridge Planned Community, Oceola County, Florida, 1980s–1990s, Glatting, Lopez, Kercher, Anglin, Associates, Inc.
- Lantana Landfill, Palm Beach County, Florida, 1984, gbs&h, landscape architects
- Mono Lake, National Forest Scenic Area, California, 1980s, Ted Rickford, landscape architect with the National Forest Service
- Effigy Tumuli Sculptures, Buffalo Rock State Park, Ottawa, Illinois, 1980s, Michael Heizer, sculptor
- Sky Mound, Hackensack Meadows, New Jersey, 1980s, Nancy Holt, sculptress

D. Vocabulary:

- American Academy in Rome
- Arabesque
- Art nouveau
- Buffer zone
- Landscape architecture
- Land use plan
- Megalopolis
- Moderne
- Chatauqua
- Civilian Conservation Corps
- Condominium
- Conurbation
- Country park
- Cul-de-sac
- Eclectic
- Ecole des Beaux-Arts
- Ecology
- Environmental impact statement
- Garden city
- Genius loci
- Green belt
- Historic preservation
- Holistic
- International style
- Interprofessional collaboration
- New town
- Open space (planning)
- Parkway
- Physiographic determinism
- Picturesque
- Planned unit development (PUD)
- Regional planning
- Romantic
- Scenic easement
- Suburban
- Super block
- Urban design/planning
- Urban renewal
- Vest pocket park
- Visual resource analysis
- Zoning

SECTION 4

MAPS OF MAJOR WORKS OF LANDSCAPE ARCHITECTURE

Maps of Major Works of Landscape Architecture

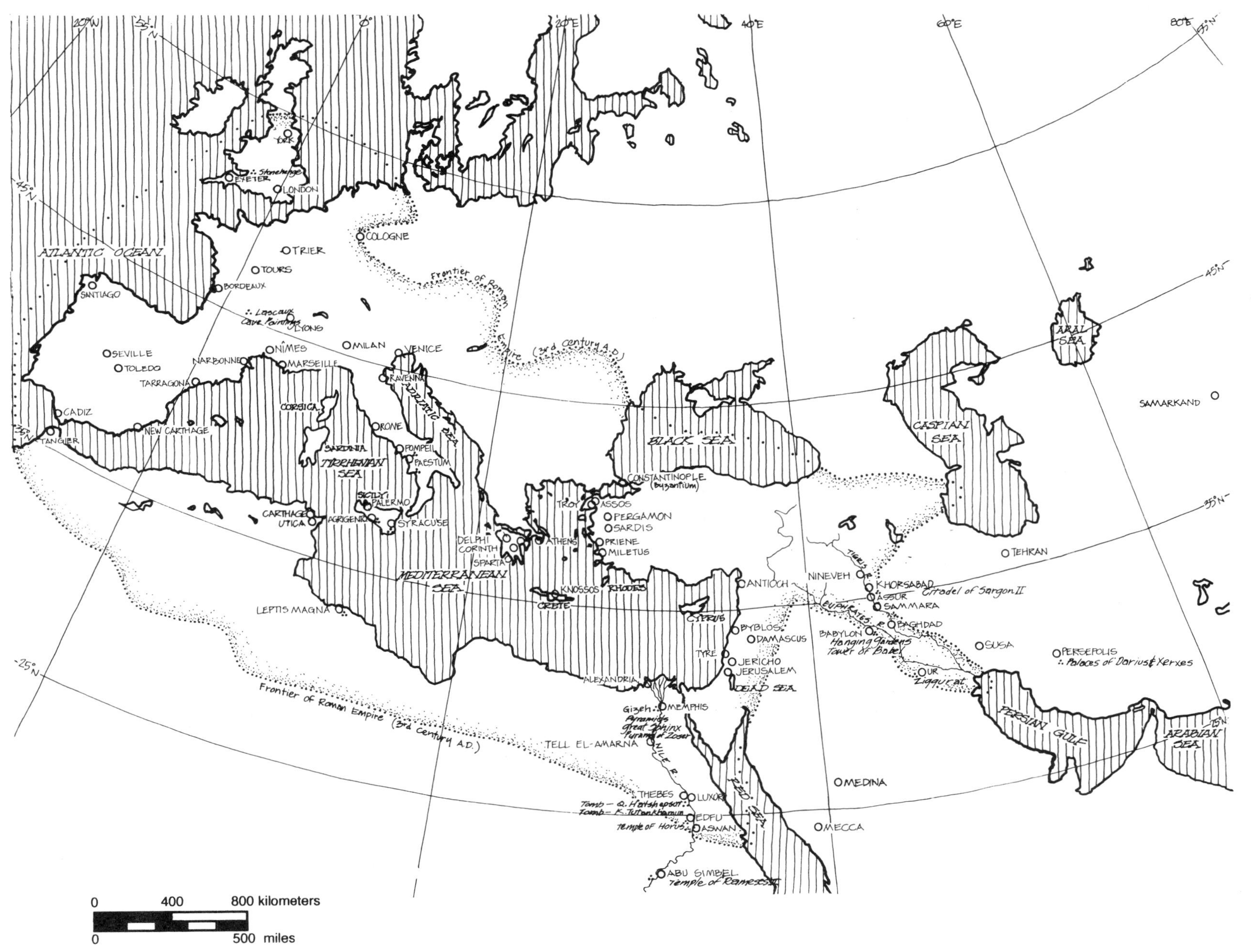

Prehistoric, Ancient and Medieval

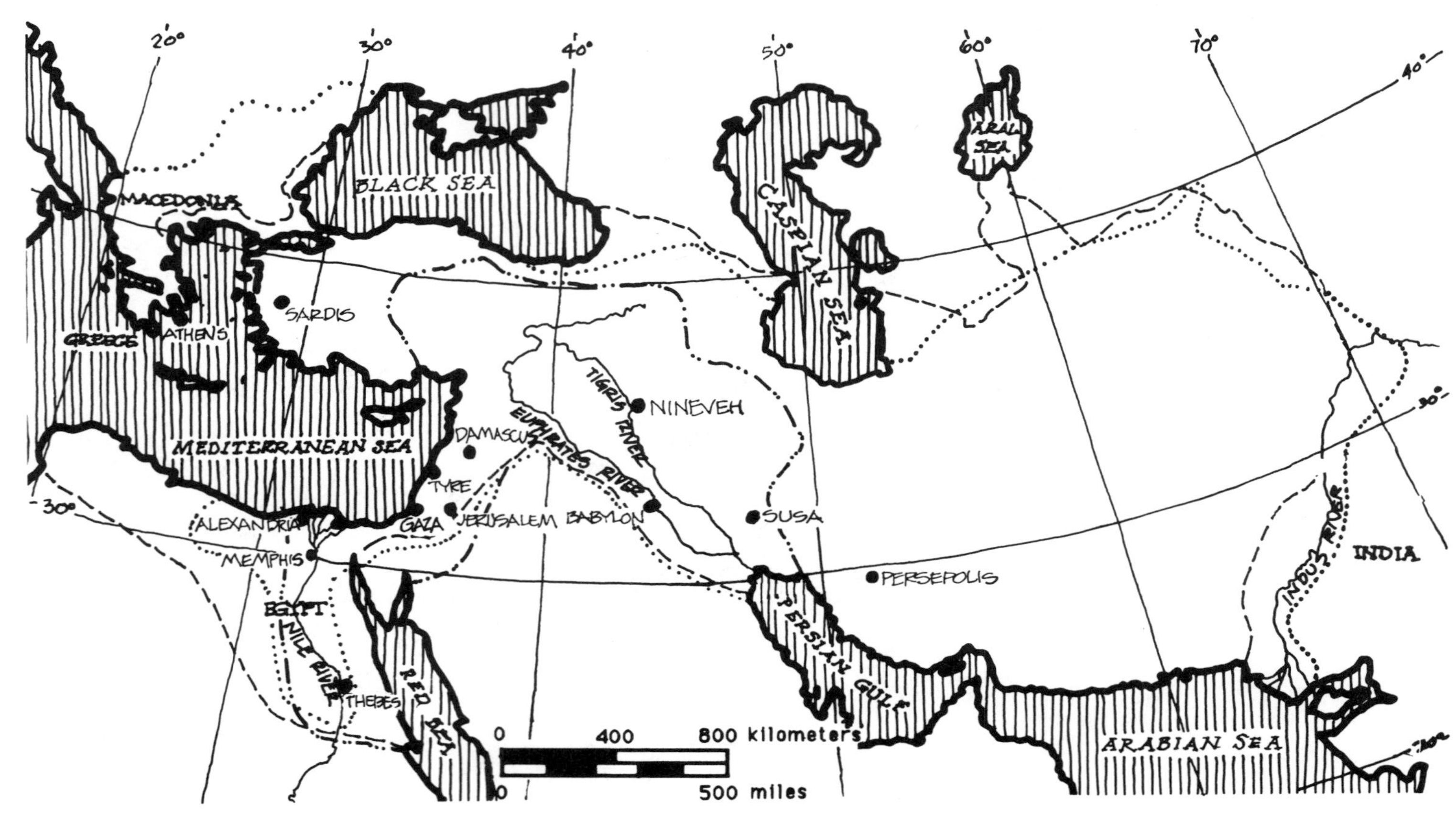

Assyrian Empire c.625 BC —··—··—··—··—··—··

Persian Empire c.490 BC — — — — — — — — — —

Conquests of Alexander 336 BC—323 BC ························

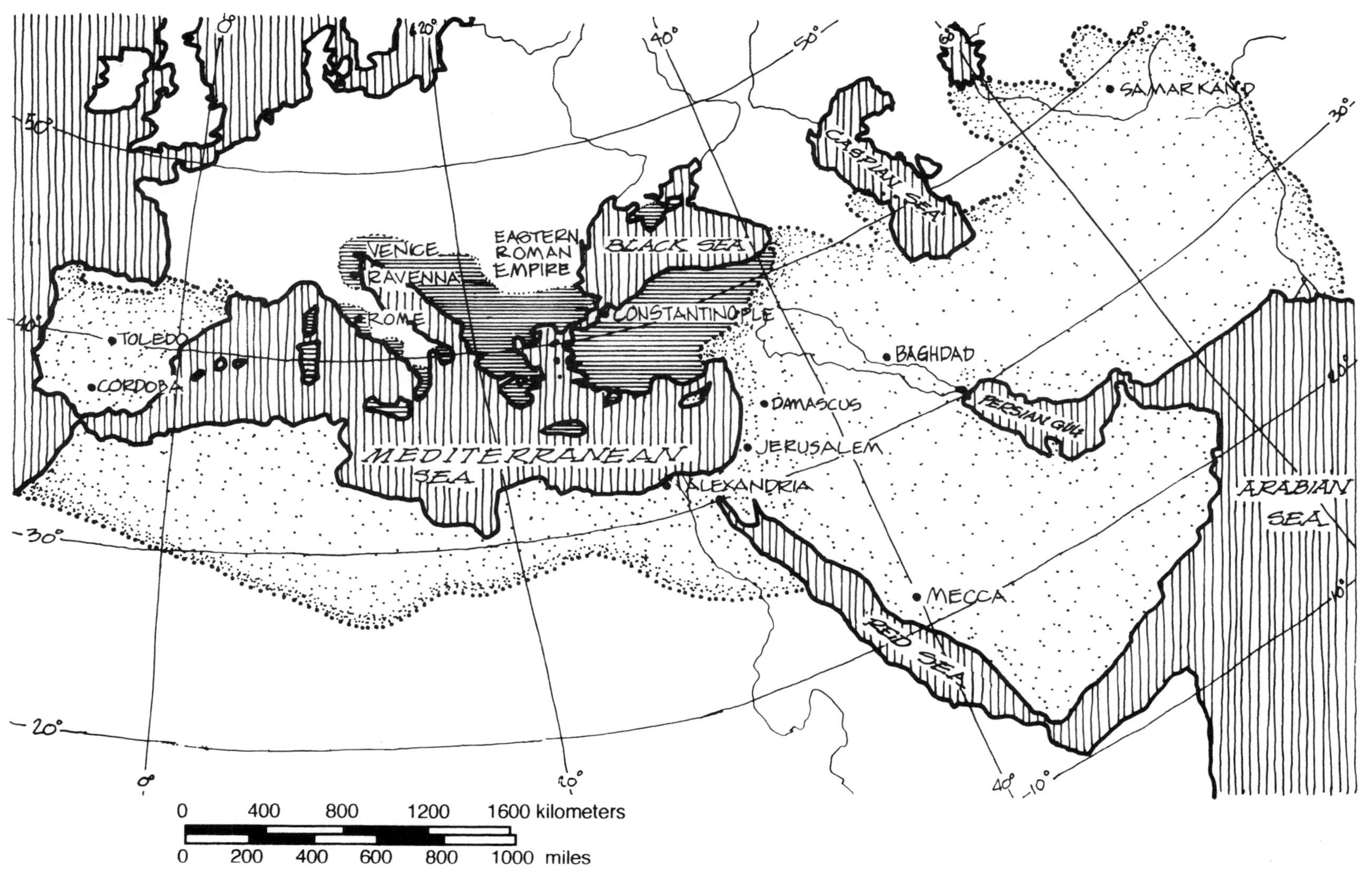

VENICE
RAVENNA
ROME
EASTERN
ROMAN
EMPIRE
BLACK SEA
CASPIAN SEA
SAMARKAND
CONSTANTINOPLE
TOLEDO
CORDOBA
BAGHDAD
PERSIAN GULF
DAMASCUS
JERUSALEM
MEDITERRANEAN
SEA
ALEXANDRIA
ARABIAN
SEA
MECCA
RED SEA
0 400 800 1200 1600 kilometers
0 200 400 600 800 1000 miles

Islamic World 622—1492

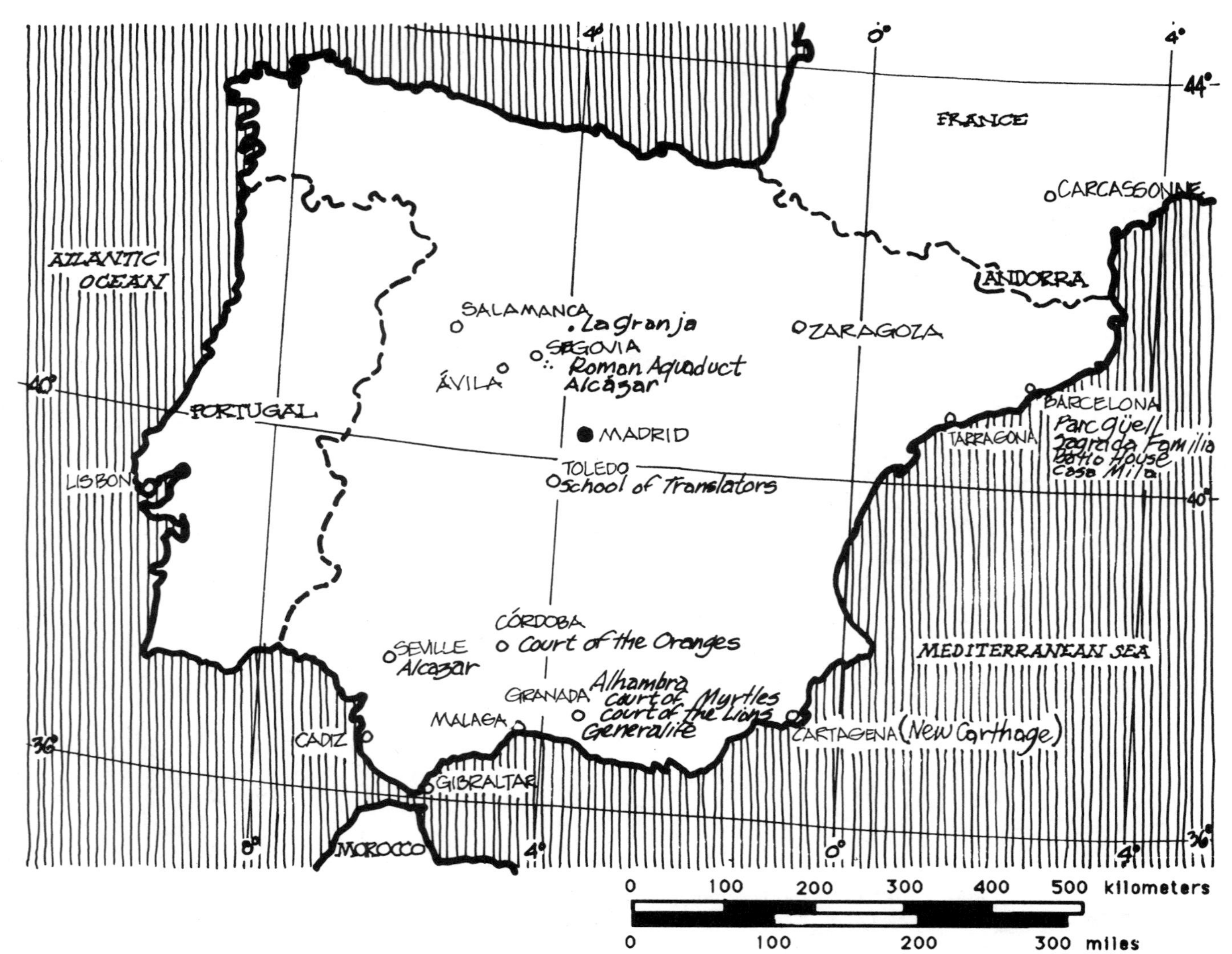

FRANCE
CARCASSONNE
ANDORRA
ATLANTIC OCEAN
SALAMANCA
La granja
ZARAGOZA
SEGOVIA
Roman Aqueduct
Alcázar
ÁVILA
PORTUGAL
BARCELONA
Parc Güell
Sagrada Familia
Batlló House
Casa Milà
TARRAGONA
MADRID
TOLEDO
School of Translators
LISBON
CÓRDOBA
Court of the Oranges
SEVILLE
Alcazar
MEDITERRANEAN SEA
GRANADA
Alhambra
Court of Myrtles
Court of the Lions
Generalife
MALAGA
CADIZ
CARTAGENA (New Carthage)
GIBRALTAR
MOROCCO
0 100 200 300 400 500 kilometers
0 100 200 300 miles

Spain

SWITZERLAND
Bern
AUSTRIA
HUNGARY
FRANCE
JUGOSLAVIA
STRESSA
Isola Bella
BERGAMO
MILAN
VICENZA
VENICE
Pza. S. Marco
PADUA
MANTUA
Palazzo Te
GENOA
RAVENNA
San Vitale
Theodoric's Tomb
S. Apollinare in Classe
NÎMES
Pont du Gard
Amphitheatre
Maison Carree
ARLES
Amphitheatre
MARSEILLE
Florence:
Giardini di Boboli
Pza. della Signoria
Pza. d. SS. Annunziata
V. Garzoni
COLLODI
LUCCA
PISA
FIESOLE
V. Medici
FLORENCE
SETTIGNANO
V. Gamberaia
URBINO
Ducal Palace
Pliny's Villa
SPLIT
Palace of Diocletian
SIENA
Pza. del Campo
CORTONA
ASSISI
ADRIATIC SEA
DUBROVNIK
ORVIETO
TODI
BOMARZO
V. Orsini
BAGNAIA
V. Lante
CAPRAROLA
V. Farnese
CORSICA (FR.)
ROME
Cortile del Belvedere
Villa di Papa Giulio
Villa Madama
Villa Medici
Villa Pia
Forum Romanum
Imperial Fora
Piazza San Pietro
Piazza dei Campidoglio
Piazza del Popolo
Nero's Golden House
TIVOLI
Temple of the Sybil
V. d'Este, Hadrian's Villa
Pliny's Villa
FRASCATI
V. Aldobrandini
V. Mondragone
MEDITERRANEAN SEA
CASERTA
Pal. Reale
NAPLES
Pompeii
Hse of Vetti
Paestum
Temples
SARDINIA (IT.)
TYRRHENIAN SEA
PALERMO
SICILY
PZA. AMERINA
V. Romana del Casale
AGRIGENTO
Temples
SYRACUSE
TUNISIA
TUNIS
0 100 200 300 kilometers
0 100 200 miles

Italy

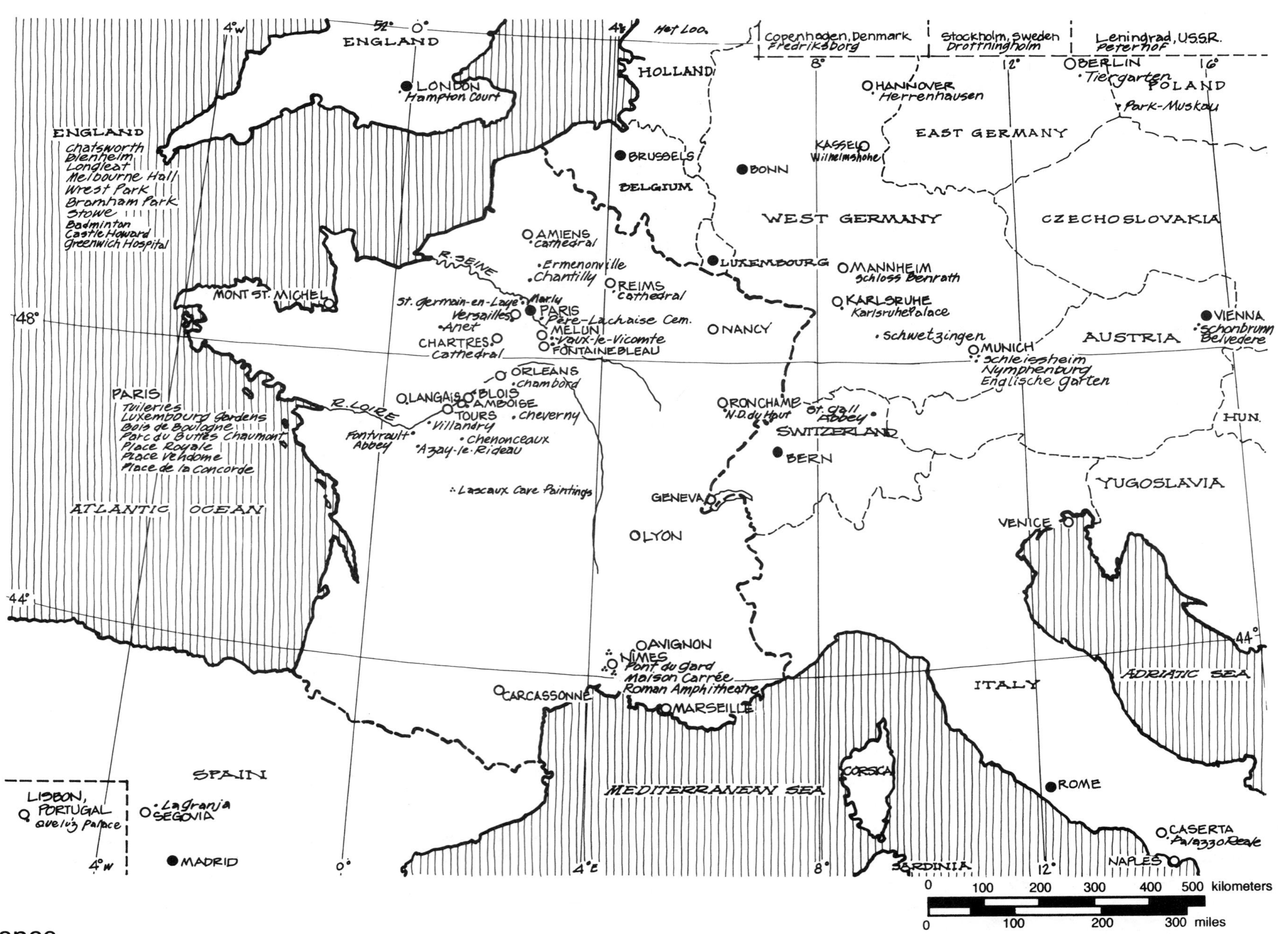
ENGLAND
LONDON
Hampton Court
Het Loo
Copenhagen, Denmark
Fredriksborg
Stockholm, Sweden
Drottningholm
Leningrad, U.S.S.R.
Peterhof
HOLLAND
BERLIN
Tiergarten
POLAND
HANNOVER
Herrenhausen
Park-Muskau
EAST GERMANY
ENGLAND
Chatsworth
Blenheim
Longleat
Melbourne Hall
Wrest Park
Bromham Park
Stowe
Badminton
Castle Howard
Greenwich Hospital
BRUSSELS
KASSEL
Wilhelmshohe
BONN
BELGIUM
WEST GERMANY
CZECHOSLOVAKIA
AMIENS
cathedral
R. SEINE
Ermenonville
Chantilly
LUXEMBOURG
MANNHEIM
Schloss Benrath
MONT ST. MICHEL
REIMS
cathedral
KARLSRUHE
Karlsruhe Palace
St. Germain-en-Laye
Marly
Versailles
PARIS
Anet
Pere-Lachaise Cem.
MELUN
Vaux-le-Vicomte
FONTAINEBLEAU
NANCY
Schwetzingen
VIENNA
Schonbrunn
Belvedere
AUSTRIA
CHARTRES
Cathedral
MUNICH
Schleissheim
Nymphenburg
Englische Garten
ORLEANS
Chambord
PARIS
Tuileries
Luxembourg Gardens
Bois de Boulogne
Parc du Buttes Chaumont
Place Royale
Place Vendome
Place de la Concorde
LANGAIS
BLOIS
AMBOISE
R. LOIRE
TOURS
Cheverny
Villandry
Fontvrault Abbey
Chenonceaux
Azay-le-Rideau
RONCHAMP
N.D. du Haut
St. Gall Abbey
SWITZERLAND
BERN
HUN.
Lascaux Cave Paintings
ATLANTIC OCEAN
GENEVA
YUGOSLAVIA
LYON
VENICE
44°
48°
52°
AVIGNON
NIMES
Pont du Gard
Maison Carrée
Roman Amphitheatre
CARCASSONNE
MARSEILLE
ITALY
ADRIATIC SEA
SPAIN
CORSICA
MEDITERRANEAN SEA
ROME
LISBON, PORTUGAL
Queluz Palace
La Granja
SEGOVIA
MADRID
CASERTA
Palazzo Reale
NAPLES
SARDINIA
4°W
0°
4°E
8°
12°
16°
0 100 200 300 400 500 kilometers
0 100 200 300 miles

France

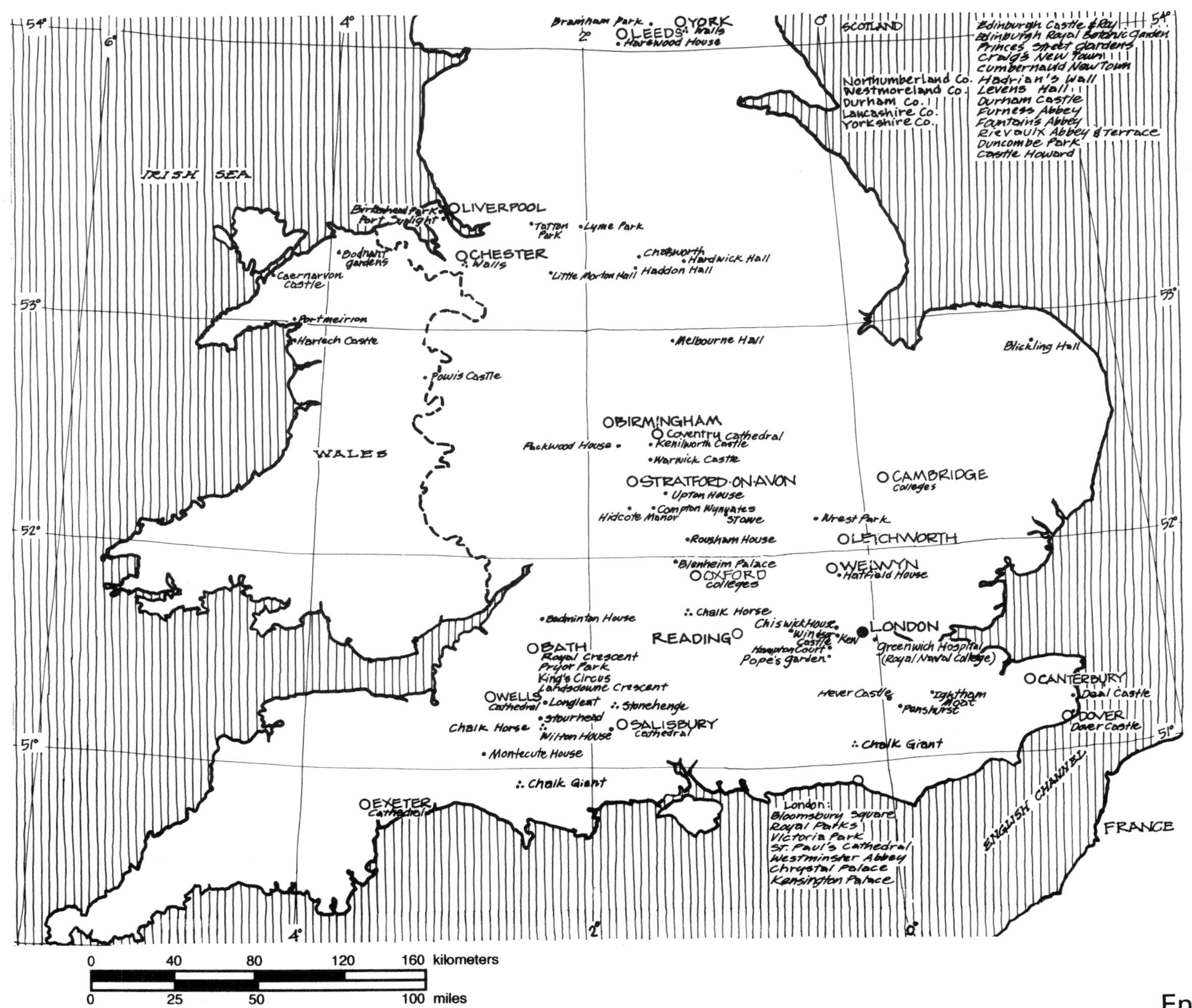

54°
6°
4°
Bramham Park
YORK
Walls
LEEDS
Harewood House
2°
0°
SCOTLAND
Edinburgh Castle & Ray
Edinburgh Royal Botanic Garden
Princes Street Gardens
Craig's New Town
Cumbernauld New Town
Northumberland Co.
Westmoreland Co.
Durham Co.
Lancashire Co.
Yorkshire Co.
Hadrian's Wall
Levens Hall
Durham Castle
Furness Abbey
Fountains Abbey
Rievaulx Abbey & Terrace
Duncombe Park
Castle Howard
IRISH SEA
LIVERPOOL
Birkenhead Park
Port Sunlight
Tatton Park
Lyme Park
CHESTER
Walls
Bodnant gardens
Chatsworth
Hardwick Hall
Haddon Hall
Little Morton Hall
Caernarvon Castle
53°
Portmeirion
Harlech Castle
Melbourne Hall
Blickling Hall
Powis Castle
BIRMINGHAM
Coventry Cathedral
Kenilworth Castle
Packwood House
Warwick Castle
WALES
STRATFORD-ON-AVON
CAMBRIDGE
Colleges
Upton House
Compton Wynyates
Hidcote Manor
Stowe
Wrest Park
52°
Rousham House
LETCHWORTH
Blenheim Palace
WELWYN
Hatfield House
OXFORD
colleges
Chalk Horse
Badminton House
Chiswick House
Windsor Castle
Kew
LONDON
READING
BATH
Royal Crescent
Prior Park
King's Circus
Lansdowne Crescent
Hampton Court
Pope's Garden
Greenwich Hospital
(Royal Naval College)
WELLS
Cathedral
Longleat
Stonehenge
Hever Castle
Ightham Moat
Penshurst
CANTERBURY
Deal Castle
DOVER
Dover Castle
Chalk Horse
Stourhead
SALISBURY
Cathedral
Wilton House
Montecute House
51°
Chalk Giant
Chalk Giant
EXETER
Cathedral
London:
Bloomsbury Square
Royal Parks
Victoria Park
St. Paul's Cathedral
Westminster Abbey
Chrystal Palace
Kensington Palace
ENGLISH CHANNEL
FRANCE
4°
2°
0°
0 40 80 120 160 kilometers
0 25 50 100 miles

England

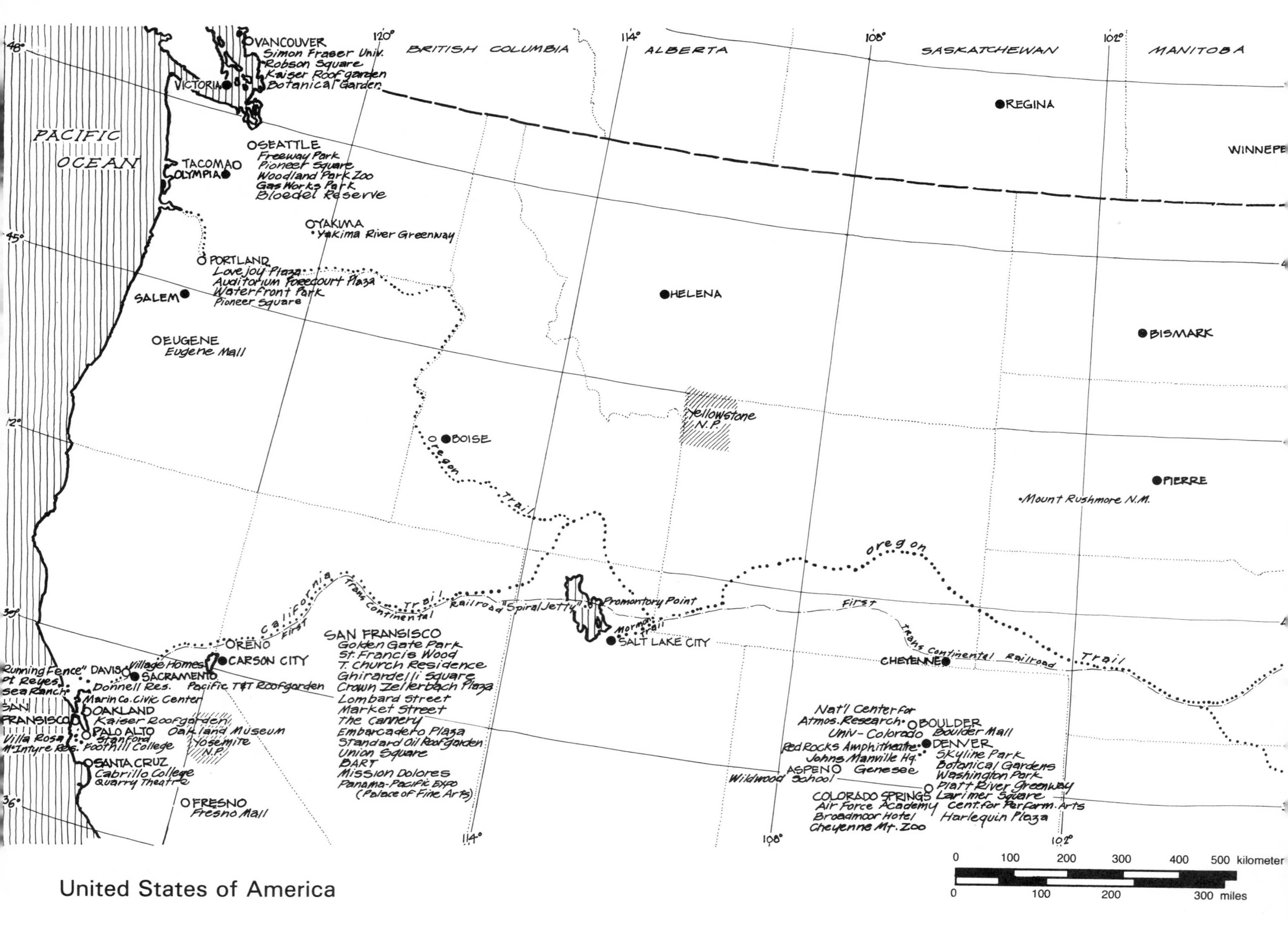

PACIFIC OCEAN
BRITISH COLUMBIA
ALBERTA
SASKATCHEWAN
MANITOBA
120°
114°
108°
102°
48°
45°
42°
39°
36°
VANCOUVER
Simon Fraser Univ.
Robson Square
Kaiser Roofgarden
Botanical Garden
VICTORIA
REGINA
WINNIPE
SEATTLE
Freeway Park
Pioneer Square
Woodland Park Zoo
Gas Works Park
Bloedel Reserve
TACOMA
OLYMPIA
YAKIMA
Yakima River Greenway
PORTLAND
Lovejoy Plaza
Auditorium Forecourt Plaza
Waterfront Park
Pioneer Square
SALEM
EUGENE
Eugene Mall
HELENA
BISMARK
Yellowstone N.P.
BOISE
Oregon Trail
PIERRE
Mount Rushmore N.M.
oregon Trail
California Trail
First Trans Continental Railroad
"Spiral Jetty"
Promontory Point
Mormon Trail
SALT LAKE CITY
First Trans Continental Railroad
CHEYENNE
RENO
CARSON CITY
SAN FRANSISCO
Golden Gate Park
St. Francis Wood
T. Church Residence
Ghirardelli Square
Crown Zellerbach Plaza
Lombard Street
Market Street
The Cannery
Embarcadero Plaza
Standard Oil Roofgarden
Union Square
BART
Mission Dolores
Panama-Pacific Expo (Palace of Fine Arts)
"Running Fence"
Pt Reyes
Sea Ranch
DAVIS
Village Homes
SACRAMENTO
Donnell Res.
Pacific T&T Roofgarden
Marin Co. Civic Center
SAN FRANSISCO
OAKLAND
Kaiser Roofgarden
Oakland Museum
PALO ALTO
Stanford
Foothill College
Villa Rosa
McIntyre Res.
Yosemite N.P.
SANTA CRUZ
Cabrillo College
Quarry Theatre
FRESNO
Fresno Mall
Nat'l Center for Atmos. Research
BOULDER
Univ-Colorado
Boulder Mall
Red Rocks Amphitheatre
DENVER
Johns Manville Hq.
Skyline Park
ASPEN
Genesee
Botanical Gardens
Wildwood School
Washington Park
Platt River Greenway
COLORADO SPRINGS
Larimer Square
Air Force Academy
Cent. for Perform. Arts
Broadmoor Hotel
Harlequin Plaza
Cheyenne Mt. Zoo
0 100 200 300 400 500 kilometer
0 100 200 300 miles

United States of America

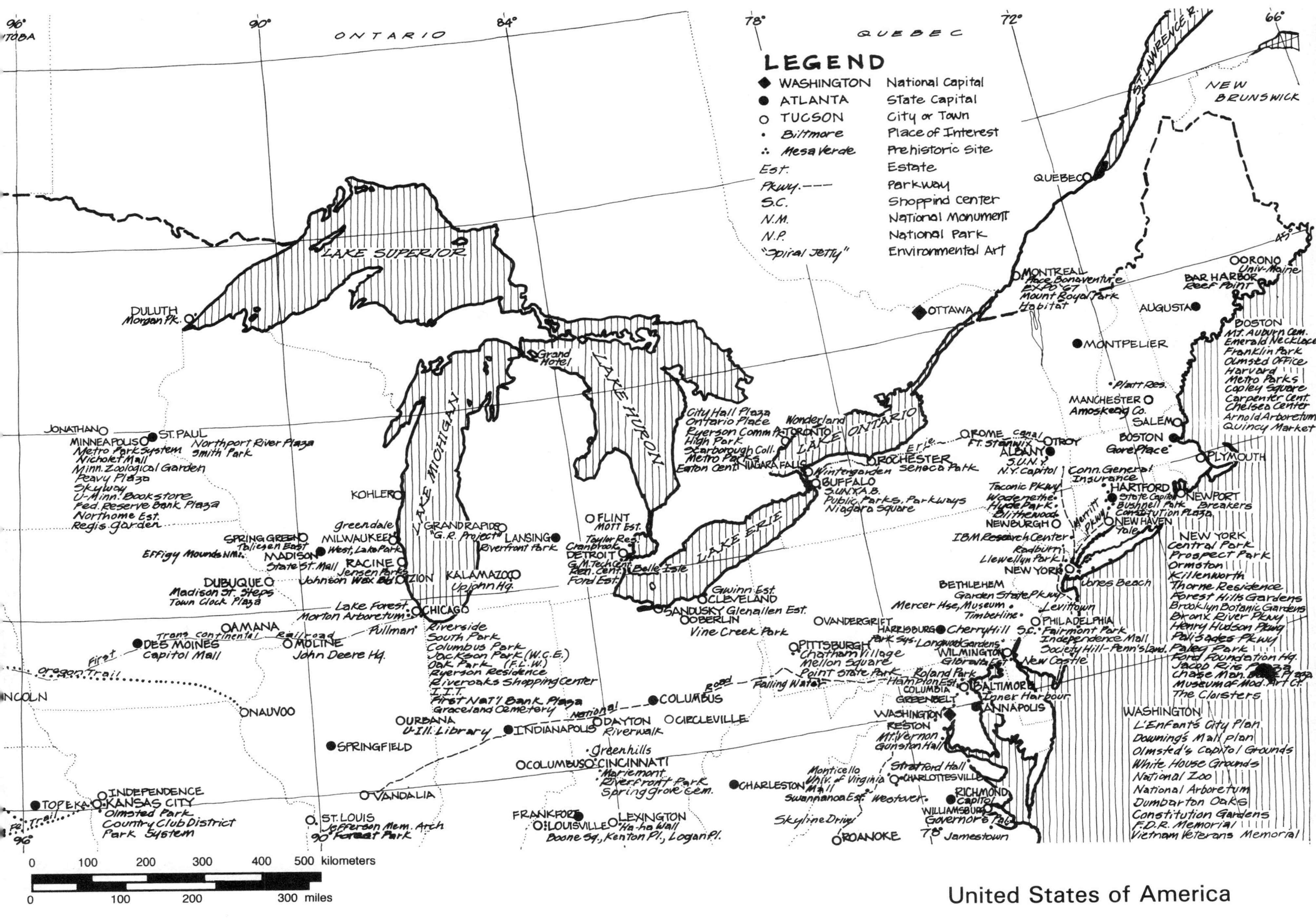

United States of America

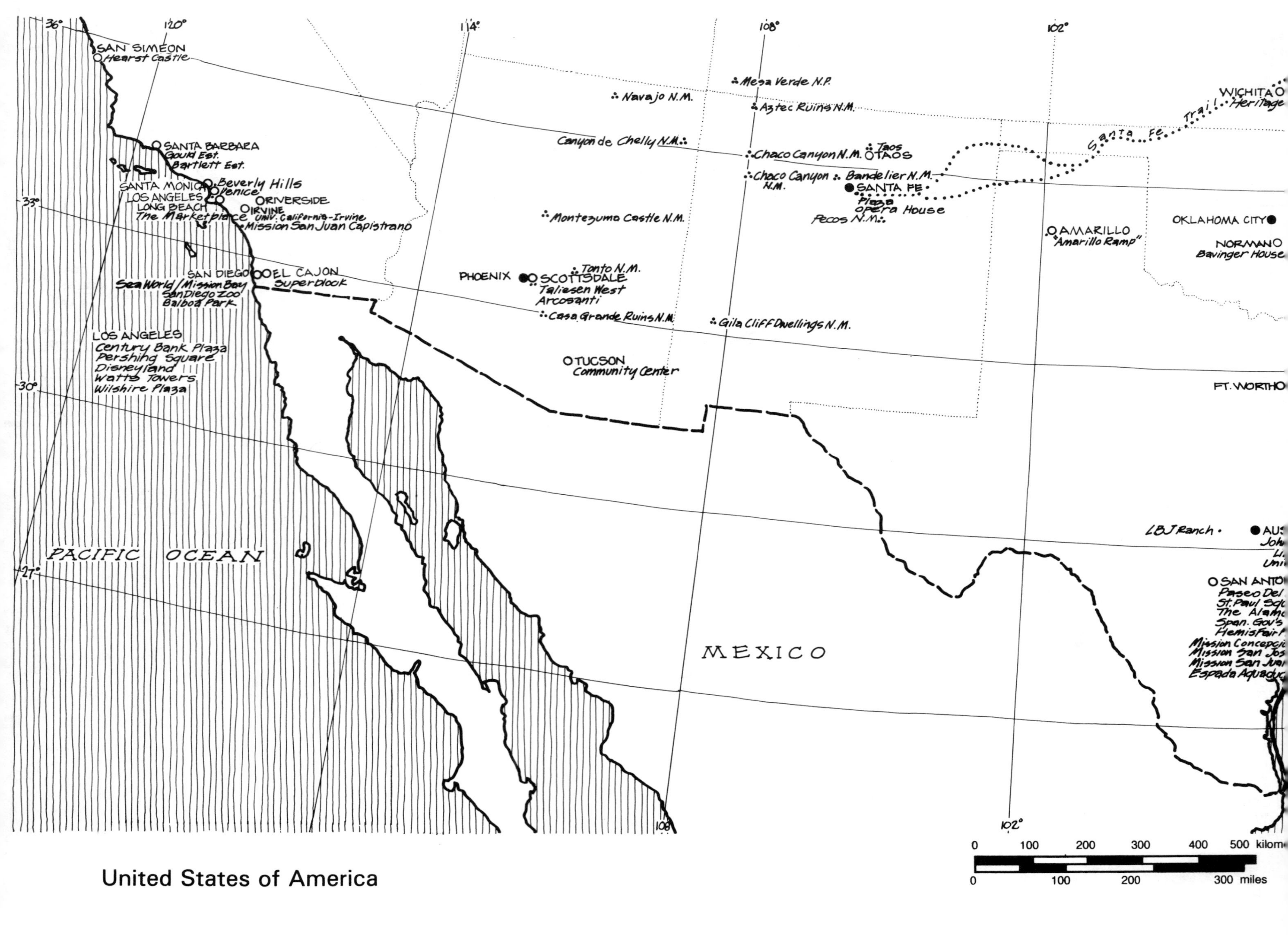
SAN SIMEON
Hearst Castle
SANTA BARBARA
Gould Est.
Bartlett Est.
SANTA MONICA
Beverly Hills
Venice
LOS ANGELES
LONG BEACH
The Marketplace
RIVERSIDE
IRVINE
Univ. California-Irvine
Mission San Juan Capistrano
SAN DIEGO
EL CAJON
Superblock
Sea World/Mission Bay
San Diego Zoo
Balboa Park
LOS ANGELES
Century Bank Plaza
Pershing Square
Disneyland
Watts Towers
Wilshire Plaza
PACIFIC OCEAN
Mesa Verde N.P.
Navajo N.M.
Aztec Ruins N.M.
Canyon de Chelly N.M.
Chaco Canyon N.M.
Taos
TAOS
Chaco Canyon N.M.
Bandelier N.M.
SANTA FE
Plaza
Opera House
Pecos N.M.
Montezuma Castle N.M.
Tonto N.M.
PHOENIX
SCOTTSDALE
Taliesen West
Arcosanti
Casa Grande Ruins N.M.
Gila Cliff Dwellings N.M.
TUCSON
Community Center
Santa Fe Trail
WICHITA
Heritage
AMARILLO
"Amarillo Ramp"
OKLAHOMA CITY
NORMAN
Bavinger House
FT. WORTH
LBJ Ranch
MEXICO
0 100 200 300 400 500 kilom
0 100 200 300 miles

United States of America

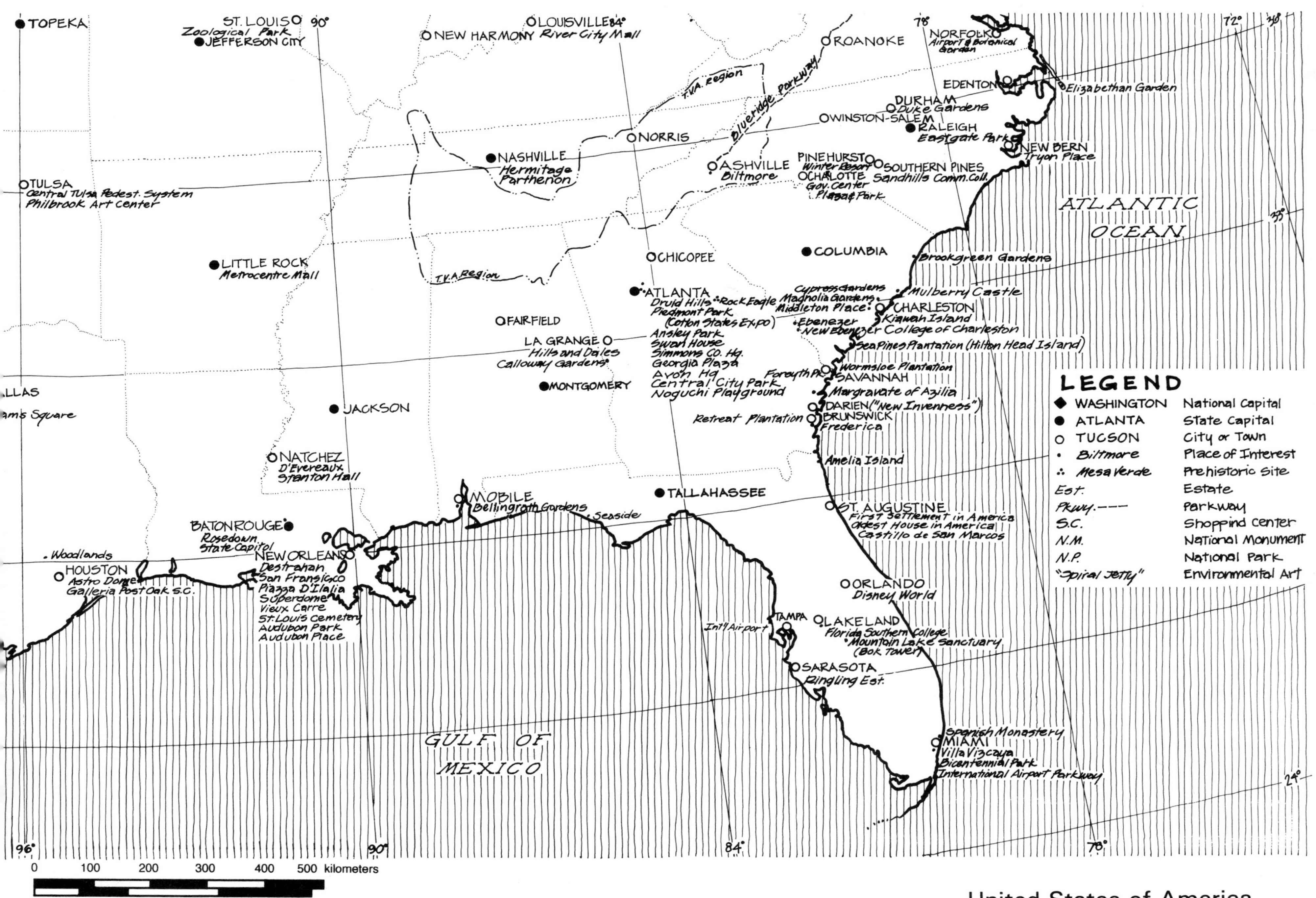
TOPEKA
ST. LOUIS
Zoological Park
JEFFERSON CITY
NEW HARMONY
LOUISVILLE
River City Mall
ROANOKE
NORFOLK
Airport & Botanical Garden
EDENTON
Elizabethan Garden
T.V.A. Region
Blueridge Parkway
DURHAM
Duke Gardens
WINSTON-SALEM
RALEIGH
Eastgate Park
NORRIS
NASHVILLE
Hermitage
Parthenon
ASHVILLE
Biltmore
PINEHURST
Winter Resort
SOUTHERN PINES
Sandhills Comm. Coll.
CHARLOTTE
Gov. Center
Plaza Park
NEW BERN
Tryon Place
TULSA
Central Tulsa Pedest. System
Philbrook Art Center
ATLANTIC OCEAN
CHICOPEE
COLUMBIA
Brookgreen Gardens
LITTLE ROCK
Metrocentre Mall
T.V.A. Region
ATLANTA
Druid Hills
Rock Eagle
Piedmont Park
(Cotton States Expo)
Ansley Park
Swan House
Simmons Co. Hq.
Georgia Plaza
Avon Hq
Central City Park
Noguchi Playground
Cypress Gardens
Magnolia Gardens
Middleton Place
Mulberry Castle
CHARLESTON
Kiawah Island
Ebenezer
New Ebenezer
College of Charleston
Sea Pines Plantation (Hilton Head Island)
FAIRFIELD
LA GRANGE
Hills and Dales
Calloway Gardens
Forsyth Pk
Wormsloe Plantation
SAVANNAH
Margravate of Azilia
DARIEN ("New Inverness")
BRUNSWICK
Frederica
Retreat Plantation
Amelia Island
MONTGOMERY
JACKSON
DALLAS
Adams Square
NATCHEZ
D'Evereaux
Stanton Hall
MOBILE
Bellingrath Gardens
Seaside
TALLAHASSEE
ST. AUGUSTINE
First Settlement in America
Oldest House in America
Castillo de San Marcos
BATON ROUGE
Rosedown
State Capitol
Woodlands
HOUSTON
Astro Dome
Galleria Post Oak S.C.
NEW ORLEANS
Destrahan
San Fransisco
Piazza D'Italia
Superdome
Vieux Carre
St. Louis Cemetery
Audubon Park
Audubon Place
ORLANDO
Disney World
TAMPA
Int'l Airport
LAKELAND
Florida Southern College
Mountain Lake Sanctuary
(Bok Tower)
SARASOTA
Ringling Est.
GULF OF MEXICO
Spanish Monastery
MIAMI
Villa Vizcaya
Bicentennial Park
International Airport Parkway
LEGEND
WASHINGTON National Capital
ATLANTA State Capital
TUCSON City or Town
Biltmore Place of Interest
Mesa Verde Prehistoric Site
Est. Estate
Pkwy. Parkway
S.C. Shopping center
N.M. National Monument
N.P. National Park
"Spiral Jetty" Environmental Art
96°
90°
84°
78°
72°
38°
33°
24°
0 100 200 300 400 500 kilometers
0 100 200 300 miles

United States of America

SECTION 5

DESIGN PLAN DRAWINGS

Design Plan Drawings

1 : 1200 SCALE

GREAT PYRAMID OF CHEOPS (KHUFU)

Location: Gizeh (Giza), Egypt

Date: c. 2700 BC

Designer: unknown

Client: King Cheops (Khufu)

Area: 13.12 acres / 5.31 hectares

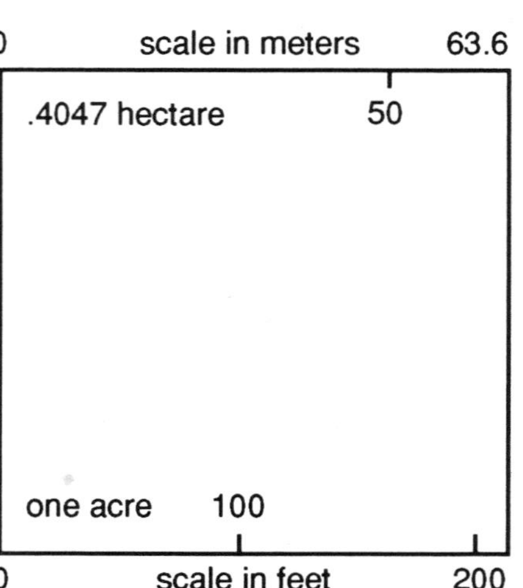

STONEHENGE

Location: Wiltshire, England

Date designed: c. 1900 BC

Designer(s): Unknown

Client: Druids

Area: 3.67 acres / 1.49 hectares

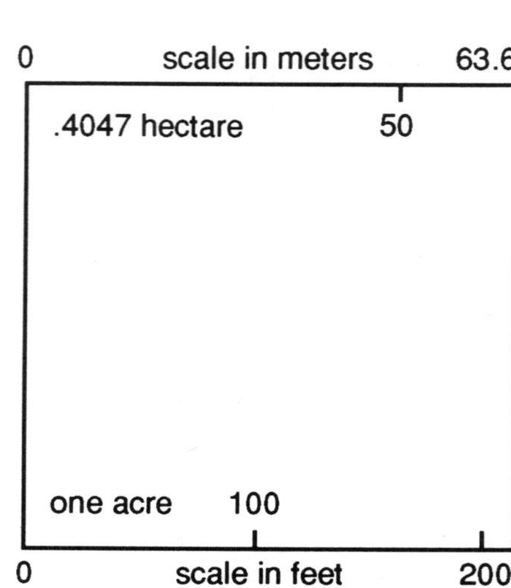

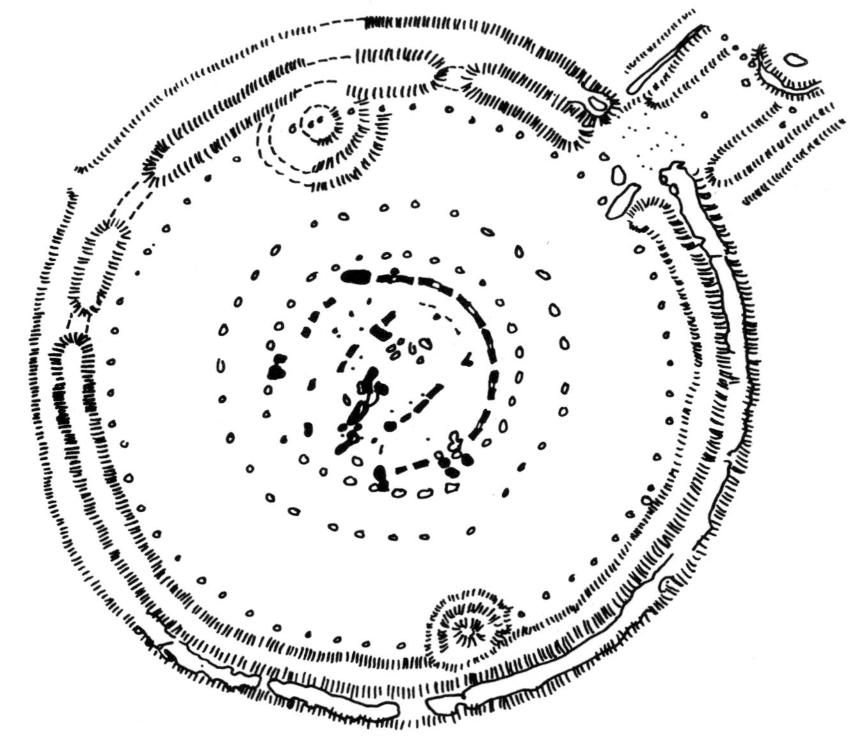

FUNERARY TEMPLE

Location: Deir el-Bahri, Egypt

Date designed: c. 1480 BC

Designer: Senmut

Client: Queen Hatshepsut

Area: 4.17 acres / 1.69 hectares

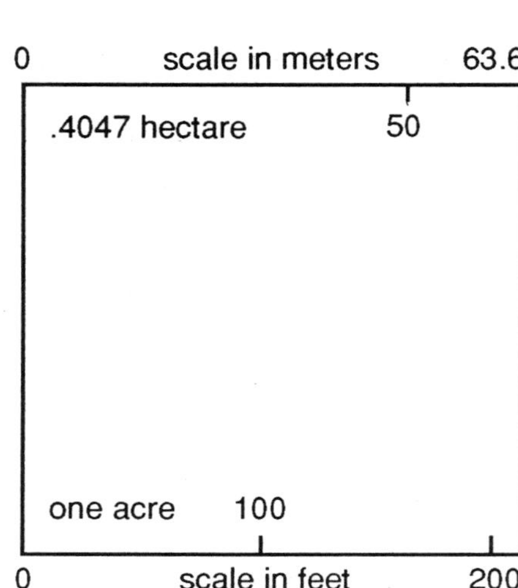

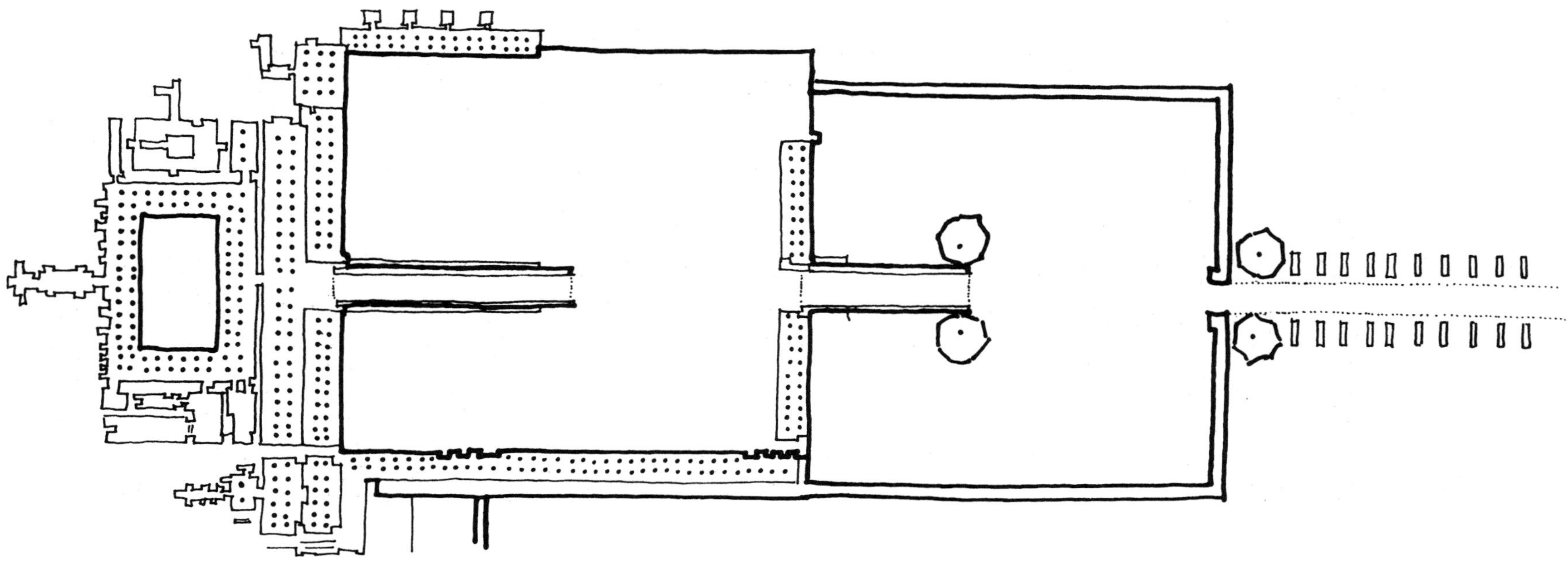

RESIDENTIAL GARDEN

Location: Thebes, Egypt

Date designed: c. 1400 BC

Designer(s): Unknown

Client: Official of Amenhotep III

Area: 1.96 acres / .79 hectares

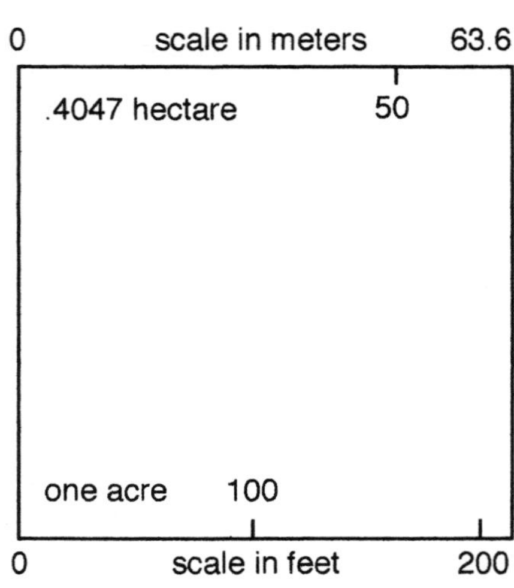

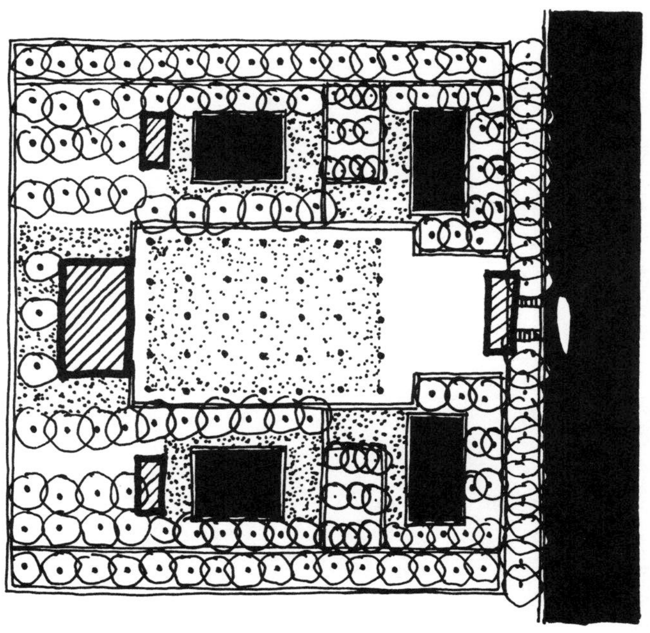

AGORA

Location: Athens, Greece

Date designed: c. 550 - 428 BC

Area: 6.3 acres / 2.55 hectares

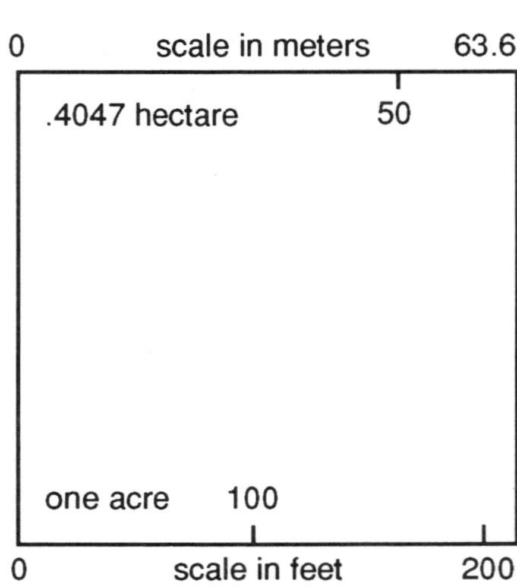

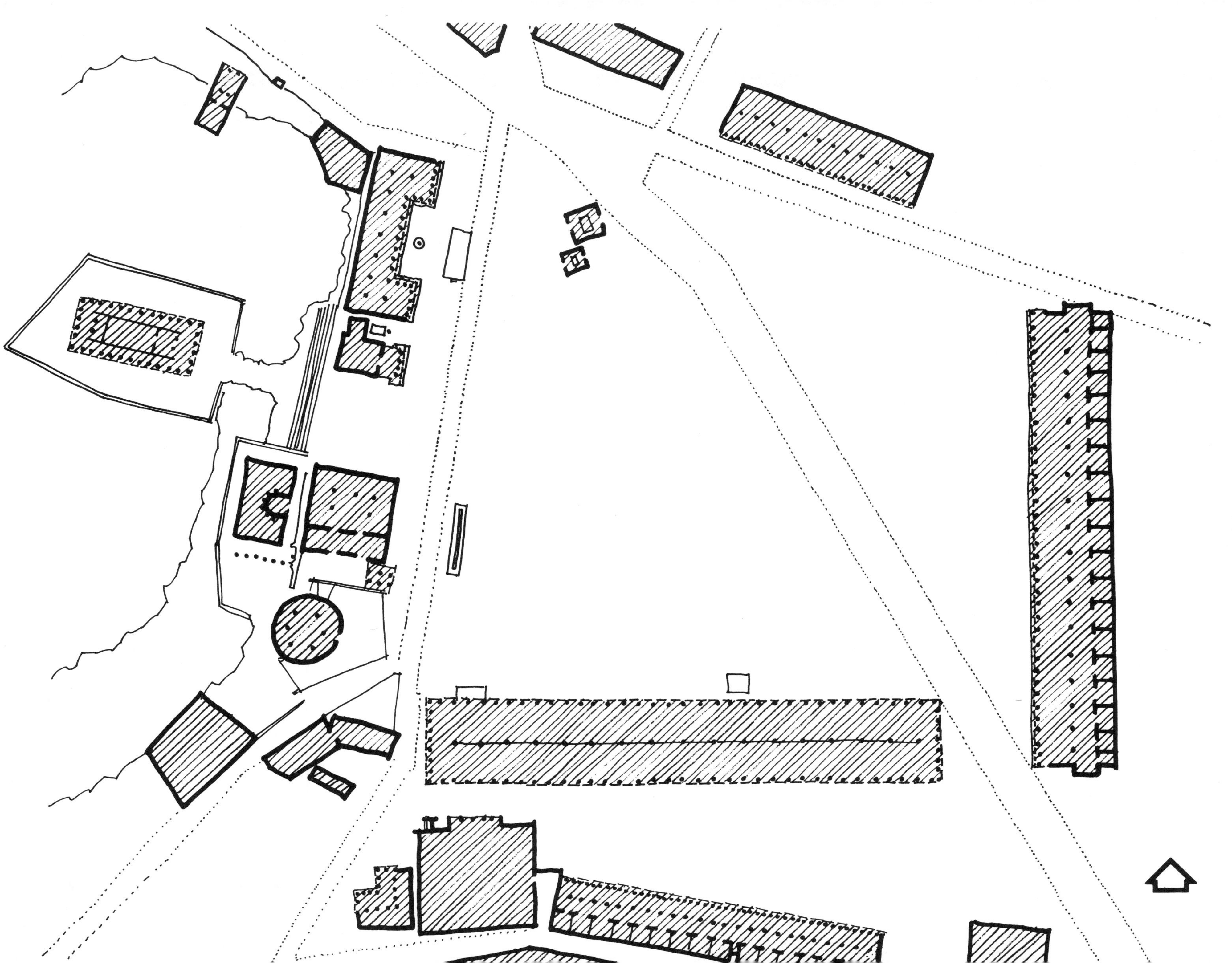

ACROPOLIS

Location: Athens, Greece

Dates: c. 480 - 393 BC

Area: 6.8 acres / 2.75 hectares

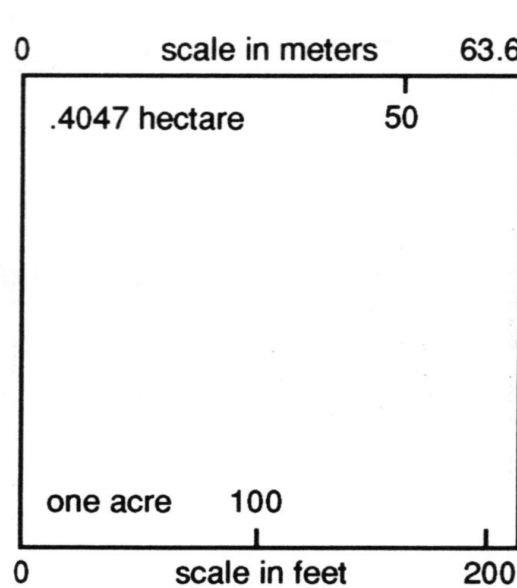

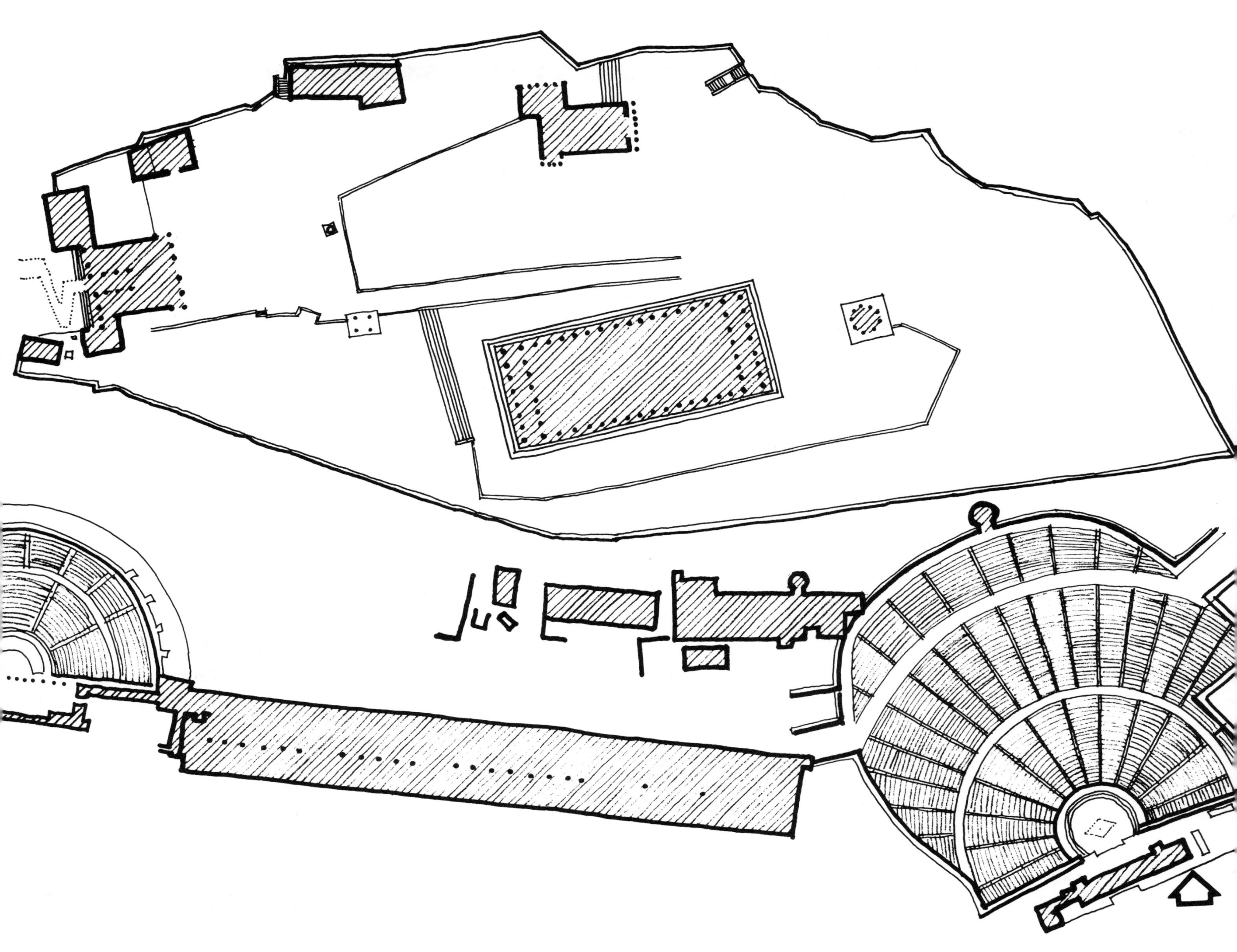

AGORA

Location: Assos, Greece

Dates: c. 450 BC

Area: .92 acres / .37 hectares

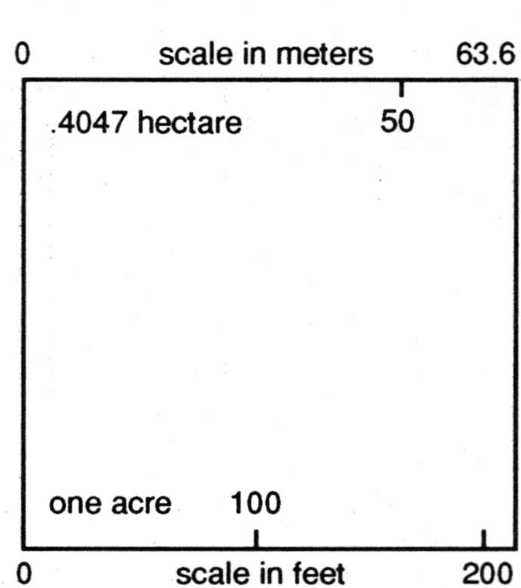

FORUM

Location: Pompeii, Italy

Dates: c. 80 BC - 79 AD

Area: 1.38 acres / .56 hectares

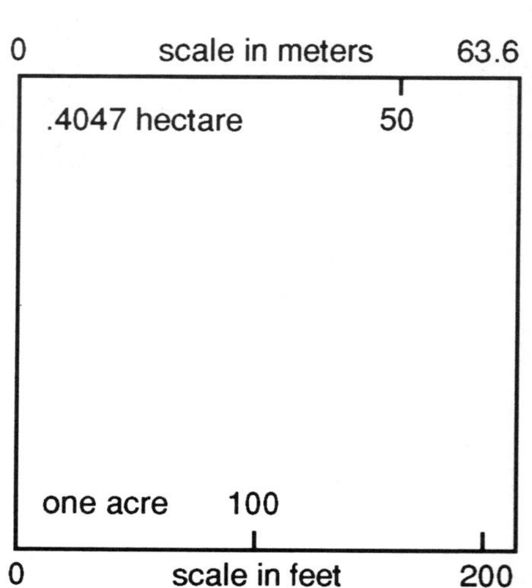

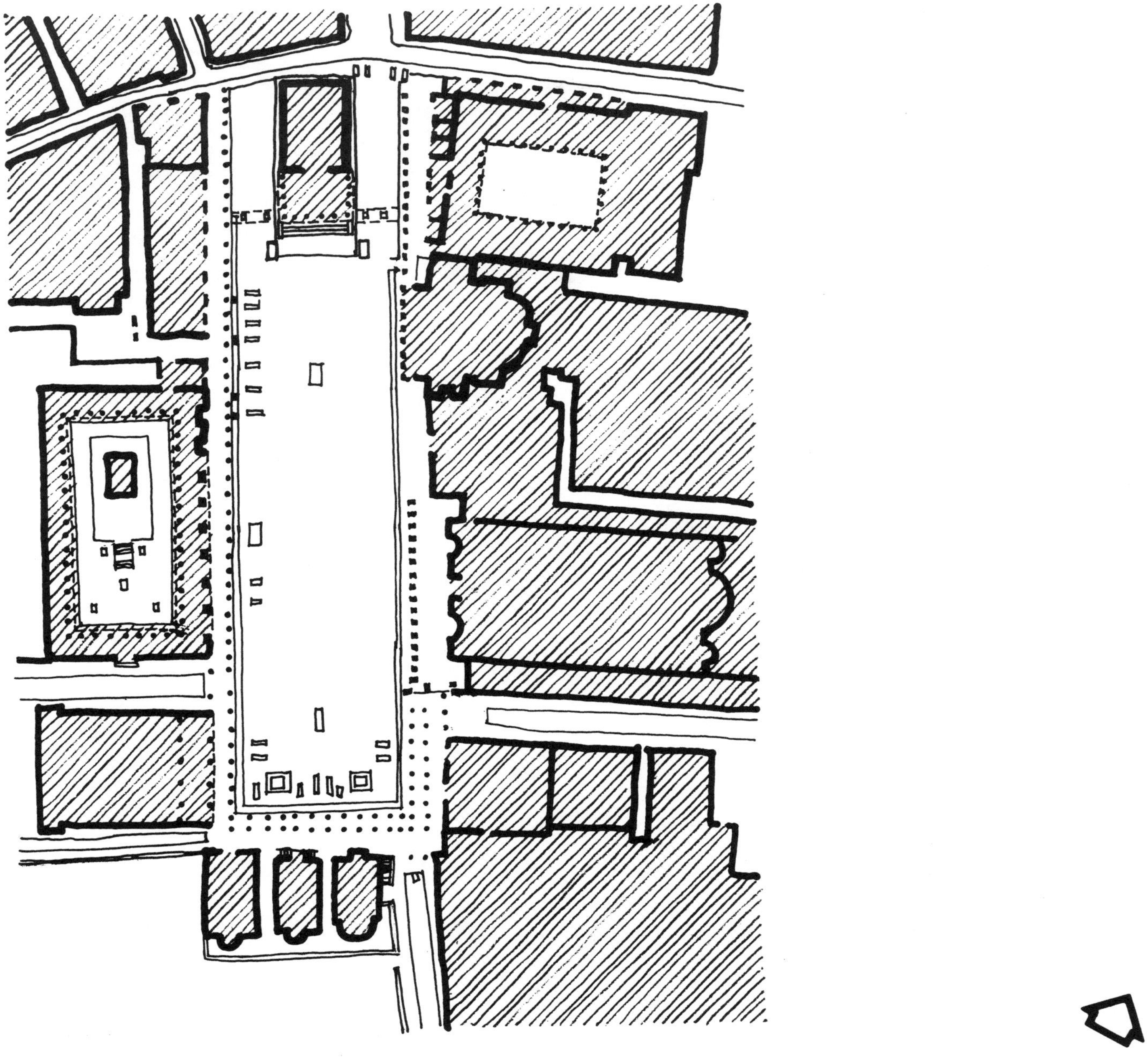

HOUSE OF THE VETTII

Location: Pompeii, Italy

Dates: c. 80 BC - 79 AD

Client: a Roman citizen named Vettii

Area: .32 acres / .13 hectares

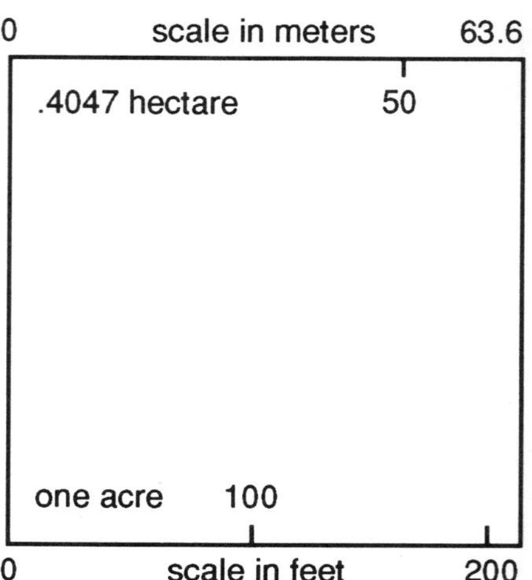

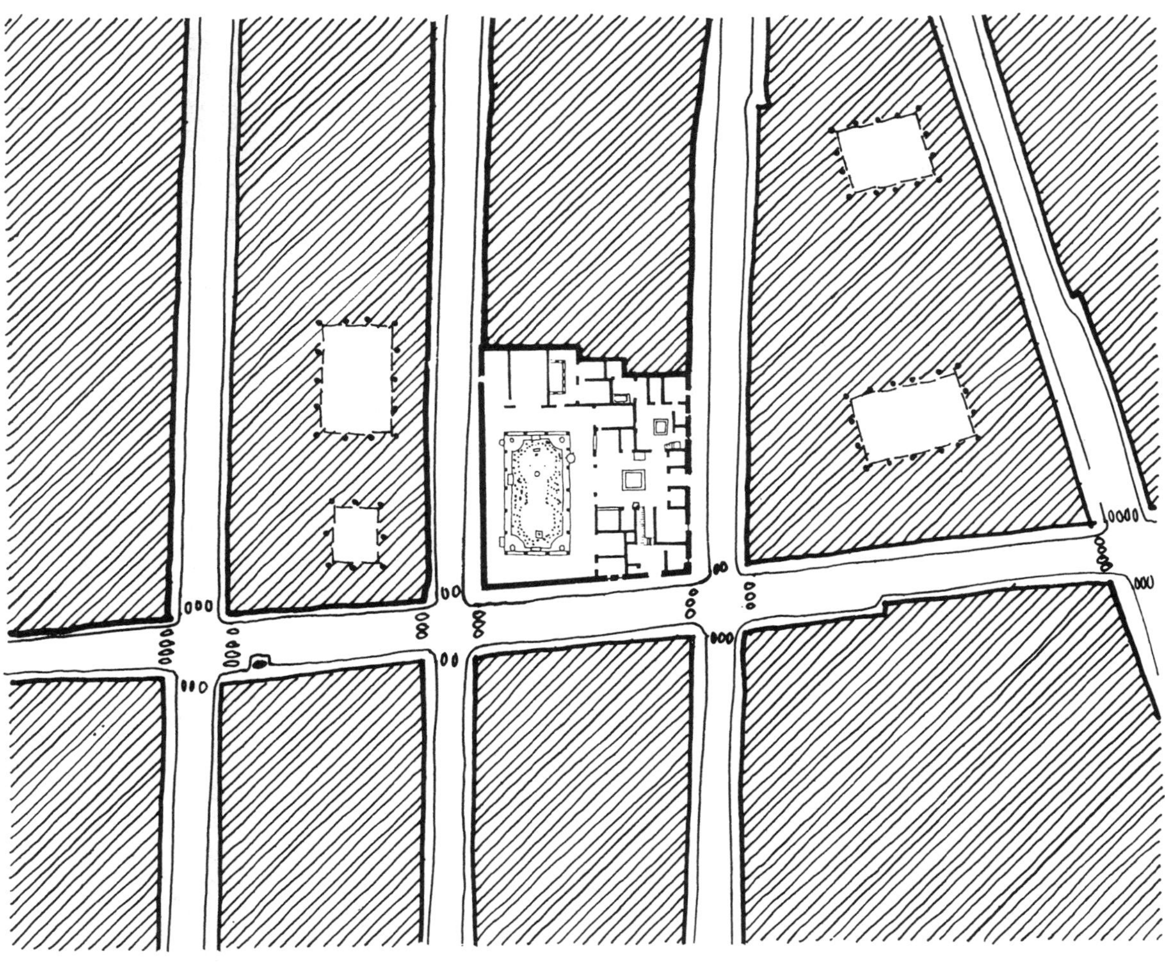

PANTHEON

Location: Rome, Italy

Dates: 27 BC - 128 AD

Designers: unknown

Clients: Emperors Agrippa and Hadrian

Area: .95 acres / .39 hectares

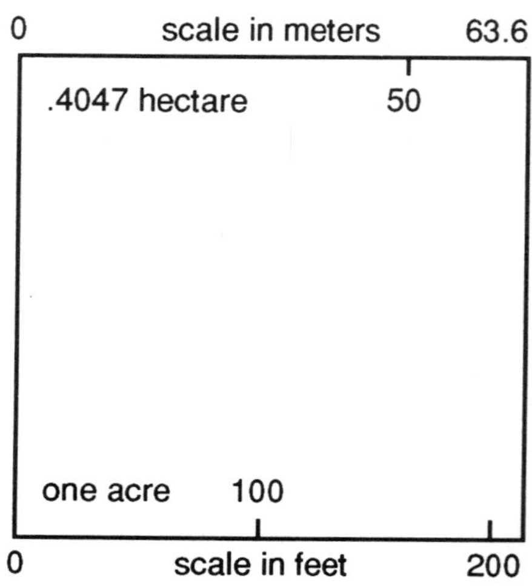

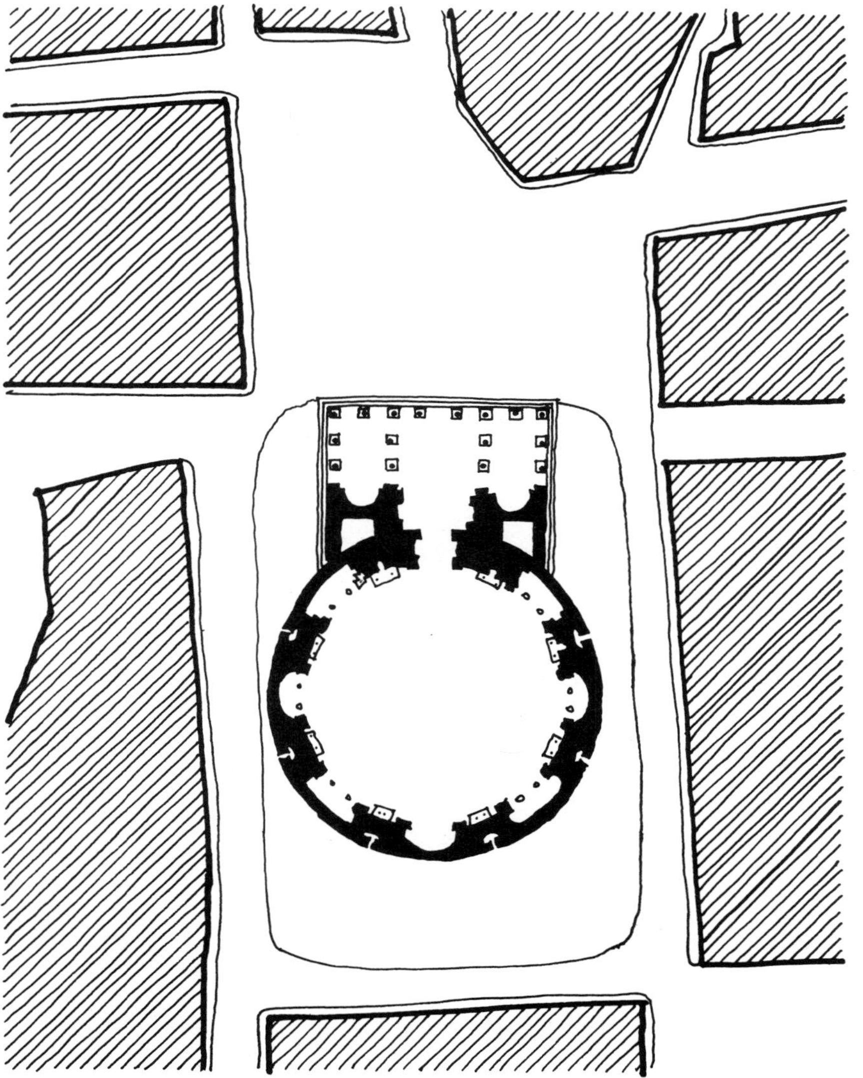

COLOSSEUM (FLAVIAN AMPHITHEATRE)

Location: Rome, Italy

Dates: 70 AD - 80 AD

Designer: unknown

Clients: Emperors Vespasian, Titus and Domitian

Area: 7.3 acres / 2.95 hectares

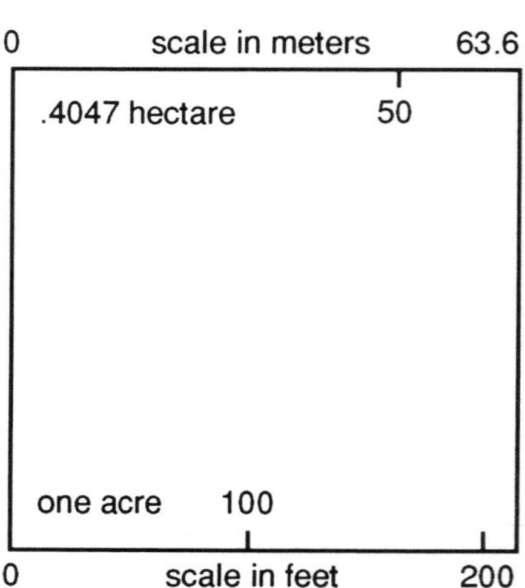

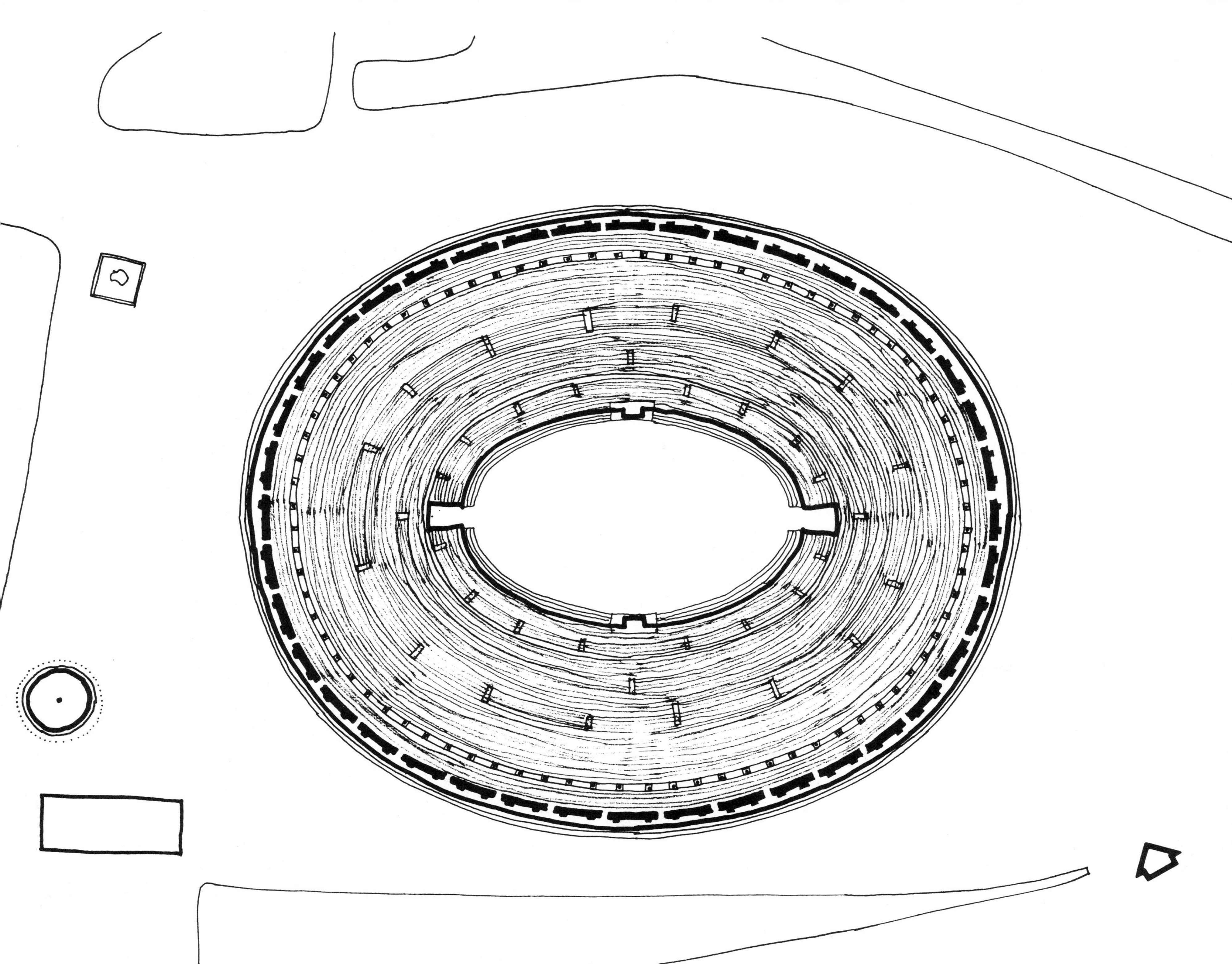

FORUM ROMANUM

Location: Rome, Italy

Dates: c. 100 BC - c. 46 BC

Clients: Emperors Sulla, Pompey and Julius Caesar

Area: 2.4 acres / .97 hectares

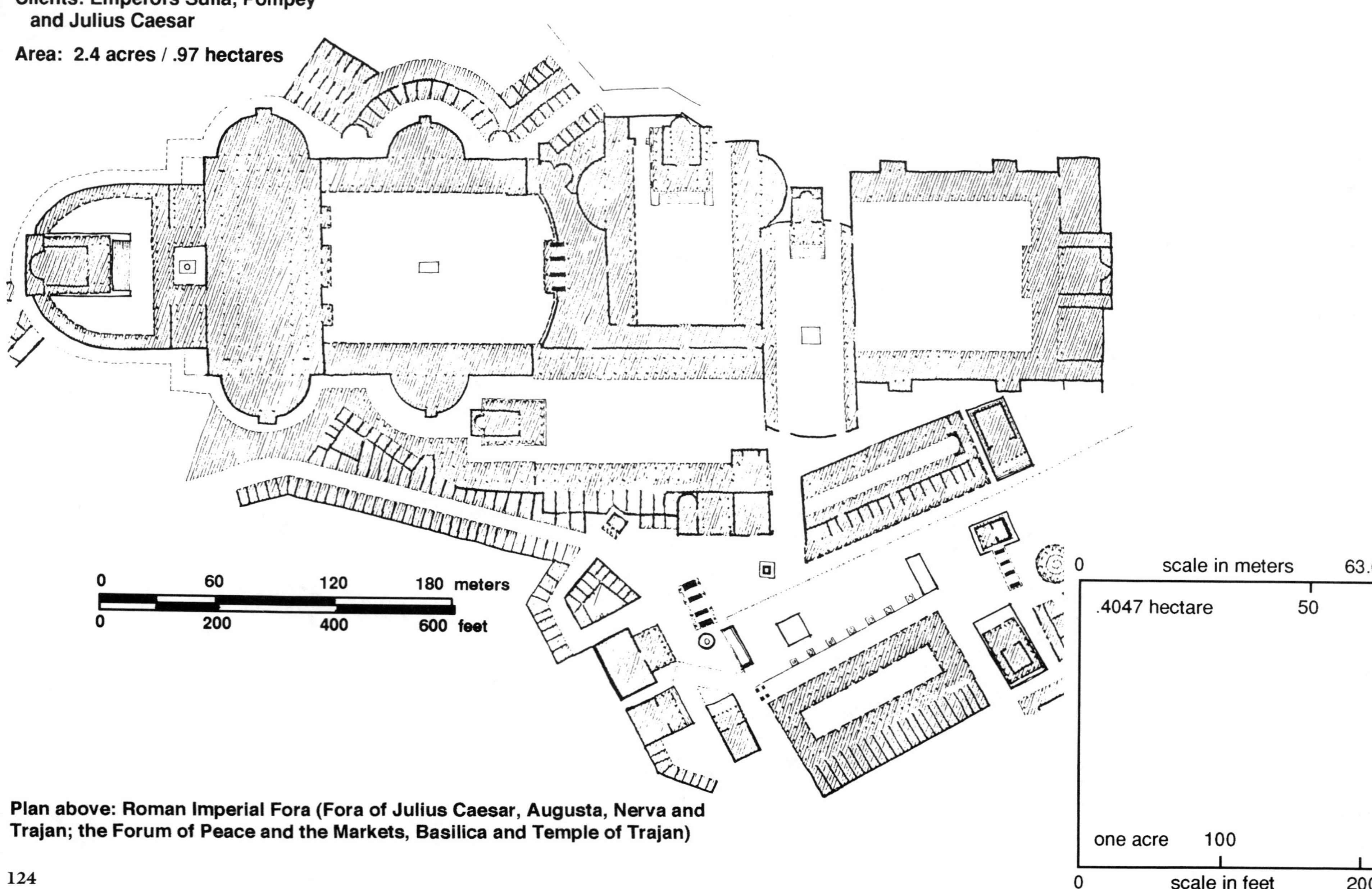

Plan above: Roman Imperial Fora (Fora of Julius Caesar, Augusta, Nerva and Trajan; the Forum of Peace and the Markets, Basilica and Temple of Trajan)

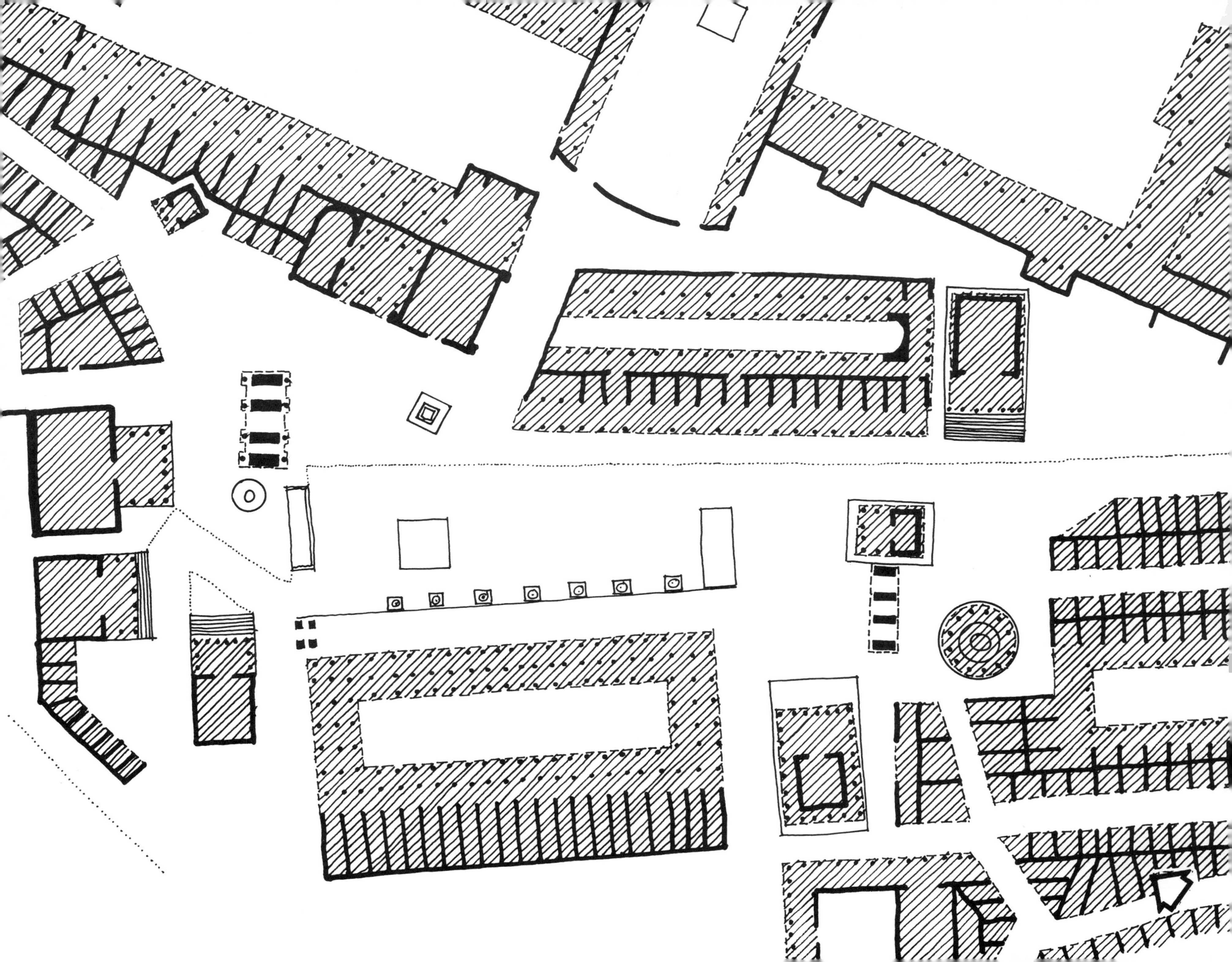

FORUM OF TRAJAN

Location: Rome, Italy

Dates: c. 100 AD - c. 112 AD

Designer: Apollodorus of Damascus

Client: Emperor Trajan

Area: 2.15 acres / .87 hectares

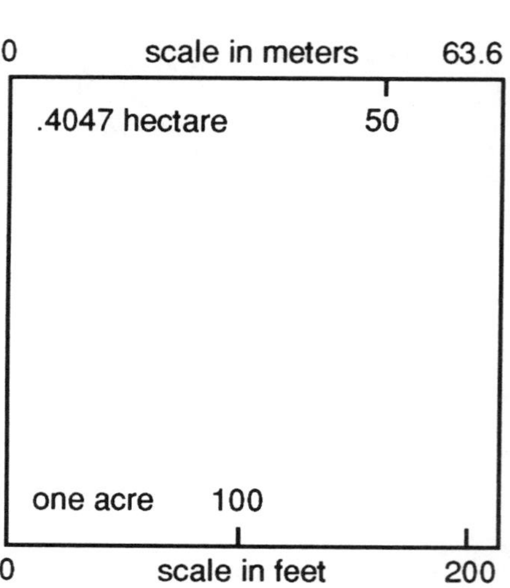

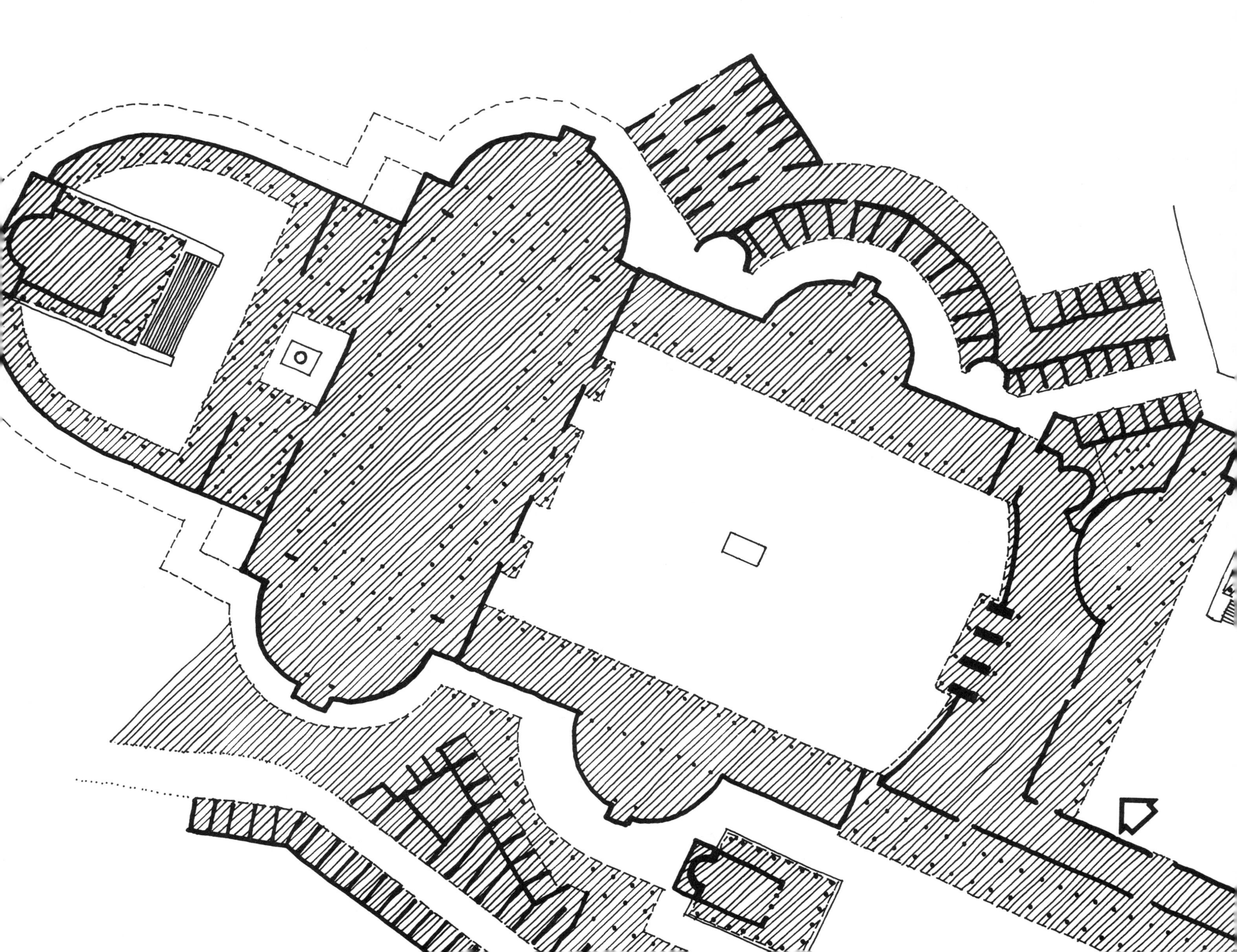

HADRIAN'S VILLA

Location: Tivoli, Italy

Dates: 117 - 138 AD

Designer: Emperor Hadrian

Client: Emperor Hadrian

Area: 125 acres / 50.59 hectares

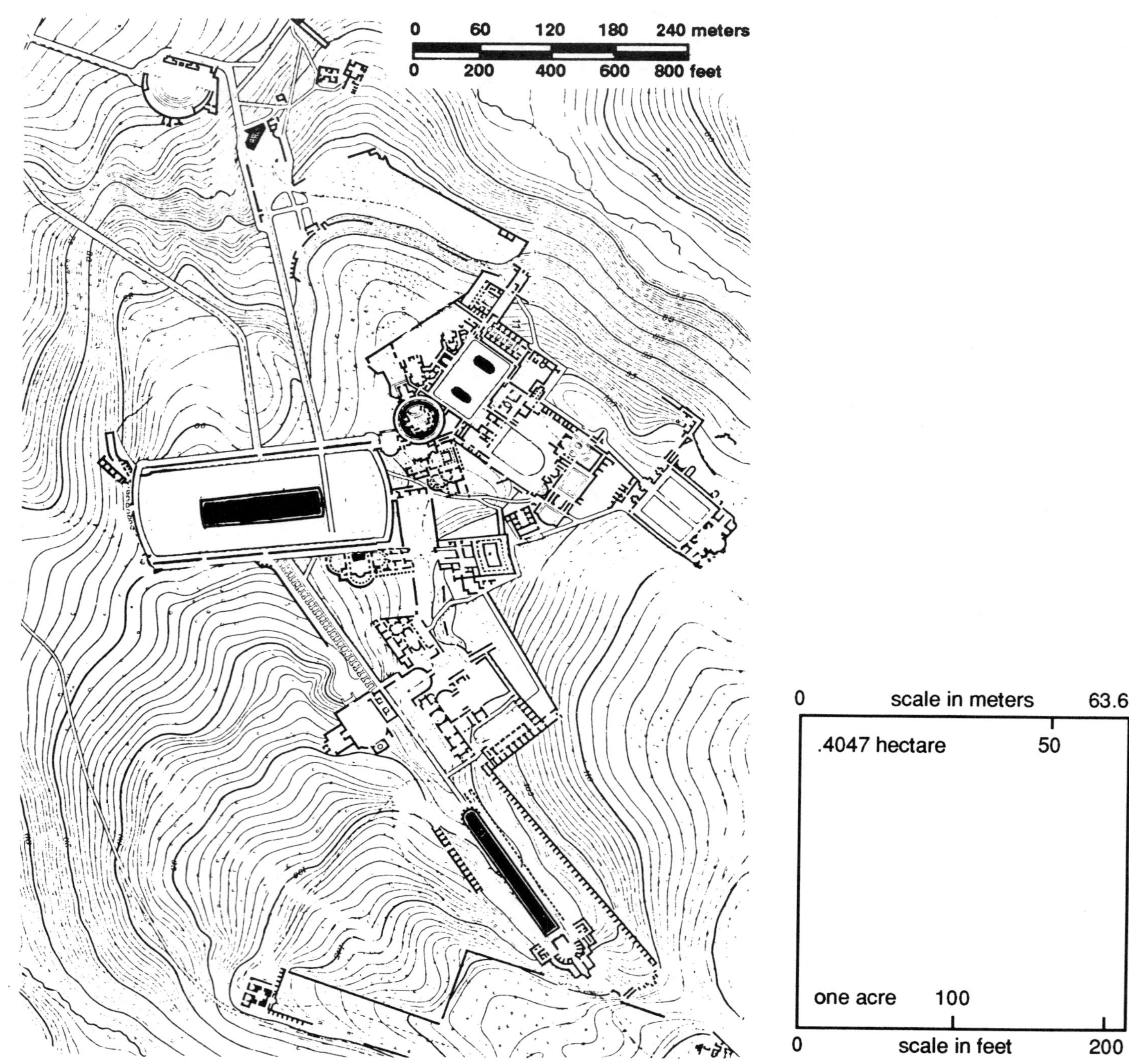

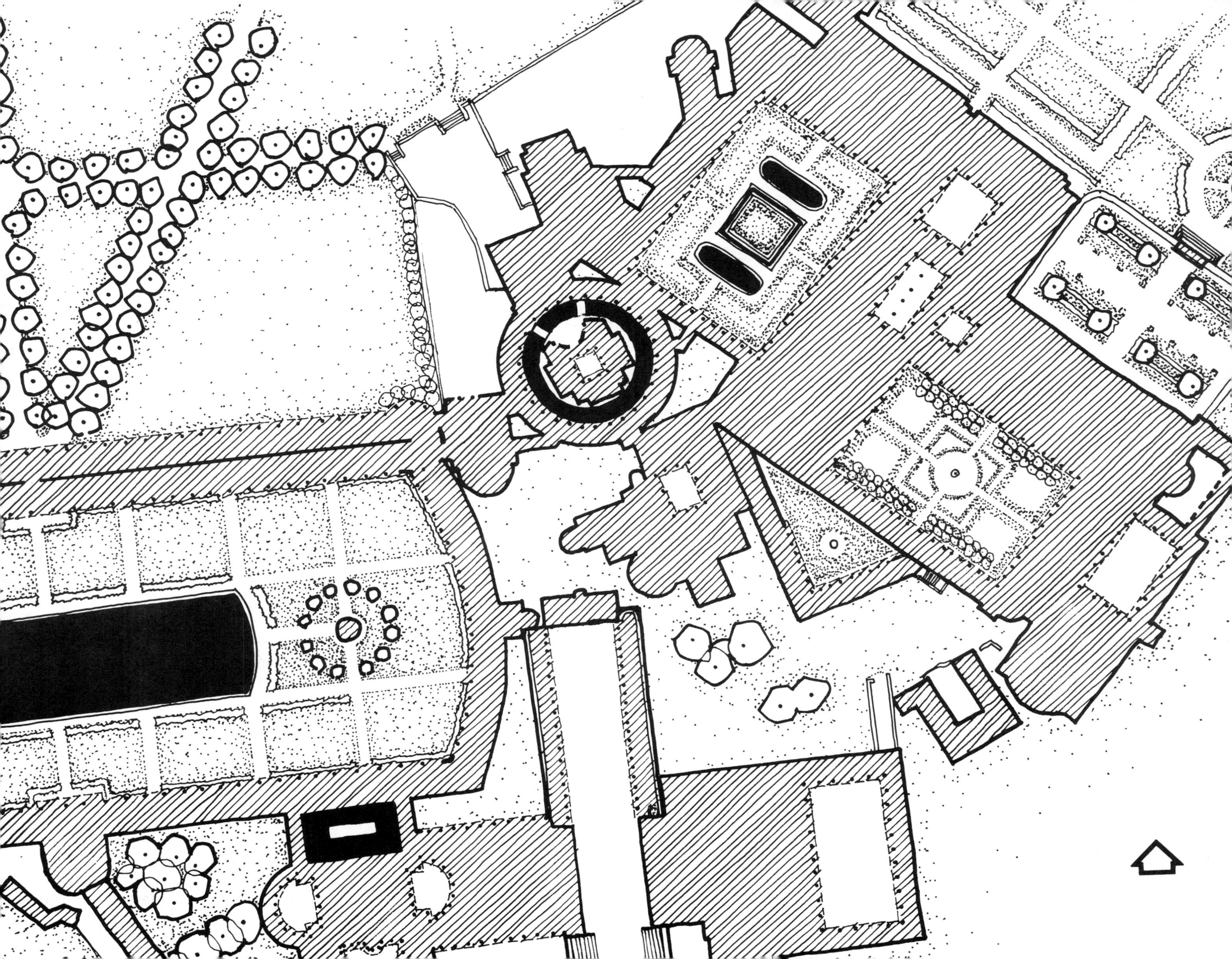

BASILICA OF SAINT PETER

Location: Rome, Italy

Dates: 320 - 330 AD

Designer: unknown

Client: Emperor Constantine

Area: 4.65 acres / 1.88 hectares

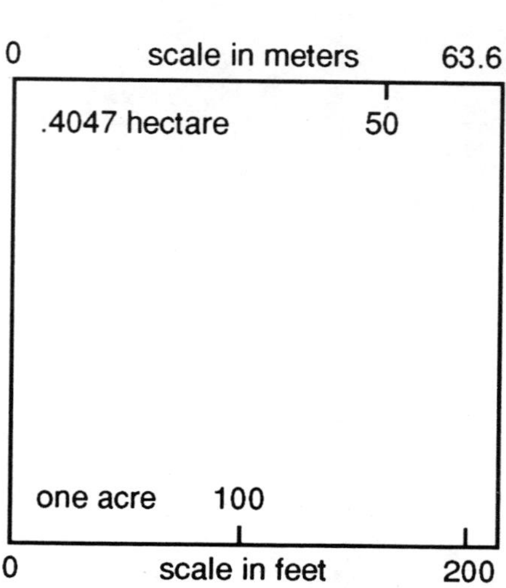

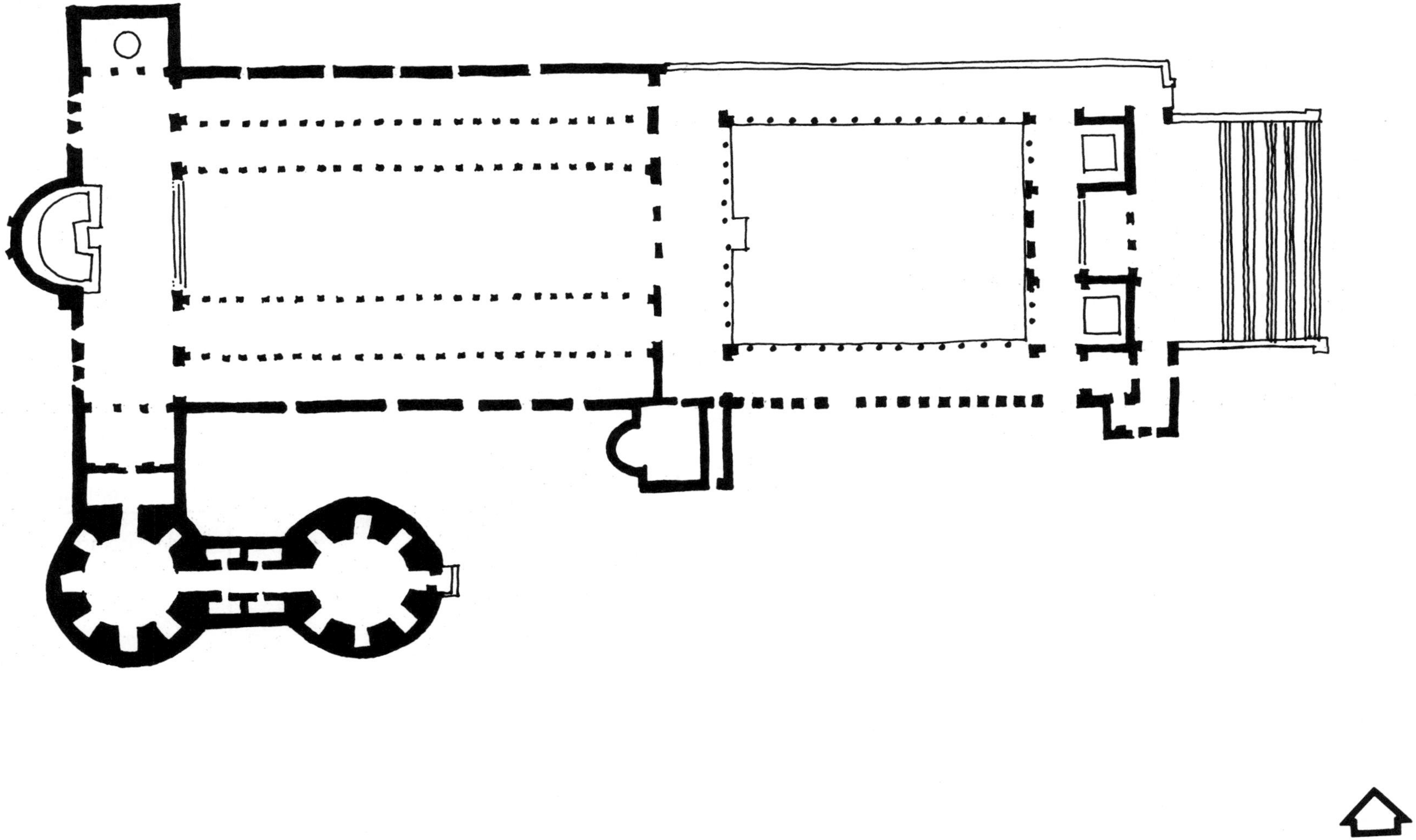

SAINT GALL MONASTERY

Location: St. Gallen, Switzerland

Date: c. 816 - 836 AD

Draftsman: Abbot Gozbert

Client: Benedictine Monastery

Area: 8.26 acres / 3.33 hectares

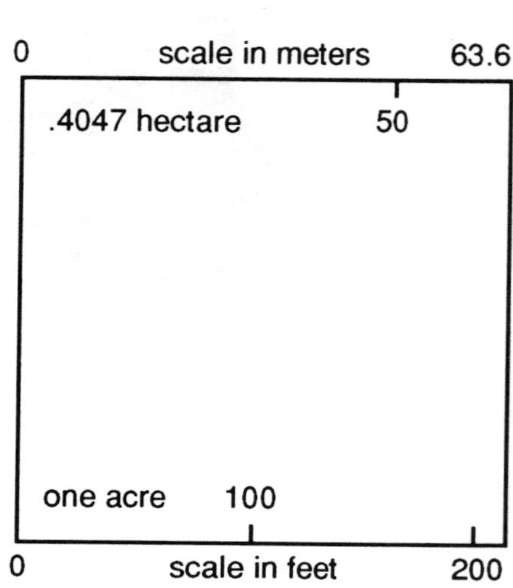

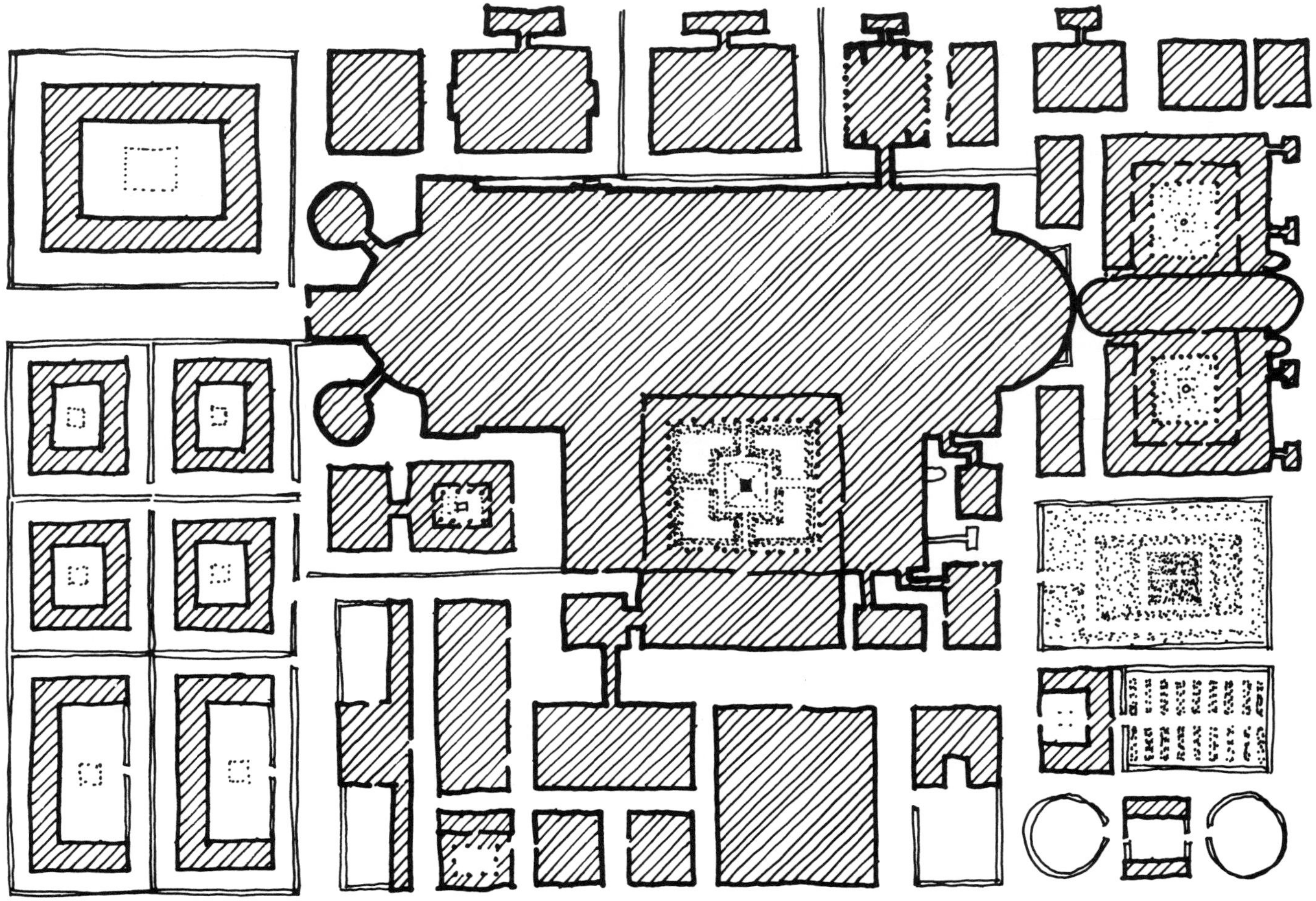

FOUNTAINS ABBEY

Location: North Yorkshire, England

Date: c. 1137 - 1536 AD

Designer: unknown

Client: Cistercian Monastery

Area: 8.75 acres / 3.55 hectares

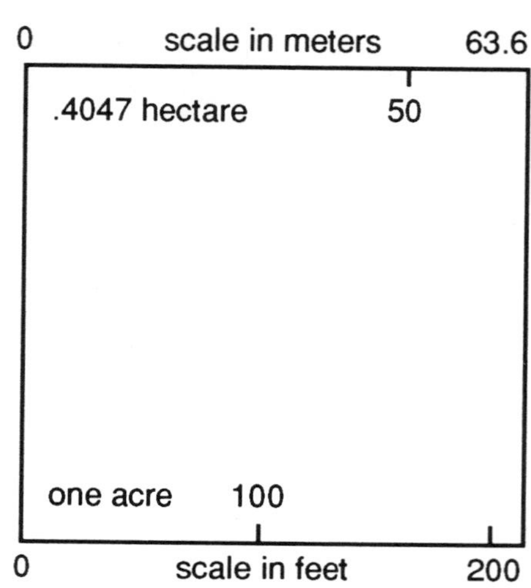

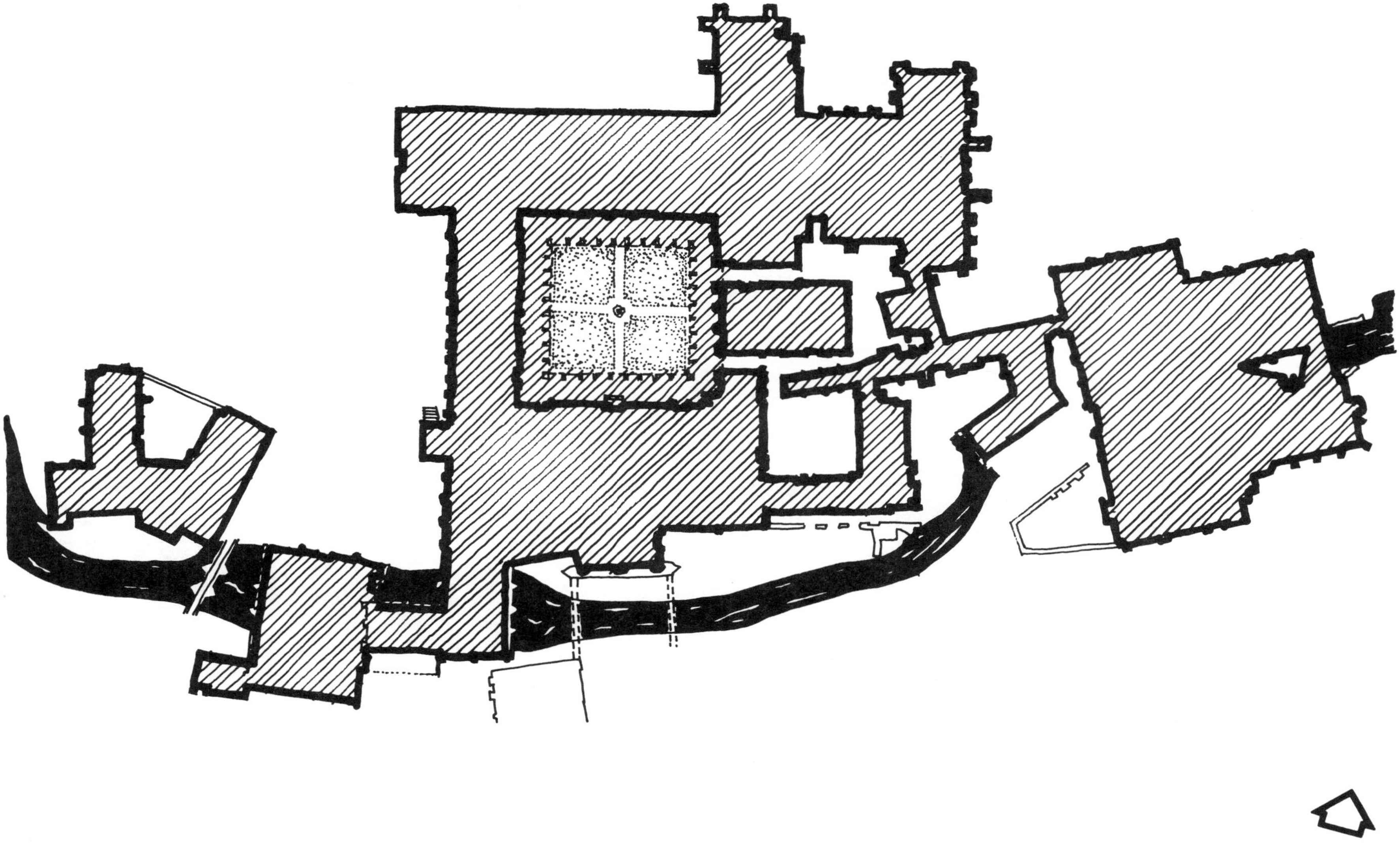

NOTRE DAME CATHEDRAL

Location: Paris, France

Date: 1163 - 1250

Designer: unknown

Client: Bishop Maurice de Sully

Area: 1.59 acres / .64 hectares

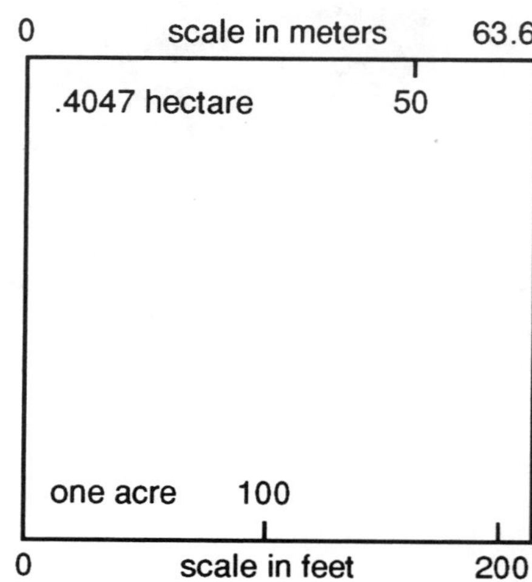

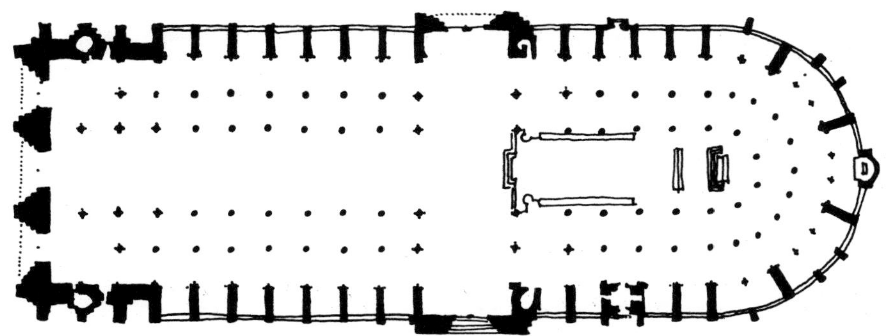

MOSQUE AND COURT OF THE ORANGES

Location: Cordoba, Spain

Date:s c. 750 - 987 AD

Designer: unknown

Clients: Caliphs Abd ar-Rahman II,
al-Hakim and al-Mansur

Area: Mosque with court (5.96 acres / 2.41 hectares)
Court of the Oranges (1.53 acres / .62 hectares)

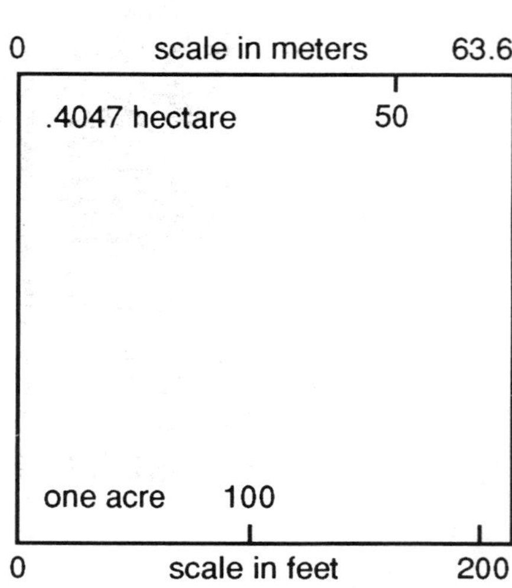

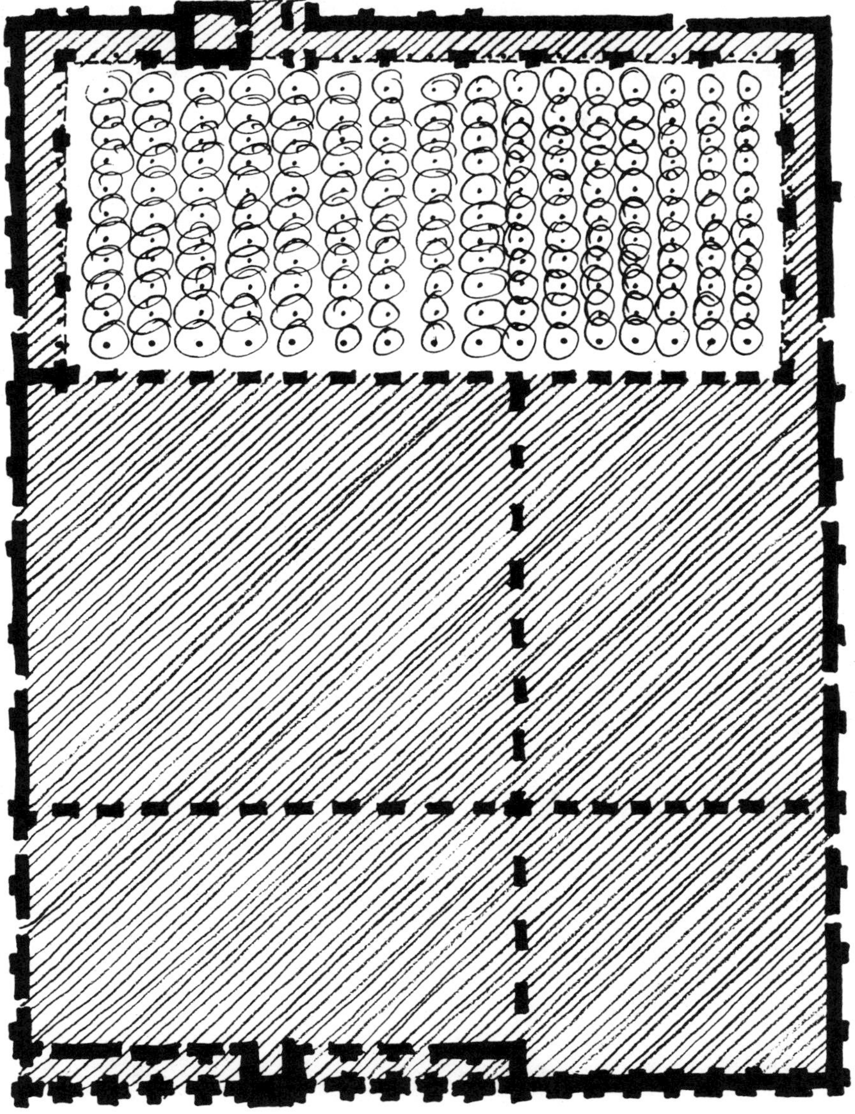

THE ALCAZAR

Location: Seville, Spain

Date: 1364

Clients: Moorish kings

Area: 4.13 acres / 1.67 hectares

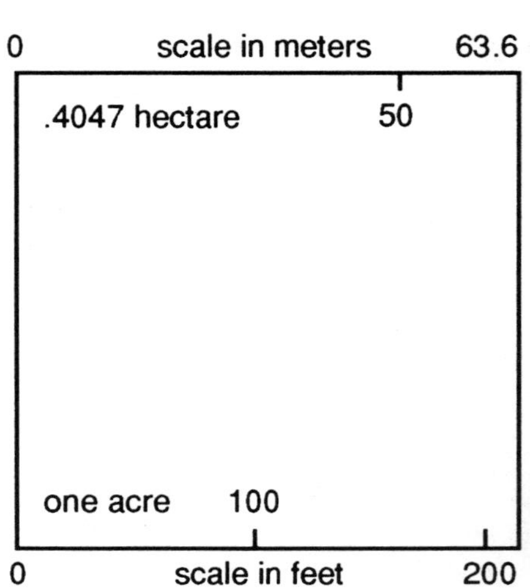

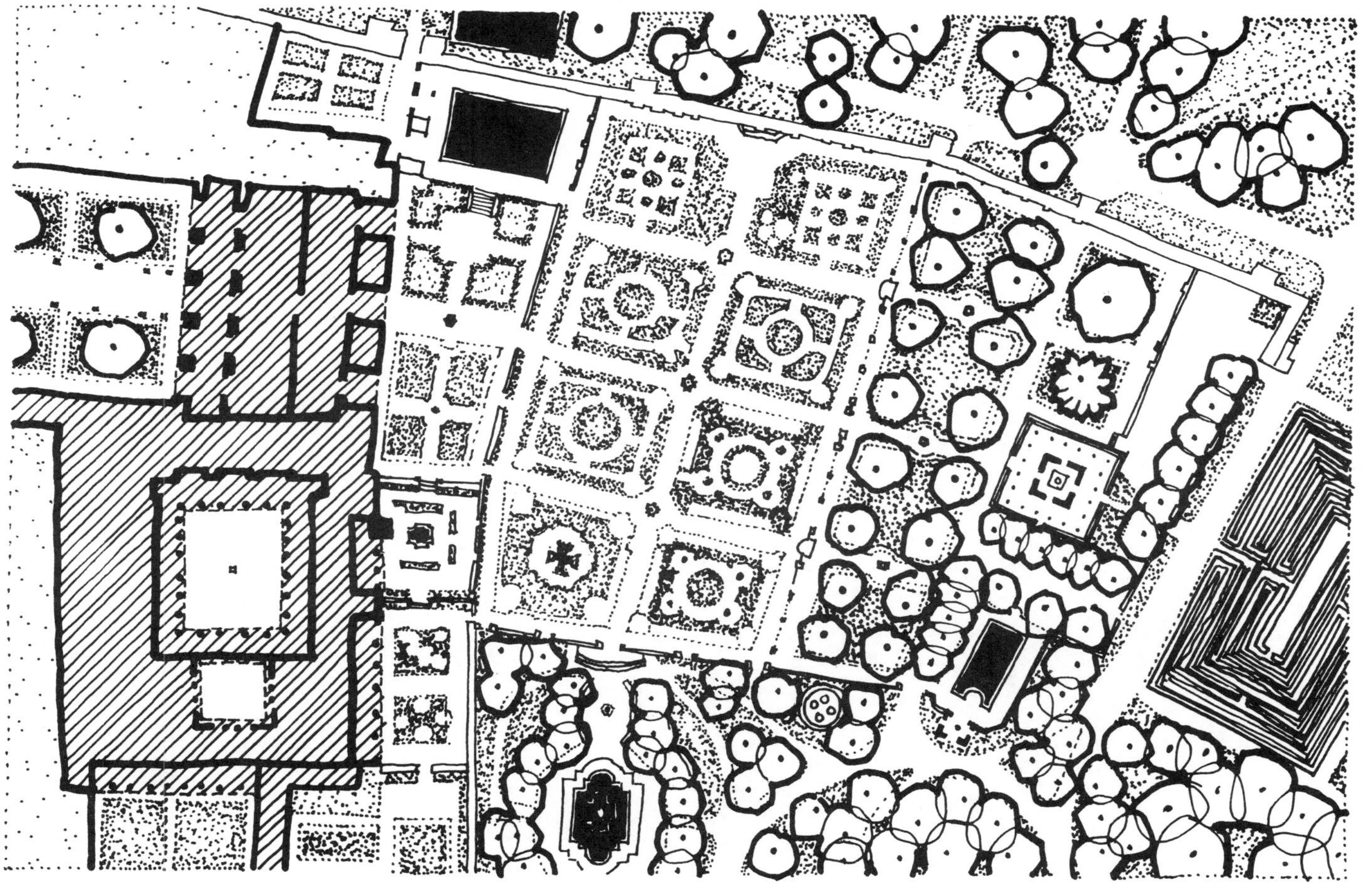

THE ALHAMBRA (COURT OF THE MYRTLES, COURT OF THE THE LIONS

Location: Granada, Spain

Dates: 1338 - 1390

Designer: unknown

Clients: Moorish King, Mohammed ben Al-Ahmar

Area: Court of the Myrtles (78.7 x 121.5 feet, .22 acres / .09 hectares)
Court of the Lions (51.8 x 125.6 feet, .15 acres / .06 hectares

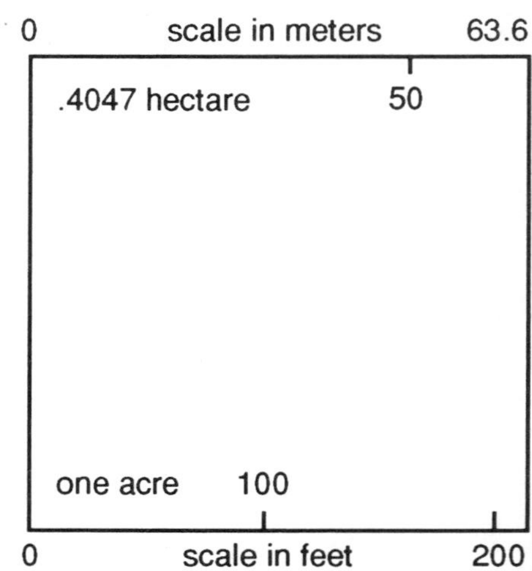

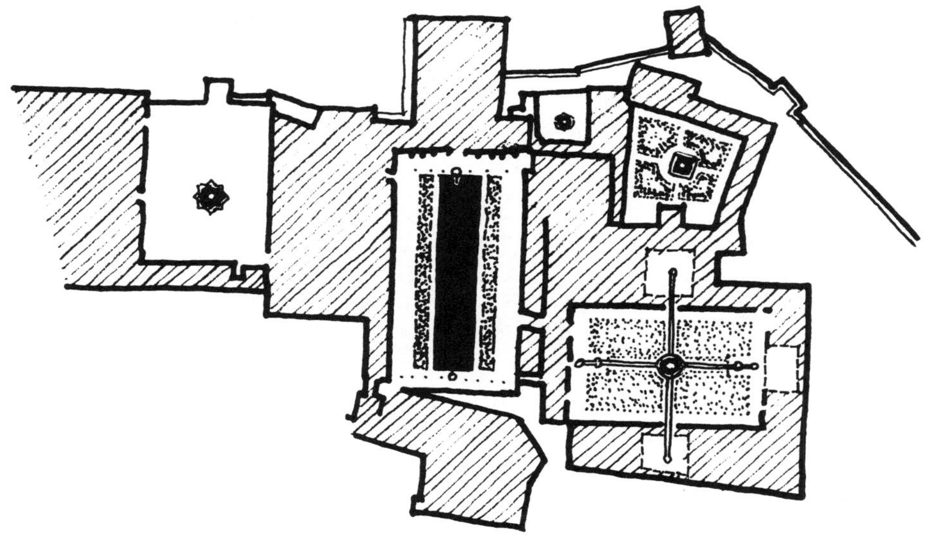

THE GENERALIFE

Location: Granada, Spain

Date: 1275

Designer: unknown

Clients: Moorish Kings, Mohammed I, Yusef I, Mohammed V

Area: 2.16 acres / .87 hectares

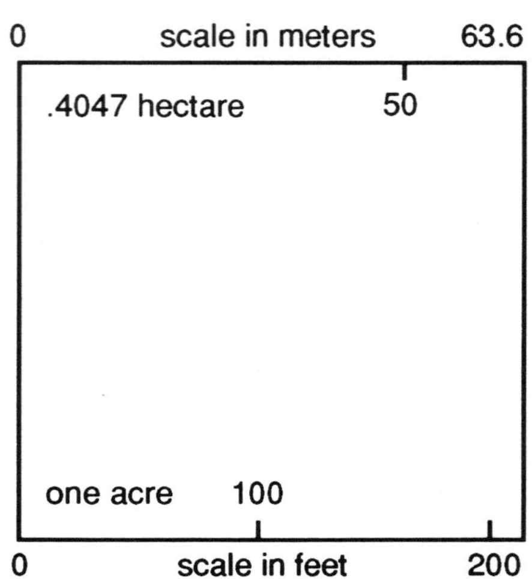

PIAZZA DEL CAMPO

Location: Siena, Italy

Dates: 1262 - 1410

Designer: unknown

Client: City Council

Area: 2.75 acres / 1.11 hectares

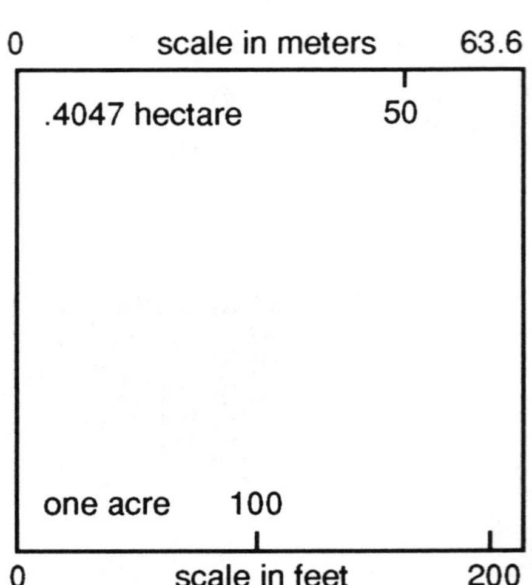

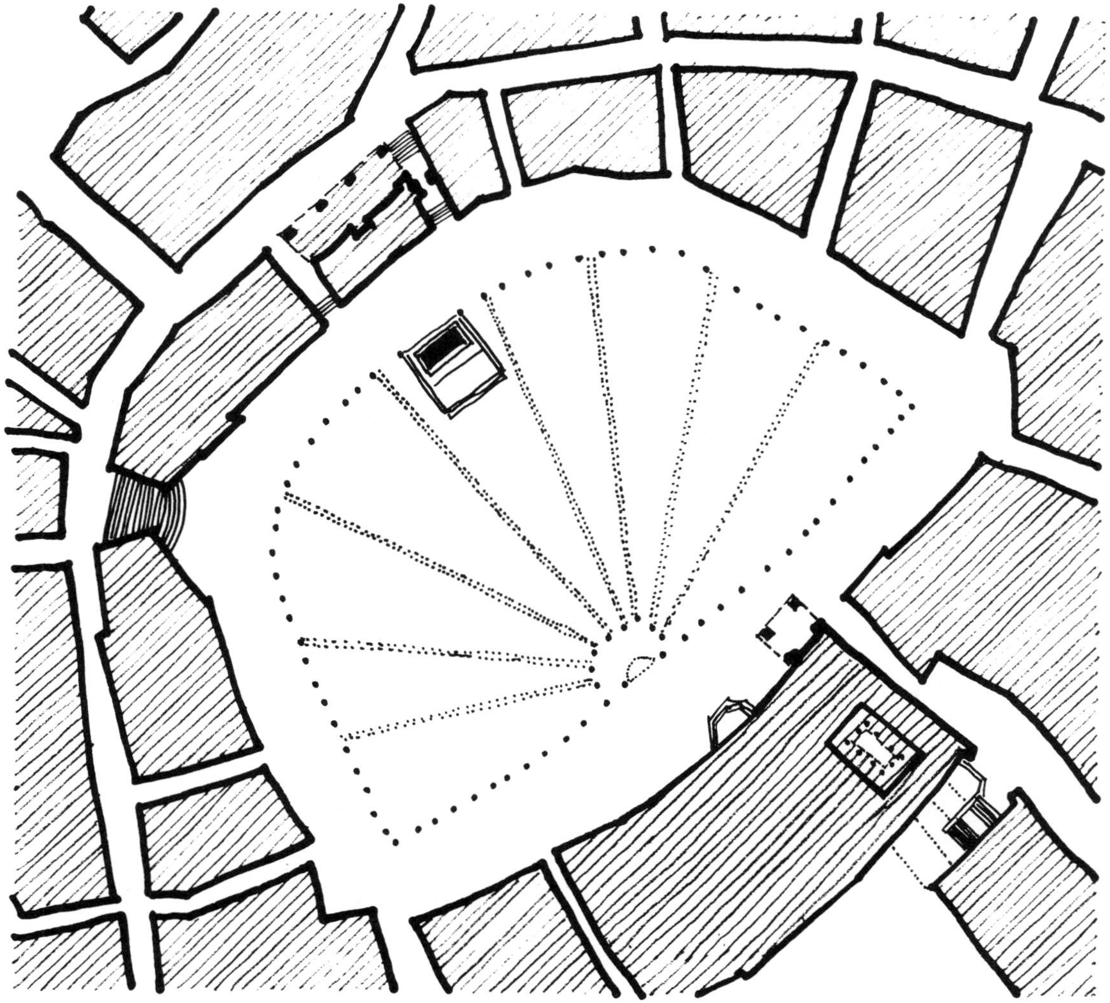

PIAZZA SAN MARCO

Location: Venice, Italy

Dates: c.840 - 1810

Designers: many

Clients: Doges (ruling familiy of Venice)

Area: 4.41 acres / 1.78 hectares

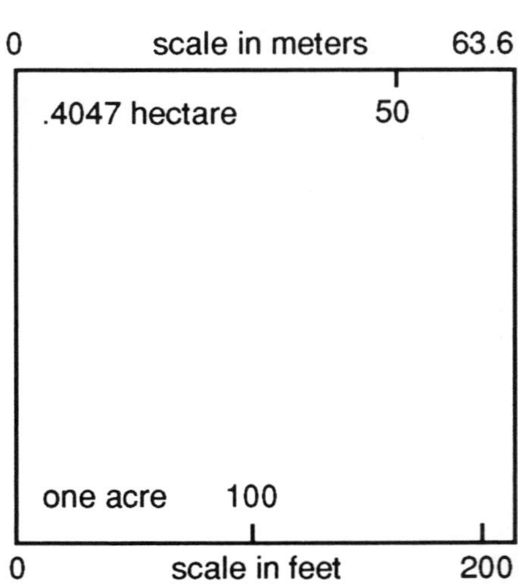

PIAZZA DEL POPOLO

Location: Pienza, Italy

Dates: 1459 - 1462

Designer: Bernardo Gambarelli, called "Rossellino"

Client: Enea Silvio Piccolomini (Pope Pius II)

Area: .16 acres / .065 hectares

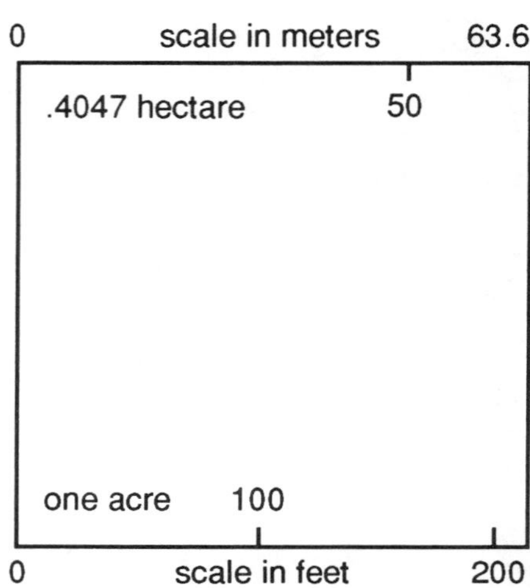

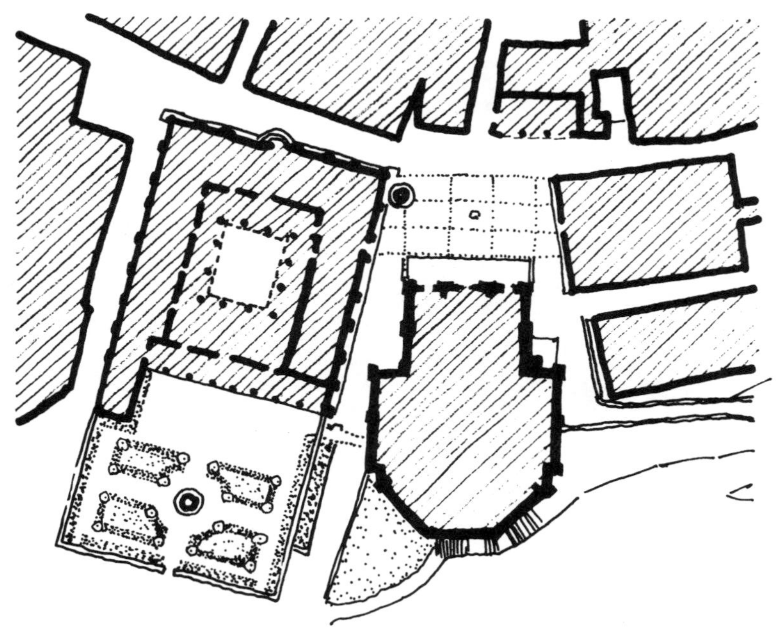

PIAZZA DELLA SS. ANNUZCIATA*

Location: Florence, Italy

Dates: 1419, 1454, 1516, 1601

Designers: Brunelleschi, Michelozzo Sangallo the Elder, Caccini

Client: City Council

Area: 1.1 acres / .43 hectares

*** SS. : Santissima (Most Holy Annunciation)**

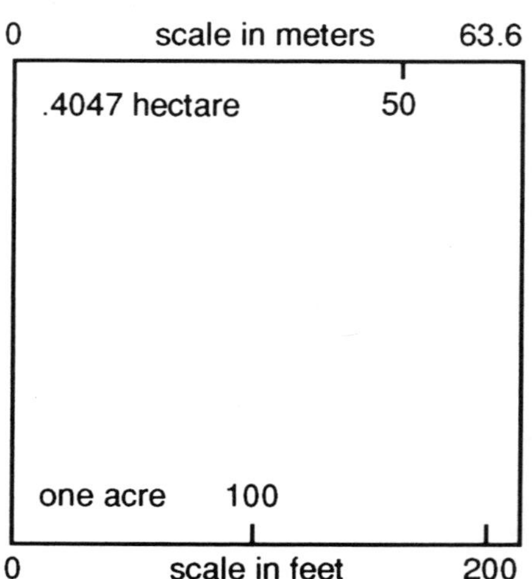

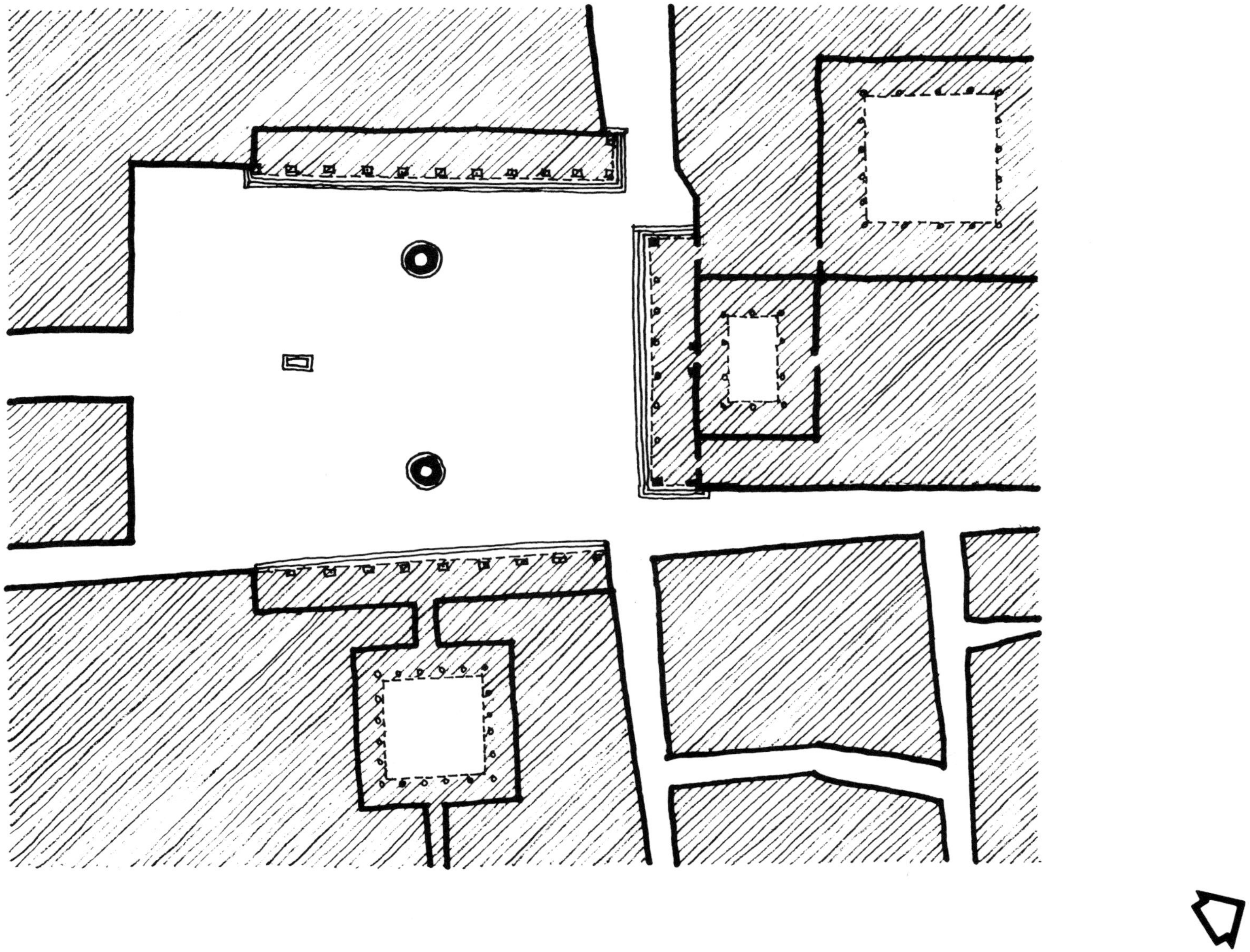

PIAZZA DELLA SIGNORIA

Location: Florence, Italy

Dates: Middle Ages; "David," by Michelangelo, placed in piazza c. 1503

Designers: many

Client: City Council (Signoria)

Area: 2.25 acres / .89 hectares

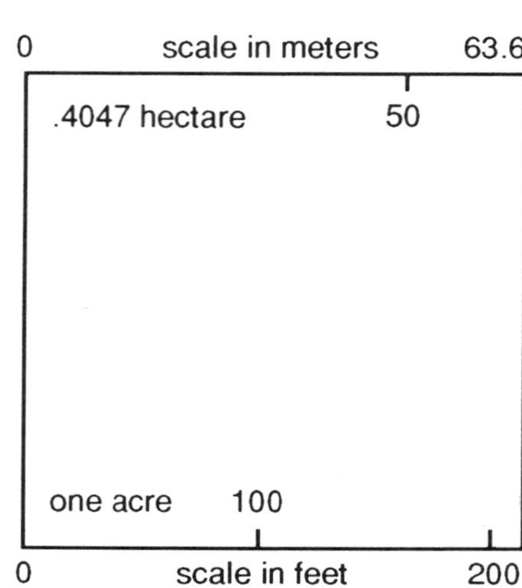

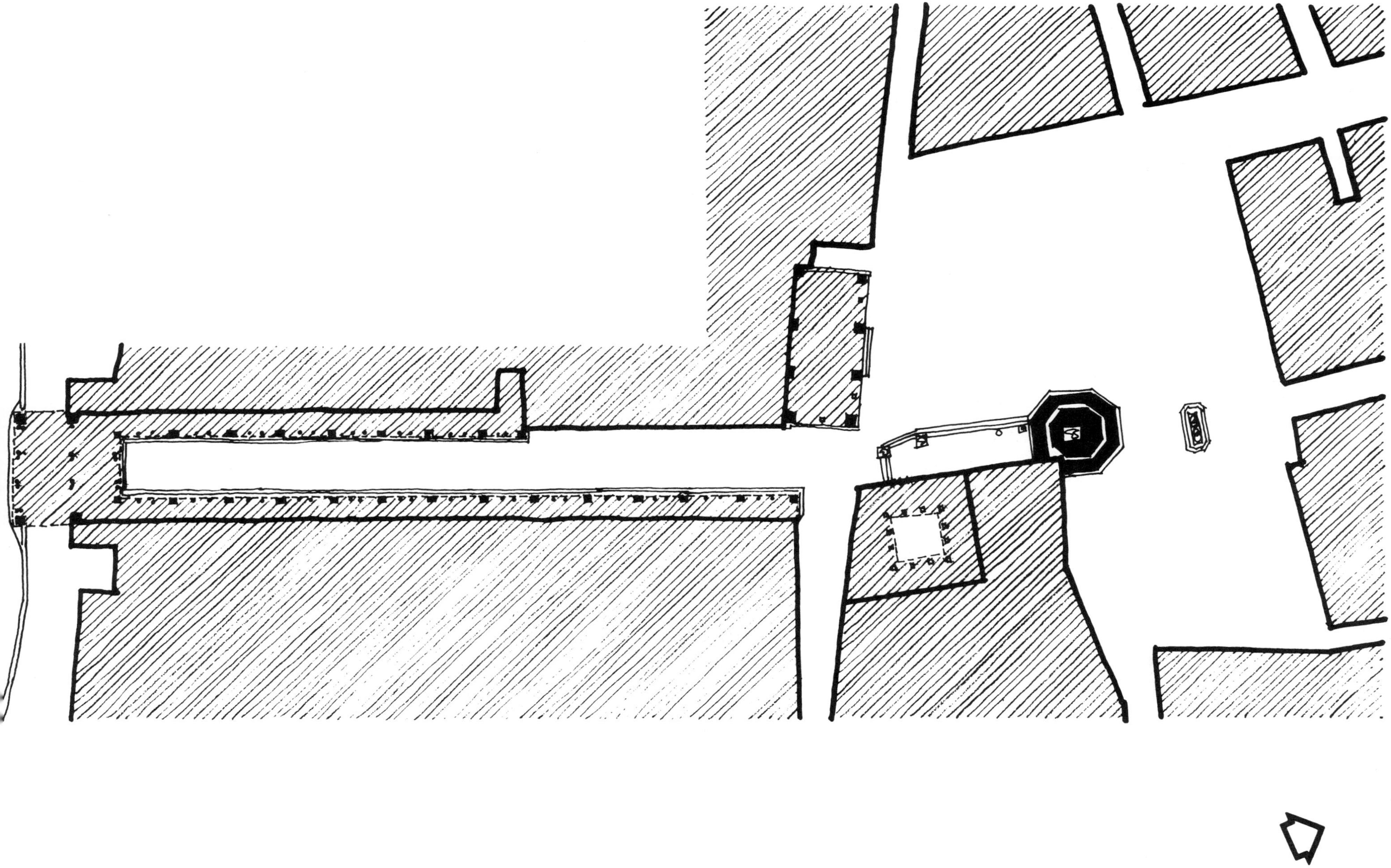

PIAZZA DEL CAMPIDOGLIO

Location: Rome, Italy

Dates: 1537

Designer: Michelangelo

Client: City Council

Area: .88 acres / .36 hectares

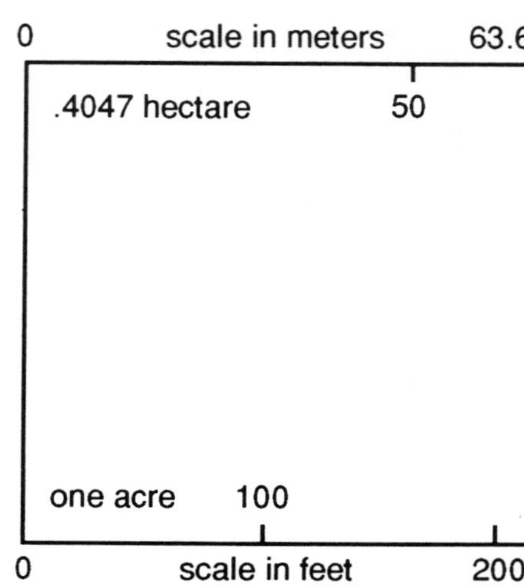

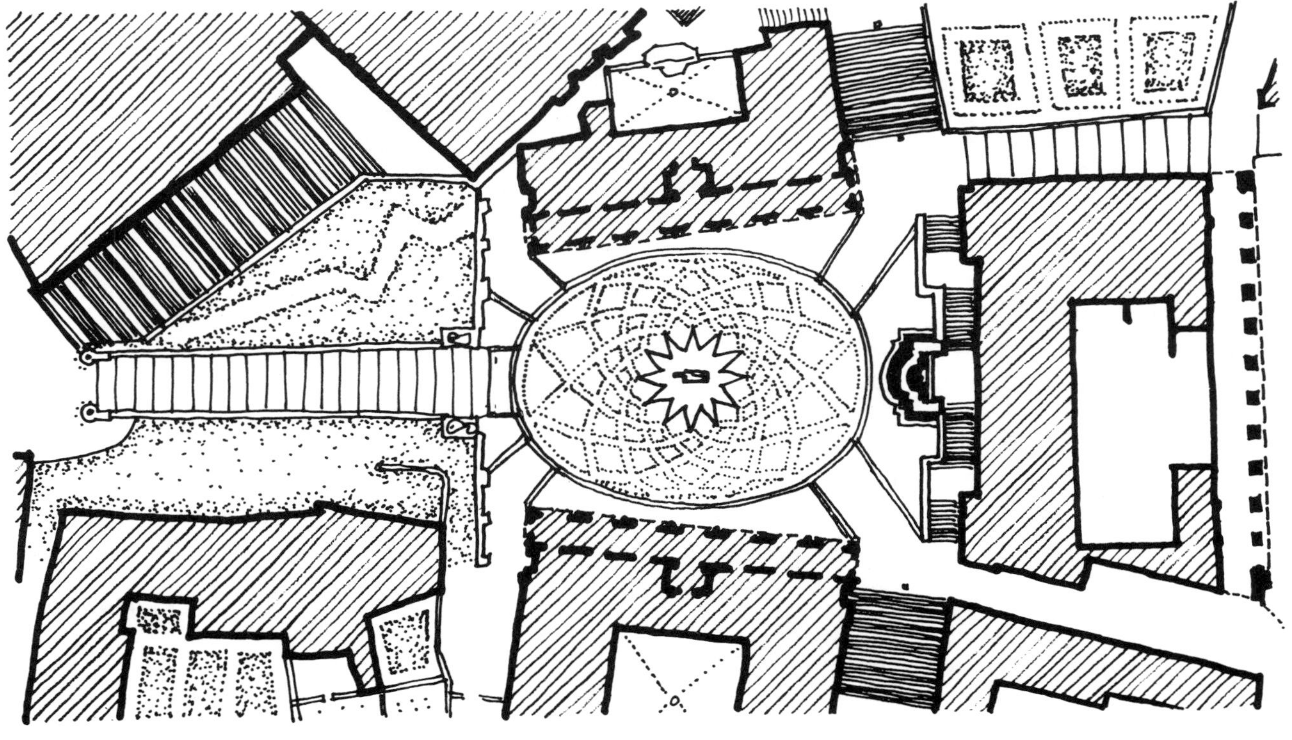

PIAZZA SAN PIETRO

Location: Rome, Italy

Dates: 1585 - 1667

Designers: Pope Sixtus V, Carlo Fontana and Giovanni Bernini

Client: Pope Sixtus V

Area: 1.1 acres / .43 hectares

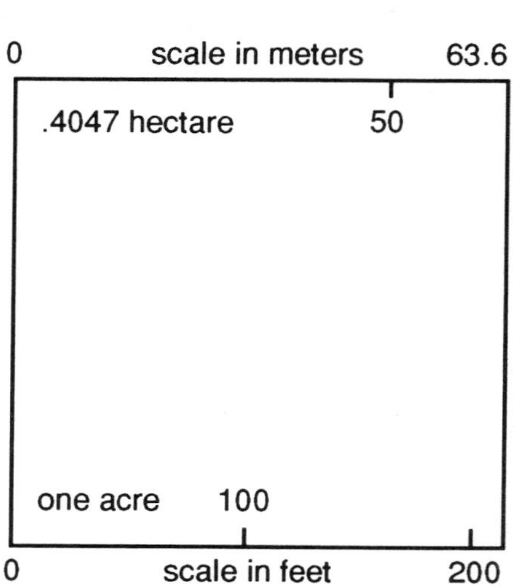

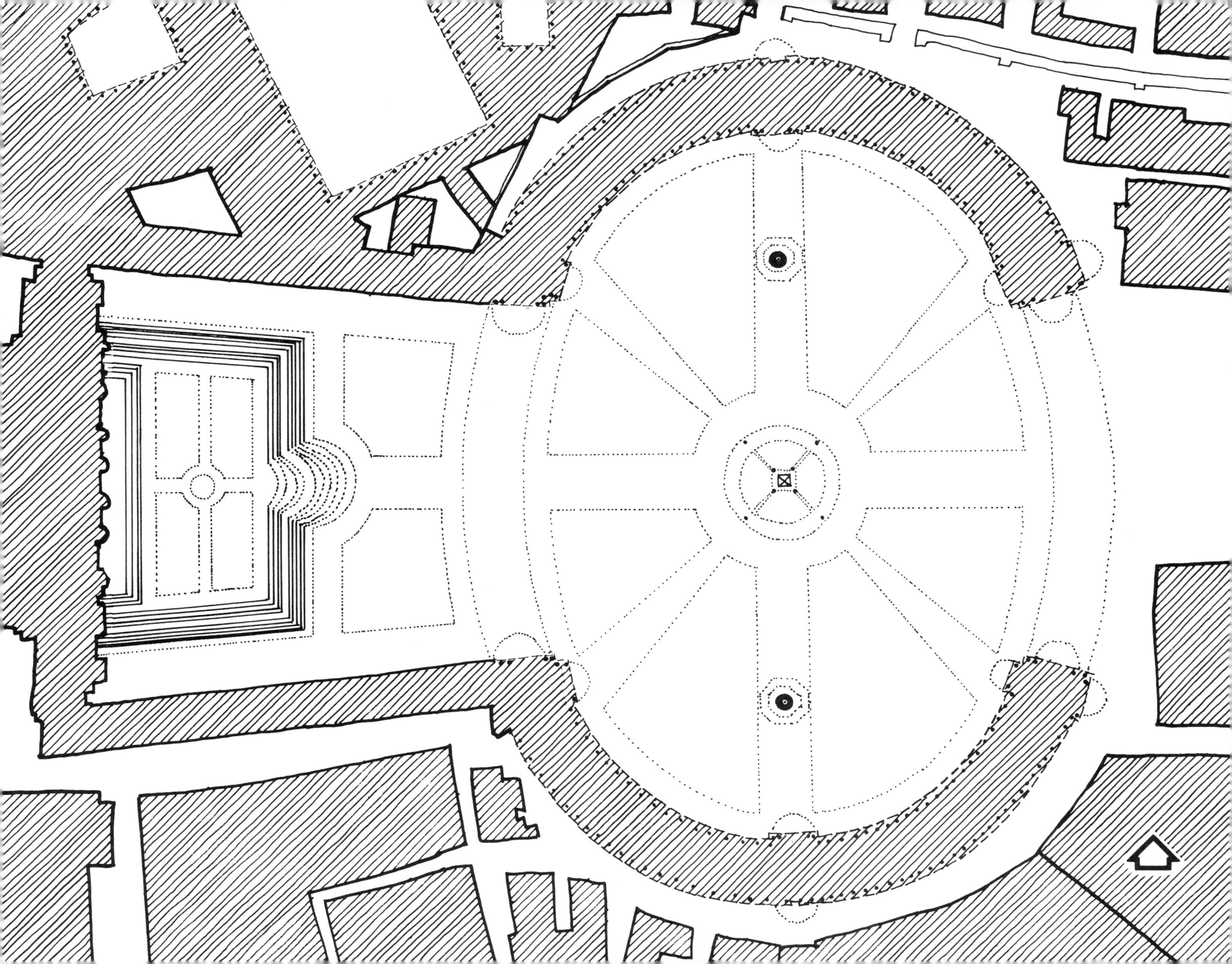

VILLA MEDICI

Location: Fiesole, Italy

Dates: 1458 - 1461

Designer: Michelozzo

Client: Cosimo dei Medici

Area: 2.79 acres / 1.13 hectares

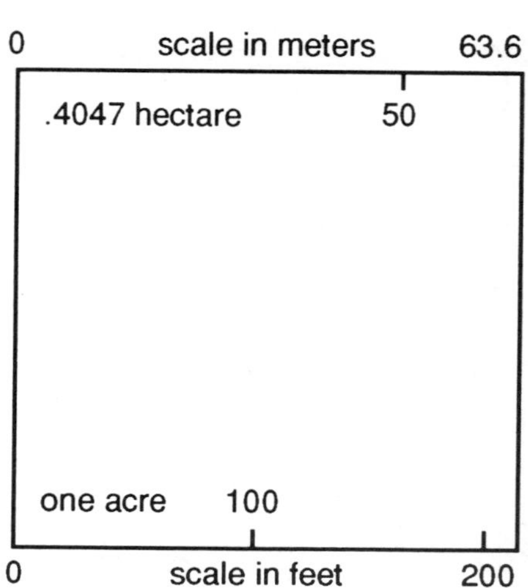

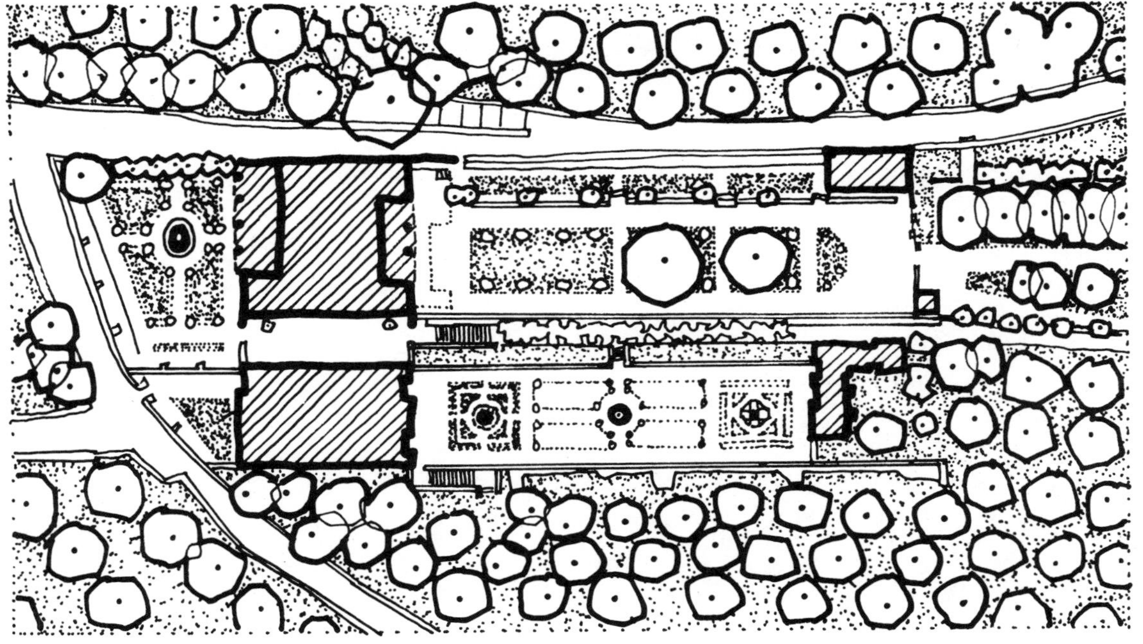

CORTILE DEL BELVEDERE

Location: The Vatican, Rome, Italy

Dates: 1503 - 1560

Designers: Bramante, Raphael, Sangallo the Younger, Michelangelo, Ligorio

Clients: Pope's Julius II, Leo X, Julius III

Area: 6.31 acres / 2.55 hectares

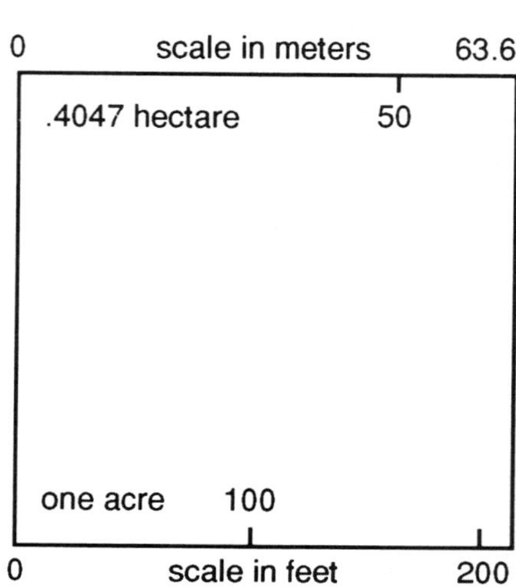

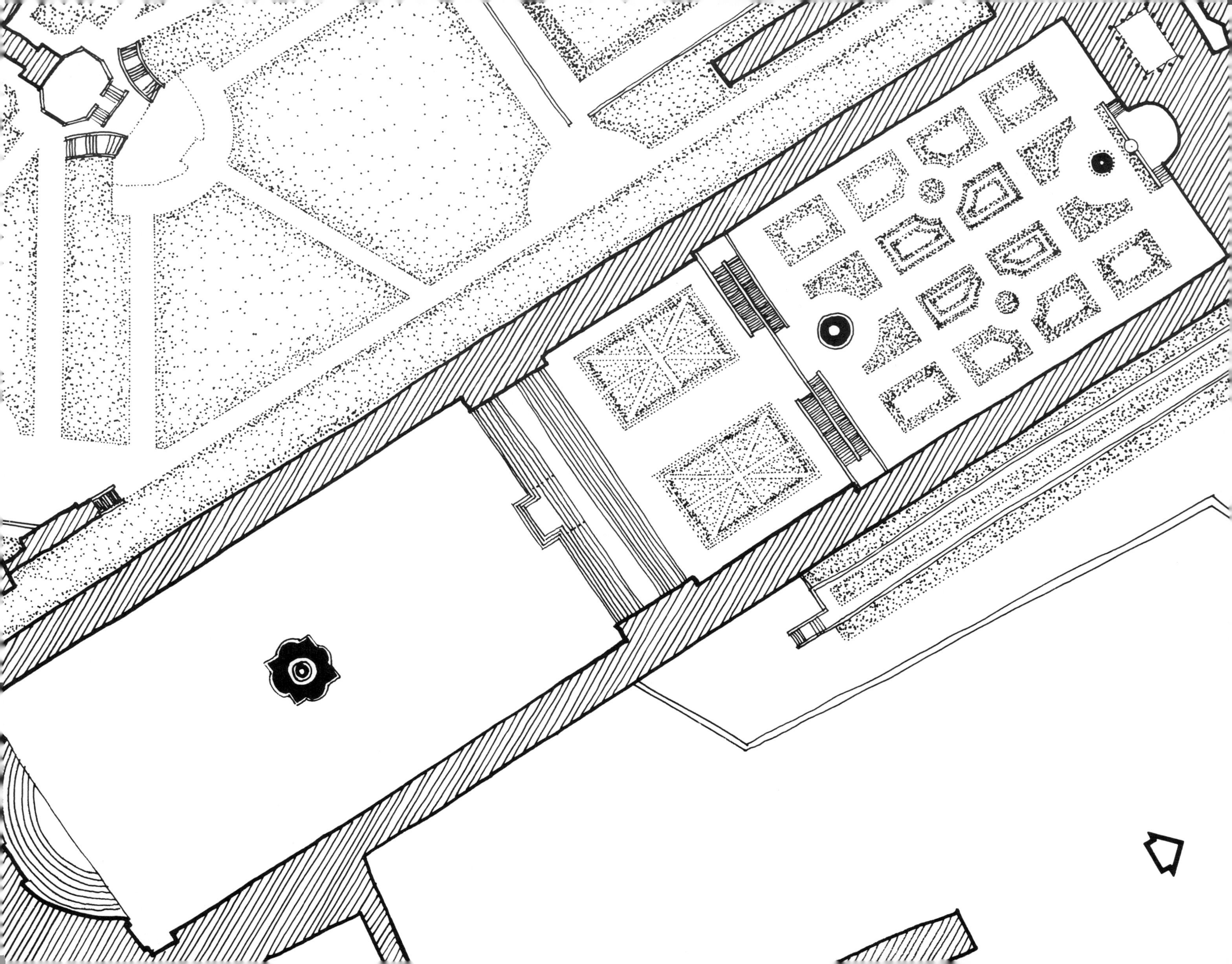

VILLA GIULIA

Location: Rome, Italy

Date: 1550 - 1552

Designers: Giacomo Vignola and Ammanati

Client: Pope Julius III

Area: .78 acres / .33 hectares

(also called Villa di Papa Giulio)

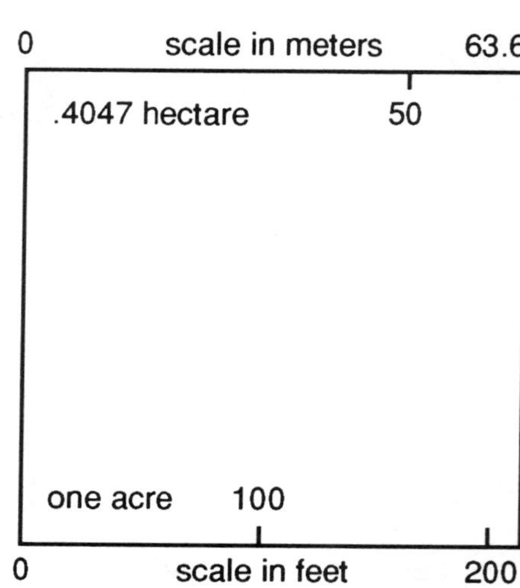

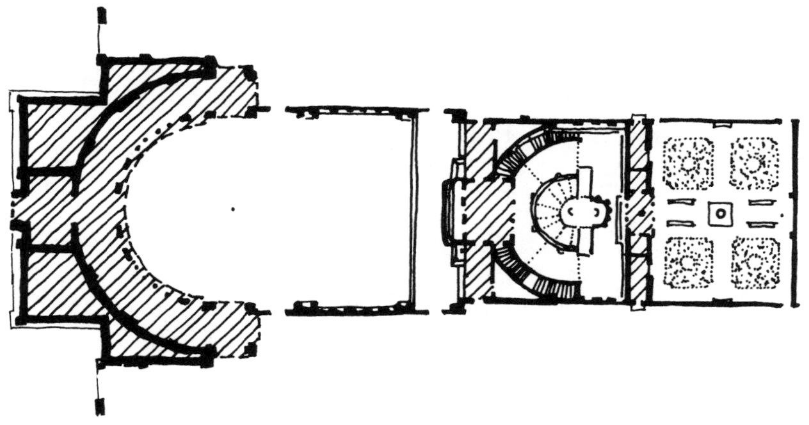

PALAZZO FARNESE

Location: Caprarola, Italy

Dates: 1556 - 1583

Designer: Giacomo Vignola

Client: Cardinal Alessandro Farnese

Area: Palace gardens, 2.52 acres / 1.02 hectares

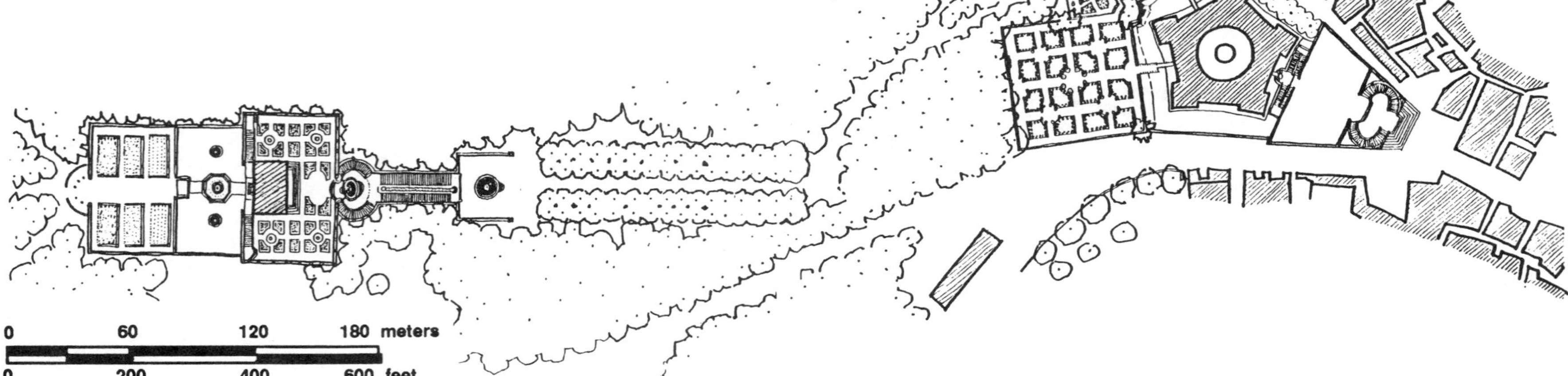

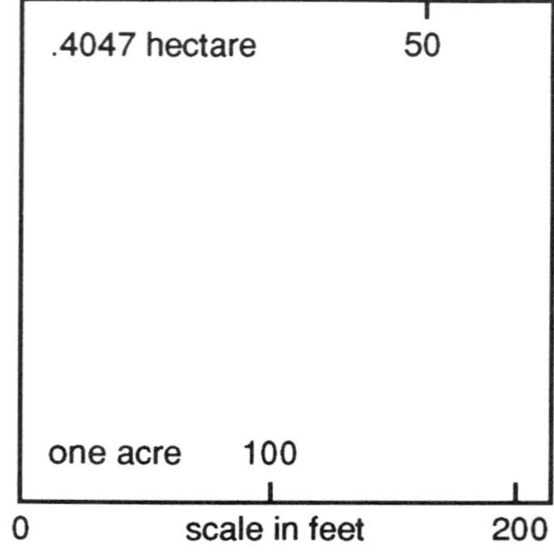

Plan above: the Palazzo Farnese and the Villino Caprarolla or Casino Villino

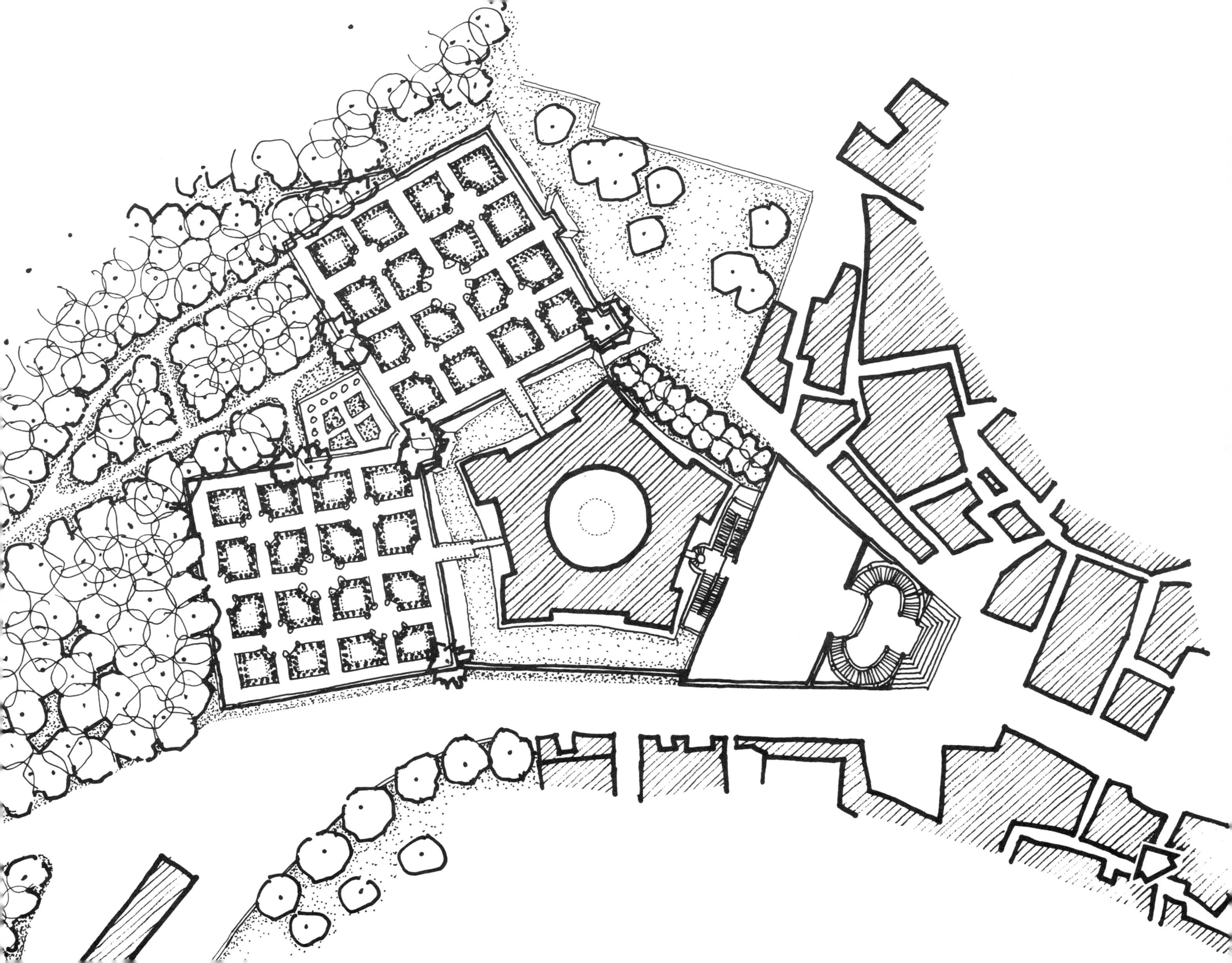

VILLINO FARNESE

Location: Caprarola, Italy

Dates: 1547 - 1620

Designer: Giacomo Vignola

Client: Cardinal Alessandro Farnese

Area: 3.64 acres / 1.47 hectares

Also called the Villino Caprarola or the Casino Villino

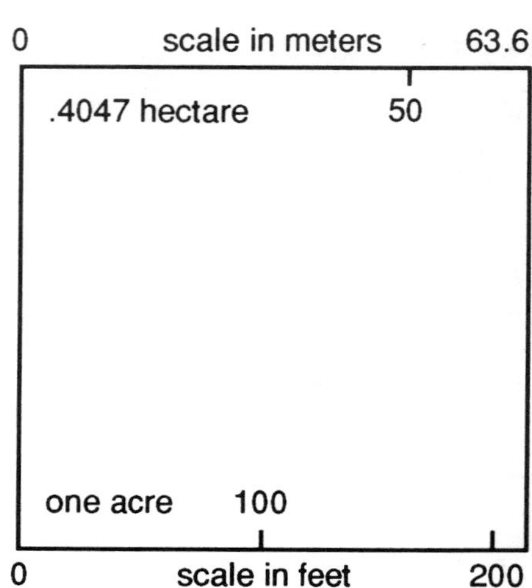

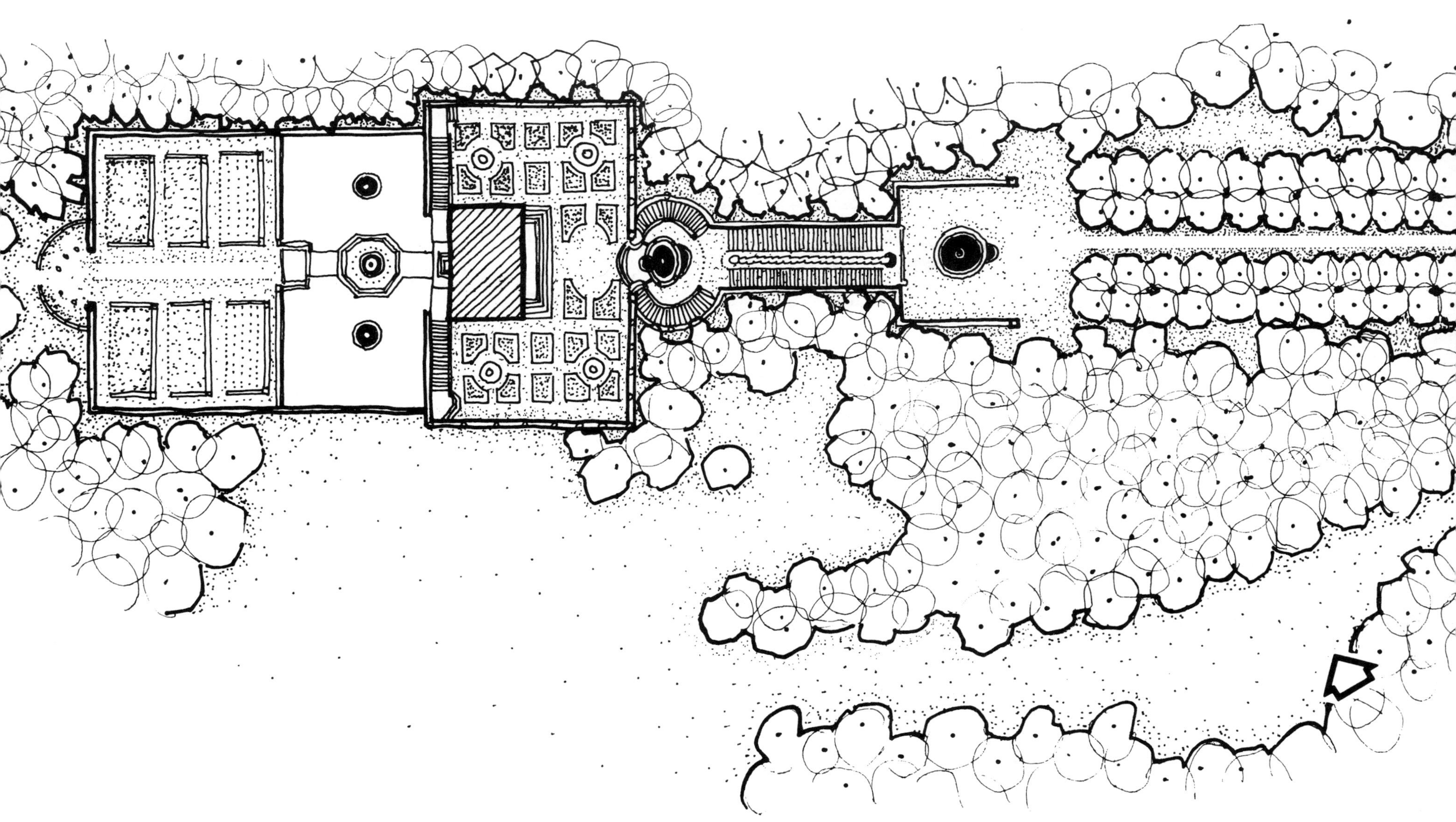

VILLA LANTE

Location: Bagnaia, Italy

Dates: 1566 - 1578

Designer: Vignola

Client: Cardinal Gianfrancesco Gambera

Area: the "barco" (hunting park), 62.0 acres / 25.0 hectares
the humanistic garden, 4.59 acres / 1.86 hectares

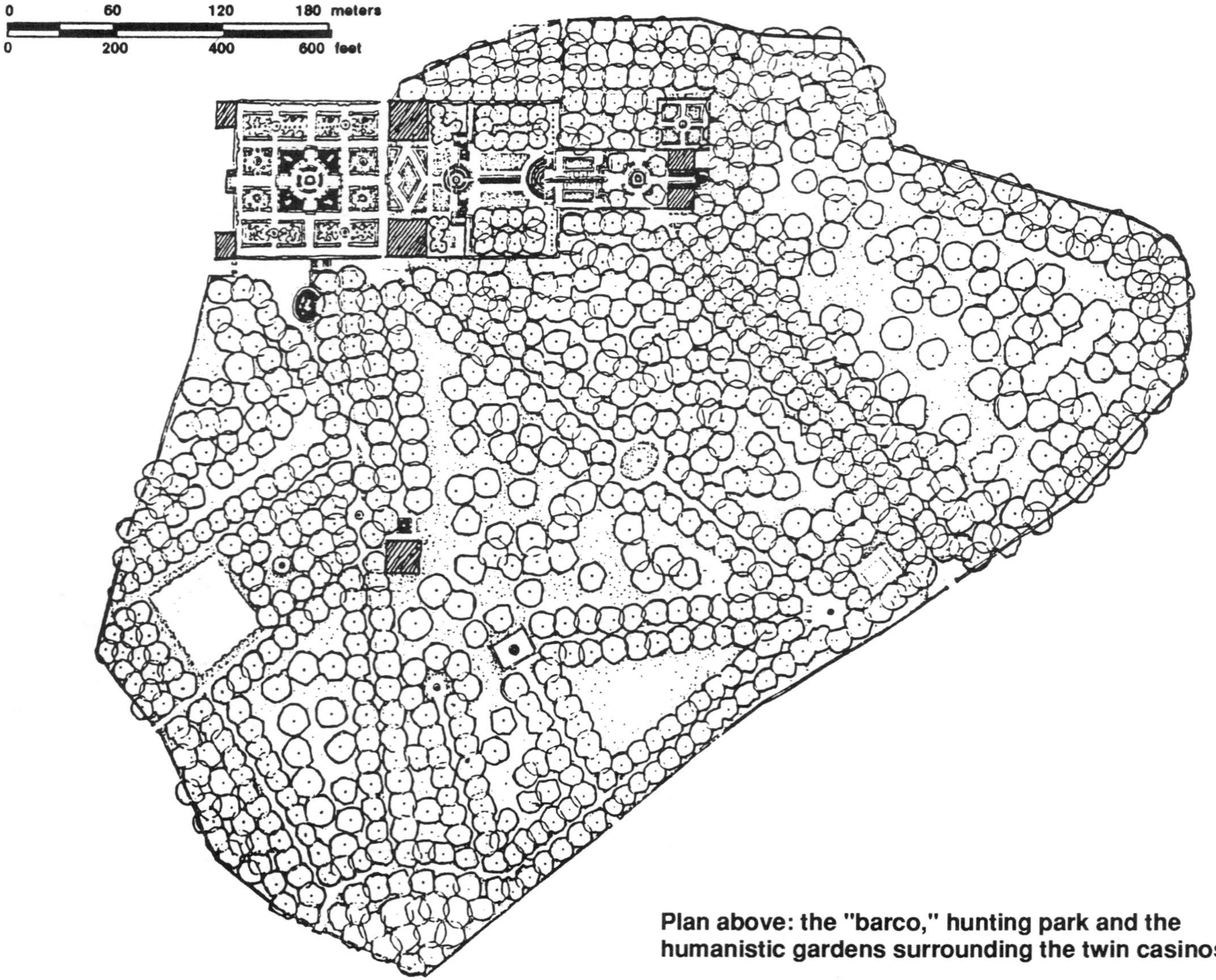

0
60
120
180 meters
0
200
400
600 feet

0
scale in meters
63.6
.4047 hectare
50
one acre
100
0
scale in feet
200

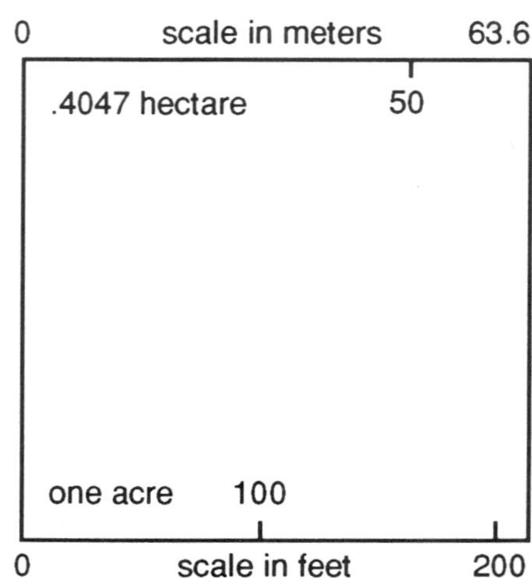

Plan above: the "barco," hunting park and the humanistic gardens surrounding the twin casinos

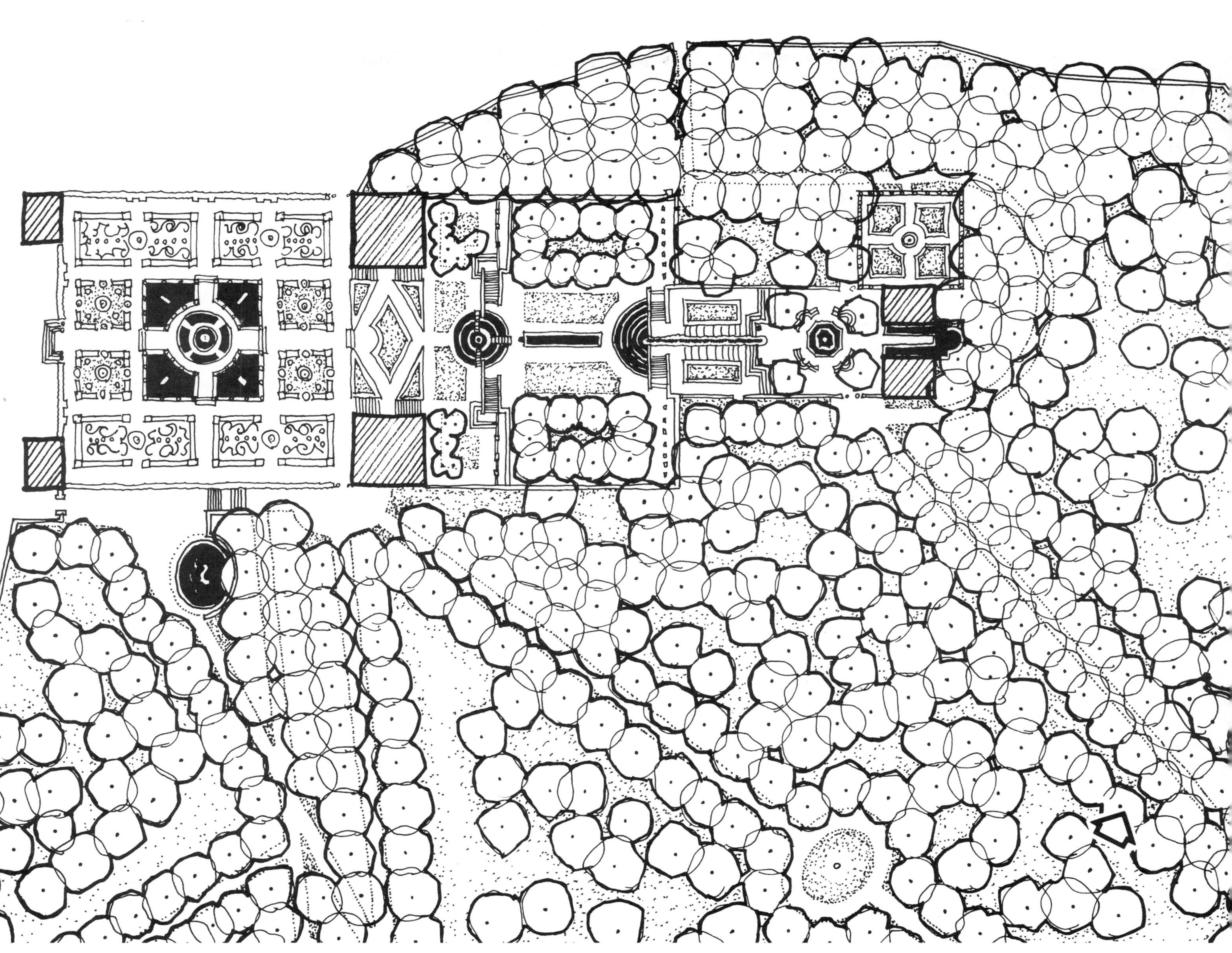

BOBOLI GARDENS

Location: Florence, Italy

Dates: 1549 - c. 1700

Designers: Tribolo, Buontalenti, Ammanati, da Bologna and Parigi

Clients: Grand Duke Cosimo I and Elenora de Medici; Cosimo III

Area: the upper and lower amphitheatres, 2.75 acres / 1.11 hectares
The park with the Piazzale dell'Isolotto: 60 acres / 24.3 hectares

Italian name: Giardini di Boboli

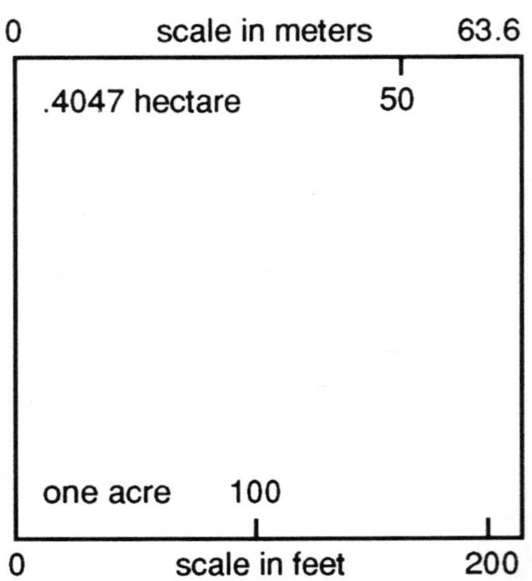

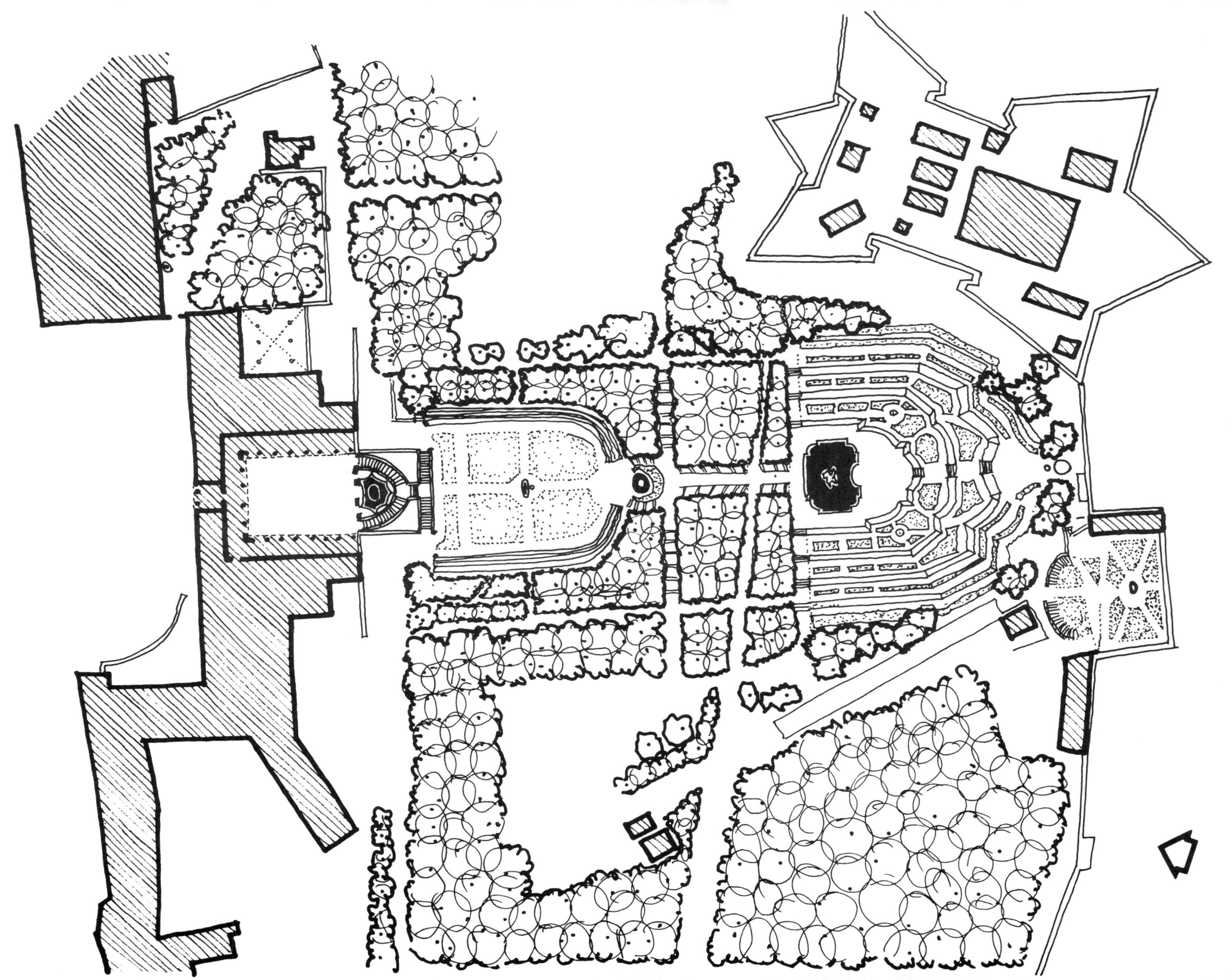

VILLA D'ESTE

Location: Tivoli, Italy

Dates: 1550

Designers: Pirro Ligorio, Giacomo della Porta, Orazio Olivieri

Client: Cardinal Ippolito d'Este

Area: 9.7 acres / 3.93 hectares

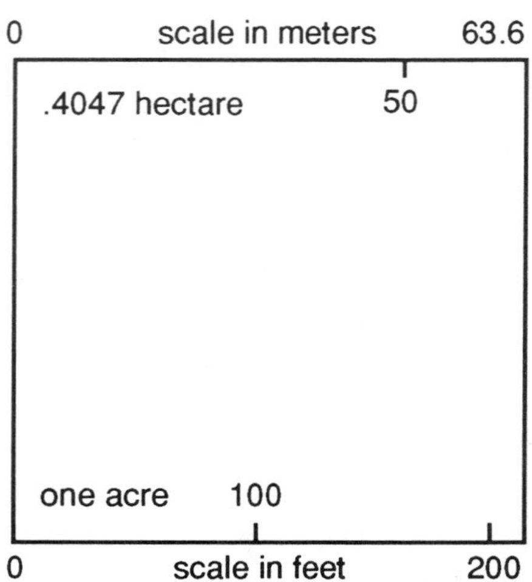

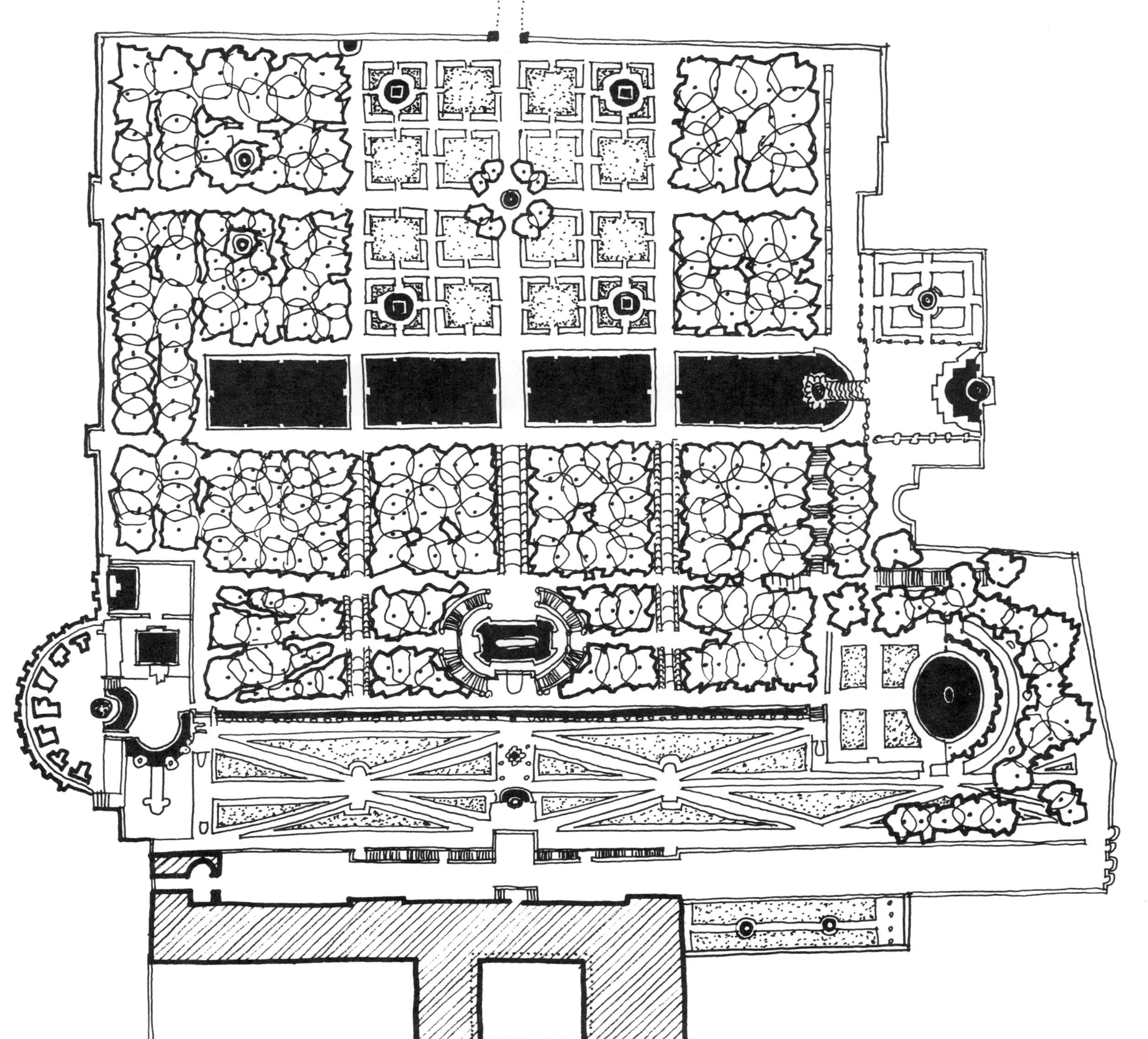

VILLA ALDOBRANDINI

Location: Frascati, Italy

Dates: 1598 - 1603

Designers: Giacomo della Porta, Carlo Maderno and Domenico Fontana

Client: Cardinal Pietro Aldobrandini

Area: 13.1 acres / 5.3 hectares

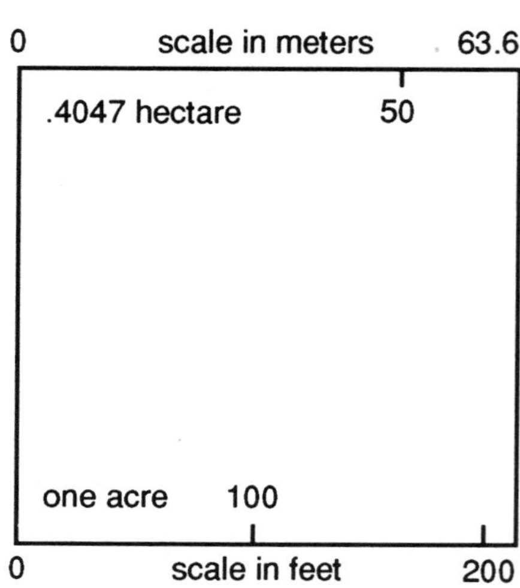

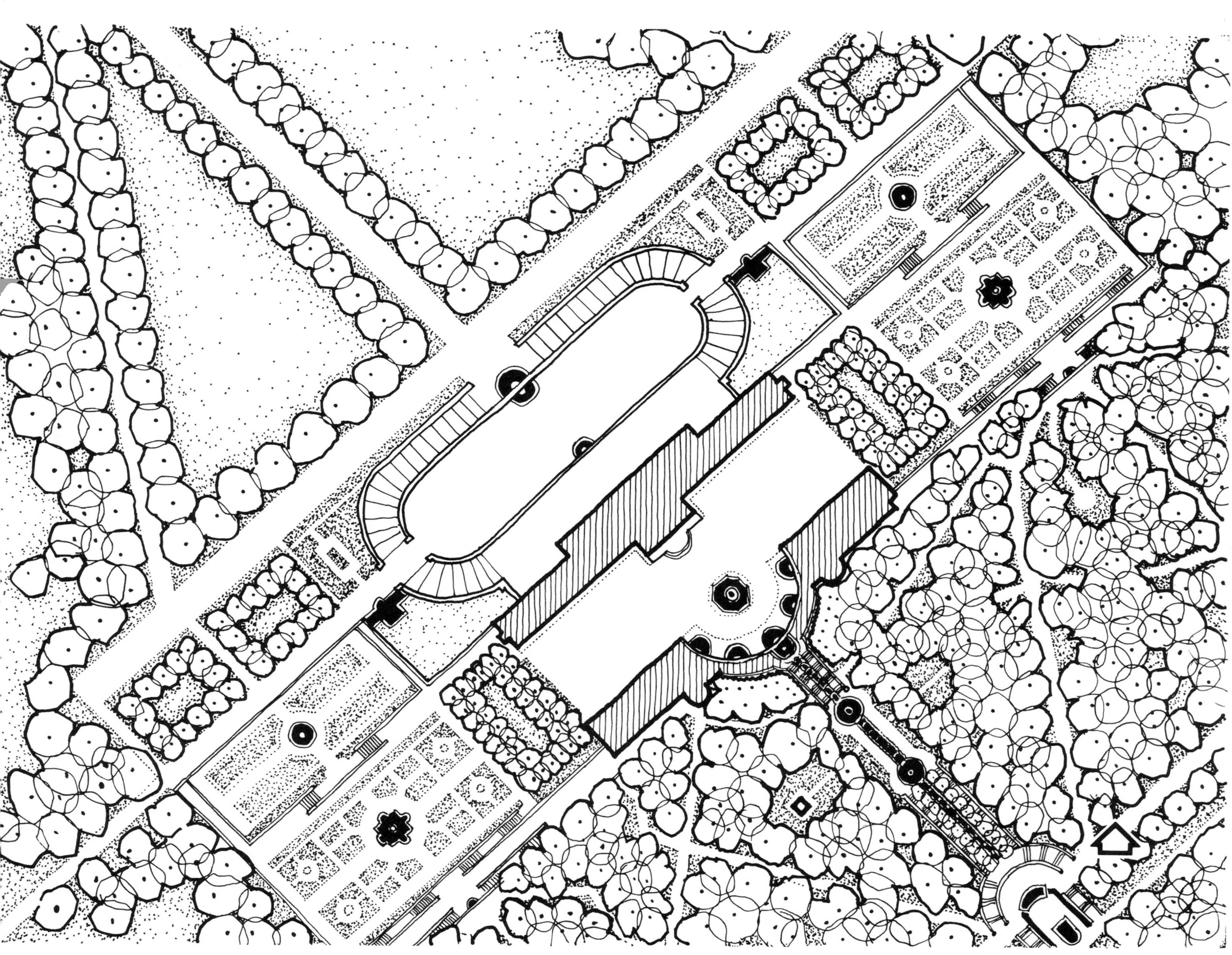

VILLA GAMBERAIA

Location: Settignano, Italy

Date: 1610

Designer: unknown

Client: Giovanni Gamberelli

Area: 3.13 acres / 1.27 hectares

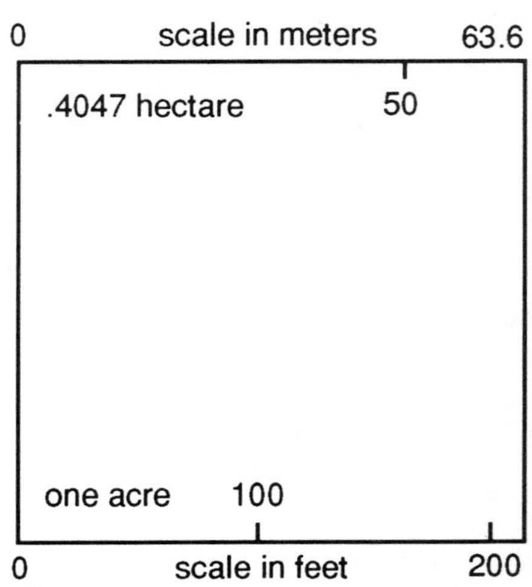

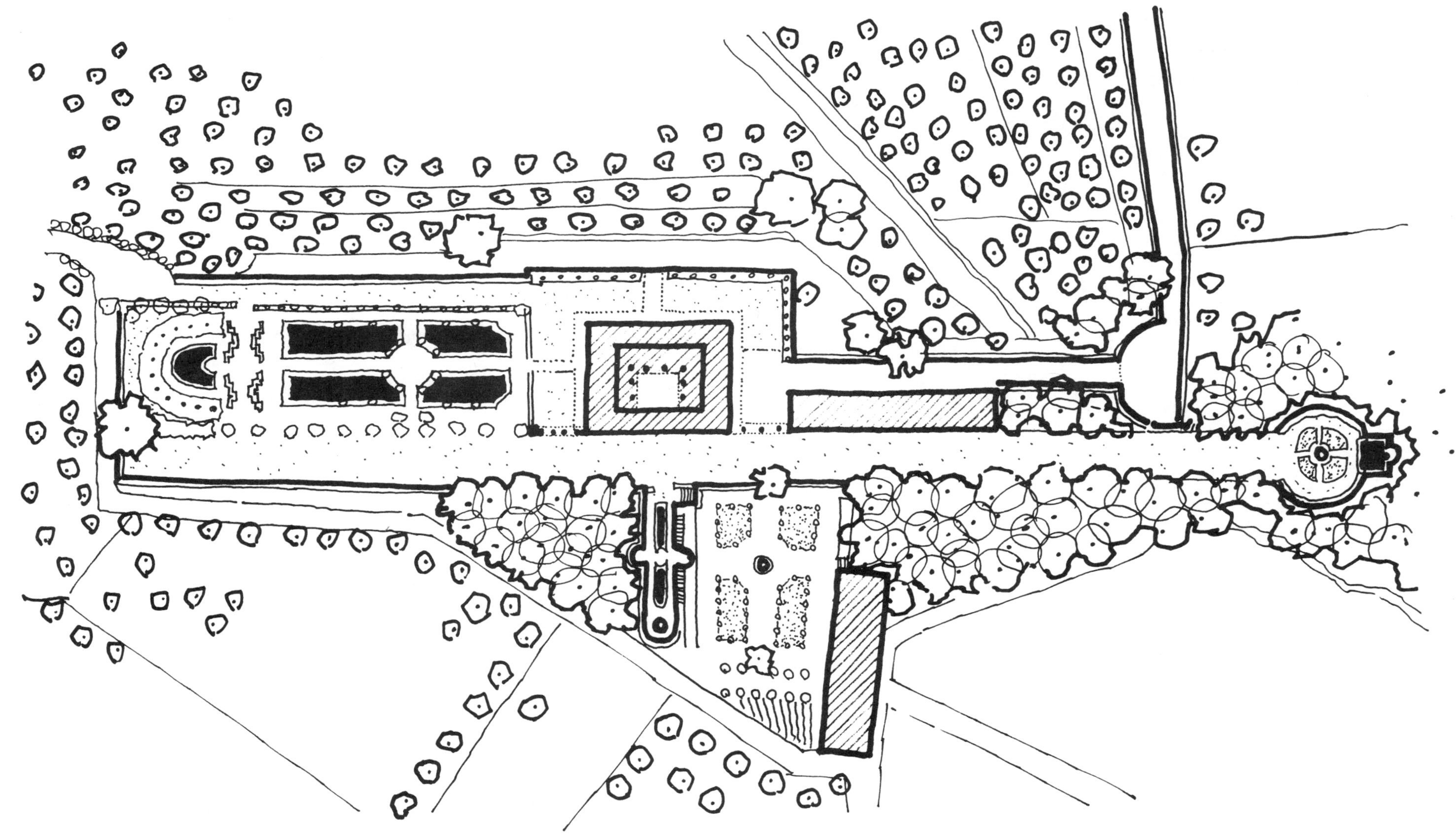

ISOLA BELLA

Location: Lake Maggiore, Italy

Dates: 1632 - 1671

Designer: Carlo Fontana

Clients: Count Carlo Borromeo and Count Vitalione Borromeo

Area: 7.35 acres / 2.97 hectares

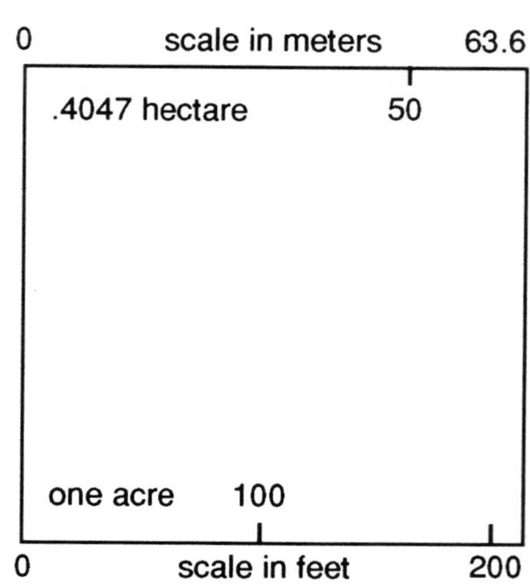

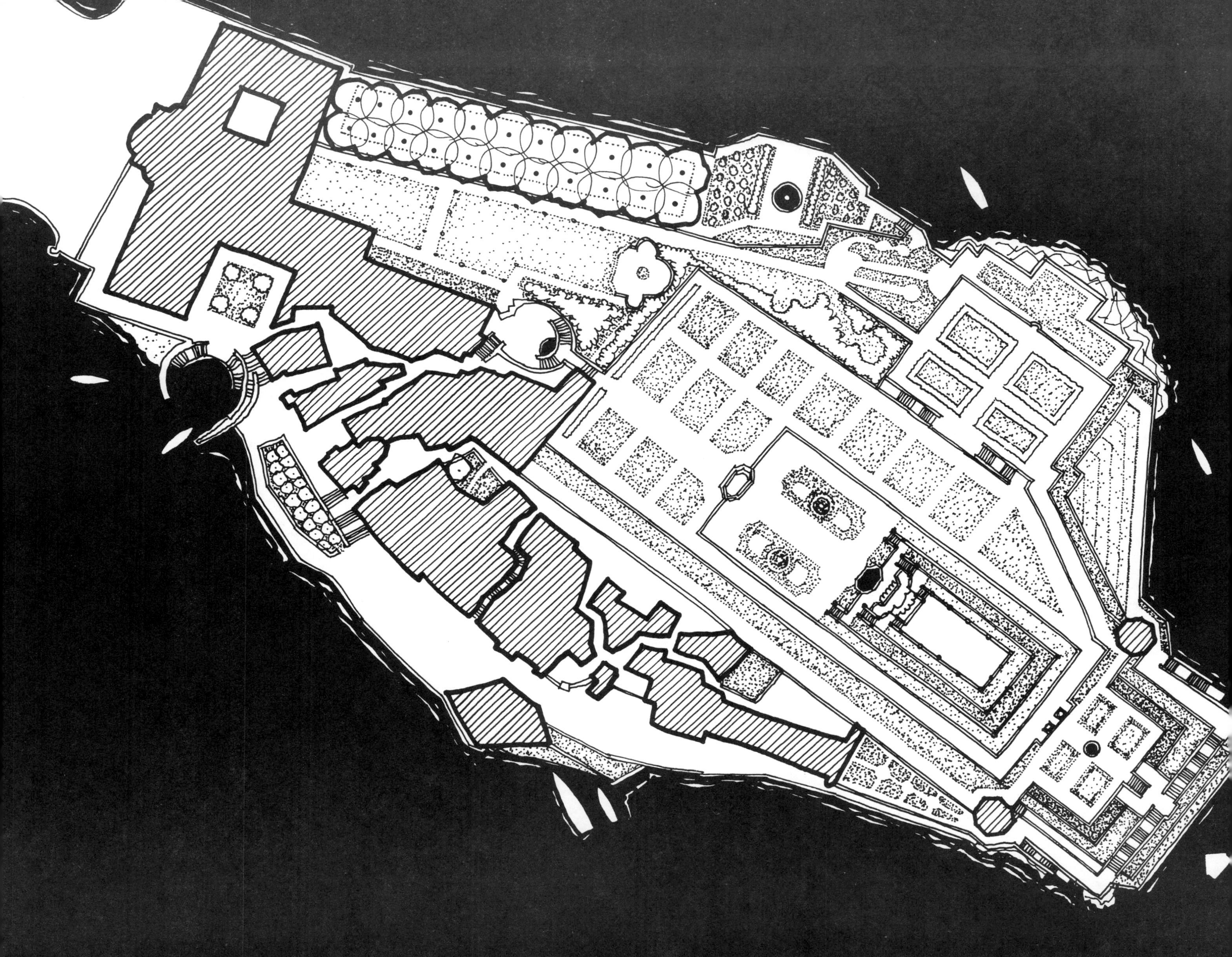

AMBOISE

Location: Indre-et-Loire, France

Dates: 1495 -1498

Designer: Pacello de Mercogliano

Client: Charles VIII

Area of the gardens: .98 acres / .39 hectares

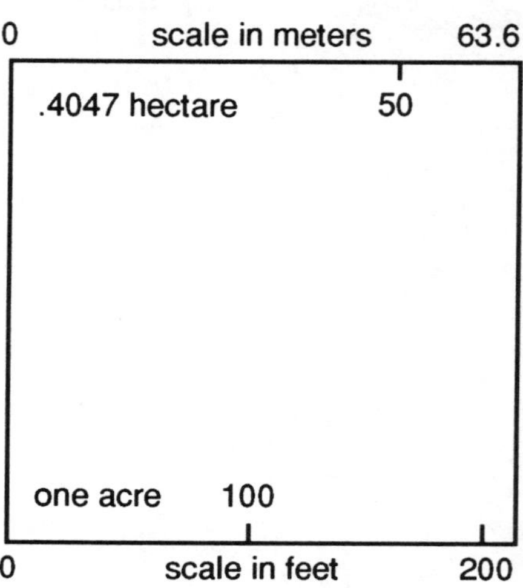

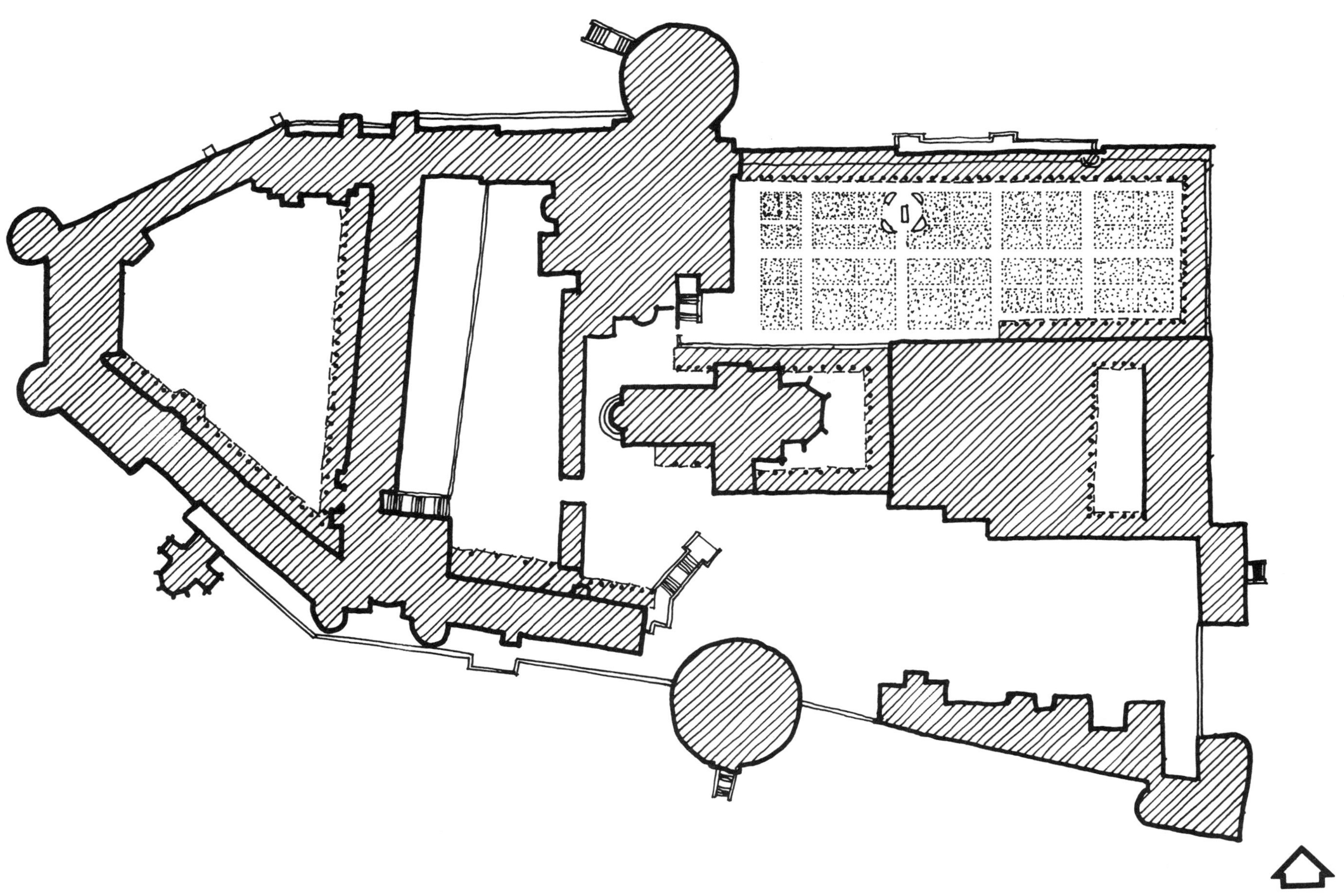

BLOIS

Location: Loir-et-Cher, France

Dates: 1498 - 1515

Designer: Francois Mansart and Pacello de Mercogliano

Clients: Louis XII and Francois I

Area of the gardens: 13.66 acres / 5.53 hectares

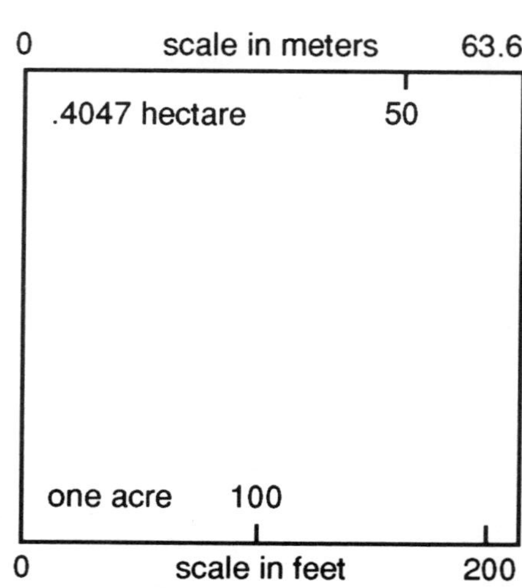

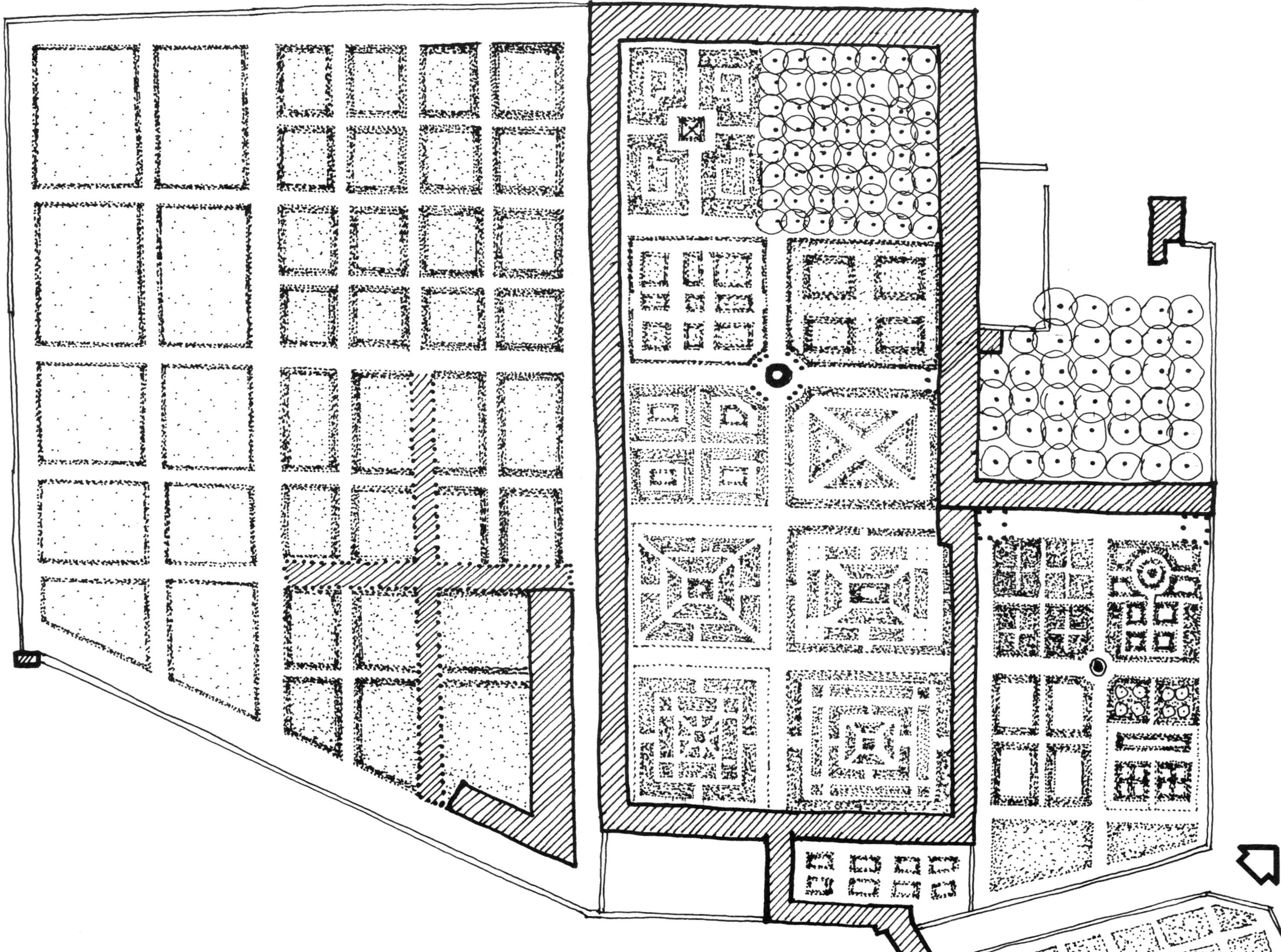

CHENONCEAUX

Location: Indre-et-Loire, France

Dates: 1551 - 1560

Designers: du Cerceau and Philibert de L'Orme

Clients: Diane de Poitiers and Catherine de Medici

Area of the gardens: 8.87 acres / 3.59 hectares

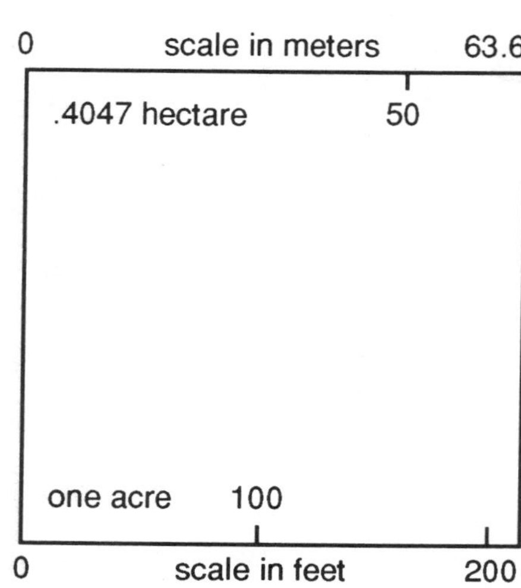

ANET

Location: Eure-et-Loir, France

Dates: 1546 -1552

Designer: Philibert de L'Orme

Client: Diane de Poitiers

Area of the Château: 9.64 acres / 3.9 hectares
area of the gardens: 2.48 acres / 1.0 hectare

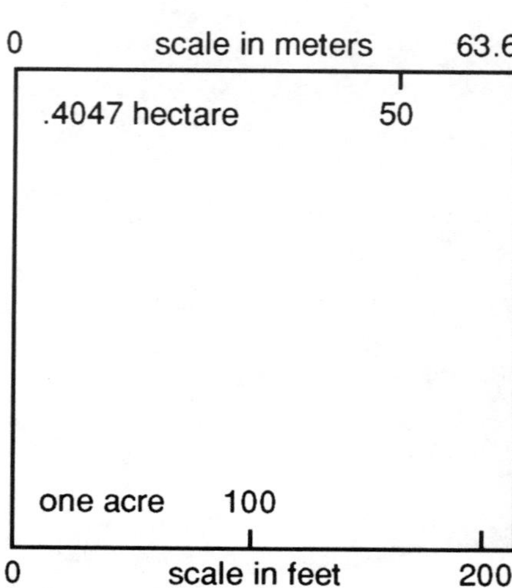

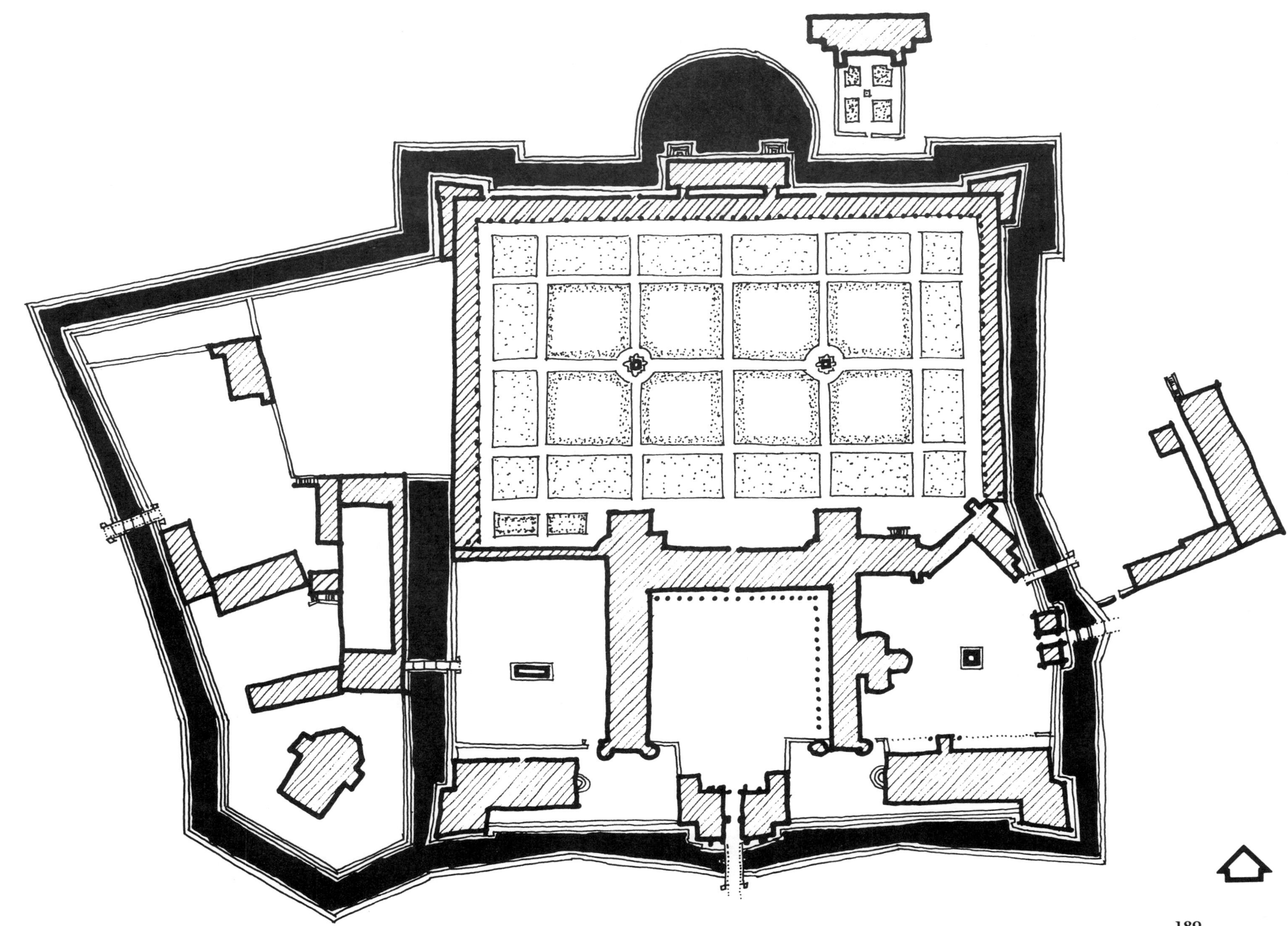

HADDON HALL

Location: Derbyshire, England

Date: c. 1480

Designer: unknown

Clients: the Dukes of Rutland

Area of the gardens: 2.2 acres / .88 hectare

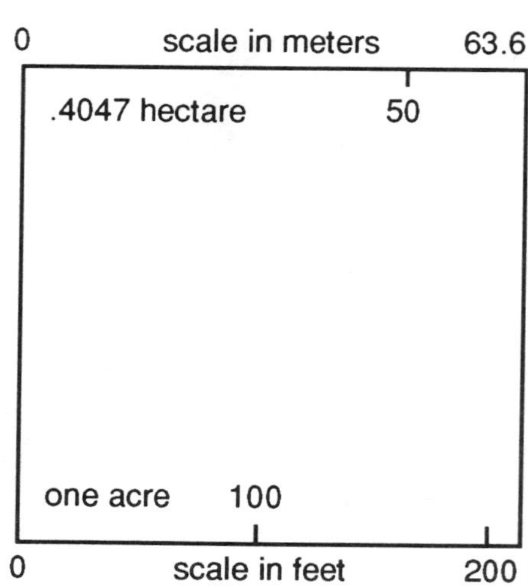

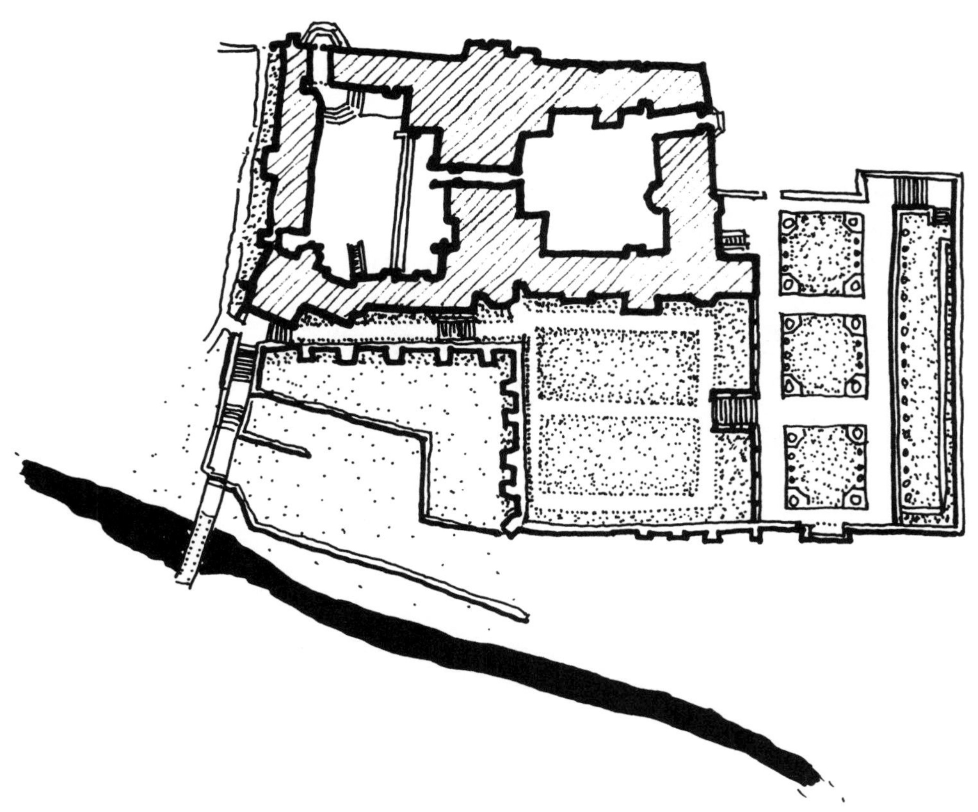

MONTACUTE HOUSE

Location: Yeovil, Somersetshire, England

Dates: 1558 - 1600

Designer: unknown

Clients: Sir Thomas Phelips; Sir Edward Phelips

Area of the gardens: 3.89 acres / 1.57 hectares

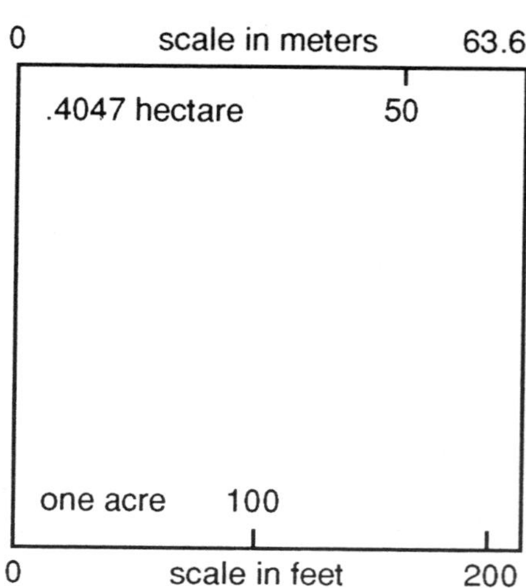

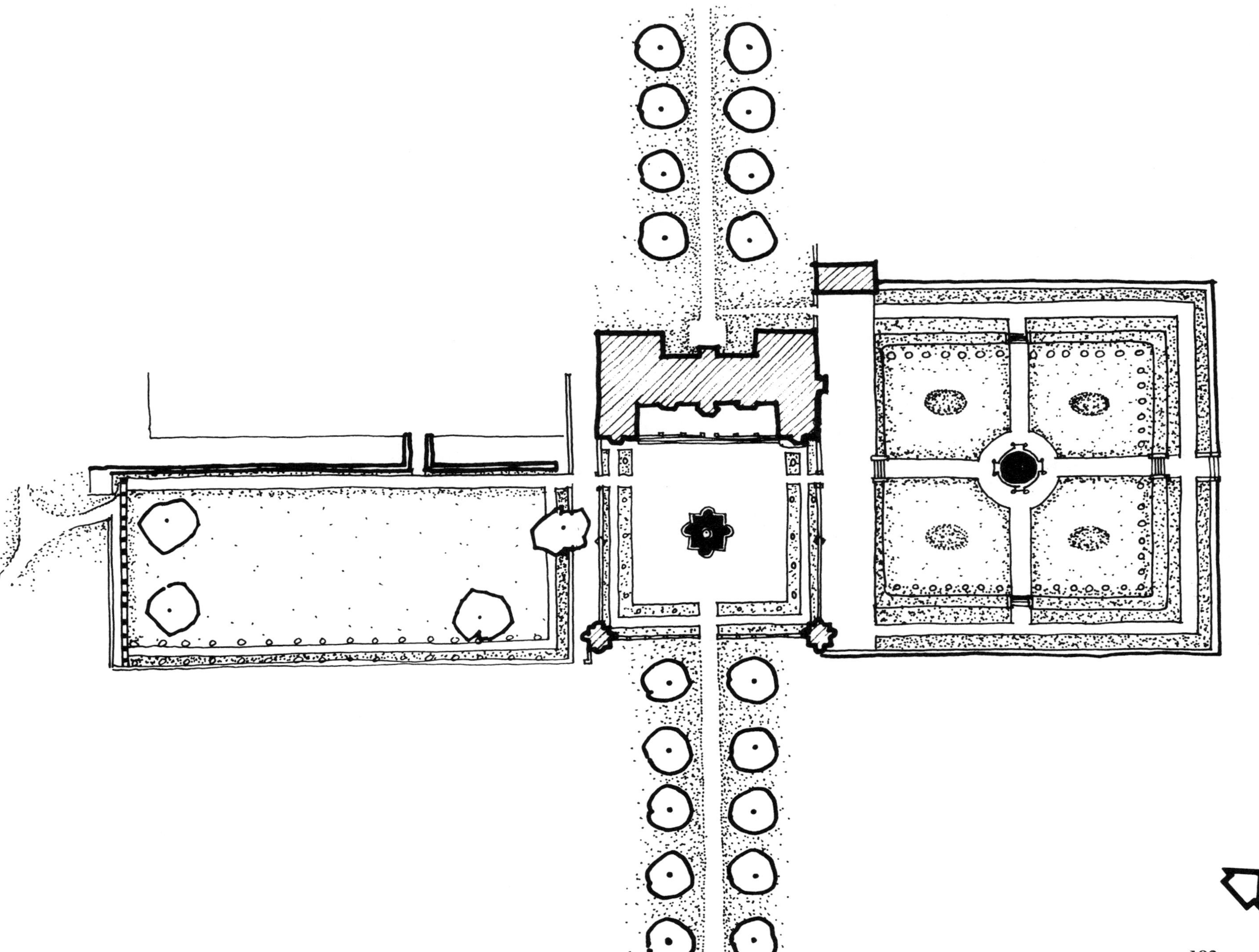

MELBOURNE HALL

Location: Derbyshire, England

Date: 1704

Designers: Henry Wise and George London

Clients: Thomas Coke

Area: 11.5 acres / 4.66 hectares

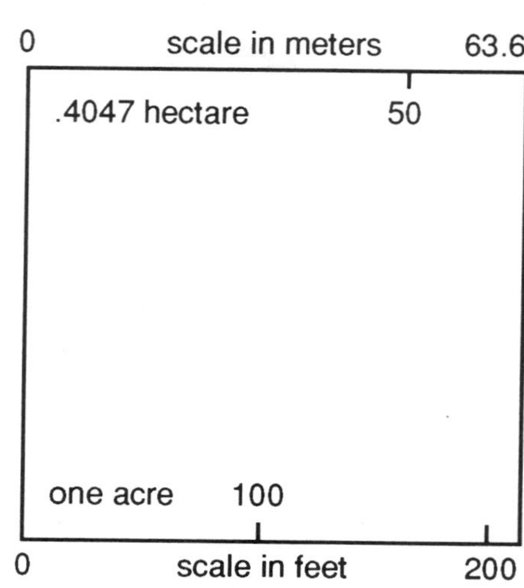

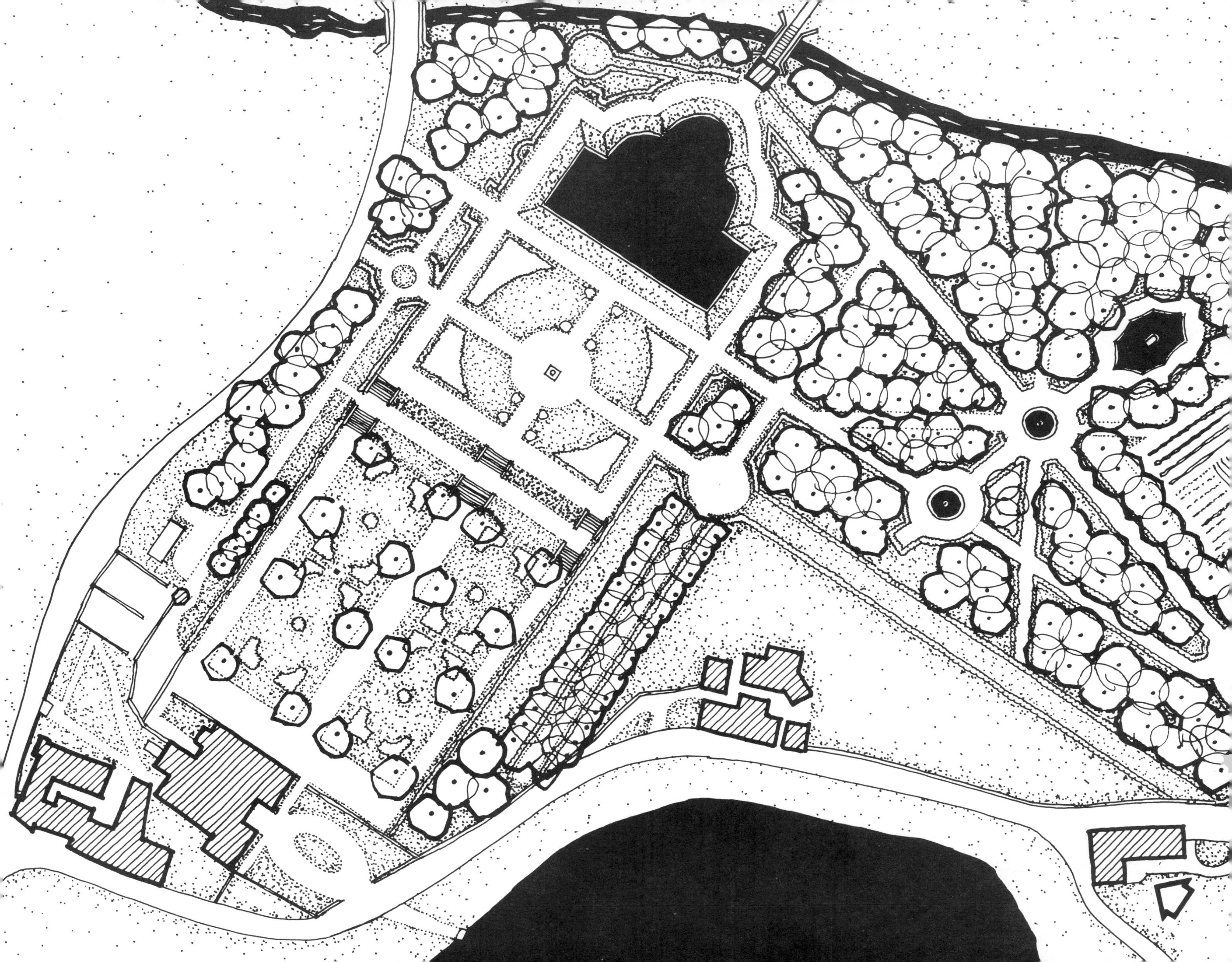

POPE'S GARDEN*

Location: Twickenham (London), England

Dates: 1719 - 1744

Designer: Alexander Pope

Client: Alexander Pope

Area: 5 acres / 2.02 hectares

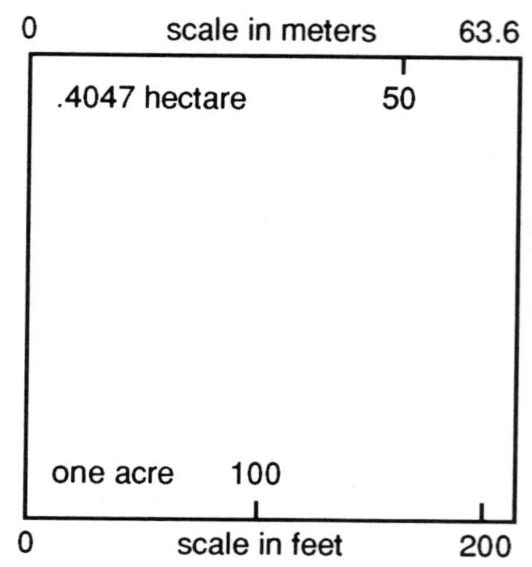

* This plan is after the modified garden plan by A. James Sambrook, *Eighteenth-Century Studies*, vol. 5 (Spring 1972): pp. 450-455.

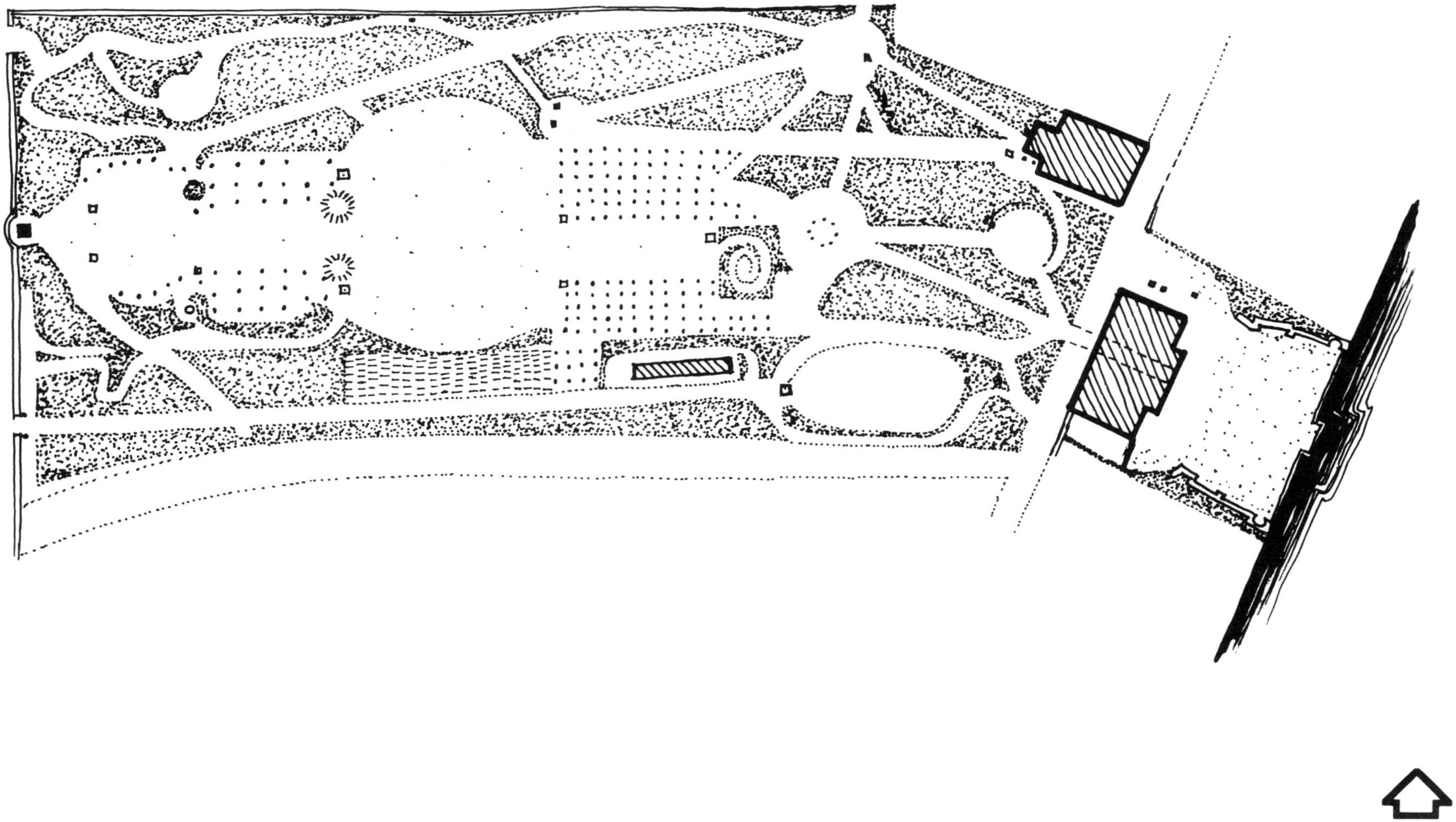

ROYAL CRESCENT

Location: Bath, Somersetshire, England

Dates: 1767 - 1775

Designer: John Wood II

Client: John Wood II

Area: 11.36 acres / 4.6 hectares

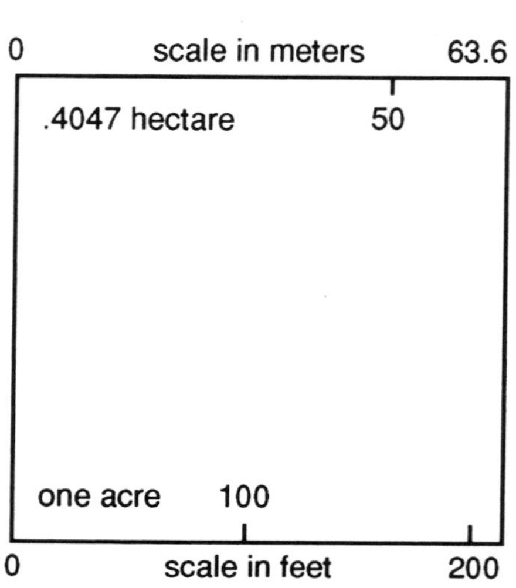

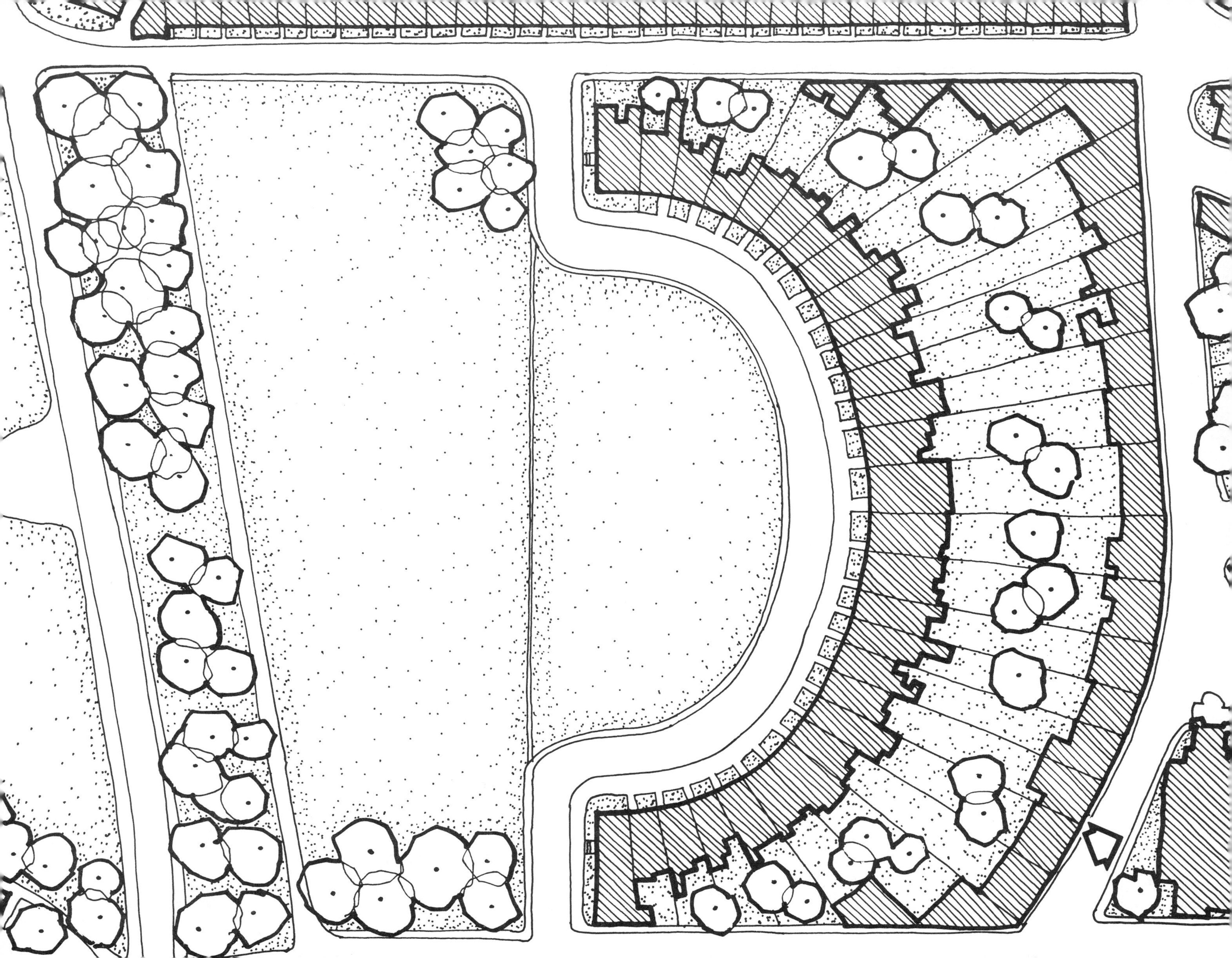

STRATFORD HALL

Location: Montross, Westmoreland County, Virginia

Date: 1730

Designer: Richard Taliaferro

Client: Governor Thomas Lee

Area of the gardens: 4.42 acres / 1.79 hectares

Also called Stratford-Lee Hall

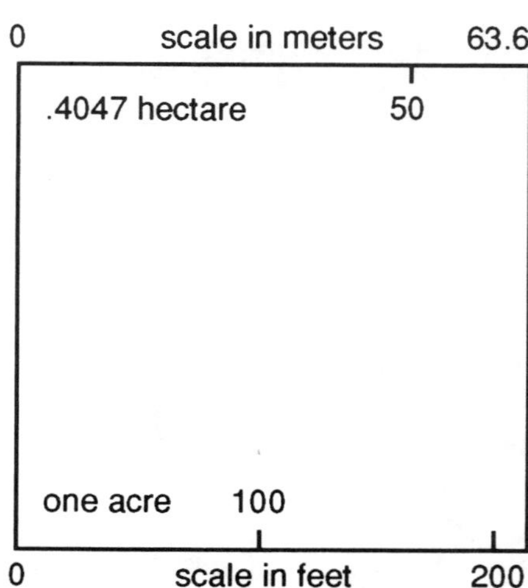

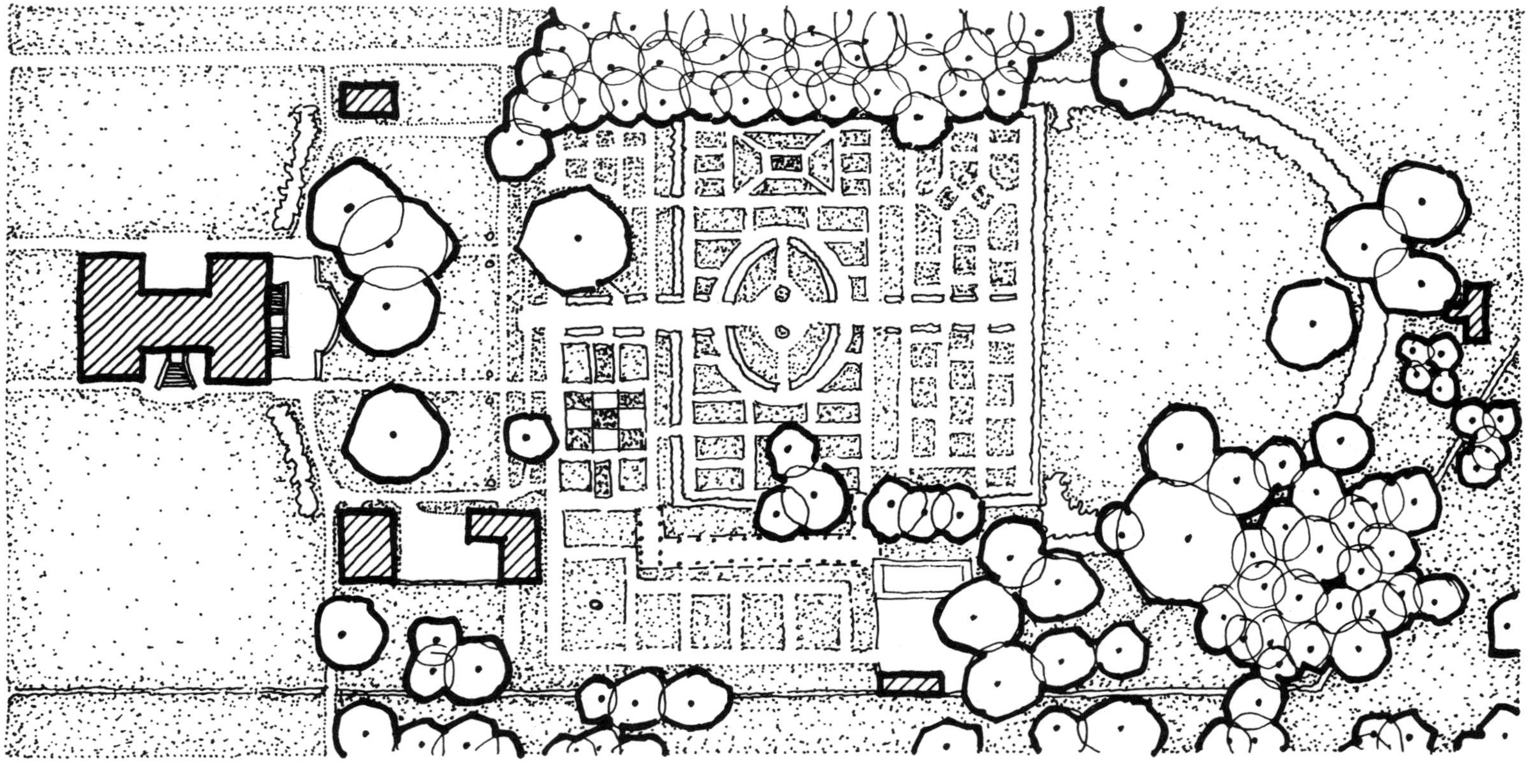

PACA HOUSE

Location: Annapolis, Maryland

Dates: 1763 -1766

Designer: William Paca

Client: William Paca

Area: 1.8 acres / .73 hectare

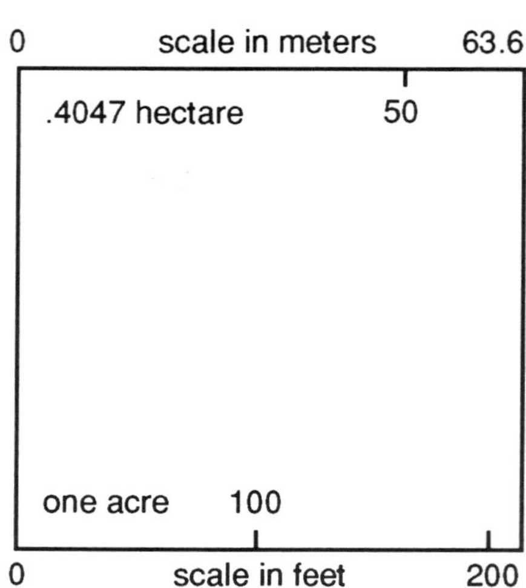

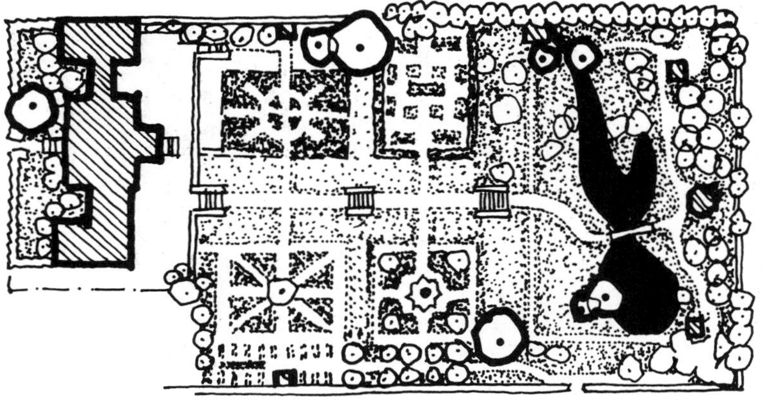

MOUNT VERNON

Location: Fairfax County, Virginia

Dates: 1759 - 1785

Designer: George Washington

Client: George Washington

Area of the plantation: 8000 acres / 3238 hectares;
area of the "Mansion House Farm": 500 acres / 202.3 hectares
area of the pleasure gardens: 14.46 acres / 5.85 hectares

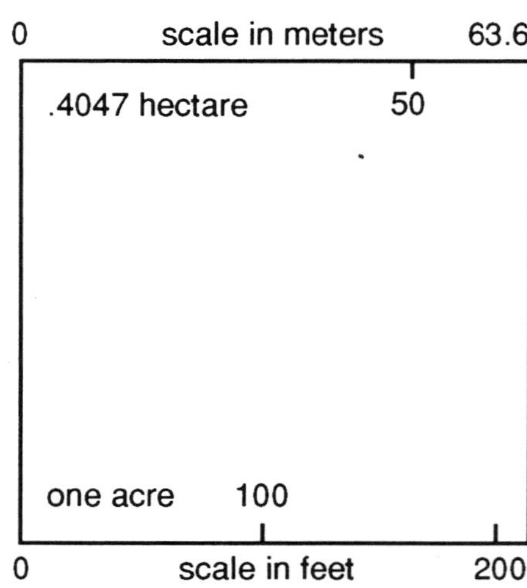

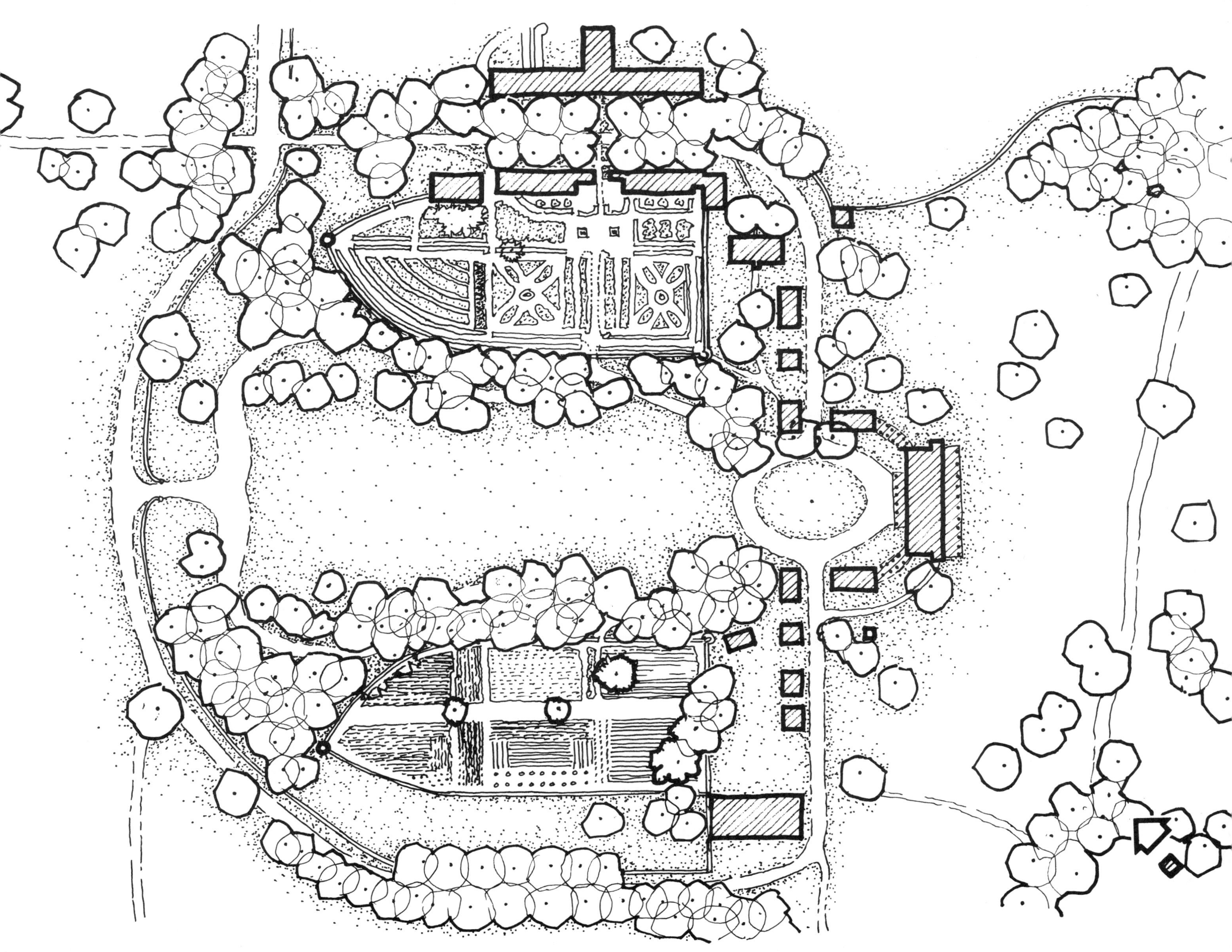

MONTICELLO

Location: Charlottesville, Virginia

Dates: 1771 - 1809

Designer: Thomas Jefferson

Client: Thomas Jefferson

Area of the plantation: 1900 acres / 769 hectares;
area of the residential gardens: 7.33 acres / 2.96 hectares

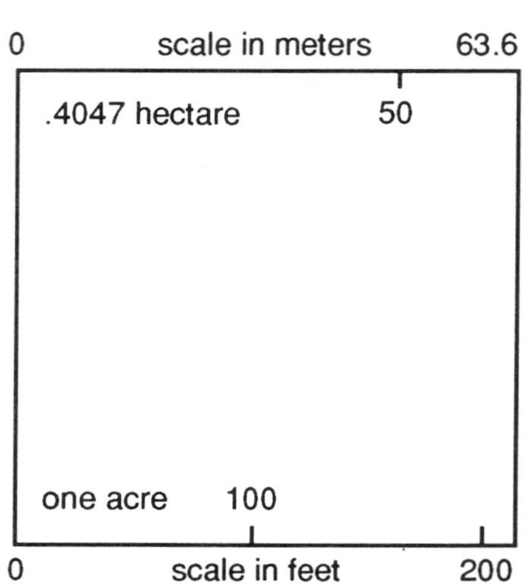

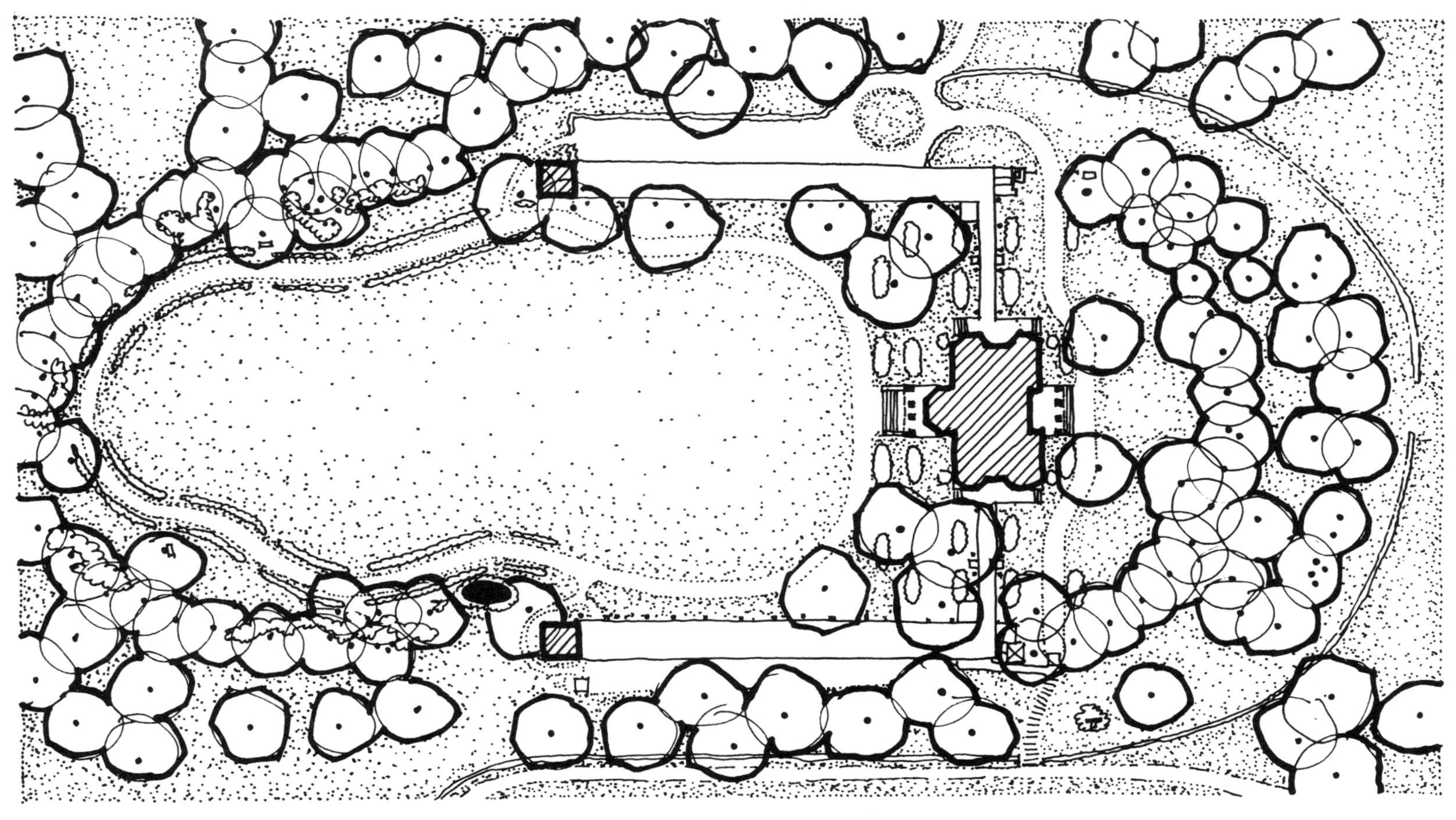

UNION COLLEGE

Location: Schenectady, New York

Dates: 1813 - 1815

Designer: Joseph-Jacques Ramée

Client: President Eliphalet Nott

Area of the campus: 67 acres / 27.1 hectares

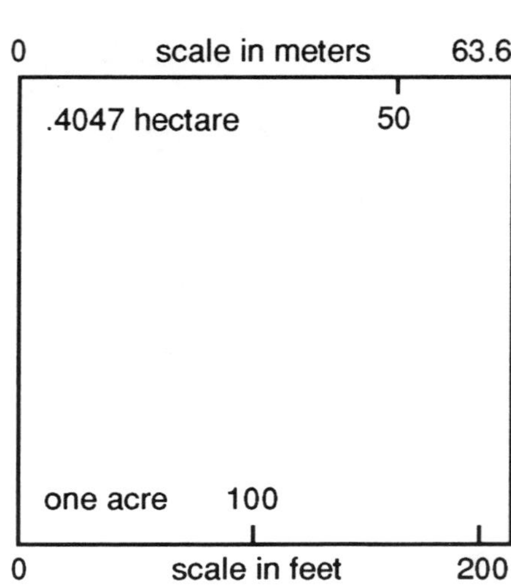

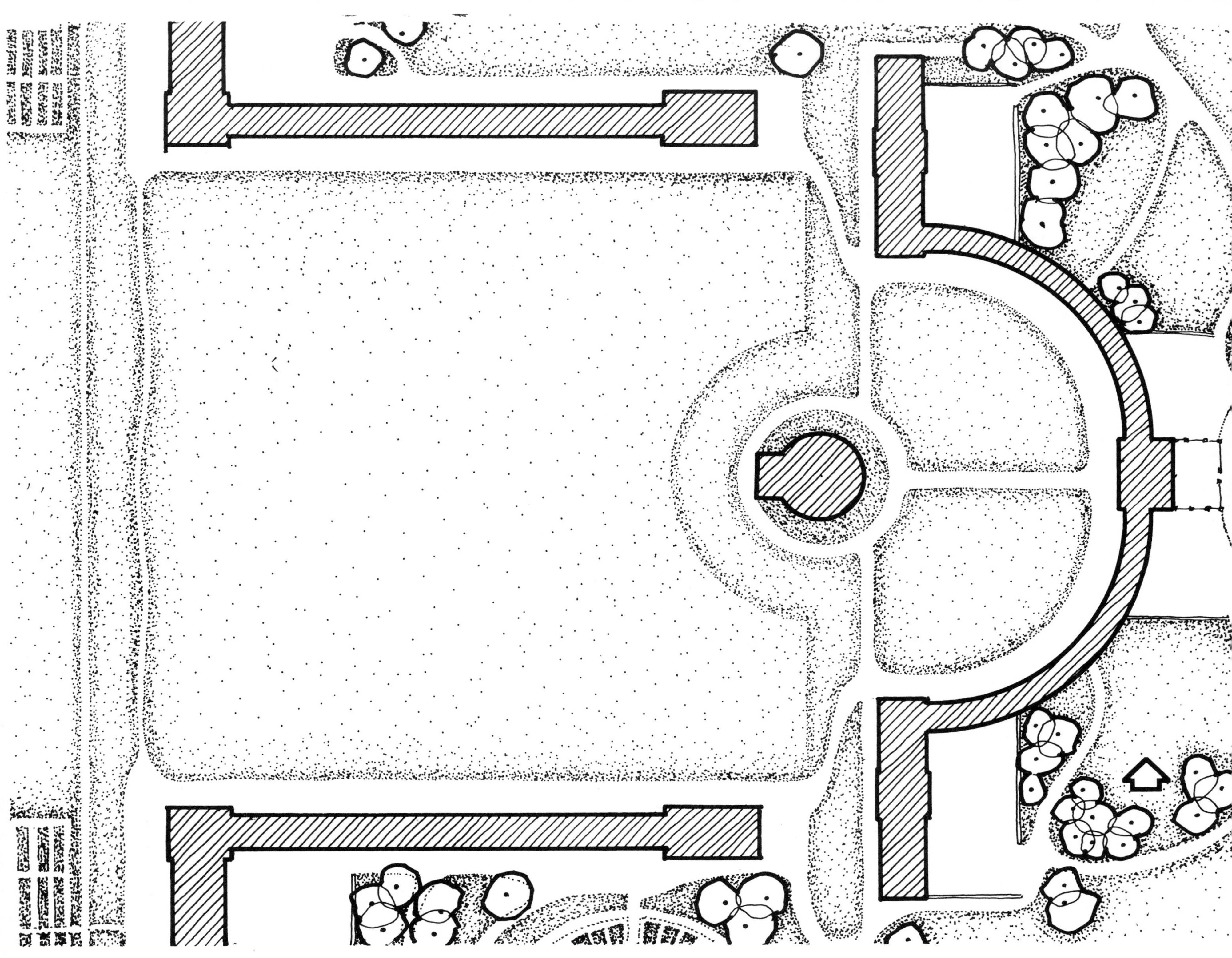

UNIVERSITY OF VIRGINIA

Location: Charlottesville, Virginia

Dates: c.1805 - 1825

Designer: Thomas Jefferson

Client: Board of Visitors, Central College of Virginia

Area of the campus: 14.6 acres / 5.85 hectares

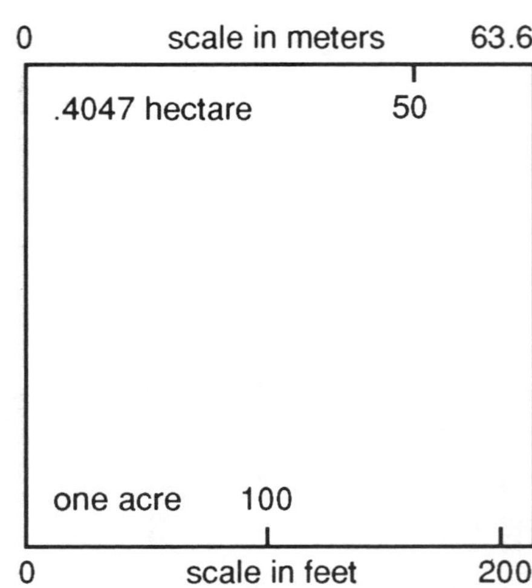

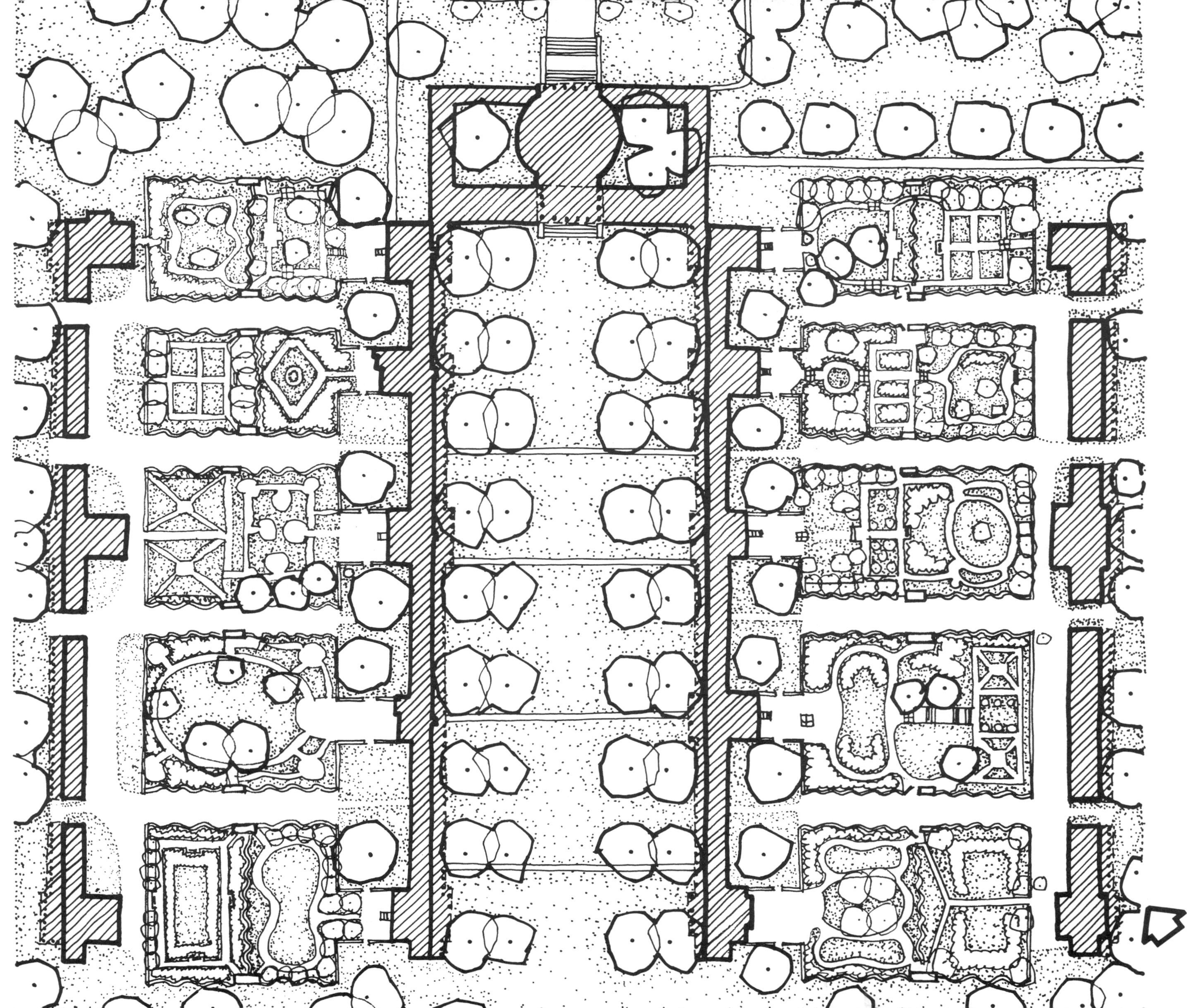

BROOKLYN BOTANIC GARDEN

Location: Brooklyn, New York

Dates: 1824 - 1830

Designer: André Parmentier

Client: André Parmentier

Area: 24 acres / 9.7 hectares

Also known as: Parmentier's Garden

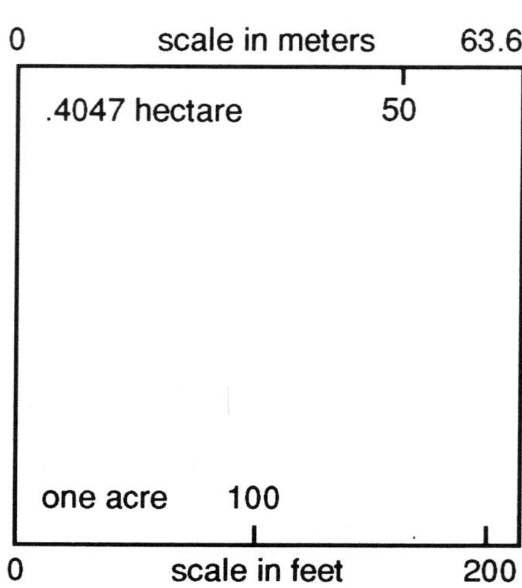

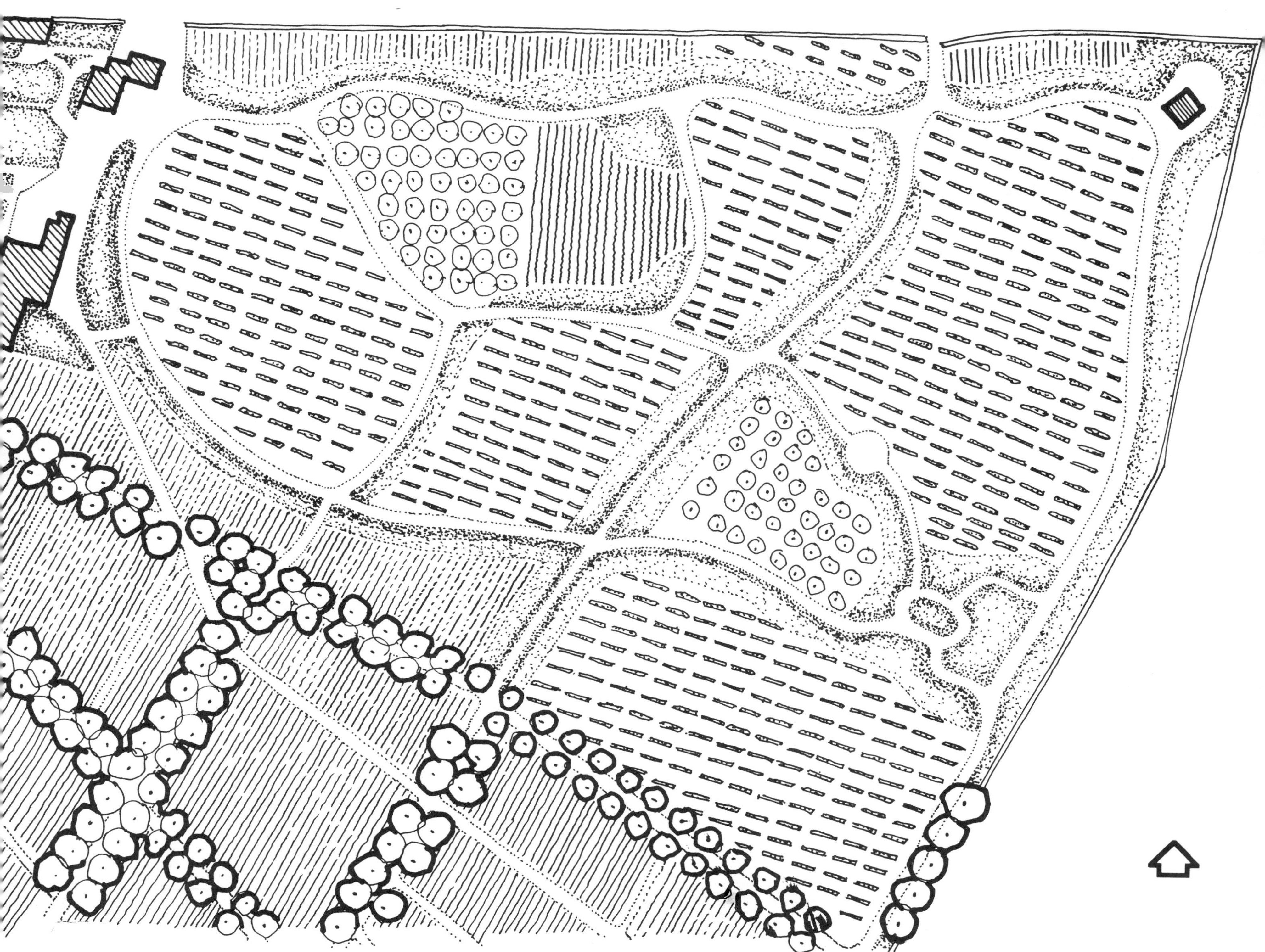

SPRINGSIDE

Location: Poughkeepsie, New York

Dates: 1850 - 1852

Designer: Andrew Jackson Downing

Client: Mathew Vassar

Area: 20 acres / 8.1 hectares

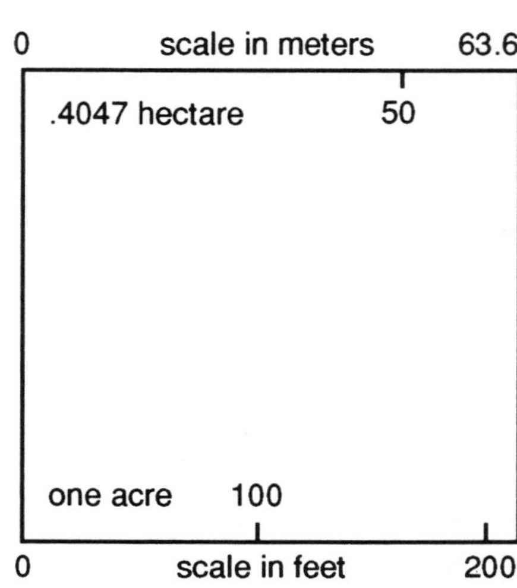

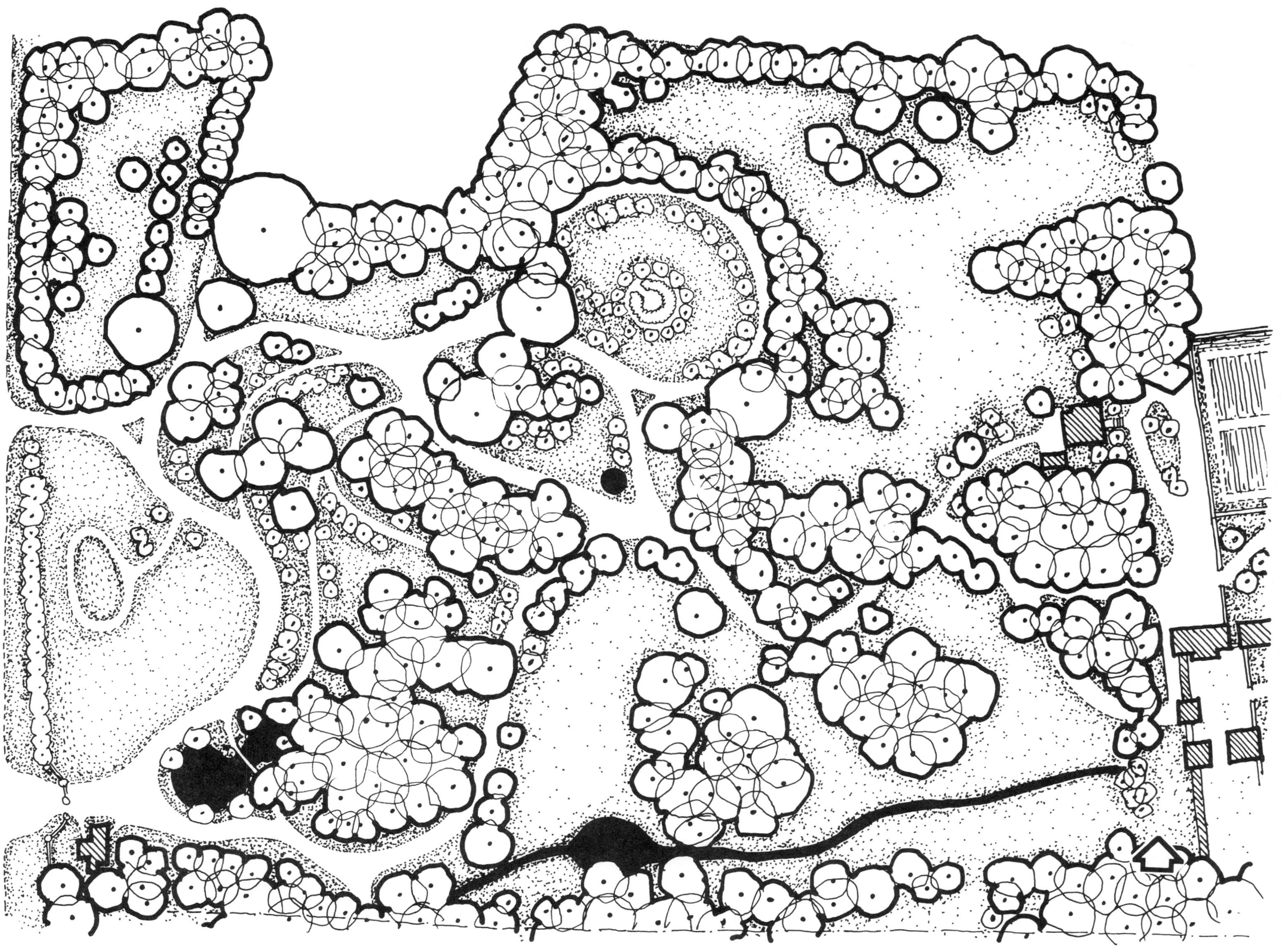

CHARLES A. PLATT RESIDENCE

Location: Cornish, New Hampshire

Dates: 1892-1912

Designer: Charles Adams Platt

Client: Charles Adams Platt

Area: 15 acres / 6 hectares

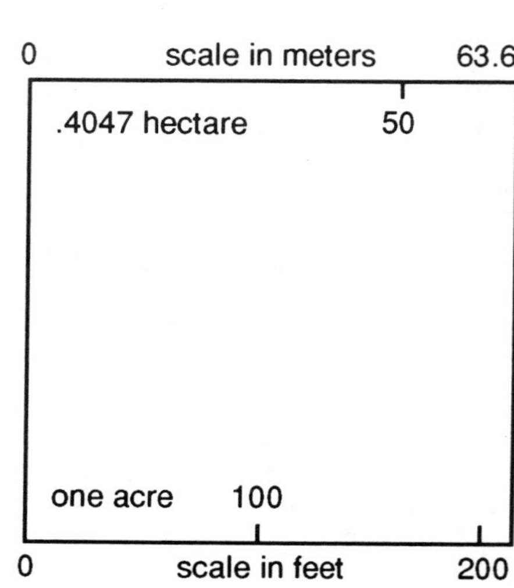

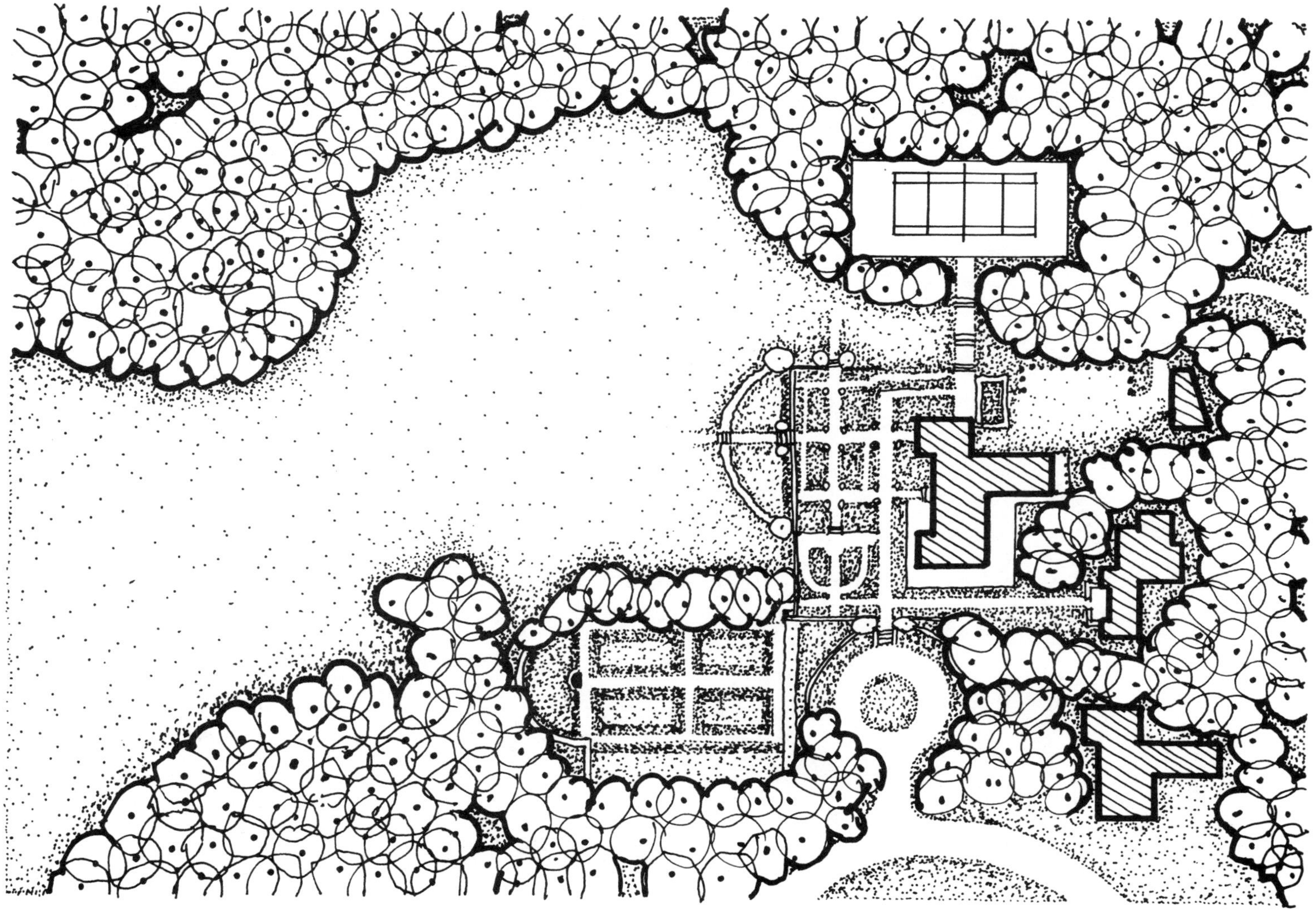

VILLA VIZCAYA

Location: Miami, Florida

Dates: 1914 - 1921

Designers: F. Burrall Hoffman, Paul Chalfin and Diego Suarez

Client: James Deering

Area: 34.59 acres / 14 hectares

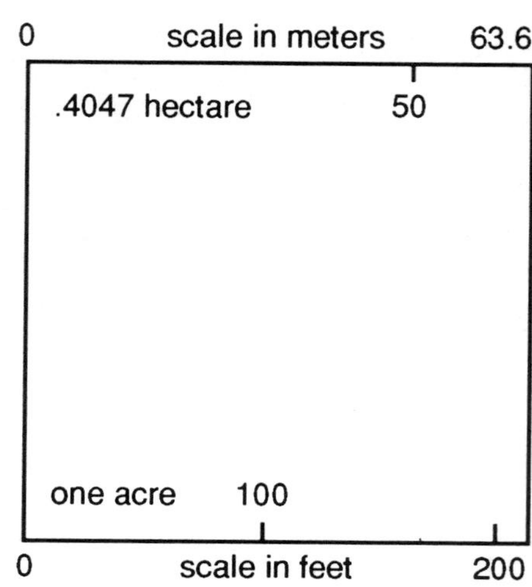

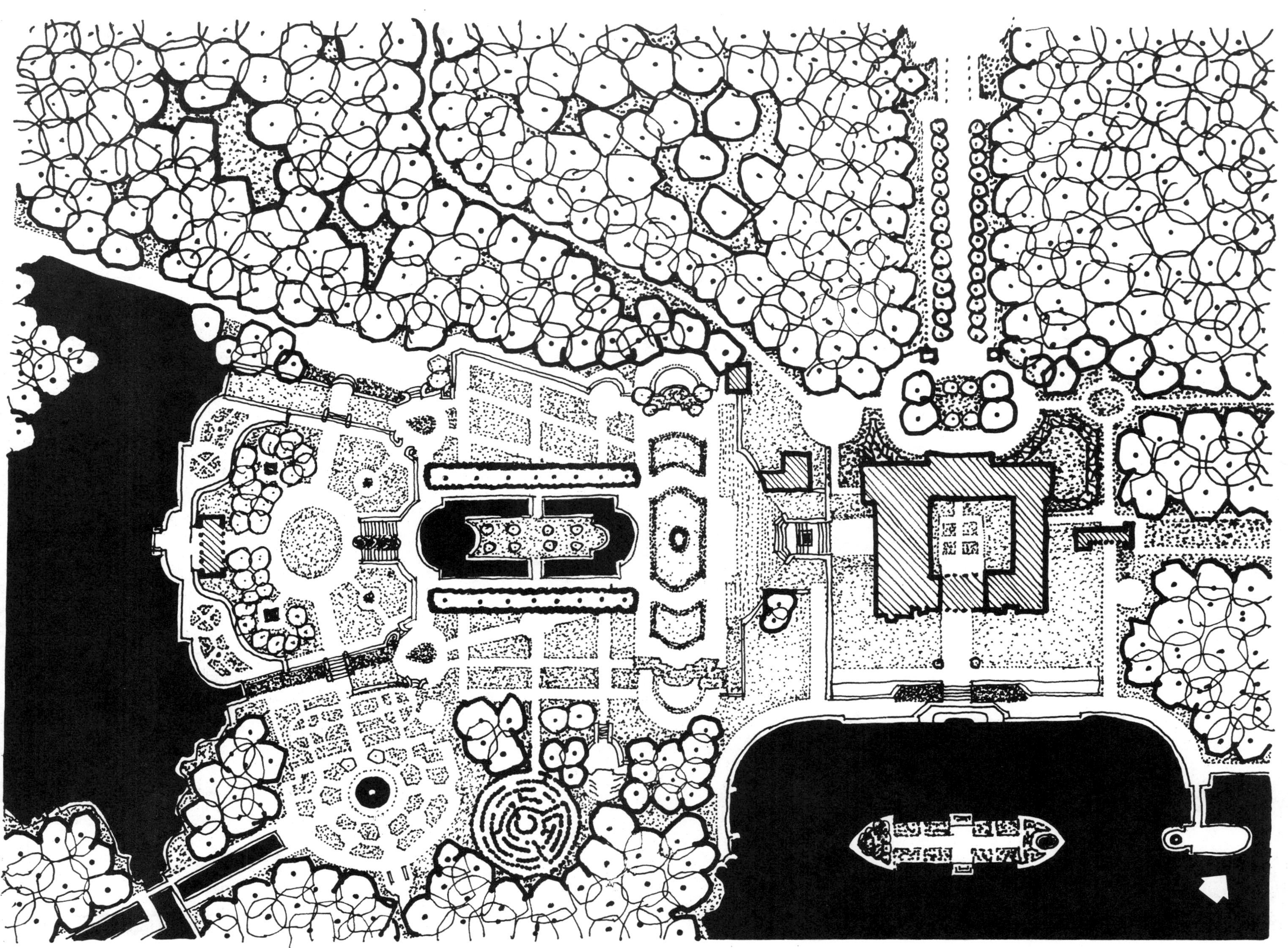

DUMBARTON OAKS

Location: Georgetown, Washington, D. C.

Dates: 1922 - 1947

Designer: Beatrix Jones-Farrand

Client: Mildred and Robert Woods Bliss

Area: 13.6 acres / 5.5 hectares

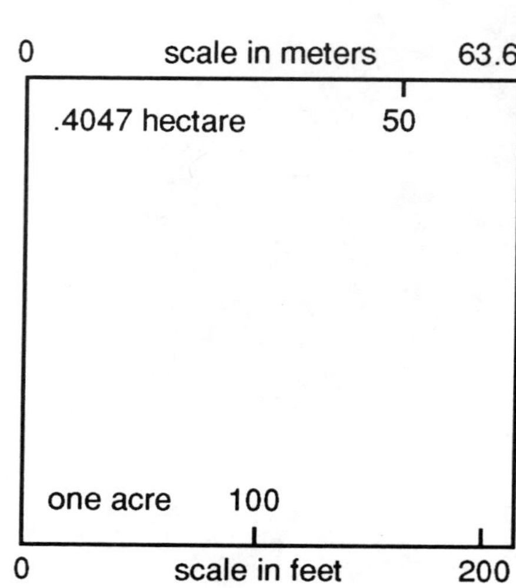

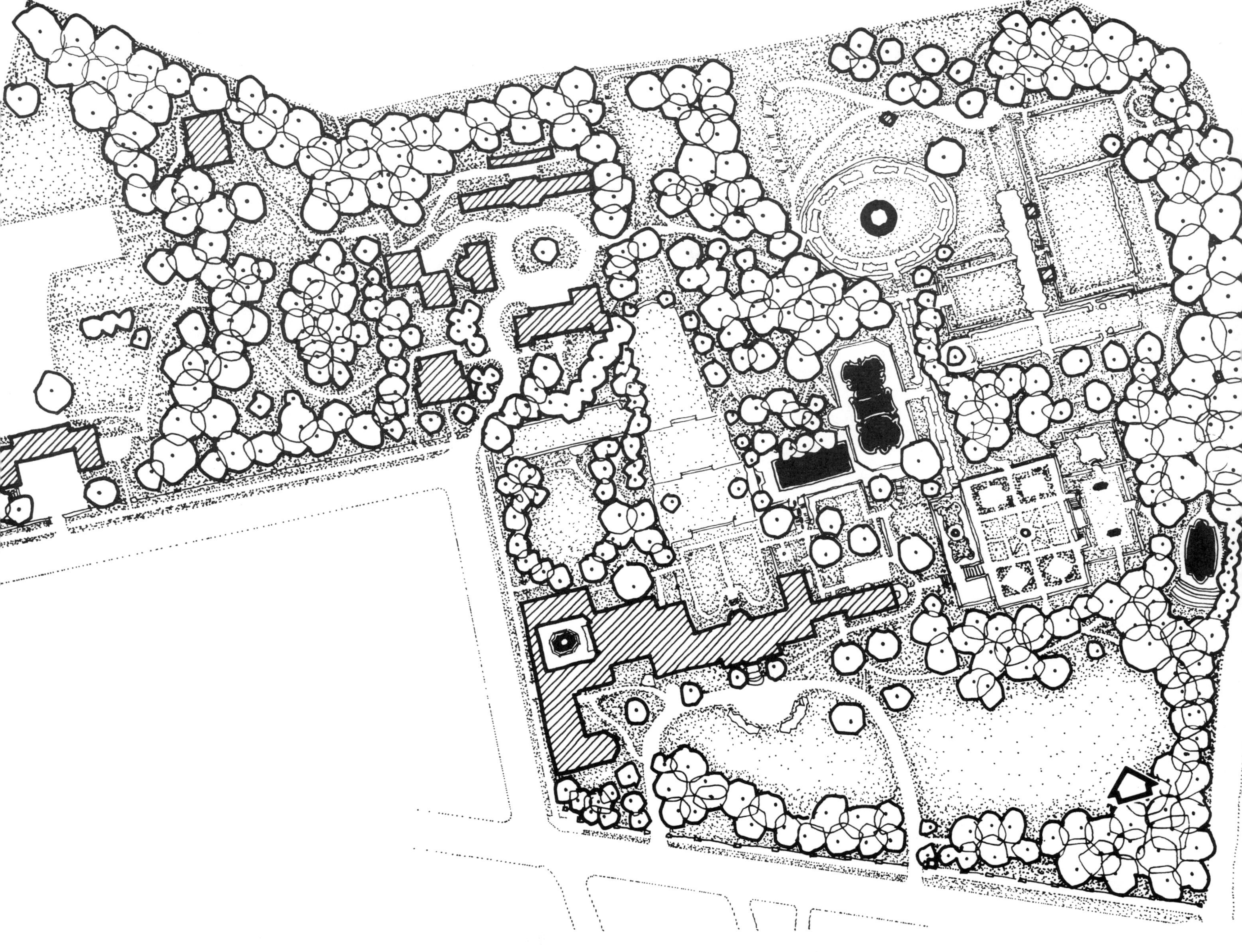

WALLACE W. GILL RESIDENCE

Location: Glencoe, Illinois

Date: 1922

Designer: Jens Jensen

Client: Wallace W. Gill

Area: 2.8 acres / 1.12 hectares

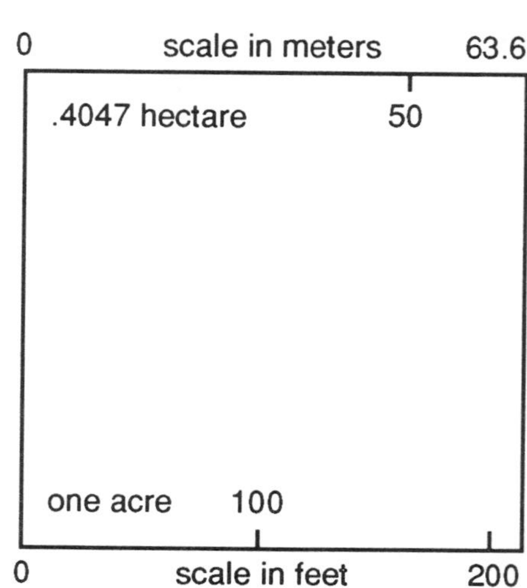

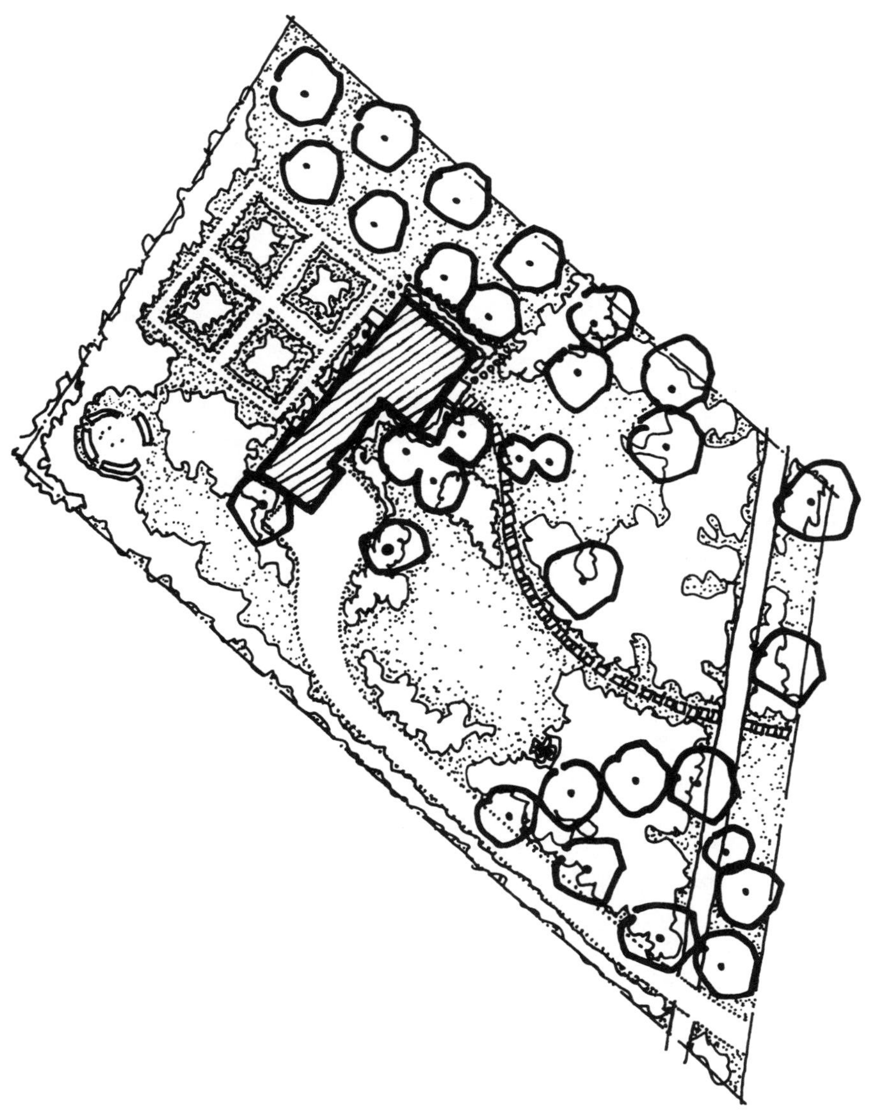

RADBURN GARDEN CITY

Location: Radburn, New Jersey

Dates: 1927 - 1929

Designers: Clarence Stein, Henry Wright and Marjorie Cautley

Client: The Radburn Corporation

Area: 1300 acres / 526.1 hectares

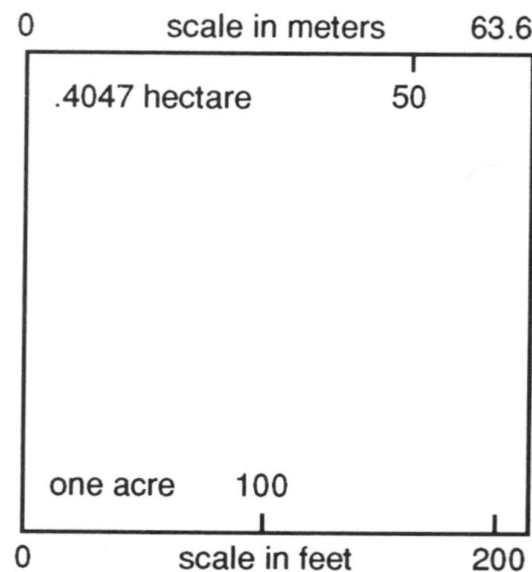

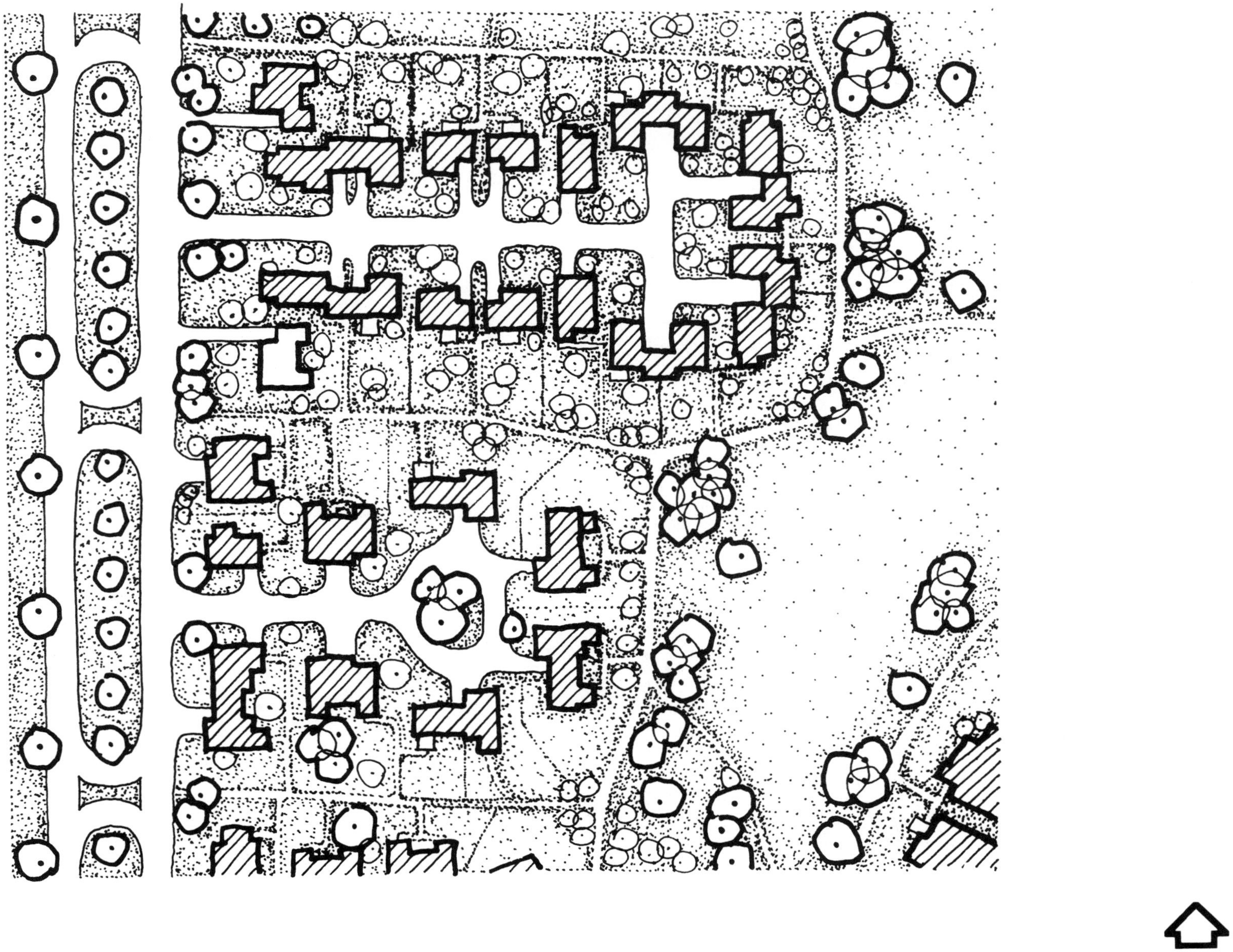

DONNELL RESIDENCE, "EL NOVILLERO"

Location: Sonoma, California

Dates: 1947 - 1948

Designers: Thomas D. Church and Lawrence Halprin

Client: Mr. and Mrs. Dewey Donnell

Area: 5.75 acres / 2.33 hectares

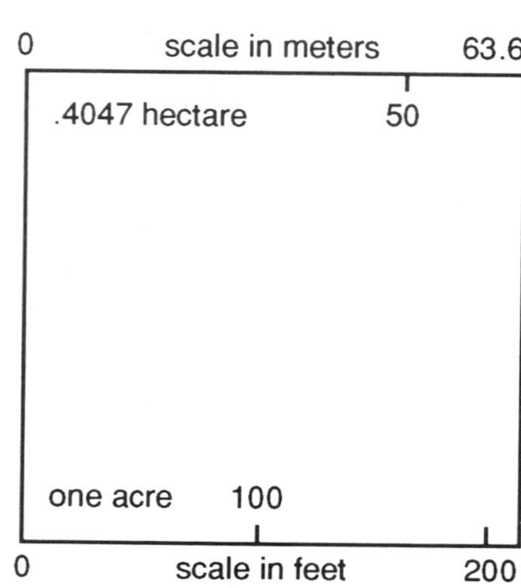

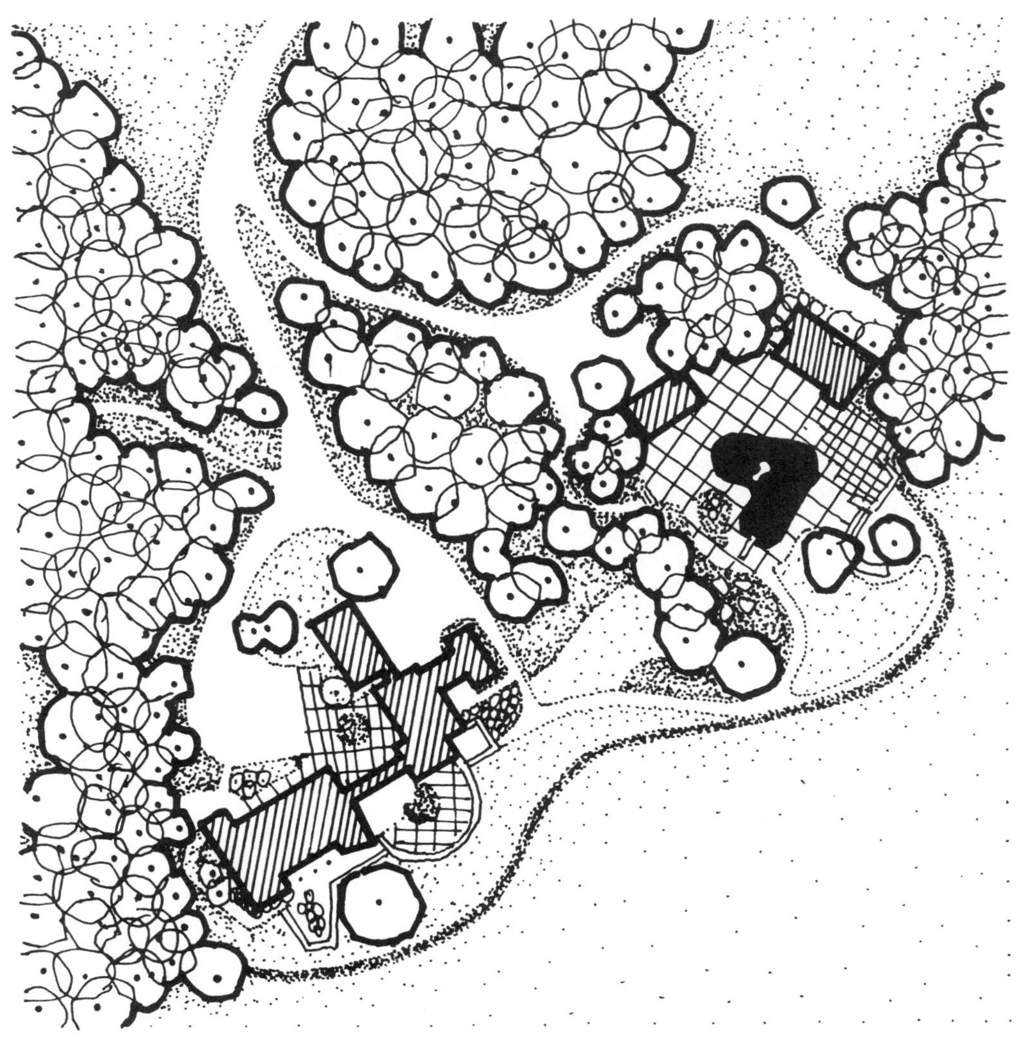

FOOTHILL COLLEGE

Location: Los Altos, California

Date: 1959

Designers: Ernest J. Kump and Mason & Hurd,, Architects
Sasaki, Walker and Associates, Landscape Architects

Client: Foothill College

Area: 122 acres / 49.6 hectares

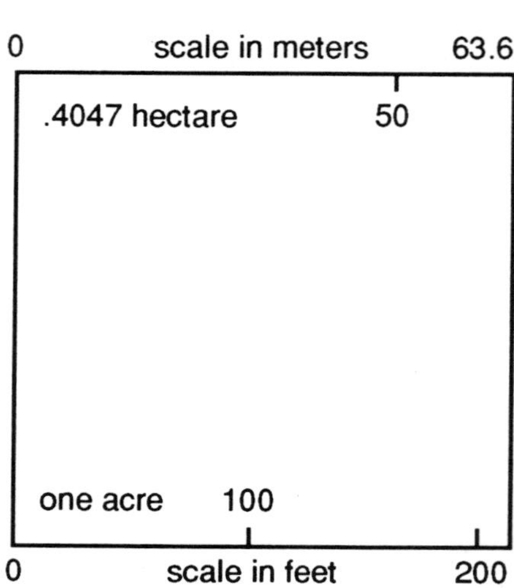

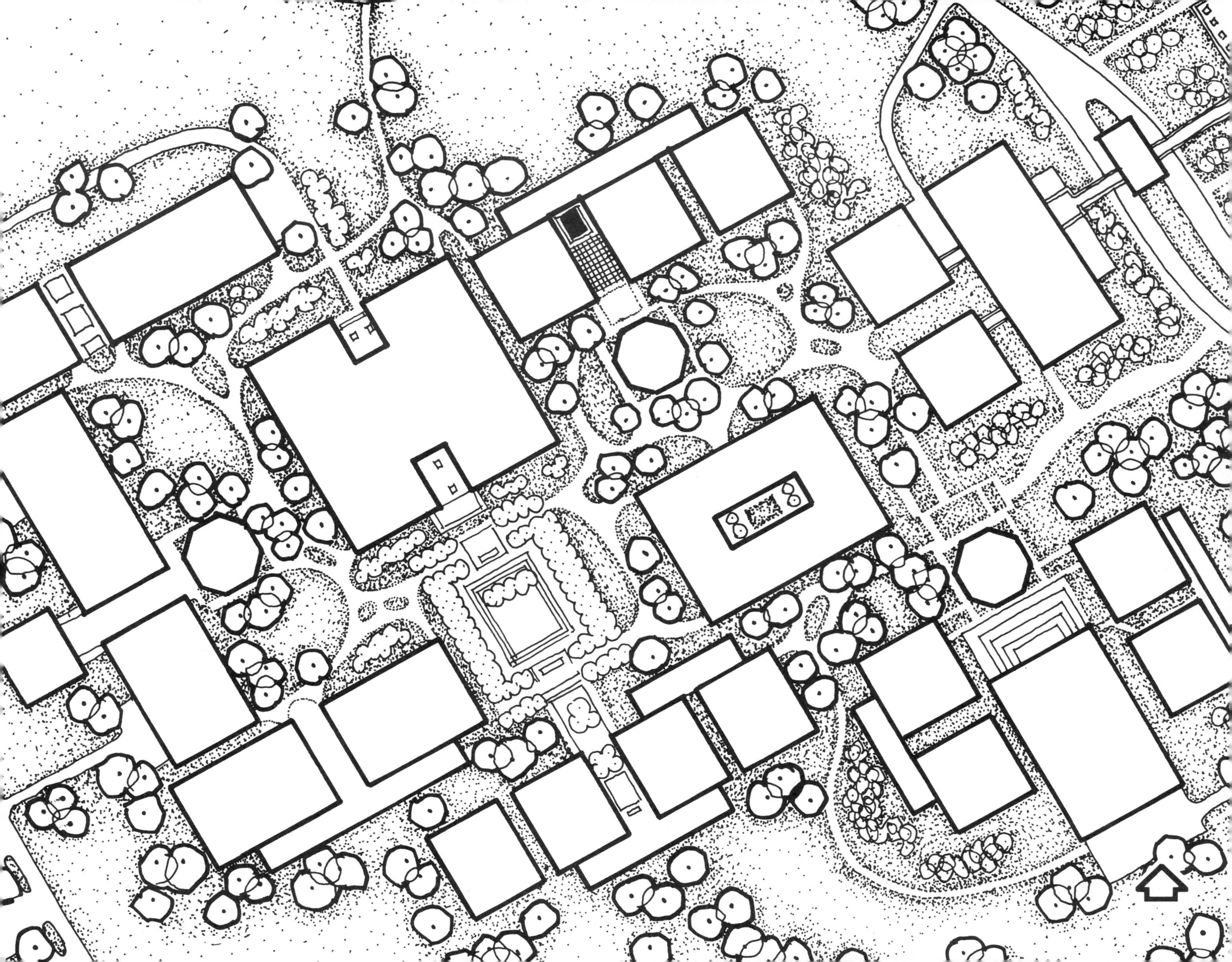

MELLON SQUARE

Location: Pittsburgh, Pennsylvania

Date: 1955

Designer: Simonds and Simonds Assoc., Inc.

Client: The City of Pittsburgh

Area of the plaza: 1.37 acres / .56 hectare

plan at left

OAKLAND MUSEUM

Location: Oakland, California

Dates: 1965 - 1969

Designers: Kevin Roche, John Dinkeloo, architects
Dan Kiley and Associates, landscape architects

Client: The City of Oakland

Area: 3.3 acres / 1.33 hectares

plan at right

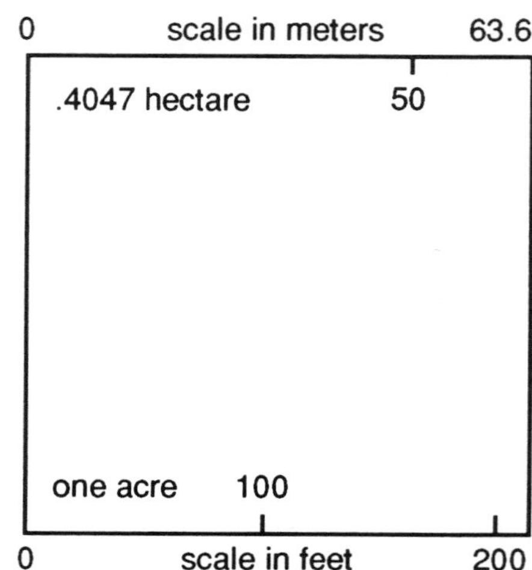

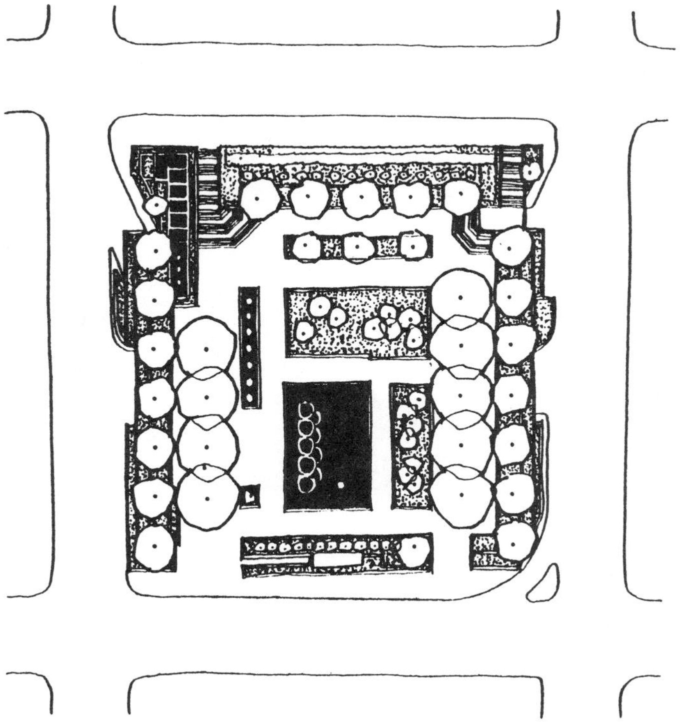

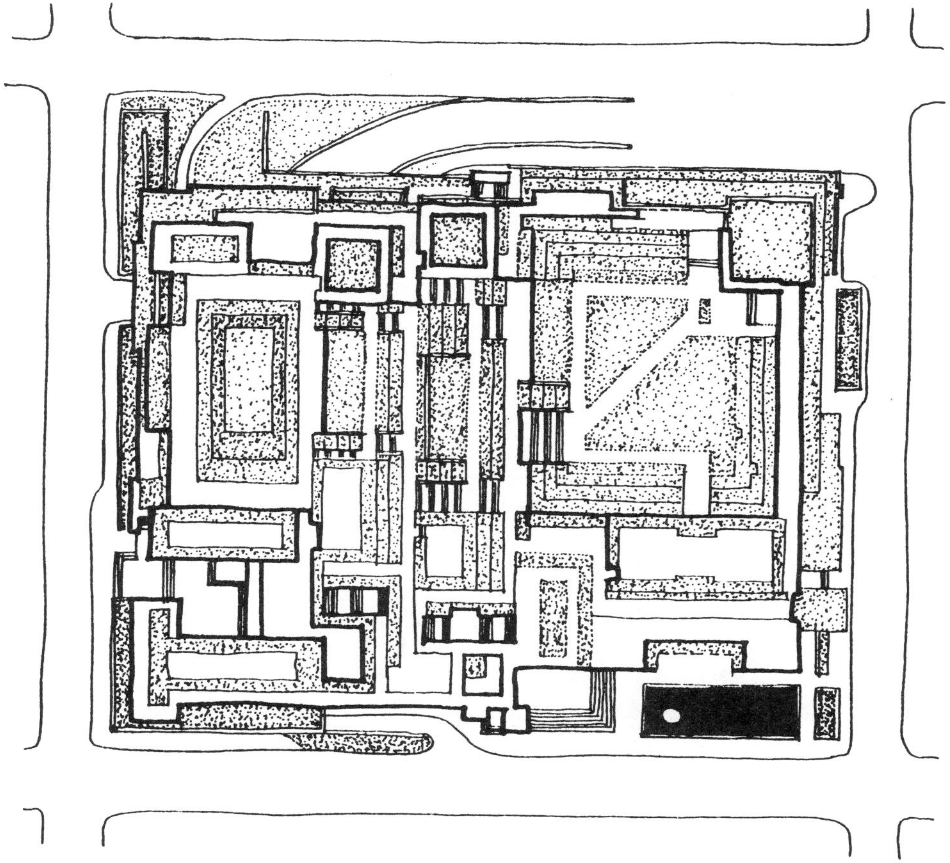

CONSTITUTION PLAZA

Location: Hartford, Connecticut

Dates: 1959 - 1963

Designer: Sasaki, Dawson, DeMay, Assoc., Inc.

Client: Broadcast Plaza, Inc.

Area of the plazas: 3.8 acres / 1.54 hectares

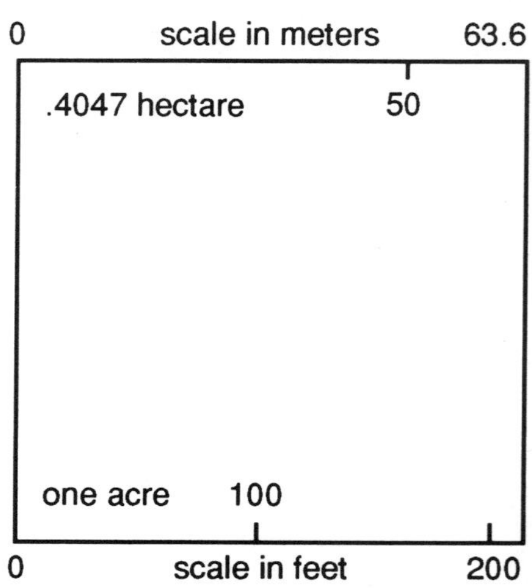

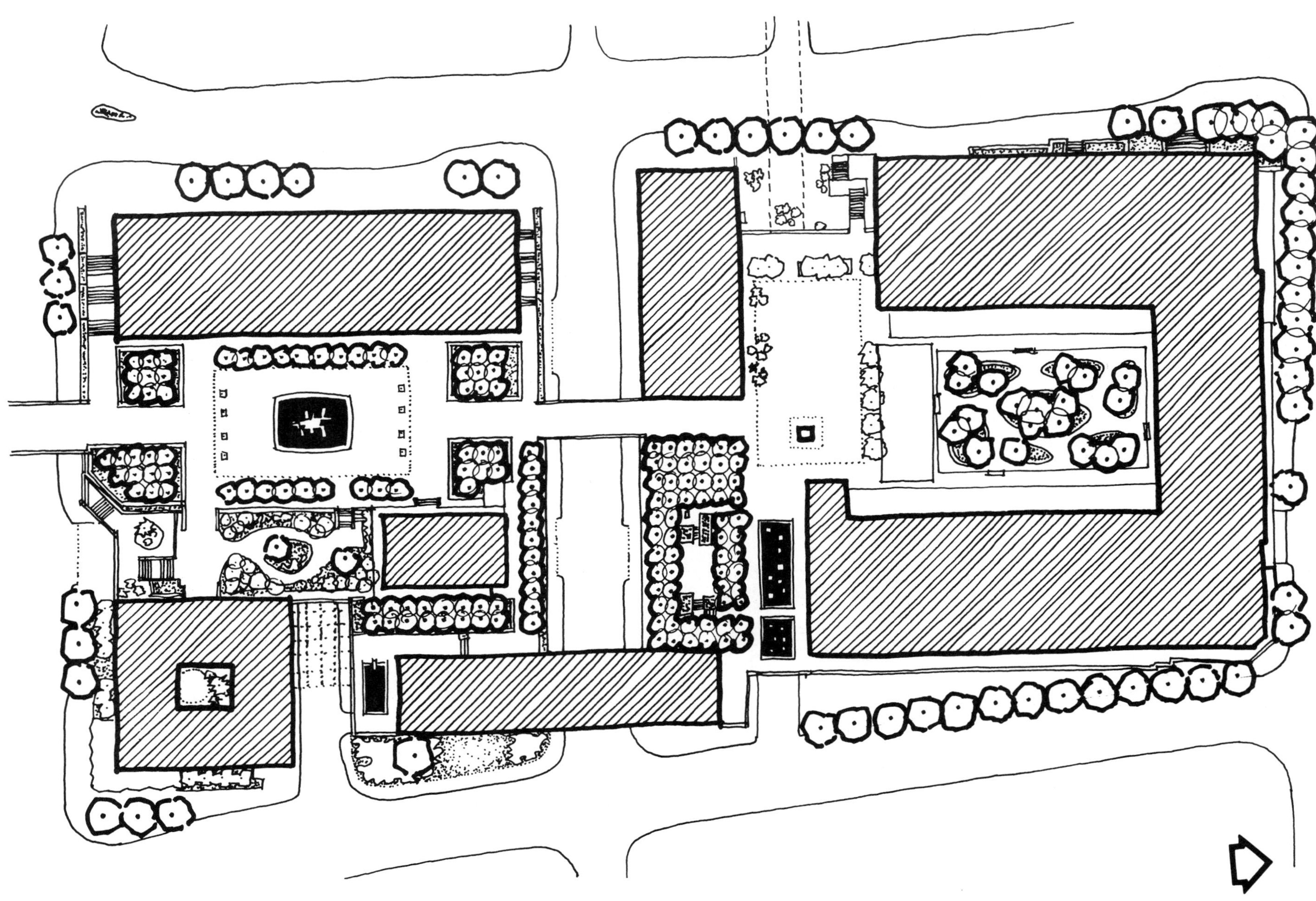

JACOB RIIS PLAZA

Location: New York, New York

Date: 1964-1966

Designer: M. Paul Fiedberg and Assoc., Inc.

Client: New York City Housing Authority

Area of the plaza: 2.8 acres / 1.13 hectares

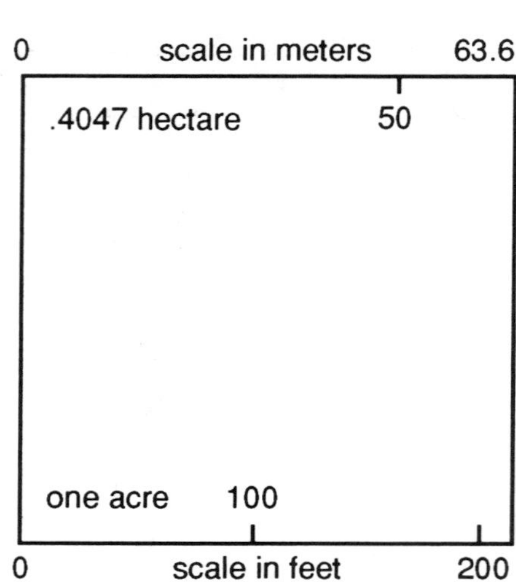

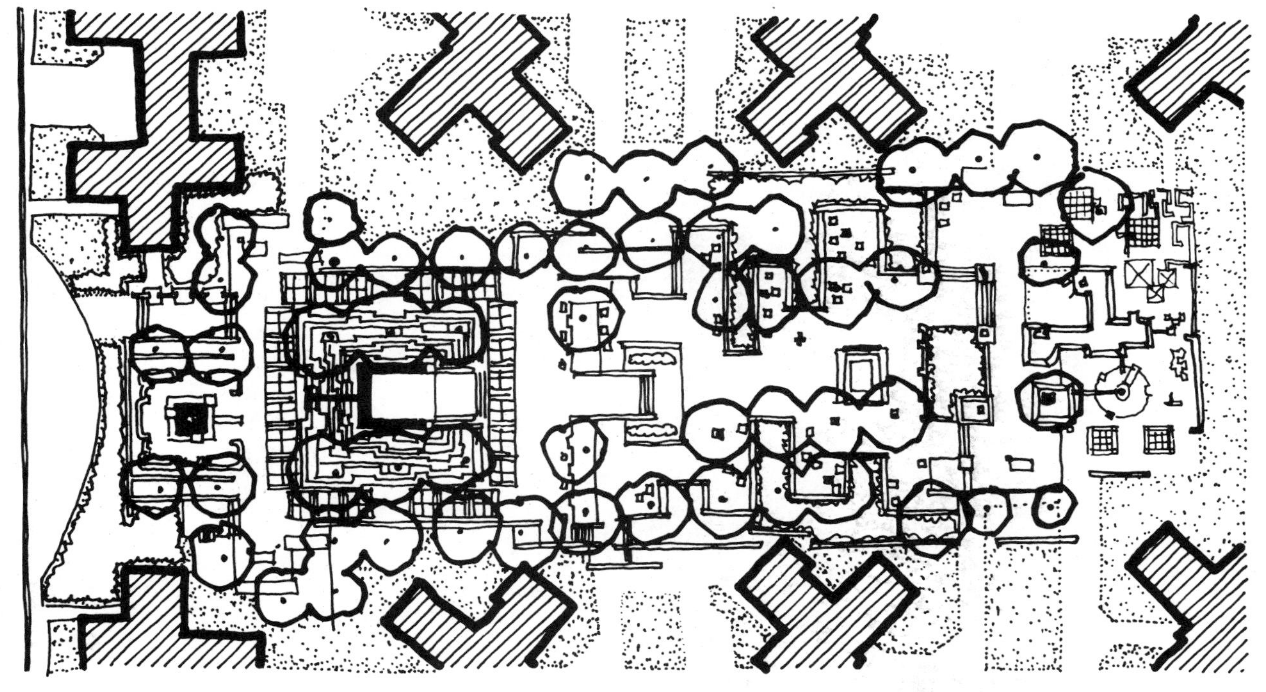

COPLEY SQUARE

Location: Boston, Massachusetts

Dates: 1966 - 1968

Designers: Sasaki, Dawson, DeMay, Assoc., Inc.

Client: The Boston Redevelopment Authority

Area: 3.66 acres / 1.48 hectares

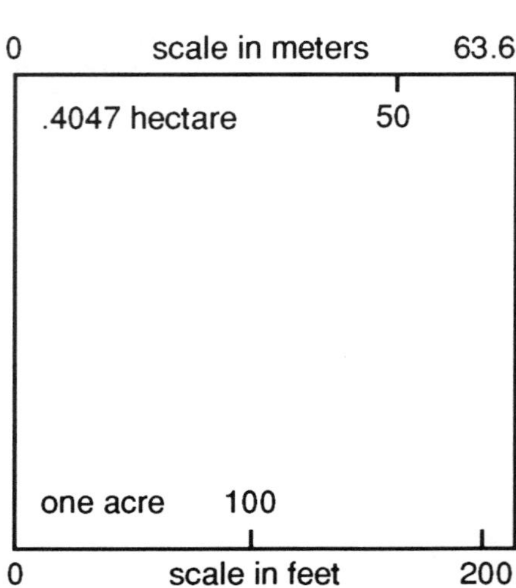

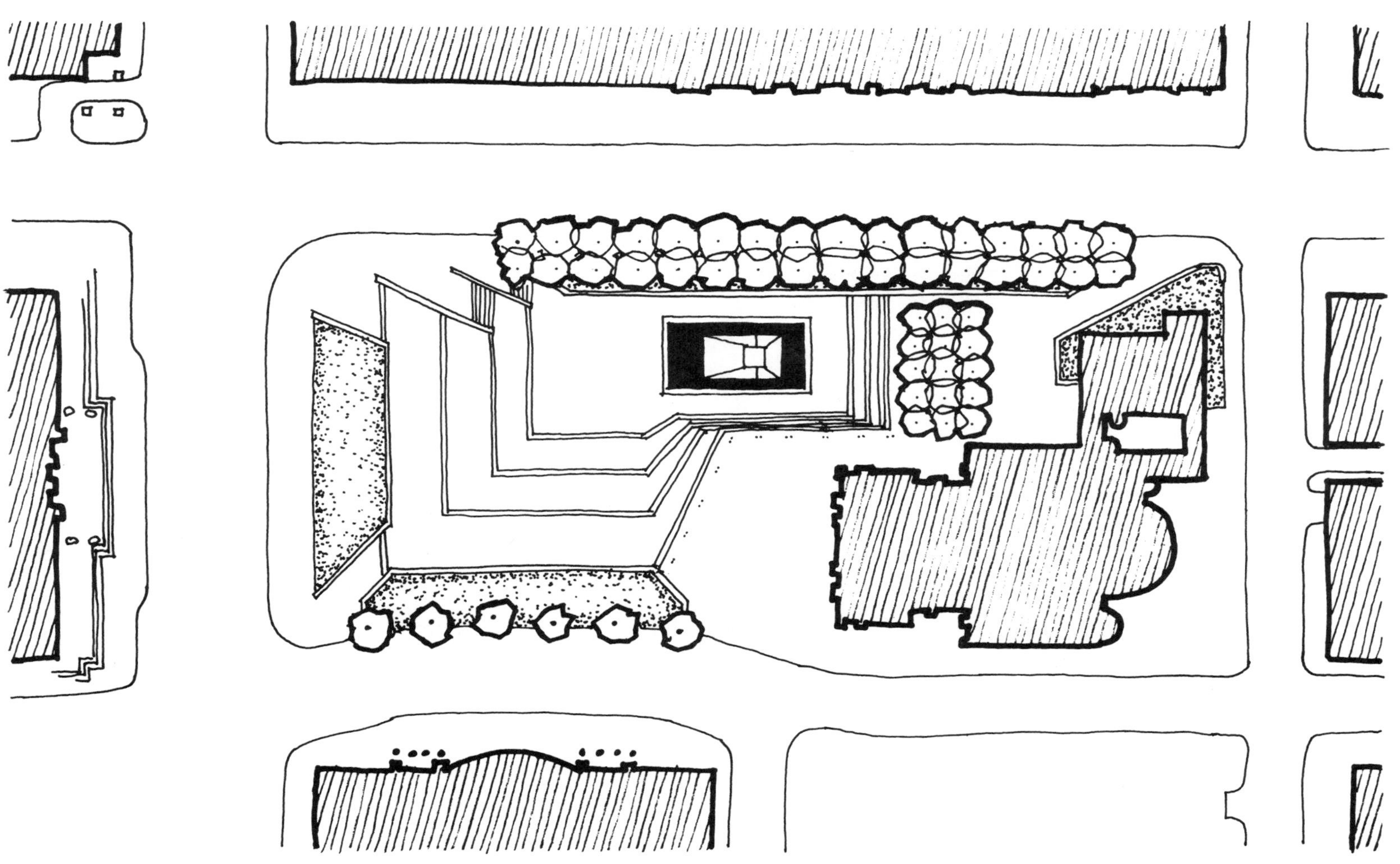

COPLEY SQUARE

Location: Boston, Massachusetts

Date: redesigned in 1984

Designers: Dean Abbott of Clarke & Rapuano, Inc.

Client: The Boston Redevelopment Authority

Area: 3.66 acres / 1.48 hectares

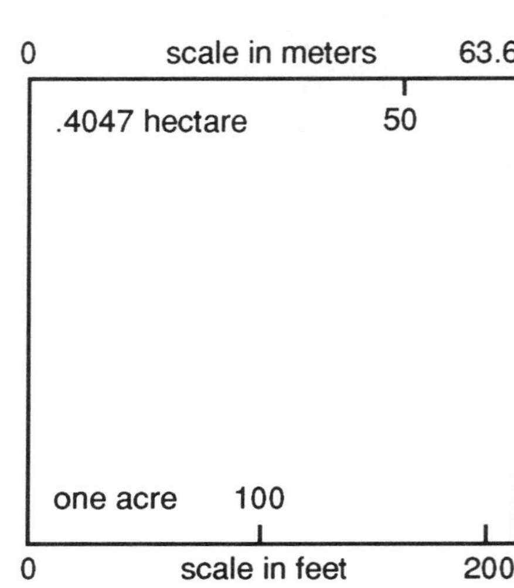

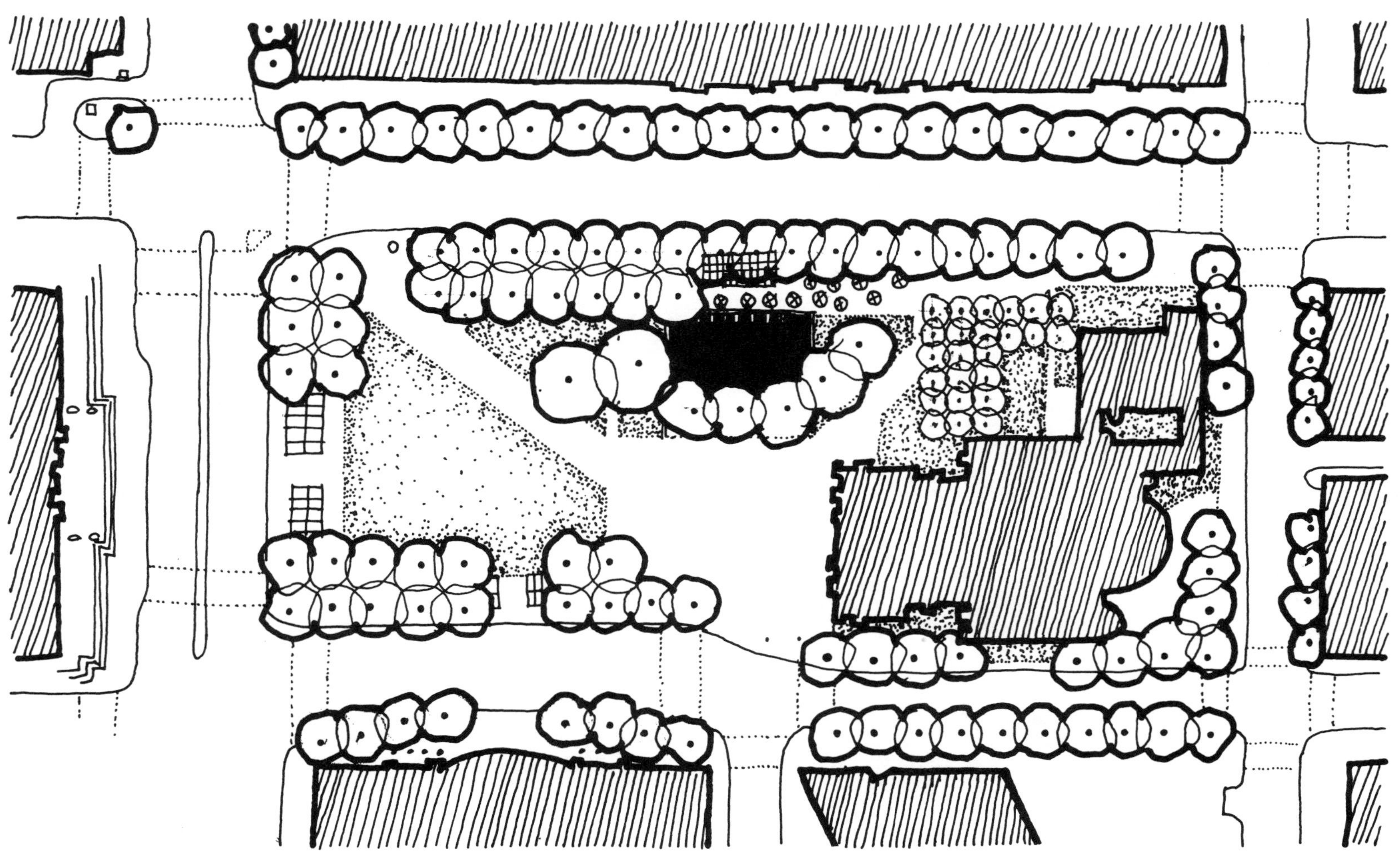

LOVEJOY PLAZA

Location: Portland, Oregon

Dates: 1965 - 1966

Designers: Lawrence Halprin and Associates, Inc.

Client: The City of Portland

Area of the plaza: 1.89 acres / .77 hectare

plan at left

IRA KELLER FOUNTAIN

Location: Portland, Oregon

Dates: 1965 - 1970

Designers: Lawrence Halprin and Associates, Inc.

Client: The City of Portland

Area of the plaza: 1.27 acres / .51 hectare

plan at right

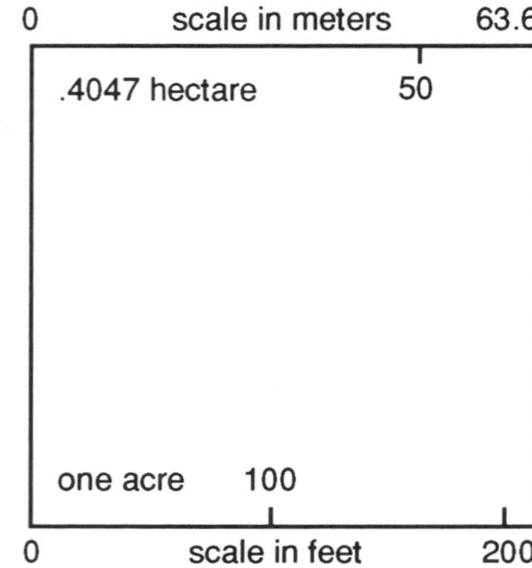

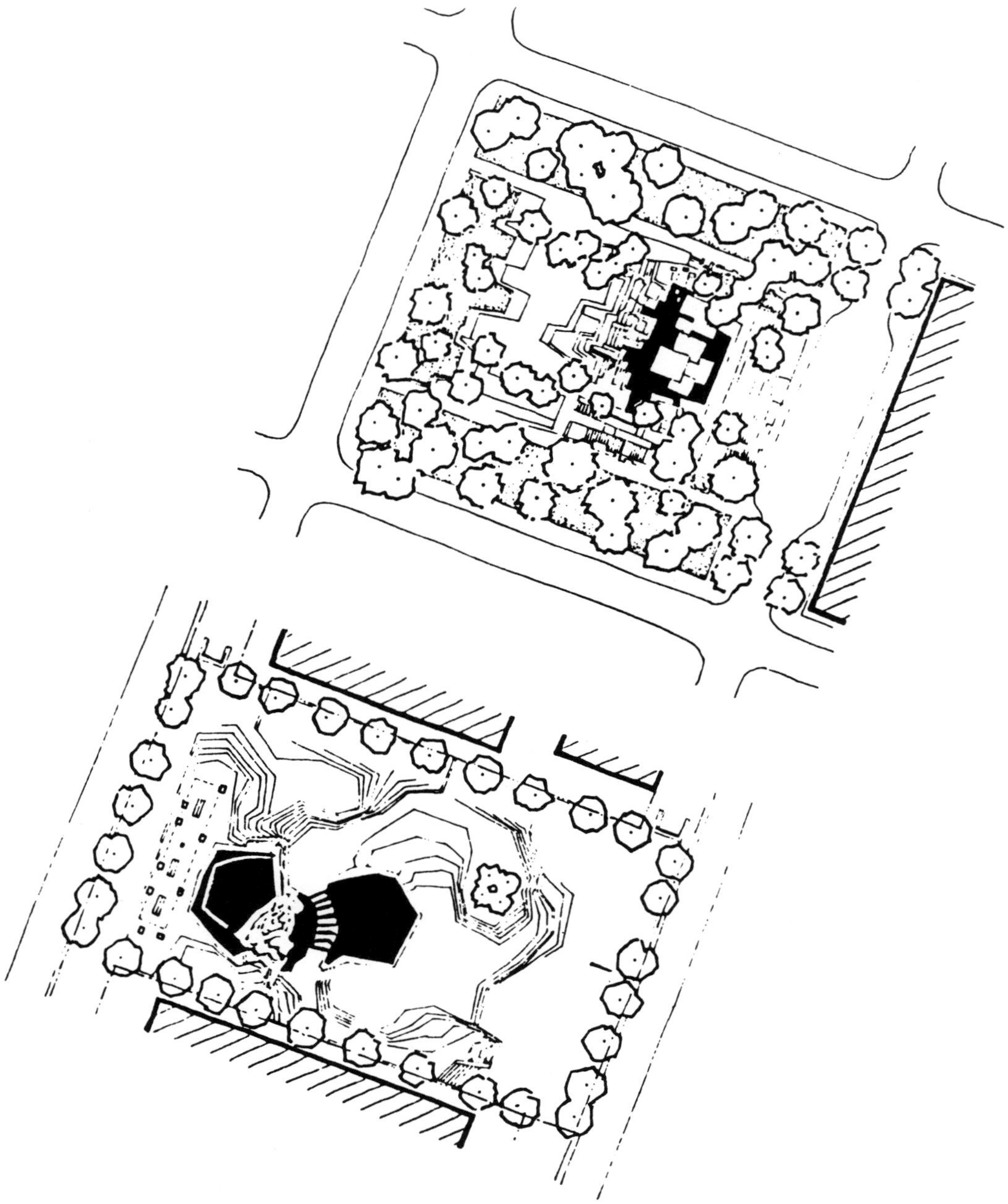

PALEY PARK

Location: New York, New York

Dates: 1966 -1967

Designers: Zion and Breen Associates, Inc.

Client: WilliamSamuel Paley

Area: 42 x 100 feet / .096 acre
12.8 x 3..48 meters / .039 hectare

plan at left

PIAZZA D'ITALIA

Location: New Orleans, Louisiana

Date: 1975

Designer: Charles W. Moore, architect

Client: The City of New Orleans

Area of the plaza: .42 acre / .17 hectare

plan at right

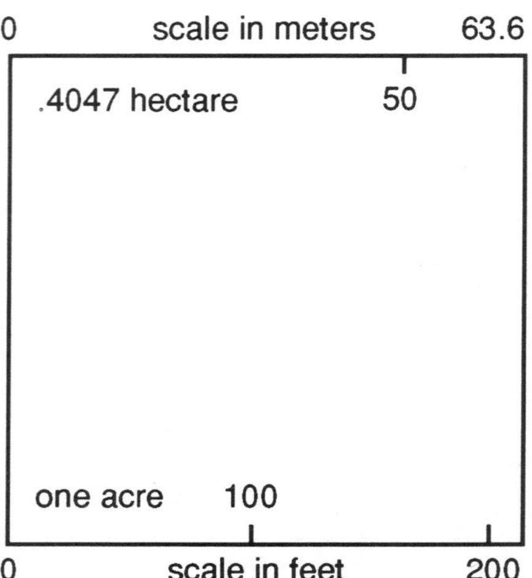

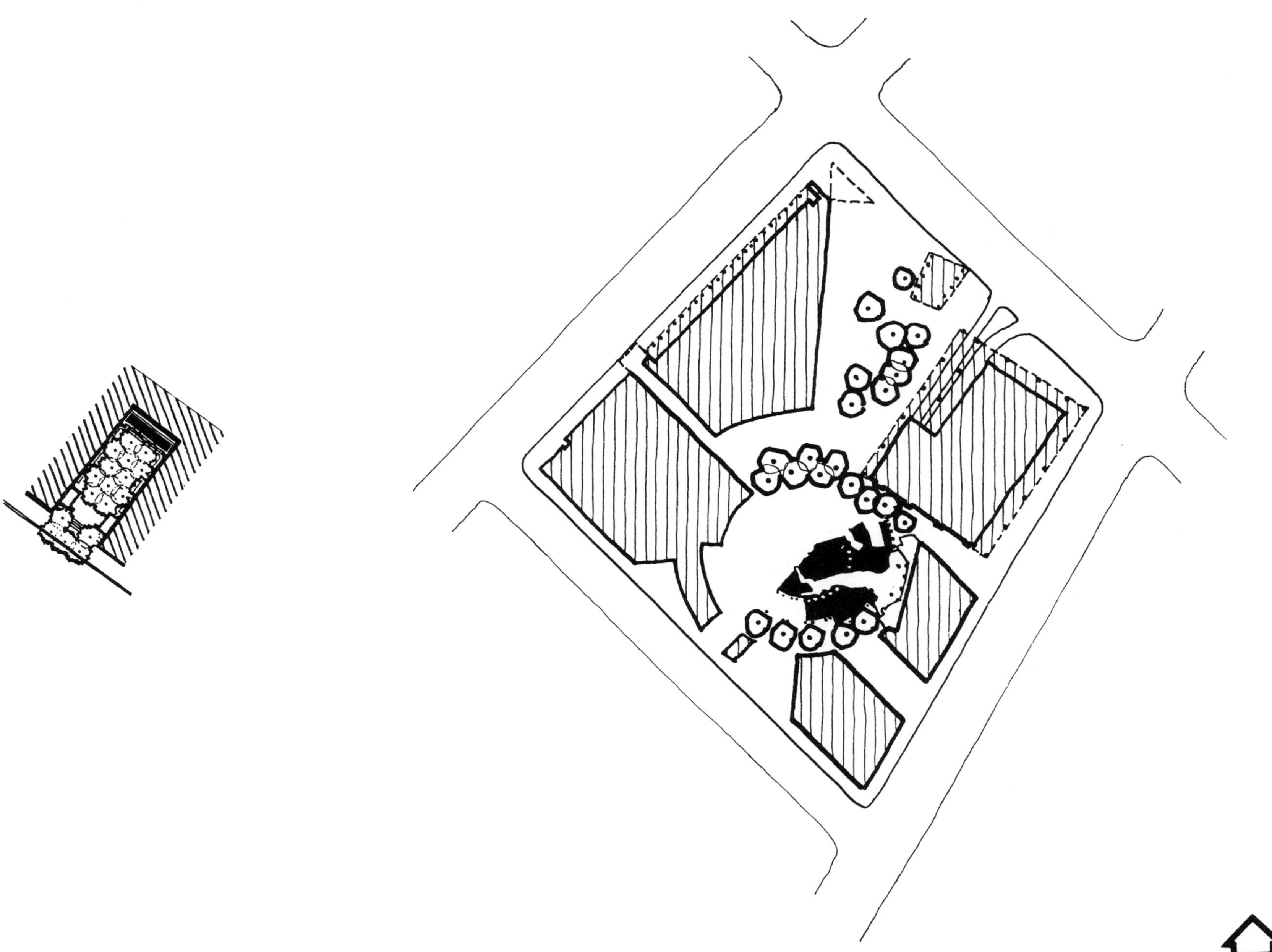

GAS WORKS PARK

Location: Seattle, Washington

Dates: 1970 - 1975

Designer: Richard Haag and Associates, Inc.

Client: The City of Seattle

Area: 20.5 acres / 8.3 hectares

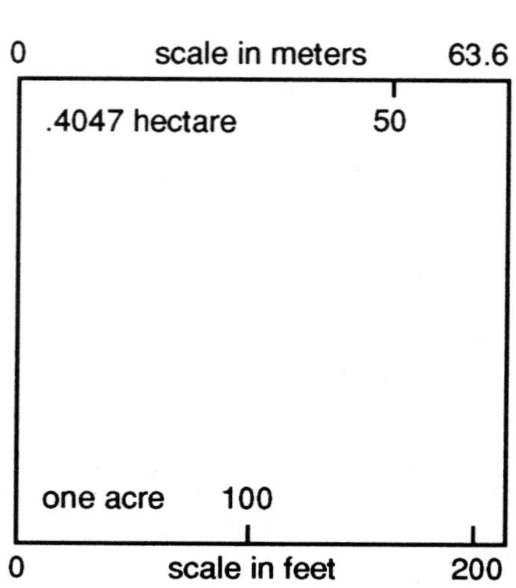

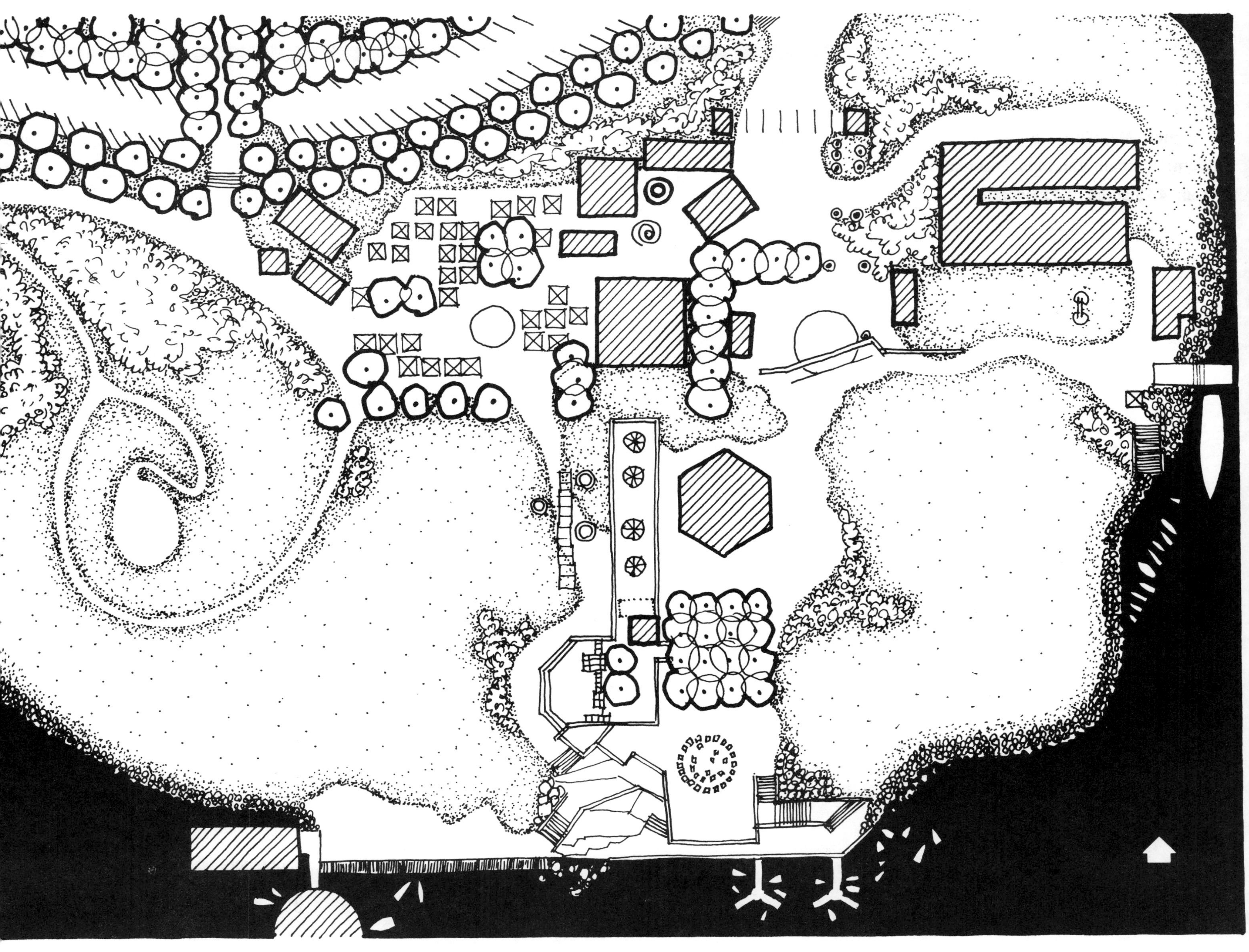

VIETNAM VETERANS MEMORIAL

Location: Washington, D. C.

Dates: 1981 - 1985

Designer: May Ying Lin

Client: Vietnam Veterans' Foundation

Area: 4.25 acres / 1.72 hectares

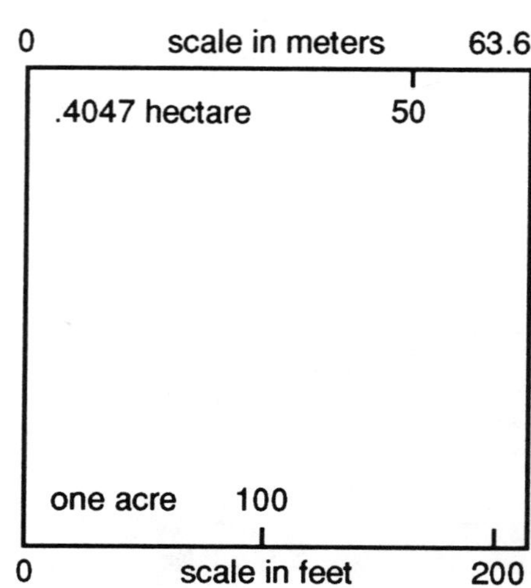

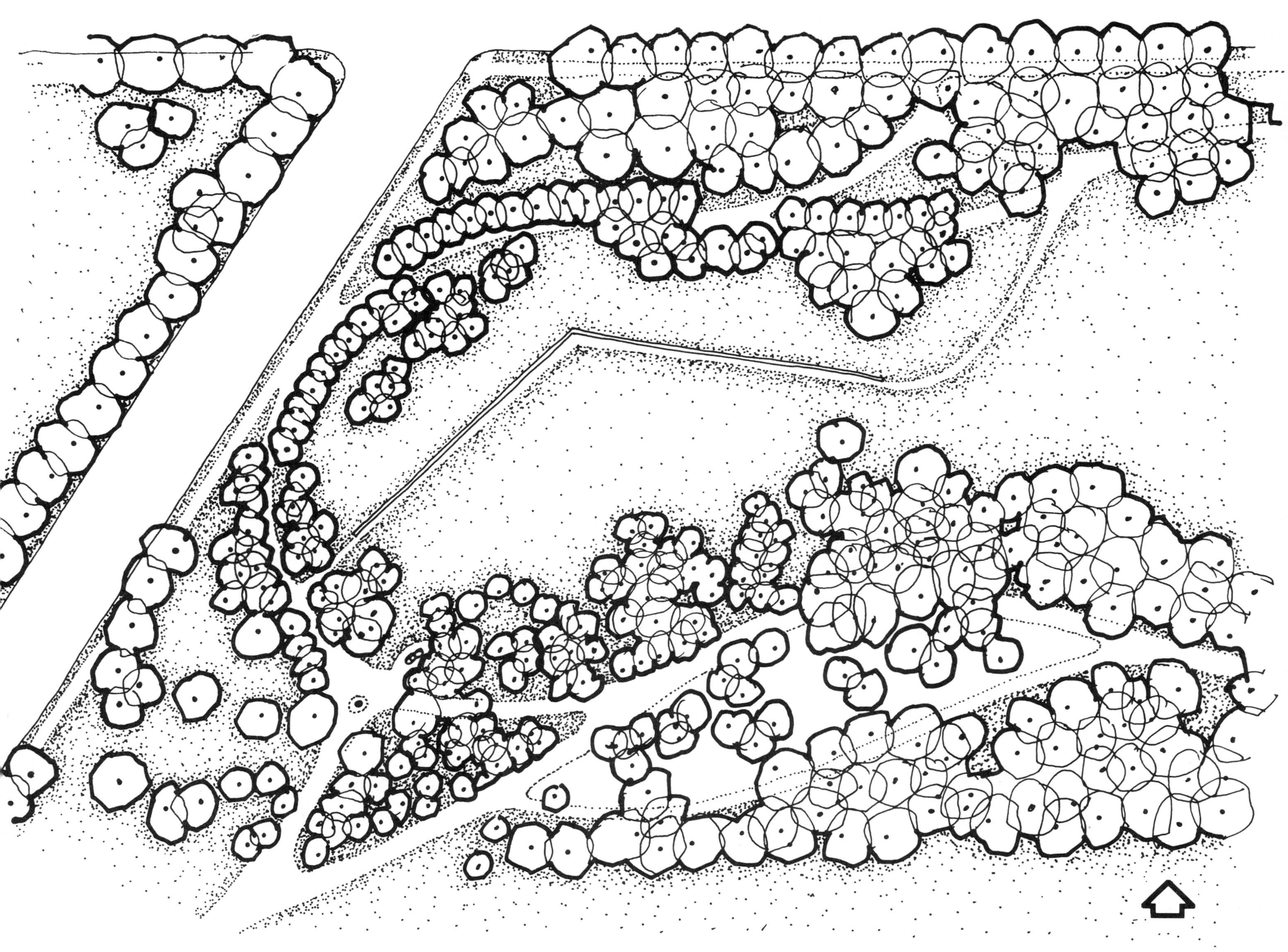

WILLIAMS SQUARE

Location: Las Colinas, Irving, Texas

Dates: 1983 - 1985

Designers: The SWA Group, Landscape Architects
Robert Glen, Sculptor

Client: Las Colinas Corporation

Area of the plaza: 1.89 acres / .77 hectare

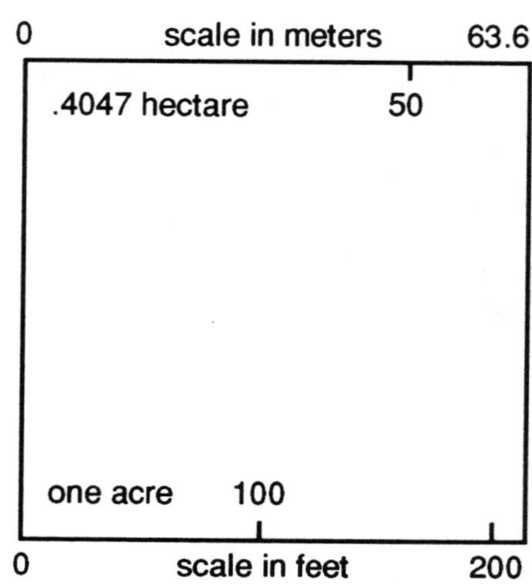

1 : 24,000 SCALE

THE PYRAMID GROUP

Location: Gizeh (Giza), Egypt

Dates: c. 2723 - 2563 BC

Designers: unknown

Clients: Kings Cheops (Khufu),
Chephren (Khafra),
Mykerinos (Menkaura)

Area of the plan: 595 acres / 241 hectares

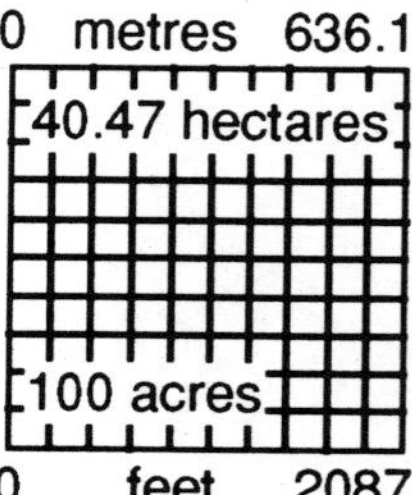

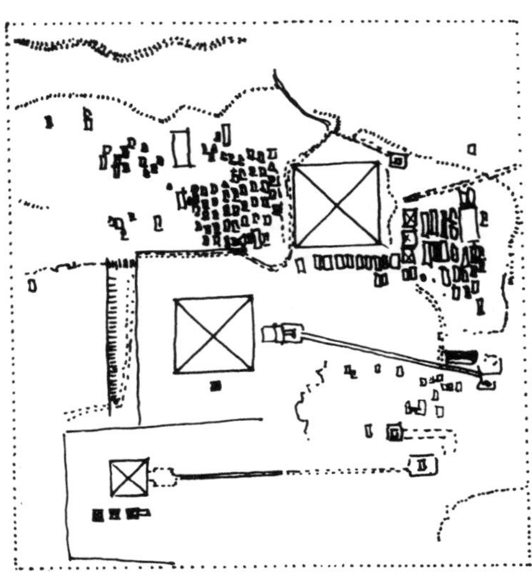

POMPEII

Location: Pompeii, Italy

Dates: founded c. 700 BC
occcupied by Greeks c. 500 BC
occupied by Etruscans c. 450 BC
occupied by Romans c. 80 BC
destroyed by earthquake in 62 AD
rebuilt and destroyed by vulcanic eruption of Mount Vesuvius in 79 AD

Designers: various and unknown

Clients: Romans, at time of vulcanic eruption

Area of the walled town: 110 acres / 44.6 hectares

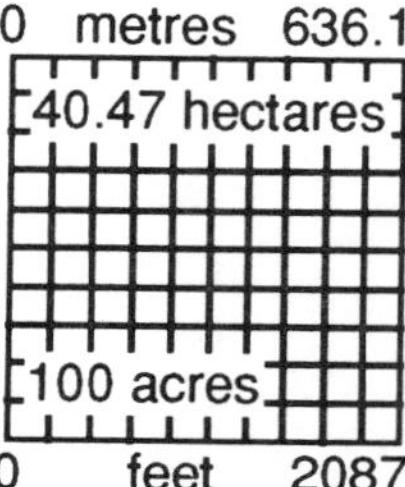

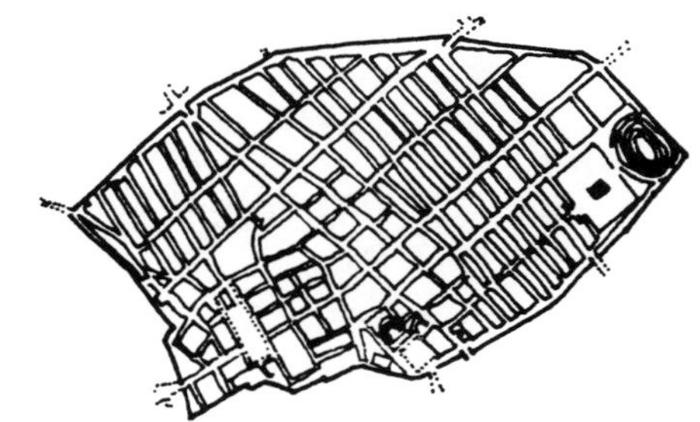

VAUX-LE-VICOMTE

Location: Melun, France

Dates: 1656 - 1661

Designers: Louis Le Vau II, Charles Le Brun and André Le Nôtre

Client: Nicolas Fouquet

Area: 887 acres / 359 hectares

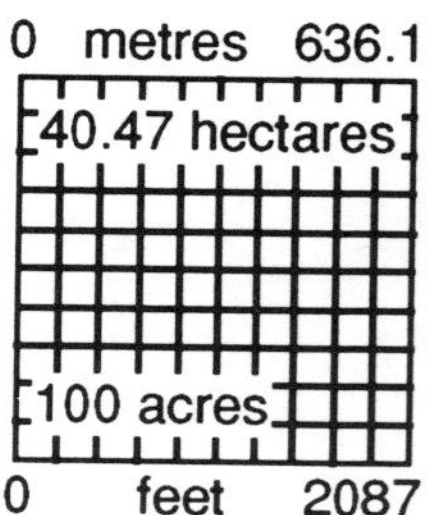

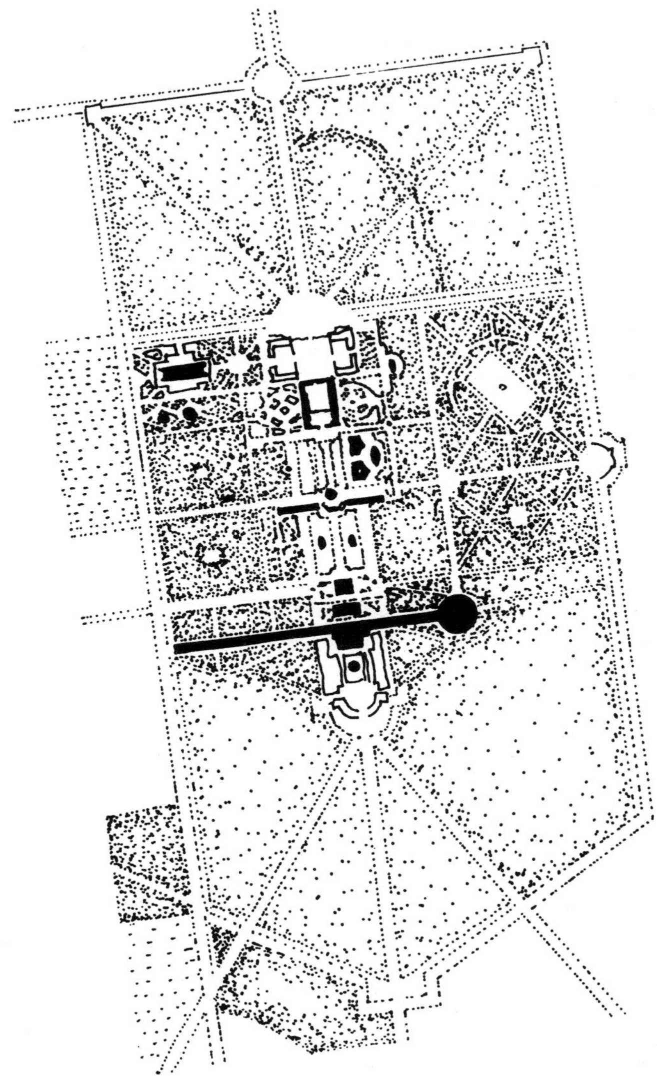

VERSAILLES

Location: Versailles, France

Dates: 1661 - 1680s

Designers: Louis Le Vau II, Charles Le Brun and André Le Nôtre

Client: Louis XIV, *Le Roi Soleil*, "the Sun King"

Area: 2985 acres / 1208 hectares

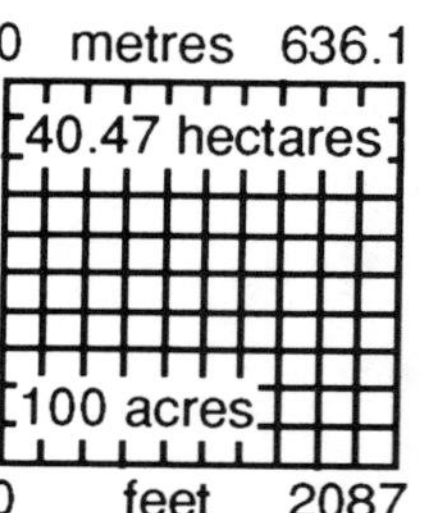

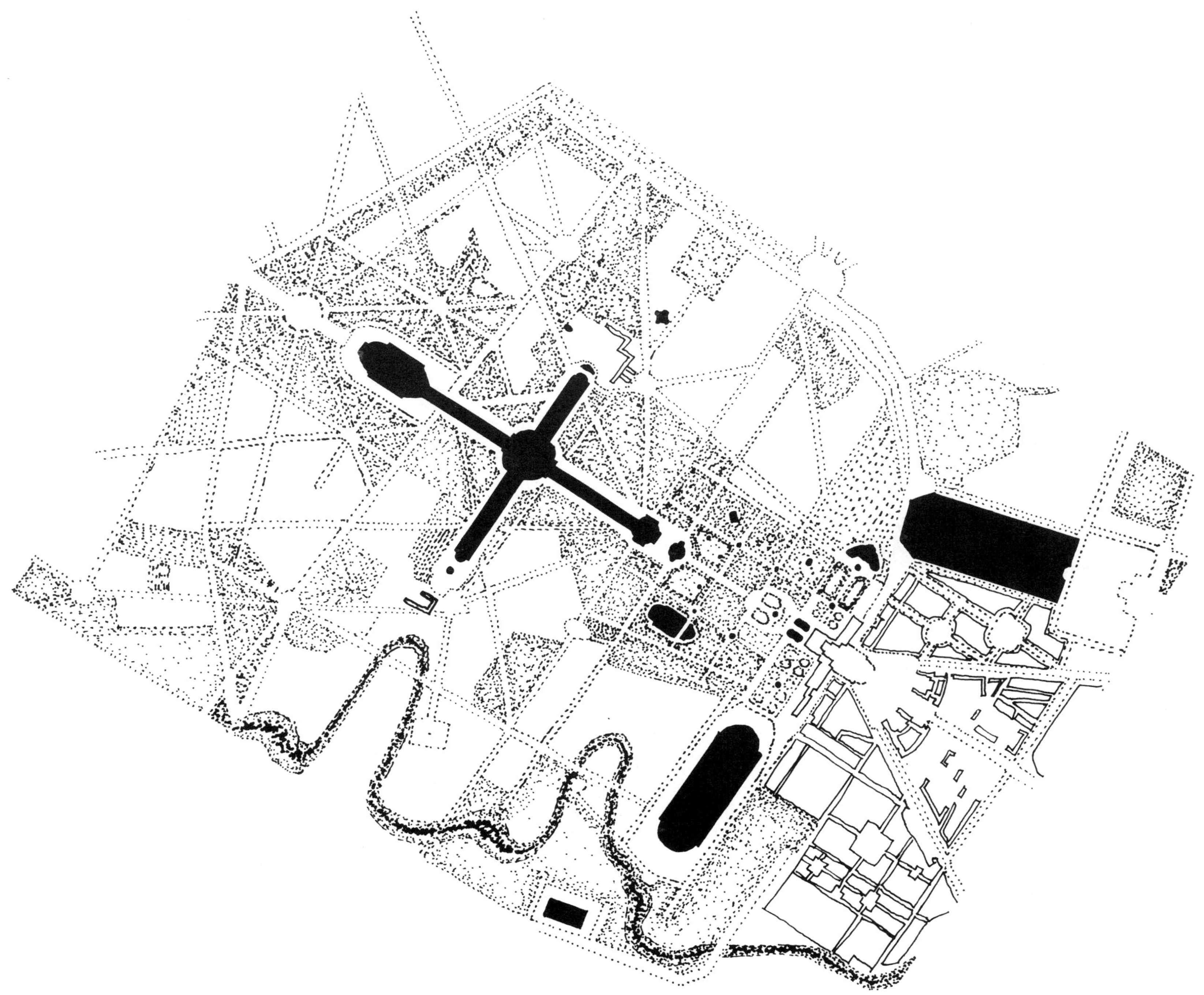

TUILERIES, CHAMPS-ELYSÉES, LUXEMBOURG GARDENS

Location: Paris, France

Tuileries

Dates: 1560 - 1670s

Designers: De L'Orme, Mollet, Boyceau and Le Nôtre

Clients: Catherine de Medici, Henri IV and Louis XIV

Area: 96.5 acres / 39 hectares

Luxembourg Gardens

Dates: 1612 - 1790s

Designers: de Brosse, Deschamps, Boutin, Boyceau, and Le Nôtre

Clients: Marie de Medici, Gaston d'Orleans and Louis XIV

Area: 115.7 acres / 46.8 hectares

Champs-Elysées (Cours de la Reine) including the Place de la Concorde and the Place de L'Etoile (Arc de Triomphe)

Dates: 1600 - 1870

Designers: Mollet, Boyceau, and Le Nôtre, Hausmann

Clients: Marie de Medici, Louis XIV, Louis XV, Napoleon I and Napoleon II

Area: 180 acres / 72.8 hectares

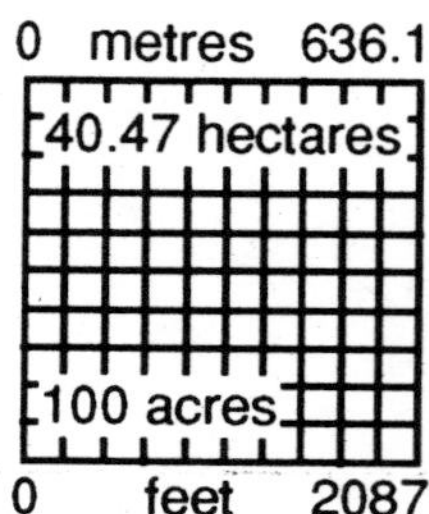

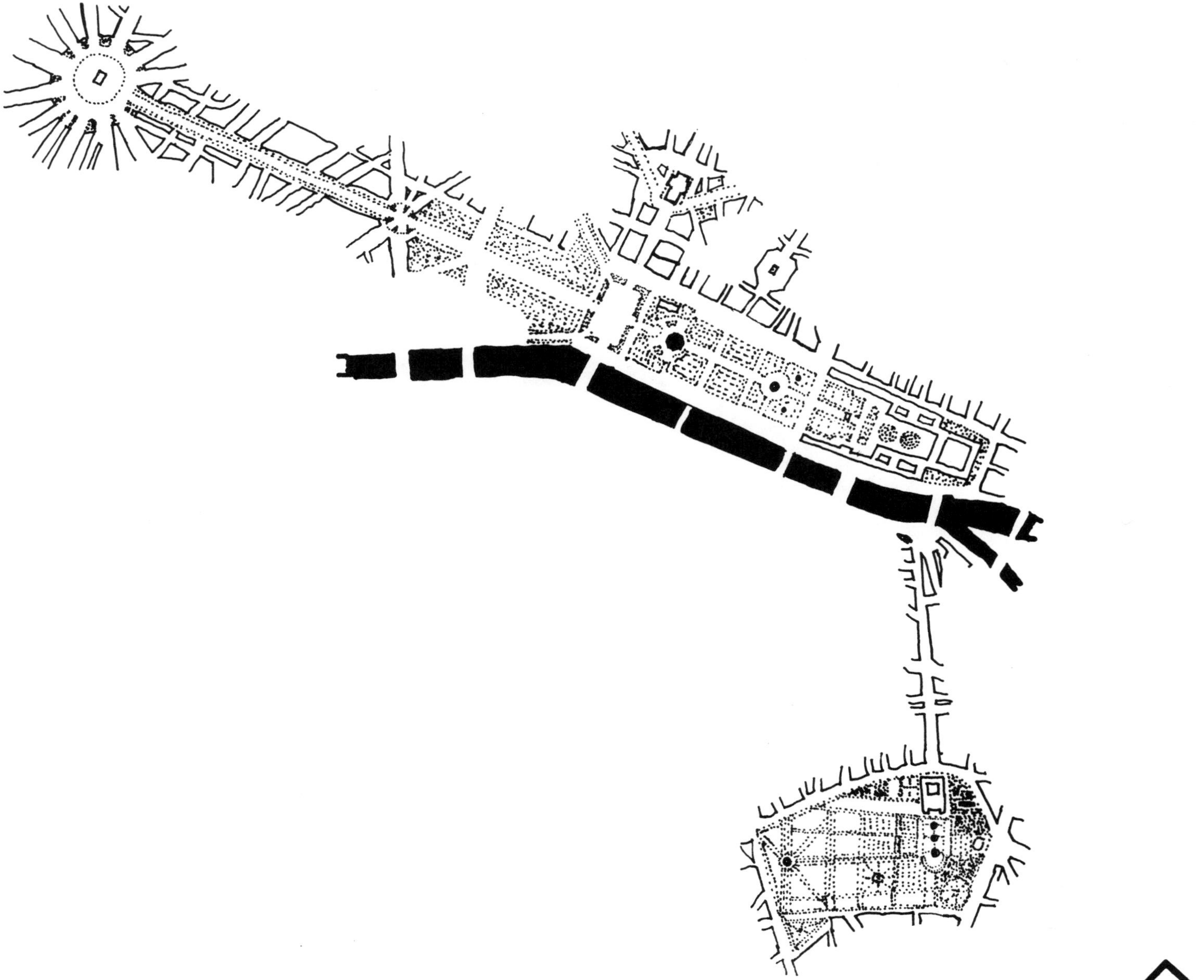

HAMPTON COURT PALACE

Location: London, England

Dates: 1515 - 1714

Designers: André and Gabriel Mollet, Sir Christopher Wren, Daniel Marot and Henry Wise,

Clients: Cardinal Wolsey, Henry VIII, Elizabeth I, Charles II, William and Mary, and Anne

Area, including Bushey Park: 1562 acres / 632.1 hectares

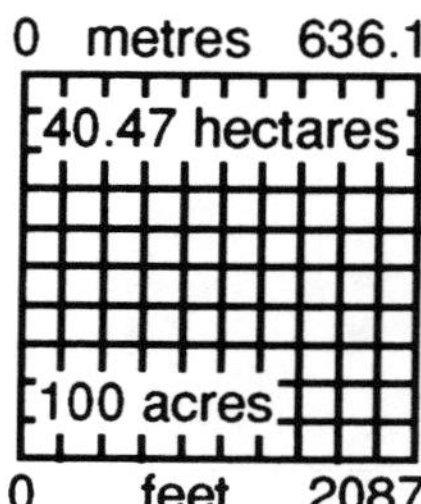

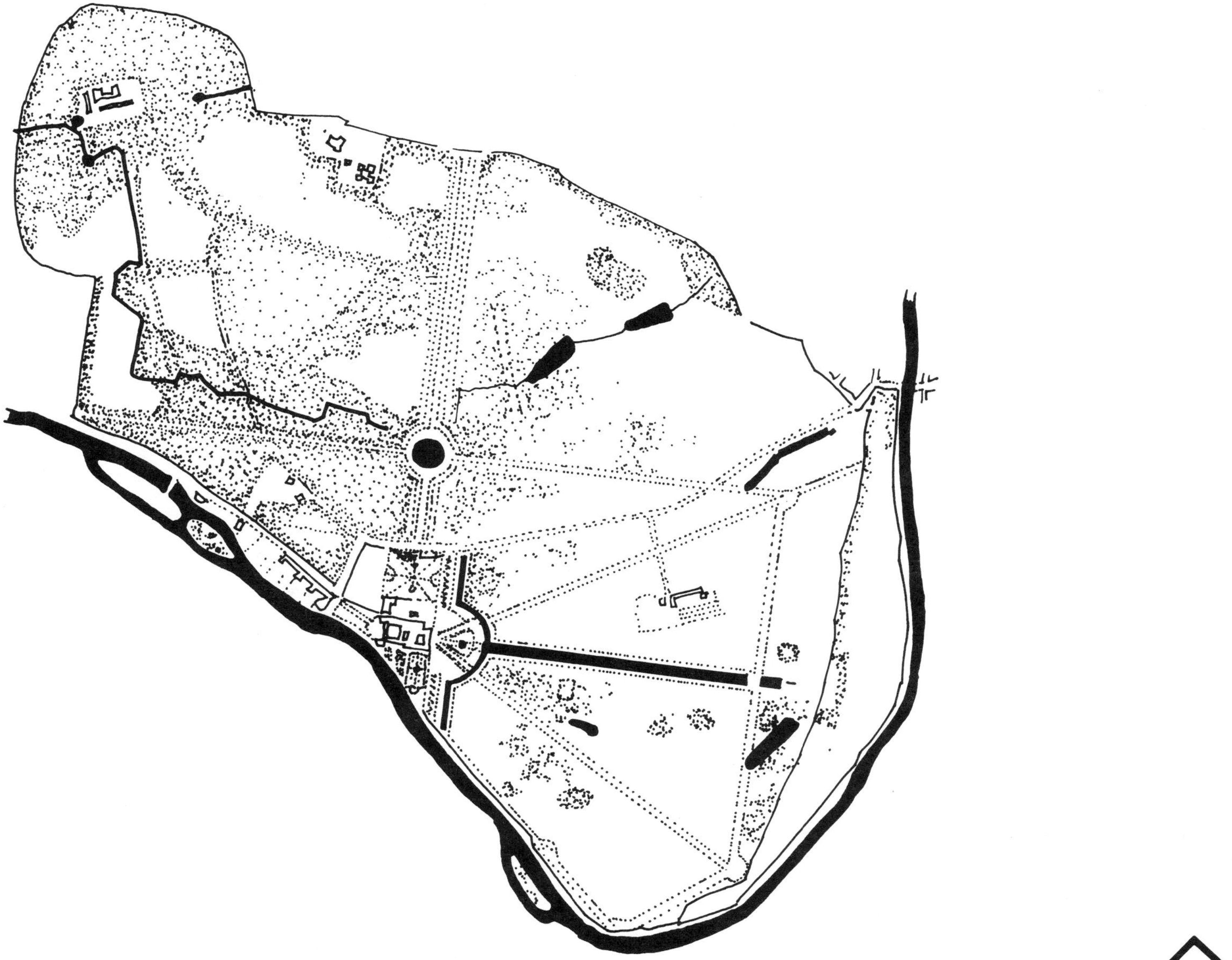

STOURHEAD

Location: Wiltshire, England

Dates: c.1743 - 1775

Designers: Henry Hoare II, Henry Flintcroft

Client: Henry Hoare II

Area: 200 acres / 81.3 hectares

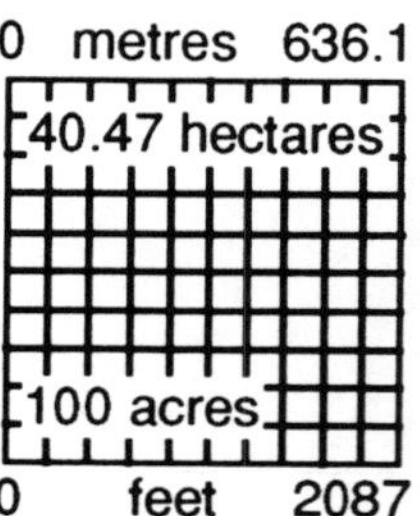

BLENHEIM PALACE

Location: Oxfordshire, England

Dates: 1705 - 1764

Designers: Sir John Vanbrugh, George London and Henry Wise, Charles Bridgeman, Lancelot "Capability" Brown, Sir William Chambers

Clients: Dukes (I and IV) of Marlborough

Area: 2168 acres / 877.3 hectares

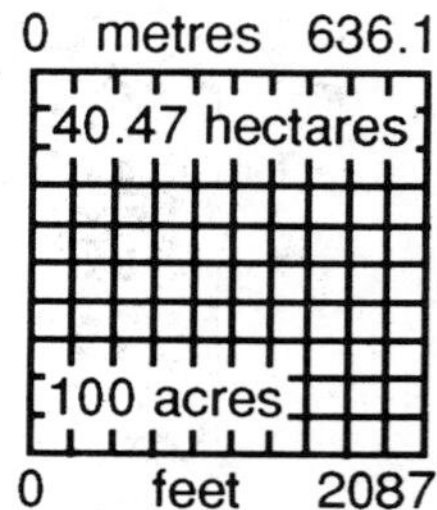

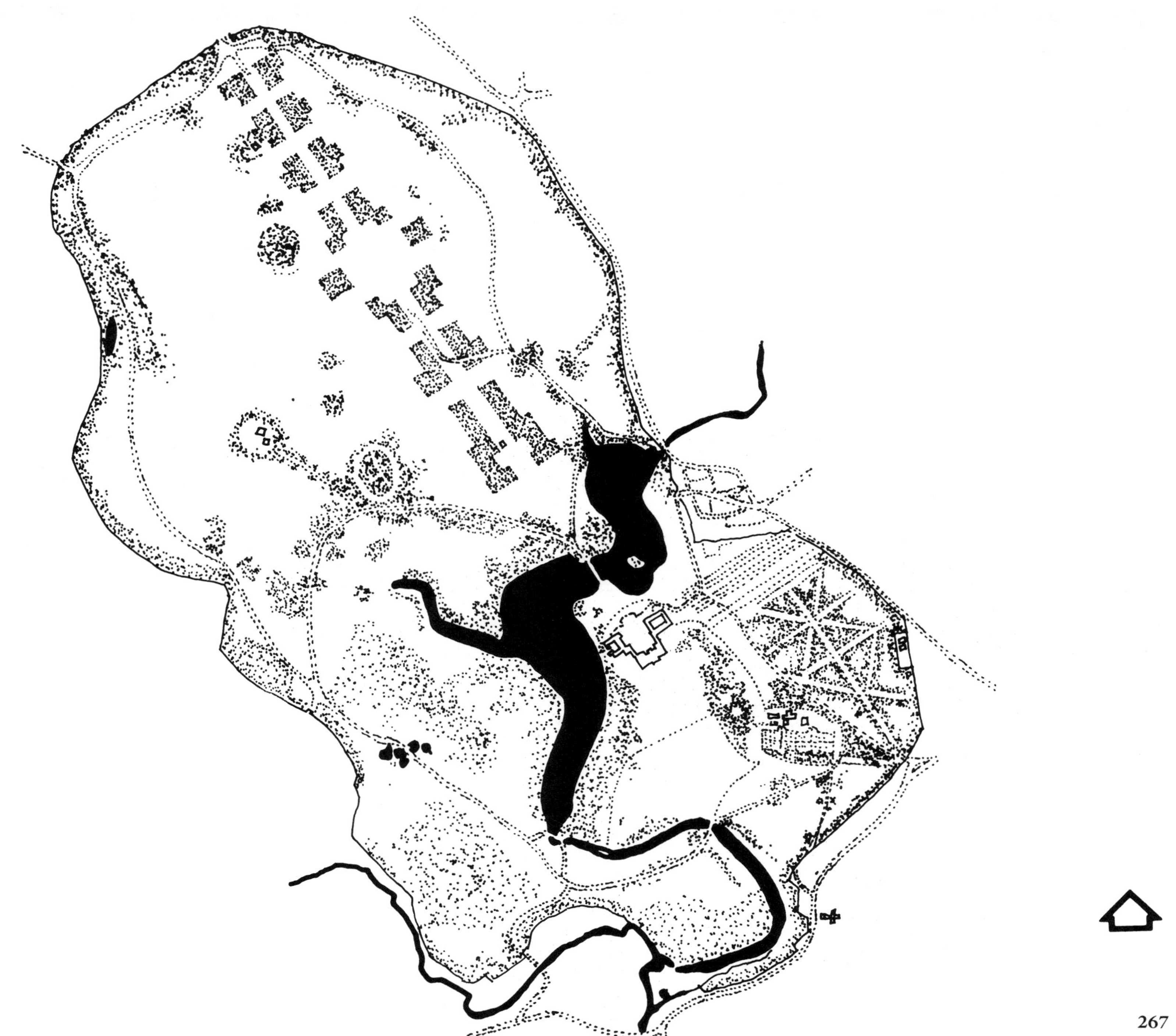

ENGLISCHE GARTEN

Location: Munich, Bavaria, Germany

Dates: 1789 - 1820s

Designers: Benjamin Thompson (Count Rumford) and Friedrich Ludwig Sckell

Clients: Prince Karl Theodor

Area: 600 acres / 242.8 hectares

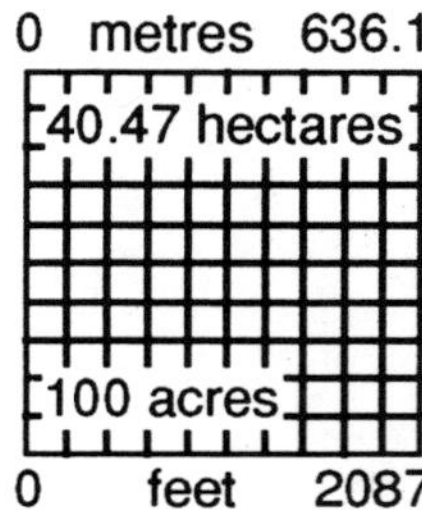

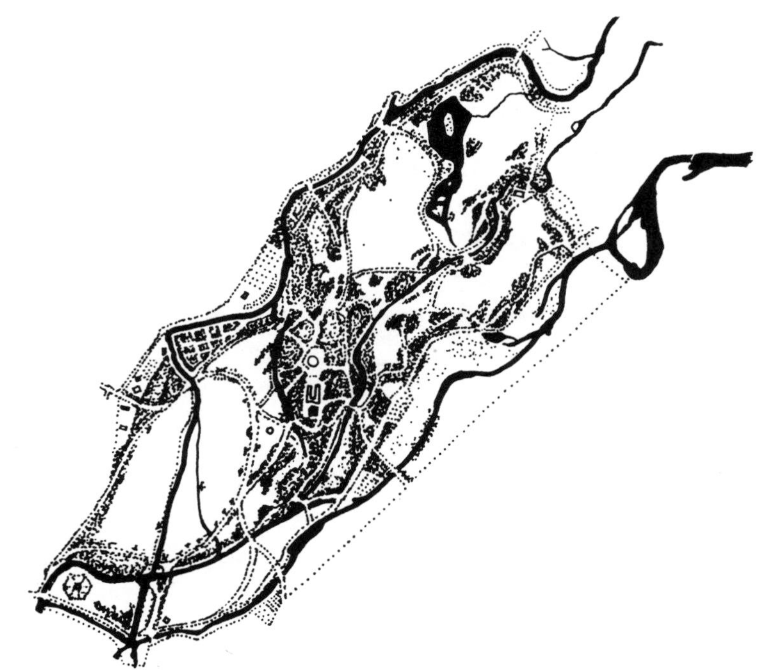

ROYAL PARKS

Location: London, England

<u>Regent's Park</u>

Date: 1811

Designer: John Nash

Client: Prince Regent (George IV)

Area: 368 acres / 149 hectares

<u>Regent's Street</u>

Dates: 1812 - 1820

Designer: John Nash

Client: Prince Regent (George IV)

<u>St. James Park</u>

Dates: 1660, 1820

Designers: André Mollet, John Nash

Clients: Charles II, Prince Regent (George IV)

Area: 86 acres / 34.8 hectares

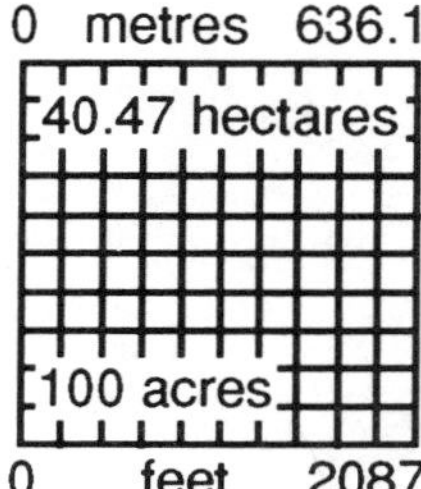

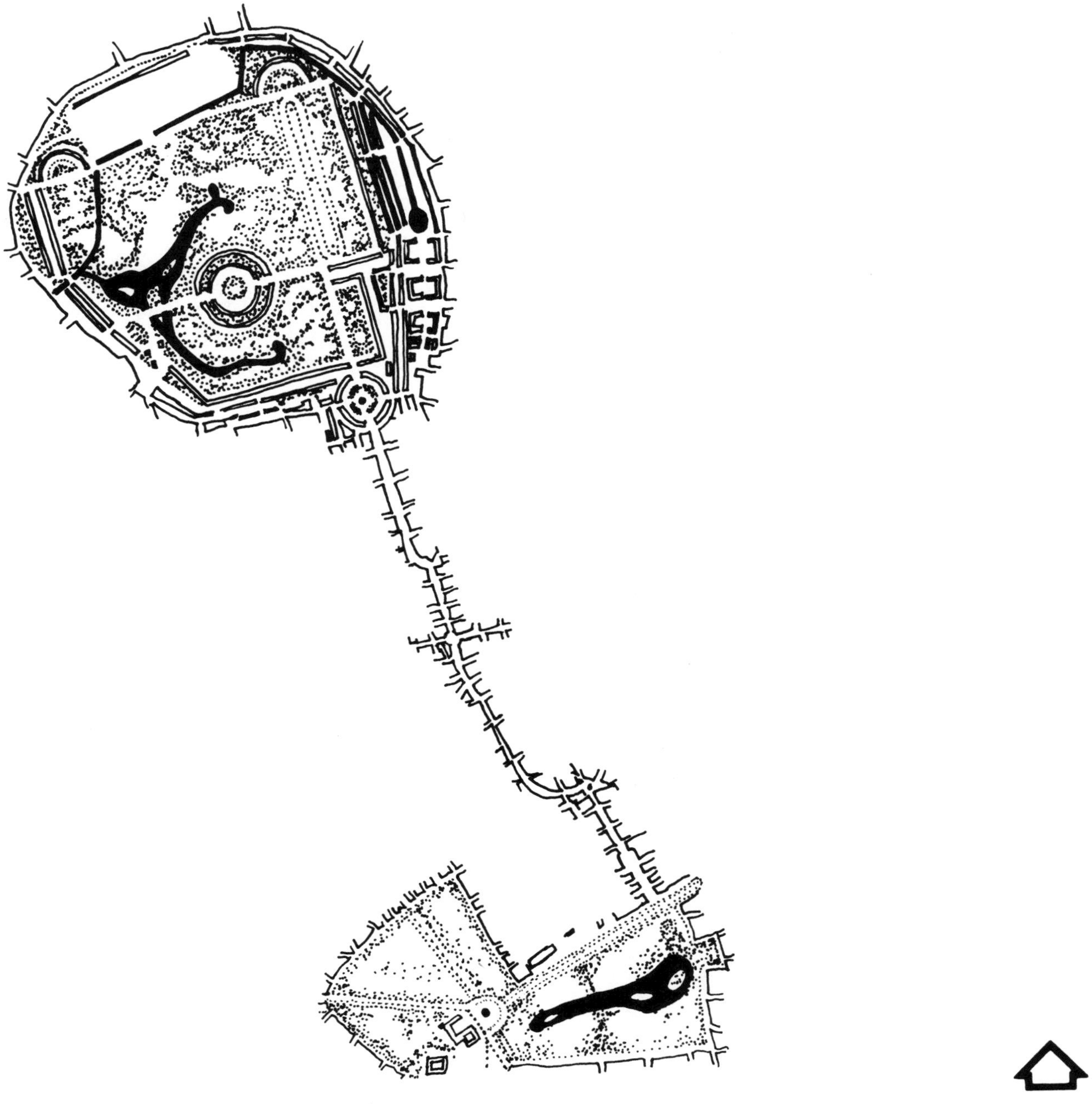

VICTORIA PARK

Location: London, England

Date: 1841

Designer: James Pennethorne

Client: The City of London

Area: 290 acres / 117.4 hectares

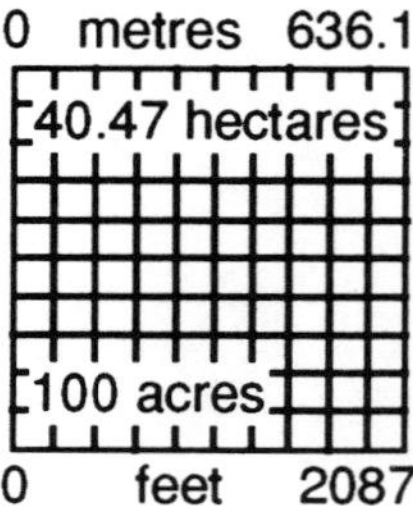

BIRKENHEAD PARK

Location: Birkenhead, near Liverpool, England

Date: 1844 - 1847

Designer: Joseph Paxton

Client: The City of Birkenhead

Area, including house lots: 226 acres / 91.5 hectares
area of public park proper: 125 acres / 50.6 hectares

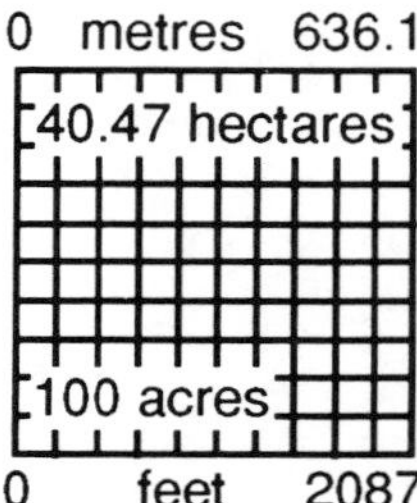

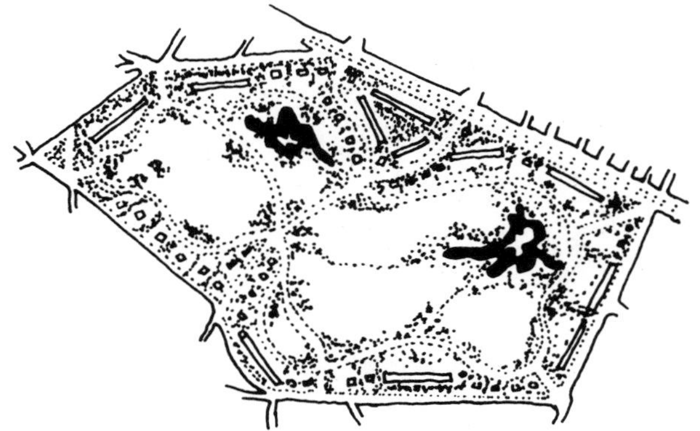

BOIS DE BOULOGNE

Location: Paris, France

Dates: 1852 - 1870

Designers: Georges Eugène von Haussmann, Adolphe Alphand and Edouard François André

Client: Emperor Louis Napoleon III

Area: 2100 acres / 849.9 hectares

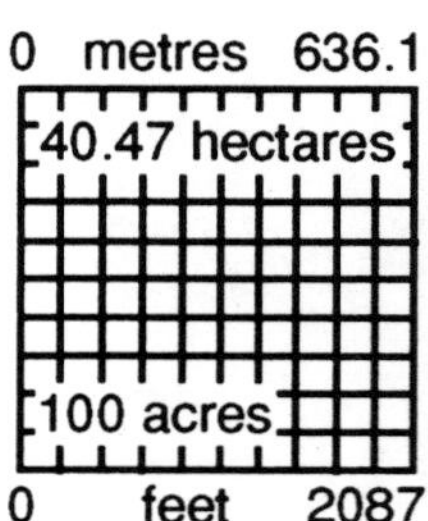

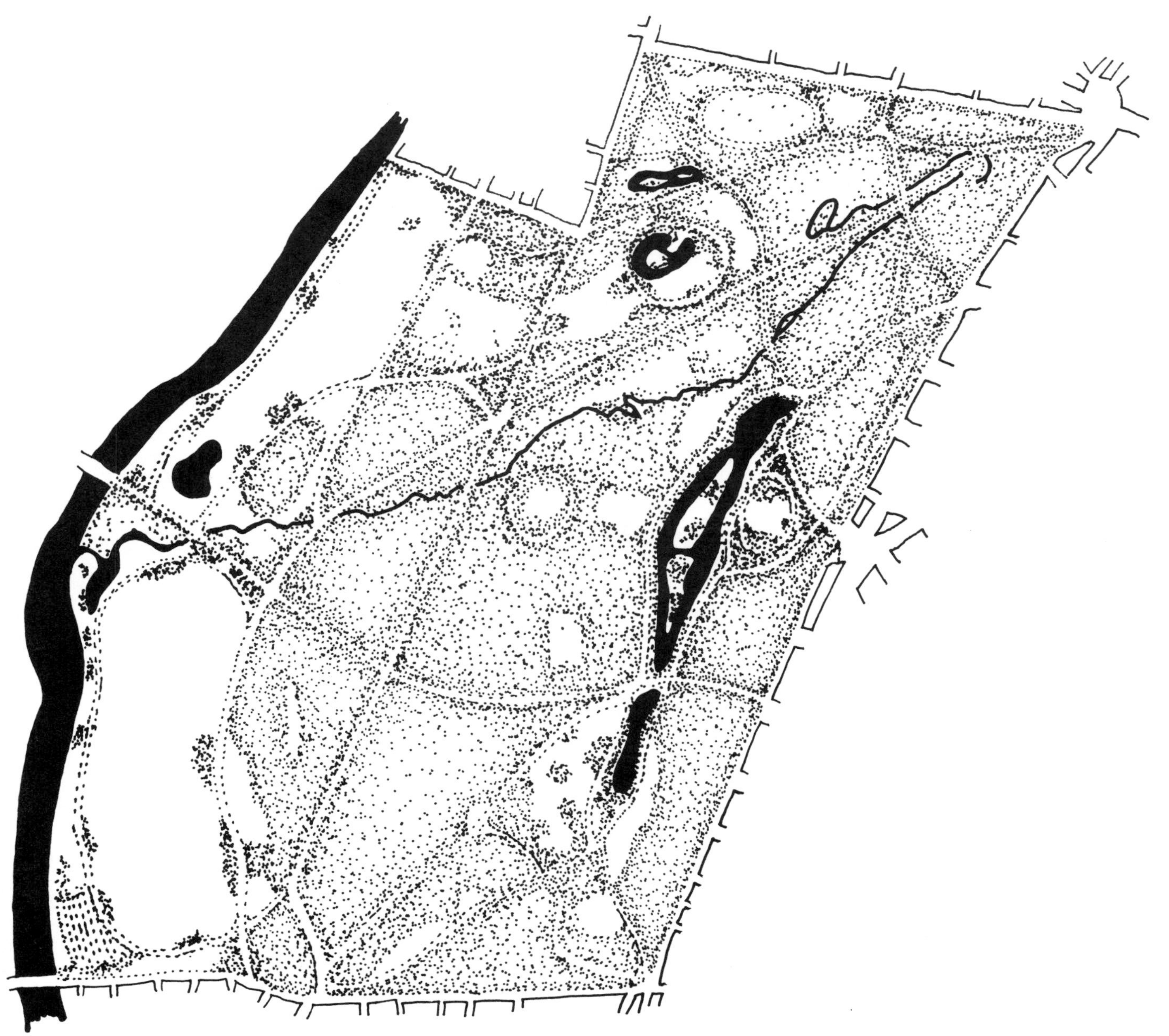

PHILADELPHIA

Location: Pennsylvania

Date: 1682

Designers: William Penn and Thomas Holme

Client: The Society of Friends

Area: 1382 acres / 559.3 hectares

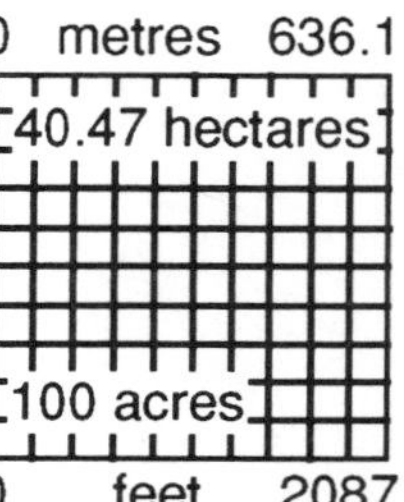

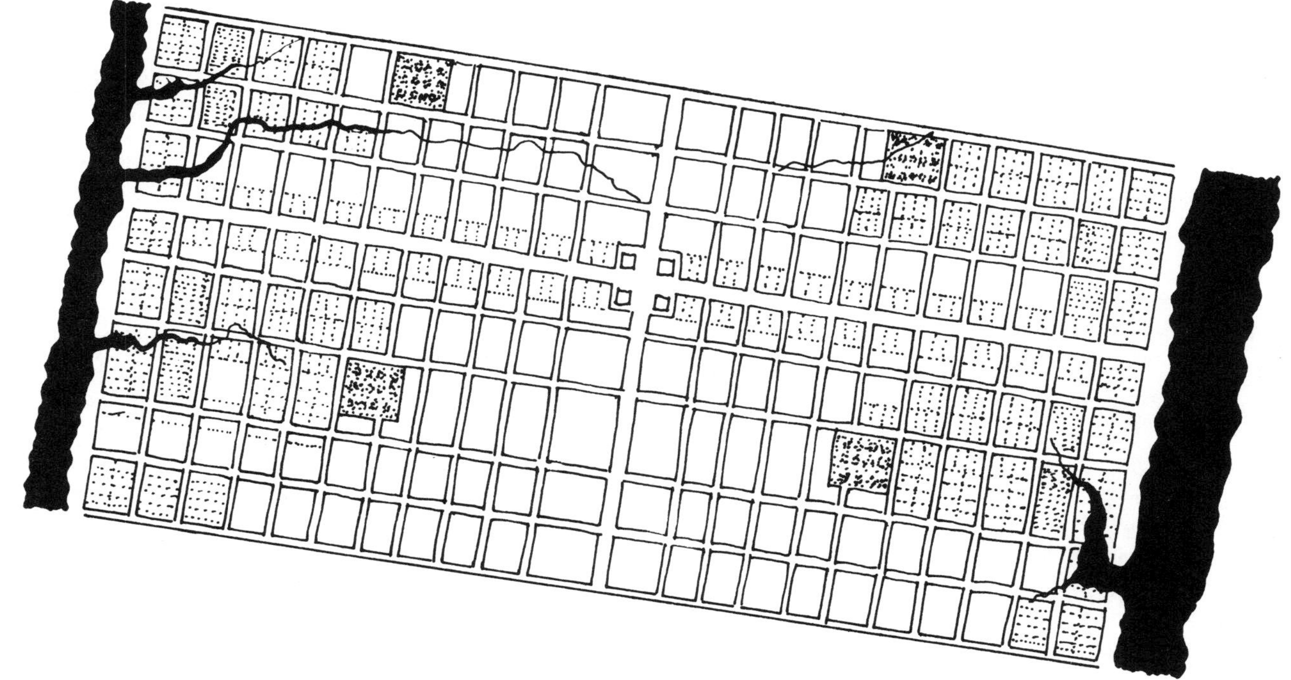

ANNAPOLIS

Location: Maryland

Date: 1695

Planner: Sir Francis Nicholson, Royal Governor

Client: King James II, The Maryland Colony

Area: 207 acres / 83.6 hectares

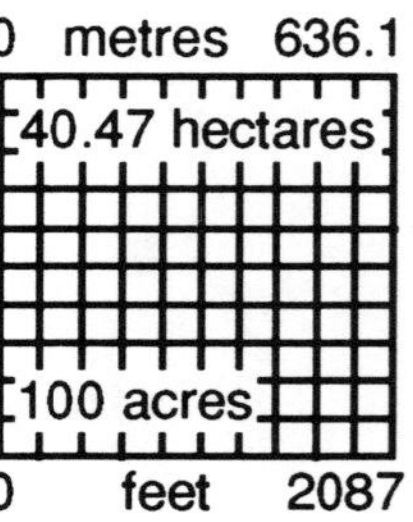

WILLIAMSBURG

Location: Virginia Colony

Date: 1699

Planner: Sir Francis Nicholson, Royal Governor

Client: King James II, The Virginia Colony

Area: 190 acres / 76.9 hectares

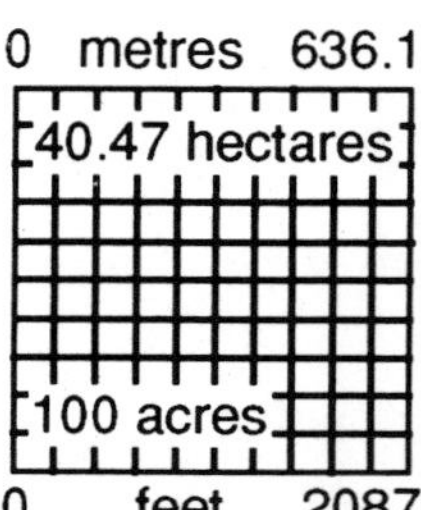

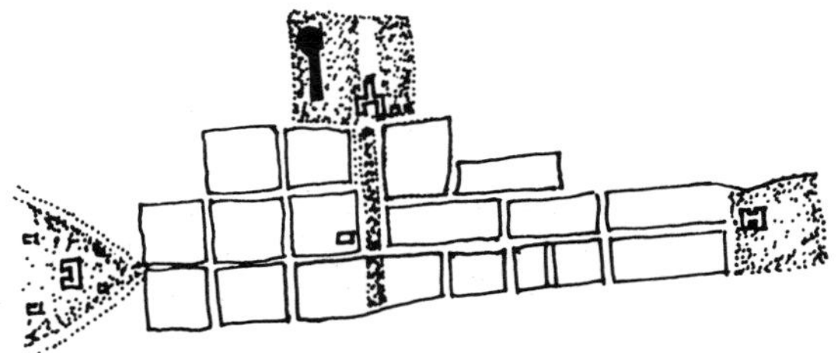

SAVANNAH

Location: Georgia Colony

Date: 1733

Planner: Gen. James Edward Oglethorpe, Royal Governor

Client: King George II, The Georgia Colony

Area: (1733, first four wards) 44.5 acres / 18.1 hectares
(1856, ward scheme abandoned) 320 acres / 130 hectares

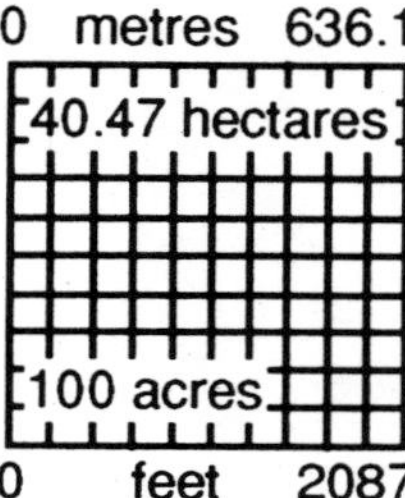

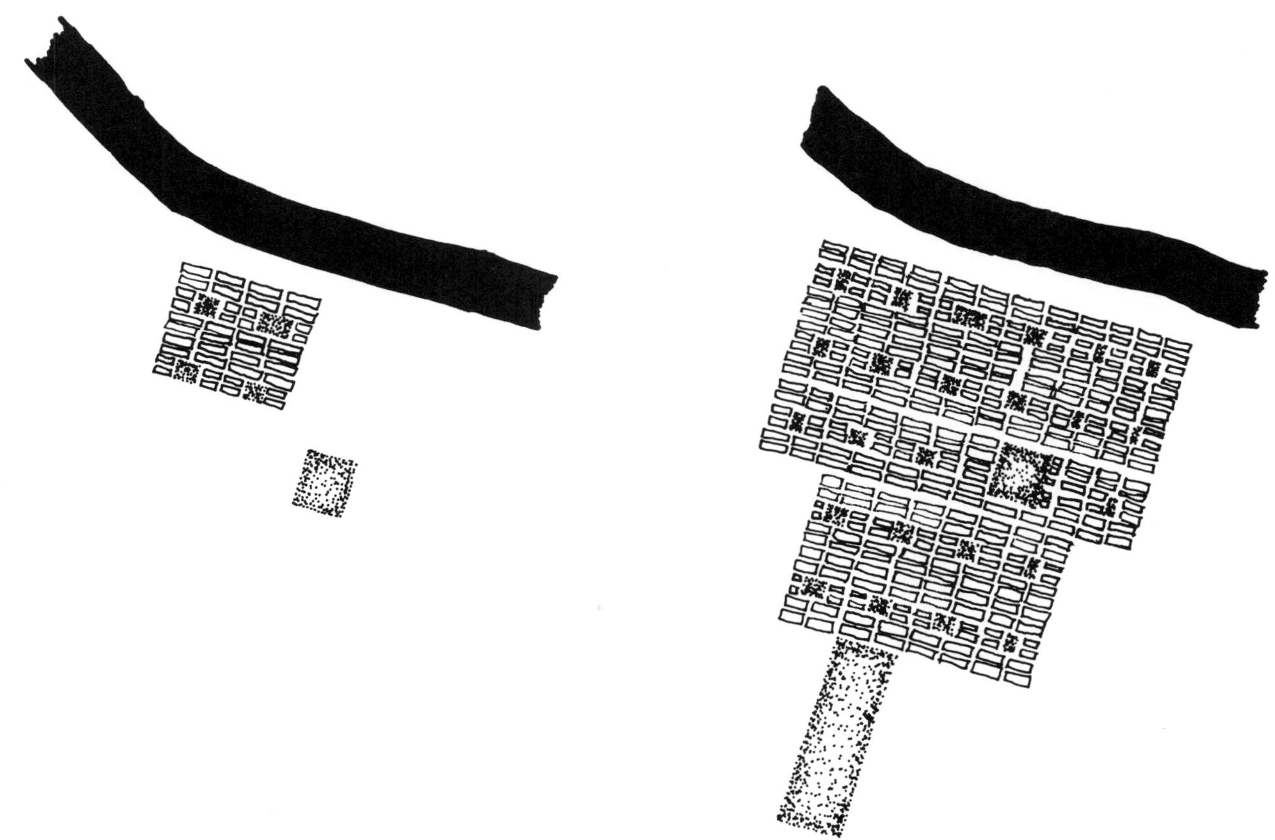

WASHINGTON, D.C.

Location: United States' National Capital/District of Columbia

Date: 1791

Planners: Gen. Pierre Charles L'Enfant, Thomas Jefferson

Client: The People of the United States

Area: (District *was* 10 miles square) 64,000 acres / 25,900 hectares
(L'Enfant plan) 7280 acres / 2946 hectares

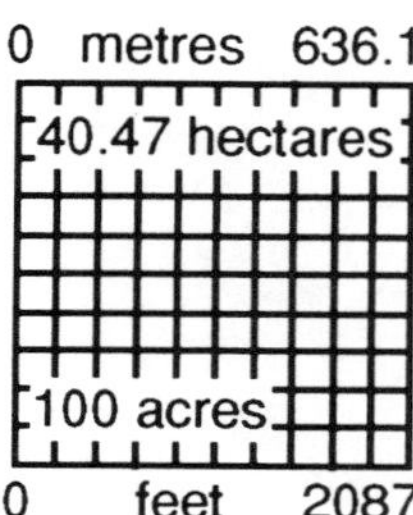

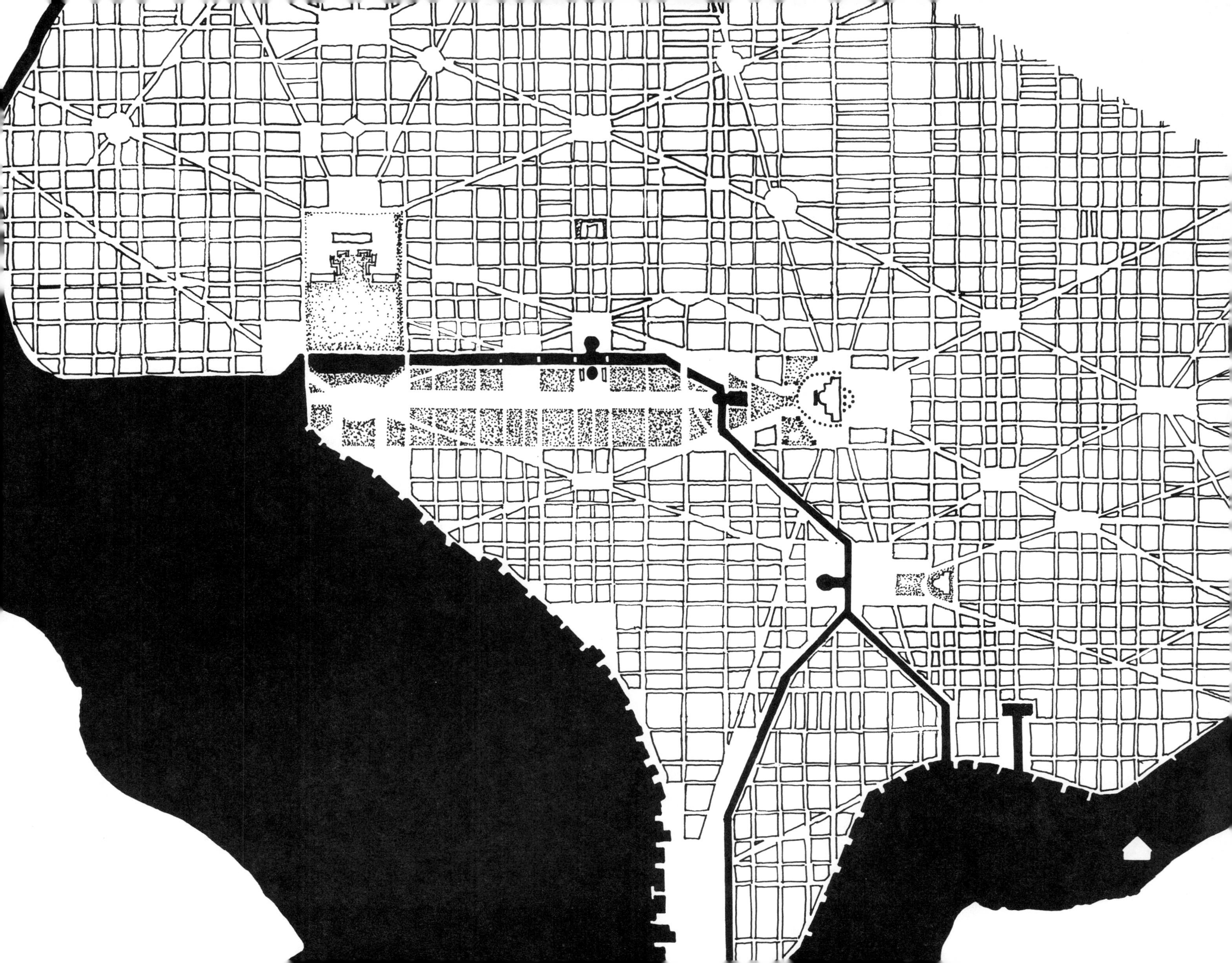

MOUNT AUBURN CEMETERY

Location: Suburban Boston (Cambridge and Watertown), Massachusetts

Dates: 1831 - 1871

Designers: Gen. Henry A. S. Dearborn and Dr. Jacob Bigelow

Client: "Cemetery and Garden Committee" of the Massachusetts Horticultural Society

Area: (1831) 72 acres / 29.1 hectares

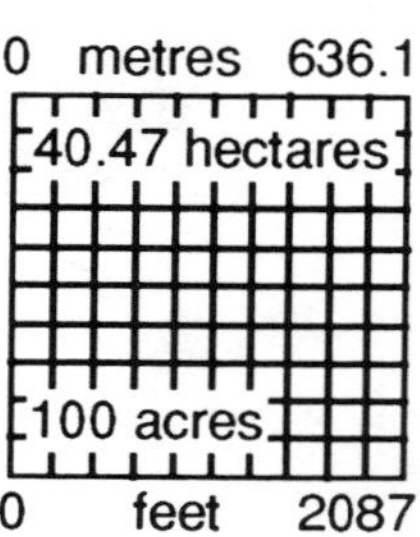

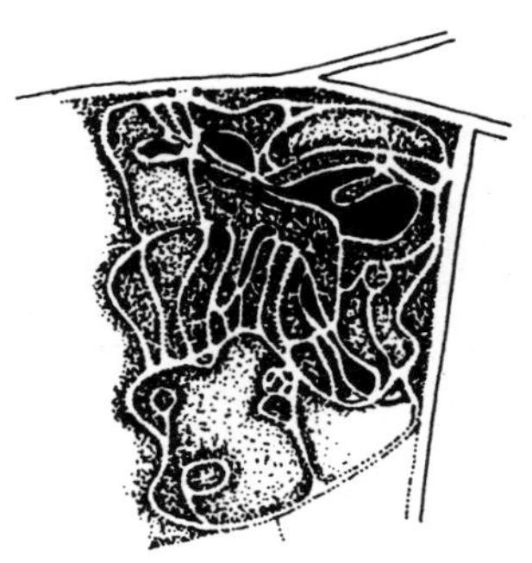

LLEWELLYN PARK

Location: West Orange, New Jersey

Dates: 1853 - 1857

Designers: Alexander Jackson Davis and Eugene A. Baumann

Client: Llewellyn Haskell

Area: 350 acres / 141.6 hectares

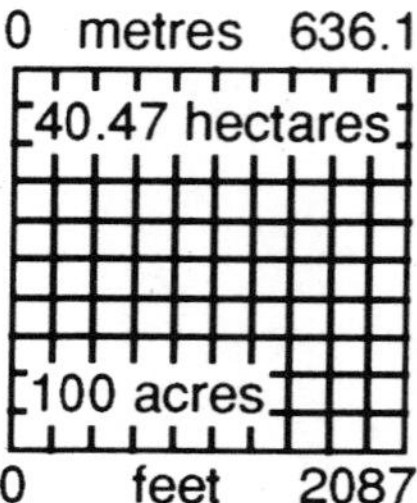

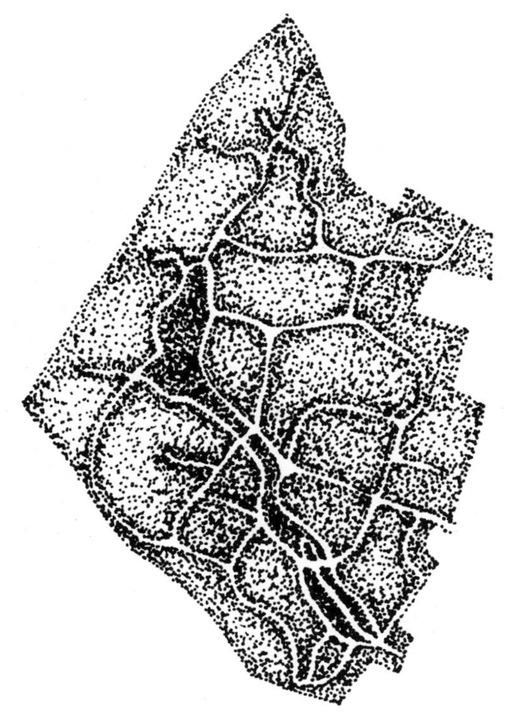

CENTRAL PARK

Location: New York, New York

Dates: 1858 - 1878

Designers: Frederick Law Olmsted and Calvert Vaux

Client: The City of New York

Area: 843 acres / 341.2 hectares

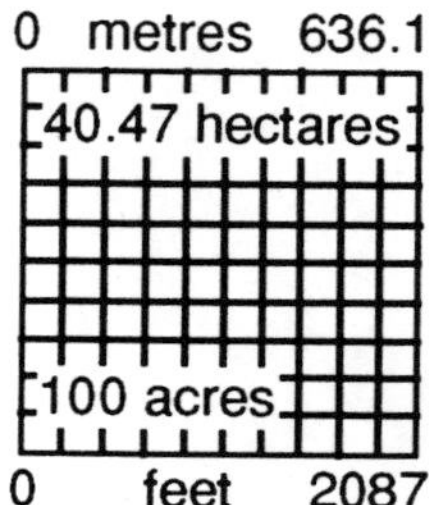

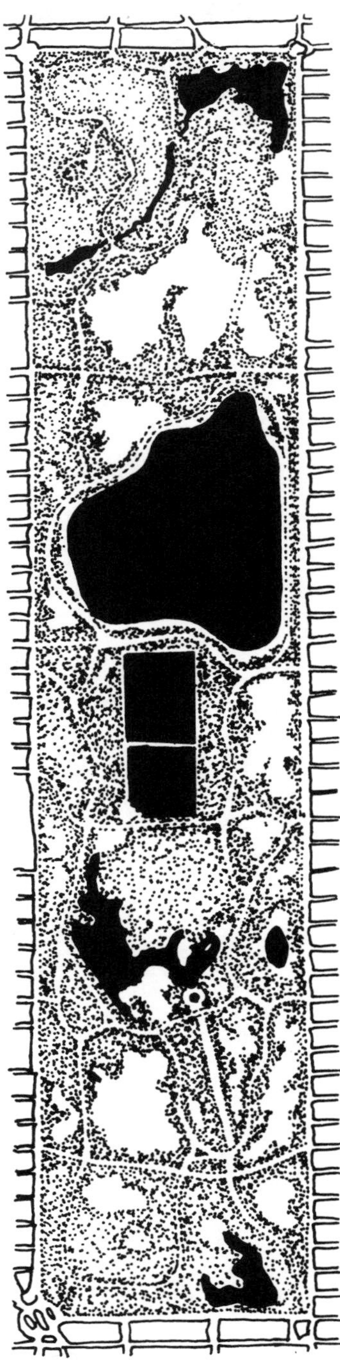

PROSPECT PARK

Location: Brooklyn, New York

Dates: 1865 - 1873

Designers: Frederick Law Olmsted and Calvert Vaux

Client: The City of Brooklyn

Area: 526 acres / 212.9 hectares

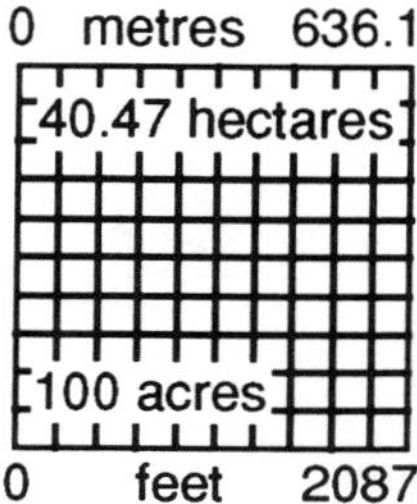

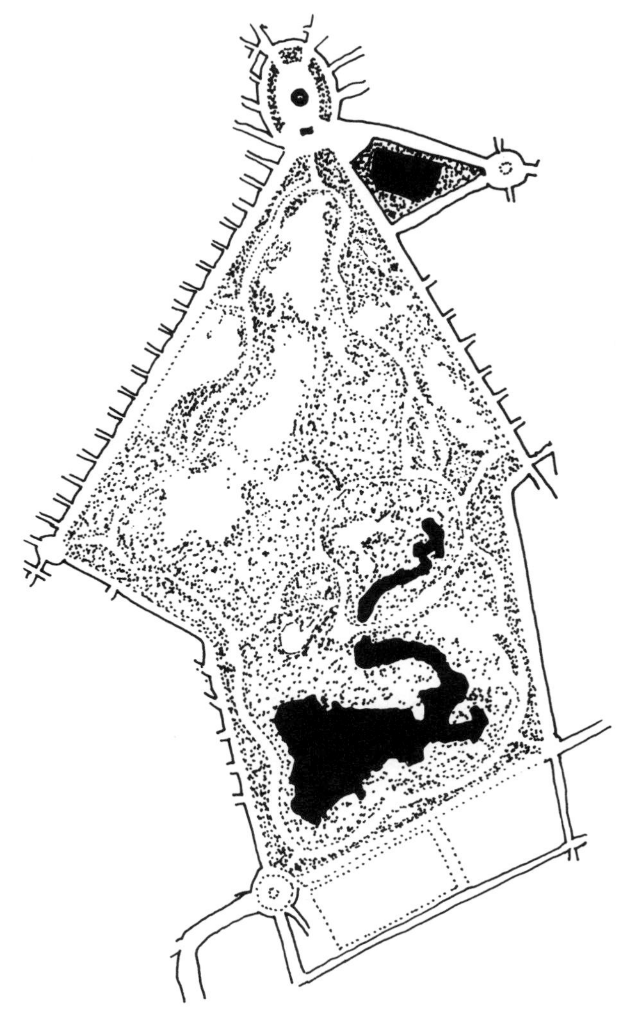

RIVERSIDE

Location: Suburban Chicago, Illinois

Dates: 1868 - 1870

Designers: Frederick Law Olmsted and Calvert Vaux

Client: The Riverside Corporation

Area: 1600 acres / 647.5 hectares

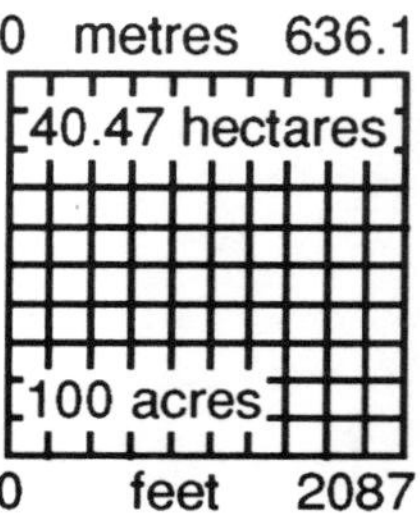

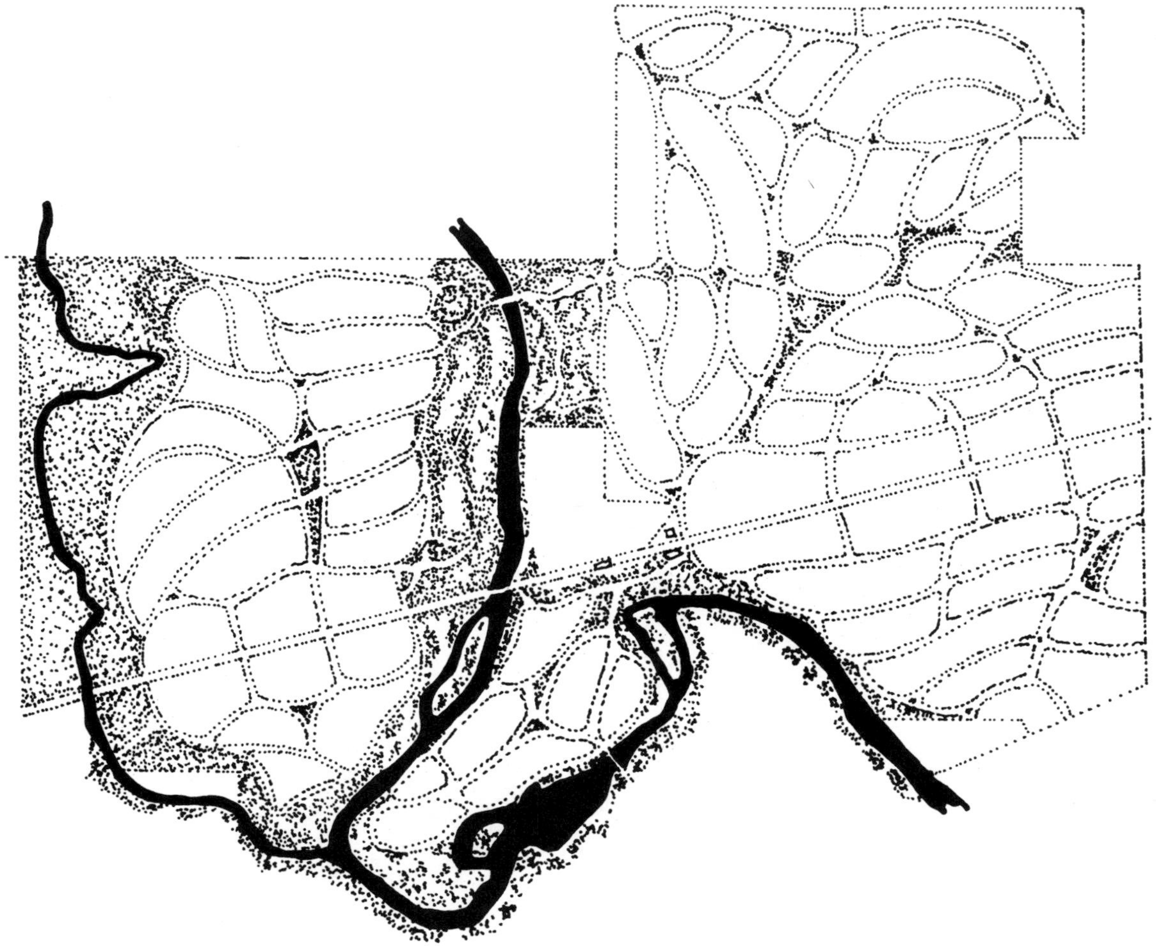

THE "EMERALD NECKLACE" PARK SYSTEM

Location: Boston, Massachusetts

Dates: 1878 - 1890s

Designers: Frederick Law Olmsted,
John Charles Olmsted
(F. L. and J. C. Olmsted, Inc.)

Client: The City of Boston

Area: Franklin Park, 545 acres / 220.5 hectares
Arnold Arboretum, 395. 4 acres / 160 hectares

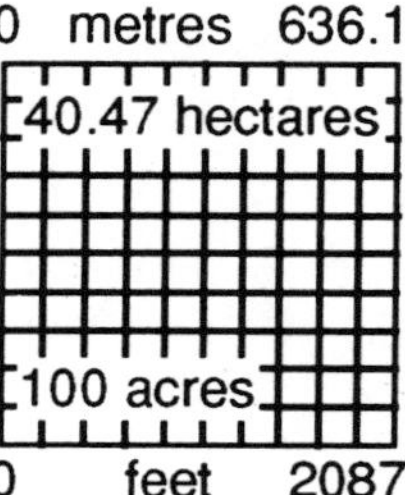

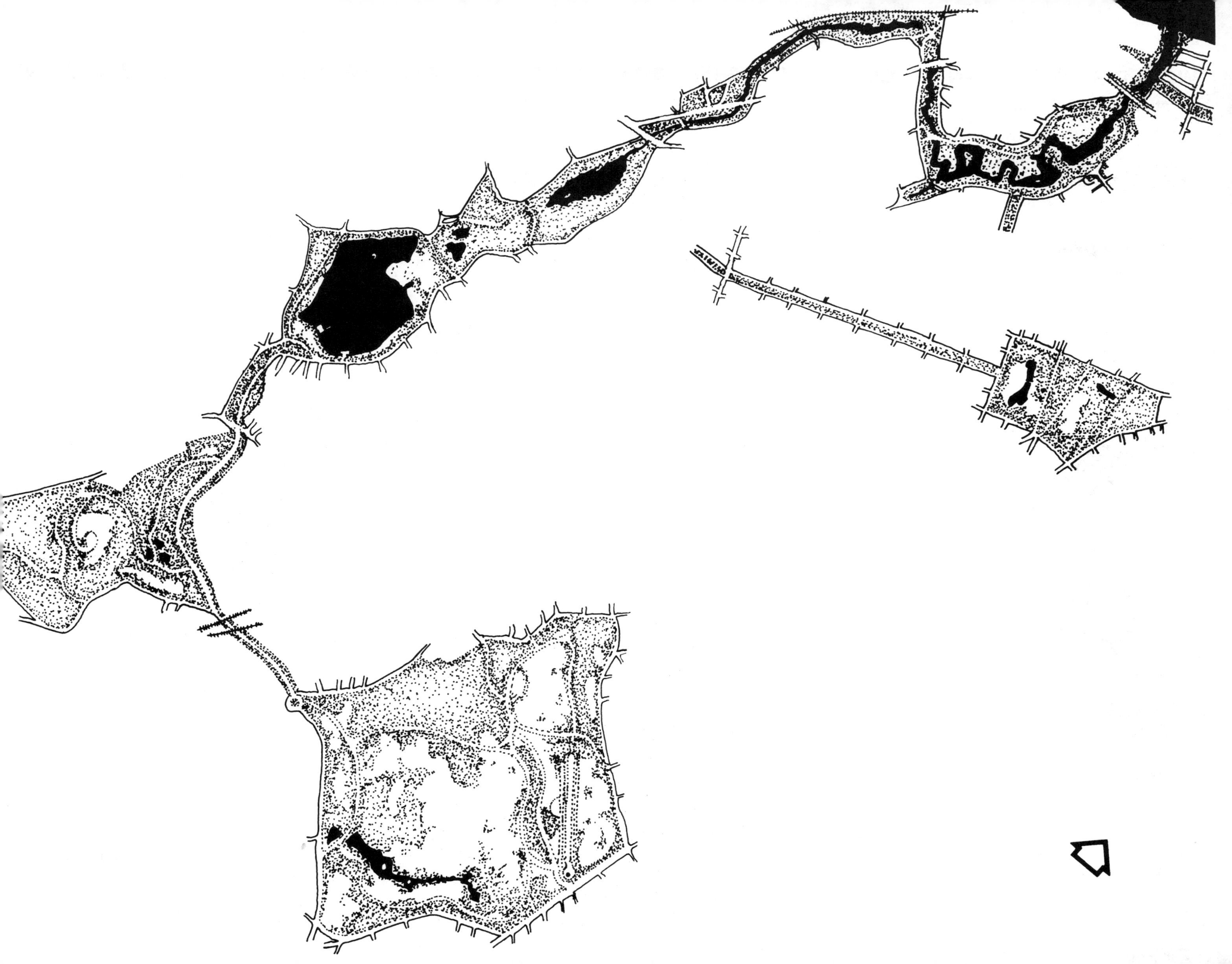

WORLD'S COLUMBIAN EXPOSITION

Location: Chicago, Illinois

Dates: 1890 - 1893

Designers: Frederick Law Olmsted
(Olmsted, Olmsted and Elliot, Associates)

Client: The City of Chicago

Area: Exposition Grounds, 593 acres / 239.9 hectares
Jackson Park, 593 acres / 239.9 hectares
Washington Park, 372 acres / 150.5 hectares
The Midway, 90 acres / 36.4 hectares

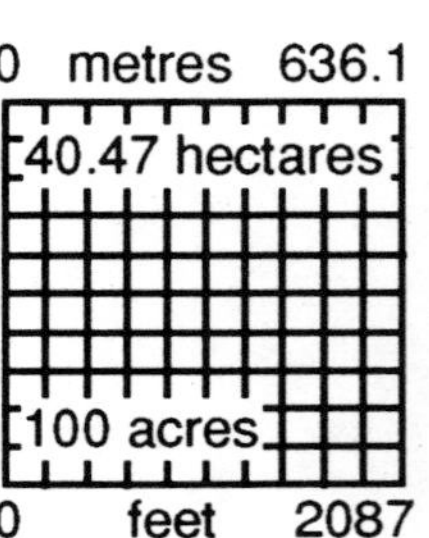

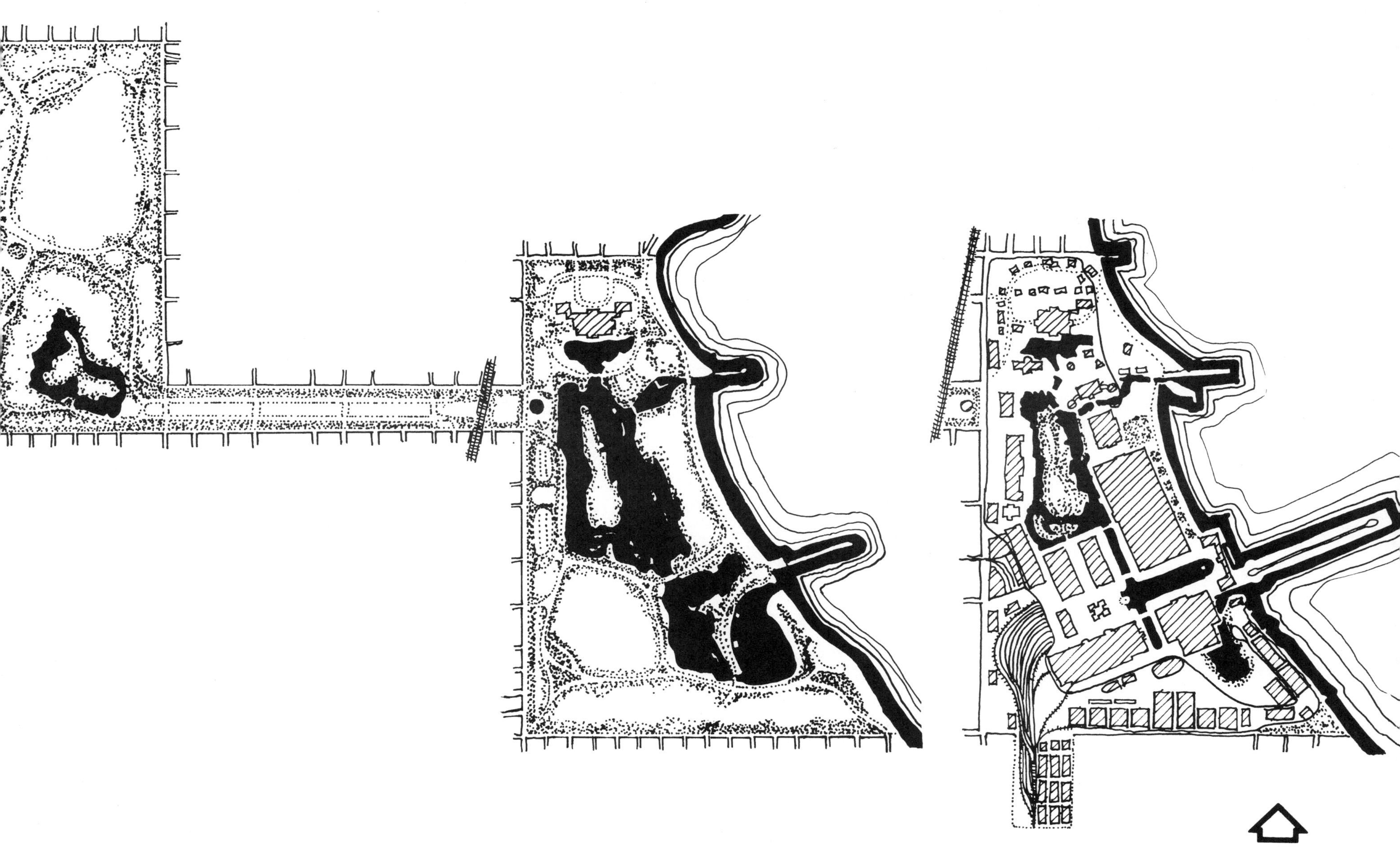

RADBURN GARDEN CITY

Location: Radburn, New Jersey

Dates: 1927 - 1929

Designers: Clarence Stein, Henry Wright and Marjorie Cautley

Client: The Radburn Corporation

Area: 1300 acres / 526.1 hectares

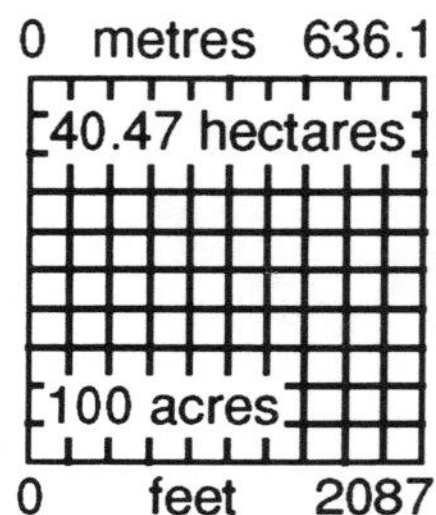

STATE UNIVERSITY OF NEW YORK AT BUFFALO

Location: Amherst, New York

Dates: 1968 - 1978

Designers: Sasaki, Dawson, DeMay, Assoc. Inc.

Client: The State University of New York

Area: 1200 acres / 485.6 hectares

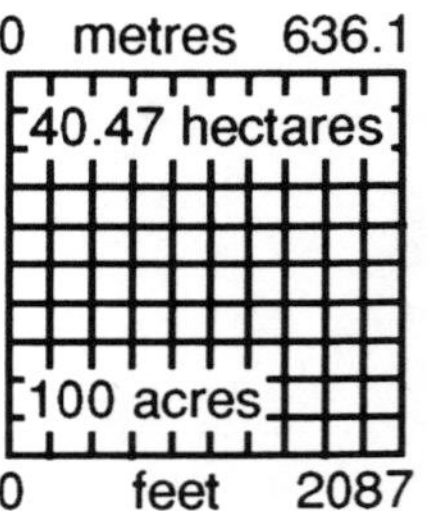

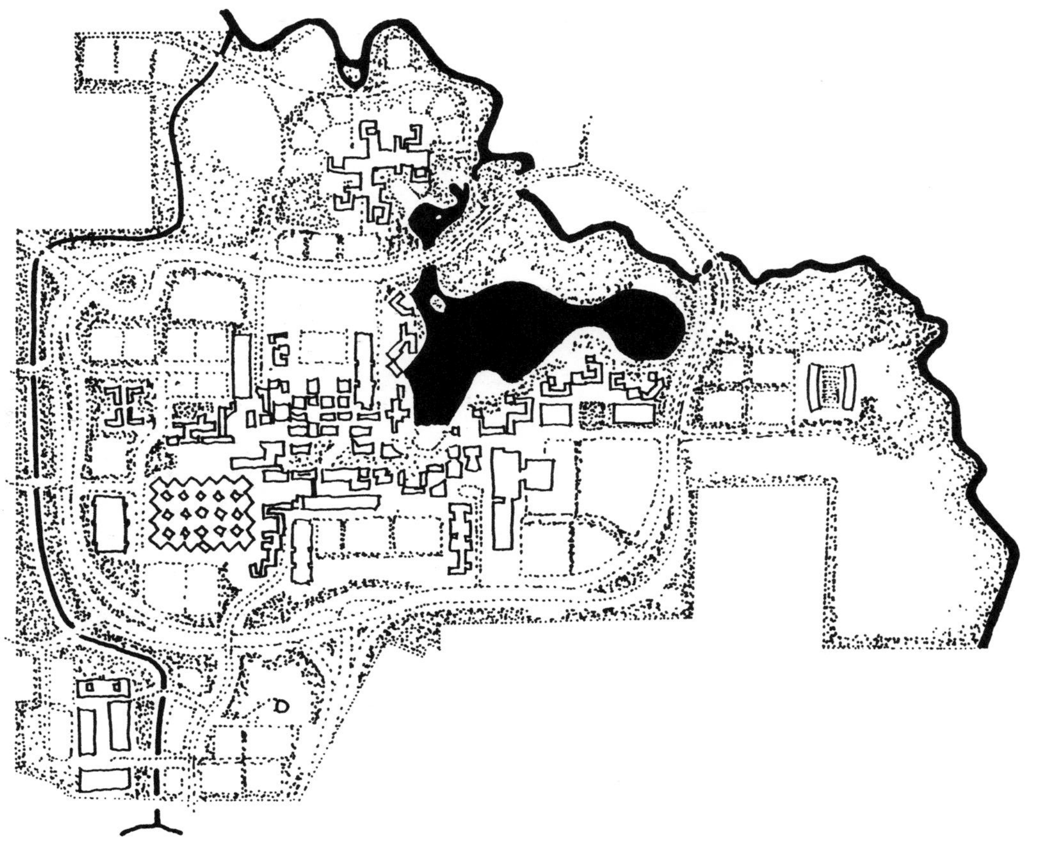

SECTION 6

BIOGRAPHICAL SKETCHES

Biographical Sketches

ABBOTT, Stanley William (1908–1975), landscape architect, was the chief planner and designer of the Blue Ridge Parkway connecting the southern end of Virginia's Skyline Drive in the Shenandoah National Park with the Great Smoky Mountains National Park to the south, a distance of 470 miles. One of the largest landscape architectural construction projects ever conceived, this was the first national parkway, built between 1935 and 1987 (with the completion of the Linn Cove Viaduct). It began as a project of the federal Public Works Administration and was intended to help rejuvenate the depressed Appalachian region through which it passed, while it served as a pleasurable driving experience for tourists. A new concept in land preservation was born with the Blue Ridge Parkway, the "scenic easement." Through contractual arrangements with landowners within the "viewshed" of the parkway, the use of private land could be controlled, maintained as rural scenic panoramic views, rather than allowing the land to become developed. When driving on the Blue Ridge Parkway, the motorist is completely immersed in truly rural, agricultural scenery with occasional overlooks placed to provide the traveler with stopping points for viewing the scenery below.

Abbott said, "I see a . . . parkway as one which has as its reason for existence none other than to reveal the charm and interest of the native American countryside . . . having selected a route, you design a road that fits as sympathetically as it can be fitted . . . into that particular piece of topography. This is almost a form of sculpture; it takes a three-dimensional mind."

He earned his degree in landscape architecture from Cornell University in 1930, and worked with Gilmore Clarke on the Westchester Park and Parkway Authority in White Plains, New York before joining the National Park Service in 1934.

In 1950 he was named supervising landscape architect for the Mississippi River Parkway and was a member of the planning group for the new Cascades National Park in Washington state. From 1953 until his retirement in 1966, Abbott was superintendent of the Colonial National Historical Park, developing plans for the observance of the 350th anniversary of Jamestown, Virginia.

In 1966 he established Abbott Associates, architects and landscape architects, specializing in master planning, design, and development of state, county, and city parks. His firm did site planning for the Homestead in Hot Springs, West Virginia and various Virginia colleges, rehabilitation of gardens at the Governor's Mansion in Richmond, and landscaping along Virginia's interstate highways.

Abbott was chairman of the Virginia Historic Landmarks Commission and a member of several civic and professional organizations, including the American Society of Landscape Architects, of which he was a fellow.

ADDAMS, Jane (1860–1935), social reformer, was the founder of Hull House in Chicago, one the most widely known settlement houses in the United States. The Chicago slums attracted her attention and she tied the issues of disease, crime, and machine politics to the living conditions of those who formed Chicago's industrial army. She believed that the development of playgrounds and parks provided one answer to the slums and their problems. She is thought to have organized the first true playground in 1894 and to have started the movement for a small park and playground system in Chicago. She served on the Chicago Playground Association Board along with Jens Jensen. Many regard her as the greatest woman of her generation, and in 1931 she was awarded the Nobel Peace Prize. Her books include *Democracy and Social Ethics* (1902), *Newer Ideals of Peace* (1907), *Twenty Years at Hull House* (1909), and *The Second Twenty Years at Hull House* (1930).

ADDISON, Joseph (1672–1719), was a poet, philosopher, playwright, statesman, and social critic. He directed his acid wit and pen at the proliferation of grandiose country estates whose grounds were, after the Restoration (1660–1688), sprawled over the countryside in the French grand style. He detested such gardens as incongruous anomalies of foreign origin and out of character with the nature of the English environment. Between 1709 and 1718, he composed a number of satirical essays, which were published in various magazines and newspapers, such as the *Tatler, Guardian,* and *Spectator.* In these articles, Addison assailed the "defective" artificiality and ostentatiousness of the "stately Palace Gardens," with their parterres, topiary, and forced geometry. He saw the formal garden, "made by too much art," as the antithesis of nature. He called the "nice touches and embellishments . . . the curiosities [and the] elegancies of art" trivial compared to the "bold and masterly . . . the rough, careless strokes of nature."

He was a student of the ancient poets and in the *Spectator* (1712) he identified his favorite writers and discussed his gleanings of the different garden types from their works. Addison was well informed about the non-formal gardens of China and in 1712 characterized Chinese design as an "imitation of nature . . . an image of landscape microcosm . . . the design of vantage points to deceive the eye and captivate the ear."

ALBERTI, Leone Battista (1404–1472), a writer, composer, architect, painter, and design theoretician, was called the "Florentine Vitruvius." His immensely influential book, which he wrote in Latin, *De Re Aedificatoria, Libri X* (Ten Books on Buildings), was written in 1452 but not published until 1485. In it, he enumerated the planning and design principles for the rural Italian villa of the Renaissance. His design guidelines were based on his understanding of those of the classical ancient Romans, especially Vitruvius and Pliny the Younger. As the basis for selecting the situation for one's rural villa, he emphasized the expansive "borrowed scenery" into the surrounding agricultural countryside. Also to be considered were the availability of good fresh water, breezes, and sun. Alberti was one of the clearest definers of design beauty when he wrote: "I shall define beauty to be a harmony of all the parts, in whatsoever subject it appears, fitted together with such proportion and connection, that nothing could be added, diminished or altered, but for the worse."

ALLEN OF HURTWOOD, Marjory, Lady. English landscape architect and author. Lady Allen studied horticulture at Reading University and worked at gardening before specializing in designing playgrounds, roof gardens, and private gardens. She served for several years as the president of the Nursery School Association of Great Britain and was the chairperson of the advisory council appointed to advise on film-making for children. In 1948–1949, Lady Allen was governor of the British Film Institute. Throughout the 1950s, she was the United Nations liaison officer with UNICEF, advising on children's welfare issues. She was the gardening correspondent of the *Manchester Guardian* for fifteen years and contributed numerous articles on her specialization to popular and professional journals in Britain. She wrote the books *The New Small Garden* (1956), *Design for Play* (1962), and coauthored *Gardens* (1953) with Susan Jellicoe.

She was vice-president of the (British) Institute of Landscape Architects from 1939 to 1946. Lady Allen received her title in 1921 when she married Clifford Allen (who later became Lord Allen of Hurtwood).

ALPHAND, Jean-Charles-Adolphe (1817–1891), was a French engineer but a person with the sensibilities of a landscape architect. Between 1852 and 1870, during the reign of Louis Napoleon, Emperor Napoleon III, he planned and supervised the transformation of the grand formal hunting park, the 2100-acre Bois de Boulogne, at the edge of Paris, into a *jardin anglais,* the French version of a Hyde Park or Regent's Park in London. He remodeled the rigid *allées* and *rond points* into meandering carriageways and footpaths, created sinuous water bodies, and opened up spacious meadows. In 1859, while his Central Park was in its second year of construction, Frederick Law Olmsted visited Paris and toured the Bois with Alphand.

Alphand also reworked a 55-acre abandoned stone quarry in Paris into an English-style pleasure park, the Parc du Buttes-Chaumont (1864–1869). He published his two-volume *Les Promenades de Paris* in 1867 and 1873, and in collaboration with Baron A. A. Ernouf, Alphand produced *L'Art des jardins* (1886).

AMENHOTEP III (c. 1417–1379 B.C.), also known as Amenophis III, was the Egyptian ruler from 1411 to 1375 B.C., during the New Kingdom's eighteenth dynasty (1574–1320 B.C.). He was worshipped as a god beside the god Amon. His reign was a time of peace and prosperity through the Nile valley and he is considered one of the greatest builders in all of Egypt's long history—especially for his ordering the erection of a great number of important and splendid public temples in Thebes. The Temple of Amun-Re in Luxor (1408–1300 B.C.) is the most notable among those built under his rule. The splendid residential gardens of the official of

Amenhotep III (c. 1400 B.C.), depicted in a well-preserved wall painting, is one of the best records left to history of this garden type.

ANDRÉ, Edouard François (1840–1911), was a French landscape architect who worked under Baron Haussmann in transforming Paris in the 1860s. He designed gardens in Luxemburg, the Netherlands, Russia, Monte Carlo, Italy (the redesigned grounds of the Villa Borghese), and England (Liverpool's Sefton Park). He was Adolphe Alphand's successor at the Bois de Boulogne and other projects in Paris. He planned the renovation of Montevideo, Uruguay and later directed the Ecole d'Horticulture de Versailles. He wrote *L'Art des jardins: traité général de la composition des parcs et jardins* (1879), discussing the aesthetic merits of adapting the English landscape garden to public parks in France.

ASPLUND, Gunnar (1885–1940), Swedish architect and landscape architect, designed the Forest Cemetery (Skogskyrko-gården, 1917–1940), at the edge of Stockholm. This spacious setting is both extremely modern in its feeling and recalls the romantic flowing landforms of "Capability" Brown.

ATTIRET, Jean-Denis (1701–1768), French painter and Jesuit priest lived in Beijing, China in the 1740s, sending back to France letters describing Chinese gardens. The French, perceiving the superficial similarities between Chinese and English gardens, with their similar rustic and natural countryside character, termed the style *le jardin anglo-chinois*. Father Attiret's writings were translated into English by Joseph Spence (under the pen name Sir Henry Beaumont) as *A Particular Account of the Emperor of China's Gardens near Pekin* (1752), stirring much interest in England for the chinoise style.

AUDUBON, John James (1781–1851), ornithologist, artist, and naturalist, (christened Fougère Rabin) was born in Haiti, the son of a French officer and a Creole woman. He was reared in France and renamed Jean Jacques Fougère Audubon. He studied painting with the French master Jacques Louis David.

In 1803 he emigrated to the United States to manage his father's lead mine in Pennsylvania. Here he took to traveling the wilds observing and painting birds. For a while he supported his family as a portraitist. During the 1820s, he produced a folio of bird paintings, which only an English publisher was willing to publish. In 1827, the first of his four-volume *Birds of America* (1827–1831) was finished and caused the British and French to hail him as a genius. In 1831 he published a five-volume *Ornithological Biography.* Returning to the United States, Audubon traveled from New England to the Carolinas, Louisiana, and the Dakotas painting birds and animals, and working on his (unfinished) *The Viviparous Quadrupeds of North America.*

AUSTEN, Jane (1775–1817), English novelist, admired the picturesque ideas of William Gilpin and Humphry Repton, quoting the former in her novels *Northanger Abbey* (1790), *Sense and Sensibility* (1811), and *Pride and Prejudice* (1813). She also discussed landscape gardening and mentioned Humphry Repton by name in *Mansfield Park* (1814). Like Gilpin, she was a devotée of "picturesque travel" and wrote about her love of highland scenery in *Tour Through Wales in a Letter from a Young Lady.* Because her writings were so popular in English-speaking countries, her concepts about landscape gardening were conveyed to the general public.

BACON, Francis, Viscount St. Albans (1561–1626), philosopher, writer, and pioneer of the scientific method in England, was lord chancellor in 1618. In his essay *Of Gardens* (1625) he discussed his basic principles of gardening and garden layout. It also contained many well-known quotable garden verses: "God Almighty first planted a garden."

BANKS, Sir Joseph (1743–1820), English botanist and naturalist, made an expedition to Newfoundland and Labrador in 1766 to collect plants and insects from Canada. Two years later he accompanied Captain James Cook on his ship *Endeavour* as he explored the Pacific islands, Australia (1768–1771), and New Zealand (1769). Because of the many plant types previously unknown to him, Banks named their landing place, near today's Sydney, Botany Bay. Many plants were named for him, including the Australian honeysuckles *(Banksia),* comprised of over forty species, and the beautiful climbing Banks, or Lady Banks, rose *(Rosa banksiae)*. Banks was president of the Royal Society for forty-two years (1778–1820).

BARRAGAN, Luis (1902–), educated as an engineer, is a Mexican architect and landscape architect famous for his "minimalist" creations. He and Roberto Burle Marx, from Brazil, are Latin America's most influential landscape architects today. Barragan's work is made up of brightly colored wall surfaces seen against foliage, water, and sky. He uses some traditional landscape elements in his gardens. In the Pedregal subdivision (1945–1950), which he developed south of Mexico City, he incorporated massive lava forms with his cubistic buildings, metal grilles, and lush vegetation.

At the Plaza y Fuente del Bebedero de los Caballos, at Las Arboledas, near Mexico City (1959), he used white and blue freestanding walls, eucalyptus trees, and *bebederos* (horse watering troughs), from which water plunged into reflecting pools to lend the sound of splashing water—"the music of the landscape." At the San Cristobal [horse] stable and pool (1968), in Los Clubes, he recalled aqueducts in his use of waterfalls and crashing water. He wrote, "The garden is a magic place for the enjoyment of meditation and companionship . . . the garden is the soul of the house" (Jellicoe et al., 1986, p. 39).

BARRETT, Nathan F. (1845–1919), was one of the twelve founders of the American Society of Landscape Architects in 1899. He learned to be a landscape gardener through working in his family's nursery on Staten Island. His practice began in 1869 with a project for the Central Railroad of New Jersey. He was the planner of the company town of Pullman, Illinois (1880–1885) and was a member of the Palisades Interstate Park Commission for fifteen years. He had a practice that was national in scope, with work from Maine to Florida in the east and as far west as California. He produced plans for Birmingham, Alabama, Fort Worth, Texas, and Chevy Chase, Maryland. He did the formal gardens for the Ponce-de-Leon Hotel in St. Augustine, Florida and, as he called them, "Reptonian" landscapes for private country estates of the wealthy in a dozen eastern states. He served as president of the ASLA from 1903 to 1907.

BARTRAM, John (1699–1777), a Pennsylvania Quaker, was one of America's greatest plant collectors. He traveled widely between 1736 and 1766 (after 1753 with his son, William), exploring for new plants, which he exchanged with the best botanists in England, Peter Collinson and Philip Miller. From his home near Philadelphia, he toured as far south as Georgia and Florida, finding such plants as the *Franklinia altamaha* (Franklin tree), the *Rhododendron maximum* (Rosebay rhododendron), and the *Dionaea muscipula* (Venus's flytrap). In all, he introduced over 200 new species into England. He was made the king's botanist in 1765—before the War for American Independence. He and William operated a plant nursery on their farm south of Philadelphia, from which they also exchanged plants and seeds all over the American colonies.

BARTRAM, William (1739–1823), the fifth son of John Bartram, traveled extensively throughout the eastern United States with his father after 1753, collecting and studying flora and fauna. He was a good artist and sent many of his very detailed drawings to England with his father's plant samples. William Bartram introduced many European plant species to the United States and exported many American species to England and Europe. His *Travels Through North and South Carolina, Georgia, East and West Florida* . . . , published in 1791, was well received in the United States and Europe.

BAUMANN, Eugene A. (1846–1896), a German landscape gardener, was responsible for much of the on-site construction and planting of Llewellyn Park, in West Orange, New Jersey (1853).

BAYLIS, Douglas (1915–1971), landscape architect, was one of the founders of the so-called "California school" of landscape architecture which emerged in the late 1930s and 1940s and had a profound effect on the profession throughout the country. Others in this movement were Thomas Church, Garrett Eckbo and Robert Royston. Baylis worked for Church from 1941, where they designed government housing communities, until opening his own office in San Francisco in 1946. Working with him for twenty-five years was his wife, Maggie, a talented graphic artist.

The "California school" approach to design was "modern" as was the work produced by that group. They eschewed the Beaux-Arts method of mimicking past historical styles, but were instead responding to the unique climate and outdoor lifestyle of California. Designs by these men where characteristically free from traditional geometry and bilateral symmetry, being much influenced by cubism, with strong abstract forms and nontraditional materials such as concrete, redwood, large boulders and modern sculpture.

Baylis' main vehicle for conveying his design philosophy and examples of his completed projects was through the numerous illustrated articles which he wrote for *Landscape Architecture* and the hundreds of conceptual "how-to" articles he wrote for popular magazines including *Sunset, House Beautiful, Better Homes and Gardens, McCalls* and *Family Circle*. He also wrote *California Houses of Gordon Drake* (1956) and *Garden Center Planning Book*.

Among the projects which Baylis designed during the 1950s and 1960s were: Foothill Farms, near Sacramento; the San Francisco Civic Center Plaza; IBM Headquarters, near San Jose; Washington Square, in San Francisco; the Monterey Freeway and the San Bruno Mountain and Housing Preserve. For three years he was the campus landscape architect for the University of California at Berkeley, where he also lectured.

BEAUMONT, Guillaume (d. 1727), French garden designer, laid out the grounds of Levens Hall in Westmoreland, England between 1689 and

1712. His yew and beech parterres there comprise some of Britain's most spectacular topiary.

BÉLANGER, François-Joseph (1744–1818), French architect and garden designer, introduced the *jardin irrégulier* into France. He spent most of the 1770s in England learning about the latest fashion in landscape gardens there. Working for the Comte d'Artois, brother of Louis XVI, he designed the pavillon and laid out the English-style Bagatelle (1777) at the edge of Paris's Bois de Boulogne. He also created the picturesque grounds of the Folie Sainte-James, near Paris, and the English gardens of the Château Beloeil, in Belgium, in 1780. He favored the use of *rocailles* (rockeries) and *fabriques* (follies) in his gardens.

BERNINI, Giovanni Lorenzo (1598–1680), was an Italian sculptor, architect, and designer. In 1665 he was commissioned by Louis XIV to remodel the Louvre palace in Paris. While his plans were not executed, his *drawings* initiated the Roman baroque movement outside Italy. Among his most notable environmental design projects were the oval-armed colonnade (c. 1656) for St. Peter's in the Vatican; the *Fountain of the Four Rivers* (1647–1652) in the Piazza Navonna in Rome; and the equestrian statue of Louis XIV, which terminates the south axis of the gardens of Versailles.

BIGELOW, Jacob (1786–1879), was the designer of Mount Auburn Cemetery, the Boston area's romantic "rural cemetery," which has been called "the first large-scale example of Romantic landscape design in this country." Not only was Mount Auburn important as an early landscape design, it was America's first rural cemetery and one of the first of its kind in the world. Its picturesque visual appeal and its feeling of security as a human-ordered and managed naturalistic public landscape, so easily accessible from a large population center helped to bring about a new, less remorseful American attitude toward death.

Bigelow was a Boston physician and respected botanist. In his day, medical doctors prepared their own remedies for their patients from plants which they grew themselves. Thus botany was a common course of study for one preparing for the medical profession. It was through this interest in plants that the doctor became involved with gentlemen of like mind in the Boston area. Together they formed the Massachusetts Horticultural Society, the organization for which the cemetery was created in 1831.

Bigelow, a native of Massachusetts and graduate of Harvard College, received his medical schooling at the University of Pennsylvania in 1810. He returned to Boston to practice medicine, and in 1815 he became a Professor of Materia Medica at Harvard Medical School, a post he held for forty years. Bigelow was named the first Rumford Professor in 1816 and held that chair until 1827. He spoke out against the widespread use of erroneous prescriptions and overdosages of drugs.

The layout of the grounds of Mount Auburn also owe much of their beauty to General Henry A. S. Dearborn, president of the Massachusetts Horticultural Society in 1831. He was a lawyer with a great knowledge of Greek architectural orders, engineering, and the English landscape garden design principles. He advised that the roads and walks should respond to the undulating landforms within the property. Avenues, he said, should run "as nearly level as possible by winding gradually and gracefully through the valleys and obliquely over hills, without any unnecessary or unavoidable bend."

When opened, Mount Auburn became an instant success, not only as a cemetery but as a manicured suburban nature playground which the public could enjoy at a time in our country's history when there were no public parks. Within that decade, dozens of other naturalesque rural cemeteries were created in cities and towns around the country. It was largely due to Mount Auburn and its imitators that the public park movement in the United States got its start in the 1840s and 1850s.

BIRCH, William Russell (1755–1834), was an English painter of portraits and landscapes as well as the designer of several landscapes in America. In 1794 he came to America and settled in Philadelphia. He published two volumes of views, *Views of the City of Philadelphia* (1798–1800) and *Country Seats of the United States* (1808). This folio of engravings portrayed and praised the design merits of twenty rural residences that he believed captured the essence of the most fashionable style in England. Birch designed his own house, Springland, and its English-style grounds near Philadelphia (1798–1805). He also advised several other country gentlemen on the layout of their estates. In his *Country Seats,* he wrote about his role in the siting and design of the home of a Virginia gentleman, George Washington Parke Custis (grandson of Martha and adopted son of General Washington). He advised against placement of the house on such a steep site. His advice was not heeded, and today that house, the Custus–Lee Mansion, is inside today's Arlington National Cemetery and commands one of the most revered panoramas in the nation's capital, overlooking the Potomac and the Mall.

BOLOTOV, Andrei Timofeyevich (1738–1833), Russian writer and theoretician on landscape gardening, founded and wrote for the journal *Ekononmichesky magzin* ("Economic Magazine") during the 1780s.

BONAPARTE, Joseph Napoleon (1768–1844), was the older brother of the emperor of France, Napoleon I. Joseph was, for a short time, king of Spain and the Kingdom of Naples. In 1815, after the fall of his brother's empire at the Battle of Waterloo, Joseph fled to America, where he settled near Philadelphia. Having designed estates for himself in France and Switzerland in the *jardin anglais* style, he worked for a quarter of a century to transform his 1800-acre estate, Point Breeze, in Bordentown, New Jersey, into a magnificent and romantic English-style country seat—but with certain French variations.

BONAPARTE, Joséphine (1763–1814), empress of France from 1804 to 1809, was married to Napoleon Bonaparte and acquired the estate Malmaison, at which she maintained a *jardin anglais.* She exchanged rare plants and garden information with friends around the world and displayed them on the grounds of her estate. The 1600-acre (726-hectare) park included a model farm, a menagerie (stocked with black swans, emus, and kangaroos), miniature cascades, and a temple d'amour atop a tall rocky mount. Her collection of roses was especially noteworthy in its day. The landscape garden at Malmaison was featured in three books. It was portrayed in 120 engravings in *Jardin de la Malmaison* (1808) by E. P. Ventenat and by 64 plates in *Description des plantes rares cultivées a Malmaison et a Navarre* (1813), by Aimé Bonplond.

BOYCEAU, Jacques (d. 1633), was a French gardener and the author of the *Traité du jardinage* (1638). He worked for Marie de Medici at the Luxemburg gardens in Paris with Claude Mollet during the reign of Louis XIII. There he developed the *parterre de broderie* ("embroidery on the ground"), named for the embroideries that its intricate patterns resembled. He also laid out the parterres at Versailles before Le Nôtre remodeled the entire place for Louis XIV.

BOYLE, Richard. *See* Burlington, third Earl of.

BRAMANTE (1444–1514) was an Italian High Renaissance architect whose real name was Donato d'Agnolo. He was schooled in Urbino and moved to Milan, where he designed several fine churches. He moved to Rome in 1499 and was made papal architect under popes Alexander VI and Julius II. He designed the Tempietto ("little temple") as a shrine in 1502 on the site of St. Peter's crucifixion. Four years later he began reconstruction of the Basilica of St. Peter and the Vatican Palace.

His design for the Cortile del Belvedere (1503) revolutionized villa site planning. It was conceived to link the papal palace with the pope's older summerhouse, the Belvedere, a thousand feet away and at the top of a small hill. Bramante did this by means of two parallel three-story corridors enclosing a long narrow space comprised of three terraces with gardens, grand stairs, and fountains. The enormity of the long axial Belvedere Court, the largest palace space since Hadrian's second-century villa, recalled the huge scale of Roman times. Thus the sixteenth-century fashion in villa design called for large, very architectonic, multiterraced ground plans, organized along a single central axis or sight line. This was also consistent with that century's fascination with one-point perspective.

BRIDGEMAN, Charles (d. 1738), English landscape gardener, apprenticed under George London and later became a partner of Henry Wise. In 1722, Bridgeman toured China and returned to write *New Principles of Garden Design* (1728), wherein he mentioned "chinoiserie" and suggested the grafting of Chinese features onto classic forms. These verbal descriptions of the Chinese gardens did not include plans or views and therefore would have had only a minor affect on the development of the natural style in England. They did, however, reflect much the same reverence for nature that the English had. Bridgeman popularized the ha-ha wall as a landscape feature, using it to separate formal garden areas from outlying grazing areas, thus allowing the surrounding pastoral scenery to be enjoyed while deterring the livestock from intruding upon the pleasure garden.

He worked with the architect John Vanbrugh at Stowe, his most successful landscape. He also designed the grounds of Rousham, Chiswick, and many other country seats. William Kent redesigned many of Bridgeman's places, replacing his formal planning with the naturalistic forms of the English landscape gardening style.

Bridgeman's authenticated projects include Stowe, 1714–1738; Eastbury, c. 1716–1738; Claremont, 1716–1738; Langleys, 1719; Wimpole, 1720–1725; Gubbins, Briggins, Purley Hall, and Carshalton, 1721; Down Hall, 1720–1727; Kedleston, 1722–1726; Marble Hill, 1724; King's College (Cambridge), 1724; Houghton, 1725–1731; Chicheley Hall, 1726; Boughton, 1726–1731; Compton Place, 1728; Bower House, 1729; Amesbury, 1730–1738; and Wimbledon House, 1732–1735. In 1727 he was placed in charge of the royal gardens: Kensington Palace, Hyde Park, Hampton Court, St. James's Park, Richmond Park, and Windsor Park. Seventeen other projects are attributed to Bridgeman but have yet to be verified (Hussey, pp. 36–37).

BROWN, Lancelot "Capability" (1716–1783), English landscape gardener, was characterized by Horace Walpole as creating *"artificial* natural-looking landscapes," when he stated, "[T]he effect of his genius [was] that when he was the happiest man, he will be least remembered; so closely did he copy nature that his works will be mistaken." In doing so, Brown dismantled some of England's most elaborate parterres and clipped allées.

As a lad, he worked as a gardener for Sir Richard Grenville and was hired in 1740 by William Kent while he was remodeling the grounds of Stowe. Working on his own after Kent's death in 1748, he demolished all formal lines and geometry in the landscape, using the ha-ha to set the mansion in a spacious park.

Brown's nickname derived from his frequent expression to each new client that he perceived great "capabilities of improvement" in the given situation of each site. He was prolific, producing 169 (authenticated) works as well as another 49 projects attributed to him, accounting for more acreage in England than all the works of Le Nôtre in France. Despite Brown's professional output, he never wrote or published a word about his design philosophy or about any of his built works. Therefore, historians can only speculate about his ideals.

Brown's basic precepts were amazingly few: augment nature wherever possible; increase natural slopes, or create them if too flat; carpet the landforms in closely cropped green turf; use mirrorlike surfaces of water wherever possible; curve drives and walks in serpentine lines; group trees and shrubs to surprise; and encircle the site with belts of trees in soft-edged masses to hide unwanted off-site views and lead the eye from one pleasure to another.

In 1782, at the end of his career, a former client wrote of Brown: "He illustrates everything he says about gardening by some literary or grammatical allusion [and] compared his art to literary composition. 'Now *there,'* said he, pointing his finger, 'I make a comma, and there . . . where a more decided turn is proper, I make a colon; at another part, where an interruption is desirable to break the view, a parenthesis; now a full stop [period], and then I begin another subject' " (*Turner*, 1984, p. 78).

At the pinnacle of his career, in the 1770s, Brown's "place-making," as he called it, came under a great storm of criticism from two sides, led by Reverend William Gilpin, Sir Uvedale Price, and Richard Payne Knight. The naturalists attacked his artificially smooth lawns and "clumps" of trees as "un-natural. . . too 'feminine'." The romantic/picturesque school found his work to be "vapid and bland," too boring and formulalike, not varied and interesting enough; not sufficiently rugged and masculine to approach the wildly dramatic diversity of true nature. His work increasingly withdrew from nature, as he evened out every intrinsic feature that had contributed to the "genius" of the places on which he worked. The "picture-garden" enthusiasts deemed Brownian landscapes to be devoid of the variety and complexity upon which good painted scenes of landscapes had come to depend. In Brown's "empty" scenes, where was the artifice, where were the traces of human involvement? Price found no "accidents" of nature in the groomed shorelines of Brown's ponds and lakes—no rotten stumps and logs, no aquatic "weeds," none of the uncouth tangled undergrowth by which nature stabilizes a real body of water.

During his nearly forty-three-year career, Brown was castigated for more destruction of historic architectural gardens than that of any other person. His admirers assert that he achieved visual harmony with each environment because he coaxed the ultimate design forms out of the natural qualities of each situation. In fact, the "great genius" recontoured each property at a scale never before imagined. He ordered a "dell" or "concave scoop" or the filling of vast areas of the ground to depths as great as 12 feet above or below the existing grade simply "to vary the ground plane" and "contain the eye." To keep the finished carpet groomed, armies of laborers daily scythed, raked, and rolled Brown's turf.

He was most masterful in his handling of water, and in every work in which water was present, it always stole the show. He seldom allowed the entire surface area of a body of water to be seen from a single vantage point, concealing parts of the lake or pond by creating an irregular shoreline relieved by a number of coves or inlets, and wrapping a stream around a slight hillock or mass of vegetation in a way that created a mystery as to the full extent of the water feature. Frequently, he impounded a stream to provide a mirrorlike surface on which he would reflect tree masses and landforms from the opposite bank. To obscure the distant edges of his lakes and to mask his clever hydraulic engineering devices, he massed shade-producing foliage around such spots, thereby darkening them as well as exaggerating the dimensions of his artificial lakes. For the pure visual enjoyment of his clients, he is known to have inundated as many as 80 acres of arable land, such as at Blenheim, where his so-called Brown's Lake is 15 feet deep. As this drastic engineering feat meant the submerging of the foundation of Vanbrugh's Grand Bridge, it resulted in a far more handsome scale relationship between the structure and the broad plane of water. As large as some of Brown's lakes were, however, often they were extremely shallow.

Brown avoided all humanmade structures in close visual proximity to his lakes, with the exception of bridges, which were a logical means of crossing over water and were acceptable in water scenes. Vanbrugh's bridge at Blenheim is the most notable of such features in a Brownian landscape.

Brown's planting palette was extremely limited and concentrated on the use of species native to England. His favorite trees were the various native oaks, beeches, birches, elms, and chestnuts. There were a few exotic exceptions, such as the Spanish chestnut *(Castanea sativa),* horse chestnut *(Aesculus hippocastanum),* European mountain ash *(Sorbus aucuparia),* scarlet oak *(Quercus coccinea),* and lime *(Tilia cordata).* His ideal was that all plants—their form, color, and size—should appear in harmony with one another and that horticultural anomalies such as purple, blue, or variegated foliage were forbidden. Preferring the "most obfuscate green[s]," broadleaved and coniferous evergreens were used sparingly in Brown's planting schemes. Of these, his favorites were those with dark green foliage, the Cedar of Lebanon, the native yew and holly, Scots pine, and the Holm oak. In the distance and behind lighter deciduous foliage, they added solidity and depth to the picture. Brown shared Shenstone's view that planting should be done "without any seeming order," and also the opinion of William Mason, who said that "trees should be planted as if the seeds had been dropped by a bird pursued by a hawk." In his later years, Brown was ridiculed for his tendency to plants trees in clumps. His, however, were not the three or four tree clusters such as Kent and others had created. Brown worked on a grander scale, as revealed by some of his 14-acre clumps recorded on nineteenth-century topographical maps. Each of Brown's pet trees was more irregular and picturesque in its habit than symmetrically conical, a form he disapproved of strenuously. His admirer, Horace Walpole, expressed Brown's concept as well as *the master* might himself: "[E]xcept as a screen to conceal some deformity, or as a shelter in winter, I am not fond of total plantations of evergreens. Firs in particular form a very ungraceful summit, all broken into angles."

In close proximity to the house, the area he called the "pleasure ground," Brown departed from his reliance on indigenous plants and embellished his "close walks" with much more variety of form and seasonal color. He used such horticultural selections—many from North America—as bird cherry *(Prunus padus),* double-flowering hawthorns *(Crataegus oxyacantha),* "Virginia schumach" (smooth sumac) *(Rhus glabra),* red and sugar maple *(Acer rubrum* and *A. saccharum),* "Cockgyreas" (smoke tree) *(Cotinus coggygria),* wax myrtle *(Myrica cerifera),* Persian lilac *(Syringa persica),* and Portugal laurel *(Prunus lusitanica).*

Among Brown's works are Petworth Park in Sussex (improved 1752), Stowe (1740–1749), Warwick Castle (1749–1751), Croome in Worcestershire (1750–1758), Moor Park in Hertfordshire (1753), Burghley House (1754–1782), Longleat in Wiltshire (1757), Prior Park in Bath (1760), Corsham Court in Wiltshire (1760), Bowood (1761), Chatsworth in Derbyshire (c. 1761), Hampton Court (1764), Claremont (1769), Harewood in Yorkshire (1772), and Blenheim in Oxfordshire (1764–1774).

BRUNELLESCHI, Filippo (1377–1446), is considered the first great architect of the Italian Renaissance. He was a student of classical Roman architecture, and this knowledge enabled him to solve the enormous technical problems involved in erecting a dome to span the unfinished cathedral of Florence, Santa Maria del Fiore (1420–1434). Among his best designs (all in Florence) were the Pazzi Chapel (1440), in the cloister of the Santa Croce; the Founding Hospital (1419); the Church of Santo Spirito (1428); the Church of San Lorenzo (1421–1425); and the central portion of the Pitti Palace. Brunelleschi established a school of architecture in Florence, through which he advanced the recently revived technique of perspective.

BRYANT, William Cullen (1794–1878), was an American poet and journalist who was taught to write in imitation of Alexander Pope. At the age of 17 he wrote *Thanatopsis,* regarded as the first important poem composed by an American. He edited the *New York Review* and later the New York *Evening Post* for over fifty years. As a friend of many of the Hudson River school landscape painters and Andrew Jackson Downing, he spoke and wrote voluminously about the importance of preserving natural wilderness and of establishing public urban parks in American cities. His efforts contributed to the ultimate establishment of the Central Park in New York City.

BUONTALENTI, Bernardo (1536–1608), Italian artist and designer of La Grotta Grande (1583–1593) at the edge of the Boboli Gardens, in Florence, and the grottoes, *automata* and *giochi d'acqua* at the Villa Pratolino (1569–1581), near Florence.

BURKE, Edmund (1729–1797), English philosopher and statesman, wrote one of the eighteenth century's seminal works on the subject of aesthetics, *A Philosophical Enquiry into the Origin of Our Ideas of the Sublime and Beautiful* (1757). Burke's sublime was characterized by large-scale elements, irregularity of form, stark contrasts between light and dark, all of which conveyed a sense of terror. His ideas set the stage for the late eighteenth-century aesthetic debate between the proponents of the beautiful, demonstrated by "Capability" Brown, with his smooth serpentine lines, and the picturesque school led by Richard Payne Knight, Uvedale Price, and William Gilpin.

BURLE MARX, Roberto (1909–), born in São Paulo, is the son of a Brazilian mother and a German father. He spent his childhood years in Germany, studying painting and music while learning Brazilian flora in the Dahlem Botanical Garden. Returning to Brazil in 1929, he designed gardens in 1932 and 1933 for clients of the noted architect Lúcio Costa. He is a talented painter, set designer, fabric and jewelry designer, authority on botany, and one of the twentieth century's most remarkable landscape architects. Burle Marx has collaborated with the modernist architects Affonso Reidy, Oscar Niemeyer, and Costa. His landscape plans for Brasilia (1960), the national capital, greatly influenced Latin American landscape architecture.

He said he wanted "above all to rid gardens of the European features with which they have always been endowed in this country. We must also eschew the romantic approach, since gardens must keep pace with human progress." He abhors the frequent labeling of his work as "stylized," because he resists formulas and treats each project as a unity between nature and art. Nevertheless, his compositions have achieved the deferential designation "the Burle Marx Brazilian Style," characterized by his liberal use of native flora and a sculptural and "painterly" arrangement of colors, free-flowing patterns of ground cover, water, and hard surfaces.

Burle Marx has discovered and collected many of the exotic jungle plants that he uses in his designs and maintains a nursery business. Among his most significant projects are the 5-kilometer-long promenade of the Copacabana Beach in Rio de Janeiro; the Municipal Gardens in Recife (1935); roof gardens for the Ministry of Education and the Resurgeros Insurance buildings in Rio (1936–1938); the Pampulha Botanical Garden in Belo Horizonte; the civic centers of Curitiba and Santo André; the Hospital Sulamerica; the Parques Este and Oeste in Caracas, Venezuela; and the botanical gardens in São Paulo and Brasilia. The career of Burle Marx is summarized in the books *The Tropical Gardens of Burle Marx* (1964) by Pietro M. Bardi and *Roberto Burle Marx e a Nova Visão da Paisagem* by Flávio L. Motta (1984).

BURLINGTON, third Earl of [Richard Boyle] (1695–1753), was a major connoisseur of the arts in the early eighteenth-century England. William Kent met and traveled for a year in Italy with Lord Burlington. While together, they studied and steeped themselves in the architecture of the sixteenth-century architect Andrea Palladio. Returning to London, Kent redesigned Burlington's summer place, Chiswick House, which was completed in 1727. Burlington was praised by the poet Alexander Pope in his *Epistle to Burlington* (1731), one of the seminal essays on the subject of the natural-style landscape garden.

BURNHAM, Daniel Hudson (1846–1912), was a Chicago architect, who with his partner John Wellborn Root is said to have originated the Chicago school of architecture. Burnham and Root developed the steel-skeleton building frame technology, which enabled the erection of "sky-scrapers." The Fuller ("Flatiron") Building (1903) in New York City is their most widely recognized creation.

Burnham was the head of design for the World's Columbian Exposition of 1893 in Chicago, for which Frederick Law Olmsted and his partner, Henry S. Codman, were the landscape architects. In 1901 the U.S. Senate appointed the Senate Park Commission with Burnham, Frederick Law Olmsted, Jr., New York architect Charles McKim, and sculptor Augustus Saint-Gaudens, as the team of designers charged with reviving the L'Enfant plan of Washington, D.C. As a major landmark in the city plan, Burnham designed the capital's romanesque revival Union Station. Following the success of that civic design effort in bringing public attention to urban design, Burnham's professional focus shifted to producing city planning and civic design proposals for a number of cities around the world—in what became known as the "city beautiful movement"—with Burnham as one of the prime movers. He produced grandiose sweeping master plans for the redesign of the central city of Chicago; San Francisco; Baltimore; Cleveland; Manila, the new capital of the Philippines; and Baguio, also in the Philippines. It was largely out of this interest in the appearance of urban centers that the new discipline, city planning, got its start, with Harvard University's Department of Landscape Architecture offering the first master's degree course in 1923. It was Burnham at his grandiose best when he said: "Make no little plans, they have no magic to stir man's blood. . . . Make big plans . . . remembering that a noble, logical diagram once recorded will never die but long after we are gone will be a living thing asserting itself with ever growing insistency."

BUSCH (or BUSH), John (1730s–1790s), was a German-born landscape gardener who emigrated to England in 1744. There he ran a nursery business in Hackney until 1771, when he accepted a commission by Catherine the Great of Russia to design an English landscape garden at her palace, Tsarskoye Selo, near Petersburg. He also designed a naturalistic park on the grounds of her Pulkova palace. He remained in Russia until 1789, when he returned to England.

BYE, Arthur Edwin, Jr. (1919–), is a landscape architect who, since 1951, has produced work all over the United States as well as in Europe and the Caribbean. His multidisciplinary practice is located in Cos Cob, Connecticut. His scope of work has included many campuses, office parks, national monuments, cemeteries, institutional sites, and residences. His most noted residence was the Roland Reisley House, in Pleasantville, New York, designed by Frank Lloyd Wright in 1957. Bye's splendid use of natural-looking, soft, undulating earth forms and native vegetation are his signature. He wrote in his handsome book, *Art into Landscape, Landscape into Art* (1983): "To create effectively, the landscape architect must work outdoors to 'feel' each rock and stone, the trees and vines, sand and earth, the sky and water, reflecting light and shadow, the mist, the snow and ice, the rain, the wind, and the odors and the noises that are all about us."

Bye was educated at Pennsylvania State University and worked in both the National Park Service and the Forest Service. In addition to the book noted above, he wrote *Abstracting the Landscape* (1990), has authored many articles, and compiled the landscape architectural entries for the *Dictionary of Architecture and Construction,* Cyril M. Harris (editor). He has been a visiting professor at many universities in this country and in 1971 was made a fellow of the ASLA.

BYRD, William II (1674–1744), born at his family's James River plantation, Westover, in Virginia, was a gentleman farmer, growing what he called "that bewitching vegetable, tobacco." He became a member of the House of Burgesses and Council of State. His library of 3500 volumes was considered the finest in the colonies. It included many volumes related to architecture, gardening, and garden design.

About 1711, he began his first improvements on the grounds of Westover, situated on the north side of the James River, one of the chief transportation arteries at the time. There was an axis from the river through the house and its grounds. The gentle slope from the house to the river was maintained as a spacious lawn with scattered trees. On the landward side was a short tree-lined avenue leading to the main entrance gate, on an axis with the symmetrical house. A combination vegetable and pleasure garden sat off to the west of the central arrival court.

Moving back and forth to England several times until his mid-fifties, Byrd was steeped in both the older French formal fashion in garden design and the new "modern" taste in gardens in Britain—the landscape garden—with its openness, inspired by natural forms and materials. This movement had been under way for less than two decades by 1726, when Byrd conceded to live out his life in Virginia. He subscribed to the preachings of the garden authorities Addison, Pope, Steele, and Stephen Switzer, who in his *Ichnographia Rustica* (1718) admonished the former generation for their land-consuming, foreign-inspired formal gardens. Byrd traveled about England a good deal and, in his personal correspondence—as early as 1706—he wrote about his admiration of many newly improved seats, commenting on several great houses [Clivedon, near Windsor; Sudbrook House, near London; Blenheim, in Oxfordshire; Durdans and Woodcote Grove, in Surrey; Whitton Park; Hagley Park; Uborn; and Woodcote Park (home of Charles Calvert, governor of Maryland, 1732–1733)], each of which was "finely situated" in a "park" with fine "prospect[s]." Byrd mentioned having strolled in gardens and parks with Horace Walpole on four occasions. It is highly probable that Byrd met the poet Alexander Pope, or as was *de rigueur* for the *cognoscenti,* visited his famous Twickenham garden (1719–44).

Byrd worked intermittently at developing his garden between 1711 and about 1740. He may have been alluding to a ha-ha wall he was beginning in his reference to a "ditch" he was having made in 1721, although no archaeological evidence indicates such on the site. He would have seen a few by that time in the places he toured in England and conceivably intended a ha-ha for Westover.

Byrd created a grottolike construction on the grounds of Westover, according to correspondence of a family friend, William Mayo, who mentioned it in 1731 (Martin, 1991, p. 203, n. 72). During the time that Byrd was in England, Pope created a sensation with his famous shell-encrusted grotto in his garden.

Extending out from Westover house were two curving lines of trees, at each end of which was a "Temple of Cloacina," a reference to the sewers of Rome—two privies. When the Marquis de Chastellux saw Westover in 1782, he noted: "The walls of the garden and the house were covered with honeysuckle . . ." (Rice, 1963, p. 432). This reference to climbing vines being in evidence suggests not that the widow Byrd was a sloppy gardener, but that she probably accepted the romantic or natural informality of such ramblers on her walls.

Among Byrd's writings about social and environmental conditions in the Virginia Colony were *The History of the Dividing Line Between Virginia and North Carolina, A Journey to the Land of Eden, Progress to the Mines,* and *Secret Desires.*

CAMERON, Charles (c. 1743–1812), a Scottish architect and landscape architect from London, went to Russia in 1779 to serve as the court architect for Catherine the Great (1729–1796). Before his Russian sojourn, Cameron had received wide acclaim for his book about Roman classical architecture, *The Baths of Rome* (1772).

He was the designer of the palace and a portion of the grounds of Tsarskoye Selo (Pushkin) and the Palladian palace at Pavlovsk. After Catherine's death, Cameron was retained by her successor, Alexander I. Between 1803 and 1805, he designed a number of important civic buildings in the capital, Petersburg.

Tsarskoye Selo ("imperial spot"), considered one of the world's greatest landscape parks, is comprised of two palaces, the Yekaterinsky ("Catherine's"), in the Italian baroque style, and the neoclassical Alexandrovsky ("Alexander's") for Alexander I (1777–1825). These both sat in forested parklike settings, each of which comprised several thousand acres. The French grand manner gardens of the former were 225 acres in extent, while the latter measured 440 acres. Catherine's palace at Tsarskoye Selo was massive, with its garden facade measuring over 900 feet in length.

The enlightened Tsarina (or Czarina, "empress") was a devotée of the *jardin anglais,* the English landscape garden style. In 1771 she hired John Busch (or Bush, 1730s–1790s), a German-born landscape gardener who moved to England in 1744, and Vasily Neyelov (1722–1782), a Russian architect, who had studied garden design in England. Between 1771 and 1780 they remodeled the park into a semblance of the English landscape garden. Its grounds included a Palladian bridge, fashioned after the one at Wilton, England; a small shrine, called the Creaking Pavilion; a classical concert hall; a Turkish kiosk; and a small pond filled with several islands, called the Archipelago.

Cameron was hired to design several Chinese-style buildings in the manner of those depicted in Sir William Chambers' books of 1763 and 1772. These comprise the Chinese village, the largest collection of buildings in Europe executed in that style. He also modified the lakes into the "natural" style and added many monuments and obelisks, commemorating important accomplishments in Russian history.

As well as making many improvements to the grounds of the palace, Cameron built several structures, most important of which was the elevated Cameron Gallery, between the formal gardens and the romantic landscape garden, with commanding views of both.

Catherine wrote to Voltaire in 1772: "I now love to distraction gardens in the English style, the curving lines, the gentle slopes, the ponds in the forms of lakes . . . and I scorn straight lines and twin allées. I hate fountains which torture water in order to make it follow a course contrary to nature . . . anglomania rules my plantomania."

Cameron worked at Pavlovsk (Paulowsky), for Grand Duke Paul I between 1780 and 1796. This palace and grounds outside Petersburg consisted of a 1300-acre park, within which were the Doric-style Temple of Friendship, the Apollo Colonnade, an aviary, the Temple of Three Graces, a rustic thatch-roofed dairy, a hermitage, and a picturesque charcoal-maker's hut. These sat amidst dense forest greenery and spacious grassy strolling spaces. This place was altered many times over the years after Cameron was dismissed. Vincenzo Brenna, Pietro Gonzaga, Carlo Rossi, and Andrei Voronikhin each built structures and attempted to improve on nature in the park.

J. C. Loudon, in his *An Encyclopedia of Gardening* (1822), devoted two pages to Cameron's Tsarskoye Selo, pronouncing its layout and maintenance "equal to any in Europe." He called Pavlovsk "the best specimen of the English style in the [Russian] empire."

CARHART, Arthur Hawthorne (1892–1978), landscape architect, graduated from Iowa State College in 1916, earning the institution's first bachelor of science degree in landscape architecture. He went on to work for O. C. Simonds in Chicago. In 1919 he became the U.S. Forest Service's first landscape architect, in charge of recreation planning. He was called the "Beauty Doctor" by many of the rangers. He prepared the first forest recreation plan, for San Isabel National Forest in Colorado in 1919. At the same time, he proposed that major tracts of Forest Service acreage around Trappers Lake in the White River National Forest of Colorado be closed to summer home construction, to be left untouched by grazing, logging, roads, or other intrusions. In essence they were to remain as pristine wilderness.

In 1919, he met Aldo Leopold, who was then an assistant forester at Gila National Forest in New Mexico [Territory]. Carhart strengthened Leopold's wilderness attitudes immensely and was a major influence on Leopold's quitting the Forest Service in 1924 to devote his life to the study of ecology and preaching about the wilderness ethic. That year Carhart wrote to Leopold, "There is a limit to the number of . . . lakes [and] mountains . . . in existence, and in each one of these situations there are portions of natural scenic beauty which are God made, and the beauties of which of right should be the property of all people."

Over the years, Carhart's planning philosophies earned for him the moniker, "the father of the wilderness concept" and were instrumental in the passage of the Wilderness Act of 1964. In the 1930s he formed his own firm in Denver and practiced as a land use planning consultant as well as serving as the coordinator of the Colorado Wildlife Restoration Program. Carhart was a prolific writer, publishing not only 500 articles on conservation, but several works of fiction. Among his books were *Water—or Your Life* (1951), *Timber in Your Life* (1954), *The Outdoorsman's Cookbook* (1955), *Trees and Game: Twin Crops* (1958), and *The National Forests* (1959).

CARSON, Rachel (1907–1964), scientist, naturalist, and author, helped enlighten an entire generation of twentieth-century Americans by changing our view of humankind's relationship to nature. This change marked the beginning of the important "environmental awakening" in the United States during the 1960s and 1970s. Her scientific expertise combined with her extraordinary skill as a writer made her most important book, *Silent Spring* (1962), an American classic within the environmental literature. It popularized the pesticide issue while defining an environmental ethic. Other books by Carson include *Under the Sea-Wind* (1941), *The Sea Around Us* (1951), *The Edge of the Sea* (1955), and *The Sense of Wonder* (1965).

CATO, Marcus Porcius (234–149 B.C.), was a Roman statesman and farmer who wrote the book *De Agri Cultura* in 160 B.C. He offered advice for the management of one's rural estate and considered the garden second only in importance to the vineyard.

CAUTLEY, Marjorie Sewell (1891–1954), was a landscape architect who, with architect Clarence Stein and landscape architect Henry Wright, was responsible for landscape planning and design at the garden cities of Sunnyside Gardens in New York's Borough of Queens (1924) and Radburn, New Jersey (1927). She was a superb detail designer and plantswoman who imbued the large public spaces in these two projects with the human qualities for which they have become so well known. Among her other projects were the Hillside Housing Project, Bronx, New York, Phipps Garden Apartments, Queens; Roosevelt Common, New Jersey; the Women's Club, Ridgewood, New Jersey; and private estates on Long Island, New Jersey, and Connecticut.

She was a graduate of Cornell University (1917) and the author of *Building a House in Sweden* (1931) and *Garden Design* (1935), as well as several magazine articles.

CHAMBERS, Sir William (1726–1796), a Scottish architect who had studied architecture in Paris and Italy, returned to England in 1757 after his second trip to China and published *Of the Art of Laying Out Gardens Among the Chinese* and an essay entitled "Designs of Chinese Buildings, Furniture, Dresses, Machines, and Utensils." He felt that there was an affinity between the British and Chinese philosophies, stating that "Chinese gardeners are like the European painters."

Following the publications, Chambers was appointed garden architect of London's Kew Gardens, where he was commissioned to "improve and embellish" the grounds. The landscape garden plan that he produced and his designs for structures such as the Pagoda were published in 1763 as *Plans, Elevations, Sections, and Perspective Views of the Gardens and Buildings at Kew in Surrey*. Nine years later he wrote a pamphlet, *A Dissertation on Oriental Gardening*. It was largely through his influence that the fashion for *chinoiserie*—buildings and furniture designed to look Chinese—caught on in England and elsewhere.

He explained that the Chinese garden is organized into "a variety of scenes, and you are led, by winding passages cut in the groves, to the different points of view, each of which is marked by a seat, a building, or some other object." He believed that the success of their gardens resulted from the number and variety of these prescribed scenes, which in England at the time were called "offskips."

Chambers was a critic of the Brownian manner of landscape design and ridiculed it in his *A Dissertation on Oriental Gardening* (1772), wherein he wrote that Brown's gardens "differ little from common fields, so closely are they copied from vulgar nature." Elsewhere, in reference to Brown, Chambers wrote, "[T]he regularly serpentine curves of which our English gardeners are so fond . . . these eternal, uniform undulating lines are, of all things, the most unnatural, the most affected and the most tiresome to pursue. . . ." It was he who initiated the late-eighteenth-century controversy about the "picturesque" versus the "beautiful." Sir William designed the New Bridge and some follies on the grounds of Blenheim.

CHURCH, Thomas Dolliver (1902–1978), was born in Boston but grew up in San Francisco, where he worked as a landscape architect for over fifty years. He is said to have been the creator of the "modern garden" style. He was educated at the University of California at Berkeley and Harvard. Following graduation in 1922, he traveled extensively in Europe. He had a special interest in the Mediterranean region because its climate was similar to that of California. Upon his return to the United States, he began teaching landscape architecture at the University of California at Berkeley. In 1929, on the eve of the Depression, he opened his office, designing small residential gardens. The economic limitations of his clientele forced him to invent many labor- and maintenance-saving garden features, such as a minimal use of mowed lawn area and an extensive use of hardscaping—patterned pavement to create visual interest—and redwood decking. The garden as an "outdoor room," was very much a California invention of Tommy Church.

His design approach drew heavily on cubism, using free-flowing abstract curvilinear lines, forms, and spaces in occult balance. Consistent with the precepts of the modern sculptors, he said, "A garden should have no beginning and no end." His work also reflected the eclectic in that he combined geometry based on the French baroque, all the while using native plantings. Above all, Church led the American landscape architecture movement away from the strict Beaux-Arts tradition of the early twentieth century. Church's designs were much publicized by a number of popular home and garden journals, chief among which was *Sunset* magazine. With his work so readily accessible in magazines, it was often copied and became known as the California style. His philosophy and principles of design were spelled out in two books, *Gardens Are for People* (1955, reprinted in 1983) and *Your Private World* (1969).

Church often carried pruning shears in his pocket and would return to visit with former clients to "whack off a few branches," because while he was making visual improvements in his previous work, he also believed that "today's humble client is tomorrow's CEO."

Among Church's most important works were his masterpiece, the Dewey Donnell garden, El Novillero, in Sonoma, California (1948), done with Lawrence Halprin, who was then working in his office; the General Motors Technical Center in Warren, Michigan (1956); portions of the campuses of Stanford University and the University of California at Berkeley and at Santa Cruz; and Longwood Gardens in Delaware. He is also known to have worked on the grounds of at least three Frank Lloyd Wright–designed houses, hired independently after the construction was under way or finished: the Smith House (1960s) in Bloomfield Hills, Michigan; the Auldbrass Plantation (1950s), near Yamasee, South Carolina; and the Walker House ("Cabin on the Rock," 1948), near Carmel, California.

CLARKE, Gilmore David (1892–1982), was a graduate of Cornell University. In 1916 he was hired by Charles Downing Lay as a landscape architect with the Bronx River Parkway Commission, whose task was to lay out a road from the Bronx Park out to the countryside—to Kensico Dam—a distance of 15 miles, specifically for pleasure driving. When completed in 1923, this was the first true parkway in America.

Clarke was the chief landscape architect for the Westchester County Park Commission from 1923 until 1933, during which time the county built a park and parkway system admired internationally. He also worked with Robert Moses on many other projects in New York City, including the Henry Hudson Parkway. Among his finest works were the Mount Vernon Memorial Parkway in Virginia, the Merritt Parkway in Connecticut, and the Garden State Parkway in New Jersey. In 1934 he opened his own office in New York City with Michael Rapuano and at the same time was made professor of city and regional planning at Cornell University. He taught there from 1935 to 1938, when he was named dean of the College of Architecture, a position in which he served until 1950. In 1932, President Hoover appointed Clarke to the national Commission of Fine Arts. He chaired the commission from 1937 to 1950. One of his major decisions in that role was the siting of the Pentagon building in Arlington, Virginia, at the edge of Washington, D.C. Clarke and Rapuano were major planners for both the 1939 and 1964 New York World's Fairs, with the centerpiece of the latter fair, the Unisphere, being his creation. The firm also planned the grounds of the United Nations Headquarters in New York City.

He was president of the American Society of Landscape Architects from 1949 to 1951. In 1950, Clarke served as the national merit badge counselor in landscaping for the Boy Scouts of America. He wrote the *Merit Badge Series Manual: Landscaping*.

CLEVELAND, Horace William Shafer (1814–1900), landscape architect, was born in Massachusetts and trained in agriculture, civil engineering, and horticulture. As a young man, he met Andrew Jackson Downing and resolved to become a landscape designer. Beginning in 1854, he worked in Boston with Robert Morris Copeland (Copeland and Cleveland), practicing "landscape and ornamental gardening" and furnishing "plans for the laying out and improvement of Cemeteries, Public Squares, Pleasure Grounds, Farms and Gardens, as well as for the construction of every species of Building connected with Agriculture, Horticulture, and general rural improvement." In 1856, they published a remarkable little pamphlet, *A Few Words on the Central Park* (1856), in which they promoted the importance of comprehensive master planning for such large and complex projects as the much discussed but yet to be designed New York Central Park. Their counseling, it can be assumed, prompted the Central Park Commission to stage the design competition, which Copeland and Cleveland entered but were not successful in winning. One of the firm's most notable projects was the layout of Boston's Back Bay section in 1856. The

Copeland–Cleveland partnership continued for a short time after that but the Civil War intervened, at which time they parted company.

Cleveland later collaborated with Olmsted and Vaux on the design of Prospect Park in Brooklyn. Cleveland, Olmsted, and Charles Eliot were major civic improvers in their day, pushing for fundamental changes in American cities, such as comprehensive planning, better sanitation, parks, and attention to the design of outdoor pedestrian places.

Cleveland moved his practice to Chicago in 1869, then to Minneapolis in the 1880s, and back again to Chicago in the mid-1890s. His practice involved the design of private estates, municipal and state government grounds, park systems, and planned residential communities. His office burned in the great Chicago fire of 1871, with most of his business records and writings—speeches, articles, and pamphlets about the value of planned suburban development—being destroyed. He wrote, "Landscape architecture is the art of arranging land so as to adapt it most conveniently, economically and gracefully to any of the varied wants of civilization."

Cleveland's work was concentrated mostly in the midwest, in Minnesota, Wisconsin, Illinois, Iowa, Nebraska, Kansas, Ohio, and Michigan. He did work elsewhere and among his most successful creations were the Roger Williams Park (1878) in Providence, Rhode Island; the Minneapolis (1872–1895) and Omaha, Nebraska park systems; and the master plan for the Jekyll Island Club in Georgia (1886).

Cleveland took his son into practice with him in 1891. His best known writing was *Landscape Architecture as Applied to the Wants of the West* (1873).

CLINTON, Dewitt (1769–1828), American statesman, was a U.S. Senator (1802–1803), governor of New York State (1817–1822 and 1824–1828), mayor of New York City (1803–1815), and ran unsuccessfully for president of the United States in 1812. He is most notable for his sponsorship of the Erie Canal, between Albany, on the Hudson River, and Lake Erie, beginning in 1810. Construction of the canal began in 1816 and it opened to traffic in 1825. More than any other single factor, the Erie Canal opened up the Great Lakes region and midwest to settlement and the exploitation of its vast resources, so much in demand by the expanding American population.

In 1816, Clinton became president of the American Academy of Fine Arts and organized a major exhibition of paintings by our three leading painters, Colonel John Trumbell, Benjamin West, and Gilbert Stuart. That event has been regarded as one of the first events signaling the new wave of cultural nationalism that began after the War of 1812. In Clinton's address to the academy, he expressed many of the same sentiments that our foremost writers, Washington Irving, James Fenimore Cooper, and William Cullen Bryant, and many of our landscape painters were soon to express. He stated that the artist's imagination "must derive its forms . . . from the country in which he was born. . . . Can there be a country in the world better calculated than ours to exercise and exalt the imagination? . . . Here nature has conducted her operations on a magnificent scale . . . this wild, romantic scenery." The arts, he said, "marked the boundary between barbarism and refinement." Since Americans could hardly afford to buy originals or even good copies of the old masters, there became a ready market for home-grown artists' work. Led by Thomas Cole, Frederick E. Church, and others, the Hudson River school of painting developed. To a great extent, the romantic painted scenes of the American wilderness brought about the change in Americans' attitudes toward natural scenery. The same wilderness that earlier generations had loathed became an object of adoration on an immense scale.

COBHAM (first Viscount, or Lord Cobham), Sir Richard Temple. *See* Temple, Sir Richard.

CODMAN, Henry Sargent (1864–1893), nephew of the renowned botanist Charles Sprague Sargent, graduated from the Massachusetts Institute of Technology in 1884 and three years later studied in Paris under Edouard André, landscape architect. Upon his return to Boston in 1889, he became a partner in the firm then named F. L. Olmsted and Company. Through his talent for elaborate formal design, he was instrumental in expanding the firm's practice in estate designing. He was made the project manager of the firm's prize commission, the World's Columbian Exposition, in 1893. Unfortunately, within four years of his joining the elder Olmsted, Codman, "the gifted young junior partner," died while supervising site construction in Chicago. In desperate need of a replacement, Olmsted rehired Charles Eliot, who had apprenticed with him between 1883 and 1885, and then, with his stepson, John Charles Olmsted, renamed the firm Olmsted, Olmsted and Eliot.

Codman is said to have owned the largest private collection of literature on landscape architecture in the country at the time of his death. He published "A List of Works on the Art of Landscape-Gardening" in *Garden and Forest* magazine (March 12, 1890, vol. 3, pp. 131–135). This identified 231 works in English, French, German, and Italian since 1625, the date of Francis Bacon's essay, "Of Gardens."

COFFIN, Marian Cruger (1880–1957), learned landscape architecture through private tutoring and studied at MIT as the only woman in the class of 1904. She opened her own office in New York City, which she was forced to do since, as a woman, no one else would hire her. She maintained her practice there until 1927, when an illness prompted her to move to New Haven, Connecticut, where she continued to work until near her death in 1957. Most of her work was designing the grounds of private residences for the wealthy, such as the E. F. Hutton estate, Wheatley Hills, on Long Island; the Marshall Field estate at Lloyds Neck, Long Island; the grounds of the University of Delaware; the New York Botanical Garden; and the "April Garden" at Winterthur, near Wilmington, Delaware, for the DuPont family.

She was also interested in painting and had held several exhibitions of her work in New York. Coffin was made a fellow of the ASLA and in 1930 was awarded the gold medal of the Architectural League of New York. In addition to her well-known book *Trees and Shrubs for Landscape Effects,* she wrote many magazine articles on landscape architecture.

COLE, Thomas (1801–1848), a Lancashire painter, came to the United States in 1818. He established his studio in the town of Catskill, New York, overlooking the Hudson River and Catskill Mountains. Although English, Cole was the first painter to interpret the American wilderness expressively as a theme. He sensitized our American eyes and enhanced our love of our own scenery. Thus began the Hudson River school of painting, the first truly American movement in painting. Within a decade, the demand for paintings that portrayed the American wilderness had flourished, prompting many aspiring painters, such as Frederick Edwin Church, John F. Kinsett, Jasper Cropsey, Albert Bierstadt, Asher Durand, David Johnson, and scores of others, to set out traveling the environs of the Hudson River to record its beauty.

Cole trekked around the wilderness, sketching studies from nature, then returning to his studio to synthesize more idealized landscapes in oil on large canvasses. He described his technique as follows: "[T]he most lovely and perfect parts of Nature may be brought together, and combined in a whole that shall surpass in beauty and effect any picture painted from a single view . . . without the objections." Perhaps his most important painting, "The Oxbow on the Connecticut" (1836), was a large "panoptic" scene of an oxbow bend in the Connecticut River as seen from Mount Holyoke. In fact, Cole synthesized this composition from several sources, sketches he had traced from a book of etchings of American scenery by Captain Basil Hall (1829), sketches he made of the Catskill Mountains, a hundred miles away, sketches he made of the Bay of Naples, and even from his trip to Africa.

The role of patrons cannot be overstated. Particularly important were Robert Gilmor and Luman Reed, both of whom were motivated by their own boundless patriotism. Typically, they dictated the themes they wished to have imbued in the works by the artists in their "stables." One such directive called for the "gorgeous colors of the forest trees in autumn. . ." Another patron urged the portrayal of "a true American landscape . . . a rich green valley just pictured after a shower in the soft repose of a summer sunset. . ." The connoisseurs, more so than the artists, wanted fine detail and realism depicted in the canvasses they commissioned. This was motivated as much by religious morality as it was by nationalism. They believed that moral excellence was akin to physical perfection and so great detail was a measure of beauty. Also, God was thought to be manifested in natural scenery, and so if America had the most beautiful, sublime scenery in the world, then God must have favored this nation over others. Cole's work had such religious qualities, and in his *Essay on American Scenery* (1836) he stated that he saw "rural nature as . . . an unfailing fountain of intellectual enjoyment where all may drink and be awakened to a deeper feeling of the works of genius and a deeper perception of the beauty of our existence." Among Cole's most important paintings were those commissioned by Reed, such as his five large canvases entitled *Course of Empire* (1832).

William Cullen Bryant was a close friend of Cole and at Cole's funeral in 1848 delivered an oration which recalled their "many frequent rambles in the Catskills."

COLLINSON, Peter (1694–1768), an English naturalist, was one of the most important plant dealers of the eighteenth century. As John Bartram's agent in London, he exchanged seeds and plants with America's foremost botanist for four decades, introducing more new North American plant species (over 200) into England and Europe than any person of his day. In turn, he helped introduce many new plants to the American plant palette.

COLVIN, Brenda (1897–1981), British landscape architect, lecturer, and author, combined her skills in landscape design and planning with her sizable knowledge of philosophy and history. She wrote two important texts, *Trees for Town and Country* (1947) and *Land and Landscape* (1947).

The former, written during World War II, became the standard reference book on trees and was used for reforestation in England following the war. The latter work became a standard text for planning authorities. It was the first book to connect natural earth sciences to the art of landscape design. She was a founding member of the British Landscape Institute (president from 1951–1953) and the International Federation of Landscape Architects. Among her works as consultant were the new military town at Aldershot, Bristol Polytechnic, several reservoirs on the River Severn, power stations for the Central Electricity Board, and several schemes for urban design, land reclamation, and private residences.

COOPER, Anthony Ashley, the third Earl of Shaftesbury *See* Shaftesbury, Anthony Ashley Cooper.

COPELAND, Robert Morris (1830–1874), was a partner in the firm of Copeland and Cleveland in Boston from 1853 to 1860. Their practice included "landscape and ornamental gardening" and furnishing "plans for the laying out and improvement of Cemeteries, Public Squares, Pleasure Grounds, Farms and Gardens, as well as for the construction of every species of Building connected with Agriculture, Horticulture, and general rural improvement." In 1856, Copeland and his partner, Horace William Shaler Cleveland, published the pamphlet *A Few Words on the Central Park* (1856), in which they promoted the importance of comprehensive master planning for such large and complex projects as the much discussed but yet to be designed New York Central Park. Their counseling, it can be assumed, prompted the Central Park Commission to stage the design competition, which Copeland and Cleveland entered but were not successful in winning. One of the firm's most notable projects was the layout of Boston's Back Bay section in 1856. The partnership continued for a short time after that, but the Civil War intervened, at which time they parted company.

Copeland graduated from Harvard College in 1851. He also wrote *Country Life: A Handbook of Agricultural, Horticultural and Landscape Gardening* (1859) and *The Most Beautiful City in the World: Essay and Plan for the Improvement of the City of Boston* (1872).

CORBUSIER, Le (Charles-Edouard Jeanneret-Gris) *See* Le Corbusier.

CROWE, Dame Sylvia (1901–), is a British landscape architect, lecturer, and author who has served as consultant for the new towns Harlow and Basildon, and prepared the master plan for Commonwealth Gardens in Canberra, Australia. She has maintained her own private practice, handling a remarkable diversity of project types, including master planning, coastal reclamation, forestry management, and urban projects. Among her works were the redesign of Banbury churchyard, the reclamation of sand dunes on the coast of Lincolnshire, the landscape of the Commonwealth Institute in Kensington High Street, and the new towns of Harlow, Basildon, Warrington, and Washington. She was appointed Design Consultant to the British Forestry Commission in 1964. In 1976 she designed a roof garden for the Scottish Widows' Fund and Life Assurance Society in Edinburgh.

She was educated at Swarley Horticultural College (1920–1921) and designed private gardens in Britain until the beginning of World War II. In 1945, Dame Sylvia resumed her practice. Her work has been honored by the British government; the Royal Institute of British Architects (RIBA), of which she is an honorary fellow; and the Australian Institute of Landscape Architects (AILA). She was the president of the British Landscape Institute from 1957 to 1959 and was one of the founders of the International Federation of Landscape Architects in 1948, once serving as acting president.

She once stated: "As long as man's activities are in sympathy with nature, or are on so small a scale that they do not interfere with nature's self-renewing cycle, the landscape survives, either in a predominantly natural form or as a balanced product of human partnership with nature. But as soon as the growth of the population or its urban activities are sufficient to upset nature's balance, the landscape suffers, and the only remedy is for man to take a conscious part in the landscape's evolution."

Dame Sylvia wrote a number of important books that have remained standard works for the profession and show her concern with the regeneration and preservation of the English landscape. They include *Tomorrow's Landscape* (1956), *Garden Design* (1958, second edition, 1981), *The Landscape of Power* (1958), *The Landscape of Roads* (1960), and *The Landscape of Forests and Woods* (1966). She was appointed the first landscape consultant to the British Forestry Commission, where she produced *Forestry in the Landscape* (1966).

She was made a Commander of the Order of the British Empire in 1967, a Dame of the British Empire in 1973, and received the American Society of Landscape Architects' medal, their highest award, in 1988. She is an honorary fellow of the Royal Institute of British Architects and an honorary member of the Royal Town Planning Institute.

CUNNINGHAM, Ann Pamela (1816–1875), historic preservation activist, was responsible for the preservation of Mount Vernon as a national shrine between 1931 and 1938. Between 1858 and 1863, under her leadership, funds were raised from across the nation to purchase Mount Vernon and to preserve, restore, and maintain "with sacred reverence, Washington's house and grounds in the state he left them." Her contribution to the historic preservation movement in the United States was to furnish imaginative and energetic leadership and help in organizing, planning, fund raising, publicizing, and lobbying for the preservation of historic structures and properties. Through her efforts, Mount Vernon is a model for similar historical projects.

DANIELS, Howard (d. 1863), architect, was hired in 1845 to lay out the grounds of Spring Grove Cemetery in Cincinnati. His scheme was an attempt to imitate the romantic rural character of Mount Auburn Cemetery, but with his fussy road alignment and excessive geometry, the plan fell far short of its model. Ten years later, the cemetery was remodeled by Adolph Strauch into America's first lawn cemetery.

Within the next few years Daniels designed fifteen rural cemeteries around the country and worked with Alexander Jackson Davis and Eugene A. Baumann on the design of Llewellyn Park in West Orange, New Jersey (1852–1853). In 1857 he submitted a proposal for the design of New York's Central Park, earning the fourth-place prize. Soon after, he laid out Druid Hills Park in Baltimore (1860).

DAVIS, Alexander Jackson (1803–1892), called himself an "architectural composer." He was a friend and occasional collaborator with Andrew Jackson Downing, landscape designer, and the Hudson River painters Thomas Cole and Asher Durand. In the 1830s he was a proponent of the Greek Revival style, designing several superb examples, including the state house in Raleigh, North Carolina. In the 1840s he shifted to the more picturesque, asymmetrical Gothic Revival style championed by Downing. Lyndhurst Mansion in Tarrytown, New York is one of his best examples of that period.

His work was so popular that he designed many homes from clients' requests sent through the mail. His buildings were produced in two dozen states which he never visited.

Among his works were Glen Ellen, the Baltimore home of one of America's foremost art connoisseurs, Robert Gilmor; the William Paulding mansion, Knoll, in Tarrytown, New York; Rokeby and Montgomery Place on the Hudson River; and Samuel F. B. Morse's house in Poughkeepsie, New York. In the 1850s, Davis widened his stylistic repertoire to include the American log cabin, English cottage, collegiate Gothic, French suburban, Swiss chalet, and others.

In 1852, Davis planned Llewellyn Park, the 350-acre property of Llewellyn Haskell, in West Orange, New Jersey, as a utopian planned romantic residential community. Many of Downing's concepts came through in the plan for the place, even though by then he was no longer alive. The site was "a wild tract of mountainous land . . . covered with thick woods . . . threaded by mountain streams and ravines, rimmed and ribbed with rocks, monumented with venerable trees. . ." The plan retained as much of the natural character of the site as possible while providing winding carriageways, abutted by fifty "villa sites" ranging from 5 to 10 acres in size. There were several rustic seats in the 50-acre common land, known as the "Ramble," and the rocky gatehouse at the neighborhood's only entrance. Davis designed about twenty houses in the project, including two for Haskell, Eyrie and Castlewood, and his own, Wildmont. He fit these masterfully with the rugged character of the site by using earthtone colors and rustic elements such as rock and rough timber.

Eugene A. Baumann, a German landscape gardener, was responsible for much of the on-site construction and planting of Llewellyn Park. Calvert Vaux, partner of Frederick Law Olmsted, designed one house there.

DEAN, Ruth (1888–1932), landscape architect and author, apprenticed with Jens Jensen in Chicago and later formed her own small office through which she designed many fine urban, suburban, and country place gardens. She was particularly admired for her respect of ecology and her use of native vegetation, creating wonderfully "livable" spaces with great originality despite the Beaux-Arts or Colonial Revival architectural backdrops within which her work was set.

Dean wrote many articles for *House and Garden, Country Life in America,* and *Garden* magazine. In 1917 she wrote the book *The Livable House: Its Garden.*

DEARBORN, Henry A. S. (1783–1851), was one of the chief designers of the grounds of Mount Auburn Cemetery at the edge of Boston. He was schooled in law, but after serving as brigadier general of the militia defending Boston during the War of 1812, he gave up that field and turned to civil engineering, architecture, horticulture, and politics. He had a great knowledge of Greek architectural orders and the English landscape garden design principles. As the first president of the Massachusetts Horticultural Society in 1831, Dearborn advised that the roads and walks in the cemetery should respond to the undulating landforms within the property. Avenues, he said, should run "as nearly level as possible by winding gradually and gracefully through the valleys and obliquely over hills, without any unnecessary or unavoidable bend."

Dearborn was superintendent of the construction work on the site and responsible for much of the natural and human-made beauty of the site. He "transplanted from his own nurseries a large collection of healthy, young forest trees, which he distributed through the entire front of the Cemetery" (Bigelow, 1860, p. 20).

DE CAUX, Salomon (c. 1576–1626), was a French engineer and garden designer. He was the designer of the castle gardens at Heidelburg, Germany; the gardens at Hatfield House in Hertfordshire, England (1611); and the waterworks of the gardens at Richmond (c. 1610). He was related to Isaac de Caus, designer of the formal grounds of Wilton House near Bath, England. De Caux wrote *Les Raisons des forces mouvantes* (1615) and *Hortus Palatinus* (1620).

DEZALLIER D'ARGENVILLE, Antoine-Joseph (1680–1765), French naturalist, was the anonymous author of the classic book *La Théorie et la practique du jardinage* in 1709. This work was influential in disseminating the French grand style of André Le Nôtre all over the continent during the eighteenth century. The book's third edition (1713) erroneously identified the author as Alexandre Le Blond, but in the fourth edition (1747) Dezallier claimed authorship and credited Le Blond with the creation of the majority of the illustrations in the book. The book was translated into English in 1712, mentioning the ha-ha for the first time and introducing to Alexander Pope his famous notion, the "genius of the place."

DOWNING, Andrew Jackson (1815–1852), nurseryman, landscape gardener, and author, was born in Newburgh-on-Hudson, New York, where he learned about horticulture from his older brother, who operated the family nursery. As important as Downing was in the history of American landscape architecture, very little is known of his career due to the loss of nearly all of his personal and professional papers. A complete and accurate list of his projects and clients has not been produced. As a young man Downing was friends with Baron de Lederer, the Austrian consul, who had a fine country estate near Newburgh. The baron was educated as a mineralogist and botanist and it was from him that Downing learned to appreciate natural science and rural scenery. Downing also knew a young English landscape painter with the fascinating name of Raphael Hoyle, from whom he learned the principles of composition that he was to apply to his study of the landscape and landscape gardens.

Through the nursery business, Downing gained access to a great number of the large and beautiful Hudson River estates with fine mansions set amidst soft natural "parks." Downing cultivated the acquaintances he made at each home with great vigor. Coming well after the careers of Kent and Brown in England, Downing was most heavily influenced by the precepts of Humphry Repton and John C. Loudon. Repton vociferously criticized Brown's cow pastures filled with scattered clumps of trees, extending right up to the steps of the English country houses. He advocated a more architectural garden in close proximity to the building; this approach is the one chosen by Downing, who adapted the writings of Repton and Loudon into his own American version of landscape design. In 1841 he published his *A Treatise on the Theory and Practice of Landscape Gardening, Adapted to North America*. It was a tremendous success, going through six printings. He urged the landscape designer to "preserve only the spirit or essence [of the place] . . . arrange materials so as to awaken emotions of grace, elegance or picturesqueness, joined with unity, harmony and variety, more distinct and forcible than are suggested by [purely] natural scenery." Consistent with Repton, he suggested the inclusion of artifice in the landscape, recommending that the reader "admit the graceful accompaniment of vases, urns and other harmonious accessories."

The *Treatise* brought Downing tremendous fame, and thus as an authority on landscape design, he was able to apply his influence toward the establishment of street tree planting societies in a number of eastern cities, the establishment of a state agricultural school, and the founding of the National Agricultural Bureau in Washington. With William Cullen Bryant and others, Downing was a driving force in the establishment of the New York City Park Commission, whose efforts led to the creation of Central Park.

In 1850 he traveled to England, where he befriended the architect Calvert Vaux, whom he prevailed upon to emigrate to America. They joined forces professionally but for less than three years. Downing was very impressed by what he saw of the English parks and private estates in the landscape garden style which he visited during his travels in Britain in 1850. He wrote much about these parks and gardens in his editorials in the *Horticulturist* magazine, which he founded in 1846.

One of Downing's major concerns about the design of one's property was that the *genius loci* (the unique character) of each site should be the basis of whatever design might be put on that land. Downing's designs include the grounds of Wodenethe at Fishkill, New York (c. 1847); Blithewood, in Dutchess County, New York; and the 20-acre estate Springside in Poughkeepsie, New York (1850–1852), the only unaltered, documented work by Downing.

The first major landscape architectural project of the Downing and Vaux partnership were the grounds of the White House and Smithsonian Museum (the "Castle") at the edge of the Mall in Washington, D.C. (1851). Today, located a few steps to the east of the Castle is the Downing Urn, a small marble memorial to the man, one of very few public tributes to the landscape architect of a specific site.

Downing collaborated with Calvert Vaux on the design of a number of houses and public buildings, including the Norman chapel and gatehouse for Evergreens Cemetery, Brooklyn, New York (1850); a summer house for Daniel Parish, Newport, Rhode Island (1855); a residence for John Angier, Medford, Massachusetts; a villa for B. Phelps, Springfield, Massachusetts; and the residence of R. P. Dodge, Washington, D.C.

In addition to the *Treatise,* Downing wrote several other books: *Notes About Buildings in the Country* (1849); *The Architecture of Country Houses* (1850); and *Cottage Residences: A Series of Designs for Rural Cottages and Cottage Villas, and Their Gardens and Grounds Adapted to North America* (posthumously in 1853).

In memory of Andrew Jackson Downing, the city of Newburgh dedicated a park in 1897, the design of which was made through the combined efforts of Frederick Law Olmsted, Sr.; his son, John C. Olmsted; Calvert Vaux; his son, Downing Vaux; and Warren Manning.

DRAPER, Earl Sumner (1893–), a planner and landscape architect, was an associate of John Nolen in Cambridge, Massachusetts. Draper moved to Charlotte, North Carolina in 1915 to supervise the Myers Park Garden Suburb in that city and the new town of Kingsport, Tennessee. Two years later he started his own office in Charlotte. He produced more than eighty master plans for new company towns. His best known is Chicopee, Georgia (1927), the factory town for the Chicopee Manufacturing Corporation, a division of Johnson and Johnson. During the Depression, Draper was head of the Division of Land Planning and Housing for the Tennessee Valley Authority. This group planned and built the town of Norris, Tennessee for the Norris Dam construction workers and their families. He later served as deputy commissioner of the Federal Housing Administration until he resumed private practice in 1945.

Draper also designed over a dozen campuses and scores of estates and public and private gardens, primarily in the southeastern United States. In 1928, in Charlottesville, Virginia, he planned a golf course subdivision on the Farmington estate, designed by Thomas Jefferson in 1802, one of Jefferson's finest building designs.

The oldest living member of the ASLA, since 1927 he has been a fellow of the society. Draper has written numerous articles for the *Landscape Architecture Magazine* as well as other publications. His professional papers are in the archives of Cornell University.

DU CERCEAU, Jacques Androuet (c. 1515–1584), French Renaissance architect, engraver, and author, his *Livre d'architecture,* written in 1539, was the first architectural handbook printed in French. He also wrote *Second livre d'architecture* (1561), *Monuments antiques* (1560), and his two-volume *Les Plus excellents bâtiments de France* (1576 and 1579). In the last work were his plans for the chateaus at Charleval and Vereuil. His plans reveal that the tight geometric medieval-like enclosed French garden was evolving to command open vistas and greater scale, reflecting the expressiveness of the villa landscape of the Italian Renaissance.

ECKBO, Garrett (1910–), California landscape architect, theoretician, and educator, was born in New York, and educated at the University of California at Berkeley and the Harvard Graduate School of Design. In the late 1930s, Eckbo and his classmates Dan Kiley and James Rose led the "Harvard revolution," ushering in the modern period in landscape design, in opposition to the traditional axial symmetry of the Beaux-Arts approach to site design. Eckbo's illustrated articles on the modern garden were the first such discussions of the new American garden expression to be published, appearing in the magazine *Pencil Points* (later called *Progressive Architecture*) in 1937 and 1938. The designs of the young trio of upstarts were bold, nontraditional and imaginative—functional outdoor rooms. They were influenced by the precepts of cubism and European (Bauhaus) architecture, led by Walter Gropius, who had arrived to teach at Harvard in 1936. To a certain extent, the intimacy of the Japanese garden and the work of Thomas Church in California in the 1930s also influenced the new movement.

Eckbo states: "The atmosphere at the Graduate School of Design was charged, controversial and exciting. [We] were so turned on by the new ideas upstairs that, on our own, we began to explore forms and arrangements which might reflect the new design ideas . . . it made it possible to eliminate preconceived design vocabularies, and to develop forms and arrangements which spoke to the specific sites, clients, users, local contexts, and regional cultures." Classmate John Simonds recalls that "Garrett discovered asymmetric geometry," and the use of the diagonal became one of his main devices for redirecting axial space.

Following graduate school, Eckbo went to work as a landscape architect for Norman Bel Geddes on the General Motors pavilion for the 1939 World's Fair in New York and for the Farm Security Administration (1939–1942), planning new communities, designing migrant housing, and redesigning older ones. He led the way for landscape architects to lessen their focus on the designing of country places for the wealthy and to respond instead to public needs, which had been the basis for Olmsted's earliest work.

Eckbo's designs have been widely hailed by his clients and the design critics and have been influential for other landscape architects all over the country. He joined with several other designers in 1945, forming the firm Eckbo, Dean, Austin and Williams (EDAW). Among the firm's many projects are the Fulton Mall, Fresno; the grounds of Ambassador College in Pasadena; Mission Bay Park; the Tucson Community Center; the Denver Botanical Gardens Water Facilities; the roof garden of the Union Bank in Los Angeles; the central campus of the University of New Mexico in Albuquerque; the Shelby Farms Public Use Plan, Memphis, Tennessee; and Lodi Park, New Delhi, India.

Eckbo taught at the University of Southern California in the 1940s and 1950s and served as chairman of the Department of Landscape Architecture at the University of California at Berkeley in the late 1960s. He is a fellow of the ASLA and the author of scores of journal articles and the books *Landscape for Living* (1950), *The Art of Home Landscaping* (1956), *Urban Landscape Design* (1964), *The Landscape We See* (1969), and *Public Landscape: Six Essays on Government and Environmental Design in the San Francisco Bay Area* (1978).

EFFNER, Joseph (1687–1745), was a Paris-trained German architect and gardener who designed the three "castles," or small pavilions, at Nymphenburg Park between 1716 and 1725. The Pagodenburg is in the chinoiserie style, the Badenburg is a bathhouse, and the Magdalenenklause is a rustic hermitage.

ELIOT, Charles (1859–1897), apprenticed with Frederick Law Olmsted in Brookline, Massachusetts between 1883 and 1885, when he began his efforts to create the Boston metropolitan park and open-space system.

Eliot, the son of the president of Harvard University, Charles W. Eliot, based much of his thinking on the English landscape garden tradition. Early in his career he traveled about America and to England and the continent, where he formed his belief in the value of naturalistic parks in American cities. He visited Birkenhead Park, many works by Brown and Repton, and Prince Pückler's park in Muskau. In his notebook he wrote, "Repton remains my master." In 1890, Eliot helped to establish the first authority for the historic preservation of natural landscapes in the United States, the Trustees of Public Reservations in Massachusetts. He identified five distinct land types that were to be preserved for their intrinsic value to society just as are libraries and museums: urban parks and commons, forest reservations, tidal estuaries, ocean beaches, and offshore islands. It is believed that in inventorying natural systems on such a regional scale, Eliot developed the technique of using translucent overlays to study the complexity of composite natural phenomena.

He was a good communicator and wrote often for *Garden and Forest* magazine as well as others. His history-making position paper, "The Waverly Oaks: A Plan for Their Preservation for the People," appeared in *G&F* in March 1890.

Eliot's early death, at age 37, meant that the man most likely to succeed Frederick Law Olmsted was gone. As a memorial to young Charles, his father established the world's first comprehensive course in landscape architecture at Harvard in 1900. (Note that other college-level courses were being taught in landscape gardening and horticulture, primarily at land-grant colleges.)

The senior Eliot wrote his son's biography, *Charles Eliot, Landscape Architect,* in 1902.

EVELYN, John (1620–1705), was an English writer, translator of garden books, and garden designer who lived for nearly fifty years at Sayes Court in Deptford, Surrey, where he developed his gardens, in the French formal style, into the envy of all his aristocratic neighbors. There he began his great book on horticulture, *Elysium Britanicum,* published in 1664. His most important work was *Sylva, or a Discourse of Forest Trees,* also published in 1664. This was reprinted many times and was, into the nineteenth century, the standard reference text on the propagation, planting, and use of trees. Evelyn's interest grew out of his concern about the demise of the nation's forests and his alarm over the government's increasing demand for timber to build its navy and for other building construction. He urged property owners each to do their part to aid in the afforestation of the countryside. His preachings did eventually catch hold and by the time of the landscape garden movement (1720–1750), arboriculture was an accepted practice on large estates.

Evelyn's influence in garden design was also considerable in his time, as his advice was often sought about matters of taste, which for him tended toward the Italian classical style in architecture and the French in gardens. In 1699 he inherited the noted Wotton House in Surrey, with its Italian villa-style gardens, from his older brother. He also wrote *The Complete Gardener* (1693), a translation of a French work by Jean de la Quintinie.

FAIRBROTHER, Nan (1913–1971), was an English author, historian, and environmentalist. Her books altered the profession's view of the landscape. In her *Men and Gardens* (1956) she explored the meaning of gardens and examined 2000 years of the "why," rather than the "how" of garden design, discussing the values and uses of gardens in the twentieth century. In *New Lives, New Landscapes* (1965), illustrated with her own photography, she documented the changes in our relationship to the land and hinted at its future. She was an advocate of land use planning in England, which respected the old while accommodating the new and fulfilling social, economic, and aesthetic criteria. In her third book, *The Nature of Landscape Design* (1974), she shifted from regionalism to the garden, focusing on site-specific design and a concern for the integration of disciplines and ideas. Rex Fairbrother, her husband, founded the landscape architecture degree program at Manchester Polytechnic Institute in 1966.

FARRAND, Beatrix Cadwalader Jones (1872–1959), was born into a family of great wealth and connections and went on to become one of the most creative landscape architects of the early twentieth century. Her aunt and frequent traveling companion to Europe was Edith Wharton. Jones studied plant material with Charles Sprague Sargent, director of the Arnold Arboretum, and began her own practice as a landscape gardener in 1895. She was the consulting landscape architect for the campuses of Yale, Princeton, the University of Chicago, Oberlin, Vassar, Cal Tech, and several others. Her greatest works were the Dumbarton Oaks estate in Georgetown, Washington, D.C., which she began in 1921 and continued with for twenty-six years, and the Abby Aldrich Rockefeller Garden at Seal Harbor, Maine (1926–1950). Her influences came from two brilliant English designers, William Robinson and Gertrude Jekyll, and her work was said to have a "freedom of scale, a subtle softness of line and an unobtrusive asymmetry," drawn from the English formal style (Tishler, p. 95). After the death of her husband, Max, she moved her practice to their estate, Reef Point, in Bar Harbor, Maine, continuing there until her retirement in 1940. Her book *Beatrix Farrand's Plant Book for Dumbarton Oaks* (1980) is a meticulous study for maintenance of a planting design.

She was a charter member of the American Society of Landscape Architects—the only woman—and was its last surviving founding member. Her personal library and extensive file of projects, including many by Gertrude Jekyll, were bequeathed to the University of California at Berkeley.

FLANDERS, Annette Hoyt (1887–1946), earned an A.B. in botany at Smith College in 1910, then went on to study landscape architecture at the University of Illinois (B.S., 1918) and later engineering at Marquette University in Milwaukee. She also studied architecture and architectural history at the Sorbonne in Paris (1919). Before completing her formal education, in 1914, she opened her own practice in her native Milwaukee, mainly doing her work for charity. She soon moved to New York and for a short time worked with Ferruccio Vitale and Alfred Geiffert, Jr. in their New York office (Vitale, Brinckerhoff & Geiffert) in charge of design and supervision of planting. She opened her own practice there in 1922 to be nearer her main source of clients. Her very diverse and busy practice involved her in nearly half of the forty-eight extant states doing subdivision design, industrial plants, parks, and exhibitions gardens such as the "classic modern garden" at the Century of Progress Exposition in Chicago in 1933. She was the designer of many residential estate gardens, such as the French-style gardens for Charles F. McCann on Oyster Bay, Long Island; the Vincent Astor estate; the Philip Armour estate, Lake Bluff, Illinois; and the Kellogg Patten Gardens in Milwaukee. In 1932, Flanders was awarded the medal of honor of the Architectural League of New York. In 1943, near the end of her career, she returned to practice in Milwaukee, but in less than three years she closed the business and died in 1946.

Flanders lectured widely to public and college audiences and taught courses at the Milwaukee Art Institute in 1941. She contributed articles on design to a number of publications, including the *Landscape Architecture Magazine, House and Garden, Country Life in America,* and *Good Housekeeping*.

FONTANA, Domenico (1543–1607), was an Italian architect and engineer whose patron in his early years was Cardinal Montalto. When the cardinal became Pope Sixtus V in 1585, Fontana was made papal architect, charged with the redesign of major portions of the Vatican and the pope's two palaces, the Quirinal and the Lateran, both in Rome. Fontana worked with Giacomo della Porta on completion of the dome of St. Peter's Basilica from a model and drawings made by Michelangelo. Most notable of Fontana's urban design work was his ingenious engineering solution to the problem of erecting the Egyptian obelisks in the Piazza del Popolo (1585) and in St. Peter's in the Vatican (1589).

FRIEDBERG, M. Paul (1931–), an American landscape architect, writer, and educator, was educated at Cornell University. He made a major contribution to the design of play environments through his innovative playground and recreation area designs in the 1960s. Jacob Riis Plaza, in New York City, a housing development that he remodeled into a series of outdoor rooms, including his seminal playscape, with its massive timber-climbing elements and stone mound, is the most notable of Friedberg's early "urban blocks."

Friedberg has been active in downtown revitalization and produced pedestrian space master plans for a number of cities, including the Monroe Center in Grand Rapids, Michigan; the State Street Mall in Madison, Wisconsin; Peavey Plaza in Minneapolis; and Pershing Square in Washington, D.C. (1980). One of his most charming spaces, Pershing Square, on Pennsylvania Avenue in sight of the White House, is a shady oasis, set below the street level with a handsome refreshment kiosk and movable tables placed around a reflecting pool.

Another of the most striking schemes designed by Friedberg is the Winter Garden, a conservatory in Niagara Falls (1976). He has collaborated with many leading architectural firms, such as Victor Gruen and Associates; Skidmore, Owings and Merrill; and I. M. Pei and Associates.

Friedberg is also founder and chairman of the Department of Urban Landscape Architecture at the City College of New York, as well as visiting professor at Columbia University and the New School for Social Research at Pratt Institute. He has lectured widely on campuses and professional meetings.

He has articulated his playground design philosophy in several books which he authored or coauthored: *Play and Interplay* (1970, with Ellen Perry Berkeley), *Playgrounds for City Children* (1969), *Creative Play Areas* (1970), and *Handcrafted Playgrounds* (1975).

GAUDI Y CORNET, Antoni (1852–1926), a Catalan from Barcelona, designed many private residences, apartment buildings, and churches, all in Barcelona, in his unique style—partially neo-Gothic, partially Art Nouveau. Included in his Barcelona work were the Sagrada Familia (1883–1926 [still in progress]), Casa Batlló (1906), and Casa Milá (1906–1910). At the edge of the city he laid out a small subdivision, Park Güell (1900–1914), and designed many of the houses within it, including his own. The centerpiece of the community is a large pedestrian plaza approached by fantastic stone causeways and surrounded by a serpentine mosaic bench comprised of pottery and porcelain dinnerware chards. This terrace space is elevated high off the ground, supported on chard-encrusted columns, with an exquisite ceiling of dazzling China platters and tea cups.

GEDDES, Norman Bel (1893–1958), was a product/industrial designer during the 1920s and 1930s. He was one of the leaders of the restyling of such things as automobiles, planes, ships, and trains into streamlined, sleek, aerodynamic instruments of great speed, or so they appeared. His energy was boundless and he even designed kitchen utensils, appliances, radios, and bathroom fittings into similarly "high-speed" sculptural wonders. He designed the General Motors pavilion at the 1939 New York World's Fair, including not only the building, but the entire exhibit and a model, Futurama, displaying the "city of tomorrow."

Not an architect, he nevertheless designed many buildings and interiors, complete with all his furniture. His repertoire included theaters, hotels, restaurants, nightclubs, and residences. He produced a master plan for Toledo, Ohio and devised a system for the manufacturing of prefabricated housing. His writings include *Horizons* (1932); *Magic Motorways* (1940); and his autobiography, *Miracle in the Evening* (published posthumously in 1960).

GEDDES, Sir Patrick (1854–1932), Scottish biologist, sociologist, educator, and urban planner, championed sociological considerations in planning and broadened its scope and purpose to include religion, history, industry, and education. One of his most notable planning reports, done for a study of Indore, India, was *Town Planning Toward City Development* (1918).

GEIFFERT, Alfred, Jr. (1890–1957), apprenticed with Ferruccio Vitale in his New York firm and was taken in as a partner in the early 1920s with the firm called Vitale & Geiffert until Vitale's early death in 1933. Geiffert continued the practice on his own until 1957. Their list of clients included many private residences during the country place era, such as the Landon K. Thorne place at Bayshore, Long Island, completed soon after Geiffert joined the partnership. Following World War II, Geiffert worked on Fresh Meadows, a 175-acre housing development in New York City developed by the New York Life Insurance Company.

GIEDION, Sigfried (1888–1968), architectural historian, educator, and an influential advocate of the modern movement in architecture, he wrote classic study of the subject, *Space, Time and Architecture: The Growth of a*

New Tradition, in 1941. He also wrote *Mechanization Takes Command* (1948), *The Eternal Present: The Beginnings of Architecture* (1964), and *Architecture and the Phenomena of Transition* (1970). He said, "For planning of any sort our knowledge must go beyond the state of affairs that actually prevails. To plan we must know what has gone on in the past and what is coming in the future. This is not an invitation to prophecy but a demand for a universal outlook upon the world."

GILLETTE, Genevieve (1898–1986), landscape architect, conservationist, and lecturer, was the one-woman force behind nature preservation and conservation in Michigan for more than sixty years. She was founder and president of the Michigan Parks Association and an effective lobbyist for park issues. Through her efforts, the acquisition of land for more than thirty state parks in Michigan was made a reality and the Sleeping Bear Dunes on Lake Michigan were designated by Congress as a national lakeshore, administered by the National Park Service.

GILPIN, William (1724–1804), English clergyman, is considered the founder and master of the "picturesque school" in the landscape gardening controversy of the late eighteenth century in England. He also was the leading popularizer of the turn-of-the-century English fashion for picturesque tourism. He wrote his *Essay on Prints* (1768) to inform the public on how to appreciate engraved or etched prints. Several years later he wrote a number of travel books, beginning in 1782 with his *Observation on the River Wye, and Several Parts of South Wales &c. Relative Chiefly to Picturesque Beauty.* His *Observation on the Lakes* (1789) and his seminal *Remarks on Forest Scenery* treated the subject of scenery of the Lakes district and the Scottish highlands. He was a skilled artist who illustrated his principles in each book with his own engraved sketches. To Reverend Gilpin, the term *picturesque* meant "depictable," or "that which is suited to pictorial representation." Earlier, in his *Essay on Prints* (1768), he referred to picturesque as "that kind of beauty which would look well in a picture." His writings spelled out the principles of painting composition that the picturesque pilgrims were to absorb *before* they ventured into the less settled areas of the country, *Claude-glasses* in hand, in search of scenes in nature which resembled painted landscape vignettes. He said, "[T]he chief object[s] of our pursuit, [are] the wild scenes of nature—the *wood,* the *copse,* the *glen,* and *open-grove.*" His wish for all travelers was that they "view the country with the eyes of persons accustomed to drawing and deciding on its capability of being formed into pictures." He went further than stylized scenery alone, discussing also the forms of individual trees, roots, rocks, and rugged landforms. He was formulating the concept of "regionalism" as opposed to Brown's systematically applying the same formulas throughout the kingdom to "improve" the spacious grounds of his wealthy patrons.

GIOTTO DI BONDONE (c. 1266–1337), an Italian painter and architect, first appeared on the art scene in 1300 with the frescoes he executed in the Upper Church in Assisi and the Arena Chapel in Padua (c. 1305). His scenes from the life of St. Francis and other saints are of "nobly humanized forms" set in spacious and inviting, rather than oppressive-looking rural landscapes as was the norm previous to his work. He is thus credited with setting in motion the more naturalistic painting style of the fifteenth century.

Just three years before his death, in 1334, he was appointed architect of the Duomo in Florence. The nearby campanile bears the name Giotto's Tower, although he may have only done rudimentary sketches of his proposal before its cornerstone was laid.

GIRARDIN, Louis-René, Marquis de Vauvray, Vicomte d'Ermenonville (1735–1808), was a French count who laid out the grounds of his 2000-acre chateau in Ermenonville as a *jardin anglais,* or *ferme ornée,* beginning about 1770. He had toured England in 1763 and 1775, specifically to examine picturesque estates—in the character of Uvedale Price—after which he might model his own. In England he saw Shenstone's Leasowes, and in France he studied J.-J. Rousseau's rustic cottage. In his Grand Parc, he incorporated the essence of the landscape garden: expanses of undulating lawn and still water; copses of trees; meandering paths and eyecatchers, such as a memorial to Shenstone; a Gothic tower; a rustic hermitage; windmills; and in homage to Rousseau, the half-built Temple de la Philosophie and the Ile des Peupliers (Lombardy poplars) with the philosopher's tomb.

By 1777, Girardin was so well versed in the picturesque that he wrote a treatise on the subject, *De la composition des paysages . . . a la nature . . . ,* which was translated into English six years later as *An Essay on Landscape.*

GORE, Christopher (1758–1827), governor of Massachusetts (1809–1810) and U.S. Senator (1814–1817), built his home, Gore Place, in Waltham, on a lofty site above the Charles River. After the Revolutionary War, he lived in England as American envoy to Britain (1796–1804), during which time he grew to admire the Repton-designed landscapes of many of the country seats he visited. Back in America, he began remodeling his fire-damaged home in 1805 and continued over the next twenty years to fashion the grounds into a romantic model of the English landscape garden. The house commands a fine broad prospect of the Charles, with its spacious lawn, here and there punctuated with majestic shade trees, extending to the water's edge. His neighbor was Theodore Lyman, noted also for his naturalistic landscape garden estate, The Vale.

GREENLEAF, James Leal (1857–1933), was a civil engineer and landscape architect, noted as the designer of many prominent country places in the mid-Atlantic region of the United States. He taught civil engineering at Columbia University's School of Mines from 1891 until 1895. He began his private practice in landscape architecture in 1894, designing many notable country places, including Killenworth, on Long Island; W. K. Vanderbilt's Hudson River estate, Hyde Park; and others in Maine, Illinois, and New Jersey. He served as town planner in the United States Housing Corporation during World War I and after the war designed American cemeteries for the war dead in several European countries.

In 1932 he designed the grounds around the Arlington Memorial Bridge in Washington. He was president of the ASLA from 1923 to 1927, during which time he served as a consultant to Stephen Mather of the National Park Service.

GRIFFIN, Walter Burley (1876–1937), a Chicago architect and landscape architect, won the international design competition for the layout of the new Australian national capital, Canberra, in 1912. The scheme is a "twentieth-century baroque" or "city beautiful" expression, with its two main concentric circles, one for governmental buildings and the other for commercial structures. It is based on the two major topographical features of the district, a small mountain and a broad flat plain in which he created a vast human-made lake, Lake Burley Griffin. His scheme also included many neighborhood parks, parkways, lakes, a botanical garden, and several residential suburbs.

Griffin, a graduate of the University of Illinois (1899), was employed in the Frank Lloyd Wright office in Chicago between 1901 and 1905, when he opened his own practice. In 1911 he married Marion Lucy Mahoney, an architect and brilliant illustrator, whose plans and perspectives of the Canberra proposal did a great deal to win the couple the top prize. He was a good friend of Jens Jensen, with whom he shared the "prairie spirit" in landscape architecture.

In 1913, the Griffins moved to Sydney, Australia to supervise the development of their grand scheme. They maintained a private practice in Melbourne until 1935, when they moved their practice to Lucknow, India, and lived there until his death two years later. Griffin-designed structures abound around the American midwest, in Australia, and in India. While he wrote nothing of his own work, it has been discussed in a great number of books and articles by other authors.

GRISWOLD, Ralph E. (1894–1981), was a landscape architect whose practice was located in Pittsburgh. He won the Rome Prize in landscape architecture (fellowship to the American Academy in Rome) in 1922.

In 1932, during the Depression, Griswold modified the small housing development in Pittsburgh, Chatham Village, which had earlier been designed by the architects Stein and Wright.

He collaborated on several projects with Thomas Church and coauthored, with Frederick Doveton Nichols, the book *Thomas Jefferson, Landscape Architect* (1977).

GROPIUS, Walter (1883–1969), was a German architect who transformed the Grand Ducal Art School at Wiemar, Germany in 1919 into the Bauhaus (*Das Staatliche Bauhaus Weimar,* "School of Building"). He moved it to Dessau in 1925, and his design for the building to house the Dessau Bauhaus (1925–1926) marks the beginning of the international style in architecture. Artists and designers who studied or taught in the Bauhaus were Paul Klee, Vassily Kandinsky, and Lászlo Moholy-Nagy, all of whom subscribed to the Gropius doctrine of functionalism: the close relationship between modern art and the machine, clean lines without ornamentation, and economy of materials. In 1928, Gropius returned to private practice, producing many of his finest designs. Adolph Hitler, who wished to become an architecture but failed in his attempts to get into school in his chosen profession, so persecuted the architects of the international style (he closed the Bauhaus in 1933) that Gropius moved to London in 1934. Three years later he joined the faculty of the Architecture Department at Harvard University and served as its chairman until 1952.

In the course of his eighty-six prolific years, Gropius profoundly influenced the course of twentieth-century design and education in the United States and elsewhere. He lured a number of designers to America to teach design at the Harvard Graduate School of Design, including the German architect Ludwig Mies van der Rohe, who succeeded Gropius at the Bauhaus; architect Marcel Breuer; and the Canadian landscape architect Christopher Tunnard, then practicing in England. In Harvard's landscape architecture department, radical design precepts of the international style were banished, thereby causing three students, Garrett Eckbo, Dan Kiley, and James Rose, to experiment surreptitiously with the new style of "modern garden." The three were reprimanded for contradicting the old guard traditions and threatened with expulsion. Their innovative work was published in 1937 and 1938 in *Pencil Points* magazine (now *Progressive Architecture*), making it the first-ever airing of ideas about landscape architecture, with the same approach to design that had been going on in Europe for a generation.

GUILFOYLE, William (1840–1912), born in Britain, moved to Australia in 1849. There he became a nurseryman and Australia's foremost garden designer of the late nineteenth and early twentieth centuries. His greatest creative work was the Royal Botanic Gardens in Melbourne, which was started in 1845 by Ferdinand J. H. von Mueller (1825–1896). Between 1873 and 1909, Guilfoyle worked on the redesign of the formal gardens, transforming them into a soft English landscape garden park. His other projects include Werribee Park, Greenoaks estate, Rippon Lea, Coombe Cottage (for Dame Nellie Melba), and the Mawallok and Turkeith gardens.

HAAG, Richard (1923–), landscape architect and teacher, was born in Kentucky and educated at the University of Illinois under Stanley White and Hideo Sasaki. He received his undergraduate degree from the University of California and earned his master's degree at Harvard University. He traveled to Japan on a Fulbright fellowship (1954–1955), where he studied Japanese landscape design and acquired the Zen spirit of what he calls "nonstriving"—less is more. In San Francisco he worked with Theodore Osmundson and Lawrence Halprin (1957–1958) and taught at the University of California. He founded and chaired the program in landscape architecture at the University of Washington. Haag's simple credo is: "There is a basic, fundamental, primordial relationship of humankind to the earth, the water, the vegetation. Much of my design is setting up situations where . . . trees are climbable . . . and play with water, earth, fire [is] allowed to happen."

Haag's two most notable works to date are his Gas Works Park in Seattle (1970–1975), an adaptive reuse of an obsolete gas generation plant on the shore of Lake Union at the edge of the city, and his design for the Bloedel Reserve of the University of Washington (1979–1984). The reserve included a series of four gardens by Haag: the garden of planes, anteroom, reflection garden, and the bird sanctuary. For these two projects and his important contributions to education, Haag is the only person ever to be twice honored with the president's medal of the American Society of Landscape Architects (1981 and 1986).

HALL, William Hammond (1846–1934), a civil engineer, was the designer of Golden Gate Park in San Francisco (1871–1876). In 1865, Frederick Law Olmsted, during his two-year sojourn in California (1863–1865), warned that San Francisco would not be able to develop a park in the image of New York's Central Park because two-thirds of the vast 1000-acre site (½ mile wide and 3 miles long) was covered by sand dunes and scattered salt-spray scrub plants. He wrote: "[T]he conditions are so peculiar and the difficulties so great . . . that it must be solved . . . by wholly new means . . . invention, not adaptation [of East Coast methods]. There is not a full-grown tree of beautiful proportions near San Francisco . . . It would not be wise nor safe to undertake to form a park upon any plan which is assumed as a certainty that trees which would delight the eye can be made to grow near San Francisco."

In 1871, the city held a design competition that was won by the 25-year-old Hall. He envisioned the park as a romantic landscape garden–style country estate, with winding carriage roads and footpaths, rolling lawns, lakes, flower gardens, a botanical garden with subtropical plants, and a 15-acre conservatory for the more exotic species. Through his understanding of the ecological constraints of the region and an exhaustive research of dune reclamation in other countries, Hall was able to stabilize the dunes and introduce new plant species to create the first romantic country park in California. More significantly, Hall's work was the first American application of such critical ecological principles to large-scale landscape design. In his transformation of the barren site into a verdant west coast version of Central Park, Hall began a "new [California] school of the art of landscape gardening," an approach based on the unique climatic characteristics of the Bay Area's Mediterranean climate.

The supervision of the park's development was done by John McLaren, a Scottish gardener. Working there from 1890 until 1943, he helped to carry out Hall's scheme, planting large masses of trees and shrubs to blur the hard edges of the long narrow park. McLaren was also responsible for much of the "Australianization" of California through his planting of so many eucalyptus trees.

Hall, authority on irrigation, was the first state engineer of California (1879–1889). In 1889–1890, he was the supervising engineer of the United States Irrigation (later named the U.S. Reclamation Service), and later was the consulting engineer on irrigation in England, South Africa, Russia, Turkey, and Panama. Other projects that Hall designed were Burlingame

Park, the Magnolia Valley subdivision in San Raphael (1888), and several large private estates.

HALPRIN, Lawrence (1916–), born in Brooklyn and educated at Cornell University (plant sciences) and the University of Wisconsin (horticulture), Halprin was "converted" to landscape architecture following his reading of Christopher Tunnard's *Gardens in the Modern Landscape*. He studied at Harvard from 1942 to 1944, just a few years after the "Harvard revolution" was begun by Dan Kiley, Garrett Eckbo, James Rose. Walter Gropius, Marcel Breuer, and Christopher Tunnard were still teaching there to instill their design philosophies in him. His classmates in architecture were Phillip Johnson, I. M. Pei, Edward Larrabee Barnes, and Paul Rudolph. Following service in World War II, he settled in San Francisco, where he worked in the office of Thomas Church (he collaborated on the design of the Donnell Garden, in 1948). He founded his own practice in 1949. His residential designs during the late 1940s and 1950s helped to establish the "California" or "modern garden" as a major outdoor design form. His McIntyre Garden in Hillsborough, California (1959), in a "Moorish style," shows Halprin's talent for the use of water and concrete, elements that have become his signature ever since. This approach can be seen in several of his public fountain plazas: Lovejoy Plaza (1965–1966) and Auditorium Forecourt (now Ira Keller Fountain) Plaza, in Portland, Oregon (1965–1970); Manhattan Square Park, in Rochester, New York (1971–1976); and the Seattle Freeway Park (1970–1976). The Keller Fountain and Seattle Freeway Park owe much of their success to Halprin's very creative design partner, Angela Danadjieva, who worked with his office for many years.

Halprin has been one of the twentieth century's most important design theoreticians. His work on the analysis and notation of movement and the "spatial experience" of people in the environment ("motation") have frequently been published. His book *The RSVP Cycles* (1969) was based on this system of motion choreography, developed with his wife, the dancer Anna Halprin. His urban work has been done out of his commitment to making cities more livable through bringing the users into personal contact with the materials with which each space is made. People are invited to climb on his sculptural forms, wade in his pools, and splash in his fountains.

Halprin's practice has included civic design as well as landscape architecture. His innovative adaptive reuse of old industrial structures, including a chocolate factory at Ghirardelli Square in San Francisco (1962–1968), is his best known example of this complex type of urban project. His firm also designed the Nicollet Mall in central Minneapolis (1962–1967) and the pedestrian mall in Charlottesville, Virginia (1973–1975). The Sea Ranch, a planned community in northern California (1962–1967), is one of his finest examples of fitting buildings into a rural landscape at the edge of the wind-swept cliffs beside the Pacific Ocean. His designs for the Levi Plaza (1978–1982) in San Francisco and the Franklin D. Roosevelt Memorial (designed 1976, under construction 1992–1995) in Washington, D.C. reflect some of the later integration of the Halprinesque stone, concrete, and water into a large people-oriented landscape.

Halprin has been of inestimable influence in the profession through his lectures, workshops, films, and numerous books and articles, including *Freeways* (1966); *New York, New York* (1968); *Notebooks* (1972); *Cities* (1963); and *Take Part* (1972).

HAMILTON, William (1730–1813), was considered one of America's foremost horticulturist of the late eighteenth century. His home, The Woodlands, at the edge of Philadelphia was called by Thomas Jefferson, "the only rival which I have known in America to what may be seen in England." Hamilton was an American Tory sympathizer who spent three years in England following the Revolution, studying the best country house architecture and landscape garden design. Between 1787 and the turn of the century, he remodeled both house and grounds into America's premier example of the English country seat. In his extensive greenhouse he amassed the largest horticultural collection in North America. Jefferson so admired Hamilton's landscape design talent that he sought his expertise when the grounds of Monticello were being remodeled in 1806. President Jefferson entrusted Hamilton with nearly half of the seeds and plants collected by Lewis and Clark on their expedition to the Pacific northwest in 1804–1806.

HAMMERBACHER, Herta (1990–1985), landscape architect and educator, was the first female German professor in landscape design at the Technical University of Berlin, where she taught for twenty-one years. She was a member of the "Bormin circle," a group of landscape architects who viewed the garden as a landscape in an ecological context in the 1930s. In her professional practice, she fit her client's gardens into their natural surroundings and used plants consistent with local habitats—at a time when baroque garden designs were popular. Environmental protection, landscape planning, habitat development, and ecology were part of her teaching objectives, and her work encompassed over 3000 planning projects throughout the world.

HARE, Sidney J. (1860–1938), and **Sidney Herbert HARE** (1888–1960) were a team of father and son landscape architects and city planners based in Kansas City, Missouri. The elder Hare was a geologist and made many important paleontological discoveries. Most of his landscape architecture work was related to cemetery design. He was landscape architect and superintendent of Forest Hills Cemetery in Kansas City from 1896 to 1902, when he opened his own office. His knowledge of geology and rock plants brought him many commissions for the design of rock gardens.

S. Herbert was a 1910 graduate of Harvard and became a partner with his father that year in the firm known as Hare and Hare. Their most notable project was the planned residential community, the Country Club District in Kansas City. This was an extended effort in which they were involved between 1913 and 1933. Hare and Hare collaborated with the Olmsted Associates on the design of Forest Hills, New York (1911); planned the mill town, Longview, Washington (1922); and designed the Waite Phillips estate in Cimarron, New Mexico (1926).

Among their other works were campus plans for the University of Texas and the University of Nebraska; the Texas Centennial Exposition in Houston (1936); and city planning, parks, and school grounds in Houston, Ft. Worth, Dallas, Oklahoma City, and Kansas City.

HATSHEPSUT (d. 1450 B.C.) was queen of Egypt from 1503 to 1482 B.C., and co-regent with her nephew, Thutmose III, until 1450, during the eighteenth dynasty of the New Kingdom. Her reign was peaceful and a time of great temple building. She had several large halls erected at Karnak along the Nile River. At Deir el-Bahri she had her architect, Senemut, lay out one of Egypt's greatest temples, her funerary temple (c. 1480 B.C.) at the base of the high cliffs facing the Nile. Historians have ranked her with the two greatest women in world history, Elizabeth I (1533–1603) of England and Catherine the Great of Russia (1729–1796).

HAUSSMANN, Georges Eugène von (1809–1891), Baron von Haussmann, was the architect of the great changes in the appearance of Paris, executed between 1853 and 1870, during the reign of Louis Napoleon, Emperor Napoleon III (1852–1870). He adapted the city planning principles of Louis XIV and André Le Nôtre with his rebuilding of Paris after the French civil war, laying out of many wide boulevards and monuments at each major *rond point*. Together with Jean Charles Adolphe Alphand, his assistant, he transformed the French grand style Bois de Boulogne into a *jardin anglais,* an English-style landscape garden park at the edge of Paris (1852–1870).

HIPPODAMOS OF MILETUS (c. 500 B.C.), who according to Aristotle was the "father of town planning," preached that good urban planning could improve society. He devised the gridiron pattern of streets and building blocks which was the formula repeated all around the shores of the Mediterranean, from today's Spain and southern France to Egypt and Asia Minor, as the Greeks colonized so much of the known world. His ideas were especially influential in the Athens of Pericles and its dependencies (c. 460–429 B.C.). This was the city planning model that the Romans adopted and perpetuated throughout their Empire, from England to old Persia, until the fifth century A.D.

HOARE, Henry II (1705–1785), a banker by profession, was the owner and designer of Stourhead, which Horace Walpole called "one of the most picturesque gardens in the world." An amateur with no prior experience in garden design, between about 1743 and 1775, Hoare remodeled his ancestral estate near Bath. While he was acquainted with the leading designers in the landscape garden movement—Pope, Kent, Burlington, and Switzer—it was through his "looking into books and [his] pursuit of knowledge" gained from studying his large and valuable collection of landscape paintings by many of the masters that he was able to design such an exquisite landscape composition.

HOGARTH, William (1697–1764), was a painter in the mid-eighteenth century who, in his book *The Analysis of Beauty* (1753), promoted the serpentine line as the "line of beauty." He discussed the various shapes and forms and asserted that certain ones were universally pleasing, especially those with graceful, waving lines—hence the serpentine. Hogarth felt that even more beautiful were three-dimensional "waving and winding" lines, which he termed the "line of grace." Good examples of these are paths and carriage roads whose horizontal and vertical alignment both meander from side to side and undulate over hills and down swales.

These forms were to be found in the designs of the leading landscape garden designers' work, such as William Kent and Lancelot Brown, and in rococo ornamentation used in architectural detailing and in furniture, where, as he wrote, "[T]he eye and the mind were lead on a wanton kind of chase following the serpentine Line of Beauty."

HOME, Henry, Lord Kames (1696–1782), was said to have been the first person to connect gardening to the fine arts. A Scotsman of many interests and vast knowledge, Kames was a lawyer, judge, and an authority on the topics of antiques, religion, literature, politics, and agriculture. He authored many essays on plant propagation and the cultivation of fruits and vegetables. He owned a large estate in Perthshire, Blair-Hammond, which he groomed into a tasteful example of the landscape garden. In 1761 he wrote, in his *Elements of Criticism* (which went through fourteen editions until 1855), "Gardening is now improved into a fine art." He further stated that landscape design does not copy nature but is "nature itself embellished." Kames believed that landscape design was related to painting, but "requires more genius to paint in the gardening way." He said that a garden should be based on "simplicity . . . as a ruling principle." He felt that "only artists destitute of genius . . . crowded their gardens with triumphal arches, Chinese houses, temples, obelisks, cascades, fountains without end." He considered the design of Versailles as "a lasting monument of a taste the most vicious and depraved."

Lord Kames thought that gardens should have ruins "to inspire a sort of melancholy pleasure." He believed, however, that Classic ruins were not desirable since they might remind the viewer that the barbarians had triumphed over the taste of the ancients. On the other hand, Gothic ruins, Kames felt, were more suitable because they "represented merely the victory of time over strength."

HOMER (eighth century B.C.) was a Greek poet whose epic poem *The Iliad,* written in the eighth century B.C., influenced later Roman poets and men of letters of the first century B.C. and A.D., chief among whom were Virgil (70–19 B.C.), the *elegiac* or nonpolitical poets Horace (65–8 B.C.) and Ovid (43 B.C.–A.D. 17), and the Roman governor Pliny the Younger (c. A.D. 61–113).

HORACE (65–8 B.C.), one of the greatest Roman lyric poets, wrote passionately about his country villa in the Sabine hills outside Rome, about 15 miles from Tivoli.

HOSACK, David (1769–1835), a medical doctor and professor of botany and materia medica (medicine) at Columbia University, was the founder of the renowned Elgin Botanic Garden of New York in 1801. At the time it was a 20-acre site 3 miles from the center of the city. Today the same land is occupied by Rockefeller Center, between Fifth and Sixth Avenues and from 47th to 51st Streets.

Hosack's picturesque Hudson River estate Hyde Park was "the resort of the learned and enlightened." An invitation by Hosack was a "must" for all dignitaries who visited New York. It was this place that inspired Andrew Jackson Downing to embark on his career in landscape gardening. In his *Treatise,* Downing called Hyde Park "one of the finest specimens of the modern style of Landscape Gardening in America . . . while the native woods, and beautifully undulating surface, are preserved in their original state, the pleasure-grounds, roads, walks, drives and new plantations, have been laid out in such a judicious manner as to heighten the charms of nature. . . . The plans for laying out the grounds were furnished by [André] Parmentier . . ." (Downing, 1841, pp. 29–30). The Hyde Park estate contained 700 acres overlooking the Hudson. Downing visited it numerous times and admired it immensely, so much so that it served as the model for much of his later design work.

When Parmentier first arrived in New York, Hosack "urgently pressed upon him" the post of superintendent of the Elgin Botanic Gardens, but he declined in favor of establishing his own commercial nursery in Brooklyn.

Hosack was a leader in many philanthropic and patriotic movements and was a connoisseur of works of art. He was Alexander Hamilton's second and attending physician when he was fatally wounded in his duel with Aaron Burr just across the Hudson River from Hyde Park.

HOSKINS, William G. (1908–), is a British historian and the leading cultural geographer of the history of the human-altered British landscape. Hoskins has taught English local history at the University of Leicester and at Oxford. His book *The Making of the English Landscape* was published in 1955. Other works of Hoskins include *Exeter in the Seventeenth Century; The Midland Peasant* and "English Landscapes," a publication derived from his BBC television series of 1973 and 1978. Hoskins and the American cultural geographer John Brinckerhoff Jackson are considered the two leading authorities on the subject.

HOWARD, Ebenezer (1850–1928), was a visionary law clerk whose interest in urban planning grew out of the philosophies of Edward Bellamy's parable *Looking Backward* and by the American transcendentalists Walt Whitman and Ralph Waldo Emerson. He rejected the deplorable living conditions in British industrial cities and espoused the development of numerous small towns of about 30,000 population arranged around the outskirts of major urban centers. His classic book *Garden Cities for To-morrow* (originally titled *To-morrow: A Peaceful Path to Real Reform*), published in 1898, proposed that such communities be surrounded in perpetuity by open, agricultural lands in order to stem the tide of urban sprawl into their productive hinterlands. As he said, "Town and country must be married and out of the union will spring a new life, a new hope, a new civilization." Thus buffered by "greenbelts," Howard called his visionary planned communities "garden cities." The greenbelt was to enable the town's residents to have immediate contact with nature. The garden city was to be self-contained, with its own industries and shops to provide employment, goods, and services for its citizens.

The first application of his theories was in the development of Letchworth, designed by Raymond Unwin and Barry Parker in 1903, and Welwyn, 12 miles away, in 1924. After World War II, the British New Towns Act (1946) was passed with more new towns, such as Harlow, Stevenage, and Crowley being built.

In the United States, the Howardian garden cities precepts were expressed in the plans for a number of Depression-era planned towns, some funded by the federal government and others developed as private company towns. Among these were Radburn, New Jersey (1927–1929); Chicopee, Georgia (1927); Greenbelt, Maryland (1935); Greenhills, Ohio (1933); Greendale, Wisconsin (1935); and Norris, Tennessee (1933). More recently, the planned towns of Reston, Virginia (1964); Columbia, Maryland (1965); and Woodlands, Texas (1972) have carried Howard's nineteenth-century principles to the brink of the twenty-first century.

HUBBARD, Henry Vincent (1875–1947), was educated as an architect at MIT and later studied landscape architect under the tutelage of Frederick Law Olmsted, Jr. at the Lawrence Scientific School of Harvard University. In 1901 he earned the first landscape architecture degree ever granted from the university. He went to work in the office of Olmsted Brothers, Inc. in Brookline, Massachusetts, before assuming a teaching post at Harvard in 1906. He initiated the use of real-world rather than hypothetical design problems in his teaching studios. In 1917, he and Harvard's landscape architecture librarian, Theodora Kimball (whom he married in 1924), wrote one of the earliest texts specifically directed toward students, *An Introduction to the Study of Landscape Design*. In 1920 he returned to practice with Olmsted Brothers Associates as a partner. Hubbard became the first chairman of the new Department of City Planning at Harvard in 1929, serving there until 1941. From 1931 to 1934 he served as president of the ASLA. He was a consultant to several federal agencies: the Tennessee Valley Authority, the Federal Housing Administration, and the National Park Service.

The Hubbards founded *Landscape Architecture* magazine of the ASLA in 1910. For thirty-seven years they served as the journal's co-editors.

HUBBARD, Theodora Kimball (1887–1935), was a librarian at the Harvard Graduate School of Design with a special interest in the subjects of the landscape architecture and city planning. The collection of literature on these subject which she assembled during her tenure, 1911 to 1935, came to be the largest in the world and the nucleus of the influence that Harvard and the profession of landscape architecture exerted all over the world. Not only did Mrs. Hubbard, née Kimball, amass all the existing literature she could obtain at the time, she coauthored with her husband, Henry Vincent Hubbard, the first student-oriented textbook on the subject, *An Introduction to the Study of Landscape Design* (1917). Together, the Hubbards founded and edited the professional journal *Landscape Architecture* from 1910 until his death in 1947. They also started the journal *City Planning*. Mrs. Hubbard also wrote *Our Cities To-day and To-morrow* and *Manual of Information on City Planning and Zoning* (1923).

HUNT, Richard Morris (1828–1895), was the first American to earn a diploma in architecture from the Ecole des Beaux-Arts, in Paris. He returned to America and secured numerous commissions from the Vanderbilt family. His favorite style was the French Renaissance, which he replicated in the design of several Vanderbilt mansions in New York City and in the palatial Biltmore House in Asheville, North Carolina for George Washington Vanderbilt, beginning in 1888. He was skilled with other styles as well, as evidenced in his schemes for the Lenox Library in New York; the Fogg Museum and other buildings at Harvard; the U.S. Naval Observatory in Washington, D.C.; the Breakers "cottage" in Newport, Rhode Island; and the Administration Building for the World's Columbian Exposition in Chicago (1893).

Hunt worked with Frederick Law Olmsted on the Breakers and Biltmore House during the latter years of the elder Olmsted's career. He was a founder of the American Institute of Architects and its president in 1888. Hunt and Henry Hobson Richardson are acknowledged as giving focus to American architecture during its wildly eclectic period after the Civil War.

JACKSON, John Brinckerhoff (1909–), invented his own discipline within the liberal arts—cultural geography—and for many decades has been an educator and author of numerous articles and books on the topic of the American landscape. His counterpart in Britain is the renowned William G. Hoskins.

He founded the journal *Landscape* in 1951 and was its editor until 1968. Jackson has taught at Harvard University, the University of California at

Berkeley, the University of Texas at Austin, and the University of New Mexico. Books by Jackson are *Landscapes* (1970), *American Space* (1972), *The Necessity for Ruins* (1980), and *Discovering the Vernacular Landscape* (1984). He was a major contributor to *The Interpretation of Ordinary Landscapes* (1979), D. W. Meining, editor.

JACOBS, Jane (1916–), planner and writer, was the associate editor of *Architectural Forum* from 1952 to 1962, during which time she wrote *The Death and Life of Great American Cities* (1961), in which she discussed the attitudes held by many American planners about the widespread practice of urban renewal. She explained that "the characteristics which conventional theory seek to reduce or eliminate—high density, narrow and congested streets, old buildings and a casual admixture of residential, commercial and industrial uses—are precisely those which create the tissue of economic and social relationship which generate city vitality and diversity." She also wrote *The Economy of Cities,* which examined the belief that economic growth depends on the increased expansion of large established institutions. She suggested that the many unpredictable, unplanned, and small offshoots of large institutions are those that promote economic growth.

She is married to an architect who influenced her to focus on architectural and environmental issues. Jacobs is the author of the chapter "Downtown Is for People" in the *Exploding Metropolis.*

JEFFERSON, Thomas (1743–1826), one of America's greatest statesmen, was also an indefatigable architect and landscape architect. Perhaps no other person has contributed more than Jefferson to the appearance of the human-made American environment. Jefferson is credited with having produced complete or partial designs for sixteen private homes; five governmental buildings, including the Virginia State House in Richmond; and proposals for both the national "Congress House" (Capitol) and "President's House" (White House) in Washington. He designed a church for Williamsburg and one in Charlottesville, two county courthouses, and one prison. While in Paris between 1785 and 1789, he redesigned his ambassador's residence and its garden, the Hôtel de Langeac. Following two terms as president he planned the campus of the University of Virginia, wrote its curriculum, and designed its seventeen original buildings. Through his examples the Virginia State House and Monticello, Jefferson popularized Classic Revival architecture in America.

Jefferson was also a planner. He advocated the shift of the Virginia state capital from Williamsburg to Richmond. For the Virginia capital, he conceived the scheme of separating the three branches of state government into separate structures, a concept not adopted until a decade later in the federal capital. Jefferson was instrumental in the selection of the site for the new national capital and was the main advocate for the adoption of a gridiron street pattern for the city. This was later merged with L'Enfant's system of baroque-style radial avenues, which were punctuated by public monuments at major intersections. Jefferson's suggestion of a "public walk" between the grounds of the executive mansion and the spacious site for the judiciary—the "Congress House"—culminated in the Mall. While he was president from 1801 to 1809, Jefferson superintended the development of the L'Enfant plan for the city, lending his design and engineering expertise to such details as grading, drainage, paving, and tree placement along the major thoroughfares. As its first resident, he collaborated with Benjamin Henry Latrobe on architectural revisions of the White House and its grounds.

Jefferson also drafted three town plans. In 1802, for Jeffersonville, Indiana, he proposed a checkerboard scheme comprised of alternating developed blocks with unbuilt blocks in order to lower the density of the town and thus combat the dreaded yellow fever. He proposed a similar arrangement for Jackson, Mississippi and New Orleans.

Jefferson's most visibly apparent imprint on our environment related to the National Survey Grid, which was set forth in the Land Ordinance of 1785. Devised to expedite the survey and settlement of the lands of the Northwest Territory, Jefferson's checkerboard scheme grew out of his belief in democratic order and equality for all landowners. In 1803, he brokered the Louisiana Purchase, which doubled the land area of the United States. That vast area extended from the Mississippi to the Rocky Mountains and was plotted into new states, most of which were delineated by rectangular boundaries.

Jefferson's most far-reaching contribution to our national landscape stemmed from his instructions to the Virginia delegates to the First Continental Congress. The feudal laws of primogeniture and entail—limiting the inheritance of land to specified heirs—were alien to the spirit of the common law. He wrote that man is endowed with the "right to possess land in absolute domain and may appropriate such lands as he finds vacant, and occupancy will give him title." This concept became the basis of our homesteading and the eventual Homestead Act of 1862.

He was obsessed with the dream of making America a self-sufficient nation. His main goal was to see to it that our agriculture capabilities enabled our farmers to produce not only sufficient food and fiber harvests for our population, but surplus yields to be sold overseas and thereby build up America's economy.

All of his adult life Jefferson loved plants and experimenting with unfamiliar species. He traded plants and seeds with friends in this country and abroad. The Lewis and Clark expedition to the Pacific northwest (1804–1806) contributed more native plants to the nation's palette than any other single event. Upon their return, Jefferson, as president, entrusted half of the seeds and plants brought back to Philadelphia botanist William Hamilton's care. The other half of the seed cache was given to Bernard M'Mahon, another Philadelphia botanist. M'Mahon had hosted the first meeting, held in 1802 at his home, Upsala, for the purpose of planning the scientific exploration of the newly purchased Louisiana Territory.

Despite political differences, Jefferson kept abreast of the unfolding romantic landscape gardening movement in England, often procuring new treatises within a year of their publication. He owned, or borrowed and read, works by Edmund Burke, William Chambers, John James, Batty Langley, William Hogarth, Lord Kames, Alexander Pope, William Shenstone, Thomas Whately, and Horace Walpole. In a letter dated 1811 to Charles Willson Peale, he revealed his calling as a landscape architect: "No occupation is so delightful to me as the culture of the earth, and no culture comparable to that of the garden. . . . But though an old man, I am but a young gardener."

In his Account Book dated 1771 were his first expressed intentions to create a garden in the modern English landscape garden style. He wrote about his ideas concerning the character of a burying place he was intending to create at Monticello:

> [C]hoose . . . some unfrequented vale in the park . . . let it be among ancient and venerable oaks . . . encircle with an untrimmed hedge . . . in the form [of a spiral]. In the center erect a small Gothic temple of antique appearance . . . let the exit of the spiral . . . look upon a distant part of the blue mountains.
>
> A few feet below the spring, level the ground . . . let the water . . . form a cascade . . . where it may fall into a cistern under a temple . . . under this may be a bath. . . . The second storey to have . . . a spacious window . . .with a small table and a couple of chairs. The roof may be Chinese or Grecian . . . plant trees of Beech and Aspen about it. Open a vista to the millpond, . . . a view to the neighboring town . . . intersperse an abundance of Jesamine, Honeysuckle, sweet briar, etc., form a cave or grotto . . . cover it with moss. Spangle it with . . . pebbles and shells. . . .
>
> [T]hin the trees. Cut out the undergrowth . . . cover the whole with grass. Intersperse with [vines]. . . . Keep it in deer, rabbits, peacocks. . . . Let it be an asylum for . . . every other wild animal. . . . A buffalo may be confined also. (Betts, 1944, pp. 26–27)

In the spring of 1786, while Jefferson was American minister to France, he and John Adams spent three weeks examining the grounds of twenty country places in England. Included in their itinerary were such places as Chiswick, Pope's garden at Twickenham, Hampton Court, Painshill, Stowe, Blenheim, and Kew Gardens.

At the end of April, Jefferson reflected on his British observations, stating that "the gardening [in England] is the article on which it surpasses all the earth. I mean their pleasure gardening. This indeed went far beyond my ideas" (Garrett, 1971, p. 98). Architectural historian Frederick Nichols of the University of Virginia stated that Jefferson's European tour "made him the . . . most knowledgeable designer of architecture and gardening . . ." in the new republic (Nichols, and Griswold, 1977, pp. 133–134).

Jefferson pursued his dream "to improve [the grounds of Monticello] in the style of the English gardens" for four decades, until 1809. That year a French nobleman, the Marquis de Chastellux, wrote, "Jefferson had set his house, like his mind, on the heights. [He] is the first American who has consulted the Fine Arts to know how he should shelter himself from the weather" (Chastellux, 1963, pp. 390–391).

Jefferson wanted to bring public higher education to the south in hopes that young men would not have to go to the colleges in the north. He began developing plans for the University of Virginia about 1805, according to a letter to Virginia Senator L. W. Tazewell, stating: "[Don't] overbuild . . . by attempting a large house . . . a plain small house for the school & lodging of each professor is best. These connected by covered ways out of which the rooms of the students should open. . . . In fact a University should not be a house but a village."

That year he produced his first drawing of the "Central College," and by 1810 he had resolved that the plan should be organized around a central lawn: "[E]rect a small and separate lodge for each professorship, with only a hall below for his class, and two chambers above for himself; joining these lodges by barracks for a certain portion of the students opening into a covered way to give a dry communication between all the schools the whole of these arranged around an open square of grass and trees would make it . . . an academical village, instead of a large and common den of noise, of filth, and of fetid air" (Padover, 1943, pp. 1063–1064).

He rationalized, "[Among] the advantages of this plan [is] the admission of enlargement to any degree to which the institution may extend in future times . . ." (Dober, 1968, p. 22). The plan was symbolically open and accessible to all who wanted to study at the university as opposed to the English system of closed cloisters welcome only to Anglicans.

The ten pavilions were to represent America's cultural ambitions and serve as "models of taste and good architecture, and of a variety of appearance, [with] no [two] alike, so as to serve as specimens for the architectural lecturer." Behind each of the ten pavilions of the East and West Lawn were ten gardens, enclosed by serpentine brick walls. These satisfied many of his purposes—stability, economy of materials, warm microclimatic niches for plants, and the suggestion of informality as they softly delineated each of the gardens.

According to Nichols, "not since Hadrian of Rome has anyone combined administrative talent with aesthetic genius more successfully than Thomas Jefferson" (Nichols and Griswold, 1977, p. 177). In 1826, Jefferson designed his own tombstone and composed his epitaph in his characteristically self-effacing manner: "Here was buried Thomas Jefferson, author of the Declaration of Independence, of the statute of Virginia for religious freedom and father of the University of Virginia" (Nichols and Griswold, 1977, p. 178).

JEKYLL, Gertrude (1843–1932), was one of the twentieth century's most important British landscape designers and writers. In her youth Jekyll was a painter, but poor eyesight forced her to choose another career. She loved the cottage garden and reinterpreted it in many medium- and small-scale landscapes in Edwardian England. She was influenced substantially by the Anglo-Irish author and designer William Robinson.

Jekyll contributed many articles to William Robinson's magazine *The Garden,* serving as its joint editor for a while. She also wrote for the *Journal of the Royal Horticultural Society* and for *Country Life*. Her many books and articles helped to popularize her ideas on "controlled" wildness and herbaceous borders, which she invented—a collection of hardy perennial flowering plants that provided a succession of flowers throughout spring, summer, and fall. Much of her design approach was developed during visits to the Austrian Tyrol and the Swiss Alps. Her studies of the tidy formalism of the vernacular (or popular) gardens she found in that region added to her design repertoire.

Her practice and writing during the late nineteenth century and the first thirty years of the twentieth century were extremely influential in opening up the question of what a garden should be. Books by Gertrude Jekyll are *Wood and Garden* (1899), *Home and Garden* (1900), *Lilies for English Gardens* (1901), *Roses for English Gardens* (1902), *Old West Surrey* (1904), *Flower Decorations in the House* (1907), *Children and Gardens* (1908), *Colour in the Flower Garden* (1908), *Gardens for Small Country Houses* (1912), and *Old English Household Life*.

In the book *Gardens of a Golden Afternoon,* the work of Miss Jekyll and Sir Edwin Lutyens, with whom she collaborated for many years, is discussed. Among the best projects by the two of them is *Hestercombe* in Somerset. A "Lutyens house with a Jekyll garden" became an important contribution to the English way of life.

JELLICOE, Sir Geoffrey Alan (1900–), is an English landscape architect, architect, and planner. He and J. C. Shepherd wrote *Italian Gardens of the Renaissance* (1925, fourth edition 1986) and *Gardens and Design* (1927, second edition 1989). In the early 1930s he and his partner Russell Page were pioneers in England of the modern movement in landscape architecture.

He planned the towns of Hemel Hempstead (1947), Guilford, and central Gloucester, England. He led the way in land reclamation efforts with his long-term master plan for the use of the lands spoiled by limestone quarrying in Derbyshire. In his eighties he continued to work and write, planning a large modern garden at Sutton Place in England (1980), two parks in Italy and the Moody Gardens, a large theme park in Galveston, Texas. His late wife, Susan, was a frequent collaborator on planting design and coauthored some of his many books, including *Modern Private Gardens* (1968), *The Use of Water in Landscape Architecture* (1971), *The Landscape of Man* (1975, second edition 1987), and *The Oxford Companion to Gardens* (1986). Alone he wrote *Baroque Gardens of Austria* (1932, second edition 1990); *Gardens of Europe* (1937); *Studies in Landscape Design,* Volumes I–III (1960–1970, updated in 1990); *The Guelph Lectures in Landscape Design* (1983); and *The Landscape of Civilization: As Experienced in the Moody Historical Gardens* (1989).

He was president of the British Landscape Institute from 1939 to 1949 and was founder-president of the International Federation of Landscape Architects in 1948. In 1979 he was knighted for his services to the profession.

JENSEN, Jens (1860–1951), was born in Denmark, immigrated to the United States in 1884, and lived briefly in Florida and Iowa before settling in Chicago in 1886. There he worked as a gardener in the Chicago West Parks. The midwestern native plants affected him greatly and his use of them became his theme—the "prairie style." He had been called the "egocentric maverick of the mid-west" because his approach was a contradiction of the eastern establishment's more traditional way of designing.

Jensen was appointed superintendent of Humboldt Park in the late 1890s but was sacked in 1900 for speaking up about the rampant graft and political meddling throughout the park department bureaucracy. He opened his private practice in landscape architecture refining his "prairie style," with its emphasis on native plant massing and wildflowers enfolding spacious lawns and woodland underplantings. Jensen scorned the use of formality or geometry in the landscape, preferring the broad horizontality of the natural midwestern landscape. Frank Lloyd Wright, whose architectural style was also called the "prairie style," was a good friend, and frequently the two men made suggestions about each other's work. Two projects on which they collaborated were the Coonley House (1908) in Riverside, Illinois and the Roberts House in Marquette, Michigan. He is believed to have designed the grounds of several other Wright-designed houses, but *after* the structures were completed. In 1906, Jensen returned to work for the sprawling Chicago West Park System, remaining in that post until 1920, when he resumed his private practice. Much of his private work was on estates for wealthy midwesterners. Among his many projects were Columbus Park in Chicago; the Ryerson estate, in Lake Forest, Illinois (1912); the Racine, Wisconsin park system; the Cook County Forest Preserve District; and Fair Lane, the Edsall Ford estate in Dearborn, Michigan.

A member of the ASLA for a brief period, he resigned due to his contempt for the attitudes of a majority of the society. In 1935, at age 75, he closed his office in Chicago and moved to Ellison Bay in Door County Wisconsin, to open a rural retreat, the Clearing, at which he taught landscape design. He began each student's schooling thus: "First grow cabbages. After that, plant a flower. When you have successfully grown a flower, then you can start to think about growing a tree. After watching a tree grow for several years, observing how its character develops from year to year, then you can begin to think of a composition of living plants—a composition of life itself. Then you will know what landscape architecture is."

In 1939, while at the Clearing, he wrote *Siftings*.

JOHNSON, Carol R. (1930–), landscape architect, opened her own office, Carol R. Johnson and Associates, in Cambridge, Massachusetts in 1959, when she was one of only a handful of women in the field. Today, hers is the largest and one of the most respected woman-owned firms in the United States. Following graduation from Wellesley (art history), she enrolled in the Harvard Graduate School of Design—where women students were kept in a separate room from the males—earning her master's degree in landscape architecture in 1957. "I'm a traditionalist, doing "mainstream" design," she says of her firm's work. Among her most important works are the John F. Kennedy Park near Harvard Square in Cambridge; John Marshall Park in Washington, D.C.; and the Lechmere Canal Park and Mystic River Reservation, both at the edge of Boston.

JOHNSON, Claudia Alta Taylor, "Lady Bird" (1912–), conservationist, wildflower expert, and wife of the late Lyndon Baynes Johnson, thirty-sixth president of the United States. She was the owner of the Texas Broadcasting Corporation, a cattle rancher, owner of cotton and timberlands, and managed her husband's congressional office in Washington, D.C. in the 1940s. As the nation's First Lady, her special interests were in beautification and conservation. She was the chair for the Committee for a More Beautiful Capital and helped organize the first National Conference on Beauty. In 1982 she established the National Wildflower Research Center near Austin, Texas. The center's aims are the preservation, propagation, and use of wildflowers, native grasses, and other plants throughout the United States.

JONES, Inigo (1573–1652), was an English architect who was heavily influenced by the designs of Andrea Palladio and was responsible for introducing Italian Renaissance design ideas into Britain. Among his works were the Banqueting House at Whitehall (1619–1622), the Queen's House at Greenwich (1617–1635), restoration of Old St. Paul's in London (1631, destroyed in the great fire of 1666), and the square at Covent Garden (1630).

KAMES, LORD Henry Home. *See* Home, Henry, Lord Kames.

KENT, William (1684–1748), was alleged to have "leaped the fence and saw that all nature was a garden." From Yorkshire, Kent was a painter, architect, furniture designer, and designer of theater stage sets, but his greatest vocation was as a garden designer. As Repton was later to do, Kent entered the arena of garden design at the advanced age of 46 (in 1727). He lived in Italy, studying painting between 1710 and 1718, where he grew to admire the paintings of Claude Lorrain, Nicolas Poussin, and Salvator Rosa.

In the last year of his Italian sojourn, Kent met and traveled for a year with Richard Boyle, fourth Earl of Burlington. While together, they studied and steeped themselves in the architecture of the sixteenth-century architect Andrea Palladio. Returning to London, Kent redesigned Burlington's summer place, Chiswick House, which was completed in 1727. He had many commissions to "improve" on the work of his predecessor, Charles Bridgeman, such as at Rousham and Stowe. Both were in the French formal style and Kent, a proponent of the modern or naturalistic style, demolished much of Bridgeman's work. His patron, the Earl of Burlington, obtained for him the titles of both Architect and Painter to the Crown, although art historians have regarded him as an "unsuccessful painter." According to Horace Walpole, it was Kent who stated: "Nature abhors a straight line."

Kent's practice of grouping trees neatly together in wide spacious meadows led others to criticize his scattering of clumps of trees all over the landscape. Despite this, many historians believe that Kent, "more than anyone else, formed Lancelot Brown's taste both in architecture and in gardening." Among his accomplishments were the grounds of Stowe; Carlton House (said by Walpole to have been modeled after Pope's garden); Holkham; Euston; Chiswick House; Claremont; Hampton Court; Esher; Rousham, referred to by Walpole as "the most engaging of all Kent's works"; Kensington Palace; Wooburn Farm; and Stanstead Park. Kent designed many garden structures, such as the "ruins" on the grounds of Chiswick House.

KESSLER, George Edward (1862–1923), German-born city planner and landscape architect, came to the United States in 1865. He was educated in this country and in Europe in forestry, civil engineering, botany, and landscape garden design. He began his practice in Kansas City, Missouri in 1882. He planned the grounds of the Louisiana Purchase Exposition in St. Louis in 1904 and was the planner of the 3471-acre park system for Kansas City, Missouri (1893). He also produced parks and city plans for: Syracuse; Mexico City; Longview, Washington; Pensacola, Florida; Indianapolis; Cincinnati; St. Louis; Memphis; Denver; Houston; Dallas; and Salt Lake City.

Over the course of his long career he laid out many private residential grounds and designed subdivisions in Baltimore and Cleveland; campus plans for Miami University in Oxford, Ohio; Mississippi College; Missouri State; Kansas University; and the Baptist College in Shanghai, China.

KILEY, Daniel Urban (1912–), is an architect, landscape architect, and urban designer who apprenticed in the office of Warren Manning in Boston and earned his master's degree at Harvard. Kiley, Garrett Eckbo, and James Rose fomented the "Harvard revolution" of the late 1930s, eschewing the Beaux-Arts tradition in landscape architecture education (and practice) in favor of the modern or more site-specific design. His work, with its crisp architectonic geometry, has been labeled "classical" or "reminiscent of the seventeenth century" because he believes the human-made landscape should "be an obvious contrast to the world of nature" (Jellicoe et al., 1986, p. 312).

Following World War II, Kiley and Eero Saarinen produced the design for the St. Louis Arch, the winning entry in the Jefferson Memorial Gateway competition. Among his other outstanding works, produced out of his farmstead office on Lake Champlain in Vermont, are the U.S. Air Force Academy in Colorado Springs; the Oakland Museum in California (1963), often cited as a twentieth-century "Hanging Gardens of Babylon"; Dulles Airport near Washington; the Ford Foundation Headquarters in New York City; the Lincoln Center in New York; the East Wing of the National Gallery of Art in Washington, D.C.; the Bank of Korea in Seoul; Arcade Center in Seattle; and the North Carolina National Bank in Tampa. Kiley's best residential design was for the Miller Residence in Columbus, Indiana, a flat site with a stark grid of trees and a Henry Moore sculpture. Kiley's gardens at the Oakland Museum spawned a number of other west coast "hanging gardens," in Portland, Seattle, Vancouver, and other cities.

Although he has not written a great deal, he has appeared widely as a speaker and his work has been published in *Landscape Architecture, Process Architecture, Inland Architect,* and elsewhere.

KNIGHT, Richard Payne (1750–1824), an English scholar and connoisseur, held the most extreme views of the three compatriots (together with Reverend William Gilpin and Sir Uvedale Price) of the picturesque school of landscape gardening in England toward the end of the eighteenth century. He was a scholar and connoisseur of the poetry of Alexander Pope. He was a member of the Society of Dilettanti and the owner of the most valuable collection of paintings by Claude in Europe. In his *The Landscape—A Didactic Poem* (1794), Knight proclaimed his contempt for Brown and his "bare and bald" designs. He was averse to the "femininity" of the Brown landscapes and claimed that a more wild, naturalistic style was in better taste. "Romantic scenery," according to Knight, was "wild, abrupt, and fantastic—in which endless intricacies discover, at every turn, something new and unexpected." Price treated the two words as nearly synonymous. To him, picturesque scenes were always well composed, whereas romantic compositions could be "odd, misshapen, and uncouth." Knight's home, Downton Castle, in Hertfordshire was developed as a prototype of the picturesque country estate.

He wrote *An Analytical Inquiry into the Principles of Taste* (1805), basing his design theories on painting and the rules of composition of the painter, saying, "[L]et us learn, in real scenes, to trace/The true ingredients of the painter's grace. . ."

KNOX, Alistair Samuel (1912–1986), Australian architect, had a great love of the native Australian environment. He was a founding member of the Australian Institute of Landscape Architects. In 1948 he began the "Eltham Movement," an Australia movement in the use of native plants and building materials. Knox designed or supervised the construction of over one thousand buildings, many of which were "environmental buildings," built of adobe or what he called "mud brick." The town of Eltham, near Melbourne, was the venue of many of his works, most of which were designed and built, by the clients, under his supervision. In his home in Eltham he provided quarters and moral support for two generations of some of Australia's finest painters, potters, sculptors, poets and thinkers.

KOBORI ENSHU (1579–1649), Japanese architect and garden designer, built many fine buildings and gardens in Kyoto. He established the Enshu school of tea ceremony and flower arranging. His most noted works were the Imperial Palace and Gardens (1596–1614), the Katsura Imperial Villa (1620), and Sento Gosho (1634), all in Kyoto.

LADY ALLEN OF HURTWOOD. *See* Allen of Hurtwood, Marjory, Lady.

LANGLEY, Batty (1696–1751), wrote *New Principles of Gardening, or, The Laying Out and Planting Parterres, Groves, Wildernesses, Labyrinths, Avenues, Parks, etc. after a more grand and rural manner than has been done before* (1728). Despite the title's inclusion of "parterres," Langley deplored what he called "that abominable Mathematical Regularity and Stiffness." He preferred to let the "site shape the form and arrangement of the landscape." He wanted the garden to be comprised of "a continued series of harmonious objects, that will present new and delightful scenes to our view at every step we take, which regular gardens are incapable of doing."

Langley declared his affinity for the utility of the *ferme ornée,* saying that "a good Garden, is to be both profitable and delightful. . . ." He condemned formal gardens because "they always deviate from Nature, instead of imitating it . . . a Garden which is regular . . . instead of entertaining the Eye with fresh Objects, after you have seen a quarter Part, you only see the very same Part repeated again, without any Variety." While many other critics of the formal style professed to love nature and venerable old trees, few of them spoke out on behalf of the monarches of the forest that were being sacrificed for the sake of making the geometric gardens. Langley was one of the first to put his feelings for the existing vegetation so clearly when he said: "What a shame it is, to destroy a *noble* OAK of two or three Hundred Years Growth . . . for the sake of making a *trifling Grass-Plot* or *Flower-Knot regular.*"

LATROBE, Benjamin Henry (1764–1820), was an English architect, engineer, and proponent of the natural style of landscape design. Born in Yorkshire, England, he was the son of a Pennsylvania mother who had returned to England. He came to the United States in 1795 to become one of our greatest architects. He championed the Classic Revival style of architecture. Among his most noted architectural works were the Bank of Pennsylvania, in Philadelphia, wherein he introduced the first Greek Ionic order into America; the façade of the Virginia state capital in Richmond (1798, the building was designed by Thomas Jefferson); the south wing (House chamber) and the north wing (Senate chamber) of the U.S. Capitol; the Roman Catholic Cathedral in Baltimore in the Gothic Revival style (1804); America's first Gothic Revival house, Sedgeley, near Philadelphia; as well as many churches, banks, academic buildings, and public monuments from the east coast to Ohio, Kentucky, and Louisiana. Latrobe completed several major engineering projects also, including America's first fully steam-powered waterworks in Philadelphia and the improvement of navigation on Pennsylvania's Susquehanna River.

In 1798–1799, Latrobe wrote "An Essay on Landscape Painting" to convey his ideas of composition to a friend who he was teaching to paint. This *composition* might have been an essay on the design of landscape gardens in that he so eloquently related his thoughts on *landscape architectural design* theory as well as pictorial composition. In doing so, he was one of the earliest thinkers in America to commit his thoughts to paper relative to the connection between painting composition theory and the actual aesthetic arrangement of natural elements on the land.

A portion of the White House grounds was planned by Thomas Jefferson with the benefit of Latrobe's suggestions. In 1807, Jefferson sketched a plan for the site which the latter amended with his own proposal drawn over that of the president's. Latrobe showed a serpentine carriageway and to the south a "park." The plan of the two men was not completed during Jefferson's term of office but did establish the general character of the White House grounds, which were slowly developed into a semblance of the English landscape garden park.

LE BLOND, Jean-Baptiste Alexandre (1679–1719), was a French architect and garden designer who apprenticed under André Le Nôtre. He laid out the grounds of Peterhof in St. Petersburg, Russia, for Peter the Great, beginning in 1716. In Paris he designed the Hôtel de Vendôme and the Hôtel de Clermont.

LE BRUN, Charles (1619–1690), was a French painter and interior designer. Working for the French court for most of his adult life, he, more than anyone else, established the taste for the Louis XIV style. He had studied with Nicolas Poussin in Italy (1642–1646) and returned to France to design the interior of the Château Vaux-le-Vicomte. Following that, he was put to work by Louis XIV on decorating the interior of his palace at Versailles.

LE CORBUSIER (Charles-Edouard Jeanneret-Gris) (1887–1965), Swiss modernist architect, painter, urban planner, and writer, was known after 1919 by his chosen professional name, meaning "The Builder." He began practicing architecture in Paris in 1916 with his cousin. His buildings were cubist-like in style, trim, clean, of modern materials such as concrete ("concret brut"), steel, glass block, and plastics—"machines for living."

Le Corbusier traveled to Rio de Janeiro, Brazil in 1936 for the Ministry of Education and left his influence on later Brazilian and Latin American architects and landscape architects Roberto Burle Marx, Lucio Costa, and Oscar Niemeyer, as can be seen in the city planning, architecture, and landscape treatment of Brasilia (1961).

Included in his best works were the Villa Savoye; the Citrohan, Monol, and Plainex houses in Paris; the Maison Laroche at Auteuil; the Pavilion de l'Esprit Nouveau at the Paris Exposition of 1925; the design of the Palace of the Nations in Geneva; the "Radiant City" apartment building in Marseilles; the master plan of Chandigarh, the new capital of the Punjab (India) begun in the 1950s; and the planning for Belmopan, the new capital of Belize in Central America.

Corbusier said: "To me the quest of harmony seems the noblest of human passions. Boundless as is the goal, for it is vast enough to embrace everything, it yet remains a very definite one. Architecture subtly and eloquently inserts itself into the site, absorbing its power to move us and in return offering to it the symphonic elements of human geometry."

His books were *La ville radieuse, Toward a New Architecture, The City of Tomorrow and Its Planning; The New World of Space, Creation Is a Patient Search,* and *When Cathedrals Were White.*

LEDOUX, Claude-Nicolas (1736–1806), the most extreme exponent of French neoclassicism, was greatly influenced by late Italian Renaissance design. Also a devotée of the *jardin anglais*—English landscape gardening style—he helped to popularize it in France and other European countries. His treatise *L'Architecture* (1804), in which he proposed a theoretical "ideal" community named Chaux, established him as an authority on urban planning. His most significant built work was the Arc-et-Senans, the Royal Saltworks (1744–1749), which was proposed to be the centerpiece of his visionary utopian city, Chaux.

He designed the Hôtel de Montmorency in Paris in 1769 and the romantic-style grounds of the neoclassical Hôtel Thelusson, also in Paris, as well as the houses and grounds of several other residential estates in the naturalistic style. One of his buildings, the Hôtel-Guimard in Paris (1770), for the famous dancer Marie-Madeleine Guimard, was so admired by Thomas Jefferson while he lived in that city that he modeled his Pavilion IX at the University of Virginia after it. Ledoux's work also influenced Joseph Jacques Ramée, French èmigrée and designer of the Union College in Schenectady, New York (1813).

L'ENFANT, Pierre Charles (1754–1825), a French soldier, engineer, and architect, spent his youth in the royal village at Versailles, where his grandfather was the court painter. The younger L'Enfant was schooled as a landscape painter and his strongest talents were in the areas of perspective, optical illusion, topography, color, and rendering of plant material. In 1776 he volunteered his services as a lieutenant of engineers in the Continental Army, serving under Baron von Steuben at Valley Forge during the American Revolutionary War. As an artist he was called upon to illustrate von Steuben's manual *Army Regulations,* and he made portraits of Washington and his officers. L'Enfant was captured by the British early in the war and held prisoner until its end, when he retired to practice architecture in New York. One of his most prominent works was the remodeling of the old City Hall, where in 1789 George Washington was inaugurated as the first president of the United States. As the original surveyor of the 100-square-mile District of Columbia, he was subsequently hired by President Washington in 1791 to master plan the new national capital. Thomas Jefferson was secretary of state and contributed his own ideas to the layout of the city—primarily, the gridiron pattern of streets, running east-west and north-south, and the "public walk," which developed into the Mall. L'Enfant's visionary proposal was to fuse the Jeffersonian grid with a network of baroque avenues running diagonally and intersecting at monumental *rond points* marked by statues and fountains. Consistent with the theme of the central axis at Versailles, the spacious Mall unified the three widely spaced branches of our government, an idea originated by Jefferson. L'Enfant's scheme was brilliant but not original. He modeled it after components of a number of European capitals, and not surprisingly, Paris in particular. It was very much a monumental piece of three-dimensional sculpture. The plan was based on landform, climate, and perspective. More than just a street map, L'Enfant's grand design called for gardens, tree-lined avenues, promenades, plazas, statues, fountains, cascades, and canals (both navigational and sculptural). At the junctions of the major diagonal avenues were to be monumental nongovernmental institutional edifices such as churches, synagogues, learned academies, and museums.

L'Enfant was an abrasive man who had many disagreements with Washington over the next three years and subsequently was sacked in 1793. The federal government was moved from Philadelphia on December 11, 1800 and Jefferson became the first president to live in the White House in the new national capital. For the remainder of his life L'Enfant continued to design forts, all of which were found to be too extravagant and therefore never built. He prepared a plan for the village of Paterson, New Jersey but never executed any other significant projects and died in poverty in Green Hill, Maryland. He is buried in Arlington National Cemetery in front of the Custis–Lee Mansion.

LENNÉ, Peter Josef (1789–1866), German landscape gardener, designed many *Englische garten*-style places, beginning in 1809. Included in his work were Sanssouci (1816–1860); Stadtschloss and the Prinz Albrecht Garten, in Berlin; many private estates and urban parks, including the Tiergarten in Berlin (1818–1840); and Volksparks in Magdeburg (1824), Frankfurt (1835), and Dresden (1859).

LE NÔTRE, André (or Le Nostre*) (1613–1700), was a French landscape designer who was the royal gardener for Louis XIV (the Sun King) for nearly half a century. He grew up in the village of Versailles and in the gardens of the Tuileries, where his father, Jean Le Nôtre, was the royal gardener to Louis XIII. Le Nôtre studied architecture under François Mansart and became the head gardener at the Tuileries in 1637. In 1657, Le Nôtre laid out the gardens of the Château Vaux-le-Vicomte for Nicolas Fouquet, the finance minister to the king. These gardens began the development of what has come to be called the French grand style, with its strong, central axis extending far into the distance, radiating and perpendicular paths traversing broad open grassy planes ornamented with low evergreen hedges called "parterres," and more upright, tightly clipped sculptural and geometric forms. These patterns were intended to be admired not only from within the gardens but from within the château.

When completed, the gardens of Vaux-le-Vicomte surpassed in elegance and size all gardens that had been created before it, much to the dislike of the Sun King. In order to best him, the king commandeered the three designers of Vaux, André Le Nôtre, Charles Le Brun, and Louis Le Vau, and put them to work remodeling and enlarging his own hunting lodge in the village of Versailles. This effort began in 1661 and continued for two decades, altering the course of garden design history. The palace and gardens at Versailles grew to be the largest (3000 acres), grandest, most awe inspiring in all of the Western world and were imitated (on much smaller scales) by many other European monarchs. Here, Le Nôtre employed the *patte d'oie* or "goose foot" liberally. This baroque design device consisted of three axes radiating from a single *rond point,* "point in space." The central sight line extended westward, perpendicular to the main facade of the palace, and at 22.5-degree angles (northwest and southwest) two diagonal allées were projected far out into the surrounding *bosques* of trees. The angles were precisely comparable to the normal person's cone of vision; thus one could scan in three directions from one vantage point. At Versailles, that focal point was the window of the king's bedroom.

Over the course of the next forty years, the king put Le Nôtre to work remodeling the gardens of many of the other royal châteaux: Marly, Grand Trianon, Saint-Cloud, Fontainebleau, Clagny, the Tuileries, Saint-Germaine-en-Laye, Sceaux, and Chantilly.

Among the Versailles imitations elsewhere in Europe were Peter the Great's Peterhof palace in St. Petersburg, Russia; La Granja, near Madrid; the Palazzo Reale, in Caserta, Italy; Hampton Court, London; Schönbrunn, Vienna; Nymphenburg, Munich; and many lesser attempts.

LEOPOLD, Aldo (1882–1948), has been called the most significant conservationist of this century. He is best known as the author of a series of essays published posthumously in book form as *A Sand County Almanac* (1949). He was a pioneer in the fields of forestry, wilderness preservation,

**According to F. Hamilton Hazelhurst, author of* Gardens of Illusion: The Genius of André Le Nostre *(1980), "the latter spelling is a child of the eighteenth century; . . . the substitution of* ô *for* os *was not in widespread use until the fourth decade of the eighteenth century" (p. viii).*

wildlife ecology, and soil conservation. With the eye and mind of a scientist, Leopold thought, spoke, and wrote like a poet, thus assuring that his *Almanac* would be considered a literary classic for many generations to come. More than any man of this century, he promoted a "land ethic" based on scientific necessity rather than on religion or sentimentality. He wrote: "[A] land ethic changes the role of Homo Sapiens from conqueror of the land-community to plain member and citizen of it. . . . A land ethic reflects the existence of an ecological conscience, and this in turn reflects a conviction of individual responsibility for the health of the land."

Born and reared in Iowa, Leopold studied forestry under Gifford Pinchot, the founder of the Yale School of Forestry. In 1908 he graduated and joined the U.S. Forest Service as a "forest assistant" in the Gila National Forest in New Mexico [Territory]. In December 1919, Leopold met Arthur H. Carhart, the U.S. Forest Service's first landscape architect. At the time when the Forest Service philosophy leaned more toward "utility" than conservation, and most foresters saw the timber in the national forests as "crops awaiting harvesting," and wildlife as "game," Carhart reinforced Leopold's wilderness attitudes immensely. Four days after their meeting, Carhart wrote a memorandum to Leopold, stating, "There is a limit to the number of . . . lakes [and] mountains . . . in existence, and in each one of these situations there are portions of natural scenic beauty which are God made, and the beauties of which of right should be the property of all people." Thus it was Carhart who was the major influence on Leopold's quitting the Forest Service in 1924 to devote his life to the study of ecology and preaching about the wilderness ethic.

In 1921, in an article in the *Journal of Forestry,* Leopold declared that wilderness is "a continuous stretch of country preserved in its natural state, open to lawful hunting and fishing, big enough to absorb a two weeks' pack trip, and kept devoid of roads, artificial trails, cottages, or other works of man."

Leopold taught at the University of Wisconsin during the 1930s. He died while fighting a brush fire in Wisconsin.

LE VAU, Louis, II (1612–1670), was a French architect who worked with André Le Nôtre on both the Château Vaux-le Vicomte (1656–1661) and enlargement of the palace at Versailles (1661–1670). Later he worked for Louis XIV remodeling the Tuileries gardens and the Louvre Palace in Paris.

LEWIS, Philip H. (1920–   ), for many years chairman of the Landscape Architecture Department at the University of Wisconsin, developed a system of regional inventory and analysis by examining patterns of natural and cultural phenomena. He states that the objective of this system is "to identify, preserve, protect and enhance the most outstanding intrinsic values and see that introduced man-made values are developed in harmony with these quality resources." This technique is not unlike those developed by Ian McHarg and the Canadian forester G. Angus Hills. See Philip H. Lewis, "Quality Corridors in Wisconsin," *Landscape Architecture,* Vol. 54, No. 2 (1964).

LIGORIO, Pirro (1500–1583), was an Italian architect and garden designer who worked with Orazio Olivieri, a hydraulic engineer, on the design of the Villa d'Este (1549) in Tivoli, the romantic Renaissance water garden commissioned by Cardinal Ippolito II d'Este. Ligorio also designed the casino, or garden house, for Pope Pius IV in the Vatican Gardens in Rome (1558–1565).

LINNAEUS, Carolus (1707–1778), was a Swedish naturalist (christened Carl von Linné, he Latinized the spelling of his name). He was the inventor of the Linnaean system of scientific plant and animal classification, using the binomial Latin delineation (genus and species). Since its invention, it has been in use worldwide to identify flora and fauna. He was the author of over 180 published titles, his major works being *Species Plantarum* (1753) and *Genera Plantarum* (1754). These are considered the standard for all botanical nomenclature. The typical Linnaean classification of red maple, for example, is *Acer rubrum.*

LONDON, George (c. 1640–1713), began a nursery in the city of London in 1681, in partnership with Henry Wise, making them the first commercial gardeners in England. They were very prolific and highly sought after in their day, due to their skill at replicating the French grand style of gardens in England.

London followed John Rose as the royal gardener to Charles II and was influenced by the design style of André Le Nôtre. He introduced many new exotic plants from North America into England. Among his most notable works were Hampton Court (c. 1689) in London and Melbourne Hall (c. 1704) in Derbyshire. Charles Bridgeman apprenticed with London and Wise.

L'ORME, Philibert de (c. 1510–1570), studied ancient Roman architecture in Italy and was the first to incorporate Italian Renaissance features into garden design in France. His inspiration was drawn from Vitruvius, Alberti, and Serlio. He was the royal architect for Henri II, beginning in 1547. Diane de Poitiers, mistress to the king, commissioned him to develop the château at Anet—the first symmetrical union of gardens and building in France. He had also worked for Mlle de Poitiers at the Château de Chenonceaux and for the king's wife, Catherine de Medici, at the Tuileries and Saint-Germain-en-Laye before Henri's death in 1560. Two of L'Orme's major contributions were that the architect was to compose building and site as a unit rather than leave the grounds to a garden designer, and his ornamental use of water in broad canals and pools. He wrote *Premier tome de l'architecture* (1567) and *Nouvelles inventions de bien bastir* (1561).

LORRAIN, Claude (1600–1682), the pseudonym of Claude Gellée (also cited elsewhere as Claude, or Lorrain, or simply, Gellée), was one of many French painters during the seventeenth century who settled in Italy to paint the *campagna,* the rural countryside. His frequent subject was the Temple of Vesta, in Tivoli, in highly romanticized surroundings. Along with Nicolas and Gaspard Poussin and Salvator Rosa, Claude was responsible for making landscape painting into a genre in its own right. His compositions possess great space, depth, light, and melancholic ruins around which are mingled grazing sheep or cattle—the icons of the English eighteenth-century romantic landscape gardens.

It was for this man that the *Claude-glass* was named. These mirrorlike devices were popular during the late eighteenth century when the British went on their picturesque outings in the countryside in search of "that kind of beauty which would look well in a picture." These picturesque pilgrims were steeped in the principles of painting composition *before* they ventured into less settled areas of the country, *Claude-glasses* in hand, to locate scenes in nature that resembled painted landscape vignettes.

LOUDON, Jane Webb (1807–1858), English writer on gardening, was the wife of the garden authority John Claudius Loudon. She assisted him in the compilation and writing of his books and periodicals, which was particularly helpful because his own right hand was nonfunctional. Mrs. Loudon published nearly twenty books on plants and gardens on her own. Her writings were addressed specifically to female readers because during her day, it was believed that women needed less technical material then men required. *Gardening for Ladies* (1840) and *The Ladies' Companion to the Flower-Garden* (1841) were comprised of practical advice, and her directions for the use of color in the garden were firm. In 1849 she established and served as editor of *The Ladies Companion,* a periodical on subjects of interest to women.

LOUDON, John Charles (1783–1843), was called by Andrew Jackson Downing "the most distinguished gardening author of our age." From Scotland, Loudon began in 1822 to call for the establishment of public urban parks such as those already in existence in Europe. It took nineteen years, until 1841, for the first such park to be developed in England—Victoria Park in London.

As a designer of parks and gardens, he followed the principles of Uvedale Price. His publishing career began in 1803 with "Hints for Laying Out the Ground in Public Squares." Over his long career he wrote many articles and books, including *A Treatise on Forming, Improving and Managing Country Residences, and on the Choice of Situations Appropriate to Every Class of Purchasers* (1806); and *An Encyclopedia of Gardening* (1822). Loudon also founded the *Gardener's Magazine* (1826–1844) and *The Suburban Gardener and Villa Companion* (1838) and published the *Architectural Magazine* (1834–1838). His monumental eight-volume *Arboretum et Fruticetum Brittanicum* (1838) was published in abridged form in 1842 as *An Encyclopedia of Trees and Shrubs.* His last work was published posthumously in 1845, *Self-Instruction for Young Gardeners, Foresters, Bailiffs, Land Stewards and Farmers.*

Loudon was one of the major advocates of the return to geometric formalism, a style termed "gardenesque," or "Victorian," because of his belief that each different plant was to be seen individually rather than in masses, as was the basis of the naturalesque style.

LOUIS XIV (1638–1715), was king of France, *Le Roi Soleil* (the Sun King), for over seventy years, beginning in 1643. His reign is referred to as the *Grand Siècle,* the great age. In 1661, he hired André Le Nôtre to enlarge and improve his gardens at the Versailles hunting lodge started by his father, Louis XIII, in 1624. For a quarter of a century, Le Nôtre worked there to create the most elaborate and impressive gardens in all of Europe.

Louis retained his royal gardener, Le Nôtre, for forty years as he transformed the gardens at several of his other châteaux in the Paris vicinity: Chantilly, Fontainebleau, Marly, Saint-Cloud, Sceaux, Tuileries, Trianon, Saint-Germaine-en-Laye, and Clagny.

LOW, Judith Eleanor Motley, was the founder of the Lowthorpe School of Landscape Architecture, Gardening and Horticulture for Women in 1901 in Groton, Massachusetts. She had studied at the Swanley College of Horticulture in England and fashioned Lowthorpe's curriculum after that program. As a young woman, she spent much of her time at her grandparents' estate, Bussey Park, in Boston. In 1872 this become the Arnold Arboretum of Harvard University. The name Lowthorpe was created in memory of her late husband, Edward Gilchrest Low.

At the time, the Massachusetts Institute of Technology had a small program in landscape design which was coeducational. When Harvard started its landscape architecture program in 1900, MIT eliminated its courses. Since Harvard admitted men only, Mrs. Low saw the need to provide for young women interested in entering into the field and thus established Lowthorpe. As Harvard's emeritus president, Charles W. Eliot (father of landscape architect Charles Eliot), stated in 1925, "Mrs. Low's efforts to start . . . a School of Landscape Architecture for Women was founded on her belief that landscape architecture was a calling especially adapted to women. . . ." Since the elder Eliot had struggled to establish the country's first program at Harvard (1900) just one year before Lowthorpe opened, he appreciated Mrs. Low's vision. In 1945, Lowthorpe was moved to Providence and formed the nucleus of the landscape architecture program at the Rhode Island School of Design, but not before 400 women had been educated at Lowthorpe in Massachusetts.

LUTYENS, Sir Edwin (1869–1944), English architect, was converted to garden design by Gertrude Jekyll. They collaborated on several projects between 1889 and the mid-1890s, when Jekyll's eyesight began to fail. Their best joint efforts were Woodside in Buckinghamshire (1893) and Munstead Wood, Jekyll's own home (1894). Between 1912 and World War I, Lutyens worked in New Delhi, the new capital of India.

LYMAN, Theodore (1753–1839), created an English-style landscape garden on the grounds of his summer home, The Vale, in Waltham, Massachusetts, beginning in the 1790s. The grounds of this romantic residential "park" were comprised of sweeping lawns bordered by native and introduced specimen trees and shrubs, a deer park, and a pond. Handsome borrowed scenery was obtained from the house and from various places along the meandering walks of The Vale. Lyman had a good deal of design skill but was also assisted in this effort by the English garden designer William Bell and the American architect Samuel McIntire.

His neighbor was Christopher Gore, noted for his similar naturalistic landscape garden, Gore Place.

MANNING, Warren Henry (1860–1938), apprenticed in the Olmsted firm for eight years. His major interest was in urban planning and park design. He learned the business through his brothers' nursery and was a proponent of the use of native plants, which he preferred to use on his residential and park sites. He opened his own office in Boston in 1896, later moving to Billerica and finally to Cambridge. Included in his works were the Jamestown Tricentennial Exposition in 1907; the campus of Hampton Institute, in Norfolk, Virginia; the park and parkway systems in Milwaukee, Minneapolis, Cincinnati, and Harrisburg, Pennsylvania; city plans for Athens, Georgia, Billerica, Massachusetts, Birmingham, Alabama, and Warren, Arizona; and plans for the Rockefeller, Seiberling, Sprague, and McCormack estates. He was a charter member of the American Society of Landscape Architects and its president in 1914. Manning wrote many articles for *Landscape Architecture, Country Life in America,* and several other journals.

He *may* have been the first person to use transparent overlay maps of the various site factors as an analysis technique. In 1923 he published a condensation of his massive 900-page "Nation Plan for America" as a "National Plan Study Brief" in *Landscape Architecture* (vol. 13, no. 4). This plan included his proposal for a coast-to-coast system of national highways, thirty years in advance of our interstate highway system. The full work was never published. The Manning office archives are kept at Iowa State University in Ames.

MARSH, George Perkins (1801–1882), was a conservationist in America in the nineteenth century. As the author of one of the earliest books on the subject of human degradation of the environment, *Man and Nature: or, Physical Geography as Modified by Human Action* (1864), he began to alter our thinking about the wanton exploitation of nature. He demonstrated that human beings had become a geological force, citing degradation of the soil, forests and even climate through overgrazing, timbering, and mining. He was trying to suggest an alternative to the American pioneer interpretation of the Old Testament book of Genesis 1:28 when he stated that "man has too long forgotten that the earth was given to him for usufruct alone, not for consumption, still less for profligate waste." Marsh served as the U.S. Minister to Italy from 1861 until his death in 1882. His book was revised and republished as *The Earth as Modified by Human Action* (1870).

MATHER, Stephen Tyng (1867–1930), an industrialist (he invented the "Twenty Mule Team" slogan for his borax company), in 1917 became the first director of the National Park Service (as a separate bureau of the Department of Interior), serving in that post under three presidents, until

1929. When Congress passed the legislation establishing the National Park Service in 1916, its express purpose was to "conserve the scenery and the natural and historic objects and wildlife therein [and] to provide for the enjoyment of the same in such a manner and by such measures as will leave them unimpaired for the enjoyment of future generations."

During Mather's tenure, he expanded the number of national parks from thirteen to twenty. He also administered the growing number of national military parks, historic sites, battlefields, monuments, seashores, national parkways, and the National Capital District, including the Mall and the White House grounds. Formerly, the national parks were administered as separate units, with no overall coordination of the activities and funding of the individual parks. Mather believed in the value of the parks as public treasures to be enjoyed by all. He pushed for increased access and facilities in the parks—roads, trails, lodging, and camp sites.

He organized the first National Conference on State Parks and was a member of the National Capital Park and Planning Commission. He was an honorary member of the American Society of Landscape Architects.

MAWSON, Thomas Hayton (1861–1933), was a prolific English landscape architect and town planner of the late nineteenth and early twentieth centuries who produced work in Britain, the Netherlands, Denmark, Germany, Greece, the United States, and Canada. He maintained offices in Lancaster, London, Vancouver and, for two years, in Athens, Greece. He was also involved in the turn-of-the-century arts and crafts movement.

In England, Mawson's most significant work was within the planned community Port Sunlight, near Liverpool (1887–1905), for Lord Leverhulme of the Lever brothers (soap magnates). In 1908, Mawson won first prize for his garden design of the Palace of Peace at The Hague, the Netherlands. He was commissioned in 1914 by King Constantine of Greece to lay out the royal palace gardens as well as tree plantings around the Acropolis, several public parks, and some work on the island of Corfu. That year Mawson also designed the grounds of the Kaiser's summer villa. After World War I, he replanned the Greek city of Salonika, which had been heavily damaged by fire.

His first book, *The Art and Craft of Garden Making* (1900), brought him considerable attention and helped launch his North American sojourn in 1910. In the United States he lectured in Chicago, New York, and Philadelphia and at Yale, Cornell, and Harvard universities. He traveled and spoke widely in Canada, speaking in fourteen cities from Halifax, Nova Scotia to Victoria, British Columbia. In Toronto he spoke to an audience of 1200 listeners about "Garden Cities and Model Housing for the Working Classes." He was commissioned in 1912 to prepare plans for the grounds of the provincial parliament in Regina, Saskatchewan, known as Wascana Centre; master plans for the University of Saskatchewan; the University of Dalhousie (Halifax, N.S.); the University of Calgary; civic improvements in Calgary and Ottawa, including the grounds of Parliament House; Stanley park in Vancouver; and a large portion of Banff National Park and the town of Banff, Alberta. He was commissioned to design a number of private residences as well. He returned to England to produce the plans above out of his Lancaster office, but in 1913 came back to Canada with his son, John, to open his office in Vancouver. The outbreak of World War I in 1914 led to the closing of his Vancouver office and a major reduction in his staff and workload.

Mawson was the leading proponent of university-level formal education in landscape architecture when there was not yet such a program in Britain. He advised that such a program should be modeled after those in the United States. In 1909, Lord Leverhulme funded a chair in civic design at the University of Liverpool, and Mawson was made a visiting lecturer there.

He was also the author of *Civic Art, Studies in Town Planning, Parks, Boulevards and Open Spaces* (1911); *An Imperial Obligation: Industrial Villages for Partially Disabled Soldiers* (1917); and *The Life and Work of an English Landscape Architect* (1927). He was the president of the Town Planning Institute in 1923 and the first president of the British Institute of Landscape Architects in 1929.

McFARLAND, J. Horace (1859–1948), was a photographer, authority on roses, writer, and almost a one-man crusader in his effort to improve the condition of the U.S. environment during the first third of the twentieth century. With the use of his photographic lantern slides, he gave illustrated lectures around Pennsylvania and elsewhere. His major campaign was for the prohibition of sewage and solid waste dumping into the nation's rivers. His efforts eventually won out and improvements were effected through a number of legislated regulations on dumping. His campaign against billboards was equally successful.

McFarland was a founder and first president of the American Civic Association (1904), serving until 1924. He lectured and wrote widely in such magazines as the *Saturday Evening Post, Century Magazine, Ladies Home Journal,* and *Outlook.*

Bolstered by the American Civic Association, he fought to control development at Niagara Falls and later in Yosemite National Park, such movements culminating in the formation of the National Park Service in 1916. McFarland has thus been called "the father of the National Park Service."

McHARG, Ian (1920–), was born in Scotland and came to the United States in 1946 to study landscape architecture and city planning at Harvard, earning the two degrees in 1950. He was the founder and chairman of the Landscape Architecture and Regional Planning Program at the University of Pennsylvania from 1957 until the mid-1980s. In 1962 he founded the Philadelphia multidisciplinary firm of Wallace, McHarg, Roberts and Todd, through which he perfected the "overlay analysis" technique, incorporating geographic, climatic, vegetative, and land use studies of a given landscape area. His book *Design with Nature* (1969) is considered a modern classic in the environmental planning literature. Perhaps more than any other person, McHarg promoted ecological planning and helped to make "ecology" the household word that it is today. His approach integrates the findings of the physical and biological sciences and terrestrial and aquatic ecology into a systematic process for land analysis and land use planning. The motion picture that he produced in the mid-1970s, *Multiply and Subdue the Earth,* has been an influential teaching tool.

Among the most important built works by McHarg and his associates are Woodlands New Town in Texas; Amelia Island Resort, Florida; the plan for the valleys outside Baltimore; Harborplace, the centerpiece of Baltimore's revitalized Inner Harbor; and the Medford Report (done through the University of Pennsylvania). In the 1970s, the WMRT firm planned a zoo, called Pardisan, for the Shah of Iran, but due to the overthrow of the Shah, that proposal was never executed.

McKIM, Charles Follen (1849–1909), was a principal architect in the New York firm McKim, Mead and White, which produced more than 500 buildings between 1879 and 1904. The work of the firm was in the Beaux-Arts style (McKim was educated there, 1867–1870), copying nearly all of the major historical styles from Europe.

Each of the partners was responsible for his own projects, with McKim in charge of the design of the Boston Public Library (1887–1892); the campus plan of Columbia University (1893–1894); the Frederick W. Vanderbilt House in Hyde Park, New York (1895–1899); Rosecliff House in New Port (1897–1902); the Low Library at Columbia University (1897); Pennsylvania Station, New York (1910); Grand Central Terminal, New York (1903); the Agriculture Pavilion at the World's Columbian Exposition in Chicago (1893); Harbor Hill House, Roslyn, New York (1899); and the J. Pierpont Morgan Library in New York (1902–1907).

McKim was the president of the American Institute of Architects from 1901 to 1903, during which time he served on the McMillan Commission, together with Chicago architect Daniel H. Burnham, landscape architect Frederick Law Olmsted, Jr., and sculptor Augustus Saint-Gaudens, charged with the replanning the federal center of Washington, D.C. according to the plan of L'Enfant in 1791. The firm also designed additions to the Metropolitan Museum of Art in New York (1904–1916).

McKim and Burnham originated the idea of the American Academy in Rome, a postgraduate school for architecture and the related arts in Italy, established in 1897.

MEADE, David (1744–1830), was a Virginia planter whose 600-acre James River plantation was called Maycox, or Maycocks, from the name of an earlier owner. The site of the house was one of the best on the river, on the opposite side of the river from William Byrd's Westover. Meade's "pleasure ground," which he began improving in 1774, is described in Reverend John Jones Spooner's *Topographical Description of the County of Prince George, in Virginia, 1793,* as follows: "These ['pleasure'] grounds contain about twelve acres, laid out . . . in a most beautiful and enchanting manner. Forest and fruit trees are here arranged, as if nature and art had conspired together to strike the eye most agreeably. Beautiful vistas, which open as many pleasing views of the river; the land thrown into many artificial hollows or gentle swellings, with the pleasing verdure of the turf; and the complete order in which the whole is preserved; altogether tend to form it one of the most delightful rural seats that is to be met with in the United States, and do honour to the taste and skill of the proprietor, who was also the architect."

Fiske Kimball wrote, Maycox "may be counted with Monticello (from 1771) and the Woodlands, as one of the first attempts in this country to make a picturesque informal arrangement [of one's residential grounds] (Kimball, 1924, p. 123).

The Marquis de Chastellux visited Maycox in 1782 and wrote, "*Maycox* is charmingly situated, for it is directly opposite Mrs. Byrd's, which with its different annexes, has the appearance of a small town and forms a most delightful prospect. Mr. Meade's garden, like the one at Westover, forms a terrace along the bank of the river."

MEDICI, a family of bankers in Florence, ruled Tuscany for several generations during the fifteenth and sixteenth centuries and as patrons of the greatest artists alive then, financed many of the greatest artistic creations of the early Renaissance. The family patriarch, Cosimo the Elder (1389–1464), commissioned Michelozzo to design an open, airy garden around his older residence at the Villa Medici in Careggi—the venue of his Platonic Academy until it was moved to the newer Villa Medici in Fiesole

(1458), also designed by Michelozzo. Situated on a hillside high above Florence, this "philosopher's garden" was the first built in keeping with the principles being translated from the first-century writings of Pliny the Younger and Vitruvius (Ten Books of Architecture) by Leon Battista Alberti (completed in 1452, but published in 1485 as *De Re Aedificatoria, Libri X*).

Lorenzo il Magnifico (the Magnificent, d. 1492), Cosimo I (1519–1574), and Francesco I (1541–1587) carried on the great humanist traditions of their ancestors, commissioning subsequent generations of artists and building great villas and palaces. Pratolino (c. 1569) and Boboli Gardens in Florence (1549) are two of the most outstanding examples.

The Italian influence was exported to France through the female side of the Medici line. Catherine de Medici (1519–1589) married Henri II and built for herself the smaller of the two gardens beside the Château de Chenonceaux (1560), enlarged the palace and gardens at the Tuileries in Paris, and built the Château Saint-Germain-en-Laye in Paris. Later, Marie de Medici (1573–1642), wife of Henri IV, ordered construction of the Luxemburg Palace and gardens in Paris (c. 1612), modeled after the Boboli Gardens. She also had her architect, Mollet, extend the Cours de la Reine beyond the gardens of the Tuileries, eventuating in the Avenue Champs-Elysées.

MICHAUX, André (1746–1802), French botanist, spent twelve years in the United States (1785–1796) collecting native plants to send to the Jardin des Plantes in Paris. He and his son, François André Michaux, settled in New Jersey and established a nursery there. André moved to Charleston, South Carolina in 1787 and developed another botanical garden. He explored from Florida to the Mississippi River and as far north as Hudson's Bay in Canada. About 1800, he presented several camellias to Arthur Middleton for his plantation, Middleton Place, near Charleston. He returned to France and wrote a large volume on American oaks . François Michaux worte *The North American Sylva* (1819).

MICHELANGELO BUONARROTI (1475–1564), Italian sculptor, painter, architect, and poet, designed the Capitaline Piazza (the Campidoglio) in Rome between 1537 and 1539, the dome of the reconstructed St. Peter's Basilica in the Vatican (1547–1564), and the Porta Pia in Rome (1561–1564). His sculpture and paintings include the Pieta (1498), the David (1501–1504), the ceiling of the Sistine Chapel in the Vatican (1508–1512), Moses (1513–1515), and the Last Judgement on the wall of the Sistine Chapel (1534–1541).

MICHELOZZO DI BARTOLOMMEO (1396–1472), architect and garden designer, was a favorite of the Medici family as they built palaces and villas around Florence in the fifteenth century. He designed the gardens at the first fifteenth-century Platonic Academy, the Villa Medici in Careggi, and the entire Villa Medici in Fiesole (1458), near Florence, for Cosimo de Medici. Michelozzo's design was based on Pliny the Younger's writings and villa designs. He used neoclassical techniques popular in his day to create a formal house and grounds in a hillside setting.

MIES VAN DER ROHE, Ludwig (1886–1969), was a German architect, many of whose early project proposals were too visionary to be funded. His ideas, however, were frequently published and thus became very influential on the development of modern architecture. His German Pavilion at the 1929 Barcelona International Exposition, with its Barcelona chairs, established him as one of Europe's leading designers. His designs were based on functionalism and geometric precision. From 1930 to 1937, Mies directed the Bauhaus, with its emphasis on the international style, a union of all the arts with twentieth-century industrial materials. Following the Nazi rise to power, in 1938 he fled from Germany to the United States and settled in Illinois as the director of the Illinois Institute of Technology. He planned the campus and designed its buildings (1939–1940). Other projects include the Farnsworth House, in Plano, Illinois (1945–1951); the Seagram Building in New York City [with Philip Johnson] (1954–1958); and a series of high-rise apartment towers on Lake Shore Drive in Chicago (1948–1951).

MILLER, Philip (1691–1771), was a Scottish horticulturist and garden planner who directed the Physic Garden of the London Apothecaries at Chelsea from 1722 to 1770. His *Gardener's Dictionary* (1731) and *Gardener's Kalendar* (1732) were *the* standard horticultural references in their day in both England and America. In the *Dictionary* he incorporated a section on garden design, which made it also the major guide to the laying out of gardens, both for pleasure and for crops. He corresponded for years with John Bartram of Philadelphia, exchanging plants and plant knowledge. He introduced many plants into England and sent some of the earliest cotton seeds to the Georgia colony.

MITCHELL, Donald Grant (1822–1908), agriculturist, landscape gardener, and man of letters, wrote a number of books about the design of rural residential pleasure grounds. He was an acquaintance of Andrew Jackson Downing and shared many of Downing's philosophies about design. His writings on the subject are considered second only to Downing's and are less technical and more literary.

Mitchell inherited his family's ancestral farm near New London, Connecticut in 1841 and at the age of 19, retired there as a gentleman farmer, living a life of leisure and writing. In 1845 and 1846, he toured around Britain and the continent on foot. His observations were composed into a number of newspaper articles from 1846 to 1855 under his *nom de plume,* "Ik. Marvel" or "Ike Marvel."

His first major literary work was published in 1847 as *Fresh Gleanings, or a New Sheaf from the Old Field of Continental Europe,* an account of his European travels. He later wrote *The Battle Summer* (1850), *Reveries of a Bachelor* (1850), and *Dream Life* (1851). He served as the U.S. consul to Venice in 1853 and 1854 and the following year lived in Paris.

Upon his return to the United States (1855), he purchased a 360-acre farm near New Haven and named it Edgewood. His years of living abroad sensitized him to the beauty of farming while leading him to detest the ugliness of the typical American farmstead. For the rest of his life he endeavored to transform his Edgewood into a model *ferme ornée,* claiming, "Good example will do very much in way of reform. . . ." Edgewood and his philosophy of landscape design became the subjects of four of his books: *My Farm of Edgewood* (1863); *Wet Days at Edgewood* (1865); *Rural Studies, with Hints for Country Places* (1867), republished as *Out-of-Town Places: With Hints for Their Improvement* (1884); and *Pictures of Edgewood* (1877). He also wrote many journal articles about agriculture for the *Knickerbocker,* the *Atlantic Monthly,* and *Harper's Magazine.*

Mitchell's design skill was demonstrated in a small number of public places, such as East Rock City Park in New Haven, and the grounds of a number of private estates in Connecticut. His books were likened to "a wood fire is on a dreary day . . . all warmth and cheer and light." Among his later works were *Fudge Doings* (1855); *Seven Stories with Basement and Attic* (1864); *Dr. Johns* (1866); *About Old Story Tellers* (1869); *English Lands, Letters and Kings* (1889–1897); and many others.

Mitchell's writings about his Edgewood convey a great wealth of information about the practical aspects of farming and a great sensitivity about the pleasures of landscape gardening in the Downing mode. The New York Agricultural Society awarded him its silver medal (1843) for his innovative plans for farm buildings, his writings, and his lectures at Yale.

M'MAHON, Bernard (also spelled McMAHON) (c. 1755–1816), was an Irish horticulturist and author of the first book on horticulture published in the United States to include a section on modern pleasure gardens. Before M'Mahon's *American Gardener's Calendar,* published in 1806, there had never been an articulation of the modern principles of landscape design aimed at the American audience. M'Mahon's *Calendar* included a section on the laying out and planting of "pleasure grounds" specifically adapted to American climatic and soil conditions. This book was reprinted eleven times and became the standard encyclopedic work for farming for more than fifty years. Until Downing's *Treatise* appeared in 1841, it was the standard reference for ornamental gardening as well. M'Mahon lived in Philadelphia and operated a successful nursery business. President Jefferson entrusted M'Mahon with nearly half of the seeds and plants collected by Lewis and Clark on their expedition to the Pacific northwest (1804–1806). Thomas Nuttall, in his *Genera of North American Plants* (1818), named the genus *Mahonia* for Bernard M'Mahon.

MOLLET, André (d. 1665), the son of Claude Mollet I, is best known as the author of *Jardin de plaisir* (1651), summarizing the basic principles of classic French formal garden design. He was a royal gardener to Louis XIII of France, for whom he developed many pleasure gardens. Mollet went to England about 1630 to work on the gardens at St. James Place and returned there in 1642 to remodel the grounds of Wimbledon House for the wife of Charles I. He worked in Holland in the early 1630s and later was royal gardener for Queen Christina of Sweden. He worked in England again in 1658 with his brother Gabriel at St. James Place. From 1661 until his death, he worked at St. James and Hampton Court for Charles II. His work in England influenced his British contemporaries George London and Henry Wise.

MOLLET, Claude, I (c. 1563–1664), was the son of Jacques Mollet I, a gardener at the Château Anet. Mollet wrote *Théâtres des plans et jardinages* (1652) and is said to have laid out the first *parterre de broderie.* In 1595 he was the gardener for Henri IV, designing the gardens at Fontainebleau, Montceau, the Tuileries, and Saint-Germain-en-Laye. He was the father of the gardeners André, Gabriel, Jacques II, Noel, and Pierre Mollet. André Le Nôtre's father, Jean, worked under Claude Mollet at the Tuileries. In his *Théâtre,* he described the *jardin français* style of his time:

> A broad avenue flanked by double or triple rows of elms or limes planted in strict line, at right angles to the building, which must look on to a spacious fore-court, either circular or square. On the opposite side of the house, parterres, with flower beds, are to be laid out where they can be enjoyed from the windows, without

trees or other obstacles to interrupt the view. Then must follow parterres with grass lawns, and hedges and palisades, and then bosquets, which have alleys arranged so that the trees converge on a statute or fountain; and finally, there may be a painted canvas that can be renewed if spoiled by rain. Statues should be ranged about, grottoes contrived, and (where level permits) terraces built. And further, there must be aviaries, fountains, jets, canals, and other decorations, the which, when all has been duly ordered, form the most perfect pleasure garden.

MOLLET, Claude, II (d. 1664), the grandson of Claude I, worked at the gardens of the Tuileries beginning in 1630. He designed the earliest version of the parterres at Versailles in the 1630s and later produced the illustrations of the parterres in Jacques Boyceau's book *Traité de jardinage*.

MOLLET, Gabriel (d. 1663), the son of Claude I, was a gardener who went with his brother André to England to work at St. James Place in the 1660s. He and André Mollet worked for Charles II at Hampton Court from 1661 until his death.

MOLLET, Jacques, I (c. 1500s), was the head gardener at the Château d'Anet. He helped to shape the early French formal garden style. He was the father of Claude I and grandfather of André, Gabriel, Jacques II, Noel, and Pierre Mollet, all royal gardeners.

MOLLET, Jacques, II (d. 1622), son of Claude I, was the head gardener at Fontainebleau.

MOLLET, Pierre (d. 1659), the son of Claude Mollet I, succeeded his father at the Tuileries.

MOORE, Charles W. (1925–), American architect, was educated at the University of Michigan and at Princeton (Ph.D. in architectural history). He has taught at the University of Utah, Princeton, Yale, the University of California at Berkeley, and UCLA. He began practicing in 1962 and has been in partnership with various people to this date. He says that architecture is "the making of places . . . its excellence [derives] from its ability to communicate and to engage the individual's mind in making connections through time and space."

His architectural and environmental design works have included many private residences, office buildings, commercial buildings, civic centers, museums, college buildings, and urban spaces. Some of his most important environmental design projects include Sea Ranch, California (with Lawrence Halprin & Associates) (1964–1965) and Piazza D'Italia, New Orleans (1975).

His work and philosophy have been widely reviewed in a variety of professional and lay publications and he has written many journal articles and the book *The Place of Houses* (1974).

MORGAN, Julia (1872–1957), architect, was the first woman accepted in the architecture section of the Ecole des Beaux-Arts in Paris and California's first licensed woman architect. Her career flourished during the building boom following the San Francisco earthquake of 1906. Her commissions, most of which were in the Bay Area, included more than 700 houses and many institutional structures such as churches, clubs, banks, schools, and hospitals. Her trademarks were the use of locally available material, fine attention to detail, craftsman-like quality of construction, and dramatic swimming pools. Her most notable clients were the Hearst family, for whom she worked for twenty-five years. For them she designed projects in Mexico, the Grand Canyon, and the most spectacular of all, San Simeon estate, at which she created a museum for the Hearst's private art collection and lavish formal gardens. When she closed her office after forty-five years of practice, she had all her records destroyed, insisting that the buildings should speak for themselves.

MORRIS, William (1834–1896), English social critic, writer, poet, and artist closely associated with the Pre-Raphaelites, began the arts and crafts movement in England with his founding of the Arts and Crafts Society and the Society for the Protection of Ancient Buildings in England. Influenced by John Ruskin, he became a major tastemaker of his day in Europe and the United States and played a major part in the elevating of the decorative arts to the status of the fine arts of painting and sculpture. He urged "art for use," and strived to demonstrate that hand-crafted art was preferable to the inferior machine-age products of his day. He helped revive the interest in preindustrial-quality objects "made by people, and for the people." A social reformer, he also wanted to elevate the status of the tradesman, stating, "It would be well if all of us were good handcraftsmen in some kind, and the dishonour of manual labour done away with . . . no master should be too proud to do [his profession's] hardest work."

In 1857, Morris established a firm designing and crafting decorative interior art objects such as furniture, stained glass, ceramics and tiles, wallpaper, tapestries, wood carvings, and engraved and forged ornamental metalwork. His creations were fabricated from natural materials and were conceived to convey the nature of those materials and the process by which they were formed. Garden designers William Robinson, Gertrude Jekyll, Edward Lutyens, and Thomas Mawson were influenced by this philosophy. They spurned carpet bedding and geometric styles in favor of craftsman-like use of "old-fashioned" plants in their cottage gardens of the late nineteenth century. Jekyll's herbaceous borders, with their soft forms and subtle color variations, are a good counterpart to Morris's wallpaper and tapestry designs.

Morris was the author of scores of poems, articles, and books, including *The Defence of Guenevere* (1858), *The Earthly Paradise* (1870), *The Aenids of Virgil* (1876), *The Odyssey of Homer* (1887), *The Tale of Beowulf* (1895), *The House of the Wolfings* (1889), and *The Roots of the Mountains* (1890).

MOSES, Robert (1888–1981), was America's greatest builder of public facilities—parks, highways, bridges, and housing. He was perhaps the most powerful person in New York state politics for two generations. Moses was the chairman of the New York State Council of Parks and commissioner of parks in New York City beginning with Mayor La Guardia in 1934 and remaining in that post until 1960. During his reign, Moses administered the construction of $27,000,000 in projects. The chief landscape architect for much of this work was Gilmore Clarke. Moses emphasized recreation and utility rather than conservation and thus introduced many sports fields and active recreational facilities into parks which were originally designed for purposes of the passive contemplation of nature. The ball fields and hard courts in Central Park are his most blatant travesty.

Moses made many enemies during his domination of New York politics, including Robert Caro, who wrote the book *The Power Broker, Robert Moses and the Fall of New York*.

MUIR, John (1838–1914), was one of America's most important naturalists and writers about conservation. Along with Frederick Law Olmsted, he helped to protect the Yosemite Valley from mining and timbering and to secure its establishment as a California wilderness preserve and later as a national park. He also led the effort to found the Sierra Club (1892), an organization of environmentally sensitive citizens united to fight the Hetch Hetchy Dam, which was proposed to be built in the Yosemite Valley in 1900. Muir was born in Scotland, grew up in Wisconsin, and graduated from the University of Wisconsin. He wrote numerous articles for the *Century Magazine* and the books *The Mountains of California* (1894) and *Our National Parks* (1901).

MUMFORD, Lewis (1895–1990), was an historian, educator (taught at Stanford and the University of Pennsylvania), urban planning authority, and author of more than thirty books, most notable of which were *Sticks and Stones* (1924), *American Taste* (1929), *The Brown Decades* (1931), *Technics and Civilization* (1934), *The Culture of Cities* (1938), *The City in History* (1961), and *The Highway and the City* (1963). He argued that the dehumanizing effects of modern technology, urbanization, and impersonal institutions were "a monster that can transform man into a passive, purposeless animal." Among his many honors, Mumford was made an honorary Knight of the British Empire in the 1930s.

NASH, John (1752–1835), English architect and town planner, was a partner of Humphry Repton until 1802. Beginning in 1811, he transformed the Marylebone Farm at the edge of London into Regent's Park for the Prince of Wales, the Prince Regent. This large tract of land (328 acres) was to be enclosed all around its boundaries by rows of "villas," or "terrace houses," which fronted on and enjoyed a commanding prospect of the sprawling naturalistic park laid out in the Repton style. This "crown park" was the model for the later public parks in England and elsewhere. It was opened to the public in 1838.

Nash also laid out a grandiose plan for the realignment of one of the major streets in London, renamed Regent's Street, along which he proposed to build all the buildings from his own designs. This connected between Regent's Park via Picadilly Circus to St. James and Green Parks and Buckingham Palace.

Nash was one of the leading architects of the picturesque school, designing country houses in the "castle" style or in the Tuscan villa manner, as depicted in the landscape paintings by Claude Lorrain and others. Among Nash's other projects were alterations to Buckingham Palace, the Royal Pavilion (in an "Indian" style) and several seaside pavilions at Brighton, and a house for the landscape critic Sir Uvedale Price.

NICHOLSON, Sir Francis (c. 1665–1728), royal governor to the colonies of Maryland (1694–1698) and Virginia (1690–1692 and 1698–1705), produced the town plans for Annapolis (1695) and Williamsburg (1699). Both plans, with their grid and radial street arrangement, reflect the baroque design character of the plan of London that was produced in 1666 by Sir Christopher Wren. Annapolis was laid out with several large circular or square public spaces designated for public purposes and named for comparable residential squares in London. In the plan for Williamsburg, Nicholson included ordinances that standardized setbacks and side yards for each house and the location and height of required fencing around each property. Nicholson placed the Governor's Palace at the north end of a long spacious axial greensward, the Palace Green, which extends perpendicular to the town's main east-west thoroughfare, the Duke of Gloucester Street. The governor achieved two objectives when he created the spacious perspective between the town center and his residence. From his residence he could enjoy the openness of the long, green lawn sprawling out in front of him, and in turn, the townspeople could clearly see the Governor's Palace and thus be reminded of his authority.

Nicholson also served as royal governor to the colonies of New York (1687–1689), Nova Scotia, Canada (1712–1717), and South Carolina (1721–1725). He was knighted by George I in 1720.

NOGUCHI, Isamu (1904–1989), Japanese-American sculptor, was born in the United States but moved to Japan and was later schooled in Paris under the Romanian sculptor Constantin Brancusi. For much of his career he maintained studios at Shikoku Island, Japan and Long Island City, New York. He designed at all scales, from paper lamps to gardens, parks, and playgrounds. Among his many executed works were the Japanese Garden at the UNESCO headquarters in Paris (1958); a series of courtyards at the Yale University Beinecke Rare Book Library (1964); the Chase Manhattan Bank in New York (1964); the "Garden of the Future" at the IBM headquarters in Armonk, New York (1964); the Hart Plaza in Detroit (1970s); and the "California Scenario" in Costa Mesa (1982). His work was characterized by his stark use of symbolic sculptural forms and a minimum of plantings.

NOLEN, John (1869–1937), was one of America's first city planners to confine his activities to that discipline alone. He began his practice in Cambridge, Massachusetts in 1903, and during his thirty-three-year career he planned more than 400 public and private projects. Among these were new towns, suburbs, parks and parkways, civic and commercial centers, campuses, and industrial sites.

He began his interest in "civic improvement" while studying landscape architecture at Harvard and in the 1920s helped to begin the first university-level city planning programs in the country at Harvard and the Massachusetts Institute of Technology. His credo was: "What is fair must be fit [and provide] fully for the plain necessities of living." His most important projects were the industrial town of Kingsport, Tennessee (1915), and Mariemont, Ohio near Cincinnati (1923). He also prepared park plans for Madison, Wisconsin (1911); Walpole, Massachusetts (1911–1935); San Diego, California (1908–1926); and Venice, Florida (1925).

Nolen joined the ASLA in 1905 and was a member of the National Conference on City Planning, the American City Planning Institute, and the International Federation of Housing and Town Planning. He wrote many articles for periodicals and the book *Replanning Small Cities* (1912). With Henry V. Hubbard, Nolen coauthored two important planning documents, *Airports* (1930) and *Parkways and Land Values* (1937).

NOTMAN, John (1810–1865), Scottish-born architect and landscape architect, came to the United States and settled in Philadelphia in 1831. He designed the grounds of Laurel Hill Cemetery, overlooking the Schuylkill River in Philadelphia (1836–1839). This was the first U.S. cemetery to be built in imitation of the romantic character of Mount Auburn Cemetery in Boston (1831). He designed the Holly-Wood Cemetery in Richmond, Virginia (1848) and several others elsewhere. In 1845, Notman prepared a plan for Spring Grove Cemetery in Cincinnati, but his scheme was rejected as too fussy. Also in Richmond, he designed the Capitol Square (1850–1860) and the Huguenot Springs estate in 1847.

Notman was a friend of Andrew Jackson Downing and worked with him on several publications, including the magazine *The Horticulturist*, after Downing's death. Downing cited two of Notman's residential works in his *Treatise* (1841), Nathan Dunn's Cottage in Mount Holly, New Jersey (1837–1838), and Riverside, residence for Bishop George Washington Doane, in Burlington, New Jersey (1839). In the latter house, Notman is credited with the first use of the Italianate, or Tuscan villa style, in the United States. More important than mere eclectic style, Notman avoided symmetry and developed the Riverside house as a picturesque, asymmetrical composition of varying structural masses, textures, and lights and shadows. These devices he took further in two houses in Princeton, New Jersey—Prospect (1851) and Fieldwood (now Guernsey Hall at Princeton University) (1853–1855).

Among his other works were the New Jersey State House, Trenton (1845); the Athenaeum of Philadelphia (1845–1847); the New Jersey State Lunatic Asylum (1845–1848); Saint Mark's Church, Philadelphia (1847–1852); and Saint Peter's Church, Pittsburgh (1851–1852).

OBERLANDER, Cornelia Hahn (1927–), Canadian landscape architect, was born near Berlin, Germany and came to America in 1939. She attended Smith College and later earned the master's degree in landscape architecture at Harvard, where Walter Gropius and Christopher Tunnard still taught. She worked in Philadelphia after World War II, collaborating with Dan Kiley, James Rose, and Louis Kahn. With her husband the Austrian-born architect–urban planner H. Peter Oberlander, she moved to

Vancouver, where he started the planning department at the University of British Columbia in 1953.

She describes herself as part artist and part technician. She is also a superb plantswoman, and as the architect Moshe Safdie described her, "She is a landscape architect in the old tradition, with a passion for plants and for gardens. In her landscapes, you get a sense that the plants are happy." Oberlander has served as the president of the Canadian Society of Landscape Architects. Among her most important works are several playgrounds for Expo '67 in Montreal (1967); the setting for the British Columbia Provincial Law Courts (Robson Square) in Vancouver (1979); the Museum of Anthropology in Vancouver (1979); the Canadian Chancery in Washington, D.C. (1990); and the National Gallery of Art in Ottawa (1992).

OGLETHORPE, James Edward (1696–1785), English general, member of Parliament, prison reformer, and founder of the Georgia Colony. His plan for the town of Savannah (1733) is unique in the history of town planning. It was based in part on the Hippodamian gridiron but was modified by means of a series of repeatable modules, called "wards," each of which was to be built as the town's population expanded and more building lots were called for. This system was adhered to until 1854, when the last ward, the twenty-fifth, was completed (six wards comprised the town until 1790 when three more were developed). In the center of each of the wards was an open space, or "square," measuring about 2 acres in area. According to William Gerard de Brahm, surveyor general in 1757, each of the six squares was to be a "marketplace" and was intended to be the social, economic, and religious focus for the population of each ward. Flanking the squares were "trust lots," dedicated to various public functions, such as churches, schools, or in some cases, the homes of the town fathers. The balance of land in each ward was divided into four clusters ("tythings") of ten house lots, making a total of forty families per ward.

Another unique feature of Oglethorpe's plan was the provision for outlying properties—in effect, a regional plan. Each family was allotted a 5-acre garden plot, triangular in shape, at the edge of town. Beyond a belt of common land but within easy walking distance from one's home, each householder received a 44.9-acre farm lot, on which he was obliged to grow mulberry trees, a source of food for the colony's fledgling silkworm industry.

Many of the first boatloads of settlers were former occupants of the overcrowded debtors' prisons in England (at a time of great economic depression); thus Savannah has had the much exaggerated reputation as a colony of convicts.

Oglethorpe was governor of the colony from 1732 until 1743, and through his military skill was able to fend off the Spanish incursions into British territory, from Florida to the south. He returned to England in 1743 and spent thirty-two years in Parliament. A man of considerable stature, among his close friends were Dr. Samuel Johnson, James Boswell, Horace Walpole, Oliver Goldsmith, and Edmund Burke.

OLDHAM, John, Australian landscape architect, architect, planner and writer, has been a major influence on the profession of landscape architecture in his native country. In 1939 he designed the Australian Pavilion at the New York World's Fair. In the 1950s, he prepared a master plan for the city parks around Perth Foreshores in Western Australia. This plan has been substantially implemented but a section immediately below the center of Perth is now the subject of controversy. Oldham was Vice-President of the International Federation of Landscape Architects from 1973 to 1977. His wife, Ray Oldham, is a noted historian and writer. Together they wrote the book *Gardens in Time* (1980), in which they indicate that the influence of Asian landscaping on Western landscape architecture is far more significant than is generally assumed. They also wrote *Western Heritage* and *Western Heritage II,* which are the standard references for the early architecture of Western Australia.

OLIVIERI, Orazio (sixteenth century), was the Italian Renaissance hydraulic engineer of the fountains at the Villa d'Este in Tivoli (1549), the site design of which was done by Pirro Ligorio.

OLMSTED, Frederick Law (1822–1903), was arguably America's most important landscape architect. His contributions to the field and to the American environment are inestimable. In addition to his monumental career as a designer, Olmsted was an extremely influential writer, journalist, and social reformer. His early experiences touring the countryside and urban parks of Britain in 1850 and meeting with Andrew Jackson Downing and Calvert Vaux at the former's home in 1851 did much to launch him into the new field of landscape architecture.

Olmsted grew up in rural Connecticut, briefly attended Yale University, and struggled to find his niche as he tinkered with earning a living as a scientific farmer, surveyor, traveling correspondent, and even merchant marine. In 1850, he visited England, touring on foot, sightseeing, and recording his observations in letters to family back home. These were subsequently published in book form as *Walks and Talks of an American Farmer in England* (1852). One of the most influential sights he examined was the just-completed Birkenhead Park, near Liverpool (1844–1847). The notion of a handsome public park created specifically to serve the working-class public transformed Olmsted into a social reforming dynamo for the rest of his life. For months, he trekked around the English countryside visiting a number of important country estates, some laid out by "Capability" Brown and/or Humphry Repton, and talking with the local landowners and laborers.

Upon his return to the United States, he was sent by William Cullen Bryant, editor of the New York *Evening Post,* to tour the antebellum south and to compose a series of articles about the social and economic conditions within the slave states. This tour, on the eve of the Civil War, culminated in his classic book *The Cotton Kingdom* (1861).

On the basis of his reputation as a social critic and man of letters, Olmsted was appointed to head the newly formed New York Central Park Commission in 1857. He teamed with the English architect (and former partner of A. J. Downing) Calvert Vaux in 1858 to prepare the winning plan for the competition for the design of the park. The competition requirements specified that the following be incorporated into the master plan: "1. four transverse roads running east and west through the park; 2. a parade grounds for the militia; 3. a fountain; 4. three playgrounds; 5. a concert hall; 6. a flower garden; 7. a site for ice skating; 8. plans to be in India ink or sepia ink at the scale of 1″ = 100′; 9. a written description of the proposed park; 10. all work due on April 1, 1858."

Olmsted and Vaux's "greensward" plan (submitted anonymously) was a brilliant solution to the monumental topographical liabilities of the site and a visionary anticipation of the city's imminent growth and transportation nightmares. Their scheme combined a multitude of environments and yet enabled the visitor to experience a great freedom of choice and movement. It called for the separation of pedestrians and vehicles by grade-separated crossings and the separation of all other means of circulation (pedestrian, equestrian, and bicycle). It provided for elegant promenading on a long axial mall and bridle and footpaths meandering throughout the 840-acre site. Lakes for boating and fishing were provided. Generous expanses of woods separated the park from the surrounding city and from place to place within the park and spacious lawns suggested pastoral rural scenery. The report stated that "the park throughout is a single work of art—subject to all laws of art requiring that there must be a single, noble motive to which all parts must agree." Central Park was a great asset to the burgeoning population of the city. It was a favorite playground even before it was finished twenty years after it began.

On May 12, 1863, Olmsted first used the term *landscape architect* in a letter of resignation to the New York Park Commission, the result of intolerable political interference. This was the professional title's first official documented usage in the United States, although it is thought to have been used casually in Britain at an earlier time.

After Olmsted's severance from Central Park, he spent two years in California, where he lent his influence to the movement that succeeded in having the Yosemite Valley and Mariposa Grove of Big [Redwood] Trees ceded to the state, planned the campus of the University of California at Berkeley, laid out the Mountain View Cemetery in Oakland, and prepared a plan for the Golden Gate Park in San Francisco (his scheme was abandoned but the park was later built). About Yosemite, he said "As civilization advances, the interest of men in natural scenes of sublimity and beauty increases."

In 1865, Olmsted returned to his partner, Vaux, and together they spent eight years designing about fifty urban parks, governmental building grounds, planned communities, and campuses around the nation. Among their jointly authored works were Prospect Park in Brooklyn (1865–1888), considered by them to be their finest; the "planned suburb" of Riverside, Illinois (1869); and parks in Albany, Buffalo, Newark, Providence, Chicago, Hartford, and many more.

During the Civil War, Olmsted served as secretary of the U.S. Sanitary Commission for the Union Army (later to become the American Red Cross). In this capacity he witnessed not only the deplorable state of the medical arts' handling of war wounds, but the problems resulting from inadequate sanitation and sewage for masses of troops living in close quarters. Olmsted wrote that the Battle of Bull Run was lost by the north not due to their lack of men or arms, but because of unsanitary conditions in the camps, dysentery, lack of discipline, and alcoholism among the officers. Olmsted later applied these realizations to the same conditions as those plaguing nineteenth-century cities. He saw public open spaces (he designed approximately 500 parks in cities in all sections of the country) as "lungs of the city." His civic improvement efforts were spurred on by the great advances being made in sanitary engineering during his career.

In 1883, Olmsted moved his office from New York to Brookline, Massachusetts, where he found a growing amount of work for himself. The major project that lured him north was the Fens and the Back Bay of Boston, nicknamed the "emerald necklace," because it encircled the city like a great green collar. From 1883 to 1885, Charles Eliot apprenticed in the Olmsted office, and from 1893 until his death in 1899, he was a partner. One of Olmsted's finest park designs, completed during the years when Eliot was with the firm, was Boston's Franklin Park.

In 1890, Olmsted was appointed the chief landscape architect for the World's Columbian Exposition in Chicago. This brought him into close collaboration with a number of America's major architects, including Chicago's Daniel H. Burnham. The architectural motif agreed upon by the architects was Beaux-Arts (Roman Revival)—monumental "mercantile classicism"—forcing Olmsted's "landscape naturalism" into small patches here and there. His two major site plan elements, the lagoon (Court of Honor) off Lake Michigan and the Wooded Isle did, however, constitute the greatest image makers of the colossal extravaganza.

Late in his career, Olmsted designed the palatial (100,000-acre) Biltmore estate in Asheville, North Carolina (1888–1895), establishing the ultimate in splendid formal grounds of country places for the following forty years. More important at Biltmore was the reforesting of thousands of acres of previously clear-cut timberland. Working with the forester Gifford Pinchot, Olmsted set in motion the founding of the first school of forestry in the country.

Among Olmsted's approximately 550 post-Vaux works (1872–1895) were Mount Royal in Montréal, Canada (1881–1884); the U.S. Capitol grounds, Washington, D.C. (1874–1891); Stanford University campus plan (1886–1891); the nationalizing of Niagara Falls (1880s); and Belle Isle Park, Detroit (1881–1884).

According to the New York City Landmarks Preservation Commission, the following fifteen elements are typical of Olmsted's park designs:

1. They are works of art.
2. They have their roots in the English romantic style.
3. They provide a strong contrast to the city.
4. They reflect a Victorian influence.
5. They are characterized by use of bold forms.
6. They provide a balance between the spatial elements of turf, wood, and water.
7. They use vistas as an aesthetic organizing element.
8. They contain a series of planned sequential experiences.
9. They provide for the separation of traffic.
10. They provide visitor services.
11. They contain artistically composed plantings.
12. They integrate the architecture into the landscape.
13. Each has provision for a formal element.
14. They are characterized by variety.
15. They were built to provide for recreation.

One of Olmsted's last design projects was the design of a park in memory of Andrew Jackson Downing for city of Newburgh, New York (designed 1889–1895 and dedicated in 1897). The design was made through the combined efforts of Olmsted, Sr. and his son, John C. Olmsted; Calvert Vaux and his son, Downing Vaux; and Warren Manning.

The Olmsted firm continued under the elder Olmsted's nephew/stepson, John Charles Olmsted, and Frederick Law Olmsted, Jr., until the latter's retirement in 1954. The Olmsted Associates firm moved to Fremont, New Hampshire in 1980 and continues to this day as "The Olmsted Office, Inc."

Olmsted's role in American landscape architecture has become better understood and valued in recent years through the establishment of his home and office, Fairstead, in Brookline as the Olmsted National Historic Site, administered by the National Park Service since 1980. The plans, documents, correspondence, reports, and photographs—the accumulation of a century of professional work—are being inventoried, catalogued, and preserved as money permits, making these materials available to scholars eager to learn and disseminate more about the man and his work. The National Association of Olmsted Parks is also contributing to the preservation and restoration of Olmsted's projects.

Olmsted's other books are *A Journey in the Seaboard Slave States* (1856), *A Journey Through Texas* (1857), *A Journey in the Back Country* (1860), and *The Spoils of the Park* (1882). In 1861, Olmsted wrote an essay entitled "Parks" for the *New American Cyclopaedia,* edited by G. Ripley and C. A. Dana.

OLMSTED, Frederick Law, Jr. (1870–1957), son of Frederick Law Olmsted, was christened Henry Perkins Olmsted, but at age 7 his name was changed by his famous father, who wished to perpetuate his own name further into history. At about the time of his father's death in 1903 and when he had achieved his own considerable stature as a landscape architect, the younger Olmsted dropped the designation "Junior" at the end of his name. Therefore, after the passing of his father, much of his work and writing is mistakenly assumed to be the product of the "elder" Olmsted when in fact he was no longer alive. The younger Olmsted graduated from Harvard University and went on to become a landscape architect and city planner in the Olmsted office (1898–1954).

Two of his earliest projects were aiding his ailing father on the design of the grounds of the World's Columbian Exposition in Chicago (1890–1893) and working on the Biltmore estate in Asheville, North Carolina from 1888 to 1895, when he was taken into the firm as a full partner.

In 1900, the president of Harvard University, Charles Eliot, hired young "Rick" to develop a curriculum for the teaching of landscape architecture at the university. This program was established as a memorial to Eliot's son (and former partner in the firm Olmsted, Olmsted and Eliot), Charles Eliot. It was the world's first comprehensive course in landscape architecture, but it should be noted that there were other ad hoc college-level courses being taught in landscape gardening and horticulture, primarily at land-grant colleges. Olmsted taught in the program he devised from 1900 until 1914.

In the centennial year of the nation's capital, 1900, the 30-year-old Olmsted, Jr. was appointed by President Theodore Roosevelt to the four-man Senate (McMillan) Park Commission. Their charge was "to restore and develop the century-old [1791] plans of L'Enfant for Washington and to fit them to the conditions of today." The other members of the group were Daniel Burnham, Charles McKim, and Augustus Saint-Gaudens. Olmsted made many major contributions to this effort, which today are so easily taken for granted. It was he who proposed that (1) the axis between the Capitol and the Washington Monument be maintained as the long tree-lined open green space that we know today as the Mall; (2) the Mall axis be extended to the shore of the Potomac River; (3) a monumental pavilion housing a statue occupy the end of the westward vista (Lincoln Memorial, 1910); (4) a long, rectangular reflecting pool lie between the Washington Monument and the Lincoln Memorial; (5) the southward axis from the White House through the Washington Monument be extended to a domed pavilion, called the "Hall to the Founding Fathers" (the Jefferson Memorial, 1933); (6) the Arlington Memorial Bridge; and (7) the Rock Creek and Potomac parkways. The 1901 plan called for the balancing of the two major axes of the city and that visual connections between all four ends of the scheme be maintained; therefore it has often been called the "Kite Plan." This large and comprehensive grand master plan for Washington initiated the "city beautiful movement," which spread to all sections of the country by the mid-1920s.

As the essence but not all of the McMillan Commission's proposals were gradually being implemented, the firm of Olmsted Brothers, Inc., was hired to do dozens of specific projects. Among their jobs were the White House grounds, Lafayette Park, Washington Monument Gardens, the Jefferson Memorial, the National Arboretum, Washington Cathedral, Rock Creek Park, the National Zoo, and the Shrine of the Immaculate Conception.

Olmsted was a charter member of the American Society of Landscape Architects and served as its president twice (1908–1909 and 1919–1923).

From 1910 to 1919, Olmsted chaired the National Conference on City Planning, and at the same time was the head of the town planning division of the United States Housing Corporation.

The younger Olmsted and Ferruccio Vitale were the main forces behind the adoption of landscape architecture as one of the disciplines at the American Academy in Rome in 1915. He was a prolific writer, publishing many articles in the *Atlantic Monthly, Landscape Architecture, American City, Parks and Recreation,* and *Journal of the American Civic Association*.

In 1922, the centennial year of his father's birth, he and Theodora Kimball (later Hubbard) wrote the book *Frederick Law Olmsted, 1822–1903*.

OLMSTED, John Charles (1852–1920), was the nephew/stepson of Frederick Law Olmsted. The son of a medical doctor, he was born in Geneva, Switzerland and was a graduate of Yale University. Upon his father's death in 1857, his widowed mother married her brother-in-law, Frederick. John began working in his stepfather's office in 1875 while it was still in Central Park in New York. When the Olmsteds moved to Brookline, Massachusetts in 1883, John was made a full partner. Eleven years later, Frederick Law Olmsted retired, leaving the firm to his two sons, John and Frederick Law Olmsted, Jr. They practiced together until John's gradual retirement in about 1918.

While his stepfather was still active, John was the stay-at-home business manager; therefore, his projects were not geographically dispersed, but he played an important role in the design of Boston's Franklin Park, the Riverway, and the Arnold Arboretum. Following the senior Olmsted's retirement (1895) and the admission of Frederick Law Olmsted, Jr. as a business partner, the firm produced work all over the United States and did a tremendous variety of project types. Among their hundreds of built works were the Seattle Exposition (1909), the Lewis and Clarke Exposition in Portland (1906), the San Diego Exposition (1915), and the Canadian Industrial Exposition in Winnipeg.

The Olmsted office planned the new towns of Vandergrift, Pennsylvania, near Pittsburgh (1895) and Kohler, Wisconsin (1913). They designed parks in Boston, Hartford, Brooklyn, Buffalo, Chicago, Milwaukee, Detroit, Seattle, Spokane, Portland, Louisville, Charleston, Atlanta, and New Orleans. The Olmsteds designed college campuses for Smith, Mount Holyoke, Ohio State, and many others. They also designed private residences from coast to coast.

"J. C. O.," as he was known, and his brother "Rick" were founding members of the American Society of Landscape Architects in 1899. John was its first president (1899–1901 and 1904–1905).

Other than a few articles for *Landscape Architecture,* he wrote very little for publication, but he did produce a great number of technical reports for clients.

OSMUNDSON, Theodore, Jr. (1921–), landscape architect, is considered one of the foremost American authorities on the design of roof gardens. He earned his degree in landscape architecture from Iowa State University. Along with the Californians Douglas Baylis, Robert Royston, and Lawrence Halprin, he worked in the office of Thomas Church in San Francisco in the 1940s. In the 1960s he became a partner in the firm of Osmundson and Staley of Berkeley, California. Today he and his son Gordon are principals in the firm Theodore Osmundson & Associates, of San Francisco. Among Osmundson's most important projects have been many urban parks, institutional grounds, residences, and office parks, with the most notable project being the Kaiser Center Roof Garden, in Oakland, California (1960). This was a 3½-acre park atop a five-story parking garage roof. Other works include the roof garden for the Standard Oil Building in San Francisco; the roof garden for the Pacific Telephone and Telegraph Company in Sacramento; Marine World in Redwood City, California; the Hearst Castle in San Simeon, California; and long-range master plans for the Chico campus of the California State University. Osmundson was the president of the American Society of Landscape Architects from 1967 to 1979 and is currently president of the International Federation of Landscape Architects. He received the ASLA medal in 1983 and the ASLA president's medal in 1987. He has taught at the University of California at Berkeley and Harvard and lectured in all parts of the country. His publications include major sections of the *Reader's Digest Practical Guide to Home Landscaping* 1972, "Roof and Deck Landscapes" in *Time-Saver Standards* (1988), *Roof Gardens* (1990), and many articles in *Landscape Architecture*.

OWEN, Robert (1771–1858), was a British textile manufacturer and utopian philosopher who formulated a form of socialism/communism and attempted in vain to apply these ideals to the development of two utopian planned communities nearly a century before Ebenezer Howard and his "garden city" concept. He believed that an improved environment would have a beneficial effect on those who lived and worked in such a setting. He developed New Lanark, Scotland in the 1820s, and in 1824 came to the United States, where he devoted three years to forming a similar community in Indiana, which he called New Harmony. By 1828 this venture proved to be unsuccessful, and in that year he returned to Scotland.

PACA, William (1740–1799), was a Maryland signer of the Declaration of Independence who designed and built both a formal geometric garden and a "wilderness" garden behind his townhouse, known as the Paca House, in Annapolis, Maryland between 1763 and 1766. This half-acre naturalistic terminus of the upper terraced garden served as a "trompe l'oeil" or visual link to the Chesapeake Bay scenery beyond it. The formal garden was based on strict rules of mathematical proportions, whereas the wilderness was evidence of his knowledge of the principles of romantic landscape painting as they were applied to the layout of ornamental residential grounds.

PACELLO DA MERCOGLIANO (d. 1534), was a priest from Naples who, it is believed, was brought back to France in 1495 by Charles VIII to remodel the gardens of the château at Amboise. He was in charge of the gardens at Blois from 1499 for Louis XII and later for François I and for Cardinal d'Amboise at Gaillon. He laid out parterres at these places and introduced the idea of growing citrus trees in movable tubs in order that they could be moved indoors in the winter.

PALLADIO, Andrea (1508–1580), Italian architect, was considered the greatest architect of the late sixteenth-century Renaissance. His neoclassical style became the most influential and imitated in European architecture. His style is known as Palladianism and is classified by some historians as Mannerist. One of his best and most influential buildings was the Villa Capra (or la Rotonda) in Vicenza. Palladio was the author of *I Quatro Libri dell'Architettura* (Four Books of Architecture) (1570). He was a sensitive landscape architect as evidenced by his comments about site selection in Book II, chapter 12: "afford a beautiful prospect. . . ."

PARKYNS, George Isham (1749–1820), was an English landscape painter, engraver, and the designer of landscape gardens in the United States at the end of the eighteenth century. He spent only six years in the United States (1794–1799), but made an important contribution to our landscape design history. He recorded several important topographical views of notable places, such as Annapolis, Mount Vernon, two views of Washington, D.C., and The Woodlands, home of William Hamilton. The books that Parkyns wrote while in England were instructional for both Jefferson and Hamilton as they endeavored to "anglicize" their country places. Both men sought the design services of Parkyns but were too late; by that time he had moved to Nova Scotia, Canada. In 1808, he returned to England.

PARMENTIER, André (c. 1780–1830), Belgian horticulturist and garden designer from a distinguished family of European gardeners, was the first to practice as a *professional* landscape designer in America. Andrew Jackson Downing claimed that Parmentier was the "first American landscape gardener known to the public as a practitioner of the art." Between his arrival in the United States in 1824 and his death in Brooklyn seven years later, Parmentier developed the nation's most famous and successful commercial horticultural nursery, the Brooklyn Botanic Garden. Through this enterprise, half of which was laid out as a demonstration naturalistic ornamental park, he promoted the qualities of the modern landscape garden style. In 1826 he wrote an eloquent review of the principles of design in the "modern" style which he incorporated into his nursery catalog. This essay, "Landscapes and Picturesque Gardens," was included in Thomas Fessenden's magazine *The New England Farmer* (1828), giving Parmentier's design theories a much wider readership.

During his brief tenure in the United States he was hired by David Hosack to manage the Elgin Botanic Garden in New York City, the first in America to be developed for medical students. He also worked for many Hudson River estate owners to design, as well as plant, their country seats, including Hosack's estate, Hyde Park. Downing reported in his *Treatise* (1841), "Two or three places in Upper Canada, especially near Montreal, were, we believe, laid out by [Parmentier's] own hands and stocked from his nursery grounds." These are actually both thought to be in Toronto, Canada: Moss Park, home of William Allan (1828), and the grounds of King's College of the University of Toronto.

He sometimes spelled his name Andrew Parmenteer.

PARSONS, Samuel H., Jr. (1844–1923), was a landscape architect in partnership with the architect Calvert Vaux, former partner of Frederick Law Olmsted, from 1880 to 1895. He was educated at Yale University, graduating in 1862, and served on the U.S. Sanitary Commission organized by Olmsted. In 1882 he was made superintendent of planting in New York's Central Park and later commissioner of the New York Parks Department. He was one of the founders of the American Society of Landscape Architects, serving as president in 1902 and 1906–1907.

PAXTON, Sir Joseph (1803–1865), English architect and landscape gardener, was a gardener at Chiswick House from 1823 to 1826, when he was appointed head gardener at Chatsworth, the estate of the sixth Duke of Devonshire. While at Chatsworth, he designed the 226-acre Birkenhead Park (1844) in the newly planned suburb by the same name at the edge of Liverpool. He remained at Chatsworth until 1858, remodeling the gardens and building glasshouses (iron and glass), including his famous Conservatory in 1836. He was the first in England to coax a blossom from the giant water lily, *Victoria amazonica,* in 1849 in a special greenhouse built for it.

Paxton's design for the Crystal Palace, centerpiece of the London World's Fair of 1851, was 1800 feet in length. For that he was knighted. Later, he planned the Crystal Palace Park in Sydenham, where the dismantled Crystal Palace was reerected. He also designed the People's Park in Halifax; Prince's Park, Liverpool (1842); Queen's Park, Glasgow (1852); Baxter Park, Dundee (1863); and Coventry Cemetery (1845).

Paxton was a friend of John C. Loudon, the author of many publications on plants and gardening. Along with his designing activities, he served briefly as a member of Parliament and was the director of the Midland Railway. He authored numerous articles and was editor of the *Horticultural Register* (1831–1834) and *Paxton's Magazine of Botany* (1834–1849) and cofounder of the *Gardener's Chronicle* in 1841. His books were *Practical Treatise on the Cultivation of the Dahlia* (1838), *Pocket Botanical Dictionary* (1840), and *Paxton's Flower Garden* (1850–1853).

In 1850, Frederick Law Olmsted toured England and was struck by the rural qualities of Birkenhead Park's layout. During the long course of his career, Olmsted referred to Birkenhead Park often.

PEETS, Elbert (1886–1968), a native of Ohio, received his master's degree in landscape architecture from Harvard in 1915 and went to work with the German city planner Werner Hegemann during the planning of the company town, Kohler, Wisconsin. His main interest was in town planning and urban design and he was one of the prime shapers of that area of specialization which had grown out of landscape architecture following the Chicago World's Columbian Exposition and the ensuing "city beautiful movement." He traveled in Europe in 1920 and 1921, studying the layout of numerous historical cities. Upon his return to America, he rejoined Hegemann in the planning of Wyomissing Park in Pennsylvania (1917–1921) and the writing of one of the best urban design books written in the United States, *Civic Art: The American Vitruvius* (1922). His city plan drawings accompanying the articles are still much in use today as references on the subject. During the Depression, Peets practiced in Washington, D.C., where he developed the master plan for Greendale, Wisconsin (1938). Many of his plans were never fully actualized, but among those completed were the plans for Santa Catalina Island, California (1938), and Park Forest, Illinois (1946–1947). During World War II he worked on many government housing developments for the military. He taught planning at Harvard and Yale in the 1950s and wrote widely on the subject.

PENNETHORNE, Sir James (1801–1871), surveyor and architect to the Office of the Woods and Forests, planned the 290-acre Victoria Park in 1841, London's first park laid out specifically for use by the public. At the time, Regent's Park, designed by John Nash, was a royal park and open to the public only on a subscription basis and was used for riding rather than strolling. It was opened to the public in 1838, making it London's first pleasure ground for the masses. Pennethorne's previous experience in park design was gained through working under John Nash on the Regent's Park (1811–c. 1828). He also worked with Nash on the remodeling of St. James's Park, the design of New Oxford Street, Buckingham Gate, and Kensington Palace Gardens. Following his association with Nash, Pennethorne laid out Battersea Park (1845) and the south entrance into Albert Park (1851). He also designed several buildings and additions, including London's National Gallery and the south wing of Buckingham Palace.

PILAT, Ignaz Anton (1820–1870), Austrian-born landscape gardener, studied at the Imperial Botanical Gardens of Schönbrunn Palace in Vienna. His lineage extended back to the infamous Roman procurator, Pontius Pilate, who presided over the conviction and crucifixion of Jesus of Nazareth.

Due to "political troubles" in Vienna, Pilat came to the United States in 1848 and spent eight years in Georgia. He was the chief gardener on Thomas Metcalf's estate near Augusta and also laid out other estates, including those of Liberty Hall, the Alexander H. Stephens plantation in Crawfordville, and the Cumming–Langdon House in Augusta.

He returned to Vienna in 1852 and four years later was appointed director of the Botanical Gardens there. The following year he was called back to New York to be made "Chief Landscape Gardener of Central Park," in charge of the preparation of a botanical survey of the site. This survey culminated in a thirty-page pamphlet, *A Catalogue of Plants Gathered in August and September 1857 in the Ground of the Central Park* (1857).

Pilat was one of the thirty-three entrants in the Central Park design competition (1857), won by Frederick Law Olmsted and Calvert Vaux. Neither Olmsted nor Vaux had sufficient knowledge of plants to be able to carry out fully their own grand scheme for the park, so Pilat, who combined his expertise in botany with his sensibilities as a landscape gardener, was the man who actually brought the "greensward" vision to reality. In 1865, when Olmsted and Vaux were reappointed to direct the development of Central Park after their three-year absence, they wrote a letter of appreciation to Pilat, the "general foreman." They said, "Before going on to the work again, we desire, as artists, to express our thanks to you, a brother artist, for the help you have so freely rendered to the design in our absence" (Olmsted, F. L., Jr. and Kimball, p. 76).

After work on Central Park slowed down, Pilat became the chief landscape gardener of the city of New York and planned the improvements of several other New York squares and parks, including Washington Square, the Battery, the New York City Hall Park, and Mount Morris and Prospect Parks. He also practiced as a private landscape architect, working for such clients as William Cullen Bryant, Cyrus W. Field, Morris K. Jessup, W. E. Dodge, and the Massachusetts Agricultural College.

Horace Greeley wrote of Pilat in his obituary in the *New York Tribune* of September 20, 1870: "To him, more than any other man, is due the credit of the Park as it appears today." Pilat's son, Carl Francis Pilat (1876–1933), was a landscape architect who worked with Warren Manning and later became the chief landscape architect for the city of New York.

PINCHOT, Gifford (1865–1946), forester, politician, and writer, worked with Frederick Law Olmsted reforesting the Biltmore estate in North Carolina in the 1890s. There began the first systematic forestry work in America and the Biltmore School of Forestry, the first in this country. Pinchot was educated at Yale and studied forestry in France, Germany, Austria, and Switzerland. He was a friend of President Theodore Roosevelt and served as his closest adviser about conservation matters. In 1898 he was appointed chief forester of the National Forest Service, where he served until 1910. During this time he insisted that the expanding federal reservations acreage should be managed to assure what he called "sustained yield." He also coined the term "conservation," in 1907. Pinchot started the School of Forestry at Yale, where he taught from 1900 to 1936. Twice Pinchot served as governor of Pennsylvania (1923–1927 and 1931–1935). He was the author of several books on forestry, including *The Fight for Conservation* (1910).

Pinchot's mother was the chairwoman of the conservation committee of the Daughters of the American Revolution, which aided in the passage of the Alaska coal bill, the La Follette legislation regulating grazing, preservation of the Appalachian watersheds, the Palisades, and Niagara Falls.

PINCKNEY, Eliza Lucas (1722–1793), at the age of 16, operated a large South Carolina rice plantation. In 1744 she perfected the process by which the indigo plant could be commercially grown and refined into blue dye, so prized by the wealthy in Europe. A nature lover and fanatical gardener, she lived in England for three years (1755–1758), where she toured the country and visited the finest country homes with their romantic landscapes. In 1758 she returned to South Carolina and began to "modernize" her plantation, Belmont, into a version of what she had so admired abroad. Her *Letterbook* (1739–1762) includes some exquisite writings about her observations of nature in this country and the "modern" gardens that she visited in England.

PIPER, Fredrik Magnus (1746–1824), Swedish landscape designer who redesigned the grounds of the royal palace, Drottningholm (1780), and the Haga Park (1780), both in Stockholm, into English-style landscape gardens. Between 1770 and 1780, he made several visits to England, France, and Germany to inspect the best of the natural-style gardens in those countries. He made measured drawings of Stourhead, Painshill, and Kew Gardens, producing some of the best records ever made of these places. In Sweden he also designed the estates, Listonhill (1790), the residence of the English ambassador, Robert Hill; Wrangelsro; Godegård; and Vällinge. In 1811 he wrote the book *A Presentation of Ideas and General Plan for an English Pleasure Park.*

PLATT, Charles Adams (1861–1933), landscape architect, architect, and painter, was one of the most important practitioners of the American Country Place Era (1880s–1930), designing both the buildings and the grounds. He was educated as a landscape painter in Paris and New York. He also studied the Renaissance villas of Italy and returned to open his practice, adapting many features of the Italian villa to the grounds of country houses he designed from New England to California.

Platt's very influential book *Italian Gardens* (1894) was the first American book to be illustrated with Renaissance gardens. It triggered the eclectic movement in that style in this country. In the book he promoted the interaction between the architect and the landscape architect on all projects and the integration of the building with the landscape. He also wrote a number of articles on the subject for *Harper's Magazine* in the 1890s. Some of his creations were his own summer place in Cornish, New Hampshire (1892); High Court, also in Cornish; the Faulkner Farm, for Charles Sargent (1897) and the "Garden of Weld," both in Brookline, Massachusetts; Villa Turicum (1908–1918) on Lake Michigan, near Lake Forest, Illinois; and Gwinn, the Mather estate on Lake Erie, near Cleveland (1908). Platt designed a number of public buildings, including the Freer Gallery of the Smithsonian Museum in Washington, D.C.

Platt did a few campuses and subdivision plans, occasionally collaborating with other landscape architects, including the Olmsted Brothers and Ellen Biddle Shipman.

PLINY THE YOUNGER (c. A.D. 61–113) was a Roman governor who owned several rural villas. The descriptions of his two favorites perhaps best conveyed the Roman love of nature and life in the country. One of Rome's greatest orators, Pliny was also a playwright, and one of his greatest pleasures at his rural retreats was the solitude that enabled him to think and compose his tragedies. He termed it "call[ing] in the country." His Tuscan villa, used for extended summer holidays from the city, was 150 miles from Rome. In letters to friends, Pliny described his villas and the country life of his time.

His and other Roman country houses not only had pleasure gardens; they were, in fact, set amidst working farms. The modern Italian custom of leaving the hot city for a summertime retreat to one's country place, called *villegiatura,* originated with this ancient practice.

Pliny's villa in Laurentinum was on the edge of the Mediterranean, 17 miles from Rome, close enough to the city that he could spend weekends there year around. Pliny's descriptions clearly reflect the Vergilian notion of the good life of the pastoralist, which greatly influenced the Renaissance writer Leone Battista Alberti, as well as foreshadowing the English *ferme ornée.*

POE, Edgar Allen (1809–1849), was an American poet, critic, and short-story writer. He was educated in Britain and at Burke's Academy in Richmond before entering the University of Virginia in 1826, the second year after the opening of Jefferson's campus. He studied there only one year.

In 1844, Poe worked on the *New York Evening Mirror* with Nathan P. Willis, the writer and pioneer in the suburban movement—he planned an utopian community of scholars on a rural site high above the Hudson River. Poe's poem "The Raven" was first published in *The Mirror,* in 1845.

In the 1840s, Poe wrote three short stories based on his admiration of landscape gardening and landscape painting. In fact, it could be said that Poe *designed* these landscapes—landscapes of the mind—having absorbed all the design principles and nuances of the English landscape garden theorists and then composing them into pictures. His were planting plans composed of words. This was not so far removed from the real-world landscape designers, who were, in fact, concocting mental images of far-away places and times, particularly Roman romantic poetry and scenes from the seventeenth-century *campagna.*

In 1842 he wrote *The Landscape Garden,* which he reissued in an expanded version entitled *The Domain of Arnheim,* two months after the death of his wife in 1847. Two years after the *Domain of Arnheim,* Poe wrote *Landor's Cottage* (1849), the last of his stories published before his death that same year. At the time he wrote these three narratives, Poe was living with his dying wife in a rustic three-room cottage in Fordham not far from the Hudson River home of Edwin Forrest, whose picturesque villa, Fonthill Castle (c. 1846), he admired very much. He also admired the poetry of the English poet and landscape gardening authority, Alexander Pope; therefore, it is safe to assume that it is inevitable that he would have read much, if not all, that Pope had to say on the subject of landscape gardening.

For each of these compositions, Poe drew his inspiration from a number of seminal writings about landscape gardening and from his knowledge of landscape painting. He clearly alluded to the design of "Capability" Brown; the various writings by Joseph Addison, Humphry Repton, William Gilpin, Uvedale Price, and Richard Payne Knight; Prince Hermann von Pückler-Muskau's *Tour of England, Ireland and France* (1833); and Andrew Jackson Downing's *Treatise on the Theory of Landscape Gardening* (1841). Poe had earlier written in "The Poetic Principle" that the "Poetic sentiment, of course, may develop itself in various modes—in Painting, in Sculpture, in Architecture, in the Dance, very especially in Music—and very peculiarly, and with a wide field, in the composition of the Landscape Garden."

The name "Arnheim" refers to a character in one of Walter Scott's novels, where sorcery was practiced. Poe noted that the theme of the *Domain of Arnheim* came straight out of Pückler-Muskau: "I first saw an account of this matter in the 'Tour' of Prince Pückler-Muskau. . . ."

Both versions of *The Landscape Garden* are a combination essay about landscape gardening and a fantastic tale in the classic Poe style. The story is a fantasy about a man who inherited $450 million and, driven by his "thirst for beauty," set out to determine to what highest purpose he should devote so large a sum. After considering all the best philanthropic and artistic alternatives, he concluded that "the richest, the truest, the most natural . . . the most extensive province [is] the creation of a landscape-garden . . . the fairest field for the display of imagination in the endless combining of forms of novel beauty. . . ." This, he stated, was "the best means . . . of fulfilling, not only his own destiny as a poet, but of the august purposes for which the Deity had implanted the poetic sentiment in man." Without actually mentioning either "Capability" Brown or Humphry Repton, Poe continued his narrative with a discussion of the merits and failings of the excessively "natural" style of Brown versus that of Repton, where "a mixture of pure art in the garden scene adds to it a great beauty. . . . A terrace, with an old moss-covered balustrade . . . is an evidence of care and human interest." In the story, Poe cited Joseph Addison, the early eighteenth-century author of many essays on the natural style of gardening, and he alluded to his friend Willis's yearning to escape the city, seeking seclusion by "retiring to the country."

The subject in this tale searched for four years and looked at a thousand sites all over the world before selecting the most sublime place to create his domain. Poe was careful not to mention the venue of the landscape garden, but his description of its setting reads like a painting by Thomas Cole, the originator of the Hudson River school of American landscape painting in the 1820s. Therefore, one can surmise that a small stream flowing into the Hudson might have been Poe's venue and inspired his passage, "[T]he river narrowed to a channel . . . the channel became a gorge, a ravine, a chasm . . . the gloom deepening every moment."

The completed landscape garden, the "domain of Arnheim," when visited by Poe's narrator, reeked of the same rusticity of the Gilpin–Price–Knight school of picturesque landscape garden. Adding to the visual scene, he titillated the other senses: "There is a gush of entrancing melody; there is an oppressive sense of strange sweet odor; . . . flocks of golden and crimson birds . . . lily-fringed lakes . . . meadows of violets, tulips, poppies, hyacinths, and tuberoses . . . silver streamlets . . . from amid all, a mass of semi-Gothic, semi-Saracenic architecture, sustaining itself by miracle in mid-air . . . with hundreds of oriels, minarets, and pinnacles. . . ."

Two years after the *Domain of Arnheim,* in the year of his death, Poe wrote *Landor's Cottage* (1849). This was more a description of one of his favorite places than a short story. That place was his own rustic "little cottage at the top of a hill," near Fordham, 12 miles from the center of New York City at the time. Today, the place is a museum of Fordham University. In the summer of 1848, Poe made a walking tour of two Hudson River counties, Putnam and Dutchess, sites of many stately mansions with landscape garden grounds described by Downing in his *Treatise.* For Poe, this was a real-life fulfillment of Washington Irving's Rip van Winkle, who trekked through precisely the same "hollows" and glades. Again in this story, he alluded to Lancelot Brown when he stated "such 'capabilities' (as they have it in the books on Landscape Gardening). . . ." Later he referred to painting: "The greatest care had been taken to preserve . . . the *pittoresque* . . . ," which is the Italian for "in the style of the painter." He also noted that the trees through which he was passing were "less lofty and *Salvatorish* in character . . . ," an allusion to Salvator Rosa, the Italian landscape painter of the seventeenth century who was most noted for his wild scenes and sublime renderings of vegetation and his sharply contrasting light and dark tones. Poe admired the alignment of the trail he was traveling, "The path was so serpentine, that at no moment could I trace its course for more than two or three paces in advance," a direct reference to the precepts of Repton, Price, Downing, and others.

In the same piece, Poe approached the edge of a pristine lake near Landor's cottage at the edge of the Hudson. What he described revived the old debate between the picturesque school and the proponents of the "beautiful." He noted, "The lake . . . if a defect could have been attributed, in point of picturesqueness, it was that of excessive *neatness* [Poe's emphasis]."

Poe discussed the vegetation in great detail: "[A]n occasional shrub, such as the hydrangea, or the common snow-ball, of the aromatic seringa [*sic,* Syringa]; or . . . a clump of geraniums . . . were carefully buried in the soil, so as to give the appearance of being indigenous." Continuing on, he observed a quintessentially English scene: "[T]he lawn's velvet was exquisitely spotted with sheep—a considerable flock . . . in company with three tamed deer. . . ." Poe next alluded to a ha-ha wall, without so naming it. Landor's domain "was crowned by a neat stone wall, of sufficient height to prevent the escape of the deer. Nothing of the fence kind was observable elsewhere; stray sheep . . . find [their] progress arrested . . . by the precipitous ledge of rock. . . ."

The cottage to which Poe eventually arrived was "of an architecture unknown in the annuls of the earth . . . its *tout ensemble* struck me with novelty and propriety." While it was "unpretending," its "effect lay altogether in its artistic arrangement *as a picture*. I could have fancied, while I looked at it, that some eminent landscape painter had built it with his brush." Here is a direct quotation from the thoughts of Shenstone and others who defined the picturesque as *"having the qualities which would look good in a painted picture."*

He disclosed that he was a student of the "panoptic" approach to landscape painting when he stated: "The point of view from which I first saw the valley . . . was nearly the best point from which to survey the house." Like Cole, Church, and others of the Hudson River school of painters, Poe could view both ways through his telescope. He could command an all-encompassing panorama while, at the same time, examining minute detail in his scene. This would be akin to reversing one's telescope and seeing a miniature, yet wide-angle image of as much as 110 degrees (*à la* the *Claude-glass*), and then sighting through the lens properly on select subjects within the whole and studying a myriad minutia.

POMPADOUR, Jeanne-Antoinette Poisson, Marquise de (1721–1764), mistress of France's Louis XV, was an important patron of the arts. She planned many of the architectural projects at the châteaux of Bellevue, Fontainebleau, Champs, Saint-Cloud, Ménars, and Versailles. For her, the Hermitage, or the New Menagery (1749), was built as a retreat from the more public parks of the Grand Trianon and Versailles. She called it her favorite spot and in her garden there flowers were arranged according to their scent.

POPE, Alexander (1688–1744), born with a curvature of the spine, was referred to as "the man who perfected the shapeliest verse of his day [but] was a malignant little hunchback [height, 4 feet 6 inches], a 'gargoyle of a man'." He was a Roman Catholic when Catholics were not accepted into universities in England. William and Mary ruled that "papists" should be removed from London, so Pope's family moved to the rustic setting of Windsor Forest. There, Pope formed the first of his attachments to rural landscapes, earning him the moniker "the poet of Windsor Forest." Despite these obstacles, at the age of 12, Pope could read Greek and Latin and wrote his celebrated poem "Solitude." He wrote four *Pastorals* in 1709, and one of his most important poems, *Essay on Criticism,* was written two years later, when he was 23. In his *Epistle to Burlington* (1731), he stated: "In all, let Nature never be forgot . . . Consult the Genius of the Place."

More than just a garden design critic, Pope influenced garden history through his 5-acre garden at his summer residence in the village of Twickenham (1719–1744). He was a friend of both William Kent and Charles Bridgeman, yet it is safe to infer, from all that he wrote about it, that much of the planning of his garden was his own. His garden was renowned during and after his lifetime.

Sir Horace Walpole wrote in the year 1760 that Pope, "undoubtedly contributed to form William Kent's taste—the design of the Prince of Wales' Garden at Carlton House was evidently borrowed from the poet's place at Twickenham. . . ." He included a grotto and a shell temple into his garden, evidence of his love of those ancient forms of artifice.

PORCINAI, Pietro (1910–1987), Italian landscape architect, architect, and artist, maintained an international practice for over fifty years from his office in Fiesole, Italy, in the shadows of the fifteenth-century Villa Medici. He was proclaimed the "greatest Italian landscape architect of our century" by the International Federation of Landscape Architects (IFLA), which he helped found in 1948. He was called Professor Porcinai because in the 1960s he began a school of design in his home. He grew up watching his father tend the grounds of the Villa Gamberaia, in nearby Settignano. He studied architecture, horticulture, and ecology in France and

Germany and at the University of Florence before opening his practice in 1935. Throughout his large body of work, Porcinai attempted to recreate the peacefulness of the Renaissance "philosopher's garden" while creating twentieth-century statements. His works achieved a fine balance between the intimate and the grand through his perceptive use of *chiaroscuro,* light and shade, his compact outdoor rooms opening onto distant prospects, and water features—often swimming pools—comfortably integrated into the pleasure garden and fringed by natural-looking vegetative associations.

Porcinai liked to joke, "In my garden the sun never sets," an allusion to both Louis XIV, the Sun King, and the fact that gardens he designed were scattered all over the globe: Italy, the United States, Canada, Albania, France, Switzerland, Germany, and Poland. Over half of Porcinai's commissions were for private residential gardens such as the Villa Riva in Saronno, the Villa Il Roseto, and the grounds of an outbuilding of the Villa Palmieri, both near Florence. He also designed such visible projects as the Mondadori Center, Milan; the Club Mediterranée, in southern Italy; four parks in Saudi Arabia; the Place Beaubourg, entrance plaza into the Pompidou Centre in Paris; and parks in Milan and Palermo, Italy.

He is the author of many articles in popular and professional journals such as *Domus* and *Architecture d' Aujourd'hui* and the book *Giardini d'Occidente e d'Oriente* (1966).

PORTA, Giacomo della (1533–1602), Italian architect, designed the Villa Aldobrandini in Frascati (1598) for Cardinal Pietro Aldobrandini. He also worked on the Villa d'Este in Tivoli somewhat after the original plan of 1549 by Pirro Ligorio and Orazio Olivieri.

POUSSIN, Gaspar(d) (1613–1675), christened Gaspard Dughet, was French but born in Rome and was the brother-in-law (or son-in-law) of the more noted painter, Nicolas Poussin. Gaspard was a distinguished landscape painter in his own right and was a close companion of Claude Lorrain, perhaps the most popular of the seventeenth-century French landscape painters. Gaspard's works were nearly as popular in England, as were those of Claude, Salvator, and Nicolas Poussin.

Because they painted under the same name, and both painted large arcadian landscape scenes of Italy, the two Poussins have frequently been confused. Gaspard's compositions were less intense than those of Nicolas, and his fame today is not at all equal to that of his in-law.

POUSSIN, Nicolas (1573–1665), was one of the seventeenth-century French landscape painters whose romantic paintings of the Italian landscape were immensely popular with British landscape connoisseurs during the eighteenth century and subsequently became influential in the popularization of the English landscape garden. He lived and painted for nearly forty years in Rome. The main themes for his landscape paintings derived from classical literature and were set in spacious pastoral scenery, with ancient Roman temples standing in ruin as cattle and sheep grazed all about them.

PRICE, Sir Uvedale (1747–1829), was a landscape critic and gentleman farmer who owned an estate, Foxley, in the west of England (Herefordshire). He was a Whig member of Parliament and a close friend of his Shropshire neighbor and ally in the picturesque cult, Richard Payne Knight. His greatest written work was *An Essay on the Picturesque,* written just a few months after his friend's *Didactic Poem, The Landscape* (1794). Price attacked the naturalistic style with which Brown and Repton had destroyed so much of the late Renaissance formalism of the earlier generation. He and his counterparts in the picturesque school, Knight and Reverend William Gilpin, saw a marked distinction between the Brownian precepts of "beauty and sublime." They characterized Brown's smooth sweeping grassy spaces as "femininity" and a destroyer of "variety." They claimed that a more wild, "naturalistic" style was in better "taste." Price treated the two words *picturesque* and *romantic* as nearly synonymous. He felt that picturesque scenes were always well composed, whereas romantic compositions could be "odd, misshapen, and uncouth."

Price spent many years "improving" the appearance of the grounds of Foxley, and his land-wealthy friends often consulted him about the modifications they could make on their land.

PÜCKLER-MUSKAU, Hermann Ludwig Heinrich (1785–1871), was a German prince, Fürst von Pückler-Muskau, and self-taught landscape gardener, who toured England twice before 1816. He visited many country estates designed by "Capability" Brown or Humphry Repton, calling such places "unattainable model[s] in the art of . . . country life." He returned home afflicted with "parcomania." A few years later he inherited the tiny principality of Muskau, on the Neisse River, running along the border of Poland and Germany. Over the following three decades, he remodeled the entire 1853 acres (750 hectares) into an Englische garten, a Reptonesque version of the English landscape garden park. In the course of the work, he returned to England again in 1826 and 1829 to refine his visions for his own park. In 1834, he wrote a superb book, *Hints on Landscape Gardening,* in which he eloquently spelled out his nine fundamental design principles. One of his major additions to the precepts of the earlier British landscape gardeners was that parks provided educational and therapeutic benefits for the public. This became a recurring theme put forth by the social reformers and proponents of urban public parks in England and elsewhere.

To finance his land improvements, the prince married a wealthy widow, Countess Lucie Pappenheim, and proceeded to bankrupt her. With his dream project halted, the prince divorced his wife and traveled to England in search of another rich dowager to marry in order to finance his park. He married again, but ultimately, in 1845, he exhausted his second wife's funds, forcing him to sell the land. This, however, did not deter him from his dream of creating an English park, there or elsewhere. Undaunted, he moved to a smaller family property of 173 acres, at Branitz, and began to remodel that in the same manner between 1846 and his death in 1871.

Pückler also counseled several other titled Germans as to improvements they might make on their land and he was called upon by Louis Napoleon (Emperor Napoleon III) to advise on the remodeling of the 2100-acre Bois de Boulogne in Paris in 1852. While he did not plan the improvements there, Pückler's writings and work at Muskau influenced the later anglicizing of the park by Adolphe Alphand.

RAMÉE, Joseph-Jacques (1763–1842), was a French èmigrée and the designer of the Union College campus in Schenectady, New York (1813) as well as of several private residences and grounds. He was an established architect and landscape designer in France as well as in Denmark, Belgium, and Germany, having designed many suburban gardens, parks, and chateaus prior to his arrival in the United States. He lived in the country for less than five years (1811–1816), but his contribution to American landscape architecture in the "modern" or naturalistic style was considerable. His Union College plan was America's first open-plan college campus, set in a romantic parklike green space.

Near the village of Ogdensburg, in upstate New York, he laid out two towns and designed several buildings and landscape garden sites. He designed the grounds of Calverton (1815), the country seat of Dennis A. Smith near Baltimore, and the Duane estate in Duanesburgh, New York. His design for the Washington Monument in Baltimore was judged second to that of Robert Mills. Ramée never really settled down in the United States, living briefly in New York City, Philadelphia, and Baltimore. Years later in France, he published his *Jardin irreguliers, maisons de campagne, de tous genres et de toutes dimensions* (1823) [Nonformal gardens, country houses of all types, and sizes], and seven years later a collection of his work, entitled *Parcs et jardins composees at executees dans differens countrées de l'Europe et des États Unis d'Amerique* [Parks and Gardens composed and executed in the different countries in Europe and the United States of America] (1830). A few years later he produced *Racueil de cottages et maisons de campagne* (1837).

REPTON, Humphry (1752–1818), a businessman, appeared on the scene one day in the spring of 1784 as a "landscape gardener . . . blessed with a poet's feelings and a painter's eye . . . determined to make that pursuit his profession which had hitherto been only his amusement." Repton explained: "I have adopted the term *Landscape Gardening* . . . because the art can only be advanced and perfected by the united powers of the *landscape painter* and the *practical gardener.*" He was the first person to call himself a "landscape gardener"—a consultant ("at a great price"), furnishing detailed proposals for the intended appearance of each given site, then moving on to the next client. His standard practice was to give each client a lengthy essay explaining his rationale and recommendations. Such reports were routinely bound in red "morocco" (sheepskin) 8 by 14 inches in size, and thus came to be called "red books." These included a number of water color scenes depicting very precisely the appearance of the place as it existed. Using a removable overlay, he called them "slides"; the same scene could be adapted to show the character following the maturation of Repton's proposed design. He said, "These slides, doubtless, a very ingenious invention [are] calculated to save a great deal of trouble in drawing; since one landscape, by means of one or two slides, may serve instead of two or three." In one of the books he wrote, *Sketches and Hints,* he included an example for his readers.

Repton was a prolific writer and willing advocate, who was as eager to commit his design theories to paper as to the ground. While Brown left us nothing of his design philosophy in writing, Repton was the author of five volumes on the subject. In 1794, he wrote: *A letter to Uvedale Price, Esq. on Landscape Gardening;* the following year came *Sketches and Hints of Landscape Gardening;* in 1803, he wrote *Observations on the Theory and Practice of Landscape Gardening;* three years later, *An Enquiry into the Changes in Landscape Gardening* was published; and in 1816, at the end of his career, he published *Fragments in the Theory and Practice of Landscape Gardening.*

While his contributions to the field of landscape gardening were many, his methods were far from original. As he stated it, "True taste in every art, consists more in adapting tried expedients to peculiar circumstances, than in the inordinate thirst after novelty, the characteristic of uncultivated minds. . . ." He admitted to relying on the examples set forth by Brown insofar as the distant natural landscape was concerned, yet turning to the formalism of the Le Nôtre approach in connection with the mansion itself. Not only did Repton visit and scrutinize many of the landscapes designed by Brown (in a handsome state of maturity, having been completed twenty to forty years earlier), he had studied many of the master's *"ground-plan"* drawings and notes. As he stated in his book, "I must . . . acknowledge my obligations to . . . the son of my predecessor for having furnished me with the maps of the greatest works in which his late father had been consulted, both in their original and improved states."

Repton prescribed to neither the Brownian manner of smooth lawns, broken here and there by clumps of trees, sweeping from the farthest horizon right up to the front steps of the house, nor the "picturesque school" led by Richard Payne Knight and Uvedale Price. Their unkempt-looking grounds were, in Repton's words, more "fit . . . for representation of the pencil" than for the comfort and convenience of strollers in the garden (Hunt and Willis, 1988, p. 358). Many of his clients were not as wealthy as those of Brown. They sought Repton's ideas about "decoration" of a smaller, more circumscribed area in the immediate vicinity of the house as contrasted to the scope of Brown's much more sprawling meadow-scale landscapes. Repton's approach was more "cosmetic." His clientele wanted, and he furnished, eclectic features from the garden types dating to before the landscape garden movement began. In the distance and middle distance, Repton adhered faithfully to the precepts of Brown (dozens of his clients had employed Brown earlier), saying that "those beautiful scenes in nature . . . defy the powers of my pencil to imitate . . ." (Hunt and Willis, 1988, p. 363).

Immediately around the house, he incorporated an architectonic foundation, or terrace, on which geometrical walks and floral beds were laid out. This was done to form a smooth transition between the geometrical verticality of the structure and the horizontality of the open grassy site—one of the greatest objections to the "Capability" Brown formula. Here, statuary, fountains, arbors, trellises (in ornamental cast iron), and *plants* were in order. Repton saw the need to reintroduce plants—including brightly colored flowering plants, so much the bane of Brown's scenes—for the variety of effects that they contributed.

He perceived the formal terrace as the English social corollary of the French *cabinets de verdure* or the Italian *giardino segreto,* saying such venues, "in the height of summer, may sometimes answer the purpose of an additional room or gallery, when there is much company. . . ."

John Nash, the English architect and town planner, was Repton's business partner until 1802. During Repton's three decades as a professional landscape garden designer, he planned approximately 200 country places, fifty-seven of which were documented with "red books." Among Repton's works that had been laid out previously by Brown were Brocklesby, Corsham, Crewe Hall, Ealing Park, Longleat, Moccas, Sheffield Park, and Wimpole.

RICHARDSON, Henry Hobson (1838–1886), was the champion of the Romanesque Revival style in American architecture during the last half of the nineteenth century. This was the first of the styles of the eclectic era (c. 1880–1930), which was not adapted from European revival models. The "Richardsonian Romanesque" was his own very personal invention, and while he built only about 100 structures during his short twenty-year career, his work was immensely influential in this country. Particularly affected by it were three architects of the Chicago school, Louis Sullivan, John Wellborn Root, and Frank Lloyd Wright.

Richardson's designs relied on the use of massive stone masonry and brick combined in a very sculptural way. He designed a great number of different building types: churches, schools, libraries, courthouses, offices, and residences. Among his most successful buildings were Brattle Square Church, Boston (1872); the Sherman House, Newport, Rhode Island (1875); Trinity Church, Boston (1877); Ames Memorial Library, North Easton, Massachusetts (1879); City Hall, Albany, New York (1882); Sever Hall (1880) and Austin Hall at Harvard University (1883); the Marshall Field Store and Warehouse, Chicago (1887); and the Allegheny County Courthouse, Pittsburgh (1888).

Richardson was a native of Louisiana who graduated from Tulane and Harvard universities before going to Paris as the second American to study at the Ecole des Beaux-Arts. He started his practice in New York in 1867 but moved to Boston in 1874. Both Charles Follen McKim and Stanford White apprenticed with Richardson, but at different times. He later took in several partners and the firm still exists today as Shepley, Bulfinch, Richardson and Abbott.

He worked with Frederick Law Olmsted on the design of the North Easton Town Hall and the Ames Estate (1880), in the same town. Here, the two combined to produce the Gate Lodge, a gatekeeper's residence, with huge boulders and a ground-hugging horizontal profile. This structure and its setting are reminiscent of the picturesque rock and shingle gatehouse at Llewellyn Park in West Orange, New Jersey (1852–1853), by Alexander Jackson Davis, with which both Richardson and Olmsted would have been familiar.

ROBINSON, Florence Bell (1885–1973), landscape architect, educator, and writer, taught courses in plant identification and planting design at the University of Illinois from 1926 to 1951. She wrote several books that expressed her design philosophy and her knowledge of plant materials. Her book *Planting Design* (1940) was the first textbook written on this topic and has been used throughout the United States and abroad. She also published *Useful Trees and Shrubs—A Card File of Data* (1960) and *Tabular Keys for the Identification of the Woody Plants* and *Palette of Plants,* which explores the characteristics of plants. Much of her highly original material has been incorporated into recently published books on planting design.

ROBINSON, William (1839–1935), was an Anglo-Irish landscape architect, author, and critic whose career paralleled and influenced that of the garden designer Gertrude Jekyll. He opposed the "gardenesque" style and has been called the "self-appointed defender of the old 'landscape school'." His work has been characterized as "Victorian naturalism"—a variation on the English kitchen garden, with an emphasis on the display of plants as specimens, particularly for their form rather than floral color, and his preference for rock gardens and herbaceous borders. Robinson worked in the Botanic Gardens at London's Regent's Park, devoting most of his attention to the native plants of England. In opposing the prevailing "carpet bedding" fashion of his time, he insisted "that the best kind of garden should arise out of its site as happily as a primrose out of a cool bank." He further stated: "Gardening is an art: the work of an artist is always marked by its fidelity to Nature." He demonstrated his principles in the garden of his own Sussex residence, Gravetye Manor.

Robinson's early writings were for the *Times* (of London). His books included *Gleanings from French Gardens; Parks, Promenades and Gardens of Paris; Alpine Flowers for English Gardens* (1870); *The Wild Garden* (1881); and *The English Flower Garden* (1883). He also began two magazines, *Gardening Illustrated,* in 1871, and *Flora and Sylva,* in 1903.

ROSA, Salvator (or Salvatore) (1615–1673), from Naples, Italy, was a landscape painter whose works, along with those of Claude Lorrain and Nicolas Poussin, influenced the romantic sensibilities of the early eighteenth-century designers and connoisseurs of the English landscape garden. Rosa's painted scenes were wilder and more sublime than those of the other two masters, with dramatic contrasts of light and dark and ruggedness of settings and elements depicted. Thus they were preferred by the later proponents of the picturesque style, Gilpin, Knight, and Price.

ROSE, James (1910–1991), along with two other avant-garde students, Garrett Eckbo and Dan Kiley, was an instigator of the "Harvard revolution" in landscape architectural design in 1936–1938. He was a catalyst for the movement toward modern landscape architectural design, rejecting the Beaux-Arts formalism in favor of an organic and informal approach. Rose's design principles were inspired by the Japanese and by cubism, particularly the paintings of Mondrian, yet his gardens were often labeled "Japanese gardens." To such ideas he said, "It used to bother me painfully. "NEVER—in my lifetime—have I studied Japanese gardens although I have often been accused of 'doing' them." He often countered, "A Japanese garden is a garden made in Japan."

In the late 1930s, he was the author of a series of six articles in *Pencil Points* magazine (now *Progressive Architecture*). These essays, together with Eckbo's in the same publication, disseminated the new way of looking at landscape design to a wide readership, including many landscape architects and clients, thus launching the modern movement. Rose's major focus was the design of private residential gardens, and his practice was largely confined to the east coast. His creations were frequently seen in many of the popular journals about the home garden, particularly the *Ladies' Home Journal,* for which in 1946 he produced a series of modular gardens designed to suit modern suburban architecture and buildings executed in the international style.

He wrote several books as well: *Creative Gardens* (1958), *Gardens Make Me Laugh* (1965), *Modern American Gardens Designed by James Rose* (1967), and *The Heavenly Environment* (1990).

ROUSSEAU, Jean-Jacques (1712–1778), was a French philosopher who thought that by living in harmony with nature, human beings could achieve spiritual nourishment. He considered nature to be both innocent and beautiful and expressed his very persuasive point of view about the human–nature relationship in 1761 when he wrote his novel *Julie, ou la nouvelle Héloïse.* Written while he was visiting friends in northern France and living in a cottage, *L'Hermitage,* this love story of sin and self-denial was set in a rural landscape—Stowe in England served as his model—where the simple peasant life was portrayed as humankind's most virtuous state. His was a paradise garden where pure, sweet streams watered the meadows, the fields were ablaze with flowers, and songbirds sang in the trees. Rousseau's views initiated the "romantic" movement, with its emphasis on emotion rather than reason.

He died while a guest of the Marquis de Girardin at his *jardin anglais,* in Ermenonville, France. In homage to Rousseau, Girardin constructed a half-built Temple de la Philosophie and on the Ile des Peupliers (Lombardy poplars) he placed the philosopher's tomb.

ROYSTON, Robert N. (1918–), landscape architect, has worked for over forty years out of his San Francisco practice, where he has received more than sixty awards for design excellence. A graduate of the University of California, he worked for Thomas Church between 1938 and his enlistment in the Navy during World War II. After the war, he formed a partnership with Garret Eckbo and Edward Williams. Church, Eckbo, Royston, and Doug Baylis were the leaders of the so-called "California school" of landscape architects, which emerged in the 1940s. Royston has taught as an adjunct professor at the University of California at Berkeley since 1948 and has lectured widely on campuses in all parts of the country.

Most of the executed work during his career has been public parks and playgrounds, not only in this country but in Malaysia, Chile, Mexico, Venezuela, Canada, and Singapore. In 1958, he formed another office, Royston Hanamoto Alley and Abey, in Mill Valley, California. One of their major projects was the University of California–San Francisco campus in 1964. In 1978 the American Institute of Architects conferred an AIA medal on Royston, "for a career of . . . creating breathing spaces in cities across the nation . . . and for turning dreams into reality." In 1989, Royston was awarded the ASLA president's medal as "the country's most outstanding landscape architect." In 1992, Royston Hanamoto Alley & Abey was selected to design one of its most challenging and meaningful projects, the National Peace Garden, to be sited on the Potomac shore near the Lincoln Memorial, in the nation's capital.

RUMFORD, Count. *See* Thompson, Benjamin.

RUSKIN, John (1819–1900), English author, art critic, and social reformer, was, together with William Morris, a founder of the arts and crafts movement in England, as a reaction against the artlessness of mass-produced decorative objects of the Victorian era.

His taste was inclined toward the picturesque in scenery and painting, leading him to admire those qualities in Gothic architecture. Ruskin's chapter "The Nature of Gothic" in his book *The Stones of Venice* (1853) focused on the natural forms and materials from which much Gothic architectural ornamentation was drawn. He inferred that the workers were happy in their work on the great cathedrals, a testament to the beauty of such structures, and that machine production was a form of slavery. This work influenced Morris, designer, craftsman, and poet, to return to traditional medieval techniques and to begin making handcrafted decorative art objects.

Following the influence of Ruskin, a small group of seven artists and writers began a new style in England in 1848 when they established the Pre-Raphaelite Brotherhood. William Morris was loosely associated with the movement. Their paintings were characterized by minute detail, based on careful studies made from nature, brilliant colors, and exotic or romantic subjects. In literature, romantic and exotic themes prevailed. Together, their works influenced the sensibility of the next quarter century in Europe and America.

Ruskin also wrote the books *Modern Painters* (1843–1849), *The Seven Lamps of Architecture* (1849), *Unto This Last* (1860), and *Praeterita* (1885–1889).

SACKVILLE-WEST, Victora (1892–1962), was an English writer and gardener, who with her husband, Harold Nicolson, created the gardens of Sissinghurst Castle in Kent County, England beginning in 1930. She was responsible for the planting design component, considered the epitome of the English garden.

"Vita" Sackville-West wrote a weekly column "In Your Garden" for the *Observer* from 1947 until 1961. A series of these were published as a book, *Victoria Sackville-West's Garden Book* (1983). She also wrote a number of books of poems, including *The Land* (1926) and *The Garden* (1946), which has been called "possibly the best evocation of the spirit and fascination of gardening in the English language."

SAINT-GAUDENS, Augustus (1848–1907), American sculptor, born in Ireland, collaborated with architect Stanford White on the Farragut Monument in New York City in 1875. He became the leading sculptor of monuments in America for the last third of the nineteenth century. He was the coordinator of the sculpture at the World's Columbian Exposition in Chicago (1893), and the sculptor on the Senate Park Commission of 1901, which was charged with reviving the L'Enfant plan of Washington, D.C.

Among his many public works were the equestrian statue of General Sherman at the edge of Central Park in New York and the Adams Memorial in Washington, D.C. Saint-Gaudens was a good friend of the architect Charles A. Platt, who designed his home and studio, Aspet, in Cornish, New Hampshire. He was a member of the first board of trustees of the American Academy in Rome in 1897.

SARGENT, Charles Sprague (1841–1927), was a professor of arboriculture at Harvard University and director of the Arnold Arboretum (founded in 1872) in Boston. He persuaded Frederick Law Olmsted to help lay out the grounds and to incorporate the Arboretum into the "emerald necklace" park system around Boston in the 1880s. Sargent taught the young Beatrix Jones (later Jones Farrand) landscape design and horticulture at the Arboretum in 1893, encouraging her to enter the profession of landscape architecture, with the advice: "Make the plan fit the ground and not twist the ground to fit the plan." Sargent was the editor of *Garden and Forest* magazine from 1887 to 1897 and wrote the books *Catalogue of the Forest Trees of North America; The Woods of the United States; The Forest Flora of Japan; Silva of North America;* and *Manual of Trees of North America.*

SASAKI, Hideo (1919–), landscape architect and educator, was born in California and educated at the University of California at Berkeley, the University of Illinois, and the Harvard Graduate School of Design. Through his teaching and his very productive professional practice, he has exerted a major influence on landscape architecture for the past thirty-five years. His firm began in Watertown, Massachusetts in 1951 and soon had branch offices in San Francisco and Toronto. Today, the multidisciplinary firm is comprised not only of landscape architects but also architects, engineers, urban and regional planners, ecologists, and interior and graphic designers. It is named Sasaki Associates, Inc., and has offices in nine U.S. cities.

The Sasaki offices have consistently produced extremely fine-quality design and planning at a wide range of scales. Their work has involved urban design, university and corporate campuses, recreation planning, new communities, and regional planning. Among the best known projects for which Sasaki has been responsible are Constitution Plaza, Hartford, Connecticut (1959); Copley Square, Boston (1966); the [John] Deere and Company Administrative Center, Moline, Illinois (1961); Greenacre Park, New York City (1971); Waterfront Park, Boston (1980s); the American Embassy in Baghdad, Iraq; and Sea Pines Plantation, with its centerpiece, Harbour Town, on Hilton Head Island, South Carolina (1958). The office has produced university campus master plans in all sections of the country, including many that have been long-term liaisons: Foothill College, Los Altos, California; the Buffalo campus of the State University of New York; and the Universities of Colorado, Virginia, Massachusetts, and Kent State. Sasaki was appointed by both Presidents Kennedy and Johnson to the U.S. Commission on the Fine Arts and was instrumental in the many landscape and urban design improvements on Pennsylvania Avenue in Washington, D.C.

Sasaki taught at the University of Illinois (1948–1950 and 1952–1953) and at the Harvard Graduate School of Design (1950–1952 and 1953–1970). He was made chairman of the Harvard Graduate School of Design in 1958, serving there until 1968. He always maintained an enviable balance between his teaching role and his professional practice. His office was a learning laboratory for the students and through his classrooms flowed a steady stream of practitioners who lectured, demonstrated, and critiqued from their real-world perspective. Sasaki claims no credit for the many outstanding teachers he helped to produce through his educational program, nor does he take credit for the massive array of built works produced by his office(s). He says: "It was a symbiotic, dynamic relationship where it wasn't pure teaching and it wasn't pure working—it was a combination of working, teaching, lecturing, visitors . . . and [thus] we were able to attract the best students. Our department was small and [yet] the most exciting . . . architecture and planning students came to our juries and seminars." He was also one of the first to bring regional planning into the educational curriculum for landscape architects, now common in most American university programs. Garrett Eckbo says that "the work turned out by his astonishing firm . . . has been of remarkably high quality . . . a little conservative from the [California] point of view, but his work is rich, strong and solid, [it has] struck the right notes at the right times and places. . . ."

Hideo Sasaki is a fellow of the American Society of Landscape Architects and in 1971 received the ASLA president's medal. Two years later, the American Institute of Architects awarded him their medal for outstanding built works.

SCKELL, Friedrich Ludwig von (1750–1823), German landscape designer, spent a few years in England, coming under the influence of the Brown and Chambers style. In Schwetzingen, Germany, he worked for Prince Karl Theodor, adapting part of his gardens there to the naturalistic style, between 1776 and 1804. At Nymphenburg Palace, Sckell created an English landscape garden around the edges of the French-style central parterre garden of the Schloss (1778), and in Munich, Sckell worked with the American Benjamin Thompson (Count Rumford) in developing the Englische Garten beginning in 1789.

SHAFTESBURY, Anthony Ashley Cooper, the third Earl of (1671–1713), was an English philosopher and politician who conceived and promoted the notion of "the Man of Taste." In 1709 he wrote *The Moralists,* followed two years later by *Characteristics of Men, Manners, Opinions, and Times.* Lord Shaftesbury associated aesthetics with moral value, saying "what is beautiful is harmonious and proportionable; what is harmonious and proportionable is true; and what is at once both beautiful and true is of consequence agreeable and good." His concept of Beautiful Nature helped foster the landscape garden as an idyllic setting for eighteenth-century man.

He announced in *The Moralists* that wilderness was more virtuous and beautiful than "the formal Labyrinths and Wildernesses of the Palace [and] the formal Mockery of Princely gardens." He claimed that in nature could be seen the divine order of God's universe when he wrote, "All Nature's wonders serve to excite and perfect [the] Idea of their Author." Nature, "the Source and Principle of all Perfection and Beauty," he insisted, should not be manipulated or "methodized" by human intervention.

He saw nature as the expression of humanist principles: "things of a *natural* kind: where neither *Art,* not the *Conceit* or *Caprice* of Man has spoil'd their genuine order. . . . Even the rude Rocks, the mossy *Caverns,* the irregular unwrought *Grottos* and broken *Falls* of waters, with all the horrid graces of the Wilderness itself, as representing NATURE more, will be the more engaging, and appear with a magnificence beyond the mockery of princely gardens" (Jellicoe 1986, p. 167).

SHENSTONE, William (1714–1763), was a struggling "melancholic" poet who Horace Walpole, in 1759, claimed was the first person to use the term *landscape* in connection with garden design. Shenstone said, "I have used the word landskip-gardeners; because in pursuance of our present taste in gardening, every good painter of landskip appears to me the most proper designer." That same year, Shenstone wrote his *Works in Prose and Verse,* which included the essay, "Unconnected Thoughts on Gardening" (published posthumously in 1764). This became among the most important writings on the topic of garden design in its time. The work summarizes his design principles as he applied them to the layout of his own *ferme ornée,* called *The Leasowes,* near Cambridge.

Shenstone was a fanatic about his 300-acre estate and it was much praised by others. He, however, was not much admired by his literary critics. One observed that his writing "is about nothing else but [The Leasowes] . . ." and Walpole said: "Poor Shenstone, his 'Correspondence' . . . like all the rest [is] insipidity itself." Shenstone's landscape garden provided him with countless surfaces on which he could place verses of his own invention, considered by some to have been too numerous for the casual visitor.

Shenstone said: "[G]arden scenes may perhaps be divided into the sublime, the beautiful, and the melancholy or pensive . . . being in some sort composed of both [of the other types]." He felt that the landscape could arouse the emotions, and said that "ground should first be considered with an eye to its peculiar character; whether it be the grand, the savage, the sprightly, the melancholy, the horrid, or the beautiful." He suggested that the designer should identify the major character of the given place and design to enhance that effect. He believed that by understanding painting composition principles, the designer of the landscape could achieve asymmetrically balanced compositions: "I believe one is generally solicitous for a kind of ballance *[sic]* in the landskip . . . the painters generally furnish one: A building . . . on one side [should be] contrasted by a group of trees, a large oak, or a rising hill on the other."

His friend, the lexicographer Dr. Samuel Johnson, said of him, "He was a lamp that spent its oil in blazing." Shenstone's biography, by Richard Graves, is *Recollections of Some Particulars in the Life of the Late William Shenstone, Esq.* (1799).

SHIPMAN, Ellen Biddle (1870–1950), landscape architect, was largely self-taught in design and horticulture, but became one of the very important women who shaped the profession during the first half of this century. She was inspired to enter the field by Charles A. Platt, with whom she later collaborated on several of his residential planting plans. Her work included many fine residences all over the eastern United States, such as Rynwood, in Glen Head, New York (1927); Longue Vue Gardens, in New Orleans (late 1930s); Wampus, in Mount Kisco, New York (1919); and Cottsleigh, in Syosset, New York (late 1920s). Women received few public commissions during Shipman's career, but she did create the Sarah Duke Memorial Garden at Duke University in Durham, North Carolina (1930s); a perennial garden in the Bronz Botanical Gardens; and Lake Shore Boulevard in Grosse Pointe, Michigan (late 1930s). Her New York office was staffed almost entirely by women landscape architects and draftswomen, many of whom were schooled at the Lowthorpe School of Landscape Architecture, Gardening and Horticulture or the Cambridge School of Architecture and Landscape Architecture for Women. Shipman taught at the former for several years. As well as designing the grounds for her clients, she frequently designed the garden structures and some residential interiors. She was named the dean of women landscape architects by *House and Garden* magazine in the 1930s.

SHURCLIFF, Arthur Asahel (born Shurtleff) (1870–1957), was the landscape architect in charge of the "historic reconstruction" (or replication) of Colonial Williamsburg, Virginia for John D. Rockefeller, Jr., between 1928 and 1937, and resuming again after World War II. The Colonial Revival movement in architecture and gardening began with this project. At the time, Shurcliff was one of the leaders in landscape architecture in America, having been the first "junior member" accepted by the original eleven founders of the ASLA. His practice in Boston was broad-based, but the Williamsburg effort consumed the greater part of his later years. Among Shurcliff's other notable works was Boston's Charles River Waterfront (1929). He published very little: *New England College Men Walking and Talking: The Annals of a Society of Saunterers* (1948), and "The Restoration of Colonial Williamsburg" (the entire December 1935 issue of *Architectural Record*).

SIMONDS, John Ormsby (1913–), landscape architect and writer, has practiced in Pittsburgh (Simonds and Simonds, Inc.) with his brother Philip since 1939. He earned degrees from Michigan State University and Harvard, where he was a classmate of Dan Kiley, Garrett Eckbo, and James Rose in the late 1930s, during the "Harvard revolution."

Since 1970 his firm has been known as the Environmental Planning and Design Partnership. They have worked on urban renewal, highway and transit systems, community planning, and landscape architecture. Among their more renowned works are the Chicago Botanic Garden, Mellon Square in Pittsburgh, and Miami Lakes new town in Florida. They have also planned 80 "ecological new towns" using the PCD philosophy of "preservation, conservation and development." Simonds says, "Preserve an area's vital ecological features, conserve its wetlands and water supplies and develop intensively on less crucial lands." He says, great design is simple, "You aren't conscious of the ego of the creator, you're conscious of the rightness of the time and place."

Simonds served for twelve years on the architecture faculty of Carnegie-Mellon University in Pittsburgh. He was president of the ASLA (1963–1965), served on President Lyndon Johnson's Task Force on Resources and the Environment (1968–1970), and is a fellow of the Royal Academy of Design in Great Britain. In 1983, he retired from the EPD firm but continues to consult on projects of his choosing.

He has written widely for many professional journals and is the author of two "semi-bibles" in the profession, *Landscape Architecture: A Manual of Site Planning and Design* (1961, revised 1983) and *Earthscape: A Manual of Environmental Planning* (1978). He edited *The Freeway in the City* (1968), a compilation of the writings of eight designers, including Michael Rapuano and Lawrence Halprin.

SIMONDS, Ossian Cole (1857–1931), was a Michigan-born landscape architect, although educated as a civil engineer. He apprenticed as an architect in Chicago, where he opened his own office as a "landscape gardener" in 1888. Among his employees was Arthur H. Carhart, who later became the first landscape architect hired by the National Forest Service and the leading proponent of wilderness preservation within the Forest Service land holdings. "O. C." designed residences, subdivisions, parks, and campuses, striving always to preserve the natural and thereby expressing the regional character of the midwest. He planned many cemeteries, earning him the title "the dean of cemetery design."

He is said to have produced work in all of the 48 states then existing. In 1908 he began teaching landscape design at the University of Michigan and helped to start its landscape architecture program. Simonds was one of the eleven founders of the ASLA and the first midwesterner to serve as its president (1913). He wrote *Landscape Gardening* (1930), in which he preached about the need for using native plants and noted that the landscape gardener must be "a dreamer, a designer, an inventor, a creator—a dreamer more than most designers because it takes years for his designs to develop."

The "masterpiece" for which Simonds is most noted is Graceland Cemetery in Chicago, with which he dealt from 1878 until the end of his career.

SITTÉ, Camillo (1843–1903), was an Austrian architect, town planner, teacher, and author. He was director of the Trades School of Salzburg from 1875 to 1893 and of the Vienna Trades School (1893–1903). His book *City Planning According to Artistic Principles* (*Der Städtebau nach seinen kunstlerischen Grundsatzen,* 1889) is a classic among writings about historical urban form and planning. He asserted that the nineteenth-century city could better serve its inhabitants through concerted open-space planning and a refinement of streetscape design detailing. He said, "The essential thing of both room and square is the quality of enclosed space."

SIXTUS V, Pope [Felice Peretti] (1521–1590), named pope in 1585, began remodeling Rome in that year by straightening out and widening numerous streets and remodeling or building several papal palaces, churches, chapels, and fountains. He had his architect, Domenico Fontana, erect ancient Egyptian obelisks at each of the seven major pilgrimage churches, thus linking them visually for the newcomers to the city. In 1587, upon the death of Cardinal Gambara, he gave Villa Lante to his nephew, who added the second casino.

SLOANE, Sir Hans (1660–1753), was one of the eighteenth-century England's most distinguished scholar-physicians and plant collectors. Sloane corresponded and exchanged plants for thirty years with two American friends, John Bartram and William Byrd II. He helped to introduce many plants into the United States while introducing numerous American species into England. He wrote a catalogue of the 800 plant specimens he collected in Jamaica in 1687, and later published the two-volume *Voyage to . . . Jamaica* (1707–1725). He purchased the Chelsea Physic Garden in 1712 and hired Philip Miller as its curator. Sloane was a founder of the British Museum and bequeathed his personal library to the institution, making it the largest natural history collection in Britain and one of the most important in the world.

SOAMI (1472–1523), also known as Shinso, was a Japanese artist and garden designer who is credited with the restoration of Ryoan-ji, in Kyoto, between 1488 and 1499. Ryoan-ji is considered the most important Zen Buddhist garden of the *kare-sansui* (dry landscape) type. This small rectangular courtyard space (2700 square feet, or 256 square meters) is comprised of swept pea gravel and five stone groupings, each fringed in moss.

SOSEKI, Muso (1275–1351), Japanese Zen Buddhist priest and garden designer who created the Silver Pavilion and the Saiho-ji ("Heart Garden") in Kyoto, Japan in 1339. He also designed the Tenryu-ji in Kyoto. He is sometimes identified as Muso-Soseki and as Muso Kokushi.

SPENCE, Joseph (1699–1768), was a professor of poetry and history at Oxford. His most noted work was *Observations, Anecdotes, and Characters of Books and Men.* Although it was not published until 1820, a half a century after his death, this essay was well known during his lifetime. Included in it are many of Alexander Pope's statements about garden design. In a letter to the Reverend Mr. Wheeler written in 1752, Spence enumerated his sixteen "general rules" about landscape design, many of which had already been put forth by his friend, Pope. Spence finished his list of rules with a two-line verse from Pope, which said, "He gains all Ends, who pleasingly confounds/Surprises, varies, and conceals the bounds. . . ."

Spence was experienced in the design of rural home grounds. He had a 17-acre estate, Byfleet, in Surrey which he had endeavored to make over into a landscape garden, or a *ferme ornée,* as indicated in his description: "[M]y fields . . . have the winding walk continued all round them. . . . I can go all round my little territory in half an hour. . . ."

Spence contributed to the notion that paintings directly influenced the design of gardens during the early eighteenth century when he attributed to Pope the comment, "All gardening is landscape-painting. Just like a landscape hung up. . . ."

SPOTSWOOD, Alexander (1676–1740), was the deputy, or lieutenant governor, of the Virginia Colony (1710–1722) and designer of the Governor's Palace grounds in Williamsburg. Proficient in mathematics, he also built the octagonal powder magazine at Williamsburg and rebuilt the College of William and Mary after it had been damaged by fire. In 1711 he wrote, "The life I lead here is . . . rather after a quiet Country manner; & now I am sufficiently amused with planting Orchard & Gardens, & with finishing a large House which is design'd . . . for the reception of their Governours."

John Reps, in *Tidewater Towns: City Planning in Colonial Virginia and Maryland* (1972), theorized that Francis Nicholson, planner of the capital, Williamsburg (1699), incorporated "landscape gardening-style vistas and perspectives" into the layout of the town. These ideas Nicholson derived from his great interest in gardening and from the many books on the subject, which he had in his personal library. According to Peter Martin of the Colonial Williamsburg Foundation, Spotswood "perpetuated Nicholson's scheme by strengthening the vistas." The main vista that Spotswood created was the palace green, a long axial greensward, which extends southward from the palace to the town's main east-west thoroughfare, Duke of Gloucester Street. Since Spotswood lived in the palace, he achieved two objectives by carving out a swath of trees to create the spacious perspective between the town center and his residence. He could enjoy the openness of the long, green lawn sprawling out from his residence, and, in turn, the townspeople could clearly see the governor's house and thus be reminded of his authority.

Behind, or north and west, of the palace were a series of formal terraced gardens which in 1716 Spotswood had shaped out of a large ravine that drained into the James River. A formal canal terminates the view from the upper level.

Under Spotswood's leadership, the frontier of Virginia was extended westward to the base of the Blue Ridge Mountains, where, in 1716, he organized the expedition that discovered the passage through "the rocky barrier" to the Shenandoah Valley.

Following his retirement in 1722, he settled as a "Virginia gentleman" on his 70,000-acre estate in Spotsylvania County, near the town of Germanna, which he founded for Germans sent to the colony by Queen Anne in 1716. This land was rich in iron ore, from which he manufactured iron for several years at his Tubal Furnace, earning for him the nickname, "the Tubal Cain of Virginia," and the distinction of being the first man to establish "a regular iron furnace in North America."

STEELE, Fletcher (1885–1971), landscape architect, completed graduate studies at Harvard in 1908 and worked for Warren Manning from then until 1914, when he opened his own office in Boston. He practiced until 1962, working on approximately 600 projects all over the United States. He was a "modernist" in the 1920s, as his probing article "New Styles in Gardening," in the March 1929 issue of *House Beautiful* attests. His design for Mabel Choate's estate, Naumkeag (Indian for "haven of peace"), in Stockbridge, Massachusetts, is one of his most notable creations. The site was laid out as an eclectic Victorian-style garden in the early 1920s by Nathan Barrett. Over three decades, Steele adapted the place into an expression of his affinity for the neoclassical forms extant on the site, yet his modern feel for space, form, and color. Steele partitioned off the garden into a series of theme gardens: the Chinese Garden, with a small temple, Moon Gate, and Devil Screen entrance; the Rose Garden; the Green Garden; the Cutting Garden; and the Afternoon Garden, with its water staircase, the "Blue Steps." This feature, in the midst of a birch grove, is a concrete adaptation of a Renaissance form, but with the steps painted blue and with graceful white painted handrails.

Steele wrote about his design ideas in *Design in the Little Garden* (1924), *New Pioneering in Garden Design* (1930), *Landscape Design of the Future* (1932), *Modern Garden Design* (1936), and *Gardens and People* (1963). He also wrote numerous articles for popular and professional journals, including *House Beautiful, Horticulture,* and *Landscape Architecture*. He was a fellow of the ASLA.

STEELE, Sir Richard (1671–1729), an Irishman and the "first of the British periodical essayists," was a member of the House of Commons, a playwright, and editor of the *Tatler* from 1709 to 1711 (under the pseudonym Isaac Bickerstaff). He wrote for the *Spectator,* a similarly short-lived publication (1711–1712) (weekly circulation, 10,000 copies) and for the *Guardian* (1713), to which Alexander Pope contributed. He was a lifelong friend of Joseph Addison as well as a friend of the architect John Vanbrugh. In the course of his career, Steele wrote over 500 essays on topics from the arts to politics to taste in gardening. He established five other periodicals between 1714 and 1720. Among the titles were *Town Talk, Tea-Table,* and *Chit-Chat*.

STEIN, Clarence S. (1883–1975), architect and regional planner, worked with Henry Wright on the planning and design of Radburn, New Jersey, America's first comprehensively planned "garden city" (1927–1929). He was schooled at Columbia University and the Ecole des Beaux-Arts in Paris. In 1924, Stein and Wright planned Sunnyside Gardens, a residential community on Long Island, New York for the City Housing Corporation. This scheme featured housing clustered around large community gardens. Radburn was developed on a 1300-acre site near Paterson, New Jersey, employing many of Sir Ebenezer Howard's standards, while also including provisions for the private automobile, a fact of life not known in Howard's day. The scheme was based on a number of "superblocks," each with its own neighborhood identity. Probable pedestrian and automobile conflicts were minimized through the use of numerous pedestrian underpasses and "cul-de-sacs," automobile courts.

During the Depression Stein and Wright planned one of the four proposed "greenbelt" towns to be built under Roosevelt's New Deal. This was the 4000-acre Greenbrook, New Jersey. It was not built due to local opposition, which tied the land up in the courts for years. The partners planned a small housing developments in Pittsburgh, Chatham Village (1930), but this was not built until 1932 from plans modified by Pittsburgh landscape architect Ralph E. Griswold. In 1941, they planned Baldwin Hills Village in Los Angeles.

Their other works include the plan for the San Diego World Fair (1915) and the master plan for the new town of Kitimat in British Columbia (1951). Stein wrote *Toward New Towns for America* (1957).

STOCKTON, Annis Boudinot (1736–1801), and **Richard STOCKTON** (1730–1781). Richard Stockton was a lawyer, landowner, and New Jersey signer of the Declaration of Independence. Annis Stockton was one of the most cultured, literary women of her day, having received more education than most young girls then. She was a poet of considerable merit who loved both romantic poetry and romantic scenery. Their home, Morven, in Princeton, New Jersey, was a center of cultural influence in its area and they wished to make their gardens into a work of art equal to their splendid house. Richard spent sixteen months in England (1766–1767), and to satisfy his wife's ambition to develop a portion of the grounds of Morven as a romantic English-style landscape garden, Richard had Alexander Pope's landscape garden at Twickenham (1719–1744) surveyed for her. He went so far as to collect a few pieces of shell and colored glass from Pope's famous grotto and obtained Pope's recipe for making mortar with which to cement the souvenirs to the interior of their proposed grotto just as the poet had. Between 1767 and the American Revolution, the two Stocktons struggled to replicate features from their favorite English model. During the Battle of Princeton, Morven was pillaged, the library burned, and furniture turned into firewood. The livestock was set free in the garden and what was not destroyed in the garden by troops, the British horses finished off. Annis and their children fled the enemy, but Richard was captured and was so poorly treated by his captors that he died a few years later. Following the war, Annis rebuilt the house and lived there for fifteen more years but gave up her dream to replicate Pope's romantic garden. Today, the house is owned by Princeton University and serves as the home of its president.

STONES, Ellis (d. 1975), Australian garden designer, worked in the Melbourne office of Edna Walling for several years before becoming one of Australia's most successful garden designers on his own. Like Walling, Stones relied heavily on the use of indigenous Australian plants and lots of rock. In the Melbourne suburban town of Eltham, Stones created many fine gardens with native materials. After World War II, the town became famous in Australia for its population of artists and writers, many of whom further popularized the native look of their country—chief among which are subdued colors and a remarkable range of plant textures. Another of his best works is the planned residential community, Elliston, outside Melbourne.

Stones was a founding member of the Australian Institute of Landscape Architects in 1968 and is a consultant to the National Trust. He is the author of *Australian Garden Design* (1971).

STRAUCH, Adolphus, or Adolph (1822–1883), was a landscape gardener from Prussia who had worked for Prince Hermann von Pückler-Muskau as well as in the royal gardens of Austria, Germany, the Netherlands, and Luxembourg. From 1848 to 1851, he worked at the Royal Botanic Gardens in London's Regent's Park. He came to the United States in 1851 and settled in Cincinnati, where in 1855 he was hired to remodel the ten-year-old "rural cemetery" Spring Grove.

In 1845, after rejecting the plan by John Notman as too geometric and lacking the desired topographical diversity, the cemetery founders settled on a scheme by a local architect, Howard Daniels. When opened, this romantic burying ground became popular immediately, not only by mourners but by droves of city dwellers seeking a quiet pastoral setting for the contemplation of nature. As with Mount Auburn Cemetery near Boston, Spring Grove was Cincinnati's first parklike public open space. However, within ten years the cemetery became a wild assortment of tombs, monuments, iron fencing, and individualized plantings, all by family plot owners. Like so many earlier rural cemeteries, its intended pastoralism was lost to so much artifice, or as Strauch said, it resembled "a marble yard where monuments are for sale." Downing criticized this practice before Strauch, saying such "hideous *ironmongery* [was a] positive blot on the beauty of the scene."

In 1855, Strauch was hired to reform the cemetery through "scientific management." Following his advice, the cemetery was enlarged to 412 acres, making it the world's largest at the time. He ordered the removal of all but the "tasteful, classical, and poetical" among the structures on the site. In the older and newer sections, the intervening spaces were shaped with plantings or left open with sweeping expanses of turf. He recontoured the ground, creating undulations and 5 acres of quiet ponds or "ornamental waters." Thus was originated the "lawn cemetery" as a new mode of landscape garden design. Soon after, Jacob Weidenmann called Strauch's innovation brilliant, with "open lawns surrounded by lofty trees and flowering shrubs, a sylvan scene of nature's loveliest productions." Lawn cemeteries became popular all over America after the Civil War.

Strauch did other work in Cincinnati, including Clifton Estates, a suburban "village park," and Eden Park. As his reputation as a cemetery and park designer quickly grew, he was hired to do similar projects in New York, Chicago, Detroit, Cleveland, Buffalo, Indianapolis, Hartford, and Nashville. In 1883, Adolph Strauch was buried in Spring Grove Cemetery.

SULLIVAN, Louis Henri (1856–1924), was one of the leaders of the modern movement in architecture in the United States. He studied at the Massachusetts Institute of Technology and the Ecole des Beaux-Arts in Paris. He apprenticed in the office of William Le Baron Jenny in Chicago. Sullivan's greatest work was completed during his partnership with the German architect Dankmar Adler (1881–1900). Both Frank Lloyd Wright and Walter Burley Griffin apprenticed with Adler and Sullivan. His best work includes some of the earliest skyscrapers, the Wainwright Building in St. Louis (1890) being the most influential. He designed the Chicago Auditorium (1889); the Transportation Building at the World's Columbian Exposition in Chicago (1893); Carson, Pirie, Scott in Chicago (1904); and the National Farmers Bank in Owatonna, Minnesota (1908).

SWITZER, Stephen (1682–1745), was a garden designer who had apprenticed from 1698 to 1705 under the great duo London and Wise, at Castle Howard and Blenheim, but his contribution to the development of the landscape garden style in England was primarily through his writings. He produced nine books and was editor of a magazine. A devotée of what he called "rural gardening," his most important work was his *Ichongraphia Rustica; or, The Nobleman, Gentleman, and Gardener's Recreation,* a three-volume tome written in 1718 and revised and expanded in 1742. In *Ichongraphia* he wrote: "A Design must submit to Nature, and not Nature to Design." He believed in the classical idea that gardening should be a balance of "the useful and the profitable." In 1715, he wrote about the necessity of liberating the garden from its confining walls. This passage was written several years *before* Kent was alleged to have "leaped the fence, and saw that all nature was garden." In 1718, Switzer used the term *ferme ornée* in connection with his description of a country seat, the first use of this expression and idea.

TAYLOR, Albert Davis (1883–1951), taught landscape architecture at his alma mater, Cornell University, from 1906 to 1908 before working for Warren Manning. He spent five years there, until he moved to Cleveland to become one of the first landscape architects to practice in Ohio. Much of his work was estate designing, for clients such as W. H. Knoll, Fort Wayne, Indiana (1919); and W. H. Albers (1925) and Julius Fleishman (1926), both of Cincinnati. He laid out the Cincinnati suburbs Rookwood (1922) and Camargo (1925). Taylor designed several parks, including Forest Hill Park at the edge of Cleveland (1937) and Maple Grove Park near Windham, Ohio, a defense housing project for the Federal Public Housing Authority in 1937. In 1942 he produced the site plan for the U.S. Defense Department's Pentagon Building in Arlington, Virginia.

Taylor and his associate Gordon D. Cooper coauthored the book, *The Complete Garden* (1921) and over three dozen articles—"Construction Notes"—for the *Landscape Architecture* magazine from 1922 to 1936. Taylor was the president of the ASLA between 1935 and 1940.

TEMPLE, Sir Richard (first Viscount, or Lord Cobham) (1669–1749), owned Stowe House during its French formal phase. Cobham became politically active in the "Patriot" or Whig party after 1733 and adapted the grounds and structures of Stowe into a liberal or reformer political statement. In the 1720s he hired Charles Bridgeman as his garden designer, and later retained William Kent in the 1730s and "Capability" Brown in the 1740s to further improve the grounds by removing the formal and reinstating the naturalistic landscape. It was Cobham who gave Brown his start as a landscape garden designer.

Cobham's niece's husband, Richard Grenville (who had the title "Lord Temple") was the major designer of the landscape garden at Stowe, after 1749—about the same time as Henry Hoare was creating Stourhead. According to the British landscape historian Michael McCarthy, "[Lord Temple] was undoubtedly the architect of the landscaping there [beginning] in 1749. . . ." Brown's employment at Stowe ended in that year, and from then until 1763 "Lord Temple worked to make the first 'natural' landscape in England, the Grecian Valley" (McCarthy, 1974, p. 37). The concepts involved in the layout of the Grecian Valley were continued into the gardens south of the house between 1753 and 1777. This area had previously been devoted to French parterres with octagonal pools.

TEMPLE, Sir William (1628–1699), made a trip to the Orient in 1685 and returned to England to write his essay *The Gardens of Epicurus; or of Gardening, in the Year 1685,* published in 1687, in which he made numerous references to the wilderness or naturalistic areas in the gardens of China, a concept that was the diametric opposite of the Euclidian geometry of the European gardens. This work began the fashion of chinoiserie in Europe. He described the palace of Peking as "a sequence of discoveries of idealized nature where the emperor's family could reside in perfect harmony with nature." To characterize the irregularity to be seen in the gardens he saw, Temple invented his own term "Sharawadgi." He wrote: "in contriving Figures, where the Beauty shall be great and strike the Eye, but without any Order or Disposition of Parts, that shall be commonly or easily observ'd . . . they have a particular Word to express it; and where they find it hit their Eye at first sight, they say the Sharawadgi is fine or is admirable. . . ."

According to Edward Hyams, *sharawadgi* was "gobbledegook." He notes that there are several other words in Chinese from which Temple might have derived his term. It may have been Temple's mistaken spelling of *sa-to-kwai-chi,* meaning "careless" or "disorderly grace"; or *san-lan-wai-chi,* "disorderly composition"; or the japanese word *sorowadji,* for "unsymmetrical design."

THOMPSON, Benjamin, Count Rumford (1753–1814), was an eighteenth-century American who planned Munich's Englische Garten, a 600-

acre park—or *ferme ornée*—conceived as an English romantic–style public park in 1789. Thus it was the first urban park in the Western world to be created specifically for the masses. More than just a romantic pastoral pleasure ground, Thompson's creation was conceived to help bring about positive social reform for the citizens of Munich. It was the social and physical design model for the later English and American public parks. When Thompson returned to England and wrote his essay on the value of public parks in 1802, he was thirty-nine years ahead of the adoption of the idea in England. London did not develop its first such public pleasure ground, Victoria Park, until 1841 and America waited another two decades until Olmsted and Vaux designed New York's Central Park.

Thompson was born in Massachusetts. A Tory, or "loyalist" to George III during the years before the American Revolution, Major Thompson was accused of being "inimical to the cause of his country." He was never convicted of actually being a traitor but was never cleared of the charges and following months of persecution, he fled to England and then to Munich.

The role of Benjamin Thompson, Count Rumford, in the history of landscape architecture and the public park movement in Europe and America is one that has been overlooked by historians. Andrew Jackson Downing often cited Munich's romantic-style Englische Garten as the model after which America should fashion similar "salubrious and wholesome breathing places." The landscape character on which Olmsted and Vaux designed New York's Central Park in 1858 was based, in many ways, on Munich's splendid Englische Garten. Within a generation, cities and towns, large and small, all over United States had built or were in the process of making parks in the mode of Munich's park and Central Park.

Thompson was knighted by England's King George III in 1785 and was made a Count of the Holy Roman Empire by Prince Karl Theodor of Bavaria in 1791.

THOREAU, Henry David (1817–1862), American transcendentalist philosopher, poet, writer, and naturalist, wrote several books about his interludes in the wilderness: *A Week on the Concord and Merrimack Rivers* (1849), *The Maine Woods* (1864), *Cape Cod* (1865), and his finest work and American classic, *Walden* (1854). His writings made a major contribution toward the growth of the American reverence for wilderness. In 1851 he declared, "In Wildness is the preservation of the World. . . . Our lives need the relief of the wilderness where the pine flourishes and the jay still screams. . . ."

TODD, Frederick G. (1876–1948), landscape architect, was born in Concord, New Hampshire and educated at the Agricultural College in Amherst, Massachusetts. He worked for the Olmsted office from 1896 to 1900, when he moved to Montréal to superintend work on Mount Royal Park for the Olmsteds. In 1900 he began his own practice there and remained in Canada for the rest of his career, making him the first resident landscape architect in Canada. By the 1920s, Todd had a nationwide practice, primarily site planning and designing urban parks and public works. He also published numerous articles in Canadian magazines and newspapers.

His most noted works include the design of a "necklace of parks" and "garden suburbs" around Montréal and other cities for the Canadian Northern Railway; the Assiniboine Park and Tuxedo Park in Winnipeg (1904–1906); Wascana Centre in Regina, Saskatchewan (1907); the parklike suburb of Vancouver, Shaughnessy Heights; the Parc des Champs de Bataille (Plains of Abraham National Battlefield, in Québec City (1909–1914); site planning and design for Trinity College, Toronto; Bowering Park, St. John's, Newfoundland (1913–1918); the restoration of St. Helen's Island, in the St. Lawrence River, within the city of Montréal (1938); and the Chemin de la Croix (Way of the Cross) at Montréal's St. Joseph Oratory (1945). Todd was made a fellow of the American Society of Landscape Architects in 1905, was a founding member of the Town Planning Institute of Canada (1922), and served as president of the Canadian Society of Landscape Architects from 1945 to 1946.

TRUMBULL, John (1756–1843), an American painter and amateur architect, planned Yale's "Brick Row" and naturalistic gardens in 1792. He was considered one of the best portrait and history painters in America during the Revolutionary period. According to campus planning authority Paul Turner, Trumbull's scheme for Yale was the first and "oldest surviving master plan for an American college (Turner, 1984, p. 38). His ground plan was also the earliest example of the application of the romantic English landscape garden principles to a college setting. It followed by only seven years the first public space to be laid out in a similar fashion—the State House Garden, in Philadelphia, designed by a visiting Englishman, Samuel Vaughan, in 1785.

Born in Connecticut and educated at Harvard, Trumbull served as aide-de-camp to General Washington during the Revolutionary War. His father, Jonathan, was the governor of Connecticut between 1769 and 1784. He studied painting under the American "master" Benjamin West (1738–1820) in London between 1780 and 1789. Trumbull's best known works were his large history paintings depicting the Revolutionary War, commissioned by the U.S. Congress for display in the Capitol Rotunda in Washington, D.C.

In 1784, British authority on aesthetics Edmund Burke advised Trumbull to pursue the field of architecture: "Architecture is the eldest sister . . . painting and sculpture are the youngest, and subservient to her; [your] young nation . . . will soon want public buildings; . . . study architecture thoroughly and scientifically, in order to qualify yourself to superintend the erection of these national buildings—decorate them also, if you will" (Verheyen, 1982, p. 260).

In 1792, Yale College hired Trumbull to design a new dormitory for its expanding enrollment. Instead, Trumbull proposed a row of three new buildings to be aligned with the two existing structures facing the New Haven town green. His "projected" buildings were two dormitories and a building to house the library and classrooms. His site plan reveals Trumbull's taste for the "naturalistic" treatment of the grounds. Behind his proposed row of buildings were the existing dining hall and three "temples of Cloacina" (the sewers of Rome were called *cloaca* in Latin, so this meant three latrines). His notation read: "The Temples of Cloacina . . . I would wish to have concealed as much as possible, by planting a variety of shrubs . . . a gravel walk should lead thru the shrubery to these buildings. The Eating Hall should likewise be hidden as much as the space will permit with similar shrubs. The walks may be irregular & winding, beginning behind the two Chapels. . . . The planting also may be irregular consisting of three groups of large Trees, Elms, Altissimas, Poplars . . . & a variety of small Shrubs interspersed" (Turner, 1984, pp. 41–42).

John Trumbull's other built works were the Meetinghouse in Lebanon, Connecticut (1804–1806); the American Academy of the Fine Arts, New York City (1831); and the Trumbull Gallery, Yale College, New Haven (1832).

TUNNARD, Christopher (1910–1979), landscape architect, urban and regional planner, educator, and writer, was born in Vancouver, British Columbia, Canada, and went to England in 1928 to study horticulture. During the 1930s he was the first landscape architect in England to design in the "modern garden style," landscapes consistent with twentieth-century architectural modernism derived from the international style in architecture. He began his private practice in 1934 and in 1938 wrote the immensely influential *Gardens in the Modern Landscape*. His seminal work includes St. Ann's Hill, in Chertsey, and Halland, in Sussex, with the architect Serge Chermayeff (1936–1937). He emigrated to America in 1939 and taught at Harvard (1939–1942) and Yale (1945–1975). He is credited with developing the concept of "regional, or linear cities," such as one he envisioned from Richmond, Virginia to Portland, Maine. Despite that, Tunnard also was quite conservative in his view of rural scenery, as he stated: "Is it not yet conceivable that a well-designed and well-placed building, a bridge or road, can be an addition rather than a menace to the countryside?"

His other built works include several residential gardens in England and the United States. He wrote numerous articles in professional journals and the books *The City of Man* (1953, with J. Pearce), *City Planning at Yale* (1954), *The American Skyline* (1955, with Boris Pushkarev), *Man-Made America: Chaos or Control* (1963), and *The Modern American City* (1968).

VANBRUGH, Sir John (1664–1726), was an English playwright and architect who designed many large and stately rural mansions, including Claremont, Blenheim, and Castle Howard. The painting critic Sir Joshua Reynolds said that Vanbrugh was "an architect who composed like a painter." He was a master at exploiting the scenic potential of each site on which he worked. He anticipated the romantic movement in his incorporation of ruins or construction of sham ancient or medieval "eyecatchers" into his panoramas, such as at Castle Howard.

VASARI, Giorgio (1511–1574), Italian painter, architect, and writer, worked in the studio of Michelangelo. He produced many fine Manneristic frescoes in the Vatican and in the Palazzo Vecchio in Florence. He is best known for his book *Lives of Excellent Painters, Sculptors, and Architects* (1550), one of the best historical records of the arts during the Renaissance. This book is the main source of information about the artists of Vasari's generation—the High Renaissance in Italy. Vasari designed several fine structures, the supreme example of which is the Uffizi in Florence (1560–1580).

VAUGHAN, Samuel (1730–1802), was an English merchant who during a brief five-year residence in the United States (1783–1787) designed two of the most visible examples of the English landscape garden in America, the Pennsylvania State House Garden (Independence Hall) and Gray's Inn Gardens in Philadelphia. At the time, Philadelphia was the national capital and these two places received a great deal of attention. The State House Garden and the ferry crossing, the most prominent crossing of the Schuylkill River into the capital, were seen by far more persons than had seen the private residential grounds of the other replicas of the "natural" or English landscape garden style. Thus Vaughan's works enlightened the greatest number of Americans to the "modern" form of design.

VAUX, Calvert (1824–1895), an English architect and landscape architect, followed the suggestion of Andrew Jackson Downing, whom he met during Downing's trip to Britain, and emigrated to the United States in 1850. The two men formed a loose partnership which lasted but two years, until Downing's drowning in 1852. Their first major landscape architectural project was the grounds of the Smithsonian Museum (the "Castle"), at the edge of the Mall in Washington, D.C. (1851).

It was Vaux who persuaded Frederick Law Olmsted to enter the competition for Central Park in 1857. That successful liaison lasted until 1872, by which time the partners had designed many other parks and public and private landscapes, including the subdivision of Riverside, Illinois; Jackson Park in Chicago; and Prospect Park in Brooklyn. Vaux designed the Belvedere and many bridges and rustic shelters in Central Park.

On his own, Vaux designed the New York Museum of Natural History, the Metropolitan Museum of Art at the edge of Central Park, and the Parliament House grounds in the Canadian capital, Ottawa (1873), thereby introducing the Olmstedian model, which was subsequently to influence Canadian landscape design. He also designed Olana, the Hudson River estate of the landscape painter Frederick Edwin Church; Blithewood estate, a villa for S. M. Fox; and Idlewild, the home of N. P. Willis, in Cornwall-on-Hudson, New York. Other residences that he designed were for Robert Donaldson, James Smillie, H. Sheldon, John B. James, Dr. Federal Vanderburgh, Joel Rathbone, Henry Delameter, Lewis B. Brown, Henry A. Kent, Henry K. Harral, William Warren, S. E. Lyon, Governor Morehead of North Carolina, and Philip St. George of Powhatan County, Virginia. He also designed the gatehouse and grounds of Wilderstein on the Hudson River.

Vaux and Andrew Jackson Downing designed a number of houses and public buildings together, including the Norman chapel and gatehouse for Evergreens Cemetery, Brooklyn, New York (1850); a summerhouse for Daniel Parish, Newport, Rhode Island (1855); a residence for John Angier, Medford, Massachusetts; a villa for B. Phelps, Springfield, Massachusetts; and a residence for R. P. Dodge, Washington, D.C.

During much of the 1880s, Vaux had a landscape architectural practice, separate from his architectural firm, with the landscape architect Samuel Parsons, Jr.

He wrote the book *Villas and Cottages* in 1857, which was a collection of essays and plans by Downing, Vaux, and Frederick Withers, another English architect, with whom they practiced. His second son, Downing Vaux, became a landscape architect and was a founding member of the ASLA. Amazingly enough, Calvert Vaux lost his life as A. J. Downing had, by drowning off Long Island.

VAUX, Downing (c.1865–1926), second son of his famous father Calvert Vaux, was a landscape architect and worked with his father from about 1885 until his father's death ten years later. He was a founding member of the ASLA.

VIGNOLA, Giacomo Barozzi da (1507–1573), Italian architect and villa designer, is most noted for his design of one of the most exquisite of the Italian Renaissance villas, the Villa Lante in Bagnaia (1560). He was influenced by the writings of the first-century Roman writer, Pliny the Younger, who had so romantically described his rural villas. Vignola's other compositions include the Villa Giulia in Rome (1555), and the "giardini segreti" (secret gardens) at the Villino Caprarola, or Villa Farnese, in the town of Caprarola (c.1547–1549).

VIRGIL, or VERGIL (Publius Vergilius Maro) (70–19 B.C.), Roman poet and gentleman farmer, wrote two books of poems, the *Bucolics* (shepherd poems) and the *Georgics* (agricultural poems). The first book of Virgil's *Georgics* deal not with the blissful life of the pastoralist but with the more arduous existence of the farmer. In this series of poems, his devotion to the soil becomes like a religious fervor. His later work, *The Æneid,* is a celebration of Roman chauvinism—a love of country. The poetry of Virgil and other Roman poets was extremely popular in England during the eighteenth century and was very influential on the romantic landscape garden movement.

VITALE, Ferruccio (1875–1933), was born in Florence, Italy, the son of a countess. He came to America in 1898 as military attaché to the Royal Italian Embassy in Washington. With a background in engineering and architecture, he took up landscape architecture after retiring from the service in 1904, opening an office in New York City with Alfred Geiffert, with whom he worked until 1933. Their office maintained a wide practice, working in most of the states east of the Mississippi, on estates, public and semipublic works, and town planning. The Italianate Meridian Hill Park (1917–1936), in Washington, D.C. is one of Vitale's most noted works.

He became a member of the ASLA in 1904 and was a major force in getting landscape architecture accepted as one of the disciplines at the American Academy in Rome in 1915. In 1927, President Coolidge appointed Vitale to the National Commission of Fine Arts. He was on the Architectural Commission of the Century of Progress Exposition in Chicago in 1933. He wrote many articles for, and had his work featured in, *Landscape Architecture, House and Garden,* and *House Beautiful.*

VITRUVIUS, Marcus Pollius (c. first century B.C.), Roman architect and city planner, lived in the time of Augustus and the greatest activity in building construction in the city of Rome. He wrote a ten-volume book of architecture, *De Architectura,* which greatly influenced the architectural design of the Italian High Renaissance.

WADSWORTH, Daniel (1771–1848), a country gentleman, philanthropist, and art collector from Hartford, Connecticut, was a friend and sponsor of Thomas Cole, the first of the Hudson River school of painters. He also commissioned many others, including Frederick Edwin Church. In 1844 he founded America's first civic, publicly incorporated art museum, the Wadsworth Atheneum, in Hartford. The building was designed by Alexander Jackson Davis in the Gothic Revival style.

Wadsworth was as interested in architecture as in painting, and consistent with his taste in painting, he preferred the romantic Gothic Revival style. Between 1805 and 1809 he designed his own house, which he built on top of Talcott Mountain near Avon, Connecticut. It was one of the first examples of the Gothic Revival style in America. The house, called Monte Video, and its environs were the subject of several of Cole's paintings during the late 1820s. This was the time and place where the fashion in large, panoramic scenery, painted from mountaintop vantage points, became popular.

The grounds of this estate, treated in the English landscape garden style, were among the most impressive to be seen in America at the time. In his *Treatise,* Andrew Jackson Downing was somewhat understated when he wrote, "Monte Video . . . is one of the most tasteful in the state [of Connecticut]." John C. Loudon, in his *Encyclopaedia* (1834), described the place: "[It] stands in a very fine situation . . . 600 feet above the Connecticut River, and its beautiful meadow scenery. The approach to the house is about three miles in length, and is carried over a succession of small hills finely wooded. There is a handsome piece of water near the house, and a hill behind it; from a tower on the top of which there is a magnificent view, bounded by the hills of Massachusetts, of [a] rich and fertile a country. . . . Advantage has certainly been taken of the natural beauties of the place in laying it out—the road, the piece of water, and the grounds . . . (Loudon, 1982, p. 402). A later traveler, Benjamin Silliman, described the tower and its view in the words of a connoisseur of panoramic scenery which was a relatively new phenomenon in the 1820s: "The tower is a hexagon, of sixteen feet diameter, and fifty-five feet high . . . the top of which is nine hundred and sixty feet about the level of the Connecticut River. The . . . view in two directions, is more than ninety miles, extending into . . . Massachusetts and New York. The little spot of cultivation surrounding the house, and the lake at your feet . . . compose the foreground of this grand panorama. . . . The whole of this magnificent picture . . . a full illustration of the beauties of this mountain, would require a portfolio of views, and would form a fine subject for the pencil of a master" (Silliman, 1824, pp. 15–16).

WALLING, Edna (1896–1973), moved from England to Australia in 1918, where she was educated in horticulture at Burnley College in Melbourne. She remained in Australia for the rest of her life, writing and practicing as a garden designer, later calling herself a landscape architect. Much of her work possessed a distinctly Australian quality, through her reliance on native plants and rock. She was also influenced by the designs of England's Gertrude Jekyll. Walling's most notable works were Cruden Farm in the state of Victoria and the Markdale estate in New South Wales, along with a great number of private residences. Working with her for several years was Ellis Stones, who went on to become one of Australia's most successful landscape architects. He further popularized the use of native Australian plants. She is the author of *Cottage and Garden in Australia* (1947) and *A Gardener's Log* (1948).

WALPOLE, Horace, fourth Earl of Orford (1717–1797), was a man of letters (he considered himself a historian), one of the eighteenth century's foremost "men of taste" and chronicler of the fashions in painting, architecture, and gardening of his time. He was the fourth son of Sir Robert Walpole, England's prime minister (1734–1742) and was himself a member of Parliament between 1741 and 1768. An enthusiast of medievalism, in 1748 he purchased Strawberry Hill, a "simple cottage" which he spent a fortune remodeling over the rest of his life into a pseudo-Gothic castle. He is considered the originator of the revival of interest in Gothic architecture and the "Goythic Tale." At his estate, he established a publishing business and wrote several books, including a Gothic tale of horror, *The Castle of Otranto* (1765); *Anecdotes of Painting in England* (1762–

1771); and in 1770 his important history of landscape architecture, *History of the Modern Taste in Gardening* (not published until 1780).

Walpole was an amateur landscape designer who contributed greatly to the transference of the principles of composition known to painters into the design principles used by landscape designers. In his *Gardening* book, he remarked that "Kent leaped the fence, and saw that all nature was a garden," a statement with great meaning relative to the landscape garden movement. The garden, from the earliest ancient models, had been a thing set apart from its surroundings. It was enclosed within a wall or fence. At an early point in the revolution from walled, formal gardens to open nature gardens, the fence was seen as the most objectionable feature that interfered with the union of the garden and its setting.

WASHINGTON, George (1732–1799), the first president of the United States (1787–1797) and the "father of our country," was a farmer and gardener at heart. Despite his political differences, he corresponded with English agriculturists all his life. His large library included many volumes devoted to animal husbandry and agriculture, but he relied primarily on his copies of Philip Miller's *Gardener's Dictionary* (London, 1731) and Batty Langley's two books, *The City and Country Builder's and Workman's Treasury of Design* (London, 1740) and his *New Principles of Gardening, or, The Laying Out and Planting of Parterres, Groves, Wildernesses, Labyrinths, Avenues, Parks, etc. after a more grand and rural manner than has been done before* (1728, London). He purchased these somewhat outdated manuals of landscape gardening principles from London in 1760. In these books Washington was able to read about "Correct Plans of Estates . . . And Grotto's, Cascades, Caves, Temples, Pavilions, and other Rural Buildings of Pleasure. . . ."

Washington undoubtedly was able to borrow other texts related to the subject of naturalizing one's home grounds, such as those by Francis Bacon, John Evelyn, Joseph Addison, Alexander Pope, and Edmund Burke, all of which were in the private collections of his neighbors. He also sought the aid of gardeners from England, saying in a 1771 letter, "I want a man that will labour hard, knowing . . . how to keep a Garden in good Order. . . ."

He had a keen interest in native trees and "shrubs" (the term he adopted from Langley), which he labored hard to find and transplant onto the grounds of his ancestral home, Mount Vernon. He set to work "improving" by "anglicizing" the grounds of his estate during the winter of 1785, when he created the "wilderness" areas at the edges of the residence. He noted that he wanted them planted "without any order or regularity . . . to consist with Nature. . . ." He placed ha-ha walls between his house and the river, the pastures and the meadows—making those areas the most closely resembling of the soft naturalistic character of the English landscape garden. The two front entrance drives were laid out in a characteristically Hogarthian serpentine alignment. The best plan view of the grounds around the house was produced in 1787, about the time that all the major modifications were completed, by a visiting English landscape gardener, Samuel Vaughan.

Near the end of his life, Washington wrote, ". . . to be a cultivator of the Land has been my favorite amusement." A European visitor praised the president's skill at creating a soft English landscape garden style setting for his home when he observed, "The whole plantation . . . prove[s] that a man born of natural taste may guess a beauty without having ever seen its model . . . he copied the best samples of the grand old homesteads of England."

WAUGH, Frank A. (1869–1943), was a landscape architect, educator, and writer. He taught at the Oklahoma Agricultural and Mechanical College (1892–1895), the University of Vermont (1895–1902), and the Massachusetts State Agricultural College from 1902, until retiring in 1939. As head of the horticulture program, he started the Department of Landscape Gardening (later, Landscape Architecture), which he headed for over three decades. He is best known for the many books and journal articles that he wrote. His *Landscape Gardening* (1899) was the standard teaching text until the Hubbards published their *Introduction to the Study of Landscape Design* in 1917. Waugh wrote seven other books, including his expanded and revised version of Downing's *Landscape Gardening* (1921), the book's sixth and last reprinting.

Waugh maintained a consulting practice while teaching. His works included campus plans for his university and the Kansas State University, as well as several projects with the U.S. Forest Service in Arizona and Oregon. In 1917 the Forest Service hired Waugh to conduct a study of the recreation potential of its lands. He reported that the "enticing wildness" and the "notable beauty" of the forests had a "direct human value" and advised that recreation be given the same considerations as logging in the use of the forests.

WEIDENMANN, Jacob (1829–1893), was a Swiss architect and engineer who practiced in Germany, Panama, and South America before coming to America in 1856. He worked for seven years (1861–1868) as the superintendent of parks in Hartford, Connecticut. He wrote *Beautifying*

Country Homes: A Handbook of Landscape Gardening (1870), which Frederick Law Olmsted later praised as "a standard book."

For several years he collaborated with Olmsted and Calvert Vaux on numerous projects, with a loose partnership arrangement extending from 1874 until Olmsted's departure for Brookline, Massachusetts in 1883. The projects included during this relationship were the Congress Park in Saratoga Springs, New York; the Schuylkill Arsenal near Philadelphia; the U.S. Capitol grounds; and the Mount Royal Park in Montréal, Québec. In 1877 he began writing *American Garden Architecture,* to be published in twelve small volumes, but this was never completed.

Weidenmann was a nineteenth-century cemetery reformer, composing many essays about the value of "modern" cemeteries and the book *Modern Cemeteries* (1888). He said that crowded graveyards should be transformed into landscaped parks. His most significant works after leaving the Olmsted firm were the Cedar Hill Cemetery, Pope Park, and Bushnell Park in Hartford; Hill Park estate on Staten Island; Henry B. Hyde's estate, Masquetux, in Babylon, New York; the Brooklyn College campus plan; and the Iowa State Capitol grounds in Des Moines. For a short time he collaborated with the celebrated Chicago architect and inventor of the "high rise," William Le Baron Jenny. It was Weidenmann who began to speak out for the establishment of professional schools in order to elevate landscape architecture, "the noblest of all Art professions," to what he called a "proper standing in science and art." Ultimately, the first comprehensive academic program in landscape architecture in the United States was established at Harvard in 1900, and soon after the Jacob Weidenmann Prize was established to honor his memory and to recognize the outstanding graduate of the program each year.

WHARTON, Edith Newbold Jones (1862–1937), Pulitzer Prize–winning American novelist and short-story writer, was the aunt of Beatrix Jones Farrand, landscape architect. Wharton is best known for her short stories and novels, but in 1904 she wrote *Italian Villas and Their Gardens,* which was richly illustrated with colored plates. This was a popular "coffee table book" and generated great interest in the creation of the eclectic gardens of the time period.

WHATELY, Thomas (d. 1772) (sometimes spelled Whateley), was a politician who served as secretary of the treasury (1765–1765) and as under-secretary of state for Great Britain (1771–1772). His greatest contribution to the landscape garden movement was the immensely popular book he wrote in 1765, *Observations on Modern Gardening* (published anonymously five years later). It was translated into French and German and was reprinted five times in English by 1793. He believed that gardening was "entitled to a place of considerable rank among the liberal arts." He stated, "Gardening . . . is as superior to landskip painting, as a reality to a representation." Whately rather simplistically categorized garden elements into ground, wood, water, rocks, and buildings. He wrote "The business of a gardener is to select and to apply whatever is great, elegant or characteristic . . . to discover and to shew all the advantages of the place upon which he is employed; to supply its defects, to correct its faults, and to improve its beauties. For all these operations the objects of nature are still his only materials . . . *ground, wood, water, rocks*" (Whately, 1770, pp. 1–2).

While this treatise, published at the height of "Capability" Brown's career, reviews what by then had become the well-established principles of design, it was extremely valuable for his readers, because many of them were versed in the rules of composition relative to painting but were not yet familiar with the same in terms of the treatment of the "pleasure grounds" of their properties. Whately had very little experience with design, except for the changes he directed at the country seat, Nonesuch. As J. C. Loudon mentioned, it is interesting that "so celebrated . . . an example of the ancient style of gardening, in the sixteenth century, should have been changed to the modern style in the eighteenth century by the first and the best of all writers on this style. . . ."

WHITE, Stanford (1856–1906), was the principal architect in the most prolific architectural firm in America at the turn of the century, McKim, Mead and White. The firm had 785 commissions during the height of its popularity, between 1879 and 1910—the period of the tremendous economic prosperity in America before the great stock market crash of 1929 and the inception of the graduated income tax, which nearly wiped out the market for great palatial buildings in America. McKim, Mead and White designed residences, offices, churches, banks, resorts, and even power stations. Most of their work was in the Beaux-Arts style.

White received no formal education in architecture, but in 1872, Frederick Law Olmsted, a friend of his father, suggested that young Stanford apprentice in the office of Henry Hobson Richardson in Boston.

White and his partner Charles Follen McKim were the chief designers in their atelier, with each of them in charge of their own projects. Works specifically from the hand of White included the Washington Memorial Arch (1892) and Judson Memorial Church (1888–1893), both in New York's Washington Square; Madison Square Garden in New York (1887–

1891); Madison Square Presbyterian Church, New York (1904–1906); the Robert Goelet Cottage (1882–1883) and the Casino (1879–1880) both in Newport, Rhode Island; the Tiffany Building, New York (1903–1906); the Boston Symphony Hall (1887–1898); the State Capitol, Providence (1891–1903); the campus plan and library at New York University (1892–1901); and the restoration of the Rotunda and Cabell Hall at the University of Virginia (1896–1907).

The firm went through many styles during this period, from Georgian to Italian Renaissance palazzo, and from Roman to French Renaissance. Among the designs produced by the joint efforts of the partners were the Agriculture Building and the New York State Pavilion at the World's Columbian Exposition in Chicago (1893) and the Villard House in New York (1915).

WHITE, Stanley (1891–1979), taught landscape architecture at the University of Illinois from 1922 until his retirement in 1959. White's students include many of the most respected names in the field: Hideo Sasaki, Peter Walker, Phil Lewis, Charles Harris, and Stuart Dawson. His contributions to the profession and to education were tremendous. His younger brother (by eight years), E. B. White, wrote of Stanley: "He was a born teacher. He imparted information as casually as a tree drops its leaves in the fall. Hardly a day passes . . . without my [remembering] something I learned from Stan. He resembled Grandfather [William] Hart [Hudson River School painter], he liked to draw and paint." E. B. White, for years an editor of the *New Yorker* magazine, also wrote the children's stories *Charlotte's Web, Stuart Little,* and *The Trumpet and the Swan.*

Stanley White earned a B.S. in agriculture from Cornell and an M.L.A. from Harvard in 1915. From there he spent a year doing "trifles" for Fletcher Steele and John Nolen before working in the Olmsted Brothers' office in Brookline (1916–1920). While working with the Olmsteds, he also taught at the Lowthorpe School of Landscape Architecture, Gardening and Horticulture for Women at Groton, Massachusetts. During the Depression, White was a consultant for the design of the New Deal planned new town, Greendale, Wisconsin.

In the classroom, White was "unconventional, humorous and sometimes shocking." He once came to class playing his violin while roller skating around the room. His educational goals and philosophies are as relevant today as when he introduced them sixty years ago. He was instrumental in establishing the National Conference of Instruction in Landscape Architecture (NCILA, now CELA) and the Landscape Exchange Program in 1924. He wrote little and published nothing but left two important manuscripts in the University of Illinois archives: "Teaching Landscape Architecture" (1953) and "A Primer of Landscape Architecture" (1956). In his diary he recorded: "Landscape architecture [is] awfully hard to do well and very costly to be without." White's further thoughts included:

> Landscape character should be intensified, not obliterated; and the ultimate harmony should emerge as a blend in which the native quality of the region and the spot still prevail. . . . These "humanized" landscapes are to us the most inviting and beloved, and we are pleased and inspired largely insofar as the whole structure and sentiment of the landscape can be preserved. . . . There can be no deviation from the rule that the newly prepared landscape must be . . . a distillate or sublimation of the original myriad forms if it is to be a work of art in the sense of a high art form, timeless and historical.
>
> The ultimate principle of landscape architecture is merely the application and adjustment of one system to another, where contrasting subjects are brought into harmonious relationship resulting in a superior unity called "order."

White was always a performer. For many years he acted in performances of the University of Illinois Faculty Players Club and played piano, viola, and cello in the University orchestra.

WILLIS, Nathaniel Parker (1806–1867), was a poet, journalist, editor of the *New York Mirror,* and pioneer in the suburban movement. The term *suburb* was first used by Willis in the 1840s in connection with his planned utopian community on a rural site high above the Hudson River. From his home near Cornwall, called Idlewild, he frequently commuted to the city to confer with his fellow writers. The steamboat made such travel possible as far up the Hudson River as Newburgh, sixty miles from New York City. By the 1820s it was possible for people of the Hudson Valley to maintain a permanent residence in a rural setting and visit the city for their cultural life. "No place," wrote Willis, "can be rural . . . where a steamer will take the villager to the city between noon and night, and bring him back between midnight and morning . . . the [steamboat] has destroyed the distance between them and the city."

In 1851, Willis conceived the idea of developing a community of scholars, called Highland Terrace, to be located on a natural plateau 120 feet above the Hudson between Newburgh and Cornwall. The wooded 30-acre site was to accommodate two or three dozen families in private houses as a retreat for persons of "rural tastes and metropolitan refinements rationally blended . . . a mixture of city and country, with the home in the country." Although Highland Terrace was never to be built, within the next few years another romantic residential community was planned and partially actualized—Llewellyn Park, in West Orange, New Jersey.

Among Willis's neighborhood friends were William Cullen Bryant, Washington Irving, Alexander Jackson Davis, and Andrew Jackson Downing. They all admired country living and watery scenery. As Willis wrote, "It is in river scenery . . . that America excels all other lands: and here the artist's labour is not, as in Europe, to embellish and idealize the reality; he finds it difficult to come up to it."

Willis published a number of essays, short stories, and poems that were much admired by his friend and neighbor, Edgar Allen Poe. He is buried in Mount Auburn Cemetery.

WIRTH, Conrad Louis (1899–), landscape architect, who after twenty years with the National Park Service was made its director in 1951, a position he held until 1964. In 1923 he graduated with a B.S. in landscape architecture from the University of Massachusetts, where he studied under Frank A. Waugh. Following his graduation, Wirth worked in San Francisco for the firm of MacGrory and McLaren, Landscape Architects. McLaren was instrumental in the development of Golden Gate Park in the 1870s and 1880s. Wirth served with the National Capital Park and Planning Commission under Stephen T. Mather between 1828 and 1931, when he was named the assistant director of the National Park Service. In 1933 he was selected to head the Department of the Interior's Civilian Conservation Corps program, where he directed more than 600 CCC camps, developing federal, state, and municipal parks all over the nation. During World War II, Wirth carried out the first nationwide inventory of recreational resources in the United States.

Among his civic activities, he was chairman of the Committee for a More Beautiful National Capital, chairman of the National Park Service Senior Advisory Committee, commissioner of the Palisades Interstate Park Commission, executive director of the Hudson River Valley Commission, vice chairman of President Johnson's National Capital Park and Planning Commission, vice chairman of the New York Natural Heritage Trust, and member of the review commission for the Kingsmill Project at Williamsburg, Virginia.

He conceived and directed Mission-66, a ten-year (1956–1966) $1 billion program to upgrade the national parks to handle the private automobile. In 1980 he wrote his autobiography, *Parks, Politics and People*.

WISE, Henry (1653–1738), English nurseryman and landscape gardener, began a nursery in the city of London in 1681 in partnership with George London, making them the first commercial gardeners in England. They were very prolific and highly sought after in their day, due to their skill at replicating the French grand style. Several of their projects, such as Chatsworth and Hampton Court, were a remodeling of the earlier work by the Mollet brothers, pupils of André Le Nôtre, who had created many grand formal gardens in England during the previous generation. London and Wise introduced numerous new exotic plant species from North America into England. Among their most notable works were the formal gardens at Hampton Court (c. 1689) in London, Melbourne Hall (c. 1704) in Derbyshire, Chatsworth in Derbyshire (c. 1710), and Blenheim in Oxfordshire (1713). After London's death in 1713, Wise became the royal gardener to Queen Anne. Much of their work was transformed into the naturalistic landscape garden style by "Capability" Brown after 1750. Charles Bridgeman apprenticed with London and Wise before beginning his own practice as a landscape gardener in 1714.

WREN, Christopher (1632–1723), was an English architect, urban designer, and scientist whose most important buildings designs were St. Paul's Cathedral (1675–1711) and the Royal Naval Hospital in London (1699–1716). He designed many other noted structures in Britain. Following the great fire of London in 1666, Wren proposed a grand baroque-style plan for the rebuilding of the city, including the realignment of a majority of the former streets. His plan was not implemented, but it did influence a few of American colonial town plans, such as Annapolis, Maryland, and Williamsburg, Virginia. Wren was a follower of the styles developed by Palladio, Bernini, and the Englishman Inigo Jones. The House of Burgesses in Williamsburg is believed to have been designed by Wren, although he never visited the colonies and no solid documentation proves conclusively that it is his work.

WRIGHT, Frank Lloyd (1869–1959), American architect, was the pioneer of the "organic architecture" style during the early years of the twentieth century. He studied civil engineering at the University of Wisconsin and worked in the architectural office of Adler and Sullivan in Chicago from 1888 until 1893, when he began his own practice. Among his most important creations that reflect his site sensitivity were his own home and studio, Taliesin East, in Spring Green, Wisconsin (1911); the Imperial Hotel in Tokyo, Japan (1915), built to withstand earthquakes; Fallingwater in Bear Run, Pennsylvania (1936), of cantilevered concrete over a waterfall; and his "atelier," Taliesin West in Scottsdale, Arizona (1937). His conceptual plan for a model rural community, Broadacres, was one of his greatest comprehensive and visionary schemes. Among his many other built works were the Johnson Wax Headquarters in Racine, Wisconsin; the Guggenheim Museum in New York City; and the Robie House in Chicago.

Wright said, "The essence of organic building is space, space flowing outward, space flowing inward." He also said, "a building should be *of* the site not *on* the site—*married* to its site." He wrote *A Testament* (1957) and *The Living City* (1959).

WRIGHT, Henry (1878–1936), was a landscape architect and town planner who worked with the architect Clarence Stein on the planning and design of Radburn, New Jersey, America's first comprehensively planned "garden city" (1927–1929). Previous to that, in 1924, they had planned Sunnyside Gardens, a residential community on Long Island, New York for the City Housing Corporation. Radburn was developed on a 1300-acre site near Paterson, New Jersey, employing many of Sir Ebenezer Howard's new town planning standards. In the plan for Radburn, Stein and Wright also included provisions for the private automobile, a fact of life not known in Howard's day. The scheme was based on a number of "superblocks," each with its own neighborhood identity. Potential pedestrian and automobile conflicts were minimized through the use of numerous pedestrian underpasses and automobile courts, or "cul-de-sacs."

During the Depression, Stein and Wright planned Greenbrook, New Jersey, one of the four proposed "greenbelt" towns to be built under President Roosevelt's New Deal. It was not built due to local opposition, which tied the land up in the courts for years. Also during the Depression, the partners planned a small housing development, Chatham Village, in Pittsburgh (1930), but this was not built until 1932 from plans modified by Pittsburgh landscape architect Ralph E. Griswold. In 1926, Wright developed a state regional plan for New York State, but this was not adopted.

Wright was a prolific writer and had many articles published in *Architectural Record, American City, Survey,* and the *National Real Estate Journal.* In 1935 he wrote the book *Rehousing Urban America.*

YOCH, Florence (1890–1972), was a California landscape architect and movie set designer. She was one of the most respected and prolific designers on the west coast during the 1920s and 1930s, designing more than 250 gardens and the sets for five films. She was often fortunate enough to master plan her client's sites *before* the architects became involved, thereby predetermining the best placement of all the structures to be built. Her great skill and sensitivity to each site and its mature vegetation led her to be a leader in the moving of extremely large trees. She designed many private estates in Beverly Hills for such luminaries as David O. Selznick. Her most memorable movie sets were for *Gone with the Wind* and *The Good Earth.*

James J. Yoch recently wrote her biography, *Landscaping the American Dream: The Gardens and Film Sets of Florence Yoch, 1890–1972* (1989).

ZION, Robert (1921–), landscape architect, is a partner in the firm Zion and Breen, Associates, whose office is in Imlaystown, New Jersey. He is noted as the designer of the first "vest pocket park," Paley Park, in New York City (1966–1976). Many designers regard this diminutive (42- by 100-foot) vest pocket park as one of the most "humane" urban spaces created in the twentieth century. Zion calls it "a room, with walls, floors, and ceiling." It is extremely simple, yet highly satisfying as a quiet sitting space with its curtainlike "waterwall" masking out street noises, its movable chairs, and the lacy, overhead canopy of honey locusts. He began his practice in 1951, taking in Harold A. Breen as a partner in 1957. Some of the firm's other projects are the American Exhibition in Moscow (1959), the redeveloped plaza around the base of the Statue of Liberty (1986), the Cincinnati Riverfront redevelopment, and the Bamboo Court in the concourse of the IBM headquarters in New York City (1983).

Zion has served as a visiting critic in landscape architecture at Harvard, the University of Pennsylvania, and Pratt Institute. He wrote *Trees for Architecture and the Landscape* (1968), as well as numerous journal articles.

GLOSSARY

Glossary

The list of words or expressions defined here is only a small portion of the words used in the design arts fields. Although many of them seem elementary to the historian or the mature designer, the selection of terms included here was based on those words that may be unfamiliar to the novice or newcomer to the field. Those words within the definitions that are shown in full capital letters are defined elsewhere in the glossary.

ABACUS (AB-e-kes)–In architecture, the flat slab atop the CAPITAL of a COLUMN, supporting the ENTABLATURE or other superstructure.

ABBEY (AB-ee)–A religious institution under the directorship of an ABBOT; a convent or MONASTERY; the church of an abbey.

ABBOT (AB-ut)–The superior or head of a MONASTERY.

ABLUTION (a-BLOO-shun)–A religious ceremonial purification by cleansing in water or other liquid; the liquid used.

ABLUTION TANK–The container that holds the cleansing liquid; may be a small or a large pool.

ABSTRACT–A work of art which in its use of lines, forms, and colors does not represent objects in nature. Expression of ideas or subject matter by means of stylized forms or geometric forms.

ABUTMENT (a-BUTT-ment) – Solid masonry that is placed so as to resist the lateral pressure (thrust) of an ARCH or VAULT; part of a building or bridge that acts as a BUTTRESS.

ACACIA (a-CAY-shuh)–1. A Tree or shrub of the *Mimosaceous* genus, native to warm geographical regions; a favorite vegetative form in much artwork in the Middle East. 2. Gum arabic.

ACADEMY–A place of study, derived from the name of the grove where Plato held his seminars on philosophy. Giorgio Vasari founded the first academy of fine arts, the Accademia di Disegno in Florence in 1563. The American Academy in Rome was founded in 1897.

ACANTHUS (a-CAN-thus)–*Acanthus mollis* a plant with large toothed, scalloped leaves. These forms were often stylized into CORINTHIAN capitals and other ornamental architectural moldings, BRACKETS and FRIEZES.

ACCRETION (a-KRE-shen)–An increase in size or extent by natural growth or by gradual external addition.

ACID RAIN–Toxic rain caused by air pollution, resulting in damage to water quality in lakes and soil in the eastern United States since the mid-1970s.

ACID SOIL–A soil with an acidic reaction in the soil HORIZONS into which roots penetrate. A soil with pH values less than 6.6. Soils with pH values between 6.6 and 7.3 are considered neutral. Soils with values above 7.3 are alkaline. Acid soils occur in areas with high rainfall, high humus content, and with very little lime being present. *See also* ALKALINE.

ACRE–The unit of land area measurement used in the United States. One square acre measures 208.71 feet by 208.71 feet, or 43,560 square feet (4840 square yards; 0.4047 HECTARE). One square mile is composed of 640 acres or 259.0 hectares.

ACROPOLIS (a-CROP-o-lis) – From the Greek, meaning "high city." Most ancient Greek cities were on hills, the CITADEL on the summit, being known as the Acropolis, containing the principal temples of the patron deity and treasure houses. In Athens, Greece, it is the location of the most famous of all temples, the Parthenon.

A.D.–Abbreviation of the Latin *anno Domini.* Since Christ was born; "in the year of our Lord."

ADOBE (a-DOE-bay)–The Spanish name for sun-dried (unbaked) brick. Adobe brick is made from soil materials, including some clay and a considerable amount of sand. This material is often used as the core of a wall behind a facing of stone or bricks; also called mud brick, rammed earth, PISÉ, and cemadobe (a portland cement–earth mixture).

ADONIS (a-DON-is) – Greek mythological character; a young male favorite of the goddess Aphrodite; slain in his youth by a wild boar. Believing that he spent half of each year on earth, the Greeks associated him with the vegetation cycle.

ADONIS GARDEN (a-DON-is) – In ANCIENT Greek times young children and women propagated herbs or flowers in pots placed on rooftops, windowsills, or balconies. These quick-growing plants symbolized the young god, ADONIS, whose short life was compared to the brief seasonal cycle of ANNUAL plants. The Adonis garden is the basis of the courtyard gardens of the Mediterranean area with their plants in pots.

AERIAL PERSPECTIVE–The technique, or compositional approach, taken to its greatest point of perfection by the Dutch LANDSCAPISTS. Its aim is to express the "expansion of the sky at the expense of land and water; the rendering of a selective view, of the sort that a window might afford; and the creation of distance by consistent application of atmospheric depth."

AEROBIC (air-O-bik)–A name applied to organisms, particularly bacteria, requiring free oxygen for their life processes.

AESTHETIC–Pertains to beauty; artistic or tasteful; also spelled *esthetic.*

AESTHETICS–A branch of philosophy dealing with beauty and the beautiful, especially with judgments of taste concerning art, nature, places, or things; relating to the beautiful as distinguished from the merely pleasing or utilitarian; that which is pleasing to the senses such as a well-designed park, recreation structure, or natural creation.

AFFORESTATION–The process of converting into a forest an area that has not been forested in recent times. The process of replacing or continuing a forest is called reforestation.

AGGER (AG-er)–Latin term for the built-up foundations of Roman roads.

AGGREGATE (AG-ri-get)–Any hard material such as sand, gravel, or crushed stone that is added to cement to form concrete.

AGORA (A-gor-a)–The open space in a Greek town used as a marketplace or open-air assembly, usually surrounded by PORTICOS, as in a FORUM.

AGRARIAN (a-GRAR-i-en)–Referring to rural, especially to agricultural land, lifestyle, economy, and so on.

AL FRESCO (AL FRES-co)–In the open air; out of doors. The ancients frequently entertained and dined al fresco; Italian for "in the fresh air."

ALABASTER (AL-a-BAST-er)–A variety of fine-grained translucent gypsum or calcite, usually white but also red, yellow, gray, and sometimes banded. It was used to a small extent as a building material in the ancient Middle East, Greece, Rome, and, in the nineteenth century, by certain Victorian architects for its decorative qualities (and Biblical associations). In Italy, a technique was evolved many centuries ago of treating alabaster to simulate marble.

ALBEDO (al-BEE-do)–The degree to which a surface reflects the solar radiation that strikes it; usually expressed as a ratio of reflected light to the total falling on that surface.

ALCAZAR (al-KA-thar)–A palace of the Spanish Moorish kings. Today a palace or castle for Spanish royalty. From the Arabic *al qasr,* meaning "fortress" or "CASTLE."

ALKALINE (ALL-ka-line)–A substance such as SOIL which has a saturation pH reading of greater than 7.0. Such soils occur in ARID areas and usually lack HUMUS; also called BASIC SOIL. *See also* ACID SOIL.

ALLÉE (al-LAY)–French term for ALLEY. A narrow passageway between walls, high fences, or tall, closely set vegetation. Since the term "alley" invokes a picture of dirt, squalor, and slums, it has become customary for garden designers to spell the word *allée* or *allee* when applying it to a narrow-way in a garden. Landscape architects define an open allée as "a narrow way framed by closely planted trees or shrubs of a height at least twice the width of the way." A PLEACHED ALLÉE is arched over by interlaced branches of clipped trees. In England, such a feature in the garden is called an *alley.*

ALLEY–In England, a narrow passageway between walls, high fences, or tall, closely set vegetation. Often called ALLÉE or allee.

ALLUVIAL DEPOSIT (al-U-vi-al)–A deposit of rock, gravel, and sand particles that have been transported and laid down by a flowing body of water.

ALPINE–The tier or zone in a mountain system that lies above the timberline, especially where the line is determined by cold and not drought. The Alps and Pyrenees have an alpine zone.

ALTAR (ALT-er)–An elevated place or structure, in a place of worship, where religious rites are performed, such as preaching or sacrificial offerings.

ALTITUDE–The height of the sun in the sky.

AMBIENT (AM-byent)–Surrounding environmental conditions such as ambient air pollution or ambient sounds.

AMBULATORY (AM-bu-la-TOR-y)–From the Latin word "to walk." A covered walkway or aisle outdoors, as in a CLOISTER, or indoors, especially the passageway around the APSE and CHOIR of a church.

AMENITY (a-MEN-i-tee)–An attractive or desirable feature of a locale such as a pleasant view or climate.

AMERICAN ACADEMY IN ROME–Established in 1894 as a counterpart of the ÉCOLE DES BEAUX-ARTS in Paris and the French Academy in Rome, this institution was founded by the architect Charles McKim, who believed that the Eternal City was the source of the greatest arts and architecture and therefore the best place to study the great works of the classical past. Landscape architecture was made one of the allied arts in 1915 through the efforts of expatiate Italian, Ferruccio Vitale, of New York City.

AMORPHOUS (a-MOR-fus)–Having no definite form or shape; formless.

AMPHITHEATER (AM-fi-theater)–An elliptical or circular space surrounded by rising tiers of seats, as used by the Romans for gladiatorial contests (e.g., the COLOSSEUM in Rome). It was first made by the Greeks as settings for their dramas.

ANAEROBIC (an-a-RO-bik)–Organisms that are able to live and grow in environments where there is no air or free oxygen.

ANCIENT–Of the time prior to the fall of the Western Roman Empire (c. A.D. 476).

ANGLE OF REPOSE–The steepest or maximum angle at which loose material on a slope will retain its position and not slide.

ANIMISM (AN-i-mizm)–The belief that all natural objects, animate or inanimate, as well as the universe itself, possess a soul.

ANNUAL–A plant whose life cycle is of one season in duration from seed to maturity. Annual plants used in gardens or as crops must be replanted each year, although certain annuals reseed themselves. Many of the most desirable and colorful garden flowers are annuals. *See also* BIENNIAL and PERENNIAL.

ANNUNCIATION–The announcement by the angel Gabriel to the Virgin Mary of the incarnation of Jesus Christ. This event is often depicted in art as Gabriel announcing the news to Mary while a white dove appears, to symbolize the Holy Ghost.

ANTE-BELLUM (AN-te-BELL-um)–Before the Civil War; referring to an American architectural style popular in the American south 1840–1860.

ANTHEMION (an-THEE-me-un)–A Greek name for a honeysuckle-like flower that was stylized into an ornament for Greek architecture, vases, and so on.

ANTHROPOCENTRIC (an-THROW-po-CEN-trik)–A philosophical concept that conceives of everything in the universe in terms of human values.

ANTHROPOLOGIC (an-THROW-po-LOG-ic)–Of, or relating to, the science of man.

ANTHROPOMORPHIC (an-throw-poh-MOR-fik)–Attributing human form or characteristics to inanimate objects, animals, or to a god.

ANTHROPOMORPHISM (an-THROW-po-MORPH-ism)–The act of attributing human form or characteristics to a god, animal, or other inanimate object.

ANTIQUITY (an-TIK-witty)–1. The quality of being ANCIENT; great age. 2. ANCIENT times; the time before the MIDDLE AGES.

APOLLO (a-PAUL-o)–A deity in the Greek and Roman family of gods and goddesses. The god of light, healing, music, poetry, prophecy, and young masculine beauty.

APPIAN WAY (AP-ee-en)–The ANCIENT Roman road from Rome to today's Brindisi (350 miles); 312 B.C. by Appius Claudius Caecus.

APPRECIATION–In real estate, the increase in the value of property flowing from general economic conditions as distinguished from increment due to physical improvements or added investment.

APPURTENANCE (a-PUR-ti-nens)–An apparatus or mechanism as a part of a network or system such as a manhole as part of a storm drainage system.

APSE (APS)–The circular or multiangular recess or termination of a church sanctuary, first applied to a Roman BASILICA. The apse is a continental feature and contrasts with the square termination of English Gothic churches. Usually the east end of a chapel or CHANCEL.

AQUA (AH-kwa)–Latin word for "water."

AQUEDUCT–Any human-made channel for carrying water by means of gravity from a distant source to a designated destination; also refers to an engineered structure that supports the channel over a valley or river.

AQUIFER (AHK-wi-fer)–Any underground geologic formation or structure of earth, gravel, or stone containing water, especially one that transmits water in sufficient quantities to supply pumping wells or springs. The terms *water-bearing bed, water-bearing stratum,* and *water-bearing deposit* are used synonymously with *aquifer.*

ARABESQUE (ayr-a-BESK)–French and English word for "in the Arab manner"; from Moorish and Persian designs, elaborate surface decoration of intertwined FOLIAGE, floral and GEOMETRICAL patterns, painted or carved in low RELIEF.

ARABLE (AIR-abl)–Land that is suitable for plowing or the production of crops.

ARBOR (AR-bor)–Literally, a place shaded by trees or shrubs, although commonly considered as an open structure, usually consisting of a horizontal framework or a lattice work supported by columns on which vines or other plants are trained. A PERGOLA or a leafy BOWER.

ARBOREAL (ar-BOR-e-al)–Pertaining to trees, or living in or upon trees.

ARBORETUM (ar-BOR-EE-tum)–A plot of land where trees or shrubs are grown for scientific or educational study either individually or in groupings.

ARCADE (ar-KADE)–A line of ARCHES resting on PIERS or COLUMNS. *See also* COLONNADE and PERISTYLE.

ARCADIAN (ar-KAY-dee-un)–PASTORAL, BUCOLIC, rural, rustic; simple or innocent. Often used in reference to the English school of landscape designers of the eighteenth century and the American movement of the nineteenth century.

ARCH–A structural device, semicircular or pointed in shape, formed of separate truncated wedge-shaped blocks to span an opening.

ARCHAIC (ar-KAY-ik)–Antiquated, old-fashioned, ANCIENT.

ARCHETYPE (AR-ke-tipe)–The original model or design from which all other things of the same kind are made; a perfect example; prototype.

ARCHIMEDEAN SCREW (AR-ke-MEE-de-un)–Named for the Greek mathematician Archimedes (c. 287–212 B.C.), a device comprised of a spiral, or screw, which turned inside an inclined closed cylinder, for raising water to a height. Such implements were used by the ANCIENT Egyptians for pumping water from the Nile into their vast system of irrigation canals. *See also* SPIRAL PUMP.

ARCHIPELAGO (ar-ke-PEL-a-go)–An island grouping or chain of islands in a large body of water.

ARCHITECTURE–Frank Lloyd Wright said "Architecture is the science of structure." Architecture is concerned with structures that enclose space for the purpose of providing a controllable climatic environment (shelter) for human activities. Architecture is also concerned with the aesthetic environment for other structures. Structures that do not enclose human-use space, such as dams and bridges, are the province of engineering. Landscape architecture is concerned with the utilization and aesthetics of all exterior space.

ARCHITRAVE (AR-ke-TRAVE)–A Greek term meaning "chief beam." The beam or lowest division of the ENTABLATURE, which extends from column to column. The term is also applied to the molded frame around a door or window.

ARCHIVES (AR-kives)–A storage place for public records or historical documents. The records or documents themselves.

ARENA–The central open space of an AMPHITHEATER; also, more loosely, any building for public contests or displays in the open air; from the Latin word for "sand."

ARES (AIR-eez)–The Greek god of war; called Mars by the Romans.

ARID–Lacking in moisture; dry; parched by heat. *See also* XERIC.

ARISTOCRACY–1. A state ruled by an upper class of nobles or elite. 2. A class standing that is socially superior.

ART NOUVEAU (noo-VO)–French term for "new art." A decorative art movement in European architecture beginning in the 1880s and reaching its peak 1893–1907, characterized by flowing and sinuous naturalistic ornament and avoidance of traditional architectural MOTIFS.

ARTICULATION–The clear definition of an idea or design MOTIF.

ARTIFACT–An object made by human craftsmanship.

ARTIFICE (ART-i-fiss)–1. An ingenious, inventive, expedient, clever, artful, sly, or tricky piece of craftsmanship or construction. 2. A person who is a master of a trade, craft, or art form who is skilled and innovative.

ASCETIC (a-SET-ik)–A person who lives a life of austerity; strict adherence to abstinence; a monk or hermit.

ASEXUAL (AY-SEX-yu-ul)–Independent of sexual processes such as in reproducing plants by CUTTINGS or grafting rather than from seeds.

ASHLAR (ASH-lur)–Cut blocks of stone or masonry that have even surfaces and square edges and are laid in horizontal courses with vertical joints.

ASPECT–1. Appearance to the mind or eye; the way in which a thing may be viewed; a view commanded. *See also* PROSPECT. 2. Exposure, or the side or face, of an object oriented to a given direction. "The building has an eastern aspect." *See also* ORIENTATION.

ASPHALT (AS-falt)–A dark-colored solid bituminous substance composed chiefly of blends of hydrocarbons, often mixed with an AGGREGATE, for paving. Also called "blacktop" or "bitumen" (in England). *See also* MACADAM.

ASSOCIATION–A term used by ecologists to indicate stabilized groups or communities of organisms that share an area and an essentially common environment.

ASSOCIATIONISM–A late-nineteenth-century philosophy whose followers believed that humankind is in a constant state of "yearning for the lost garden," Eden. They regarded gardening "as being, next to religion, the great humanizer of the age." When one perceived beauty in natural scenery, it was because of its association with other pleasurable experiences from one's life. A variation on associationism was formulated by Emanuel Swedenborg, an eighteenth-century Swedish scientist and mystic, who believed in a "great chain of being" or "grand harmonic system" composed of three corresponding states, the material, the spiritual, and the divine. Americans who followed this thinking were Ralph Waldo Emerson, Washington Irving, William Cullen Bryant, Andrew Jackson Downing, and the architect Alexander Jackson Davis.

ASYMMETRY–Without bilateral symmetry. This term applies to anything that has no point, line, or plane about which parts are arranged in a regular or geometrical fashion. Asymmetry in a landscape or an artistic design does not imply a lack of balance among the parts of the composition. An asymmetrical composition may possess OCCULT BALANCE.

ATELIER (AT-el-yay)–The studio or workshop of an artist or designer. This term came into popular use in Europe and America during the glory days of the ÉCOLE DES BEAUX-ARTS, in Paris, during the late nineteenth century.

ATHENA (a-THEE-na)–A Greek goddess, patron of the city of Athens, Greece, associated with wisdom, arts, industry, and prudent warfare. The Roman counterpart was Minerva.

ATLANTES (at-LAN-teez)–Carved male figures that functioned as PILLARS or COLUMNS; also called telamones.

ATMOSPHERIC PERSPECTIVE–A scene, whether real, photographic, or painted, that possesses an exaggerated effect of great distance because of the atmospheric conditions such as haze or mist.

ATRIUM (AY-tree-um)–A portion of a Greek or Roman house forming an enclosed entry hall or small court or courtyard with the roof opening to the sky in the center. Also in early Christian BASILICAS or churches, the open COLONNADED forecourt, often CLOISTERED. Plural, *atria*.

AUTOMATA (aw-to-MAH-tah)–Water jokes or surprise amusement features in a garden that are operated by hydraulic pressure; GIOCHI D'ACQUA or BURLADORES. Such devices were in use in the Roman times. Villa D'Este and Villa Lante have especially fine examples.

AVENUE–A broad roadway usually bordered by trees and terminating at a prominent structure such as an estate or civic building.

AXIAL PLANNING–The placing of several elements along a single centerline or at cross AXES to a main AXIS.

AXIS–A real or imaginary straight line on which an object rotates or is perceived to balance; a centerline along which the parts of an object are SYMMETRICALLY balanced. Plural, *axes*.

AXONOMETRIC PROJECTION (AX-on-o-ME-tric)–A three-dimensional-looking aerial view, or "bird's-eye" drawing, which is constructed from a scaled plan with structures and other site features projected vertically at a true scale. Since in a PERSPECTIVE picture, all forms diminish in size as they recede into the distance, an axonometric drawing is not a perspective and therefore tends to appear somewhat unreal and distorted.

AZIMUTH (AZ-i-muth)–A horizontal angle measured clockwise between a true north-south line and a line to an observed or designated point.

AZULEJOS (a-zu-LAY-hos)–Glazed pottery tiles usually painted in bright colors with floral and other patterns, much used on the interior and exterior of Spanish and Portuguese buildings.

BABYLON (BAB-i-lon)–An ANCIENT city in the Middle East on the Euphrates River, 50 miles from today's Baghdad, Iraq. Famed for its culture and magnificence, it was the capital of the Old Babylonian Empire, c. 2800–1600 B.C. Nebuchadnezzar II later ruled the New Babylonian Empire, 612–539 B.C., between 604 and 562 B.C., when he built the city into its greatest glory, including the Hanging Gardens.

BAGH (BAHG)–Persian word for GARDEN, especially one that is QUADRIPARTITE or subdivided into four quadrants by water channels crossing at its center. Baghdad, the capital of Iraq, gets its name from the same, hence "Garden City."

BAILEY–An exterior wall around an open area or enclosed courtyard of a fortified CASTLE during the MIDDLE AGES. *See also* MOTTE.

BALLOON FRAME–A method of light timber framing originated in the United States for domestic buildings. The corner posts and studs are continuous from sill to roof plate. The JOISTS are carried on girts or ties that are spiked to the studs and all these elements are secured by simple nailing.

BALUSTER (BAL-u-ster)–A rectangular or cylindrical vertical post, COLUMN, or PILLAR which supports a handrail or COPING. A continuous line or series of balusters forms a BALUSTRADE; also *bannister*.

BALUSTRADE (BAL-us-TRADE)–A series of BALUSTERS, bannisters, or small pillars that support a handrail or stair rail.

BAPTISTRY (BAP-tis-tree)–A building adjacent to, but usually separate from, a church in which is contained the baptismal FONT or tank, where baptismal rites or ceremonies are conducted; also *baptistery*.

BARBARIAN (bar-BAIR-ee-un)–Originally, the Greek for non-Greek or foreigner; an uncivilized person; rude; savage; primitive. The nomadic tribes of northern Europe, the GOTHS, VISIGOTHS, VANDALS, and so on, were considered barbarian by the peoples of the Roman Empire.

BARCO (BAR-ko)–Italian for an enclosed parcel of land used for hunting.

BARGE BOARD–A carved wooden member affixed to a roof to conceal the ends of the rafters.

BAROQUE (be-ROKE)–A style of art and architecture characterized by extensive or extravagant ornamentation, curved rather than straight lines, and CLASSICAL forms of the High RENAISSANCE; of the period, 1575–1750, in which these styles flourished.

BARREL VAULT–A continuous VAULT that is semicircular in section used during most periods and in many countries from Roman times to the present; also called a *tunnel vault*.

BASIC SOIL–A SOIL with an ALKALINE reaction in the soil HORIZONS into which roots penetrate. A soil with pH values greater than 7.3. Soils with pH values between 6.6 and 7.3 are considered neutral. Soils with values above 7.3 are ALKALINE or basic. Basic soils occur in areas with low rainfall, low humus content, and where lime is present.

BASILICA (ba-SILL-ica)–From the Greek word *basileus* for "a king." 1. A large public hall in Roman times for use as a hall of justice. 2. In early Christian architecture, a church with a NAVE and aisles and with CLERESTORY windows in the nave above the aisle roofs.

BAS-RELIEF (BAH ree-LEEF)–From the Italian basso rilievo meaning low relief; sculpture or carving of shallow depth usually on a flat or curved surface of stone; figures project only minimally from the MONOLITHIC background stone.

BASTIDE (bah-STEED)–A small fortified town laid out during the MIDDLE AGES on a GRIDIRON plan by the English in the parts of France which they occupied.

BASTION (BAHS-chun)–One of a series of projections from the main CURTAIN WALL of a fortress placed at intervals in such a manner as to enable the garrison to fire upon the adjoining sections of wall.

BATTER–A term applied to a wall with a slight inward slope to its face.

BATTERING RAM–An ANCIENT or MEDIEVAL device for military usage with a heavy horizontal BEAM for smashing through walls, gates, or doors; used to supplement the CATAPULT. Large models required as many as 100 soldiers to initiate the ram's swinging motion.

BATTLEMENT–As part of a fortress or fortified town wall; a PARAPET wall with a continuous series of indentations or openings between which are higher sections called MERLONS. The openings, called CRENELS, provided shooting positions for defenders.

BAUHAUS (BOW-house)–The common name of *Das Staaliche Bauhaus Weimar,* the school of design founded in Dessau, Germany, in the Wiemar Republic, in 1918 by the architect Walter Gropius (1883–1970) to teach experimental functional design (industrial and graphic, painting, sculpture, photography, and architecture) based on modern science, technology, and materials. Here the principle "form follows function" prevailed in all fields. This led to the INTERNATIONAL STYLE of architecture. Other teachers there were Ludwig Mies van der Rohe, Lazslo Moholy-Nagy, Josef Albers, Adolf Meyer, Paul Klee, Herbert Meyer, and Wassily Kandinsky. With the rise of the Nazis in the 1930s, the teachers fled to other countries, primarily the United States.

BAY–A compartment of a large building; in churches, the space between one COLUMN or PIER and the next, including the wall and the VAULT or ceiling over it. By extension, any unit of a wall surface divided by large vertical features or on exteriors by windows. Also the angular or curved outward projection of an interior room beyond the face of an exterior wall, usually *bay windows.*

B.C.–Before Christ.

BEAM–The structural members in a building or other structure that span horizontally and support a roof, floor, or deck. A simple beam is supported on each end; a CANTILEVERED beam projects beyond its supports; a continuous beam rests on three or more supports.

BEAUTIFUL–That which has qualities that give pleasure to the eye, ear, or mind. The term had special meaning for English ROMANTICISM as a visual and intellectual concept related to the SUBLIME and PICTURESQUE.

BEAUX ARTS (BOZE ahr)–French for the fine arts; associated with design that is formal, axial. The ÉCOLE DES BEAUX-ARTS in Paris was the oldest and most celebrated center of architectural education in the world.

BED–An area of ground in a garden in which plants are grown. *See also* CARPET BEDDING.

BEDROCK–The term for the solid rock lying below the soil and loose material; sometimes refers to rock OUTCROPS that have become exposed by soil erosion.

BEDDING PLANTS–Flowering or foliage plants planted in patterned BEDS for their temporary seasonal effect. They are a remnant of the parterre and formal gardens of the seventeenth to nineteenth centuries. Today, bedding plants are more often used in public grounds and parks than in private gardens. Many typical bedding plants may be incorporated into informal PERENNIAL and shrub borders. ANNUALS and subtropical plants are frequently employed for bedding plants. Started in greenhouses, hotbeds, or cold frames, they are then planted out in the garden just prior to blooming and removed and replaced as soon as their season is over.

BEESTE–In TUDOR England, 1485–1603, a figure, often in the form of a HERALDIC beast, of carved wood, stone, or lead, placed atop a post in the garden; used as an accent or focal point; often painted with bright colors.

BELVEDERE (BELL-ve-DARE-ay)–Italian word for beautiful view. A roofed but open-sided porch or turret structure affording an extensive view; usually located at the rooftop of a dwelling but sometimes an independent tower on an eminence in a landscape or formal garden.

BEMA (BEE-ma)–Greek for a raised platform; speaker's platform in the Greek AGORA or Roman FORUM. A raised stage reserved for the clergy in early Christian churches.

BENCHMARK–A point of known location and elevation above a DATUM; used as a point of reference in determining the geographical position and elevation of other points; sometimes referenced to sea level. It is usually marked by very durable materials, such as a brass plate embedded into a large rock.

BENEDICTINE – A French MONASTIC ORDER based on the teaching of Saint Benedict, beginning in A.D. 529.

BERM–A horizontal mound of earth; an embankment. In highway or landscape construction, this term is applied to the ridge of earth at the top of a slope to divert the flow of surface runoff water and prevent erosion of the slope.

BIANNUAL–Occurring twice each year; distinguished from BIENNIAL, which designates anything that occurs once in two years.

BIAXIAL (bi-AX-ee-al)–Possessing two AXES. *See also* QUADRILATERAL SYMMETRY.

BIAXIALLY (by-AXY-elly)–The adverb of BIAXIAL.

BID–v., To submit a price or fee as terms in a competition to secure a contract; n., the actual document that sets forth the price or fee.

BIENNIAL (BI-EN-ee-el)–A plant whose life cycle is of two seasons. There are a number of excellent flowering plants among the biennials. However, they are used rather sparingly by landscape architects because they are usually at their best only for the second season.

BIJOU (BEE-zhoo)–A jewel; something small and pretty; an exquisite trinket.

BILATERAL (bi-LAT-er-al)–Two-sided or arranged on opposite sides of an AXIS; SYMMETRICAL; adv., bilaterally symmetrical.

BIOMORPHIC (bi-o-MORF-ik)–Literally from nature; ORGANIC form.

BIOSPHERE–That part of the earth's crust and surrounding air layer that is inhabited by living beings.

BIOTA (bi-O-ta)–The vegetative and animal life of a given region or time period.

BIRD'S EYE–Colloquialism for a picture or view, the vantage point of which is from above the ground level; "bird's-eye view of the city."

BISYMMETRICAL–Having two symmetrical planes at right angles to one another; distinguished from BILATERALLY symmetrical, wherein the two parts are opposite one another along a central AXIS.

BLACK DEATH–The epidemic of bubonic plague that occurred in Europe in the fourteenth century.

BLIGHT–1. A cause of decay or decline. 2. A destructive disease in plants such as chestnut blight.

BOLE–1. A tree trunk. 2. A type of easily pulverized reddish clay.

BOLLARD (BOL-erd)–1. A nautical post to which mooring ropes are fastened. 2. Any short vertical post of stone, metal, or wood used to inhibit vehicular passage while allowing free movement by pedestrians.

BOND–The pattern in which bricks are laid for the sake of solidity and design. Four basic bonds used in the United States are: English, rows of ends or headers alternate with rows of sides or stretchers; Flemish, headers and stretchers alternate in each course with the center of each header over the center of the stretcher below; American, rows of four or five stretchers between a row of headers; and common, American bond without a course of headers.

BOREAL (BOR-ee-al)–1. Northern. 2. Boreal forest—A northern forest characterized by a predominance of CONIFEROUS trees.

BORROW–Earth material obtained from a borrow pit; used in earthwork operations; also FILL material.

BORROWED SCENERY–The appropriation, or taking advantage, of desirable views or scenery that are visible from one's own property but are, in fact, outside one's ownership. Thus they are borrowed for the pleasure of the viewers in a specific place; OFFSCAPE. *See also* SHAKKAI.

BOSCO (BOS-ko)–Italian for grove of trees; thicket. A boschetto is a small grove.

BOSKET (BOS-kit)–In England, a grove of trees; a thicket that furnishes a shaded place away from the formal geometric portion of a garden. Also, *bosquet* (French), *bosque* (Spanish), or *bosco* (Italian). The French counterpart was more ordered, with geometric paths and clearings, or CABINET de verdure. *See also* COPSE.

BOSQUET (bos-KAY)–French for grove of trees; thicket.

BOTANIC GARDEN–A public or private garden devoted to the CULTIVATION of plants for scientific or educational purposes. Botanic gardens are distinguished from other gardens by the practice of arranging plants by some scheme that is helpful to the student of botany or horticulture and by complete and accurate labeling of all plant specimens.

BOTTEGA (boh-TAY-ga)–A studio or workshop in which the master worked with the help of assistants and apprentices who he trained in their craft and provided with food and lodging.

BOTTEGA SYSTEM–During the RENAISSANCE, the Italian system of apprenticeship for the crafts. It was an all-round fine-arts training.

BOULEUTERION (BOO-leuw-TER-yon)–Greek senate building or council house.

BOULEVARD–A French term originally applied to the broad way or parade within the RAMPART of a fortified town. When these were demolished in the nineteenth century, they were often replaced by wide streets, hence its present meaning; now applied to any broad way or thoroughfare, particularly if it is bordered by important structures. In the United States, any thoroughfare larger than a lane may be called a boulevard.

BOWER–A leafy shelter; an ARBOR.

BOWLING GREEN–A game area of finely maintained, nearly level turf devoted to the sport of bowls or lawn bowling "on the green."

BOX–A broadleaf evergreen SHRUB or small tree of the *Buxus* genus; used for ornamental borders and hedges; frequently clipped into geometric or sculptured forms; also *boxwood,* which more accurately refers to the wood from the *Buxus* plant.

BRACKET–An architectural member of wood or stone that projects beyond a wall to support a weight such as a roof or balcony; generally formed of scrolls or VOLUTES; when supporting the upper portion of a CORNICE, brackets are called consoles; also BRACKETING.

BRICK–Regularly shaped block of hardened or baked clay. Glazed—brick with a polished, glassy surface, as distinct from a matt or rough surface. Mud—brick molded by hand and hardened without artificial heat, usually bound with straw or hair (e.g., ancient Mexico); also called ADOBE. Vitrified—brick burned to a hard glossy consistency; water and dampproof.

BRISE-SOLEIL (BREE-so-LAY)–French term for a screen, baffle, or louvres to block the direct rays of the sun against the windows of a building.

BRODERIE PAR TERRE (brow-DREE pahr TAIR)–French expression for embroidery on the ground; decorative arrangement of ornamental flower BEDS with intervals of gravel or turf. Also expressed as parterre de broderie. *See also* PARTERRE.

BROKEN PEDIMENT–A PEDIMENT in which one or both of the CORNICES are not continuous; much used in BAROQUE architecture.

BROWNSTONE–Reddish-brown sandstone found primarily in New Jersey, Connecticut, and Pennsylvania; a popular building material in the nineteenth century in New York City and the eastern United States; also refers to the buildings themselves when constructed of the brownstone.

BROWSE LINE or BROWSING LINE–A horizontally nibbled line beneath the canopy of certain trees whose foliage serves as browse or grazing matter for cattle, deer, or other animals. The browse line indicates the uppermost point on the tree that can be reached by the grazing animals; often a very distinctive landscape feature in the eighteenth-century English landscape.

BUCOLIC (byoo-KAH-lik)–1. A PASTORAL poem. 2. Relating to shepherds or herdsmen; typical of rural life.

BUFFER STRIP–In ecological terms, an area that functions as a transition zone or ECOTONE between two communities of organisms; also used in city planning or design for a transition area between two land uses. Thus a park or parkway may serve as a buffer strip between an industrial zone and a residential district.

BUFFER ZONE–A transition area between two land uses or zones.

BURLADORES (boor-la-DOR-ace)–The Spanish counterpart of "water jokes," or the Italian GIOCHI D'ACQUA; literally, "practical jokers." Originated by the MOORS in Spain, such features were humorous surprise sprays of water concealed in the garden and intended to sprinkle unsuspecting visitors, catching them offguard.

BUTTRESS–A mass of masonry constructed to project from an architectural wall to counterbalance the lateral pressure of an ARCH or VAULT. *Flying buttress:* An arching extension from a detached PIER or foundation abutting against a wall to receive the THRUST of the vaulting.

BYZANTINE (BIZ-en-teen)–Pertaining to the design style originating in Byzantium, the Eastern Roman Empire ruled from Constantinople, now Istanbul, Turkey, following the fall of the Roman Empire in A.D. 476 until A.D. 1453, when the city was captured by the OTTOMAN TURKS. The style, evolved at Constantinople, included architectural forms such as the OGEE ARCH and DOME, colorful MOSAICS, and rich use of light and decorations. Still the style of the Eastern or Greek Orthodox Church.

CABINET (ka-been-AY)–French term for a clearing in a grove of trees in a formal garden; serves as an outdoor amusement area. Sometimes, *cabinet de verdure* (vayr-DUR). *See also* COMPARTMENT.

CAESAR (SEE-zer)–1. Gaius Julius, 100–44 B.C., Roman general and statesman known as Julius Caesar. 2. A title for Roman emperors from Augustus to Hadrian, 27 B.C.–A.D. 138; same as *czar* or *kaiser*.

CAIRN or KAIRN (KAYRN)–A pile of stones created as a landmark or memorial in ancient Britain.

CALDARIUM (KAL-i-DAR-ium)–In a Roman public bath, the hot-water room; distinguished from the TEPIDARIUM (moderately warm) and the FRIGIDARIUM (cool room).

CALIPER (KAL-i-per)–1. A tool used for measuring inside and outside dimensions of such forms as cylinders. 2. The term used for the measurement of the trunk diameter of trees.

CALIPH (KAY-lif)–The head of a MOSLEM state.

CAMERA LUCIDA (LOO-si-duh)–The camera lucida, as contrasted with the camera obscura, literally means light chamber. It is an instrument used during the late eighteenth and nineteenth centuries to assist the artist in drawing from life. The rays of light from an object are reflected by a prism producing an image on the paper placed beneath the instrument. At the same time, the eye can see directly the pencil with which the image is being traced.

CAMERA OBSCURA (ob-SKOOR-uh)–Literally, dark chamber; an instrument consisting of a darkened chamber or box into which light is admitted through a double convex lens forming an image of external objects on the surface of paper, glass, and so on, placed at the focus of the lens. Its other, more relevant meaning is a dark chamber or room. Alexander Pope's letter of 1725 states, "When you shut the doors of this grotto, it becomes on the instant, from a luminous room, a Camera obscura." (OED, vol. 2, p. 806).

CAMPAGNA (kahm-PAN-ya)–Italian for a flat open plain; the countryside; same as CAMPO or French CHAMPAIGN.

CAMPANILE (kamp-an-EEL-ay)–From the Italian word *campana* for "bell"; Italian for a bell tower, which is usually detached from the main building or church.

CAMPO (KAHM-po)–Italian or Spanish for an extensive flat grassy plain. *See also* CAMPAGNA, CAMPUS, and CHAMPAIGN.

CAMPUS–Latin for a field used for military drill; today used to mean the grounds of school, college, public building, or lately, the grounds of an industrial park.

CANOPY–1. Utilitarian or decorative covering over a small open structure such as a tomb or NICHE or over a PATIO, TERRACE, or deck; may be supported on posts or COLUMNS, or CANTILEVERED from an adjacent structure or wall. 2. Term used for the overhanging portion of a shade tree or large shrub.

CANTILEVER (KANT-i-LEEV-er)–A projecting BRACKET, BEAM, or girder that is supported in its middle or along half its length and weighted at one end to support a corresponding weight on the projecting end.

CAPITAL–1. The city that is the seat of government of a country, state, or province. 2. Any form of wealth (money or property) capable of being employed in the production of more wealth. 3. The topmost feature of a COLUMN, post, or PILASTER. In CLASSICAL architecture, capitals followed various ARCHETYPICAL ORDERS. *See also* DORIC, IONIC, and CORINTHIAN.

CAPITOL–From the ANCIENT temple of Jupiter on the Capitoline hill in Rome, any building utilized by a state legislative body; state house.

CARDINAL–1. Deep-rich red color. 2. Member of the 70-man sacred college of the Roman Catholic Church, ranking immediately beneath the pope. 3. A prime or fundamental number.

CARDINAL POINTS–The four chief directions of the compass: north, south, east, and west.

CARDO AND DECUMANUS (KAR-do and day-ku-MAIN-us)–From Latin, the two major streets that formed cross AXES of an ORTHOGONALLY laid-out community of the ETRUSCANS and Romans. The cardo was aligned north-south, while the decumanus was oriented east-west.

CAROLINGIAN (kare-o-LIN-jun)–1. Having to do with the Frankish dynasty in France A.D. 751–987. 2. The design style originating under Charlemagne c. A.D. 800 and evolving into ROMANESQUE.

CARPET BEDDING–A VICTORIAN, nineteenth-century style popular in England and borrowed elsewhere with massed BEDDING PLANTS arranged in geometric patterns within a grass LAWN. The plants were typically ANNUALS, which were alternated into the scheme based on their time of bloom.

CARRARA MARBLE (kar-AHR-a)–A snow white marble from the Carrara district of Tuscany (northwestern Italy). It was the favored stone of Michelangelo and is still being quarried today.

CARRYING CAPACITY–The normal maximum number of organisms that an area can support; generally expressed in terms of population per acre or per square mile for larger organisms and per square foot or per cubic foot for microorganisms and soil organisms; for reproduction and other environmental factors. It is dependent on the least abundant LIMITING FACTOR of the environment.

CARTOUCHE (kar-TOOSH)–An ornament irregular or fantastic in shape on which armorial bearings or symbols are sometimes carved; frequently found in BAROQUE architecture.

CARYATID (kar-YAT-id)–From Greco-Latin, a sculptured female figure employed as an architectural supporting member. Plural, *caryatids* or *caryatides. See ERECHTHEUM.*

CASA (KAH-sa)–Italian and Spanish for house. CASINO is Italian for small house, usually in the country.

CASCADE (kas-KAYD)–A natural or human-made waterfall; a series of small waterfalls or steeply inclined rapids.

CASINO (ka-SEE-no)–1. A summer or garden house of ornamental character for amusement purposes. 2. A small country house or lodge.

CASTELLATED–A structure that is built like a castle or fortress, with TURRETS and BATTLEMENTS.

CASTLE–From the Latin word *castellum* for "fortress" or CASTRUM for "fortified place"; a fortified residence of a prince or noble in FEUDAL times.

CASTRUM–Latin for "fortified place"; a Roman legion camp that evolved into a fortified walled town; usually rectangular in outline with a GRIDIRON street arrangement within; much copied in later colonial towns. *See also* CASTLE.

CATACOMB (KAT-a-kome)–An underground burial place, especially one that consists of a network of subterranean tunnels and chambers for coffins; originally referring to those 3 miles south of Rome for entombment of Christian martyrs of the first and second centuries.

CATAPULT (KAT-a-pult)–An ANCIENT military device for throwing stones, darts, or flaming projectiles over distances or high fortress walls.

CATCH BASIN–A small underground reservoir or sump in an engineered storm drainage system where surface water enters the underground portions of the system either by gravity or pumping.

CATHEDRAL–The major church of a diocese, which contains the cathedra or throne of a bishop.

CBD–An abbreviation for "central business district"; the business core of a city with the major concentration of retail, office, and service functions; sometimes referred to as downtown, although it may in fact be located uptown or midtown. The CBD is the city's principal magnet, its mainstay and principal tax generator.

CCC—CIVILIAN CONSERVATION CORPS–Formed out of President Franklin Delano Roosevelt's NEW DEAL legislation and enacted in the 1930s to overcome the economic depression, the CCC was a civilian army of young military-age men who were organized into task forces to produce conservation and environmental projects. Such creations of the corps were countless camp structures, roads, trails, bridges, dams, and so on, in our national and state parks.

CEDAR OF LEBANON–A coniferous tree *(Cedrus libani)* with evergreen needlelike leaves, cones, and a characteristic fragrance; regarded as sacred in much of the ANCIENT Near East. *Cedrus libani sterrocoma* is the hardier strain grown more widely in America.

CELLA (SEL-a)–In CLASSICAL temples, the enclosed central room containing a statue of the divinity.

CEMENT–Any substance used as a binder for other substances. Portland cement, so called because it resembles a building stone quarried near Portland, England, is most often used. Portland cements are manufactured from limestone. Clay, cement rock, and blast furnace slag are also utilized. Portland cements are used extensively for making CONCRETES with AGGREGATES of sand and rock.

CENOTPAH (SEN-o-taff)–A monument to a person buried elsewhere.

CENTRIFUGAL (sen-TRIF-uh-gal)–1. Tending to move away from a center. 2. Developing outward from a center as in the growth of a flower or urban growth. 3. In design of spaces for people, a scheme that tends to cause an outward rather than an inward focus. Antonym, centripetal (sen-TRIP-eh-tal).

CERES (SEE-rees)–The goddess of agriculture in Roman mythology.

CHABUTRA (sha-BOOT-ra) – In Indian (MOGHUL) gardens, a small square elevated structure; an open DAIS or GAZEBO; often placed over a water channel and large enough for at least two persons to sit on, cushioned by ornate carpets and pillows.

CHADAR (she-DAR)–A large square cloth worn by women in India. The Hindu word for "shawl"; used to describe the carved marble water chutes in the MOGHUL gardens of India and Pakistan, where water is made to flow from a pool over a rippled incline to appear to sparkle as it descends to a lower pool; *also chador, chuddar,* and *chuder*.

CHADAR-BAGH (she-DAR-BAHG)–Persian for "fourfold water garden," where four water channels symbolize the four rivers of the world.

CHAMFER (CHAM-fur)–A square object such as wood, stone, or concrete whose corners are beveled at a 45-degree angle.

CHAMPAIGN (SHAM-PANE)–A broad flat plain; open country; related to campaign, the French *campagne* meaning open country suited to military maneuvers, the Italian CAMPAGNA meaning open level country, and CAMPUS, literally a field.

CHANCEL (CHAN-sel)–The part of a church near the altar, often at the east end and set apart by a rail, which is for the use of the clergy and the choir.

CHANIWA (chahn-EE-wah) – Japanese for TEA GARDEN.

CHARNEL HOUSE (CHAR-nel)–A tomb or vault for the dead; a place where corpses or bones of the dead are deposited. Sometimes, when older burial places were cleared out for the use by newer burials, the only remains, bones, were stockpiled in such places.

CHARRETTE (shah-RETT)–A rush to complete a design project. At the ÉCOLE DE BEAUS-ARTS, in nineteenth-century Paris, when the deadline for projects came due, a two-wheeled cart was wheeled around the ATELLIER, design studio, for collection of the completed projects of the students. If one's work was finished, it was placed on the cart and thus would be given full credit. If one's work was not placed on the cart at the time that it passed through the studio, that student's work was considered unfinished and not meeting the deadline. Like the train leaving the station, the charrette cart waited for no one or his work. Thus, in American design schools of today, the word *charrette* has come to be used to mean a great pressure-packed flurry of design activity directed toward completing a project by a given completion date.

CHATAUQUA (shu-TAW-kwuh)–Originating in the town of Chautauqua, New York in 1874, community meetings or assemblies with educational courses for the study of topical subjects; came to mean a group of traveling lecturers.

CHÂTEAU (sha-TOW)–French word for a CASTLE or a fine country ESTATE, including the residence and grounds. Plural, *châteaux*.

CHEEK WALL–Any two walls that form the two opposite sides of a structure, such as landscape steps or a ramp.

CHENAR (she-NAR)–The Persian word for "plane tree"; *Ficus sycomorus;* akin to our American plane tree or sycamore.

CHIAROSCURO (KEY-ar-o-SKOO-ro)–1. Italian for treatment of light and shade in a drawing or painting to suggest an illusion of depth. 2. In architecture, to create light and shadow patterns on a surface.

CHICAGO SCHOOL OF ARCHITECTURE–The term applied to the group of architects working in Chicago in the late nineteenth century, including Louis Sullivan, Dankmar Adler, William Le Baron Jenney, and Daniel Hudson Burnham. Their work was characterized by its freedom from historical ornamentation and its use of innovative industrial technologies such as steel construction and high-rise structures, or "skyscrapers."

CHINOISERIE (she-NWA-za-REE)–French term referring to anything made by, or imitated from, the Chinese; a popular motif for landscape and architectural furnishings during the eighteenth century in Europe and England.

CHIVALRY–From the old French word for "cavalry knight"; the noble qualities a KNIGHT was supposed to possess; courage, honor, grace.

CHOIR–The place in a church occupied by the choir; a CHANCEL.

CINQUECENTO (CHEEN-kway-CHAIN-toh)–Italian for the 1500s; the sixteenth century in Italian art.

CINQUEFOIL (SANK-foil)–In architecture, a circular design consisting of five converging arcs; also a plant with leaves composed of five leaflets; five-finger.

CIRCA (SUR-ka)–From Latin, literally means "about"; used with approximate dates. Abbreviated, c. or ca. (e.g., c. 1993).

CIRCUS–In the ANCIENT Roman Empire, a large open-air ARENA in the shape of a horseshoe, open at one end and surrounded by tiered seats for spectators. These were for public spectator sports, especially chariot racing. Such a structure was called a HIPPODROME by the Greeks, who used it for the same events. Rome had several circuses, the *Circus Maximus* being the largest (150,000 seats). In Britain, a circular range of buildings with an open center such as the King Circus in Bath; a place, usually circular, where several streets intersect, such as at Piccadilly Circus in London.

CISTERCIAN ORDER (sis-TUR-shen)–A French MONASTIC ORDER founded in 1098, which follows a strict interpretation of BENEDICTINE rule.

CISTERN (SIS-turn)–A tank or reservoir for holding water or other liquid, often below ground.

CITADEL (SIT-e-del)–A fortress or fortified place such as a town with a commanding height for military advantages.

CITY–Generally refers to any large or important human settlement. The term is also used to distinguish such areas from the countryside or rural districts. In ancient Greece, the polis was a city-state, while a Biblical city such as Bethlehem we might describe as a village. The word *city* is derived from the Latin *civitas,* "city-state." The Latin word for "city" was *urbs*. The French word *ville* comes from people grouping around the villa or MANOR of the FEUDAL lord. *See* HAMLET, MEGALOPOLIS, METROPOLIS, and POLIS.

CITY BEAUTIFUL–A term often used by advocates of an influential movement in urban improvement and city planning during the late nineteenth and early twentieth centuries. The expression had its origin in the "white city" concept of the World's Columbian Exposition of 1893 in Chicago. This movement inspired the preparation of countless beautification plans for civic centers, monuments, BOULEVARDS, waterfronts, and NEOCLASSICAL architecture as part of a fresh image for urban settings. The majority of the schemes were of such GRANDIOSE character and scale that they were, at most, only partially realized. The concept was a ROMANTIC expression of an age of great national optimism that declined when individual profit motivations began to dominate civic development forces after 1920.

CITYSCAPE–This term serves as a counterpart to the term LANDSCAPE. The form of a city that is observable to the human eye, especially from a distant vantage point. Manhattan's skyline is an example.

CIVILIAN CONSERVATION CORPS–Formed out of President Franklin Delano Roosevelt's NEW DEAL legislation and enacted in the 1930s to overcome the economic depression, the CCC was a civilian army of young military-age men who were organized into task forces to produce conservation and environmental projects. Such creations of the corps were countless camp structures, roads, trails, bridges, dams, and so on, in our national and state parks.

CLAIREVOIE or CLAIR VOYÉE (KLARE-vo-YAY)–French expression for a clear view; used to refer to prescribed vantage points in a garden, often as a windowlike clearing with a grillwork screen.

CLASSIC–Literally, of the highest class of Roman people, hence superior; also, that which is of, or characteristic of, Greek and Roman, especially relating to the arts and literature. Classic architecture evolved rules and forms or ORDERS that have been revived during later periods, such as the RENAISSANCE in Europe.

CLASSICAL–In accordance with the Greek and Roman CLASSIC ORDERS in the arts and literature.

CLASSICAL ARCHITECTURE–The design style that was popular from c. 1770 to c. 1840 in Britain, France, and central Europe.

CLAUDE-GLASS–A device used by members of the picturesque cult of the late eighteenth century that sought to find existing scenes in nature that resembled the compositions of their favorite paintings, such as LANDSCAPES by Claude, Poussin, and Rosa. A somewhat convex, dark or colored hand mirror used to concentrate the features of a landscape in subdued tones, sometimes applied to colored glass through which a landscape is viewed. William Gilpin wrote in *The Analysis of Beauty* in 1792, "The only picturesque glasses are those, which the artists call Claude Lorraine glasses. They are combined of two or three different colours; and if the hues are well sorted . . . give the objects of nature a soft, mellow tinge, like the colouring of that master."

CLAY–A natural earthy material that is composed of hydrated silicates of aluminum, which is plastic when wet and is used for making bricks, pottery, tiles, and so on. Clay, SILT, and sand are the three major components of SOIL.

CLERESTORY (KLEER-stor-ee)–The upper window level in a building, rising above adjacent roofs of the other parts, such as the aisles in a church; *also clearstorey, clearstory,* or *clerestorey*.

CLIMATE–The usual succession or generalization of states of weather conditions in a region through the course of a year.

CLIMAX–The plant community which, in a given area, perpetuates itself indefinitely on the best-drained landform and the most differentiated soil (e.g., sugar maple forests in the New England lowlands); the final stage of SUCCESSION; a mature ECOSYSTEM.

CLOISTER (KLOY-ster) – A rectangular courtyard surrounded by an open ARCADE; also, the covered passages around an open space or GARTH connecting the church to the chapter house, refectory, and other parts of a MONASTERY. They tend to be south of the NAVE to maximize sunlight; similar to the PERISTYLE court in Roman houses which were enclosed by COLONNADES rather than arcades. The covered walks are referred to as AMBULATORIES.

CLONE (KLONE)–A plant, or other organism, reproduced by asexual means from rooted cuttings or buds. Therefore, it has the same genetic heritage as its parent plant. In horticultural writing, such plants are identified by placing their names in quotation marks, (e.g., *Picea pungens* 'glauca"). *See also* CULTIVAR.

CLOSED GARDEN–"A garden enclosed is my sister, my spouse; a spring shut up; a fountain sealed" (Song of Solomon 4:12); a HORTUS CONCLUSUS, used as a symbol of Mary's virginity.

COBBLESTONE–A small, natural, roughly squared, or ovoid, stone large enough to be used for paving. Belgian blocks are rough-cut stones of a more rectangular form about twice the size of common bricks.

COEVAL (KO-EE-vel)–Of the same time, age, date, or duration; equally old, coincident; contemporary.

COFFERING–The treatment of architectural ceilings and dome interiors with a network of sunken panels (coffers); sometimes utilized as pure ornamentation; however, coffering has great structural efficiency and an economy of materials.

COGNOSCENTI (koh-NYOH-shen-tee)–Connoisseurs; those in-the-know; well informed; cognizant or being knowledgeable about matters of importance, especially about that which concerns a particular interest group.

COLLAGE (ko-LAHJH)–A composition made by mounting together on a flat surface various materials, such as newspaper, wallpaper, printed text, illustration, photographs, and cloth.

COLONNADE–A series or row of COLUMNS spanned by LINTELS.

COLONNETTE–A small COLUMN.

COLOSSEUM–The Flavian AMPHITHEATER in Rome, built c. A.D. 78–80. The name derives from a colossal statue of Flavius Valerius Aurelius Constantinus (Emperor Constantine I, c. A.D. 280–337 that was placed nearby in the fourth century A.D. Our word *coliseum* stems from that structure.

COLUMN–A vertical, weight-carrying architectural support or PILLAR, circular in cross section, and consisting of a base (sometimes omitted), a shaft, and a CAPITAL; also, columns are erected as freestanding monuments.

COMMON–An open place for public assembly in an urban area; also called an AGORA (Greek), GREEN or square (English), PIAZZA (Italian), and PLAZA (Spanish).

COMMUNITY–An aggregation in definite proportions of more or less interdependent organisms utilizing the resources of a common HABITAT which they either maintain or modify.

COMPARTMENT–1. A division or separate part of a building or an element of a building. *See also* BAY. 2. A French term for a clearing in a grove of trees or BOSQUET, typically developed as a sitting or amusement area in a French formal garden. *See also* CABINET.

COMPLEMENTARY COLORS–Pairs of colors, such as blue and orange, that together embrace the entire spectrum. The complement of a PRIMARY COLOR is a mixture of the other two. In pigments, they produce a neutral or gray when mixed in the correct proportions.

COMPOSITE–An architectural ORDER invented by the Romans that combined the ACANTHUS leaf MOTIF of the CORINTHIAN ORDER with the VOLUTES of the IONIC CAPITAL.

COMPOST–A combination of soil and decomposing organic matter used as a fertilizer or MULCH. Almost all organic wastes can be converted into compost.

CONCENTRIC ZONE THEORY–A theory of urban growth developed by Ernest W. Burgess in the 1920s which states that predominant land uses tend to be arranged in a series of concentric circular rings or zones about a city's central core.

CONCRETE–A mixture of fine and coarse AGGREGATES bound into a monolithic mass by a CEMENT. The aggregates used are sand and crushed rock or gravel.

CONDOMINIUM (kon-do-MIN-ee-um)–A multifamily dwelling, apartment, or rowhouse project in which each dwelling unit is owned and financed by the resident, who actually holds the deed enabling him or her to sell, mortgage, or exchange his or her unit independent of the owners of other units in the structure or project. The corridors, entranceways, and underlying land are owned jointly by all the occupants. It is different from a cooperative, in which residents own only a divided share of the whole.

CONIFEROUS (KAHN-i-fur-us)–Cone-baring; conifers are trees or shrubs, primarily EVERGREENS, which produce cones and have needle-shaped foliage. The wood of conifers tends to be softer than that of DECIDUOUS trees and is therefore known as SOFTWOOD. Typical examples: pine, fir, spruce, yew. DECIDUOUS CONIFERS such as the bald cypress have cones and needlelike leaves but shed as HARDWOODS do.

CONSERVATION–The protection of natural resources, especially the renewable ones, for purposes of maintaining a sustained yield: for example, maintenance of forest along stream borders to control water levels for the benefit of fish and game and at the same time for regeneration of the forest itself.

CONSTRUCTIVISM–A twentieth-century movement with Naum Gabo and Antoine Pevsner (Russian brothers) and Laslo Moholy-Nagy as its chief proponents. Their three-dimensional ABSTRACT sculptures abandoned the MONOLITH as the central core around which volumes were organized and constructed and instead, harmonized with new concepts in physics, mathematics, and materials of modern technology.

CONTOUR–An imaginary or implied line on the surface of the earth, all points of which are at the same elevation above sea level. The location of contour lines is frequently indicated on maps. For mapping and engineering purposes these lines are indicated on paper as dashed or continuous lines designating 1-, 2-, 5-, 10-, or 25-foot intervals.

CONTOUR INTERVAL–The predetermined consistent differential in elevation between each of the contour lines shown on a map. This difference is usually 1, 2, 5, 10, or 25 feet, depending on the given TERRAIN or degree of precision necessary for their usage.

CONTOUR PLOWING–An agricultural practice that has been employed in this century for plowing along the natural CONTOURS around a hillside rather than in rows that run up and down the side slopes. This is done to minimize rainwater RUNOFF and the subsequent SOIL EROSION from excess runoff.

CONTRAPPOSTO (kon-tra-PAHS-to)–The term, from Italian, is used in art for "counterpoise." In sculpture, a standing figure shown at rest is poised with a slight to exaggerated S-curve to the spine or main AXIS through the body. Such a stance expresses freedom of motion and grace as contrasted to the earlier portrayal of figures standing erect and SYMMETRICAL or soldierlike.

CONURBATION (kon-ur-BAY-shun)–A term first used in England in 1915 by Sir Patrick Geddes to describe the essentially unplanned aggregation of urban communities to form a continuous urban sprawl. METROPOLITAN New York is an example. *See also* MEGALOPOLIS.

COOL COLOR–Colors, such as blue, green or violet, which are psychologically calming, unemphatic, depressive; optically, they generally appear to recede. They are called cool because they are emotionally associated with objects such as ice or water as opposed to warm or hot colors (red, orange, yellow), which are associated with fire or the sun. *See also* WARM COLOR.

COORDINATE LINES–In surveying, the imaginary lines that form a GRID of north-south and east-west alignment. From these lines or MERIDIANS can be measured distances to any points on the ground. The point of intersection of the measurements from the two perpendicular coordinate lines is a coordinate or coordinate point.

COORDINATES–In surveying, the linear or angular measurements that locate a point in space with relation to an established reference. Rectangular coordinates locate a point by measuring the rectangular distance from two established lines which are at right angles to each other. The global system of latitude and longitude is a spherical coordinate system.

COPING–Brick or stone used to cap the top of a wall to prevent weathering or for ornamental purposes.

COPPICE (KOP-iss)–A small woodlot, especially one that has been cut down and is regrowing from stump sprouts. From such a stand of trees, small shoots are periodically harvested for firewood, fencing, or other uses. *See also* COPSE.

COPSE (KOPS)–A grove of small trees or shrubs. *See also* COPPICE.

CORBEL (KOR-bel)–A COURSE of masonry material, such as stone or bricks, which projects from a wall as a horizontal support for another architectural member such as a BEAM or RIB of a ceiling. These are occasionally elaborately carved or molded.

CORBEL ARCH (KOR-bel)–An ARCH that is formed by a series of successively projected COURSES of MASONRY ultimately joining at a central point to form a complete ARCH. Also CORBEL VAULT, which is a linear expression of the corbel arch.

CORINTHIAN (kor-IN-thyan)–The third variation of the three CLASSICAL Greek design ORDERS; characterized by COLUMN CAPITALS of ornamentally stylized ACANTHUS leaves and curled fern fronds. The columns were slender with FLUTED SHAFTS and FILLETS and a base or PEDESTAL.

CORNICE (KORN-iss)–In CLASSICAL or RENAISSANCE architecture, the topmost projecting portion of the ENTABLATURE; also refers to any CROWNING projection of a building.

CORTILE (kor-TEEL-ay)–The Italian word for an interior courtyard, usually surrounded by a COLONNADE or an ARCADE in a palace or other building.

COST–BENEFIT ANALYSIS–An analytic method developed to evaluate alternative results in terms of their potential benefits and costs to assist decision maker's selection. When this method is utilized in the environmental sciences, it considers the social, ECOLOGICAL, and AESTHETIC as well as economic factors and takes account of the indirect consequences of different courses of action.

COST–BENEFIT RATIO–The numerically expressed relationship between the probable dollar and related costs to anticipated beneficial results of a course of action (e.g., 1:1.5).

COTTAGE GARDEN–Small residential gardens, utilitarian and ornamental, popular in England from the middle of the nineteenth century. These gardens were generally ASYMMETRICAL in design but made considerable use of formal features such as clipped hedges, BEDDING PLANTS, flowers for cutting, TURF, gravel or paved paths, sundials, small fountains, and TRELLISES. From about 1800 to 1910, these gardens were much imitated in the eastern United States.

COULISSE (koo-LEECE)–Originally a theatrical term denoting scenery which projects from the wings onto the stage; applied in painting criticism to any lateral projections from the flanks of a painted landscape, hence a particular form of interface between voids and masses. The same effect can be seen in real landscapes, especially when a path or sweep of lawn meanders from left to right around masses of trees and or shrubs.

COUNTRY PARK–Beginning in Britain in the mid-nineteenth century; situated in or at the edge of a large urban area which due to its size and NATURALESQUE character, was a reminder to urbanites of countrylike scenery.

COUNTRY PLACE–An American term of the late nineteenth century for what are known in Britain as ESTATES or COUNTRY SEATS; a large rural property with an impressive mansion.

COUNTRY PLACE ERA–A period in American history marked by the creation of many large residential properties in the countryside; 1880s–1930s.

COUNTRY SEAT–A place of residence, especially a large house that is part of a country ESTATE. *See also* COUNTRY PLACE.

COUR D'HONNEUR (KOOR DON-oor)–Literally, the court of honor. The French expression for the most handsome court of a CHÂTEAU or other great house where visitors were formally received.

COURSE–A horizontal layer of MODULAR units such as bricks or stones, which form a vertical wall. The courses may be laid with a layer of MORTAR between each (masonry wall) or without mortar (DRY WALL).

COURT–Any chamber that is open to the sky and is partially or entirely enclosed by building walls or fences. In some countries it is the central open space of a building compound; also called courtyard, PATIO, or ATRIUM.

COVENANT–An agreement between two or more parties that is written into a deed or other legal document promising to do or refrain from doing certain acts. It aims to achieve desired results through mutual agreement and may include an owner's agreement to have certain types of structural details such as roofs or green spaces, or to support common services.

CREEPER–A term used for low-growing plants, SHRUBS, vines, or GROUND COVERS, which grow in a spreading fashion close to the ground, over rocks, or cling to supporting elements such as walls by TENDRILS or rootlets (e.g., English ivy and Virginia creeper).

CRENEL (KREN-el)–One of several openings in the PARAPET wall of a BATTLEMENT in a fortified structure. The solid portions are MERLONS. A crenellation is a battlement, notch, or indentation.

CRENELLATION (kren-el-AY-shun)–The opening in the topmost part of a PARAPET. Furnished with CRENELS or indentations. *See also* BATTLEMENT.

CRINKLE-CRANKLE WALL–In eighteenth-century England, SERPENTINE walls were called crinckle-crankle walls and were designed that way to enhance the growing of fruit, ESPALIERED against their south-facing surface. Such structures were more stable and economical than ordinary walls since they required fewer materials. Thomas Jefferson's walls at the University of Virginia (1816–1826) are good examples.

CROMLECH (KROM-lek)–From the PALEOLITHIC era; a large horizontal slablike stone that spans several DOLMEN as a prehistoric monument or tomb.

CROWN–1. The topmost part of an ARCH, including the KEYSTONE, or an open FINIAL of a tower. 2. The CANOPY or FOLIAGE mass portion of a tree or shrub.

CROWN COLONY–A colonial possession of the British Empire, such as the American colonies before the Revolution.

CROWN LAND–In Britain, a Canada, and other countries of the former British Empire, property owned by the government.

CRUCIFORM (KROO-si-form) – Cross-shaped. Maybe GREEK or LATIN CROSS.

CRYPT (KRIPT)–A subterranean cell or cave, especially one constructed for the interment of bodies; in medieval churches generally under the east end (CHANCEL or APSE).

CRYPTO PORTICUS (KRIP-TO PORT-i-kus)–A passageway wholly or mainly below ground.

CUBISM (KEW-bism)–An artform popular between 1909 and 1914. In analytical cubism, the first state of cubism, forms were analyzed and reduced to their basic geometric constituents. In synthetic cubism, the fragmental forms were reorganized into novel, many-faceted configurations. Gris, Leger, Picasso, and Braque were influenced by the movement. Cubism first appeared in American landscape architecture with the HARVARD REVOLUTION in 1936–1937 led by Garrett Eckbo, Dan Kiley, and James Rose.

CUL-DE-SAC (KULL-de-sac)–A French term that literally means "bottom of bag," for a short dead-end street. Cul-de-sacs are used widely in suburban residential layouts today. They minimize the danger, noise, and nuisance of through traffic.

CULT (KULT)–1. A system of religion or worship. 2. Devoted or extravagant admiration for a person or principle, especially when regarded as a fad. 3. The followers or sect.

CULTIVAR (KULT-i-var)–A horticultural variety of plants that can only be reproduced or propagated asexually; such plants cannot be reproduced from seeds. A CLONE is a cultivar.

CULTIVATE–1. To till or loosen SOIL in preparation for planting or to eliminate weeds in a planting bed. 2. To foster the growth of plants. 3. To refine or further encourage. 4. To seek the society of, make friends with.

CULTURAL LANDSCAPE–A term used by anthropologists for a LANDSCAPE in which a human CULTURE survives or flourishes. This term may be applied to a natural landscape that provides the resources required by a primitive people or to a landscape as modified by a highly organized agricultural or urban population. The city is the most specialized cultural landscape. The term *landscape,* in this meaning, includes not only the visual aspects of the area to which it is applied, but the climatic aspects and resources as well. Natural landscapes that are unmodified by any human activity are rare today.

CULTURE–The collective total of ways of living developed by a group of people or of humankind as a whole. The arts, ARTIFACTS, skills, and technology that is transmitted from one generation to another.

CULVERT–A human-made channel to convey surface RUNOFF under a roadway embankment or other obstruction in a natural or human-made drainage course; a sewer; a conduit.

CUNEIFORM (kyoo-NEE-i-form)–Literally having the form of a wedge; the system of writing in Babylon–Assyria using wedge-shaped characters, carved into clay tablets.

CUPOLA (KU-po-la)–From the Latin word *cupa* for "cup"; a hemispherical roof or DOME situated atop a circular or polygonal base and crowning a roof or TURRET; a towerlike structure with LANTERN windows projecting above a roof. *See also* DOME.

CURTAIN WALL–In contemporary architecture, an exterior wall that performs no load-bearing function but is a screen-like curtain of glass or brick on the surface of a building.

CUTTING–In horticulture, the portion of a plant such as a root, shoot, or leaf cut from the main plant to be used for ASEXUALLY PROPAGATING an entirely new plant.

CYCLOPEAN (sike-lo-PEE-an)–Gigantic; vast and rough; massive. Cyclopean architecture is a style of stone construction using large irregular blocks without MORTAR.

DADA (DAH-DAH)–An art movement that took its name from a review published in 1917 by a group of Dutch painters, architects, and sculptors. Mainly inspired by the work of Mondrian, its design was orderly, intellectual, and impersonal.

DADO (DAY-doh)–1. A horizontal band, often decorated, at the base or lower portion of a wall or pedestal; sometimes referred to as WAINSCOTING. 2. A wood joining technique by means of a square-sided notch that is routed across the grain of a piece of wood.

DAIS (DY-is)–A raised platform as in a MEDIEVAL hall, where the head table was elevated above all the others.

DARK AGES–Referring to the period in history known also as the MEDIEVAL period or MIDDLE AGES; between the fall of the CLASSICAL Roman Empire and the RENAISSANCE, c. A.D. 476–1350.

DATUM (DAY-tem)–A reference point or BENCHMARK of known location; used in land surveying from which elevations (vertical) and linear (horizontal) distances are measured and calculated.

DE STIJL (deh STILE)–Dutch word for "style." The expression through artforms, painting, or assemblages showing disdain for current cultural standards or modes of design. The movement began during World War I and was revitalized as funk art in the 1960s.

DECIDUOUS (dee-SID-yu-us)–A term referring to trees and shrubs that shed their leaves each autumn or at the end of their active growing season. The opposite of EVERGREEN. Often called HARDWOODS.

DECUMANUS AND CARDO (day-ku-MAIN-us and KAR-do)–From Latin; the two major streets that formed cross AXES of an ORTHOGONALLY laid-out community of the ETRUSCANS and Romans. The cardo was aligned north-south, while the decumanus was oriented east-west.

DEMESNE (de-MAIN)–An ESTATE in the possession of its owner; the land attached to a MANOR house, reserved for its owner's use; one's personal domain.

DEMOGRAPHY (dem-o-GRAF-ee)–The science of vital statistics, such as births, deaths, population, ethnology.

DENSITY–The average number of organisms, persons, families, or dwellings per given unit of area, such as an acre, square mile, and so on.

DENTILS (DEN-tills)–From the Latin word for "teeth." The small cubes into which the square member in the bed molding of an IONIC, CORINTHIAN, COMPOSITE, and occasionally DORIC CORNICE is divided.

DEPRECIATION–Loss in property value due to numerous causes, including functional and economic obsolescence and deterioration.

DESERT–An area of extremely infrequent rainfall, sparsely occupied by vegetation and wildlife; an area with few forms of life because of the lack of water, permanent frost, and the absence of soil.

DESIGN–1. To form a plan or scheme of something; to conceive and arrange in the mind; to originate mentally, plan out, contrive. 2. To synthesize a set of PROGRAM requirements into a workable solution of the said problem. 3. To sketch, delineate, draw; to fashion artistically; to make the preliminary sketch of a work of art, building, or area of land; to make the plans and drawings necessary for the construction of a structure, a landscape, and the features within it.

DI XUE (DY-ZOO)–Chinese for "moon door" or MOON GATE, a decorative feature in a walled garden or courtyard. Usually circular in shape (symbolizing heaven), but sometimes octagonal; often leading to a vista.

DIAGRAM–A graphic representation of an existing or proposed set of conditions or activities.

DIURNAL (DI-UR-nal)–Occurring daily.

DIVINE–1. Godlike; heavenly; sacrosanct; excellent in the highest degree. 2. A theologian. 3. To prophesy; to foretell; to know by intuition.

DOLMEN (DOHL-men)–Large upright stones capped with a covering slab, CROMLECH, erected in prehistoric times as a monument or tomb.

DOME–A hemispherical VAULT; an ARCH rotated on a vertical AXIS. *See also* DUOMO.

DOMESTIC–From the Latin *domus,* for house; pertaining to the house or one's place of residence; not foreign; tamed animals or plants; not wild or EXOTIC.

DOMESTICATE–To tame or nurture animals or plants; to make them no longer wild; to civilize.

DOMINANT–A term used in ECOLOGY for an organism or ASSOCIATION of organisms that in a COMMUNITY exert a great degree of influence or control the HABITAT of other organisms.

DOMUS (DOME-us)–Latin word for the Roman single-family house.

DOORYARD GARDEN–In colonial America, the small enclosed garden developed adjacent to the kitchen or front door for the cultivation of herbs, medicinal plants, or flowers.

DORIC–The earliest and simplest of the CLASSICAL ORDERS, characterized by columns having no base, relatively squatty SHAFTS that were FLUTED, and simple undecorated CAPITALS.

DOVECOTE (DUV-kote)–A small house or box with chambers for nesting pigeons or doves, usually above the ground, on the grounds of an English estate to provide a ready source of a favorite delicacy, roasted dove. *See also* PIGEON COTE.

DOWNS–In Britain, grassy uplands with gentle undulations.

DRESSED STONE–Smoothly finished stonework used externally at corners, doors, and windows of brick and stone buildings.

DRUM–In a COLUMN, the circular disks that make up the SHAFT; also used with reference to the circular or POLYGONAL wall on which a DOME is placed.

DRY LANDSCAPE–In Japan, a ZEN form of garden dating from the seventeenth century A.D.; a small garden, with a few plants, rocks, and sand or fine gravel that is meticulously manicured by raking. Such a composition is intended to suggest a larger landscape with hills or mountains; called *Kare sansui.* Ryoan-ji in Kyoto is the best known example.

DRY WALL–A wall of stone or rubble laid without mortar.

DUECENTO (doo-ay-CHAIN-toh)–Italian for the 1200s; the thirteenth century; pre-Renaissance.

DUOMO (DWO-mo)–The Italian word for CATHEDRAL. Since cathedrals usually were domed, *duomo* came to mean "cathedral." *See also* DOME.

DUPLEX–Term used in the United States to describe a two-family or semidetached house.

DUST BOWL–An expression for the areas of the United States where winds cause soil erosion when the natural or agricultural vegetation is reduced by long periods of drought. Dust storms and dunes are characteristics of the dust bowl.

DUTCH GARDEN–A type of COTTAGE GARDEN originating in Holland but little distinguished from its English and German prototypes. Dutch gardens consisted largely of trimmed box hedges and semiformal plantings. They were created primarily during the nineteenth century when the Dutch were developing numerous horticultural varieties of flowers.

DWELLING–A residence or living quarters.

DYNAMIC (DY-NAM-ik)–Characterized by energy or effective action; active; forceful. As opposed to STATIC, a process or force that is not in equilibrium.

EASEMENT–A right-of-way for public or quasi-public use, such as for public utilities, bike paths, parkways, drainageways, and so on. Easements are frequently obtained by highway departments because they involve smaller payments than would be required for full purchase, yet satisfy a road's land requirements. A scenic easement is granted by a landowner to a highway department for the right to use the land for scenic enhancement.

EAVE–The lowest edge of a roof which overhangs beyond the vertical side wall of a structure; for purposes of extending roof surface to project rainwater away from a wall.

ECLECTICISM (ek-LEK-ti-sism)–The practice of selecting from various sources, usually in order to form a new system or STYLE of design; combining historical styles of various types.

ÉCOLE DES BEAUX-ARTS (e-KOL day BOZE ahr)–The oldest and most celebrated center of architectural education in the world, located in Paris; established in 1819.

ECOLOGY–The science that deals with the interrelationships between organisms and their ENVIRONMENT; from the Greek word *oikos* for "house," meaning the study of the home.

ECOSYSTEM (EK-o-sis-tem)–A self-sustaining community of organisms plus their inorganic environment. An ecosystem must have an adequate resource of chemical nutrients, energy, and a balanced population of organisms, including energy accumulators (chlorophyll plants), primary consumers (fungi, microorganisms, herbivores), second-order consumers (carnivorous predators, parasites, scavengers), and decomposers (bacteria, fungi, etc.), which complete the regeneration of the chemical resources. All of these organisms are tied together in interlocking food chains.

ECOTONE (EEK-o-tone)–In ECOLOGY, the edge or transition zone between two different plant communities, such as the margin between a prairie and a forest.

EDEN–A place of delight; a terrestrial PARADISE. In the Christian Bible, the garden of Eden, which was said to be in the eastern part of the world and surrounded by a high wall or mountains; the place where Adam and Eve encountered the Tree of Life, or the Tree of Knowledge, and the serpent. Here is the fountain that divides into four streams that go forth and water the world. Outside this paradise were trackless wastes infested with wild beasts and serpents.

EDWARDIAN (ed-WAR-di-an)–In the style of the reigns of the English kings named Edward; especially Edward VII, 1901–1910, the son who succeeded Queen Victoria.

EFFLUENT (e-FLU-ent)–The liquid waste discharged by a collection network or a treatment plant. The liquid, solid, or gaseous wastes discharged or released from any process.

ELEVATION–1. In architectural design drawing, the proportional projection of a structure or composition onto a plane perpendicular to the horizon; a vertical projection. 2. On a survey or design plan, the ELEVATION points refer to measurable heights above a given DATUM, such as sea level or a known BENCHMARK.

ELIZABETHAN–The term applied to the Early English Renaissance; of the period when Elizabeth I was Queen of England, 1558–1603.

EMINENT DOMAIN–The right of a government to acquire private property for public use or benefit upon payment of just compensation.

ENAMEL (ee-NAM-el)–A vitreous opaque or transparent substance that solidifies when fired and fuses to surfaces of glass, pottery, or metal as a colorful ornamental coating.

ENCLOSURE ACTS–*See* PARLIAMENTARY ENCLOSURE ACTS.

ENGAGED COLUMN–A half-round semicolumn that when attached to a wall forms a projecting but nonfunctional visual articulation.

ENGRAVING–The process of cutting a design with a sharp instrument on a metal plate from which, after being inked, impressions are made on paper; also applied to such an impression or printed image.

ENTABLATURE (en-TAB-li-chur)–The horizontal top part of an order of CLASSICAL architecture supported by COLUMNS and consisting of ARCHITRAVE, FRIEZE, and CORNICE.

ENTASIS (en-TAY-sis)–The very slight convex swelling used on the shaft of Greek and later columns to counteract the illusion of concavity.

ENTROPY (EN-tro-pee)–A physical quantity or measurement of the degree of disorder in the matter and energy in the universe, each of which tend to degrade over time to the ultimate state of inert uniformity. Disorder tends to increase as isolated systems or natural processes continue. *See also* SECOND LAW OF THERMODYNAMICS.

ENVIRONMENT–The total of all external conditions that influence the growth and development of an organism. Also, all that is apart from and surrounds an observer or something being observed.

ENVIRONMENTAL IMPACT STATEMENT–The federal government, through the National Environmental Policy Act of 1970, requires that environmental impact statements be prepared by an agency, public or private, for projects that may significantly affect the quality of the environment. Many states have adopted similar requirements for projects involving permanent improvements and/or federal funds. An environmental impact statement is a detailed evaluation of the ecological, physical, cultural, socioeconomic, and aesthetic effects of a project. Its primary purpose is to disclose the consequence of a proposed action, thus alerting public decision makers to the environmental risks involved. The environmental impact statement considers both long- and short-term impacts as well as alternative courses of action and their probable impact.

EPOCH (EHP-ek or EE-pahk)–A particular period of time marked by distinct character or events; usually spanning a great period such as the time required for geological occurances.

EQUINOX (EE-kwin-ox)–The time when the sun crosses the equator making night and day of equal length in all parts of the earth. The vernal, or spring, equinox occurs about March 21 and the autumnal equinox about September 22.

ERA (AIR-uh)–A distinctive period of time during which events, artifacts, and manners have a distinct character; an age or EPOCH.

ERECHTHEUM (e-REK-thee-um, or e-rek-THEE-um)–An Ionic-style temple on the ACROPOLIS in Athens, Greece, built c. 420 B.C.; notable for the six CARYATIDS, female figures serving as COLUMNS on its south porch. The Greek spelling is *erechtheion* (e-REK-thee-un).

ERGONOMICS (er-gun-AH-miks)–The study of work; related to design, the study of the fitness or suitability of furniture, and so on, for its intended human activities or its ease and comfort for the performance of human functions.

ERICACEOUS (air-i-KAY-shus)–1. Plants that require or tolerate ACID SOIL. 2. Plants in the health family, *Ericaceae,* comprising over 1700 species; azalea, rhododendron, and laurel are among the most widely known for their ornamental qualities.

EROSION–The natural process by which matter is worn away, deteriorated, or disintegrated by the action of running water or windborne particulate matter such as in SOIL erosion.

ESPALIER (es-PAL-yay)–A tree, shrub, or vine trained to grow flat against a wall or on a TRELLIS. Fruit trees are frequently espaliered.

ESPLANADE (ES-plah-nahd)–Any open, level space, walkway, or roadway in or near a town often along the seashore; a PROMENADE.

ESTATE–1. Property; possessions; capital fortune. 2. Landed property; individually owned piece of land containing a residence, especially one that is large and maintained by great wealth.

ESTUARY (ES-tyoo-a-ri)–The mouth of a river where the ocean's saltwater tides ebb and flow to meet the river's fresh water; a FIRTH.

ETHEREAL (eh-THEER-ee-al)–Very light, airy, delicate; not earthly; heavenly.

ETRUSCAN (ee-TRUSS-kan)–The people or design style originating in Etruria, west central Italy, eighth century B.C.

EUCLIDEAN (yoo-CLID-e-an)–Adjective to characterize severely geometrical design patterns; named after the Greek mathematician Euclid, 300 B.C.

EVERGREEN–A plant that retains its FOLIAGE and remains green throughout the year;

all plants with persistent leaves; may be trees, shrubs, grasses, or succulents; may be CONIFEROUS (cone-bearing with needles) or broad-leafed.

EXEDRA (EX-ee-dra)–In Greek buildings, a recess or alcove with raised seating where the discussions among scholars were held. The Romans applied the term to any semicircular or rectangular recess with benches. It is also applied to an APSE or NICHE in a church.

EXODUS (EX-e-des)–1. A mass departure; emigration. 2. The second book of the Jewish and Christian Scripture.

EXOTIC (ek-ZOT-ik)–1. Of foreign origin or character; a term applied to a SPECIES of plants or other organisms which are not native to an area; the opposite of INDIGENOUS. 2. Colloquialism meaning strikingly unusual or colorful in appearance or effect.

EXPRESSIONISM–A term applied to art when form, line, and color are governed by an artist's need to express emotion. Distortion, exaggeration of form, marked simplification of line, and strong color are frequently present. The works of Van Gogh, Munch, and El Greco are representative.

EYECATCHER–In the English ROMANTIC LANDSCAPE GARDEN, a feature in the scene that is intended to attract the attention of the viewer; a focal element; a FOLLY.

FACADE (fa-SOD)–The front face of a building; also, the other sides when they are emphasized architecturally.

FAUX (FOH)–French for "false"; in architectural ornamentation, artificial material such as wood artfully painted to fool the eye and the mind into thinking it is marble or other expensive stone; inexpensive wood or plaster painted to look like expensive wood in window, door, and other trim.

FEASIBILITY STUDY–A preliminary design to determine the practicality of a proposed scheme before a commitment is made.

FENESTRATION (fen-es-TRAY-shun)–The arrangement of all openings such as windows, doors, or arcades in the surfaces or FACADES of a structure.

FENG-SHUI (FENG-SHOOEE)–A Chinese philosophy about the forces of nature and the influences from nature in rocks, plants, water, and so on, found on a site to be consulted when planning where to site structures and other features in the landscape; from *feng* (winds) and *shui* (waters) as well as *kan* (hills) and *yu* (valleys). *See also* GEOMANCY.

FERME ORNÉE (FAYRM or-NAY)–French expression for "ornamental farm"; a type of PICTURESQUE, ROMANTIC rural LANDSCAPE GARDEN popular during the eighteenth century in England and on the continent. The term was first used in England by the poet William Shensone in about 1730, in describing his farm, the Leasowes, which he embellished with FOLLIES and meandering paths. At the edge of Versailles, Marie Antoinette play acted as a milkmaid in her HAMEAU, a sham peasant hamlet, created in the late eighteenth century after the English LANDSCAPE GARDEN became popular in France.

FERRO CONCRETE (FAYRO)–Concrete that has been strengthened by casting into it iron, steel mesh, or reinforcing bars.

FÊTE (FAYT)–French word for "festival," gala entertainment, usually held outdoors.

FEUDALISM (FYOO-del-izm)–The social, political, and economic system in medieval Europe. The land was worked by SERFS, who were bound to the land which was held by VASSALS in exchange for military and other services provided by the lord of the land.

FIEF (FEEF)–Under the FEUDAL system land held from a lord in return for service.

FILIGREE (FILL-i-GREE)–Lacelike ornamental work of intertwined silver or gold wire; any delicate design resembling filigree. *See also* TRACERY.

FILL–In earthworks, the mass of earth, soil, stones, and so on, used to fill in a hollow or low place. *Filldirt* is also used to mean the same.

FILLET (fil-AY)–1. In architectural ornamentation, a flat square molding separating other moldings. 2. A narrow band between two FLUTINGS in a COLUMN.

FINIAL (FIN-ee-al)–A knoblike decorative feature that terminates the top of an architectural pinnacle, GABLE peak, or bannister. Typically with FOLIAGE motif.

FIRTH–The Scottish term for the mouth of a tidal river or an arm of the sea; an ESTUARY; also spelled *frith;* comparable to the Scandinavian *fiord,* or fjord.

FLAGSTONE–Any stone that can be split into large flat slabs suitable for paving or for stepping stones. Most flagstones are fine-grained sandstones.

FLOODPLAIN–A low plain along a streambed or channel that is subject to flooding. SOIL is composed of sediments deposited by the stream. *See also* ALLUVIAL DEPOSIT.

FLORA–A term applied to the plant population of a region or of a geological period. The sum of all plant populations occupying a certain region at a certain time.

FLOWERY MEDE (MEED)–An arrangement popular during MEDIEVAL times with flowering ANNUAL plants scattered in a grassy area.

FLUTE, FLUTING–Vertical channeling or grooves, semicircular in cross section, used principally on COLUMNS and PILASTERS.

FLYING BUTTRESS–*See* BUTTRESS.

FOLIAGE (FO-lee-ej)–Leaves of a tree, shrub, or vine; mass of leaves.

FOLIE D'AMOUR (fah-LEE DAHM-OOR)–The French term that means, literally, a FOLLY in which romance was conducted.

FOLLY–A structure built solely for decorative effect in the LANDSCAPE GARDEN of the eighteenth century (e.g., a GOTHIC style ruin or tower). *See also* EYECATCHER.

FONT–The ARCHAIC word for "fountain," usually of stone; a receptacle for holy water used in baptism.

FOOTING–A course of brick, stone, or concrete at the bottom of a wall made wider than the wall itself in order to distribute the weight over a larger area.

FORESHORTENING–The apparent visual contraction of an object viewed as extended in a plane perpendicular to the line of sight; the apparent spatial depth in a two-dimensional picture.

FORMAL–According to prescribed rules; very regular or orderly in pattern; rigidly symmetrical.

FORMALISM–Strict adherence to prescribed forms of execution and traditional rules of composition.

FORTHRIGHT–Noun that in old English referred to a straight path; in High Renaissance, a wide gravel PROMENADE running parallel to the main garden FACADE of the house.

FORUM–The public open space for social, civic, and market purposes found in every Roman town; normally surrounded by public buildings.

FOSSE (FOSS)–A ditch, trench, or canal; specifically, the MOAT around a CASTLE. This feature may have been the origin of the HA-HA.

FRESCO–Painting made by applying pigments to a wall while the plaster is still wet.

FRIAR (FRY-er)–A man who as a member of a MONASTIC religious ORDER living under vows of chastity, poverty, and obedience according to rules set down by that order has withdrawn from society at large; also called a MONK.

FRIEZE (Freez)–The portion of the ENTABLATURE between the ARCHITRAVE and CORNICE in CLASSICAL architecture.

FRIGIDARIUM (frig-i-DAIR-ee-um)–A room in a Roman bath building with a large cold bath. *See also* TEPIDARIUM and CALDARIUM; THERMAE.

FUNCTIONALISM–A theory that emphasizes the need to design or adapt structures to their ultimate functions, the ways in which they are to be used. "Form follows function" was a popular expression of this school of thought among designers, led by architect Louis Sullivan of the Chicago School at the turn of the twentieth century.

FUNERARY (FOO-ner-ary)–Pertaining to a funeral or burial.

FUTURISM–An Italian movement, 1850–1915, which embraced the machine AESTHETIC and interpreted its dynamism, speed, power and motion through a continual transformation of forms. This movement placed great faith in industrial technology to solve society's problems.

GABLE–In CLASSICAL architecture, it is called the PEDIMENT; the triangular portion of the end wall between the sloped sides of the roof.

GALLERY–From the old French *galerie;* a covered space for walking in with one side open.

GAMBREL ROOF (GAM-brel)–A roof, the ends of which are cut off vertically and with sides that have two slopes, the lower of which is steeper; the form of the traditional American barn roof.

GARDEN–A place where plants are cultivated for pleasure or domestic use. In gardens, the plants are arranged in an orderly or planned fashion.

GARDEN CITY–A concept proposed by Sir Ebenezer Howard in 1898. The garden city concept was a reaction against the congested slum cities of the industrial revolution in England. The scheme calls for city dwellings on individual garden plots, with commerce and industry in separate zones and surrounded by GREENBELTS.

GARDEN THEATER–A popular feature in Italian RENAISSANCE gardens, usually enclosed by walls and/or clipped evergreen hedges. Modeled after the Roman AMPHITHEATER, such divisions, or outdoor rooms in the garden were the setting for musical, dance, or theatrical performances. The Villa Madama, in Rome, has a fine example. The French CABINET is comparable. *See also* WATER THEATER.

GARDENESQUE (garden-ESK)–Having gardenlike qualities; being like a designed garden.

GARGOYLE (GAR-goyl)–A roof drainage spout typically carved into a grotesque figure and extending out from the roof edge to project rainwater away from the building walls.

GARTH–A MEDIEVAL enclosed yard or CLOISTER garden; a HORTUS CONCLUSUS.

GAZEBO (gaz-EE-bo)–The Dutch name for a summer house, garden shelter, or open pavilion from which to view the surrounding landscape or garden. Cast iron was a favorite material during the VICTORIAN era.

GENIUS LOCI (GEE-ni-us LO-sy)–The spirit of a place; the unique atmosphere of a site or area. The phrase "genius of the place" first appeared in book five of Virgil's (or Vergil's) *Æneid,* from the first century B.C. William Kent also frequently used the term in the eighteenth century.

GENUS–A category of closely related organisms which is smaller in scope than the family and more inclusive than the SPECIES. The plural is *genera.* Taxonomic binomials used for the identification of organisms consist of the generic name and the specific name (e.g., *Acer rubrum*).

GEOMANCY (JEE-OH-men-see)–A form of DIVINATION, or foretelling, done by interpreting the patterns formed by casting a handful of earth onto the ground.

GEOMETRICAL–Patterns that are based on regular geometric forms.

GEOMORPHIC–Resembling the INDIGENOUS earth forms of a given site. Geomorphic planning describes designs or forms fitting into the pattern of the landscape on which the development is built. Machu Picchu in Peru is an exemplary case.

GEORGIAN–Designating the artistic style of the period when the four kings of England, George I–IV reigned, 1714–1830.

GEOTECTURE (JEE-o-TECK-ture)–1. Literally, "earth-architecture"; a structure that is built of earth and/or built entirely or partially underground. 2. The study and practice of working with earth structures.

GESTATIO (jest-AH-tee-o)–Italian word for an area designated for exercise such as a part of a VILLA landscape.

GIARDINO INGLESE (jar-DEEN-o in-GLAY-seh)–Italian for "English garden," particularly those developed in the naturalistic landscape garden style as popularized by the English in the eighteenth century.

GIARDINO SEGRETO (jar-DEEN-o say-GRET-o)–Italian for "secret garden"; a small garden set apart from the main garden of a rural RENAISSANCE garden, providing greater privacy than available in the larger, more crowded areas of the VILLA during times of festive social gatherings.

GIOCHI D'ACQUA (JOK-ee DAHK-wa)–Italian expression for "water joke." Originated by the MOORS in Spain, such features were humorous surprise sprays of water concealed in the garden and intended to sprinkle unsuspecting visitors, catching them offguard. The Spanish term is BURLADORES.

GLADE–An opening in a forest.

GLEBE (GLEEB)–1. Turf; soil; ground; especially CULTIVATED land. 2. The land belonging to a parish church or parsonage.

GLEN (GLEN)–A small, secluded mountain valley.

GLORIETA (glor-ee-EH-ta)–Spanish for a traffic circle or a round junction of paths in a garden; the equivalent of the French ROND POINT.

GNOMON (NOH-mahn)–From the Greek "to know"; a vertical feature such as a pin, column, blade, or upright fin of a SUNDIAL, which casts a shadow indicating the time of day. For centuries, the sun's shadow was the universal means of telling time and the ANCIENT Egyptians used such features as their giant PYRAMIDS and OBELISKS to cast shadows on a flat plane calibrated with the hours of day.

GOLDEN MEAN or GOLDEN SECTION–A proportional relationship obtained by dividing a line so that the shorter part is to the longer as the longer is to the whole. These proportions have an aesthetic appeal that has led artists of various periods and cultures to employ them in determining basic dimensions.

GOOSE FOOT–The English expression for radiating avenues through a garden. *See also* PATTE D'OIE.

GOTH (GAWTH)–One of a Teutonic people of the third to fifth centuries A.D. who invaded and settled in the Roman Empire.

GOTHIC–Named after the BARBARIAN tribe the GOTHS; the style of MEDIEVAL architecture in Europe from the mid-twelfth century to the Renaissance; characterized by an emphasis on the skeletal structure and thin-walled planes, pointed ARCHES, flying BUTTRESSES, RIB VAULTS, and steep roofs. Gothic Revival began in the late eighteenth century and in the United States was popular from about 1815 to 1860.

GOTHIC ARCH–A style of ARCH popular in France and elsewhere in Europe from the twelfth to the sixteenth centuries; tall and pointed.

GRADE–1. In surveying, mapping, and designing, the noun for the ground level usually expressed as feet above sea level; also called "spot elevation." 2. In construction, the verb for the act of altering the ground's level. 3. Sometimes used as a synonym for GRADIENT or degree of slope.

GRADIENT–The rate of ascent or descent in the land's surface expressed in percent; for example 10 percent gradient is a 10-vertical-foot rise or drop in a 100-foot horizontal distance; can also be expressed as a ratio, 1:10 or 10:1 or 1 on 10 or 10 on 1.

GRADING–The act of moving and reforming portions of the earth; the arrangement of the surface of the earth to suit human purposes.

GRAFTING–A method of plant reproduction by ASEXUAL means where cions or SCIONS of one plant are attached to the living stock of a different plant.

GRAND MANNER–Representation during the High Renaissance period of human figures in noble and exalted themes as prescribed by the academics. Subject matter for painting was codified in order of ideal preference with historic painting ranked first and genre painting low. Numerous rules were devised that included how to depict sentiment and passion.

GRANDIOSE (gran-DEE-OSE)–1. Impressive due to being affectedly grand, stately, or uncommonly large. 2. Characterized by excessive size and splendor; pompous.

GRAPHIC SCALE–Used in mapping or on design drawings to represent the relative sizes of the features depicted on the drawing. Used along with written scale designation (1 inch = 100 feet, etc.) to enable scale to be interpreted upon enlargement or reduction of the drawing.

GRECO (GREE-ko)–Greek or pertaining to Greece; HELLENIC; eighth to fourth centuries B.C.

GRECO-ROMAN–Of, or influenced by, both Greece and Rome; HELLENISTIC; after the reign of Alexander the Great (336–323 B.C.)

GREEK CROSS–A cross that has four arms all of equal length as distinguished from the Latin cross of Christianity.

GREEK REVIVAL–The style of architecture popular in America from about 1810 to about 1860; characterized by the use of Greek ORDERS.

GREEN–1. An early English word meaning a central public open space in a town known as the village green; in New England, referred to as the "town common." 2. The relatively level turf area used for the game of bowls; a bowling green; also golf green.

GREEN THEATER–In Italian RENAISSANCE or BAROQUE gardens, an outdoor "room" formed by clipped evergreen plants, together with statuary; was occasionally used as the setting for open-air musical or dramatic performances.

GREENBELT–An OPEN SPACE, especially densely vegetated or in agricultural use, in which building is generally banned; functions to separate an urbanized area from the surrounding RURAL countryside; may be designated as a parkland. The concept is of British origin. A BUFFER ZONE. *See also* GARDEN CITY.

GREENBELT TOWN–New communities planned and built as part of the NEW DEAL

(1933–1938) under President Franklin Delano Roosevelt. The first three were Greenhills, Ohio (5930 acres); Greendale, Wisconsin (3500 acres); and Greenbelt, Maryland (2100 acres). Greenbrook, New Jersey (4000 acres) was also planned but never built.

GREENSWARD–An open area of well-tended, manicured grass. *See also* SWARD.

GREGORIAN CALENDAR (gri-GOR-yen)–The reformed Roman (Julian) calendar in use today in Christian countries with the year divided into 365 days and a leap year of 366 days.

GRID–In surveying, a system of two sets of equidistant parallel lines running north-south and east-west and intersecting at right angles.

GRIDIRON–Term used to describe regular arrangement of streets in planned towns from ANCIENT Greek times; like a checkerboard.

GROIN–In architecture, the ridge made by the crossing of two ceiling VAULTS.

GROTTO (GRAH-to)–The Italian word for a natural or artificial cave built as a shady moist retreat from the heat. Grottoes have been popular features in the garden from the time of the ancient Romans. The word stems from the Latin *crypta,* or crypt, meaning "a cave or cavern, especially one which is picturesque . . . an agreeable retreat . . . an excavation . . . made to imitate a rocky cave, often adorned with shell-work and serving as a place of . . . cool retreat." The French word *grotesque* comes from the kind of mural painting appropriate for grottoes. From this, it has evolved into the present meaning, "absurd," "repulsive." Another French word, *rocaille,* meaning a surface encrusted with shells, pebbles, and coarse, rough-hewn rocks, was the origin of the word ROCOCO.

GROUND–1. The surface of the earth. 2. The background or surface over which other parts are put such as the main surface of a painting.

GROUND COVER–Low-growing, typically less than 12 inches tall, plant material placed close together to form a carpetlike effect; utilized to yield continuous green ground covering as well as natural erosion control and natural MULCH.

GROUNDWATER–Water that saturates the soil below the WATER TABLE.

GROVE–A grouping of trees without undergrowth. *See also* BOSKET and COPSE.

GYMNASIUM (jim-NAY-zee-um)–A place, especially a building, in which young Greek men gathered for physical exercise and education.

HABITAT–The natural place of residence of a species of plants or other organisms where all essentials for its development and existence are present.

HACHURES (HAA-shurrs)–Short pencil or ink strokes on a drawing or map to indicate a slope or depression, especially when "hach marks" are shown inside a closed contour line.

HA-HA–An eighteenth-century English expression, of unknown origin, for a trench with one vertical side and one gently sloping side which served as a barrier for grazing animals both domestic and wild, such as deer. A creative adaptation of the MOAT or a device designed for military purposes, the ha-ha was the means by which all garden designers could "leap the fence" in the early eighteenth century. As it was alternatively called, the fosse, fuassee, fossee, fowsie, sunk-fence, or a number of other terms, it was the single most important device that enabled the borders of the English LANDSCAPE GARDEN to, in fact, be blurred and off-site views incorporated into the composition. Nature could be made to "appear" to merge with the human environment if one cleverly disguised the animal barrier in a trench at the appropriate distance from the house. Thus the "specific garden," when viewed from the residence, appeared to be a continuum. It could be seen, and thought of, as a part of its surroundings. Charles Bridgeman began the construction of the ha-ha (still standing) at Stowe in 1725, although an earlier form is known to have been placed on the grounds of Levens Hall by the French gardener M. Beaumont c. 1695, and there were probably others built elsewhere.

HALF-TIMBERED–A system of building construction exposing the timber skeleton with spaces between BEAMS being filled with STUCCO or BRICK.

HAMEAU (ahm-OH)–French for "hamlet." An artificial grouping of peasant buildings to be seen in, or from, a landscape garden in England and elsewhere, such as at the Petit Trianon at Versailles, where Marie Antoinette had made a "model farm" for her and her court to play at the PASTORAL pleasure of shepherding.

HAMLET (HAM-let)–A very small village; a small cluster of houses in the country. In Britain, a village without a church of its own but belonging to the parish of another town.

HARDINESS–The adaptation of a plant or other organism to the stresses of climate, particularly to the occurrence of freezing but also to conditions of moisture and extreme heat that affect its ability to survive. The United States and Canada are divided into ten plant hardiness zones based on the average annual minimum temperature of the area.

HARDPAN–The relatively hard or impervious layer beneath the SOIL, or in the subsoil, that offers exceptionally great resistance to digging or drilling.

HARDWOOD–The hard compact wood or timber of various trees such as oak, cherry, maple, and mahogany; also trees yielding such wood. In general, the term tends to be associated with DECIDUOUS trees.

HARVARD REVOLUTION–In the 1930s, it was common for students in American university courses in landscape architecture to produce designs that were ECLECTIC or BEAUX-ARTS in character. These were simply a reapplication of old traditional forms and materials to each class assignment. This was no different than what was happening throughout the profession at the time. Following the arrival at Harvard in 1936–1937 of Walter Gropius, Ludwig Mies van der Rohe, Christopher Tunnard, and others from war-torn Europe, many of whom came through the BAUHAUS modern architectural design, the INTERNATIONAL STYLE began to be taught in the architecture classes at the Harvard Graduate School of Design. "The landscape architecture faculty," according to one of the students, John Simonds, "had the axis up their spines. Every park design had to be a little Versailles." Radical, modernist thinking was banished, thereby causing three students, Garrett Eckbo, Dan Kiley, and James Rose, to experiment surreptitiously with the new style of "Modern Garden." For their transgressions, the three were reprimanded for contradicting tradition and threatened with expulsion. Their innovative work was published in 1937 and 1938 in *Pencil Points* magazine (now *Progressive Architecture*), making it the first-ever airing of ideas about landscape architecture with the same approach to design that had been going on in Europe for a generation. Their design solutions were heavily influenced by CUBISM as it was appearing in modern sculpture and painting and FUNCTIONALISM in outdoor spaces as reflected by architects.

HECTARE (HEK-tare)–A metric measurement of land area; 10,000 square meters; 100 ares; 2.471 ACRES. One acre equals 0.4047 hectare; 1 square mile equals 259 hectares.

HEDGE–A row of woody plants used as a barrier. The plants may be trimmed or not. The term *hedgerow* is used in England for untrimmed hedges along roads and the boundaries of fields. Requiring more land width than fences, they are often preferable for their aesthetic values, for protection and breeding places for birds and small animals, and to reduce soil EROSION.

HEGIRA (he-JY-ruh)–1. The EXODUS, or escape of the prophet Mohammed, from persecutions in Mecca (in today's Saudi Arabia) to Medina. The date, 622 A.D., marks the beginning of the Mohammedan calendar. 2. The era of Mohammed. 3. A journey, especially when undertaken to escape from danger.

HELLENIC (he-LENN-ik)–Of the Greek culture from the late eighth century B.C. to the death of Alexander the Great, 323 B.C.

HELLENISTIC (he-len-IS-tic)–Of, or characteristic of, the HELLENIC after the death of Alexander the Great, 323 B.C.

HEMICYCLE (HEM-i-cy-le)–Semicircular part of a building with a semidome over it; APSE.

HENGE–A circle of wooden or stone uprights enclosed by a bank of earth or stone usually with an internal ditch, forming a part of ceremonial structures found in Britain, Scotland, and Ireland; of the late NEOLITHIC or Bronze Age.

HERALDRY (HAIR-ul-dree)–Pertaining to armorial bearings, such as a coat of arms and other symbols of genealogy, emblazoned on armor, banners, and other objects of adornment or public display.

HERB (URB)–A seed plant with little or no woody fiber in its structure, which after forming seed dies or withers away to the ground in temperate climates. In tropical or subtropical areas, it may be evergreen or arborescent. The term is also applied to any plant used for medicine, food, flavor, or scent; sometimes pronounced *herb*.

HERB GARDEN–A garden developed for the cultivation of herbs used for medicine, food, flavor, or scent; often laid out FORMALLY and ornamental in appearance.

HERBACEOUS (her-BA-shus)–Pertaining to herbs; herblike. A PERENNIAL border may sometimes be called a herbaceous border. Plants, all of whose parts are not WOODY, but are soft, as the texture and color of FOLIAGE.

HERM or HERMA–Named for the Greek god Hermes; related to the worship of stone. The bust or legless torso of a male figure emerging from a square pedestal; sometimes used as a PILASTER or monument in ANCIENT Greece and Rome placed as milestones at the crossings of roads or at the boundaries of one's property to demarcate ownership. Hermes was the god of travelers and herms were considered good-luck charms. *See also* TERM.

HERMITAGE–The house or hut wherein dwells a hermit; a secluded retreat away from people.

HERRINGBONE–Timber blocks, brickwork, or similar materials laid diagonally, creating zigzag patterns on the FACADE of a building or in a paved area.

HIEROGLYPHIC (high-er-O-GLIPH-ic)–An ANCIENT Egyptian system of writing using pictures, called pictographs, as words.

HIGH RISE–A tall building of many stories; skyscraper.

HINTERLAND–The region surrounding a city or cities; the back country or area inland from the coastal region. The hinterland of a city may consist of the area of commerce or trade from that city.

HIPPED ROOF–A TRUSS roof with slopes on all four sides. The hip is the external angle formed by the meeting of two roof surfaces rather than GABLE ends.

HIPPODAMIAN (HIP-o-DA-mi-an)–System of town planning using the GRIDIRON system of streets; named for the Greek Hippodamos, c 450 B.C.

HIPPODROME (HIP-uh-drome)–In ANCIENT Greece, an oval track for horse and chariot races, surrounded by tiered seats for spectators. This form was adapted by the Romans for use in their gardens. It was used on a grand scale by Hadrian at his VILLA in Tivoli and later, during the Renaissance, it was the central feature of the Boboli Gardens in Florence, 1550, and the Piazza di Siena, in the gardens of the Borghese villa in Rome.

HISTORIC PRESERVATION–A broad term meaning to save or protect from destruction, structures, and settings that have historic value for our society, often achieved through the combined efforts of experts such as historians, archaeologists, architects, landscape architects, planners, lawyers, craftspersons, conservators, and realtors. The Department of the Interior defines preservation as "the process of sustaining the existing form, integrity and material of a structure and the existing form and vegetative cover of its setting. It may include ongoing maintenance of the same."

HISTORIC RECONSTRUCTION – The Department of the Interior defines preservation as "the process of reproducing by new construction the exact form and detail of a vanished structure, or part thereof, as it appeared at a specific period of time."

HISTORIC RESTORATION–The Department of the Interior defines preservation as "the process of accurately recovering the form and details of a property and its setting as it appeared at a particular period of time by means of removal of later work or by the replacement of missing earlier work."

HIVING OFF–An expression used in early New England for the formation of a new community by people no longer able to be sustained by the original town; usually, second generation from the original settlers of a community.

HOLISTIC (ho-LIS-tik)–From holism, the theory that wholes, more than the sum of the parts, are fundamental ASPECTS of the real. Emphasizing the organic or functional relationship between parts and wholes. Holistic planning attempts to see its subject as a single integrated system of mutually interdependent parts.

HOLY ROMAN EMPIRE–The empire comprised of a group of European lands ruled over by Frankish (French) and German kings for ten centuries, beginning with the coronation of Charlemagne (800) until it was dissolved by Napoleon I in 1806. It represented the continuation of the Western Roman Empire but was led by the pope as its spiritual head.

HOMESTEAD–A 160-acre tract of public land in an unsettled area granted by the government for development as a farm under the Homestead Act of 1862, enacted to open up the midsection of America by pioneers or homesteaders; also a place where a family makes its home including the land, house, and outbuildings.

HORIZON–1. The line demarcating the plane of the earth from the sky. 2. A layer in the soil that is distinct in its composition and structure from adjacent layers of soil. A vertical section through various horizons is called a *profile*.

HORTICULTURE–The science or art of propagating and cultivating plants for produce or for ornament.

HORTUS CONCLUSUS–Literally, "enclosed garden" in Latin. In the Song of Solomon (4:12), "A garden enclosed is my sister, my spouse; a spring shut up; a fountain sealed." A CLOSED GARDEN, used as a symbol of Mary's virginity. *See also* CLOISTER

HUE–The name of any of the colors as they appear in the SPECTRUM of sunlight. The PRIMARY COLORS (blue, red, and yellow) together with the SECONDARY COLORS (green, orange, and violet) form the chief colors of the SPECTRUM. Many thousands of tints and shades of these hues are recognized and named.

HUMAN SCALE–1. The dimensions of the parts or totality of a building or object in relation to its function or use by humans. In design, the size of parts relative to the whole or to the human figure. In an environment, the size of all the components must be in appropriate scale relationship with one another and with the users of those features. 2. That combination of qualities that give man's work a comfortable relationship to his size and feelings. Great height and bulk are thought to be the prime destroyers of human scale in cities. *See also* SCALE and ERGONOMICS.

HUMANISM–Any system of thought in which humanitarians predominate; the taste for and practice of literate humanitarism; of a CULTURE based on the study, spread, and use of the ANCIENT Greek and Roman authors. The movement stemmed from Petrarch. Its first real effect was on moral philosophy. After 1450–1460, it spread to each cultural discipline in turn until it became the characteristic flavor of the cultural phase of the RENAISSANCE.

HUMUS–Dark-colored, organic, well-decomposed SOIL consisting of the residues of plant and animal matter together with synthesized cell substances of soil organisms and various inorganic elements. *See also* PEAT.

HYBRID–A plant or animal offspring from a cross between parents of different SPECIES or varieties.

HYDRIC (HY-drik)–An ECOSYSTEM that tends to be excessively moist; plants that are adapted to survive in such places of extreme moisture are *hydrophytes* (HY-dro-fites).

HYDROLOGIC CYCLE–The never-ending transference of water through evaporation, transpiration, atmospheric circulation, and precipitation.

HYDROLOGY–The branch of physical geography that studies water distribution, movement, and quality.

HYDROPONICS–The system of growing plants in a nutrient solution rather than in SOIL

HYPOSTYLE (HY-po-stile)–A colonnaded hall comprised of many rows of columns that support the roof, such as the Temple of Amon at Karnak.

ICON (EYE-kon)–An image, especially in the Greek church; a panel with a painting of sacred personages. In the visual arts, a painting, piece of sculpture, or even a building regarded as sacred.

ICONOGRAPHY (eye-con-OG-rafy)–The study that deals with the symbolic meaning of objects, persons, or events depicted in works of art or ICONS.

IDYLLIC (eye-DIL-ik)–Having the nature of the PASTORAL, PICTURESQUE, or simple.

IMPACT–In environmental terms, to infringe upon the ecological equilibrium; to disturb or upset an existing set of environmental conditions that were previously in balance.

IMPERIAL–Literally means "of an empire," such as the Roman Empire, 48 B.C.–A.D. 476.

IMPLUVIUM (im-PLOO-vee-um)–In Greek and Roman houses, a shallow tank or pool under the opening in the roof of an ATRIUM.

IMPRESSIONISM–A type of artistic realism whose aim is to render the immediate sensory impression of the artist. It originated in nineteenth-century France, 1865–1875, with the work of Edouard Manet, was developed and altered by Claude Monet, Renoir, and others. A main concern of the Impressionists was the study and representation of light rather than of detail.

IN SITU (IN SY-too)–Latin for "in its original place"; usually referring to rock carved in the place where it occurs naturally, such as the CATACOMBS in Rome.

INDICATOR–In ecology, an organism whose presence under natural conditions indicates the existence of certain requisite environmental conditions.

INDIGENOUS (in-DIJ-in-us)–Native or produced naturally in a region; not EXOTIC.

INFORMAL DESIGN–The PLAN or development of a given area to follow natural or irregular lines; not FORMAL.

INSULA (INN-su-la)–Latin word for a multifamily residential structure, often including shops aligned along one or more of its outside walls and may have achieved five stories in height; an apartment building.

INTAGLIO (in-TALL-yo)–In design, the forms carved or engraved out of the surface like

RELIEF in reverse; signet ring, as opposed to *cameo*.

INTERFACE–A surface that occurs between two parts of space or matter and functions as their common boundary. In planning jargon, the meeting point of two different LAND USES or DEMOGRAPHIC zones.

INTERNATIONAL STYLE–An architectural design style based on a departure from the old principles of design in favor of a fresh approach to the ideas of FUNCTIONALISM, structure, SPACE, and the PLAN of buildings. Popularized by Mies van der Rohe, Wright, Gropius, and Corbusier, 1910–1935, at the BAUHAUS in Germany.

INTERPROFESSIONAL COLLABORATION–The combined efforts of a number of experts from different creative disciplines, such as architecture, landscape architecture, urban planning, and engineering, working mutually on a common project.

IONIC (eye-ON-ik)–The second of the three CLASSICAL ORDERS; characterized by CAPITALS with spiral scrolls (called VOLUTES), tall, graceful FLUTED shafts, and molded bases. *See also* ORDER.

IRRIGATION–The engineered distribution of water onto land to promote the growth of vegetation where insufficient natural rainfall limits plant growth.

ISLAM (IZ-LAHM)–The religious system of the Almighty Potentate, Allah, begun by Mohammed in A.D. 607–612, in today's Saudi Arabia; Mohammedanism. The entire geographical area of the believers of the Islamic religion. The holy book, the KORAN, with the revelations by Allah, was written in Arabic by Mohammed. The adherents are called MOSLEMS or MUSLIMS.

JACOBEAN (JOK-uh-BEE-un)–Pertaining to the time of James I of England, 1566–1625, who reigned 1603 to 1625.

JAPANESE GARDEN–The Japanese garden principles were adapted from the Chinese. The many types include *tsuki-yama,* hill garden; *hira-niwa,* flat garden; *kare-sansui,* garden of contemplation; and *shakkei,* borrowed view garden.

JARDIN (jhahr-DAN)–French for "garden."

JARDIN ANGLAIS (jhahr-DAN-ahng-GLAY)–French term for "English garden"; ROMANTIC, NATURALESQUE, LANDSCAPE GARDEN. Designated the opposite of the *jardin régulier* or the *jardin a la française,* with its grand and geometric gardens in the style of Le Nôtre.

JARDIN ANGLO CHINOIS (jhahr-DAN-AHNG-lo-SHEEN-WAHZ)–The French term for gardens designed in the English natural style with Chinese features such as PAGODAS and Chinese bridges placed in the landscape.

JARDINIÈRE (JHAHR-din-eer)–An ornamental container, usually ceramic, for growing and displaying plants, flowers, and so on; an urn.

JARGON (JAR-gun)–Unintelligible or meaningless language; the vocabulary peculiar to a specific trade or discipline; uncommon or unfamiliar words or expressions, hence sometimes thought of as esoteric, exclusionary, gibberish, or gobbledegook.

JET D'EAU (JHAY DOE)–French for "jet of water"; an upright spray or fountain.

JETTY–A pier or structure of stones extending into a body of water; a wharf; used to protect a harbor from strong wave action of an exposed shoreline.

JIA-SHAN (JEE-uh- SHAHN)–Chinese for artificial hill or false mountain, created in a garden to conjure thoughts of mountain walks or looking at scroll paintings. Such places were the abodes of mythical Chinese Immortals. These may be small, but some gardens during the Ming dynasty had huge assemblages, the size of buildings, through which strollers could move. The solid, coarseness of the rock served as the *yang,* which was balanced by soft vegetation and still water as the *yin*.

JIE-JING (JY-JING)–the Chinese term for BORROWED SCENERY; the counterpart of the Japanese, SHAKKEI. Viewed from within an enclosed garden or courtyard, desirable outside scenery, buildings, and so on, are incorporated into the composition, to lend a sense of a larger space.

JOIST–One of the horizontal timbers or BEAMS laid parallel to support a floor or ceiling.

JULIAN CALENDAR–The calendar established by Emperor Julius Caesar in 46 B.C. and made up of twelve months or 365 days, with leap year having 366 days.

JUXTAPOSE (JUKS-tuh-pose)–To place various objects side by side or in close proximity.

KARE-SANSUI (KAHR-e-sahn-SOO-ee)–Japanese term for "dry rock garden."

KEEP–The innermost part of a castle; often the living quarters in a tower surrounded by walls.

KEYSTONE–The central uppermost VOUSSOIR or stone in an ARCH. When in place, the arch is stabilized.

KINETIC (ki-NET-ik)–Movable; resulting from motion; DYNAMIC or energetic.

KIOSK (KEE-osk)–1. A light open pavilion in Turkey and Persia. 2. Small open structure used as a bandstand or newsstand; cylindrical, octagonal, and so on, structure for posting notices.

KITCHEN GARDEN–A garden developed for the production of edible vegetables. They were sometimes adjuncts to the pleasure gardens of the aristocracy in ancient and medieval times. *See also* DOORYARD GARDEN and POTAGER.

KNIGHT–In the Middle Ages, a mounted soldier serving under a king or lord.

KNOT GARDEN–From the word for any figure made up of frequently intersecting lines, as in embroidery. An early English expression for a garden composed of small hedges, bedding plants, and other ground covers in elaborate designs and patterns reminiscent of the designs and knots used in embroidery. *See also* PARTERRE.

KORAN (ko-RAN)–The sacred book of the ISLAMIC religion; the revelations to Mohammed by Allah, written in Arabic. Spelled *Qur'án* in Arabic.

L-SHAPED PIAZZA–A PIAZZA, or urban space in Italy, which is shaped like the letter L; a rectangular space with a structure protruding into one edge, forming a "dogleg," or two-armed public area.

LABYRINTH (LAB-i-rinth)–A place full of intricate passageways; a MAZE; a maze of paths in a PARK or GARDEN.

LAND USE–The utilization of a site, such as designation of industrial, residential, commercial, recreational, or other uses, under a master plan.

LAND USE PLAN–The official formulation of the future uses of land, including the public and private improvements to be made on it and the assumptions and reasons for arriving at the determinations. A land use plan is not to be confused with the land use map, which describes how the land and buildings are or have been used, a zoning plan that regulates use, density, coverage, bulk, and so on, or with the comprehensive plan of which it is often a part.

LANDFORM–A TERRAIN feature that has been sculpted by natural processes and has a definable composition and range of characteristics that occur wherever that landform is found. Landforms may be classified as depositional, diastrophic, erosional, or residual.

LANDMARK–A fixed object used to mark a boundary; a prominent feature of a landscape or cityscape that is the emblem or symbol of a place and helps the traveler to know where he or she is, such as a capitol dome or church steeple; spots or structures particularly valued because of their historic or cultural interest.

LANDSCAPE–1. The noun *landscape* evolved from the Dutch *landschap* and the German *landschaft,* meaning a place that is both human-altered or inhabited and surrounded by forest or WILDERNESS. It did not mean natural per se, but a parcel of land with its distinguishing characteristics and features as modified or shaped by processes and agents of human beings. 2. A view or PROSPECT of natural inland scenery such as can be taken in at a glance from one point of view; a piece of country scenery. The use of the word *natural* in the previous definition is, unfortunately, misleading since it implies that such a view must be natural, when, in fact, "natural-looking" or "naturalesque," an imitation of nature, might be more accurate. 3. Landscape also means the type of picture or painting that depicts a rural or countryside view as distinguished from a seascape or portrait. When, in eighteenth-century England, it became fashionable to collect and display seventeenth-century romantic paintings of Italian rural scenery, the English called these landscapes or the older word *landskips,* just as a portrayal of a person is called a *portrait*. The merging of the words *landscape* and GARDEN into a characterization of the design style used to treat the grounds around a country house came about during the mid-eighteenth century (c. 1759). It is assumed to have been the invention of the poet and garden critic William Shenstone. It was meant that the appearance of the residential site, both at a distance and near the house, had the pictorial qualities of the paintings. Thus it looked like a landscape picture. Since all grounds around English houses are called gardens, whether or not they consist of plant BEDS, the expression meant a site treated in the manner of the romantic paintings, predominantly NATURALISTIC in character. 4. The use of landscape as a verb, meaning "to embellish the grounds around a structure by making it part of a continuous and harmonious landscape," is primarily an Americanism, barely used by other English-speaking societies.

LANDSCAPE ARCHITECT–A person skilled in the science and art of designing within the landscape. The right to use this title is restricted by law to licensees in most states.

LANDSCAPE ARCHITECTURE–The art of space utilization in the landscape. Landscape architecture is concerned with the use to which landscape space is put, the creation of controlled environments within the landscape space, the adaptation of organisms to both the natural and the controlled environment, and the conservation of the aesthetic values and resources of the landscape. The definition of the field was stated in 1917 by Henry V. Hubbard and his wife, Theodora Kimball, in their book *An Introduction to the Study of Landscape Design*. They wrote: "Landscape Architecture's most important function is to create and preserve beauty in the surroundings of human habitations and in the broader natural scenery of the country; but it is also concerned with promoting the comfort, convenience and health of urban populations, which have scanty access to rural scenery, and urgently need to have their hurrying workaday lives refreshed and calmed by the beautiful and reposeful sights and sounds which nature, aided by the landscape art, can abundantly provide." Garrett Eckbo wrote about the profession in his *Landscape for Living* (1950): "It is the establishment of relations between building, surfacing, and other outdoor construction, earth, rock forms, bodies of water, plants and open space, and the general form and character of the landscape; but with primary emphasis on the human content, the relationship between people and landscape, between human beings and three-dimensional outdoor space quantitatively and qualitatively."

LANDSCAPE CONTRACTOR–A contractor who specializes in constructing or installing landscape architectural projects.

LANDSCAPE GARDEN–A NATURALISTIC garden style popular in the eighteenth and nineteenth centuries. It came about as a reaction against the grand formal styles common in England and Europe during and after the Renaissance. The landscape garden style had perhaps its finest development in England under "Capability" Brown and Humphrey Repton, and later in America under Andrew Jackson Downing, Frederick Law Olmsted, Jens Jensen, and others.

LANDSCAPIST–A painter of scenes of the landscape. Among the most noted and influential relative to the romanticization of nature scenery and the profession of landscape architecture were the great seventeenth-century masters Claude Lorraine, Nicholas Poussin, and Salvator Rosa, the English masters John Constable and J. M. W. Turner, and the American Hudson River School painters Thomas Cole, Frederick Edwin Church, and Albert Bierstadt.

LANDSKIP (LAND-skip)–A painted scene of rural countryside. *See also* LANDSCAPE.

LANTERN–In architecture, a small decorative structure atop a DOME, CUPOLA, or roof. It has windows for admitting sunlight. Thus it resembles a lantern from which it takes its name.

LATH HOUSE–A structure enclosed with narrow parallel slats; used to produce a partial shade for the CULTIVATION of plants.

LATIN CROSS–A cross whose vertical member is longer than the horizontal member through whose midpoint it passes; the traditional cross of Christianity. *See also* GREEK CROSS.

LATTICE (LATT-iss)–A structure made of flat, narrow wooden strips (lath) or metal straps that are crossed at right angles and usually with small square openings; typically used as a screen and/or as a support for climbing plants.

LAWN–An expanse of closely mowed TURF or grass. See SWARD.

LE GRAND SIECLE (luh-GRAHN-see-EH-kl)–French for the great age, century, or generation during which King Louis XIV (1638–1715) reigned as LE ROI SOLEIL, the Sun King; from 1643 to 1715.

LE MOYEN AGE (luh-mwa-yah-NAJH)–The French expression for the MIDDLE AGES.

LE ROI SOLEIL (luh-RWAH-so-LAYL)–French for the Sun King; pertaining to King Louis XIV (1638–1715), who reigned from 1643 to 1715, the longest of any French monarch. He was absolute ruler of France and was the center of all aspects of French life, as the sun is the center of our solar system. His court was the most splendid of all royal courts in Europe. He built the palace and gardens of Versailles into the most GRANDIOSE royal residence of all time.

LEACHING–The process by which soluble matter in the SOIL such as nutrients, chemicals, or contaminants percolate or are filtered into a lower layer of soil or are dissolved and carried away by water.

LIMITING FACTOR–The least abundant of the essential factors in an environment and therefore the one that determines the existence or survival of each organism or a related group of organisms within that environment.

LINE OF BEAUTY–In 1753, the English painter William Hogarth defined the curve or SERPENTINE line as the "line of beauty" in his book *The Analysis of Beauty*.

LINEAR PERSPECTIVE–A scene, whether real, photographic, or painted, that possesses perspective formed by the use of lines which appear to extend from foreground into the background or to a vanishing point as opposed to ATMOSPHERIC PERSPECTIVE.

LINNAEAN SYSTEM (lin-EE-en)–The system of classifying plants and animals that uses a two-part name. The first word is the GENUS, the second is the SPECIES, with all or part of each word having a descriptive meaning in Latin. Thus *Acer rubrum* is known by its common name, red maple; named for the Swedish botanist, Carl von Linne, 1707–1778, who Latinized his own name to Carolus Linnaeus. *See also* TAXONOMY and NOMENCLATURE.

LINTEL–A horizontal BEAM of any material, such as stone or wood over a door or window in the POST AND LINTEL system; also called ARCHITRAVE in CLASSICAL architecture.

LITHOTECTURE (LITH-o-tek-chur)–Architecture made from living rock, or carved out of rock IN SITU; an underground structure formed by excavating the rock in that place.

LITTORAL (LIT-o-ral)–Pertaining to the shore of a sea or lake; sometimes used as a name for the strip of land between low and high tides.

LOAM–A fertile SOIL composed of sand and CLAY particles with some SILT and HUMUS.

LOCUS AMOENUS (LO-cuss uh-MOAN-US)–The "pleasant place"; unspoiled; untended.

LOESS (LESS)–Windborne SOIL made up of SILT or dust; highly fertile when mixed with HUMUS.

LOGGIA (LO-jhah)–The Italian word for a covered GALLERY or PORTICO with an open ARCADE or COLONNADE on at least one side. A small loggia is a loggetta.

LOT–A parcel of land; a PLOT; a property; from allotment, or the drawing of lots, as in a raffle. In colonial America, lots were once distributed by this system.

LOTUS (LOHT-us)–A tropical water lily, genus *Nymphaea,* believed to be sacred by the Egyptians. Eating the fruit was supposed to induce a dreamy euphoria.

MACADAM (mek-AD-um)–A type of road construction and surfacing formed by laying down and successively rolling graded-size crushed stone or AGGREGATE. The largest sizes are placed at the bottom and each layer is composed of smaller rock fragments, with sand-sized particles being used as the topmost COURSE. It is named for its inventor, Thomas MacAdam, 1756–1836, a Scottish engineer. Roads today are made in much the same manner with a top binder layer of ASPHALT, or bituminous material, used to seal the entire road; sometimes called *blacktop*.

MACROCLIMATE–The pattern of atmospheric conditions within a given locality as measured over open ground; data obtained by local meteorological stations. See MICROCLIMATE.

MALTHUSIANISM (mahl-THOO-ze-an-ism)–Thomas R. Malthus, 1766–1834, a British political economist conceived the theory that human population, if uncontrolled, can increase at a rate faster than the means of subsistence by agriculture.

MANNERISM–A characteristic manner or style carried to excess; a term used to generalize about a sixteenth-century style in art.

MANOR–1. A mansion or large house as the main residence of an estate. 2. In FEUDAL England, the district or land over which the lord had authority, partially divided among his peasants in return for rent or crop sharing.

MANSARD ROOF (MON-sard)–A roof with a steep, almost vertical, lower slope and flatter upper portion; named after French architect, F. Mansarde, 1598–1666; similar to a GAMBREL roof except for its sloping ends.

MARBLE–The metamorphic form of limestone, including dolomites and magnesias in which the calcite and mineral dolomite are recrystallized. True marble is a granular crystalline rock made up of calcite or dolomite grains cemented or intergrown and interlocked by additional calcite. It is white. The mottling, banding, and colors of ornamental varieties are due to impurities such as oxides of iron and organic matter. Also, a tradename for any carbonate rock of good color and texture which is hard enough to take a polish. It is one of the favorite carving stones used by sculptures.

MASONRY–A structure made by a mason or masons; brickwork, stonework, or structures of concrete block.

MASTABA (MAH-sta-ba)–An ANCIENT Egyptian rectangular, flat-topped FUNERARY mound with BATTERED (sloping) sides covering a subterranean burial chamber; the forerunner of the PYRAMID.

MASTER PLAN–A term in widespread use for any plan that is assumed to be comprehensive; to depict or describe an ultimate development, whether it be for a region, city, or specific site.

MATRIX (MAY-tricks)–1. In mathematics or statistical analysis, a set of numbers arranged in horizontal rows and vertical columns for purposes of comparison of given variables. 2. The natural material in which a fossil, metal, gem, crystal, or pebble is embedded.

MATTE, MAT (MAHT)–Dull surface finish; without luster; produced on metal, pottery, photography, paper, and so on.

MAUSOLEUM (MAW-ze-LEE-um)–A rich and elaborate tomb; from the tomb of Mausolus at Halicarnassus, Asia Minor in 550 B.C.

MAZE–A network of interconnecting passages, either carved in the stone floor of a MEDIEVAL church or formed of clipped evergreen hedges, a LABYRINTH.

MAZE GARDEN–A garden consisting of hedges or other barriers of varying heights arranged as a LABYRINTH. Mazes were popular in large public and private gardens in England and Europe from the MIDDLE AGES to the nineteenth century.

MEADOWS–A grassland, especially one suited for growing hay.

MECCA (MEK-uh)–A city in western Saudi Arabia; one of two federal capitals; birthplace of MOHAMMED; the religious capital of ISLAM.

MEDIEVAL, MEDIAEVAL (mee-dee-EE-vel)–A term taken to comprehend the ROMANESQUE and GOTHIC periods of architectural development; pertaining to the period of the MIDDLE AGES between the fall of the CLASSICAL Roman Empire and the RENAISSANCE, c. A.D. 476–1350.

MEDITERRANEAN CLIMATE–The type of climate that is found in the countries bordering on the Mediterranean Sea as well as in South Africa and southern California. The climatic conditions, determined by their proximity to a large sea or ocean, are characterized by warm, dry summers with low humidity, and wet winters.

MEDIUM–The material(s) such as oil paint, marble, or clay in which an artist works. In painting, the vehicle, usually liquid, that carries the pigment. Also, the vehicle through which information is communicated such as film, newspaper, books, and so on.

MEGALITH (MEG-a-lith)–A single huge stone, especially one used in the construction of an ANCIENT MONUMENT.

MEGALOPOLIS, MEGAPOLIS (Meg-uh-LOP-oh-lis)–The combined urbanized area resulting from the gradual merging of many cities into one great urban sprawl. Ancient Greece had a city by the name. A contemporary meaning was given it, in 1961, by Jean Gottman in his book *Megalopolis*. The subject of this book, the northeastern U.S. coastal region lying between Boston and Washington, or "Bowash," is the most striking example of such an area. It is characterized by an almost continuous string of cities.

MEGASTRUCTURE–A very large structure that is larger than a single building; a consolidation of several buildings.

MERIDIAN–1. An abstraction; a true north-south line running through the earth's poles from which longitudes, AZIMUTHS, or township lines are measured. 2. Of or pertaining to noon or midday; the "meridian hour."

MERLON (MER-len)–One of the teeth forming BATTLEMENTS atop a fortified structure.

MESIC (MEE-zik)–An ECOSYSTEM that tends to be neither excessively dry, XERIC, nor excessively wet, HYDRIC; plants that are adapted to survive in such places of moderate moisture are *mesophytes* (MEEZ-o-fites).

MESOLITHIC (mez-oh-LITH-ik)–Literally, "Middle Stone Age"; pertaining to the period between the PALEOLITHIC and NEOLITHIC; characterized by food gathering and the emergence of agriculture.

METES AND BOUNDS–Areas of the United States settled and surveyed prior to the establishment and use of the rectangular National Survey Grid, 1785, contain parcels of land recorded by metes (meaning "to measure") and bounds, the length of each side of a property. They were more often than not irregular in outline and were noted along with the compass bearing or direction of each boundary line. This is an imperfect system of land surveying because it was based on the use of existing topographical features such as rocks, trees, water bodies, or other distinctive features as corner monuments to demarcate properties or even political boundaries. State lines were often established in such a manner and have subsequently been contested due to such natural occurrences as a change in the course of a river used as the boundary between contiguous states.

METROPOLIS (me-TROP-oh-lis) – The chief city of a country, state, or region. The word derives from the Greek *meter* meaning "mother" and POLIS meaning "city" (i.e., the mother city); used to denote any large city.

MICROCLIMATE–Succession of atmospheric conditions measured within a given locality (e.g., meteorology at different places within a city or other specific environment). See MACROCLIMATE.

MIDDLE AGES–The time in European history between CLASSIC ANTIQUITY and the Italian RENAISSANCE, c. A.D. 476–1350; also called the DARK AGES or the MEDIEVAL period. This period is sometimes considered from c. A.D. 1100 to as late as c. 1500.

MILE–A unit of distance equal to 5280 feet or 1.60935 kilometers. The geographical mile, which is also called the nautical mile or knot, is equal to 6080 feet in England.

MINARET (min-a-RET)–In Islamic architecture, a slender tower, with a balcony at its top, built near, or as part of, a MOSQUE from which a MUEZZIN, or crier, calls the faithful to prayer.

MIRADOR (MEER-a-dore)–Spanish word for "window" or "balcony" that commands a VIEW, especially from a garden or courtyard.

MOAT–A trench, usually filled with water, around a fortified structure or position.

MODERN–From the French word *moderne,* for "mode" or "of recent times"; having to do with the latest styles or ideas; up to date; the current fashion.

MODULE (MOD-YOOL)–A basic unit of which the dimensions of the major parts of a work are multiples; used in sculpture and other art-forms. It is most often employed in architecture. The module may be the dimensions of an important part of a building, such as a COLUMN; some commonly accepted unit of measurement such as the centimeter or inch; the average dimensions of the human figure, as with Le Corbusier's "Le Modular."

MOGHUL (MOH-guhl)–From the Persian word for "Mongol"; refers to any of the Mongolian conquerors of India or their descendants; also spelled "Mogol."

MOHAMMED (mo-HAH-med) – (c. A.D. 570–632) The English spelling of the Arabian prophet and founder of the Mohammedan religion between A.D. 607 and 612. The sacred book, the KORAN, with the revelations by Allah, was written in Arabic by Mohammed. His followers are called MOSLEMS or MUSLIMS. His name means "to praise," and is spelled Muhammad or Mahomet in Arabic as well as many other spellings in the various Moslem countries. The HEGIRA or escape of Mohammed from persecutions in Mecca to Medina in A.D. 622 marks the beginning of the Mohammedan calendar.

MONASTERY–A place of residence occupied by MONKS who have retired from the world under religious vows. *See also* ABBEY.

MONASTIC (mun-AS-tik)–Characteristic of MONASTERIES.

MONK–A man who, as a member of a MONASTIC religious ORDER living under vows of chastity, poverty, and obedience according to rules set down by that order, has withdrawn from society at large. Also called a FRIAR.

MONOCHROME (MON-o-KROME)–A painting or other composition executed in varying VALUES of one HUE or color.

MONOCULTURE–A single crop grown over an area for varying periods of time; a relatively unstable plant COMMUNITY. A grass lawn is a monoculture.

MONOLITH (MAHN-o-lith)–A single large piece of stone as used in architecture or sculpture.

MONUMENT–1. In surveying, a tree, river, stone, or other permanent object demarcating property lines under the system of METES AND BOUNDS. 2. An enduring object erected as memorial to a person or event.

MOON GATE–A Chinese decorative feature, called DI XUE, in the walled garden or courtyard. Usually circular in shape (symbolizing heaven), but sometimes octagonal; often leading to a vista.

MOOR (MUUR)–1. A MOSLEM of Arabic and Berber racial mix living in the area of Morocco in northwestern Africa. 2. A person from Morocco who invaded and settled in southern Spain in the eighth century. They controlled the region of Andalusia until driven out by the Christians in 1492. Moorish kings built many splendid palaces and gardens in Spain. They originated many playful uses of water in the garden.

MORTAR–A viscous mixture of CEMENT, or lime with sand and water, used to bond units such as concrete blocks, bricks, or stones together; also used as a plaster or STUCCO.

MOSAIC (mo-ZAY-ik)–Patterns or compositions formed by embedding small pieces of stone or glass (tesserae) in MORTAR or wet plaster on surfaces such as walls and floors.

MOSLEM (MAHZ-lum)–The English spelling of MUSLIM; pertaining to MOHAMMEDISM; a believer in MOHAMMED; an adherent of the ISLAMIC religion. Also spelled *Muslem.*

MOSQUE (MOSK)–A place of adoration; a Moslem or Islamic temple or place of worship.

MOSS HOUSE–A rustic or primitive type of small garden structure popular in the English Victorian era (1837–1900); made of logs with the bark remaining on them and frequently covered in moss and roofed in thatch. Also called a bark house. Akin to the HERMITAGE of the eighteenth century.

MOTIF (mo-TEEF)–A main element, idea, or feature of a composition or design. A main topic or subject in a story, piece of music, building design, or garden. A design pattern or elements, such as polka dots, in a fabric design or in MOSAIC tiles which are repeated throughout.

MOTTE (MOT)–The earthen mound of a castle; usually has a related BAILEY, thus a walled courtyard.

MOUNT–A raised place or small hill, usually human-made, designed to give a view of the estate. ELIZABETHAN gardens of any importance had a mount upon which one could climb "to view a fair prospect." At the top there was usually an ARBOR or sitting place.

MUDEJAR (mood-AY-har)–A vernacular style of Spanish architecture, particularly of the Aragon and Castile regions, of the twelfth to sixteenth centuries blending Moslem and Christian characteristics. Its influence survived into the seventeenth century.

MUEZZIN (MOO-ez-en)–In the Islamic religion the crier who, from a MINARET, calls the faithful to prayer five times each day.

MULCH–A layer of leaves, straw, or other semidecomposed organic material placed on the surface of the SOIL. Mulches reduce evaporation. They also reduce water runoff, prevent EROSION, and improve soil structure by reducing compaction, controlling weeds, and insulating against freezing. Materials such as paper, rocks, and vermiculite may also be used.

MULLION (MULL-yun)–A vertical divider in a window.

MURAL (MYOOR-al)–Literally, pertaining to a wall; a painting on a wall; a FRESCO is a type of mural executed in wet plaster.

MUSLIM–*See* MOSLEM.

MYRTLE (MERT-uhl)–An evergreen SHRUB or tree of the GENUS *Myrtus,* native to southern Europe and Asia, with glossy leaves, small inconspicuous flowers, and aromatic berries. In ANCIENT times it was considered sacred and emblematic of Venus and love.

MYSTICISM (MIS-teh-siz-um)–Obscure thought or speculation; occult; transintellectual and intuitive; the belief that a human's chief end lies in seeking an intimate union of the soul with the Divinity, with nature, or the world soul, achieved through contemplation.

NARTHEX–An entry porch or vestibule of a church, usually COLONNADED or ARCADED and preceding the NAVE.

NATURALESQUE–In landscape architecture, the manner of, or having the quality of, nature but contrived; consciously composed by human beings to look like a natural setting; popularized in eighteenth-century England.

NATURALISTIC–The quality of being like nature and not of human-made appearance; a carefully organized planting of INDIGENOUS plant materials.

NAVE–The part of a church between the entrance and the CHOIR flanked by PIERS or COLUMNS that separate it from the aisles.

NECROPOLIS (neh-KROP-o-liss)–A large burial area; a city of the dead such as Thebes or Memphis in ancient Egypt.

NEGATIVE SPACE–A SPACE without a definite, consciously intended purpose; accidental; a SPACE that is not bounded by definite edges such as walls, dense vegetation, or landforms. A negative SPACE feels ambiguous and lacks clarity or integrity.

NEOCLASSICISM–Literally, "new classicism"; a style following the BAROQUE; characterized by a more academic use of CLASSICAL features.

NEOLITHIC–New Stone Age. Of or pertaining to the later period of the Stone Age, which saw the first elements of a farming economy and human settlements.

NEW DEAL–Legislation passed in 1933, in the first year of President Franklin Delano Roosevelt's administration, 1932–1945, enacted to overcome the economic depression; the CCC and TVA were among the programs began then.

NEW TOWN–A community developed according to a comprehensive master plan and design of its component parts. The Greeks of the fifth century B.C., in the time of Hippodamus, formulated some of the earliest town planning principles related to the establishment of their colonial towns all around the shores of the Mediterranean Sea. Sir Ebenezer Howard promoted the concept of "garden cities" in his book *Garden Cities for To-morrow* (1898). Radburn, New Jersey (1927–1929) is one of America's most influential new towns. During the Great Depression of the 1930s, the federal government developed three important "greenbelt" towns, Greenbelt, Maryland; Greendale, Wisconsin; and Greenhills, Ohio.

NICHE (NICH or NEESH)–1. A recess in a wall, hollowed like a shell, for a statue or ornament. 2. The particular role or job of an individual species or organism in its community and its environment, including its position in the food cycle.

NODE–1. The knot on a stem of a plant from which a leaf or leaves sprout. 2. A point of intersection or tangency of two or more linear elements.

NOMAD (NO-mad)–Any wanderer who has no permanent home; tribal person who moves constantly in search of food.

NOMENCLATURE (no-men-KLAY-chur)–The system of naming and the names related to a specific discipline, such as design or botany; the names or vocabulary of a field of interest; closely related to TAXONOMY, the science of ordering; the botanical classification system that is in use today. *See also* LINNAEAN SYSTEM.

NORMAN–The style, also termed English ROMANESQUE, of the eleventh and twelfth centuries.

NUMINOUS (NUM-i-nus)–1. Supernatural; mysterious. 2. Filled with the sense of the presence of divinity. 3. Appealing to the higher emotions or to the aesthetic sense.

NYMPHAEUM (nim-FAY-um)–A sanctuary of the nymphs; a building in classic architecture for plants and running water ornamented with statues.

OASIS (o-AY-sis)–A green, sometimes moist and cool, fertile place in a desert area.

OBELISK (OB-e-lisk)–Of Egyptian origin; a tall vertical monument, usually MONOLITHIC, square in section and tapering up toward a PYRAMIDAL apex. The most notable examples were created by the ANCIENT Egyptians.

OBJET D'ART (O-JHAY DAR)–French expression for "object of art"; a small object of artistic value.

OCCIDENTAL–Characteristic of Western cultures; non ORIENTAL.

OCCULT BALANCE–A characteristic of an ASYMMETRICAL composition when the eye or mind gives equal weight to objects perceived on either side of an assumed AXIS.

OFFSCAPE (OFF-scape)–Referring to taking advantage of desirable views or scenery beyond the boundaries of one's own property; BORROWED SCENERY. *See also* SHAKKAI.

OGEE (OH-jee)–A molding formed by a convex and concave curve; also an S-curved form.

OPEN SPACE–A land area free of building coverage and open to passage; used as a park, COMMON playground, garden, or even natural clearings; usually public and recreational in character.

ORACLE (OR-e-kel)–1. In ANCIENT Greece, an obscure utterance given by a medium, priest, or priestess at a shrine as the response of the god to whom an inquiry was given. 2. The place or shrine at which an inquiry to one of the Greek gods is given: *the oracle of Apollo at Delphi*. 3. A divine communication or vision. 4. The person serving as the agent for a divine communication.

ORANGERIE or ORANGERY (o-RAHNJ-ree)–French word for a garden structure, hothouse, or sheltered place within a garden for the protected growth of citrus trees in cooler climates; popular in England, c. seventeenth to nineteenth centuries.

ORDER–1. A system governing the design of COLUMNS and ENTABLATURES in CLASSIC architecture. In Greek architecture there are two main orders, the DORIC and IONIC, and one subordinate, the CORINTHIAN. To these the Romans added the TUSCAN, somewhat resembling the DORIC, and the COMPOSITE, a combination of IONIC and CORINTHIAN. 2. A religious order; a MONASTIC society or fraternity; a society of persons living under the same religious, moral, or social regulations (i.e., the Franciscan order).

ORDINANCE (ORD-i-nence)–An authoritative rule or law; a decree or command; a regulation.

ORGANIC–1. Derived from living organisms. 2. Planning jargon for resultant built forms derived from a response to localized conditions of the TOPOGRAPHY and growth by ACCRETION.

ORIENT–1. The East; to the east and south of the Mediterranean; the countries of Asia. 2. The literal verb meaning to face toward the east; to site or align features on the land according to some reference or influencing factor, such as the points of the compass, the sun, a view, or a slope of the land. ORIENTATION, the direction that a feature on the land faces.

ORIENTAL–Characteristic of the Eastern cultures; Asian. *See also* OCCIDENTAL.

ORIENTATION–Literally, "alignment east-west"; used for any deliberate placing of a building in relation to the points of the compass. The pyramids at Gizeh, Egypt were sited so that the north star could be seen through the long, narrow entrance corridor. During the MIDDLE AGES it was customary to position the ALTAR end of churches toward the rising sun, the east. The term for east, "orient," came to mean the alignment of such structures toward the east.

ORTHOGONAL(S) (or-THAHG-e-nel) – Having to do with right angles, rectangular, linear, or axial.

OSTRAGOTH (AH-struh-gawth)–A person of the eastern tribe of BARBARIANS, the GOTHS, which kept a monarchy in Italy between A.D. 493 and 555.

OTTOMAN TURKS (OTT-uh-mun)–The people of the Turkish dynasty or empire founded in c. 1300 by Osman I and was replaced by modern Turkey in 1922. The Ottoman Empire, populated by 150 million people, was comprised of major portions of Asia, Africa, and Europe until after World War I.

OUTCROP–A part of a larger rock mass that appears exposed at the surface of the ground.

PADDOCK–A small enclosed field, pasture, or stable yard where horses are exercised or grazed.

PAGODA (pa-GO-da)–A multistoried Oriental building built in the form of a pyramidal tower; also applied to a garden structure that resembles such a temple.

PALAESTRA or PALESTRA (pa-LAY-stra)–A Greek public building for the training of athletes.

PALAZZO (pah-LOTS-o)–Italian word for palace in an urban setting. Plural, palazzi.

PALEOLITHIC (pay-leo-LITH-ic)–Old Stone Age. Of or pertaining to the period preceding the MESOLITHIC; characterized by stone implements and cave painting. Lower Paleolithic man, to 32,000 B.C., was a nomadic hunter; Upper Paleolithic man, 32,000–8000 B.C., was a specialized hunter.

PALIMPSEST (PAL-imp-sest)–1. To rub smooth. 2. A parchment, tablet, and so on, that has been written upon or inscribed two or three times, the previous text or tests having been imperfectly erased and therefore remaining visible.

PALING–A vertical fencing slat for a paled fence.

PALLADIAN (pa-LAY-dyan)–Relating to, or typical of, a CLASSICAL Roman style of architecture popularized by Andrea Palladio, an Italian architect, 1518–1580.

PANATHENAEA (PAN-a-then-AY-uh)–The most important festival of ANCIENT Athens held to commemorate the goddess Athena.

PANATHENAIC WAY (PAN-a-then-AY-ik WAY)–The religious route through the ANCIENT city of Athens, Greece, along which the citizens traveled each year during the panathenaic procession. This event featured the delivery of a new robe to the statue of Athena in the PARTHENON. The route, lined with statues and dedications, began at the Altar of the Twelve Gods in the AGORA and led to the PARTHENON on the ACROPOLIS.

PANORAMA–1. A VIEW whose dominant characteristic is its breadth. 2. A series of pictures of a LANDSCAPE displayed on a continuous surface.

PANTHEISM (PAN-THEE-ism)–The doctrine that God is not a single personality but that all laws, forces, and manifestations of the universe are God.

PANTHEON (PAN-thee-on)–1. All the gods of a people. 2. A temple dedicated to all such gods, especially the Pantheon in Rome, although it is not certain that this was its function, erected A.D. 120–124 by Hadrian.

PAPYRUS (pa-PIE-rus)–Aquatic plant, *Cyperus papyrus,* used by the Egyptians for a great variety of purposes, including the construction of primitive reed huts; a recurrent motif in Egyptian architectural sculpture; used to make a paperlike writing material.

PARADIGM (PAIR-eh-DIME)–A model or pattern; an example of good quality or taste.

PARADISE–The Old Persian word *pairidaeza,* meaning "fence" or "enclosure," was passed to the Greeks as *paradeisos,* who called it "park" or "garden"; the Romans defined it as "abode of the blessed," park or orchard; in Arabic it means "enclosure" or "walled around"; the Garden of Eden; heaven; any place of great beauty and perfection; a place or condition of great happiness.

PARADISE GARDEN–A garden created to symbolize the qualities of Eden or heaven.

PARAMETER (pa-RAM-e-ter)–A variable that can be held constant while the effect of shifting other variables is investigated. The word is used in experimentation of many kinds, including simulation for planning to test traffic, density, and other factors on given land areas.

PARAPET (PAIR-a-pet)–The portion of a wall above the roof gutter, sometimes BATTLEMENTED; also applied to the same feature, rising breast high, on balconies or bridges.

PARK–In English law, an enclosed area of land held by authority of the king which is preserved and stocked with game animals for hunting; a large enclosed piece of land, usually with woodland and pasture, attached to a country house or laid out in towns for public recreation. It derives from Old French and Middle English *parc,* "preserve for beasts of the chase." This is related to the Gallo-Roman word *parricus,* meaning "fence." The word *paddock* also comes from the same source. The Old Persian word *pairidaeza,* meaning "fence" or "enclosure," gave us our word *paradise.*

PARKWAY–A strip of public land devoted to recreation and pleasure traffic. It is essentially an elongated park with a road running through it. Parkways serve both a highway function and a recreation function.

PARLIAMENTARY ENCLOSURE ACTS–A series of laws enacted in Britain from the late fifteenth century to the middle of the nineteenth century for purposes of bringing about reforms in agriculture and rural land management. The late seventeenth century was a time of particularly significant enclosure and agricultural improvement. The new laws enabled wealthy landowners to enclose their open land; which led to the fencing, or enclosing in stone walls or hedgerows, and the reforestation of large areas of open, treeless countryside. The resultant subdividing of rangeland and the return of forests changed the scale and appearance of the rural landscape and brought about an increase in the number of habitats for wildlife and a resurgence in the populations of many desirable game animals. The acts helped to "sow the seeds" for the eighteenth-century design revolution from formal to "natural" landscaping. As the rural landscape began to change in appearance, the large number of sprawling French-style gardens began to be criticized as wasteful uses of prime agricultural land—the antithesis of good husbandry in the age of enlightenment.

PARQUET (par-KAY)–Wood flooring with small sections, often different colors, arranged in an intricate geometric pattern.

PARQUETRY (PAR-ke-tree)–Paving composed of intricate interlocking patterns of paving stones or precast unit pavers.

PARTERRE (par-TARE)–From the French BRODERIE PAR TERRE, meaning "embroidery on the ground"; an ornamental arrangement of flowerbeds with paths of gravel, pavement, or turf; a KNOT GARDEN; literally in French, *par* meaning "on" and *terre* meaning "earth." Jacques Boyceau popularized the parterre in seventeenth-century France. Also expressed as parterre de broderie.

PARTERRE D'EAU (par-TARE-DOE)–French garden feature with water, fountains, and sculpture as the major design elements. Typically open and spacious. The Parterre d'eau at Versailles is the most impressive of the seventeenth-century examples.

PARTHENON (PAHR-theh-NON)–The temple of the patron goddess, Athena, on the ACROPOLIS in Athens, Greece. Completed c. 438 B.C., it is considered the finest of all the Doric-style structures built during the golden age of Greece.

PARTY WALL–A wall dividing two properties or houses and forming a common boundary to both.

PARVIS (PAHR-vis or par-VEE)–From the Latin word *paradisus,* meaning an enclosed garden; an enclosed court in front of a church, sometimes including a garden.

PASTORAL (PASS-te-rel)–Pertaining to shepherds; having the charm or simplicity of rural pastureland; pertaining to life in the country; BUCOLIC scenery.

PASTORAL LANDSCAPE–A human-made landscape of meadows, open woodlands interspersed with hedgerows, small gardens, and farmsteads; sometimes called a ROMANTIC landscape. The grazing of flocks and herds is the primary agricultural use of this landscape.

PATINA (pa-TEEN-a)–1. A film or incrustation, usually green, resulting from oxidation that forms on the surface of bronze and copper; regarded as an enhancement by time and natural processes. 2. A similar film or coloration on other surfaces.

PATIO–Of Spanish origin; a residential courtyard surrounded by low buildings or walls; a paved area adjoining a house used for outdoor living.

PATTE D'OIE (POT DWAH)–French expression for "goosefoot"; used in reference to the radiating avenues in a garden which were popular during the French BAROQUE and English High Renaissance.

PAVILION (pe-VILL-yen)–From the French word *pavillon* for a lightweight open structure used for shelter, pleasure, exhibits, and so on, in a park or garden.

PEAT–Peat is a highly organic soil, comprised of greater than 50 percent combustible matter, made of partially decomposed plant matter. It is formed in damp or marshy places. When drained, cut, and dried out, it is used as a fuel. Peat is widely used as a somewhat ACID humus additive to planting soil.

PEAT MOSS–Sphagnum moss that grows in peat bogs used to amend SOIL by adding HUMUS to enhance its water retention properties.

PEDESTAL–The foot or bottom support of a COLUMN, PILLAR, statue, and so on.

PEDIMENT–In classical architecture, the triangular space, GABLE, at the end of a building; formed by the ends of the sloping roof and the CORNICE; also an ornamental feature having this shape.

PERCOLATION–Downward flow of liquid through the pores or spaces of a rock or soil.

PERENNIAL (per-EN-i-al)–An herbaceous or nonwoody seed plant that survives for more than two years.

PERENNIAL BORDER–A long narrow planting BED with PERENNIALS or HERBACEOUS plants; typically used as an edging or divider between a LAWN and a WOODY planting area.

PERGOLA (PER-go-la)–A garden structure consisting of a TRELLIS supported by posts or columns and upon which vines or other plants are trained; an ARBOR.

PERISTYLE (PAIR-i-style)–A COLONNADE, or rows of COLUMNS, around the outside of a building such as a Greek temple or around the inside of a courtyard in a Greek or Roman residence; the enclosed SPACE is also referred to as a peristyle.

PERPENDICULAR (per-pen-DIK-yoo-lar)–At right angles (90 degrees) to a given plane or line; vertical to the horizon.

PERRON (PAIR-en)–A French word for an exterior set of steps up a sloped terrace; ramped steps.

PERSPECTIVE–A system for projecting an illusion of the three-dimensional on a two-dimensional surface. In LINEAR perspective, all parallel lines or lines of projection appear to converge on a single point on the horizon (the vanishing point) and associated objects are shown smaller the farther from the viewer. ATMOSPHERIC or AERIAL PERSPECTIVE creates the illusion of distance by the muting of color intensity toward an almost neutral blue and the blurring of contours as the intended distance between eye and object increases.

pH FACTOR–The chemical symbol for the hydrogen ion concentration in a substance such as SOIL. The pH scale measures the relative acidity or alkalinity of the substance. A reading of 0.0 is pure ACID and 14.0 is pure ALKALINE, with 7.0 as neutral. SOILS of 4.5 or less are very acid and those greater than 7.0 are ALKALINE.

PHARAOH (FAYR-o)–The title of the rulers of ANCIENT Egypt.

PHILOSOPHER'S GARDEN–A pleasure garden created during the earliest Italian RENAISSANCE stage of VILLA garden development for purposes of gathering together people to enjoy the pleasures of the garden and to conduct polite philosophical conversation; an adaptation of the earlier Greco-Roman ACADEMY or aristocratic VILLA setting of Imperial Roman times.

PHOTOSYNTHESIS (foto-SIN-the-sis)–The production of organic substances, chiefly sugars, from carbon dioxide, water, and sunlight.

PHYSIC GARDEN–A small MEDIEVAL garden for the cultivation of medicinal plants;

often associated with a CASTLE or MONASTIC CLOISTER. *See also* HORTUS CONCLUSUS.

PHYSIOGRAPHIC DETERMINISM (fizzy-oh-GRAFF-ik)–A theory that the natural elements and processes in the environment should be regarded in planning and given priority in arriving at policy or planning decisions.

PHYSIOGRAPHIC PROVINCE (fizzy-oh-GRAFF-ik)–Portions of the earth's surface that are generally uniform in geological characteristics. These can readily be distinguished from their surrounding areas. Also called a *physiographic region*.

PIANO NOBILE (pee-AH-noh NOH-bee-lay)–Italian for the main floor, which is actually one floor above the ground floor; the second floor, where the main residential apartments are located.

PIAZZA (pee-OT-za)–1. An Italian name for a public open square in an urban area. A small space of similar function is a piazetta. The Spanish name is PLAZA. 2. A roofed walkway along the side of a building; in the United States, sometimes applied to a VERANDA or roofed porch; the space under a PORTICO. Plural, *piazze*.

PICTOGRAPH–A graphic stylized representation of ideas using pictures; also writing can be pictographic. *See also* HIEROGLYPHIC.

PICTURESQUE–The term to describe one of the attitudes of taste toward architecture and landscape gardening between 1785 and 1835. Buildings and landscapes were to have the compositional qualities and informality of a painted picture. *An Essay on the Picturesque* by Sir Uvedale Price in 1794 was the publication responsible for much of its popularity. It expresses that peculiar kind of beauty that is agreeable in a picture, natural or artificial; striking the mind with great power or pleasure in representing the objects of vision as clearly as if delineated in a picture.

PIEDMONT (PEED-mont)–From the French for "foothill," as at the base of a mountain. In the United States, this region extends along the eastern edge of the Appalachian Mountains from New York State to Alabama. It lies between the coastal plain and the mountains.

PIER (PEER)–Freestanding masonry support for an arch, usually square in section; performing the same function as a COLUMN or PILLAR.

PIGEON COTE–A nesting house or DOVECOTE for pigeons or doves placed on the grounds of an English estate to provide a ready source of a favorite delicacy, roasted dove.

PILASTER (pi-LAS-ter)–A flat, rectangular COLUMN or PILLAR attached to a wall as decoration rather than structure; usually of the same design ORDER as its structural counterparts; an attached COLUMN.

PILING–Wooden, steel, or concrete post driven vertically into the ground or river bed to support a superstructure or wall.

PILLAR–A load-bearing structural shaft such as a PIER or COLUMN; sometimes a freestanding monumental structure.

PINWHEEL PIAZZA–The general description for an Italian urban space that has no streets extending directly through the space. The sight line of each street entering the space is terminated in the piazza, thus creating a greater sense of enclosure than otherwise.

PISCINA (pee-SHEE-na)–From the Latin word *piscis* for "fish," now the Italian word for a pool or fish pond; also used for the disposal of holy water in the sacristy of a church.

PISÉ (PEE-ZAY)–A wall-building technique done by pounding or ramming clay down between temporary board forms, hence RAMMED EARTH. As each course is completed and the clay is partially dried, the forms are raised to form the next layer. Distinct from ADOBE in that there are no individual building blocks to be formed or laid.

PISSOIR (pee-SWAHR)–In France and other countries, a streetside public urinal, the users of which are only partially screened from view by a knee-to-shoulder baffle.

PITCH–The degree of slope or steepness of a roof or incline of the ground or paved surface.

PLACE (PLAHSS)–The French word for an open space or SQUARE in an urban setting; seldom used in English; PLAZA in Spanish; PIAZZA in Italian.

PLAN–1. A drawing or DIAGRAM made to SCALE to show the horizontal arrangement of the features of a building or land area. 2. To formulate a project.

PLANNED-UNIT DEVELOPMENT (PUD)–A residential development in which the subdivision and zoning regulations apply to the project as a whole rather than to its individual lots as in most tract housing. Densities are calculated on a project-wide basis permitting, among other things, the clustering of houses and provision of common open space.

PLANTATION–1. An estate or farm on which cash crops are cultivated for profit. 2. In Britain, a group of ornamental or cash crop trees.

PLAT–A precisely drawn and labeled scale map or plan of a piece of land divided into building lots, placed on file in the public records of the governing body, which has jurisdiction over the land in which the property occurs; also means "to plat or draw the above map." *See also* PLOT.

PLAZA (PLAH-zah)–The Spanish word for a public square in an urban area used as a marketplace, park, or for assembly. See also PIAZZA, PLACE, and GREEN.

PLEACH (PLEECH)–To interlace the tops of trees or other plants to form a tunnel-like archway over a walkway.

PLEACHED ALLÉE–A passageway or VISTA between SYMMETRICAL rows of closely planted trees or tall shrubs whose top branches are intertwined.

PLEASANCE (PLAY-zhans)–From the French word for pleasure; a garden created for pleasure; a "pleasure garden" during MEDIEVAL times; enclosed within the walls or RAMPARTS of a castle; also *pleasaunce*.

PLINTH–The square block at the base of a COLUMN or PEDESTAL; the course of brick or stone along the base or foundation of a building or wall.

PLOT–A small parcel of land. A plot PLAN indicates the location and boundaries of individual properties or plots for development or sale. *See also* PLAT.

POCKET PARK–*See* VEST POCKET PARK.

PODERE (POH-de-ray)–The Italian word for the portion of the VILLA that functions as a farm.

PODIUM–1. A low continuous platform or STYLOBATE on which a temple is built. 2. A raised platform surrounding the ARENA of an ANCIENT AMPHITHEATRE.

POLIS (PO-lis)–The Greek word for "city-state." The root word in *metropolis, politics, police,* and so on.

POLLARD (POLL-erd)–A tree whose main branches are cut back to near the trunk to form a crown of many small dense branches. The practice is common in European cities.

POLLEN–Fine grains consisting of the male fertilizing cells of plants.

POLYCHROME (POLLY-KROAM)–Decorated in many colors, including sculpture and architectural detail elements.

POLYGON (POLLY-GON)–A closed figure having more than four sides and angles.

POLYTHEISM (POLLY-THEE-izm)–The belief in many gods.

POMEGRANATE (PAHM-e-gran-it)–The shrub or small tree, *Puncia granatum,* that bears a round fruit with red leathery rind and many seeds covered with edible juicy red flesh; possessing many symbolic meanings to early civilizations. Due to its many seeds, it often symbolized fertility.

POPULATION DENSITY–The relation of population to area or the number of individuals of a population within a unit of area.

PORCELAIN–Translucent and impervious pottery made of kaolin; sometimes any pottery that is translucent, whether made of kaolin or not; china.

PORTAL–A doorway, gate, or entrance, especially a large and imposing one. *See also* PYLON.

PORT-COCHERE (PORT-ko-SHARE)–A porch at the entrance to a house or mansion large enough to accommodate passage of a horse and carriage; an all weather dropoff PORTICO.

PORTICO (POR-ti-ko)–A porchlike structure consisting of a roof supported by COLUMNS and attached to a building.

POSITIVE SPACE–A SPACE with a definite character; one that is consciously intended or appears to be purposeful and not accidental; a SPACE that is bounded by definite edges such as walls, dense vegetation, or landforms. A positive SPACE feels unambiguous and has an unmistakable clarity or integrity.

POST AND LINTEL–An ANCIENT structural system comprised of vertical supports, POSTS, spanned by horizontal BEAMS or LINTELS.

POTAGER (pote-ah-JHAY)–The French word for vegetable garden or KITCHEN GARDEN; from the word *potage,* meaning soup in French.

POTENTATE–A person of great power; a sovereign, monarch, or ruler.

PRE-RAPHAELITES (PREE-RAF-ee-el-ites)–A small group of artists and writers that began a new style in England in 1848, when they established the Pre-Raphaelite Brotherhood. Following the influence of John Ruskin, the movement was a rejection of the scientific, utilitarian, and commercial emphases of the everyday world of their Victorian period. The principal members of the group were Dante Gabriel Rosetti, painter and poet; William Holman Hunt, Edward Burne-Jones, and John Everett Millais, painters; and some consider William Morris, designer, craftsman, and poet, a loosely associated member of the movement. Their paintings were characterized by minute detail, based on careful studies made from nature, brilliant colors, and exotic or romantic subjects. In literature, romantic and exotic themes prevailed. Together, their works influenced the sensibility of the next quarter century in Europe and America.

PRESERVATION–*See* HISTORIC PRESERVATION.

PRIAPUS (PREE-uh-pus)–The god of gardens or fertility in both Greek and Roman mythology. He carried a pruning sickle and his image placed in the garden was thought to ward off birds; the origin of our scarecrow.

PRIMARY COLORS–The HUES red, yellow, and blue, which, when mixed, can produce any HUE in the SPECTRUM.

PRIVY GARDEN (PRIV-ee)–English expression for a hidden or secret garden.

PROGRAM–The functional design requirements of a proposed project. All the client's physical and AESTHETIC needs that are to be synthesized into a final development.

PROMENADE (prom-e-NAHD)–1. Noun, a walk, especially in a public place, for pleasure strolling. 2. Verb, (pronounced prom-e-NADE), to take a walk or to parade along a promenade.

PROPAGATE (PROP-eh-GATE)–To reproduce an organism, such as a plant, either sexually or ASEXUALLY; to breed; to reproduce.

PROPAGATION–Multiplication of plants or other organisms by seeds and asexual means such as the rooting of cuttings, GRAFTING, or budding.

PROPINQUITY (pro-PING-kwe-tee)–Physical proximity or nearness.

PROPYLAEUM (pro-pi-LAY-um)–Greek word for front PORTAL. A monumental structure forming an important entrance or gateway in front of a sacred enclosure.

PROSPECT–The VIEW available from a specific vantage point; outlook; PANORAMA or VISTA. *See also* REFUGE.

PROSPECT-REFUGE THEORY–The theory that the ability to see without being seen is conducive to the exploitation of environmental conditions favorable to biological survival and is therefore a source of pleasure.

PRUNING–The removal of diseased, dead, or unwanted twigs and branches from WOODY plants. Pruning is essential to the proper maintenance of plants.

PUEBLO (PWAY-blo)–A Native American tribe of the southwest United States that made houses and multifamily dwellings of multiple stories out of ADOBE; also the name of their structures.

PYLON (PIE-lon)–The MONUMENTAL entrance of an Egyptian temple or other wall enclosed space. *See also* PORTAL.

PYRAMID–Regular structure with a square base and sides sloping inwards to meet at an apex, such as built by the ANCIENT Egyptians as royal burial MONUMENTS.

QANAT (ka-NAHT)–Persian word for underground water canals that were constructed through the desert to bring water from a remote source to irrigate cultivated lands.

QUADRANGLE–1. A four-sided or rectangular enclosure or court defined by buildings. 2. A unit area that is standardized as to form and orientation for the purpose of systematic mapping. It is bounded on the east and west by lines of longitude (MERIDIANS) and on the north and south by lines of latitude (parallels).

QUADRIGA (kwah-DREE-ga)–In monumental sculpture, a four-horse chariot.

QUADRILATERAL–A geometric figure having four sides and four angles.

QUADRILATERAL SYMMETRY–A composition that consists of two AXES intersecting at right angles and resulting in all four subdivisions or quadrants being equal; BIAXIAL.

QUADRIPARTITE (KWAHD-ri-PAR-tite)–A form divided into four parts.

QUATTROCENTO (KWAT-tro-CHAYN-to)–Italian for the 1400s; the fifteenth century.

QUICKSET–1. In Britain, a plant CUTTING such as hawthorn planted with others to form a hedge. 2. A hedge in Britain.

QUINCUNX (KWIN-KUNKS)–Five objects set so that four are at corners of the square and the other at its center; tree plantation laid out in the diagonal, with cross lines given by combining quincunxes.

QUOIN (KOIN)–Large, sometimes RUSTICATED, usually slightly projecting stones that form the corners of the exterior walls of masonry buildings. These are often made of more durable material than the wall itself.

RADIAL (RAY-dee-el)–A composition, usually circular, which is comprised of radii, rays, or lines extending outward from a center point, like the spokes of a wheel. This was a popular MOTIF used in BAROQUE compositions. The French ROND POINT is an example.

RAISED BEDS–Rectangular plant BEDS, typically seen in the MEDIEVAL garden, with wooden planks used to retain the mounds of soil from being eroded away. The purpose is to obtain better drainage and be able to maintain the beds without excessive stooping.

RAMMED EARTH–A wall-building technique done by pounding or ramming clay down between temporary board forms. As each course is completed and the clay is partially dried, the forms are raised to form the next layer; distinct from ADOBE in that there are no individual building blocks to be formed or layed; also called PISÉ.

RAMPART–An earthen mound surrounding a castle, fortress, or fortified city sometimes, including a stone PARAPET.

RECONSTRUCTION–*See* HISTORIC RECONSTRUCTION.

RED BOOKS–During Humphrey Repton's three decades as a professional landscape garden designer, 1784–1818, he planned approximately 200 country places, fifty-seven of which were documented with "red books." These manuals were bound in red morocco (sheepskin leather) and were usually approximately $8\frac{1}{2}$ by 14 inches in size. They included written recommendations for improvements to each COUNTRY SEAT and a number of watercolor perspectives depicting very precisely the appearance of the place as it existed. Using a removable overlay that he called a slide, the same scene could be adapted to show the character following the completion, and maturation, of Repton's proposed design. He said, "These slides are calculated to save a great deal of trouble in drawing; since one landscape, by means of one or two slides, may serve instead of two or three."

REFUGE–A place that affords protection, shelter, or a feeling of security; seclusion. *See also* PROSPECT.

REGIONAL PLANNING–An outgrowth of landscape architecture and city planning, concentrating on the larger, more geographically broad-based issues of land use, both existing and proposed; involves analysis of existing physical, social, and economic factors, leading to physical planning. City and regional planning emerged as special disciplines in the United States in the late 1920s with the establishment of the Harvard School of City Planning under the direction of Henry Vincent Hubbard in 1929 and the Cornell Department of City and Regional Planning under Gilmore Clarke in 1935.

REINFORCED CONCRETE or FERRO CONCRETE–Concrete whose tensile strength is increased by iron, steel mesh, or bars embedded in it.

RELIEF–1. The collective elevations, slopes, and inequalities in a land surface; referred to as TOPOGRAPHICAL RELIEF. 2. In sculpture, figures projecting from a background of which they are a part. The degree of relief is designated high, low (BAS), or sunken (hollow).

RELIQUARY (RELL-i-kwary)–A small container for the sacred remains of saints, etc.

RENAISSANCE (REN-e-sahnss)–French for a new birth or revival. The term used for the revival of CLASSICAL learning and art in Europe during the fourteenth to sixteenth centuries.

RESTORATION–In its fullest meaning, the term applies to the reigns of Charles II, 1660–1685, James II, 1685–1688, and William and Mary, 1688–1702. If England had not had its republican Commonwealth period, the landscape garden style might never have been developed there. In 1649, King Charles I was accused of inciting civil war between Scotland and England. He was found guilty of this crime against his subjects and was separated from his head by the guillotine. For the ten years of the interregnum, Great Britain, including Ireland at that time, was governed by the Lord Protector, Oliver Cromwell, until his death in 1658. During that time the royal family was exiled in France. These were the years of the flowering of the French grand style of gardens. Known as Le Grand Siecle, this was the era of Louis XIV and his royal gardener, André Le Nôtre. The gardens of the Chateau Vaux le Vicomte for Louis' finance minister, Nicholas Fouquet, were completed and unveiled in 1661. The subsequent enlargement of the palace and the creation of its unparalleled gardens at Versailles were in progress by the end of the royal family's sojourn in France. After the death of Oliver Cromwell, his son Richard ruled, but in 1660 the Commonwealth collapsed. That date marks the beginning of the period known as the Restoration, the return of the British "royals" to England and Charles II's resumption of monarchical rule over the country. Upon their return, the members of the royal family and, in turn, their admirers in the aristocratic class, began to create French grand style places and gardens throughout England. *See also* HISTORIC RESTORATION.

RETAINING WALL–A wall that retains an earth embankment or change in levels; constructed of stone, MASONRY, concrete, timbers, or metal units. A HA-HA is often a retaining wall.

RETROFIT (RE-tro-fit)–Literally, to add a feature to another feature after the fact; to refit, or reequip, an object with a new part or parts after it has been completed; to improve a design by incorporating later improvements.

RETROGRESSION–To move backward into less complex or worse conditions; to decline or to degenerate.

REVEAL–The gap between any two planes, such as the plane of a wall and the plane of a floor. Such narrow spaces are typically in shadow, thus emphasizing the contrast between the two surfaces.

RIB–A relatively slender molded MASONRY band that projects from the surface. In Gothic architecture, the ribs form the framework of the VAULT.

RIGHT-OF-WAY–Any area that is reserved by law, or by common consent, to public or semipublic use; streets and easements are typical examples. Plural, rights-of-way.

RILL–A small stream; rivulet; RUNNEL.

RIPARIAN (ri-PAIR-ee-en)–Pertaining to land on either side of a nonnavigable stream. Riparian rights are those associated with streamside property, especially related to the use and restriction of use of the water flowing in such a stream. Riparian vegetation is that which grows adjacent to a stream.

RIP-RAP (RIP-rap)–Coarse stones, natural boulders and cobbles, or artificially broken fragments, laid either loosely or cemented against the slope of a bank or on the bottom of a channel to prevent wave or runoff erosion.

RISER–The vertical portion of a step.

ROCAILLE (RO-KAY)–French for "rock work;" ROCKERY, an assemblage of rocks.

ROCKERY (ROK-er-ee)–A rock garden; a feature in a garden which may be a natural rock outcropping, entirely artificial, or a combination of the two. Modern rock gardens are typically created for the display of Alpine plants or other plants that tolerate dry rocky situations. Similar features, called either *jai-shan* or *shi-feng*, have been in wide use in China and Japan, where they are called *kare-sansui*. During the eighteenth-century CHINOISERIE period in England, rockeries reached the peak of their popularity.

ROCOCO (RO-KO-ko)–From the French ROCAILLE meaning "rock work." A term applied to a type of RENAISSANCE ornament in which rocklike forms, scrolls, and shells are used together in a confusion of detail often without organic coherence but presenting a lavish display of decoration, especially popular in France, Germany, and Switzerland during the late eighteenth century.

ROMANESQUE–Literally, "Roman-like." The style of architecture based on Roman architecture prevalent in Western Europe during the ninth to twelfth centuries; characterized by heavy MASONRY, thick proportions, the round ARCH, and VAULT.

ROMANTIC–Idealistic; fanciful; not practical; characterized by romance or passion as contrasted with classical realism. In landscape expression, the stylization of idealized scenery to suggest a natural or BUCOLIC quality.

ROND POINT (RONE PWAHN)–French for the point of intersection of a number of AXIAL paths or ALLÉES; originally, an open space in forest parks where ladies and courtiers of the French RENAISSANCE CHÂTEAUX could sit and watch the comings and goings of the hunt;

later employed by Hausmann in Paris for traffic circles at the intersection of streets; in England, a roundabout.

ROSE WINDOW–In GOTHIC architecture, a large round window with TRACERY and stained glass.

ROSETTA STONE (ro-ZETT-uh)–A stone slab, c. 196 B.C., discovered in 1799 near Rosetta, a town on the Nile, bearing inscriptions in Egyptian HIEROGLYPHICS (sacred-character writing of the priesthood), demotic characters (popular Egyptian cursive writing of the second century B.C.) and Greek, enabling translation of the ANCIENT Egyptian writings.

ROSTRUM (ROS-trum)–Latin for the prow of a ship. The raised platform in the Forum Romanum from which orators addressed the people. So called because it was decorated with the prows of ships taken in war.

ROTUNDA (ro-TUN-da)–Any round building; not necessarily domed.

RUBBLE–A MASONRY wall built of rough broken stone.

RUNNEL–A small stream or rivulet; RILL.

RUNOFF–The rainwater that flows off the surface of roofs, paved surfaces, or the land; also the quantity of water that thus runs off. It may be expressed in gallons, cubic feet, or acre feet.

RUSTICATION (rust-i-CA-shun)–A method of forming stonework with roughened surfaces and recessed joints, employed principally in RENAISSANCE buildings to give an appearance of great strength.

SACRO BOSCO (SOK-ro BOS-ko)–Italian for sacred grove. Often an undeveloped or wild area set in contrast to a more formally designed garden; derived from the ancient tradition of the Greek sacred grove, where one could experience natural surroundings rather than human-made surroundings.

SANCTUARY–1. Literally, a holy or consecrated place. The most secret part of a church or temple containing the main ALTAR. 2. A place of REFUGE or immunity.

SARCOPHAGUS (sar-COF-a-gus)–A stone coffin, often elaborately ornamented in ANCIENT Greek and Roman times.

SCALE–1. The dimensions of the parts or totality of a building or object in relation to its use or function. In design, the size of parts relative to the whole or to the human figure. 2. In design drawings, the relation of the actual size of a composition to the size of its graphic representation. *See also* HUMAN SCALE.

SCARIFY–To loosen, scratch, or stir the TOPSOIL.

SCENIC EASEMENT–An easement established for the protection of scenic values along parkways, rural limited-access highways, etc. Generally, an easement on each side of the highway right-of-way, 300 or more feet in width, is acquired by an appropriate government agency. On this easement, the landowner is not permitted to alter the vegetation or change the land use without the consent of the government agency.

SCION (SY-un)–A twig or shoot, especially those selected for use in grafting onto other plants. Also spelled cion.

SEAT–A place of residence, especially a large house that is part of a country ESTATE. *See also* COUNTRY PLACE.

SECOND LAW OF THERMODYNAMICS–Formulated in 1850 by Rudolf Clausius, it states that the ENTROPY, or degree of disorder, in an isolated system tends to increase; this is an atypical law of nature since it holds true in the majority of cases but not always.

SECONDARY COLORS–The colors (green, orange, purple) that result from a mix of any two of the three PRIMARY colors.

SECTION–In design, a diagram or graphic representation of a part of a composition along an imaginary vertical plane passing through it.

SEDIMENT–Mineral or organic material transported from one place to another and deposited by water, wind, or ice.

SEEDLING–1. A plant grown from a seed as distinguished from other means of PROPAGATION. 2. A young tree under 3 feet in height.

SEICENTO (say-CHAIN-toh) – The Italian word for the 1600s; the seventeenth century.

SENSIBILITY–In AESTHETICS, the ability or capacity for being affected intellectually or emotionally, pleasantly or unpleasantly, by stimuli; the capacity to respond intelligently and perceptively to intellectual, moral, or aesthetic events or values, especially to those of refined quality or tastefulness; sharp intellectual responsiveness.

SERF (SURF)–A person in FEUDAL servitude, bound to the master's land and transferred with the land from owner to owner.

SERPENTINE (SUR-pen-teen)–Something that twists or coils like a serpent; winding. This was a favorite form of the painters and the landscape designers of the eighteenth century, such as William Hogarth, who felt that even more beautiful were three-dimensional "waving and winding" lines, which he termed the "lines of grace." Good examples of these are paths and carriage roads whose horizontal and vertical alignment both meander from side to side and undulate over hills and down swales. In England, serpentine walls were called CRINKLE-CRANKLE WALLS, and were designed that way to enhance the growing of fruit, ESPALIERED against their south-facing surface. Such structures were more stable and economical than ordinary walls since they required fewer materials. Thomas Jefferson's walls at the University of Virginia (1816–1826) are good examples.

SETBACK–A restriction placed on the use of land referring to the distance a structure must be from a lot line. The purpose of setbacks arises from the desire to provide for greater space for light, air, fire protection, off-street parking, visual clearance at intersections, and from historical attitudes about providing distance between land uses or structures.

SETT–A small stone paving unit, usually granite; typically, a 4-inch cube shape; often placed in a fish scale or fan pattern.

SGRAFFITO (skra-FEE-toh)–From the Italian word for "to scratch"; a process of incising or scratching the outer surface of a MURAL or clay vessel to produce design; source of word *graffito* or *graffiti*—To scribble on a wall or public surface.

SHADE–1. The partial or complete obstruction of direct sunlight. 2. In graphic representation, the relatively dark portions of an image.

SHADUF (sha-DOOF)–A device invented in Egypt for raising irrigation water from one level to another using a bucket and fulcrum.

SHAFT–In architecture, the part of a COLUMN between the CAPITAL and BASE.

SHAKKAI (shuh-KY)–A Japanese design technique or principle that takes advantage of a given place's visible surrounding landscape attributes, such a mountains, trees, etc., to suggest infinite views from a garden. In streetscape design, the term in Japanese is YAMAATE. In Western thought, both devices are expressed as BORROWED SCENERY; also *sakkai.* The Chinese equivalent is JIE-JING.

SHARAWAGGI or SHARAWADGI (shar-a-WAD-ji)–A term coined by an Englishman, Sir William Temple, in his book on Chinese gardens in 1687, to mean "where beauty is great but where no ORDER is observable." According to Edward Hyams, *sharawadgi* was "gobbledegook." He noted several other words in Chinese, from which Temple might have derived his term. It may have been Temple's mistaken spelling of *sa-to-kwai-chi,* meaning "careless or disorderly grace"; or *san-lan-wai-chi,* meaning "disorderly composition"; or the Japanese word *sorowadji,* for "unsymmetrical design."

SHELTER BELT–Trees planted along the edges of fields to protect crops from wind damage or to reduce wind EROSION of SOIL.

SHI-FENG (SHEE-FENG)–Chinese for the arrangement of rocks as natural sculptural forms in a garden or courtyard design. These may suggest distant mountains. The best of such rocks come from Lake Tai and are valued for their unique forms and textures. Sometimes they resemble animate objects.

SHRUB–A woody bushy plant, smaller than a tree, generally with multiple stems; a bush.

SIENNA (See-en-uh)–The name for a yellowish-brown pigment, raw sienna, made from ferruginous earth found near Siena, Italy. The same material when baked is called burnt sienna.

SIGHT LINE–The line along which a person in a SPACE looks; the ordering element of the AXIAL, FORMAL GARDEN, or LANDSCAPE composition, allowing one to see through a series of SPACES. A VISTA is an extended example.

SIGNORIA (seen-yor-EE-a)–Italian word for lordship; refers to the governing bodies of Florence.

SILT–A very fine sand, or earth material, which is transported by running water and deposited in another location as a SEDIMENT.

SITE–A PLOT of land intended or suitable for development; also the ground or area on which a building or town has been built.

SITE ANALYSIS–The collection and organization of data pertinent to the landscape design and development of a site. Such data include information about boundaries, drainage, topography, soil, vegetation, scenic qualities, cultural features, proposed uses, and surrounding land uses.

SLOPE–An incline. The inclination or angle of slope is measured as a ratio between vertical and horizontal distance on the slope or as degrees of arc with the horizontal. *See* GRADIENT.

SOFFIT (SOF-it)–The underside of an overhanging architectural member, such as an ARCH, LINTEL, CORNICE, or stairway.

SOFTWOOD–1. A CONIFEROUS tree such as a pine, spruce, fir, and so on. 2. Any tree whose wood is light and easily cut. This, however, can be erroneous since some CONIFERS have wood that is harder than DECIDUOUS trees, and vice versa.

SOIL–The unconsolidated mineral matter that has originated from rocks by the action of weathering processes and organic matter, both living and dead, that has usually accumulated on the earth's surface.

SOLSTICE (SOL-stiss)–Two points in the earth's path around the sun, June 21 and December 22, where the earth is tipped toward or away from the sun; the sun is at its greatest distance from the equator; the longest and shortest days of the year.

SPACE–The interval or area between or within things which has length, breadth, and height. For practical purposes, the three-dimensional working area within which landscape architects may construct gardens and landscapes. Landscape architecture is the art of space utilization. The adjective is spatial. *See also* POSITIVE SPACE and NEGATIVE SPACE.

SPAN–The distance between the supports of an ARCH, roof, or BEAM.

SPANDREL (SPAN-drel)–The roughly triangular space enclosed by the curves of adjacent arches and a horizontal member connecting their vertexes; also the space enclosed by the curve of an arch and an enclosing right angle.

SPECIES (SPEE-sheez)–The basic unit in the classification of plants and animals; a group of individuals with so many common characteristics as to indicate a high degree of relationship and common descent. *See also* GENUS.

SPECTRUM (SPEK-trum)–Bands of color made visible to the human eye when white light rays (sunlight) are transmitted through a prism or similar transparent device. The color spectrum is made up of rays of different wavelength, varying from long (red) to short (violet). This is only a portion of the entire light spectrum.

SPHINX (SFINKS)–Egyptian and later Greek HERALDIC creature with a combination of a lion's body and the head of a human being or other animal.

SPINA (SPEE-na)–The central island or wall running nearly the length of the floor of the ANCIENT HIPPODROME or CIRCUS.

SPIRAL PUMP–The device for raising water invented by the people of Mesopotamia c. 1000 B.C. The Hanging Gardens of Babylon were irrigated by this means. The ARCHIMEDEAN SCREW, named for the Greek mathematician, Archimedes (c. 287–212 B.C.), was such a device, comprised of a spiral, or screw, which turned inside an inclined closed cylinder, for raising water to a height. Such implements were also used by the ANCIENT Egyptians for pumping water from the Nile into their vast system of irrigation canals.

SQUARE–An open place, usually an open block bounded by four streets, in an urban area; used for public assembly, a marketplace, or as a park; also called an AGORA (Greek), PIAZZA (Italian), PLAZA (Spanish), or COMMONS or GREEN (English). Squares are not necessarily square but may take any form.

STALACTITE WORK–Especially in Islamic architecture, a decorative, honeycomb-like treatment to the undersides of DOME, NICHES, ARCHES, and so on, made up of small prismatic indentations and projections, such as occur in a natural cave with stalactites suspending from its ceiling.

STATIC (STAT-ik)–As opposed to DYNAMIC; a fixed, stationary condition; without action, motion, or force.

STATIONS OF THE CROSS–A series of fourteen scenes from the passion of Christ ranged around a church before which devotions are performed.

STELE (STEE-lee)–An upright carved stone slab or post used by the ANCIENT Greeks for grave or monumental site markers.

STILE–A set of steps for ascending and descending a wall or fence without an opening or gateway.

STOA (STO-uh)–In ANCIENT Greek architecture, an open COLONNADED space or PORTICO that forms an open building for public use.

STREET FURNITURE–The furnishings of the street, such as lights, signs, benches, bus shelters, canopies, KIOSKS, planters, and so on, placed in the RIGHT-OF-WAY.

STRING COURSE–Projecting horizontal band along the wall of a building.

STRUCTURE–1. Something composed of component parts such as a plant. 2. Something constructed such as a building, bridge, and so on.

STUART–A term for the English Late RENAISSANCE architecture style of the period 1675–1702 when the Stuart family ruled England and Scotland.

STUCCO (STUCK-o)–The Italian word for a fine quality of plaster used in Roman and RENAISSANCE architecture for ornamental modeled work in low RELIEF on walls.

STYLE–1. A manner of treatment or execution of works of art that is characteristic of a civilization, a people, or a single individual; also a special and superior quality in a work of art. 2. The vertical fin or GNOMON of a SUNDIAL.

STYLOBATE (STY-lo-bate)–The top step of the base of a Greek temple, which forms a platform for the columns.

SUBDIVISION–The division of a given area of land into SITES, blocks, or lots with streets or roads and open spaces; also an area so divided.

SUBLIME (se-BLIME)–1. Majestic; noble; inspiring awe through grandeur and beauty. 2. In romantic painting, a genre that was characterized by vivid irregularity of form and texture with sharp contrasts of dark shadows and strong lights and by feelings of obscurity, vastness, terror, pain, and transcendent forces of destruction.

SUBURB–A district, usually residential, on the edge of a city. A suburb can be a village or a legal city. A suburb cannot exist without an "urb." But it can grow into an "urb" itself and in turn have suburbs around it.

SUCCESSION–The process through which a plant community invades and eventually replaces another; for example, on a wet substratum, a bog sequence, and on a dry site, old-field invasions by shrubs and eventually by trees until a stable or CLIMAX equilibrium is achieved for that ENVIRONMENT.

SUCCULENT–A plant with thickened juicy stems and/or leaves that act as a reservoir of moisture during periods of drought. Succulents are to be found in most of the major families of plants. Many succulent plants are unusual or even fantastic in form such as the cactus.

SULTAN (SUL-tun)–The sovereign, or ruler, of a MOSLEM country.

SUNDIAL–A device that indicates the time of day by the position of the sun's shadow cast by a GNOMON onto a dial calibrated in daylight hours.

SUPERBLOCK–A consolidation of a number of smaller blocks and the interstitial streets into one large block, thus creating a much larger area free of through traffic.

SUPERIMPOSED ORDERS–ORDERS of architecture placed one above another in an ARCADED or COLONNADED building; usually in the following sequence, DORIC (the first story), IONIC, and CORINTHIAN. Superimposed orders are found in Greek STOAS and were used widely by Roman and RENAISSANCE builders.

SURREALISM (suh-REEL-ism)–A movement launched in 1924 to indicate a super reality, that of the unconscious: dreams and fantasies. The surrealist manifesto assigned the artist the task of liberating the soul of man from the chains of reason and inhibition. Max Ernst, Salvador Dali, and Marc Chagall were active surrealists.

SURVEY–1. A critical examination of facts or conditions to provide information on a situation such as a survey of the housing in an area or a survey of living conditions. 2. A determination of the boundaries, form, area, contours, existing TOPOGRAPHICAL features, and so on, of a tract of land by means of measurements and observations.

SWALE–A shallow linear depression in approximately level land area, particularly one that may accumulate RUNOFF water; a shallow valley.

SWARD (SWORD)–A grassy surface of the ground; a stretch of TURF grass; a LAWN.

SYCAMORE–The name originally applied to *Ficus sycomorus,* a species of small fig tree native to ANCIENT Egypt and Mesopotamia. It was much-used by the Egyptians and peoples of Mesopotamia in their gardens. The name is used for todays' Anerican native tree, *Platanus occidentalis*. The Oriental sycamore, *Platanus orientalis,* was crossed with the American sycamore to produce the London plane, *P. acerifolia,* one of the most widely used street trees in English and European cities.

SYMBIOSIS (SIM-bi-O-sis)–The living together of two dissimilar organisms because they have developed some mutual dependence. The algae and the fungi that form lichens are *symbiotic*.

SYMMETRY (SIM-e-tree)–Compositional balance achieved by placement of forms about a real or imaginary AXIS so that those on one side correspond more or less with those on the other. The correspondence may be in terms of size, shape, color, texture, and so on. Symmetry may also be achieved by a RADIAL geometry, such as in the flower blossom. See BILATERAL SYMMETRY.

SYNERGISM (SIN-er-jism) – The simultaneous action of separate agencies which together have greater total effect than the sum of their individual effects.

TABLINUM (ta-BLYN-um)–Latin for the room in a Greek or Roman house with one side open to the ATRIUM or PERISTYLE courtyard.

TACTILE–Perceivable by touch; relating to the sense of touch.

TAPIS VERT (TOP-ee VAYR)–A French term for a square or rectangular manicured grass area; "green carpet."

TAXONOMY (TAKS-ON-uh-mee)–The science of ordering; the botanical classification system, the universal Linnaean system using Latin names, which is in use today. The world's plant collection is organized into families, genera, species, and varieties, each with its own system of describing plant characteristics. *See also* NOMENCLATURE.

TEA GARDEN–In Japan, the garden associated with a tea house designed with elegance and simplicity to lend a contemplative frame of mind to the guest's partaking of the tea drinking ceremony; called *cha-niwa* or *cha-seki.*

TELL–In Near Eastern archeology, a hill or mound; usually ANCIENT sites of habitation.

TEMPERA–Of Italian origin, a technique of painting using as a MEDIUM pigment mixed with egg yolk, glue, or casein; also the medium itself.

TENDRIL (TEN-drill)–A threadlike prolongation or offshoot, of a stem or leaf, of a climbing plant usually supporting the plant by growing in a clinging or twining form around a structure or other plants. Some coil in a clockwise direction, others always in a counterclockwise movement.

TENNESSEE VALLEY AUTHORITY (TVA)–One of many federal projects initiated under President Roosevelt's Depression-busting legislation of the 1930s. This program included an entire PHYSIOGRAPHIC PROVINCE (39,000 square miles), the Tennessee River WATERSHED, comprised of parts of seven states: Alabama, Georgia, Kentucky, Mississippi, North Carolina, Tennessee, and Virginia. The authority was empowered to "promote the economic and social well-being of the people of the entire valley," a region of great poverty, which had been devastated by generations of careless timbering and wasteful agricultural practices. The TVA built hydroelectric generating plants and dams for the production of electricity for a region that had so little; built the town of Norris, Tennessee, to house the families of construction workers of the Norris Dam; improved the navigation of the rivers of the region; began reforestation and SOIL conservation programs through the introduction of scientific farming practices such as CONTOUR PLOWING and crop rotation; built outdoor recreation facilities; manufactured fertilizer; and provided employment for an untold number of jobless inhabitants of the region. The TVA demonstrated successful regional planning, with interdepartmental cooperation among many governmental divisions, while it provided multiple benefits to the population of the region.

TEPIDARIUM (tep-i-DAR-i-um)–A chamber in a Roman bath building, THERMAE, equipped with warm baths; between a FRIGIDARIUM, a cold bath and a CALDARIUM, a hot bath.

TERM–A landmark or boundary post in ANCIENT Roman times in the form of a head of the god TERMINUS atop a stone PILLAR.

TERMINUS–1. The Roman god of boundaries, private property, municipal or national. His image, in statue, was placed at the edges of gardens or property lines. *See also* TERM. 2. An endpoint; extremity of an AXIS; often a focal point.

TERRA COTTA–1. Italian for baked earth; hard-baked clay of reddish or yellowish-brown color used for sculpture, flower pots and as a building material. It may be glazed or painted. 2. The expression for the color of hard-baked clay.

TERRA FIRMA (TAIR-a FUHR-ma)–The solid earth; dry land as differentiated from water surfaces.

TERRACE–An approximately level area constructed on a slope; used as sites for STRUCTURES, for agricultural crops and for soil and water conservation. On steep slopes they may require RETAINING WALLS to maintain them.

TERRAIN–Relative to the usefulness of a specific portion of the earth's surface for specified functions or uses. This is to be differentiated from the word *terrane*—the LANDFORM or TOPOGRAPHICAL features of a tract of the earth's surface. *See also* PHYSIOGRAPHIC PROVINCE.

TERRANE–A geological formation, or group of formations, in a region in which specific rock types predominate.

TERRAZZO (tair-AHT-zo)–Of Italian origin; a flooring material composed of small marble chips set in cement and ground to a smooth, polished finish.

TESSERA (TESS-e-ruh)–Small cubic pieces of multicolored stone or glass cemented together with MORTAR to form a MOSAIC.

TEXTURE–The property of a surface deriving from the material of which it is composed; the visual or TACTILE surface characteristics and appearance of an object; surface texture is visually perceived by the way it reflects light.

THEODOLITE (thee-AHD-e-lite)–A surveying instrument used to measure vertical and horizontal angles.

THERMAE (TAIR-may)–Latin for a large complex of Roman public baths or exercise rooms (PALAESTRAE) surrounding wall-enclosed gardens as well as shops, restaurants, libraries, and occasionally a stadium.

THRUST–Force exerted by a mass of masonry and tending, if not resisted, to compress, displace, or distort part of a building. In walls and rigid sections, the thrust is downward. In arches and vaults, the thrust is downward and sideways (lateral thrust), hence the need for BUTTRESSES, ABUTMENTS, and so on.

TITLE AND PRACTICE LAW–In the states that have professional licensing for landscape architects, the use of the title *landscape architect* and the performing of certain specified design services is to be limited to only those persons so certified by the state board of licensing.

TITLE LAW–In the states that have professional licensing for landscape architects, the use of the title *landscape architect* is to be used only by persons so certified by the state board of licensing.

TOPIARY (TOE-pee-ary)–The Latin word *topia* meant the paintings that adorned the walls of porticos. Such images, known as *trompe l'oeil,* which is the French term for "trick of the eye," depicted garden scenes and served to merge the exterior setting of a building visually with the interior. In the Roman peristyle house, this effect was carried out by laying out the space as a miniature garden with small manicured evergreen plants, sculpture, and fountains. The Romans coined the word *topiarius,* meaning the person who designed or made a such a garden. Our word *topiary,* meaning evergreen plants carved into geometrical or sculptural forms, derives from this source.

TOPOGRAPHIC MAP–A graphic representation of an area of the earth's surface showing all important physical features, including relief or the configuration of the earth's surface in hills, valleys, plains, and so on; water and other natural features, such as trees, streams, lakes, ponds, rivers, and swamps; and human-made physical changes such as houses, roads, railroads, canals, and so on.

TOPOGRAPHY–The physical features, both natural and human-made, on the earth's surface; RELIEF, drainage, surface materials, vegetation, special physical phenomena, and human-made (cultural) features.

TOPSOIL–A term applied to the surface portion of the soil, including the average plow depth. It cannot be defined precisely as to depth or productivity except in reference to a particular soil type.

TOWNSHIP–1. In old England, an administrative unit of land; a parish or division of a parish. 2. In many former British colonies and in New England today, a township means a town. 3. The system of land surveying and the basis of local government in the portion of the United States that had previously been settled and surveyed by the earlier METES AND BOUNDS system, west of central Ohio to the Rocky Mountains, which was established in 1785 as the National Survey Grid. A township measures 6 by 6 miles, is comprised of thirty-six sections each of which is 1 square mile, with the number 16 section being dedicated to public educational purposes. Each 640-acre section may be further subdivided into half (320 acres), quarter (160 acres), or one-eighth section parcels, and so on. Thus this resulted in the checkerboard pattern of property ownership and county roads in that region of the United States.

TRACERY (TRAY-sury)–Any delicate pattern of interlacing lines, threads, wires, slender ribs of wood, or stone; in GOTHIC architecture.

TRANSCENDENTALISM (tran-sen-DENT-el-izm)–The philosophy that places emphasis on the spiritual and the intuitive rather than the material and empirical. Popular in New England in the nineteenth century, Emerson and Thoreau asserted that the devine presence within each person was the source of truth and the guide to action.

TRANSEPT–Part of a CRUCIFORM church at right angles to the NAVE and CHANCEL. The north and south arms are always called north transept and south transept. Some cathedrals have two additional transepts east of the crossing.

TRANSPIRATION–The loss of water vapor to the atmosphere through leaves in the growth process of plants.

TRANSPLANT–To relocate a plant or other organism from one growing area to another.

TRAVERTINE (TRAV-er-teen)–A calcareous metamorphic rock deposited in geysers and hot springs; used as a building material; also called TUFA; yellowish in color.

TREAD–The horizontal part of a stair on which the foot steps as distinct from the RISER or vertical part.

TRECENTO (tray-CHAIN-toh)–Italian for the 1300s; the fourteenth century in Italian art.

TREILLAGE (TRAIL-AHZH, or TRAIL-ij)–French term for a LATTICE for vines; TRELLIS.

TRELLIS–An open framework or LATTICE used as a support for growing vines or other plants.

TRICLINIUM (try-CLIN-i-um)–A Roman dining room with couches on three sides.

TRIGLYPH (TRY-glif)–Thrice-grooved; a structural member of a DORIC FRIEZE comprised of a pattern of rectangular blocks each with two vertical grooves, or glyphs, and half grooves at their edges; used to separate consecutive metopes, square decorative spaces between triglyphs.

TRILATERAL (TRY-LAT-er-al)–A three-sided object.

TROMPE L'OEIL (TROHMP LOY)–A form of illusionistic painting that attempts to represent an object as though it existed in three dimensions at the surface of the painting; literally, "eye-fooling"; also, employed in architecture or landscape architecture by converging and/or diminishing the size of elements in the composition to suggest exaggerated depth. *See also* FAUX.

TRUSS–A rigid triangular framework designed to span an opening and to carry roofing sheathing. Most wooden roofs are trussed.

TRUST LOT–In colonial Savannah, each WARD included four plots for public use or buildings enclosing the central SQUARE.

TUDOR (TOO-der)–1. Pertaining to the Tudor family. The line of English sovereigns, Henry VII, Henry VIII, Edward VI, Mary, and Elizabeth I, which reigned from 1485 to 1603. 2. A term applied to English Late Gothic architecture of the period 1485–1558.

TUDOR GARDEN–A style of garden popular in England during the sixteenth and seventeenth centuries. During this period, the nobility and the landed aristocracy developed pretentious country estates with extensive gardens. Although these gardens borrowed to some degree from the Italian and French styles, they acquired a flavor of their own. Tudor garden designs were divided into a number of large rectangles separated from each other by walls, ornamental fences, or hedges.

TUFA (TOO-fah)–A calcareous rock deposited by geysers and hot springs; also called TRAVERTINE; a building stone of rough or cellular texture.

TURF–A thick matting of low plants, mostly grasses, on the surface of the ground; also called sod.

TURF SEAT–Popular in MEDIEVAL England, a garden seat with a grass or TURF sitting surface.

TURRET (TURR-et)–A small tower; often built over a circular staircase or as an ornamental feature.

TUSCAN (TUSS-can)–From the Latin for ETRUSCAN; a Roman addition to the three Greek classical ORDERS; resembling the DORIC but with a base and without FLUTES and TRIGLYPHS. Tuscan columns are seven times greater in length than in diameter.

TVA–*See* TENNESSEE VALLEY AUTHORITY.

TYMPANUM (TIMM-pa-num)–1. The triangular area enclosed by a classical PEDIMENT. 2. Space between the LINTEL of a doorway and an arch over it.

TYTHING or TITHING (TIE-thing)–1. The paying of tithes. 2. From the English unit of civil administration, consisting of ten families; in Savannah, each ward contained forty house plots in four groups of ten each, called *tythings*.

UNDERSTORY–The small trees, shrubs, and other vegetation growing beneath the CANOPY of forest trees.

UNDRESSED–In MASONRY, untrimmed stone; rough cut.

URBAN DESIGN–The discipline that deals with the process of giving form to ensembles of STRUCTURES, to whole neighborhoods, or to the city at large. Urban designers blend the skills of the architect and city planner in an effort to make an urban area comprehensible, functional, and aesthetically pleasing through articulation of its parts.

URBAN PLANNING–Also called city planning, an outgrowth of landscape architecture, concentrating on the urban issues of land use, both existing and proposed; involves analysis of existing physical, social, and economic factors, leading to physical planning. Urban and regional planning emerged as special disciplines in the United States in the late 1920s with the establishment of the Harvard School of City Planning under the direction of Henry Vincent Hubbard in 1929 and the Cornell Department of City and Regional Planning under Gilmore Clarke in 1935.

URBAN RENEWAL–The upgrading of urban environments through public initiative and assistance in clearing of slums, rehabilitating or conserving existing structures, and providing for better housing, commercial, industrial, and public buildings, and for greater amenities according to comprehensive plans and programs.

UTOPIA–Any place, state, or system of ideal perfection. Utopias are social romances that have usually appeared during some period of disaffection or crisis which prompted dreams of an imaginary situation where the social ideal could be achieved.

VALUE (OF A COLOR)–The amount of light reflected by a HUE; the brilliance or dullness of a color. Brilliant (light) colors of a hue are called tints and are said to be high-value colors. Dull (dark) colors of a hue are called shades and are said to be low values of a color.

VANDAL (VAN-dl)–A person of the Germanic tribe that in the fifth century A.D. ravaged Gaul (France) and Spain, sacking Rome in 455. Because of their wanton disregard for the beautiful and valuable artworks created by the Romans, they destroyed many of the world's greatest art and architecture treasures. Therefore, destructive behavior of the property of others is known by their name.

VANISHING POINT–In LINEAR PERSPECTIVE, that point on the horizon toward which parallel lines appear to converge and at which they seem to vanish.

VASSAL (VASS-el)–In the Middle Ages, a person who held land under the FEUDAL system; a person beholden to a landlord and to service in his military for protection in return.

VAULT–A masonry roof or ceiling constructed on the ARCH principle. A BARREL vault, semicylindrical in cross section, is in effect a deep arch or an uninterrupted series of arches one behind the other. A *fan vault* is a development of linear vaulting characteristic of English Perpendicular Gothic, in which radiating ribs form a fanlike pattern. A GROIN vault is formed at the point where two BARREL vaults intersect at right angles. A ribbed vault is one in which there is a framework of ribs or arches under the intersections of the vaulting sections.

VEGETATION–The plant life that covers land areas of the earth. *See also* FLORA.

VENTURY–From the physicist, G. B. Venturi; short tube with a constricted passage that increases the velocity and lowers the pressure that flows through it. Now the word has come to be used for any environmental narrow passage that results in a constriction of things moving through it such as a narrow passage between buildings causing a wind tunnel effect; a "bottleneck."

VERANDA–A Portuguese name for an open balcony attached to the side of a dwelling; in the United States, a porch or a stoop. *See also* PATIO and PIAZZA.

VERNACULAR (ver-NAK-yu-lur) – Built objects and landscapes that result from traditions unique to a particular region or culture. These are created by local craftspersons rather than professionals and are typically made from local materials.

VEST POCKET PARK–A park or playground built on a small plot; often erected in built-up areas on vacant or abandoned lots; sometimes in private ownership for the exclusive use of the surrounding residents. *Also called* a pocket park.

VIADUCT–A bridge to carry a thoroughfare over a valley or over an obstacle such as a railroad.

VICTORIAN–Characteristic of the reign of Queen Victoria of England, 1837–1901.

VICTORY GARDEN–A type of vegetable garden popular during World War II for the production of produce for home consumption.

VIEW–A scene observed from a given vantage point.

VIGNETTE (vin-YET)–Originally, a decorative element of vine leaves and tendrils; hence any rather small decorative design in a book or manuscript that has no definite boundaries or frame.

VILLA–From the Latin for "village"; in Roman times, a self-contained farmstead serving a country estate and containing accommodation for the employees as well as the owner; in the Italy of the Renaissance, a country house surrounded by formal gardens; also *Villa RUSTICA*-(ROOS-ti-ca).

VILLA URBINA (ur-BAH-na)–The Roman residential structure located within the city.

VILLEGGIATURA (vill-ayj-yea-TUR-a)–Italian for the custom of going to the country to escape the summer heat of the city; a Roman practice that became popular again during the fifteenth century.

VISIGOTH (viz-i-GAWTH)–A Teutonic person of the western group of the GOTH tribe of central Europe. Visigoths invaded the Roman Empire in the late fourth century A.D. and established their own kingdom in France and Spain until A.D. 700.

VISTA–A confined segment of a view usually toward a terminal or dominant element or feature. A vista may be a natural or completely human-made view.

VOILE (VWAHL)–French word for a screen or visual baffle.

VOLUME–The manner in which SPACE is organized by mass; descriptive of enclosed three-dimensional space either solid or hollow.

VOLUTE (vo-LUTE)–A spiral scroll-like form characteristic of the Greek IONIC CAPITAL.

VOUSSOIR (voo-SWAH)–A wedge-shaped block used in the construction of a true ARCH. The central voussoir, which sets the arch, is the KEYSTONE.

WAINSCOTING (WAINS-coat-ing)–Wooden paneling on the walls of a room, often on the lower portion of the walls only.

WARD–A district or division of a city or town, for purposes of administration, voting, and so on. In colonial Savannah (1733), James Oglethorpe laid out a series of similar wards, each with an open SQUARE at its center.

WARM COLOR–Red, orange, or yellow. Psychologically, warm colors tend to be exciting, emphatic, and affirmative. Optically, they generally seem to advance or project.

WATER ORGAN–In sixteenth-century Italy and elsewhere, elaborate RENAISSANCE gardens such as Villa D'Este in Tovoli had very complicated mechanical devices built into some of their fountains which were capable of producing a full range of musical notes from hydraulic pressure, much as a pipe organ operates on valves regulating air pressure as it passes over perforated tubes.

WATER TABLE–The upper surface of a zone of SATURATED soil. No water table exists where the upper surface of a zone of saturation is formed by an impermeable body.

WATER THEATER–A popular feature in the Italian RENAISSANCE gardens, where water in pools and fountains was the major design feature. Usually, enclosed by walls and/or clipped evergreen hedges. The Villa Gamberaia has a fine example. The French PARTERRE D'EAU is comparable. *See also* GARDEN THEATER.

WATERSHED–The entire area that contributes water to a particular river, lake, or drainage basin; bounded by a divide or ridge of land from which the natural drainage flows in opposite directions.

WATTLE AND DAUB (WATT-ul and DOBB)–Primitive technique of wall building. Wattles, or reeds, were woven together and covered with daub, mud, or plaster, which then dries and becomes hard. This is held up by a wooden framework.

WATTLING–An erosion control technique that uses live branches, cut from such trees as willow and alder, bundled together and laid horizontally along a slope perpendicular to the RUN-OFF to intercept it and to retard gullying. Eventually, the wattles take root and grow into mature trees, thereby stabilizing the bank with their living mass of roots and the leaf litter and HUMUS, which they contribute to the SOIL.

WEEP HOLE–A small hole at the base of a retaining wall for the drainage of standing water from behind the wall, thereby reducing hydrostatic pressure at the foot of the wall.

WEST FRONT–The principal FACADE of a big church at the west end of the NAVE; conventionally used even when the church does not face east, such as St. Peter's in the Vatican. *See also* WESTWORK.

WESTWORK–A multistoried mass, including the FACADE and usually surmounted by towers, at the western end of a Medieval church. *See also* WEST FRONT

WILDERNESS–1. A region uncultivated and uninhabited; a waste; wild; barren; a tract of solitude and savageness suggesting the unpleasantness of such places. The wilderness of the Bible was condemned by God as a place of desolation, a vile place outside the Garden of Eden to which Adam and Eve were banished after committing their transgression against God. Cotton Mather preached to the American colonists that the wilderness was filled with demons and "fiery, flying serpents." 2. A piece of ground in a large garden or PARK which is planted with trees and shrubs arranged in an ornamental or NATURALISTIC style such as a MAZE or LABYRINTH. Olmsted designed such a feature in New York's Central Park in the area called The Ramble.

WOODY PLANTS–Plants that have wooden shoots, twigs, or stems; as distinguished from HERBACEOUS plants, which lack hard woody parts.

XERIC (ZARE-ik)–ARID, desertlike conditions; an ECOSYSTEM that tends to be dry or is periodically deficient of water. Plants that are adapted to survive in such places are xerophytes (ZARE-o-fites).

XERISCAPE (ZARE-i-scape)–1. n., A naturally occurring, or human-made, area of land that is dry and inhabited by plants and animals that are adapted to such conditions. 2. v., Occasionally used as a verb, as in the expression "to landscape"; meaning, literally, to create, artificially, a place composed of xerophytes or plants able to tolerate dry conditions.

XYSTOS or XYSTUS (ZIS-tus)–The Greek and Latin word for an enclosure, COLONNADE or PORTICO used for athletic exercises. The Romans also used the word *xystus* for the rear garden, outside the house but enclosed within walls.

YAMAATE (ya-MAHT-ay)–A Japanese design technique or principle that takes advantage of a given street's visible surrounding landscape attributes such as mountains, trees, and so on, to suggest infinite views. In Western thought, this device is expressed as BORROWED SCENERY. *See also* SHAKKAI.

YIN-YANG–Japanese term for the balance of principles, complementarity or harmony of things in nature (i.e., active–passive, earth–sky, rock–water, etc.).

ZEN (ZEN)–A Japanese Buddhist sect that prescribes to a philosophy or outlook based on antirationalism. Believers seek enlightenment through introspection and intuition.

ZIGGURAT (ZIG-oor-at)–A pyramidal staged tower, of which the angles were oriented to the cardinal points, which formed an important element in ancient Mesopotamian temple complexes. The number of stages rose from one to seven in the course of time. Often, each stage was faced in a stone of a different color, with the topmost shrine being the most brilliant in tone. In the Assyrian version, the stages were developed into a continuous inclined ramp circulating the four sides in turn.

ZONE–1. n., From the Greek and Latin for girdle or belt; to gird. A region that is distinct from those around it due to its particular use(s), status, or other PHYSIOGRAPHIC conditions. 2. v., To designate specific uses and/or restrictions for specific land areas.

ZONING–Generally, the demarcation of a city ORDINANCE into zones, the establishment of regulations to control the use of the land (commercial, industrial, type of residential, etc.) and the location, bulk, height, shape, use, and coverage of structures within each zone.

ZOOMORPHISM (zo-oh-MORF-ism)–The representation of gods in the form of or with the attributes of animals; the use of animal forms in art or symbolism.

Illustration Credits

All illustrations in this book were drawn by William A. Mann, with the exception of the following, which were obtained from other sources. The author and publishers would like to express our appreciation to the following for permission to reprint the illustrations:

Front cover: View at Woodenethe, Hudson River, New York. Andrew Jackson Downing, *A Treatise on the Theory and Practice of Landscape Gardening,* 6th ed. New York: A. O. Moore & Co., 1859, p. 440.

Page:

14. Fig. 1. Ziggurat of Ur, Sumeria. Courtesy of the British Museum, London, England.

18. Fig. 6. Greek Agora, Assos, Turkey. Trewin Copplestone, ed. *World Architecture.* London: Paul Hamlyn, 1963, p. 51, fig. 124.

34. Fig. 18. Plan of Versailles. Marie Louise Gothein. *A History of Garden Art.* ed., Walter P. Wright. London: J. M. Dent and Sons, 1928, p. 68.

36. Fig. 19. Palazzo Reale, Caserta, Italy. Marie Louise Gothein, *A History of Garden Art.* ed., Walter P. Wright. London: J. M. Dent and Sons, 1928. p. 208.

40. Fig. 21. Hampton Court, London. Marie Louise Gothein. *A History of Garden Art.* ed. Walter P. Wright. London: J. M. Dent and Sons, 1928, p. 118.

44. Fig. 24. Cumberland Terrace, Regent's Park, London. James Elmes. *Metropolitan Improvements of London in the Nineteenth Century.* London: Jones & Co., 1827 (reissued, London: Benjamin Blom, 1968), p. 22.

44. Fig. 25. Regent's Park, London. A. E. J. Morris. *History of Urban Form.* New York: John Wiley & Sons, 1972, p. 203, fig. 8.17.

46. Fig. 26. Virginia Colony Map, drawn by John Farrar, published in London, 1650. Courtesy of The Huntington Library, San Mateo, California.

48. Fig. 27. Governor's Palace, Williamsburg, Virginia. Arthur Shurcliff, "Gardens of the Governor's Palace, Williamsburg, Virginia," *Landscape Architecture,* 27: 2 (January 1937), p. 70.

50. Fig. 28. Central Park, New York City. Julius Gy Fabos, Gordon T. Milde and V. Michael Weinmayr. *Frederick Law Olmsted, Sr.* Amherst: University of Massachusetts Press, 1968, p. 24.

52. Fig. 29. Donnell Residence, Sonoma, California. Thomas D. Church. *Gardens Are for People.* New York: McGraw-Hill, Inc., 1955 (revised 1983), p. 182. Courtesy of Mrs. Elizabeth Church.

52. Fig. 30. Park Furniture Details, National Park Service. "Details of Construction—Bench and Table." *Landscape Architecture,* 24: 3 (April 1934), p. 160.

56. Fig. 33. Locational Score, Sea Ranch, California. *Lawrence Halprin: Changing Places.* San Francisco: San Francisco Museum of Modern Art, 1986, pp. 26–27. Courtesy of Lawrence Halprin, Lawrence Halprin Associates.

208. Plan of Union College Campus, 1813, by Joseph Jacques Ramée. Courtesy of Schaffer Library, Union College, Schenectady, New York.

References

Abrams, Charles. *The Language of Cities: A Glossary of Terms.* New York: Viking Press, 1971.

Appleton, Jay. *The Experience of Landscape.* New York: John Wiley & Sons, 1975.

Bacon, Edward N. *The Design of Cities,* rev. ed. New York: Viking Penguin Press, 1974.

Bazin, Germain. *Baroque and Rococo Art.* New York: Frederick A. Praeger, 1964.

Berrall, Julia S. *The Garden: An Illustrated History.* New York: Viking Penguin Press, 1978.

Betts, Edwin M. *Thomas Jefferson's Garden Book—1776–1824: With Relevant Extracts From His Other Writings.* Philadelphia, American Philosophical Society, 1944.

Beveridge, Charles E., and David Schuyler. *The Papers of Frederick Law Olmsted,* Vol. III, *Creating Central Park, 1857–1861.* Baltimore: Johns Hopkins University Press, 1983.

Beveridge, Charles E. "Frederick Law Olmsted's Theory of Landscape Design." *Nineteenth Century,* Summer, 1977.

Beveridge, Charles E., et al. *The Master List of Design Projects of the Olmsted Firm: 1857–1950.* Boston: National Association for Olmsted Parks, 1987.

Bigelow, Jacob. *A History of the Cemetery of Mount Auburn.* Boston and Cambridge, James Munroe & Co., 1860.

Blum, John M., et al. *The National Experience,* Part One. New York: Harcourt, Brace & Jovanovich, 1973.

Bord, Janet, and Colin Bord. *Mysterious Britain.* St. Albans, England: Granada Publishing, 1972.

Bronowski, Jacob. *The Ascent of Man.* Boston: Little, Brown & Co., 1973.

Brownell, Morris R. *Alexander Pope and the Arts of Georgian England.* Oxford: Oxford University Press, 1978.

Burn, A. R. *The Pelican History of Greece.* Harmondsworth, England: Penguin Books, 1974.

Burnham, Patricia M. "John Trumbull," in *International Dictionary of Art and Artists,* Vol. 1. Ed. James Vinson, Chicago: St. James Press, 1990.

Bye, A. E. *Art into Landscape: Landscape into Art.* Mesa, Ariz.: PDA Publishers, 1983.

Campbell, Craig S. *Water in Landscape Architecture.* New York: Van Nostrand Reinhold, 1978.

Chadwick, George F. *The Park and the Town: Public Landscape in the 19th and 20th Centuries.* New York: Frederick A. Praeger, 1966.

Chambers, Sir William. *A Dissertation on Oriental Gardening.* London, 1772.

Chase, Isabel Wakelin Urban. *Horace Walpole: Gardenist.* Princeton, N.J.: Princeton University Press, 1943.

Chastellux, Marquis de. *Travels in North America in the Years 1780, 1781, and 1782,* 2 vols. Ed. Howard C. Rice, Jr. Chapel Hill, N.C.: University of North Carolina Press, 1963.

Chinchilla, Jesus Nunez. *Copan Ruins.* Tegucigalpa, Honduras: Tegucigalpa Press, 1975.

Church, Thomas. *Gardens Are for People.* New York: Reinhold, 1955.

Clark, Kenneth. *Civilization: A Personal View.* New York: Harper & Row, 1969.

Clark, Kenneth. *Landscape into Art.* Boston: Beacon Press, 1949.

Clay, Grady. *Close-Up.* New York: Frederick A. Praeger, 1973.

Cleveland, H. W. S. *Landscape Architecture as Applied to the Wants of the West,* 1871, Ed. Roy Lubove. Reprinted, Pittsburgh, Pa.: University of Pittsburgh Press, 1965.

Clifford, Derek. *A History of Garden Design,* rev. ed. London: Frederick A. Praeger, 1967.

Coe, William R. *Tikal.* Philadelphia: University of Pennsylvania Press, 1975.

Conklin, Paul K., and David Burner. *A History of Recent America.* New York: Thomas Y. Crowell Co., 1974.

Constitution Plaza (office brochure). Watertown, Mass.: Sasaki, Dawson, Demay Associates, 1969.

Cooney, Loraine M. *Garden History of Georgia*. Atlanta, Ga.: Peachtree Garden Club, 1933.

Cooper, Helen A. *John Trumbull: The Hand and Spirit of a Painter*. New Haven, Conn.: Yale University Press, 1982.

Copplestone, Trewin, Ed. *World Architecture*. London: Paul Hamlyn, 1963.

Crandell, Gina. *Nature Pictorialized: "The View" in Landscape History*. Baltimore: Johns Hopkins University Press, 1993.

Creese, Walter L. *The Crowning of America: Eight Great Spaces and Their Buildings*. Princeton, N.J.: Princeton University Press, 1985.

Crisp, Frank. *Medieval Gardens*. New York: Brentano, 1924.

Crowe, Sylvia. *Garden Design*. London: Country Life, 1958.

Cullen, Gordon. *Townscape*. New York: Van Nostrand Reinhold, 1961.

De Jongh, Brian. *Southern Greece*. London: Collins, 1972.

"Details of Construction: Bench and Table," *Landscape Architecture*, Vol. 24, No. 3 (April 1934), p. 160.

Dober, Richard. *Campus Planning*. New York: Reinhold, 1968.

Dober, Richard P. "An Endowment of Styles," *Landscape Architecture*, Vol. 79, No. 10 (December 1989), pp. 44–45.

Downing, Andrew Jackson. *A Treatise on the Theory and Practice of Landscape Gardening as Adapted to North America*. New York: Wiley and Putnam, 1841.

Duruy, Victor. *The World of the Romans*. Trans. Swenn Lansdell. London: John Gifford, 1972.

Eaton, Leonard K. *Landscape Artist in America: The Life and Work of Jens Jensen*. Chicago: University of Chicago Press, 1964.

Eckbo, Garrett. "Landscape for Living," *Architectural Record* (1950).

Eliot, Charles W. *Charles Eliot, Landscape Architect*. Boston: Houghton Mifflin, 1902.

Elliott, Clark A. *Biographical Dictionary of American Science: The Seventeenth Through the Nineteenth Centuries*. Westport, Conn.: Greenwood Press, 1975.

Elmes, James. *Metropolitan Improvements or London in the Nineteenth Century*. London: Jones & Co., 1827. Reissued, London: Benjamin Blom, 1968.

Fabos, Julius Gy, Gordon T. Milde, and V. Michael Weinmayr. *Frederick Law Olmsted, Sr.* Amherst, Mass.: University of Massachusetts Press, 1968.

Favretti, Rudy F., and Gordon P. DeWolf. *Colonial Gardens*. Barre, Mass.: Barre Publishers, 1972.

Favretti, Rudy J., and Joy P. Favretti. *Landscapes and Gardens for Historic Buildings*. Nashville, Tenn.: American Association for State and Local History, 1978.

Fein, Albert. *Frederick Law Olmsted and the American Environmental Tradition*. New York: George Braziller, 1972.

Fitch, James Marston. *American Building: The Historical Forces That Shaped It*. New York: Schocken Books, 1973.

Fletcher, Sir Banister. *A History of Architecture*. New York: Charles Scribner's Sons, 1975.

Gallion, Arthur B. *The Urban Pattern*. Princeton: D. Van Nostrand Co., 1963.

Garden Club of America. *Gardens of Colony and State*, 2 vols. Ed. Alice G. B. Lockwood. New York: Charles Scribner's Sons, 1934.

Gardner, Helen. *Art Through the Ages*. New York: Harcourt, Brace and World, 1970.

Garrett, Wendell. *Thomas Jefferson, Redivivus*. Barre, Vt.: Barre Publishers, 1971.

Giedion, Sigfried. *Space, Time and Architecture*. Cambridge, Mass.: Harvard University Press, 1941.

Gilpin, William. *Observations on Several Parts of England*, 3rd ed. London: T. Cadell & W. Davis, 1808.

Gilpin, William. *Remarks on Forest Scenery*, 3rd ed. London: T. Cadell & W. Davis, 1808.

Gothein, Marie Louise. *A History of Garden Art*, 2 vols. Ed. Walter P. Wright, trans. Mrs. Archer-Hind. London: J.M. Dent and Sons, 1928.

Great People of the Bible and How They Lived. Pleasantville, N.Y.: Reader's Digest Association, 1974.

Guralnik, David B., Ed. *Webster's New World Dictionary of the American Language*. Englewood Cliffs, N.J.: Prentice-Hall, 1970.

Hadfield, Miles. *Gardening in Great Britain*. London: Hutchison, 1960.

Halprin, Lawrence. *Cities*. New York: Reinhold, 1963.

Halprin, Lawrence. *The RSVP Cycles*. New York: George Braziller, 1969.

Hardoy, Jorge. *Urban Planning in Pre-Columbian America*. New York: George Braziller, 1968.

Harris, Charles W., and Nicholas T. Dines. *Time-Saver Standards for Landscape Architecture: Design and Construction Data*. New York: McGraw-Hill, 1988.

Hartt, Frederick. *History of Italian Renaissance Art*. Englewood Cliffs, N.J.: Prentice-Hall, 1969.

Hawking, Stephen W. *A Brief History of Time: From the Big Bang to Black Holes*. New York: Bantam Books, 1988.

Hazelhurst, Franklin Hamilton. *Jacques Boyceau and the French Formal Garden*. Athens, Ga.: University of Georgia Press, 1966.

Hazelhurst, Franklin Hamilton. *Gardens of Illusion: The Genius of André Le Nostre*. Nashville: Vanderbilt University Press, 1980.

Hoskins, William G. *The Making of the English Landscape*. London: Hodder & Stoughton, 1988.

Howard, Sir Ebenezer. *Garden Cities for To-morrow*. London: Faber & Faber, 1946.

Hubbard, Henry Vincent, and Theodora Kimball. *An Introduction to the Study of Landscape Design,* rev. ed. Boston: Hubbard Educational Trust, 1967.

Hume, Ivor Noël, "First Look at a Lost Virginia Settlement," *National Geographic,* Vol. 155, No. 6 (June 1979), pp. 735–767.

Hunt, John Dixon. *Garden and Grove: The Italian Renaissance Garden in the English Imagination—1600–1750.* Princeton, N.J.: Princeton University Press, 1986.

Hunt, John Dixon, and Peter Willis, Eds. *The Genius of the Place: The English Landscape Garden 1620–1820.* Cambridge, Mass.: MIT Press, 1988.

Hussey, Christopher. *English Gardens and Landscapes: 1700–1750.* New York: Funk & Wagnalls, 1967.

Hussey, Christopher. *The Picturesque: Studies in a Point of View.* Hamden, Conn.: Archon Books, 1967.

Huth, Hans. *Nature and the Americans: Three Centuries of Changing Attitudes.* Berkeley, Calif.: University of California Press, 1957.

Hyams, Edward. *Capability Brown and Humphry Repton.* New York: Charles Scribner's Sons, 1971.

Hyams, Edward. *The English Garden.* New York: Harry N. Abrams, 1960.

Ito, Teiji. *Space and Illusion in the Japanese Garden.* New York: John Weatherhill, 1973.

Jackson, John B. *American Space.* New York: W. W. Norton & Co., 1972.

Janson, H. W. *History of Art.* Englewood Cliffs, N.J.: Prentice-Hall, 1969.

Jekyll, Gertrude. *On Gardening.* New York: Charles Scribner's Sons, 1964.

Jellicoe, Geoffrey, and Susan Jellicoe. *The Landscape of Man.* London: Thames and Hudson, 1975, 2nd ed., 1987.

Jellicoe, Geoffrey, Susan Jellicoe, Patrick Goode, and Michael Lancaster. *The Oxford Companion to Gardens.* Oxford: Oxford University Press, 1986.

Jellicoe, Susan, and Geoffrey Jellicoe. *The Use of Water in Landscape Architecture.* New York: St. Martin's Press, 1971.

Jensen, Jens. *Siftings.* Chicago: Ralph Fletcher Seymour, 1939.

Kassler, Elizabeth B. *Modern Gardens and the Landscape.* Garden City, N.Y.: Doubleday & Co., 1964.

Kelly, Bruce, Gail Travis Guillet, and Mary Ellen W. Hern. *Art of the Olmsted Landscape.* New York: New York City Landmarks Preservation Commission, 1981.

Knight, Richard Payne. *An Analytical Inquiry into the Principles of Taste.* 1805. Reprinted, Westmead, Farnborough, England: Gregg, 1972.

Kramer, Jack. *The New Gardener's Handbook and Dictionary.* New York: John Wiley & Sons, 1992.

Kronenberger, Louis, Ed. *Quality.* New York: A Balance House Book (Atheneum), 1969.

Kuck, Loraine E. *The Art of Japanese Gardens.* New York: John Day Co., 1940.

Laurie, Michael. *An Introduction to Landscape Architecture.* New York: American Elsevier Publishing Co., 1986.

Leighton, Ann. *American Gardens in the Eighteenth Century: For Use or for Delight.* Amherst, Mass.: University of Massachusetts Press, 1986.

Leighton, Ann. *American Gardens of the Nineteenth Century: For Comfort and Affluence.* Amherst, Mass.: University of Massachusetts Press, 1987.

Linden-Ward, Blanche, "Cemeteries," in *American Landscape Architecture: Designers and Places.* Ed. William H. Tishler. Washington, D.C.: Preservation Press of the National Trust for Historic Preservation, 1989.

Linden-Ward, Blanche. *Silent City on a Hill: Landscapes of Memory and Boston's Mount Auburn Cemetery.* Columbus, Ohio: Ohio State University Press, 1989.

Lindgren, Karen. *Fredrik Magnus Piper and the Landscape Garden.* Katrinholm, Sweden: Royal Academy of Fine Arts, 1981.

Louden, James C. *Observations on Laying Out the Public Squares in London.* London: Longman & Co., 1803.

Loudon, John Claudius. *An Encyclopaedia of Gardening,* 2 vols. 1822. Reprinted, New York: Garland Publishing, 1982.

Loudon, John Claudius. *The Landscape Gardening and Landscape Architecture of the Late Humphry Repton, Esq.* London: Longman & Co., 1840.

Lynch, Kevin. *What Time Is This Place?* Cambridge, Mass.: MIT Press, 1972.

Lynes, Russell. *The Tastemakers.* New York: Harper & Brothers, 1955.

Malone, Dumas, Ed. *Dictionary of American Biography.* New York: Charles Scribner's Sons, 1936.

Marsh, G. P. In *Man and Nature.* Ed. David Lowenthal. Cambridge, Mass.: Belknap Press of Harvard University Press, 1967.

Marsh, Warner L. *Landscape Vocabulary.* Los Angeles: Miramar Publishing Co., 1964.

Martin, Michael R. *A Graphic Guide to World History.* New York: Henry Holt & Co., 1959.

Martin, Peter. *The Pleasure Gardens of Virginia: From Jamestown to Jefferson.* Princeton, N.J.: Princeton University Press, 1991.

Martin, Peter. *Pursuing Innocent Pleasures: The Gardening World of Alexander Pope.* Hamden, Conn.: Archon Books, 1984.

Marx, Leo. *The Machine in the Garden: Technology and the Pastoral Ideal in America.* New York: Oxford University Press, 1964.

Masson, Georgina. *Italian Gardens.* London: Thames & Hudson, 1966.

McCarthy, Michael. "Eighteenth Century Amateur Architects and Their Gardens." *The Picturesque Garden and Its Influence Outside the British Isles: Dumbarton Oaks Colloquium on the History of Landscape Architecture.* Ed. Nikolaus Pevsner, Washington, D.C.,: Dumbarton Oaks, 1974, pp. 33–55.

McEvedy, Colin. *The Penguin Atlas of Ancient History.* Harmondsworth, England: Penguin Books, 1974.

McGuire, Diane Kostial. *Beatrix Farrand's Plant Book for Dumbarton Oaks*. Washington, D.C.: Dumbarton Oaks/Trustees for Harvard University, 1980.

McHarg, Ian. *Design with Nature*. Garden City, N.Y.: Doubleday, 1969.

McNeil, W. H. *A World History*. New York: Oxford University Press, 1967.

Mead, Robert Douglas, Ed. *Hellas and Rome*. New York: Mentor Book, 1972.

Michelin Green Guide: Chateaux of the Loire. London: Dickens Press, 1967.

Michelin Green Guide: Spain. Nancy, France: Berger-Levault, 1974.

M'Mahon, Bernard (McMahon). *The American Gardener's Calendar Adapted to the Climates and Seasons of the United States,* 2nd ed. Philadelphia: T.P. M'Mahon, 1819.

Moholy-Nagy, Sibyl. *Matrix of Man*. New York: Frederick A. Praeger, 1969.

Moore, Charles W., William J. Mitchell, and William Turnbull, Jr. *The Poetics of Gardens*. Cambridge, Mass.: MIT Press, 1988.

Morris, A. E. J. *History of Urban Form*. New York: John Wiley & Sons, 1972.

Morrow, Baker H. *A Dictionary of Landscape Architecture*. Albuquerque, N. Mex.: University of New Mexico Press, 1987.

Mosser, Monique, and Georges Teyssot, Eds. *The Architecture of Western Gardens: A Design History From the Renaissance to the Present Day*. Cambridge, Massachusetts: The MIT Press, 1991.

Mumford, Lewis. *The Culture of Cities*. New York: Harcourt, Brace & Co., 1938.

Nash, Roderick. *The American Environment*. Reading, Mass.: Addison-Wesley Publishing Co., 1976.

Newcomb, Rexford. *Outlines of the History of Architecture*. New York: John Wiley & Sons, 1931.

Newton, Norman T. *An Approach to Design*. Cambridge, Mass.: Addison-Wesley Press, 1951.

Newton, Norman T. *Design on the Land*. Cambridge, Mass.: Belknap Press of Harvard University Press, 1971.

Nichols, Frederick D., and Ralph E. Griswold. *Thomas Jefferson, Landscape Architect*. Monticello Monograph Series. Charlottesville, Va.: University Press of Virginia, 1977.

Norwich, John Julius, Ed. *Great Architecture of the World*. New York: Random House, 1975.

Nuttgens, Patrick. *The Landscape of Ideas*. London: Faber and Faber, 1972.

Nygren, Edward J. *Views and Visions: American Landscape Before 1830*. Washington, D.C.: The Corcoran Gallery of Art, 1986.

Okamoto, Toyo. *Invitation to Japanese Gardens*. Kyoto, Japan: Mitsumura Suiko Shoin Co., 1960.

Oldham, John, and Ray Oldham. *Gardens in Time*. Sydney, Australia: Lansdowne Press, 1980.

Olmsted, Frederick Law, Jr., and Theodora Kimball, Eds. *Frederick Law Olmsted: Landscape Architect, 1822–1903*. New York: G.P. Putnam's Sons, 1928.

Olmsted, Frederick Law. *Walks and Talks of an American Farmer in England*. London, David Bogue, 1852.

Padover, Saul K., Ed. *The Complete Jefferson*. New York: Duell, Sloan & Pearce, 1943.

Petulla, Joseph M. *American Environmental History*. San Francisco: Boyd and Fraser, 1977.

Pevsner, Nikolaus. "The Genesis of the Picturesque," *Architectural Review,* Vol. 96 (November 1944), pp. 139–166.

Pevsner, Nikolaus. *An Outline of European Architecture*. Baltimore: Penguin Books, 1963.

Pevsner, Nikolaus, Ed. *The Picturesque Garden and Its Influence Outside the British Isles: Dumbarton Oaks Colloquium on the History of Landscape Architecture*. Washington, D.C.: Dumbarton Oaks/Trustees for Harvard University, 1974.

Placzek, Adolf K. *Macmillan Encyclopedia of Architects*. New York: The Free Press of Macmillan Publishing Co., 1982.

Pond, Bremer W. "Outline History of Landscape Architecture," unpublished class lecture notes. Cambridge, Mass.: Landscape Architecture Department, Harvard Graduate School of Design, 1936.

Pregill, Philip, and Nancy Volkman. *Landscape in History: Design and Planning in The Western Tradition*. New York: Van Nostrand Reinhold, 1993.

Price, Uvedale. *An Essay on the Picturesque*. London, 1794.

Ranney, Victoria Post, Gerald J. Rauluk, and Carolyn F. Hoffman. *The Papers of Frederick Law Olmsted,* Vol. V, *The California Frontier, 1863–1865*. Baltimore: Johns Hopkins University Press, 1990.

Reps, John William. *The Making of Urban America*. Princeton, N.J.: Princeton University Press, 1965.

Reps, John William. *Tidewater Towns: City Planning in Colonial Virginia and Maryland*. Williamsburg: The Colonial Williamsburg Foundation, 1972.

Repton, Humphry. *Observations on the Theory and Practice of Landscape Gardening*. London, 1803.

Repton, Humphry. *The Art of Landscape Gardening*. Ed. John Nolen. Boston: Houghton Mifflin, 1907.

"Restoration of Colonial Williamsburg," *Architectural Record* (December 1935), pp. 78, 359–458.

Reynolds, Myra. *The Treatment of Nature in English Poetry*. Chicago: University of Chicago Press, 1909.

Rice, Howard C., Ed. *Travels in North America in the Years 1780, 1781 and 1782 by the Marquis de Chastellux: A Revised Translation,* 2 vols. Chapel Hill, N.C.: University of North Carolina Press, 1963.

Rice, H. C., Jr. *Thomas Jefferson's Paris*. Princeton, N.J.: Princeton University Press, 1976.

Roper, Laura Wood. *FLO: A Biography of Frederick Law Olmsted*. Baltimore: Johns Hopkins University Press, 1973.

Rothe, Anna, and Evelyn Lohr. *Current Biography: Who's News and Why*. New York: H.W. Wilson Company, 1952.

Rutz, Miriam, Ed. *Landscape and Gardens, Women Who Made a Difference*. Proceedings of the Conference on Women in Landscape Architecture, Michigan East Lansing, Mich.: State University, 1987.

Saalman, Howard. *Medieval Cities*. New York: George Braziller, 1968.

Sambrook, A. James. "The Shape and Size of Pope's Garden," *Eighteenth-Century Studies,* Vol. 5 (Spring 1972), pp. 450–455.

Schuyler, David. *The New Urban Landscape: The Redefinition of City Form in Nineteenth-Century America*. Baltimore: Johns Hopkins University Press, 1986.

Shepard, Paul. *Man in the Landscape: A Historic View of the Esthetics of Nature*. New York: Alfred A. Knopf, 1967.

Shepherd, J. C., and Geoffrey A. Jellicoe. *Italian Gardens of the Renaissance*. London: Alex Tiranti, 1953.

Shurcliff, Arthur A. "The Gardens of the Governor's Palace, Williamsburg, Virginia," *Landscape Architecture* (January 1937), pp. 27, 70–76.

Silliman, Benjamin. *Remarks Made on a Short Tour Between Hartford and Quebec, in the Autumn of 1819*. New Haven, S. Converse, 1824.

Simonds, John O. *Earthscape: A Manual of Environmental Planning*. New York: McGraw-Hill, 1978.

Simonds, John O. *Landscape Architecture,* 2nd ed. New York: McGraw-Hill, 1983.

Simpson, J. A., and E. S. C. Weiner, Eds. *Oxford English Dictionary,* 2nd ed. Oxford: Clarendon Press, 1989.

Sitté, Camillo. *The Art of Building Cities*. New York: Reinhold, 1945.

Sizer, Theodore. *The Works of Colonel John Trumbull: Artist of the American Revolution*. New Haven, Conn.: Yale University Press, 1967.

Sizer, Theodore, Ed. *The Autobiography of Colonel John Trumbull: Patriot-Artist, 1756–1843*. New York: Kennedy Graphics/Da Capo Press, 1970.

Snow, Marc. *Modern American Gardens: Designed by James Rose*. New York: Reinhold Publishing Co., 1967.

Speiregen, Paul D. *Urban Design: The Architecture of Towns and Cities*. New York: McGraw-Hill, 1965.

Spirn, Ann Whiston. *The Granite Garden: Urban Nature and Human Design*. New York: Basic Books, 1984.

Stein, Clarence S. *Toward New Towns for America*. New York: Reinhold Publishing Corp., 1957.

Stevenson, Elizabeth. *Park Maker: A Life of Frederick Law Olmsted*. New York: Macmillan, 1977.

Stilgoe, John. *Common Landscape of America, 1580 to 1845*. New Haven, Conn.: Yale University Press, 1982.

Subject Outlines: Uniform National Examination for Landscape Architects. McLean, Va.: Council of Landscape Architectural Registration Boards, 1976.

Takakuwa, Giesei, and Kiichi Asono. *Japanese Gardens Revisited*. Rutland, Vt.: Charles E. Tuttle Co., 1963.

Thacker, Christopher. *The History of Gardens*. Berkeley, Calif.: University of California Press, 1979.

Tishler, William H., Ed. *American Landscape Architecture: Designers and Places*. Washington, D.C.: Preservation Press of the National Trust for Historic Preservation, 1989.

Tobey, George B., Jr. *A History of Landscape Architecture*. New York: American Elsevier, 1973.

Tompkins, Peter. *Secrets of the Great Pyramid*. New York: Harper & Row, 1971.

Trancik, Roger. *Finding Lost Space: Theories of Urban Design*. New York: Van Nostrand Reinhold, 1986.

Triggs, H. Inigo. *The Art of Garden Design in Italy*. London: Longman's, Green & Co., 1906.

Trowbridge, Peter, Ed. *Public Space*. Cambridge, Mass.: Harvard Graduate School of Design, 1975.

Tuan, Yi-Fu. *Topophilia*. Englewood Cliffs, N.J.: Prentice-Hall, 1974.

Tunnard, Christopher. *Gardens in the Modern Landscape*. Westminster, England: Architectural Press, 1938.

Tunnard, Christopher. *The City of Man*. New York: Charles Scribner's Sons, 1970.

Tunnard, Christopher, and Boris Pushkarev. *Man-Made American: Chaos or Control*. New Haven, Conn.: Yale University Press, 1963.

Turner, Paul V. *Campus: An American Planning Tradition*. Cambridge, Mass.: MIT Press, 1984.

Urdang, Laurence, Ed. *The Timetables of American History*. New York: Simon & Schuster, 1981.

Verheyen, Egon. "John Trumbull and the U.S. Capitol," in *John Trumbull: The Hand and Spirit of a Painter*. Helen A. Cooper, Ed. New Haven, Conn.: Yale University Press, 1982.

Walmsley, Anthony. *Made Landscapes*. Philadelphia: Falcon Press, 1975.

Way, Douglas S. *Terrain Analysis*. Stroudsburg, Penn.: Dowden, Hutchinson & Ross, 1973.

Wells, H. G. *The Outline of History*. Garden City, N.Y.: Doubleday & Company, 1971.

Whately, Thomas. *Observations on Modern Gardening*. Ed. John Dixon Hunt, 1770. Reprinted, New York: Garland Publishing, 1982.

Who Was Who in America. Chicago: A.N. Marquis Co., 1942.

Who's Who in America, 40th ed., 1978–1979. Chicago: Marquis Who's Who, 1980.

Whyte, William H. *The Social Life of Small Urban Spaces*. Washington, D.C.: Conservation Foundation, 1980.

Wiggenton, Brooks E. *Japanese Gardens*. Marietta, Ohio: Richardson Printing Corp., 1963.

Williams, Morley J. "The Gardens at Monticello," *Landscape Architecture* (January 1934), pp. 24, 65–71.

Wright, Richardson. *The Story of Gardening*. New York: Dover, 1963.

Yoshida, Tetsuro. *Gardens of Japan*. New York: Frederick A. Praeger, 1957.

Zube, Ervin H. *Landscapes: Selected Writings of John Brinkerhof Jackson*. Amherst, Mass.: University of Massachusetts Press, 1970.

Zucker, Paul. *Town and Square*. New York: Columbia University Press, 1959.

Index

(Note: Figures in **bold** type refer to illustrations)